'By Honour and Dishonour'
The Story of the Evangelical Presbyterian Church

Ernest C Brown

The Evangelical Presbyterian Church

The Evangelical Book Shop Belfast

"We give no offence in anything, that our ministry may not be blamed. But in all things we commend ourselves as ministers of God: in much patience, in tribulations, in needs, in distresses, in stripes, in imprisonments, in tumults, in labours, in sleeplessness, in fastings; by purity, by knowledge, by longsuffering, by kindness, by the Holy Spirit, by sincere love, by the word of truth, by the power of God, by the armour of righteousness on the right hand and on the left, by honour and dishonour, by evil report and good report; as deceivers, and yet true; as unknown, and yet well known; as dying, and behold we live; as chastened, and yet not killed; as sorrowful, yet always rejoicing; as poor, yet making many rich; as having nothing, and yet possessing all things."

(2 Cor 6.3-10)

© Ernest C Brown, 2016

ISBN: 978-0-952266-22-8

All rights reserved. No part of this publication may be reproduced, stored in or introduced into a retrieval system, or transmitted, in any form or by any means (electronic, mechanical, photocopying, recording or otherwise) – except for quotations for the purposes of comment or review – without the prior written permission of the copyright owner.

Unless indicated otherwise, all Scripture quotations are taken from the New King James Version. Copyright © 1982 by Thomas Nelson. Used by permission. All rights reserved. The British Text edition (formerly Revised Authorised Version) published by the Bible Societies, by kind permission of Thomas Nelson, Inc, in 1991.

Published by
The Evangelical Presbyterian Church
www.epcni.org.uk

and

The Evangelical Book Shop, Belfast BT1 6DD
www.evangelicalbookshop.co.uk

Printed by
Kingsbridge Press, Cookstown, Northern Ireland
www.kingsbridgepressltd.com

Cover Design
David Watson

The Burning Bush motif taken from the Pulpit Fall at Knock Evangelical Presbyterian Church

To the memory of the IEC-EPC Founding Fathers

Rev James Hunter and Rev W J Grier

Rev James Hunter

Rev William James Grier

Contents

Foreword	11
Preface and Acknowledgements	13
List of Abbreviations	16
Select Bibliography	18
Introduction	23

Part 1 - The Background Centuries

1	**The Pre-Presbyterian Era**	27
	Patrick, Columba and Others (400-800 AD)	28
	Vikings, Anglo-Normans and Tudors (800-1600 AD)	28
2	**The Presbyterian Church Begins**	31
	Introducing Presbyterian History	32
	Early Blessing (1610-1630)	32
	Laud, Wentworth and Repression (1630-1642)	33
	Presbyterian Church in Ireland - Phase 2	34
	Civil War, Westminster and Cromwell (1642-1690)	35
3	**Doctrinal Surrender, Counteracting Grace**	37
	Non-Subscription and Arianism	38
	Blessings from Without	41
	The Reformed Presbyterian Church of Ireland	45
4	**Counter-Offensive, Returning Life**	47
	The Battle Joined with Arianism	48
	Returning Life	52
	Great Expectations	55

Part 2 - The Developing Crisis

5	**The Broadening Church**	59
	Lefferts A Loetscher	60
	Irish Presbyterian Colleges and Biblical Criticism	61
	Free Church of Scotland (1900-1905)	63
	Code Revision (1904-1911)	66
	Rev F W S O'Neill, China	67
	Publications	69
6	**The IEC Founding Fathers**	75
	James Hunter	76
	John Richard Gillespie	80
	William James Grier	81
	The Family Trees	86
7	**The Princeton and Machen Input**	87
	The Princeton Controversy	88
	The Princeton Influence	89

	Summers in Canada 1924-25	91
	The Machen-Grier Correspondence	92
8	**The Nicholson Missions**	**95**
	The First W P Nicholson Campaign	96
	The Second W P Nicholson Campaign	101
9	**The Leaders Engage**	**105**
	Hunter and Grier Join Forces	106
	The Cape Breton Call	110
10	**The Battle is Joined**	**111**
	SOS to Irish Presbyterians	112
	Presbyterian Bible Standards League	117

Picture insert – The Earlier Days

Part 3 - The Heresy Trial and Appeal

11	**The Heresy Trial**	**131**
	Formal Indictment	132
	Trial Overview	133
	Charge 1 - Imputation	135
	The Verdict	149
	W J Grier's Notebook	149
	Charges 2-5	152
	Notice of Appeal	153
12	**From Trial to Appeal**	**155**
	The Public Meetings	156
	Ulster Pamphlets	159
	The Days Before …	160
13	**The Appeal**	**163**
	The Appeal Structure	164
	The Case for the Prosecution	165
	The Defence: Discrediting the Accusers	167
	The Defence: Vindicating the Accused	170
	Put to the House	175
	Verdict	176
14	**Post-Mortem**	**177**
	The Combination of Factors	178
	Davey Theology - Irish Presbyterian Comment	185
	Denial	188
15	**Theological Review**	**191**
	Charge 1 Plea – Imputation – Derek Thomas	192
	Charge 2 Plea – Christology – John Grier	196
	Charge 3 Plea – Scripture – David McKay	199
	Charge 4 Plea – Sin – Iain D Campbell	204
	Charge 5 Plea – The Trinity – Andrew Woolsey	208

Picture insert – Church and Evangelical Book Shop

Part 4 – The Irish Evangelical-Evangelical Presbyterian Church

16	**Severing the Bonds (1927)**	**223**
	The Local Press	224
	Severance	226
17	**Constituting the Trust (1927-28)**	**229**
	The *Chat Noir* 'General Meetings'	230
	A Union Church?	230
	A New Denomination	232
	Early Restraints	237
	"Let Israel now Say"	242
18	**Gaining a Foothold (1928-39)**	**243**
	Industrialisation and Depression	244
	Announcing IEC	244
	The Irish Evangelical	247
	The First Congregations	249
	The First Ministers	251
	Home Missions – Mainly Colportage	255
	Foreign Missions – First Steps	260
	Council and Constitution	261
	Youth Work – in Embryo	266
	Ladies United Monthly Prayer Meeting	268
	The Emergent W J Grier	268
19	**... And Experiencing Pain (1933-34)**	**271**
	The Dispensationalist Controversy	272
	James Hunter Gillespie	275
20	**Forging the Identity (1940-64)**	**281**
	The International Scene	282
	Interceding for the Nation	283
	The Presbyterian Journey	284
	Inter-Church Relations – First Affiliations	288
	Commemorations	293
21	**Consolidating the Position (1940-67)**	**295**
	Church Extension: Phase 2	296
	Ministry Pressures and Progress	297
	Home Missions – Old and New	298
	Foreign Missions – Free Church of Scotland	302
	Youth Work – Becoming Established	303
	The Evangelical Presbyterian – Tributes and Changes	306
	Council Committees Begin	308
	Finance	311
	The Grammar School Syllabus	312
	The Free Presbyterian Church of Ulster	315
	Visitors	316
	Early Anniversaries	316
	These Forty Years	317

22	**Paying Tribute (1940-67)**	**319**
	Rev James Hunter	320
	Dr John Richard Gillespie	321
	Mr James A Kell	321
	Mr John J Patterson	321
	The First Four Ministers	321
	W J Grier	322
23	**Developing in Troubled Times (1968-1989)**	**329**
	Old Attacks Renewed	330
	Ministry Changes and Development	333
	Church Extension – Phase 3	334
	Developing Committee Structures	338
	Annual Presentation of Presbytery Reports	341
	Developments in Praise	342
	Foreign Missions – An Era Concludes	342
	Inter-Church Relations – The Changing Scene	343
	Youth Work – Developing	347
	Commitment to Prayer	349
	Ministers' and Office Bearers' Conferences	350
	50th-60th Anniversaries	351
24	**Engaging with Strategy and Change (1980-2014)**	**353**
	Strategy and *Vision for the Nineties*	354
	Further Church Development	358
	Ministry Growth and Standards	359
	A Busy Presbytery	361
	Youth Work – New Activities	363
	Autumn Evening Lectures	364
	The Book of Praise	364
	Ladies United Monthly Prayer Meeting – Its 70 Years	365
	The Evangelical Presbyterian – A New Chapter	366
	Inter-Church Relations – Expanding	366
	International Missions – A New Phase	372
	The Evangelical Book Shop – Changes	376
	Recurrent Censure	377
	75th Anniversary	381
	The Legacy of J G Machen	382
	Looking Back – and Forward – and Upward	384

Picture Insert – Missions and Youth

Part 5 – Learning from History

25	**Identifying the Issues**	**395**
	Drift	396
	Semper Reformanda	398

	The Right of Private Judgement	399
	Reaction to Change	405
	Secession	407
	The Internal Lessons	416
26	**Living to the Standard**	**419**
	The Confessional Church	420
	Church Worship	422
	Church Leaders	425
	Church Members	426
	Covenant Youth	428
	'Faith and Life'	430

Appendices

1	Heresy Trial Charges	434
2	Articles of Faith of the Irish Evangelical Church (1927)	441
3	Form of Government (1930)	442
4	Ministers – Alpha	443
5	Ministers – Congregation	449
6	Ministers' Service Chart	454
7	Congregations Chart	455
8	Congregations-Ministers Chart	456
9	Office Bearers – Congregation	457
10	Membership-Attendance Statistics	463
11	**A** Member Long-Term Missionary Service	464
	B Member Missionary Service Chart	465
12	Council-Presbytery Appointments	466
13	IEC-EPC Member Publications	469
14	Conferences	473
15	Autumn Evening Lectures	476
16	Sunday School Projects – Subject	478
17	YPA Projects	480
18	Camp Venues	481

Endnotes — 483
Index — 519

Foreword

Ireland in the 1920s had its share of trouble. The Irish Free State was proclaimed in 1921 and the following year Michael Collins was assassinated: civil war threatened. Spiritually the times were equally turbulent. Evangelicalism, typified by the Nicholson campaigns, impacted many; but the Higher Critical rationalistic approach to Scripture, as being fallible and unreliable, was propagated by others. There were clashes!

All around the world this critical view of Scripture, presented as moving with the times, infected confessional Churches; secessions occurred, often 'the size of a man's hand'. The impact on Presbyterianism in Scotland, Ireland and America, as well as the various mission fields including Manchuria (of particular significance to Irish Presbyterians), was not insignificant. Amy Carmichael, from our own shores, also had to deal firmly with this problem in her work at Dohnavur, south India in 1925. It was during these times, and with sufficient reason, that the Irish Evangelical Church (Evangelical Presbyterian Church) came into being. In summary, the full trustworthiness of Scripture and allegiance to it was at stake.

The Presbytery of the Evangelical Presbyterian Church appointed Ernest Brown to write the history of our denomination. As a son of the church, an elder, a former moderator, a missions' ambassador and a preacher of the Word of God, he is better qualified for this task than anyone we know. He knew the majority of the players and has lived through the unfolding years. We thank him sincerely for completing this massive project; for him it was a labour of love. The result is comprehensive, detailed and honest.

A factual and chronological approach is taken, but throughout the book the issues at the heart of our existence are addressed clearly and biblically. Though EPC is very far from being a perfect church (as the book points out), this fact does not negate the conviction that a stand for biblical truth is fundamental in seeking to be obedient to the God we worship. Some may say the issues of the 20th century are not necessarily the issues of the 21st century; and yet for us key issues such as Scripture and the doctrine of the church, remain. It reminds us of what Charles Hodge warned in 1869: *"if truth be lost, all is lost. Our numbers, wealth and influence will avail nothing."*

Our Church is both ordinary and extraordinary: ordinary in that it ministers in the struggle and busyness of everyday life; extraordinary in that it has more than survived, despite its smallness. The ebb and flow over the years has brought joy and pain, praise and ridicule. The story tells that however we are perceived and whatever the circumstances, whether "by honour or dishonour", we have sought to maintain a constancy and integrity befitting the Gospel as the apostles and reformers did in their day, and as our forerunners did in 1927.

We commend this history to the study and ownership of the whole Church, many of whose members are now separated from the life and times of our founding fathers but are building on their foundation. Current generations serve in a day when EPC, through the blessing of God, has its earlier development phases behind it and is well established in the local and international reformed constituency. We commend the book also to the interest of the wider church with the hope that many will find it profitable in some way for their own situations.

Church History Editorial Committee
Evangelical Presbyterian Church
January 2016

Preface and Acknowledgements

My original mandate was to complete this work in time for the Church's 75th Anniversary in 2002. The task turned out to be significantly greater than I anticipated and when I finally completed it in 2015, the members of Presbytery, as they had done in 2002, graciously accepted my apology for the delay. Furthermore, they were readily willing to proceed with publication jointly with the Evangelical Book Shop. I sincerely thank them for their sustained generosity of spirit, their confidence in the project and their practical help.

Historians try to see the 'big picture', understand what was going on, the reasons, justifications, trends, pressures, strategies, successes, failures, highs and lows. I hope I have had some success. This is not an academic work and much of it is written at the popular level. But since Church History is within the academic discipline it is necessary to relate to this genre – a number of ecclesiastical and socio-political academics have commented about EPC directly or indirectly and not always favourably.

I have tried to tell the story chronologically. The great advantage is the progressive sense of story. The disadvantage is that recurring subjects need to be linked with what has gone before. Few see Church History as exciting! Probably the events that surround our founding have the highest claim to that category, but I trust that many will receive it as an engaging story of faithfulness, hard years, sacrificial hard work and the steady development that becomes apparent with backwards perspective. There is much evidence of grace and of the Lord's favour, presence and leading throughout. To me it also carries a strong sense of potential future blessing. We look to the Lord that it may be so and that "both he who sows and he who reaps may rejoice together." (John 4.36)

Two elements prompted my choice of title, 'By Honour and Dishonour' (2 Cor 6.8). First, it captures key features of the story of the Evangelical Presbyterian Church. Second, it charges the church to be faithful in its ministry whatever the circumstances and whatever the cost, and to be steadfast whatever the response, not inflated by praise or disabled by distain.

I wish to thank Presbytery additionally for its appointment of the final editorial committee to assist me – John Grier and David Watson. They were particularly appropriate choices since we were each born into Church families and have been together in most aspects of the work of the Church and its bookshop since our youth. We each knew the Church's forefathers, apart from James Hunter who died in 1942, and absorbed from them much of the spirit, ethos and sense of identity that motivated them.

John and David each brought specialist gifts to the publication project and it has been the privilege of a lifetime for me to work with them in the completion of our Church history. I will remain very grateful for their thorough study of the manuscript and for their input which enhanced the work significantly in particular areas. And it was always given in a spirit of concern for my privilege as author, with a kind recognition that no two people would approach the work or present the story in the same way.

John Grier was manager of the Evangelical Book Shop for 35 years and possesses a renowned knowledge of Christian books and all things related. He brought this experience of his life's calling to the project, including his keen awareness of the wider church scene. His 'feel' for the years under consideration in this book is of exceptional value. Over a period he brought to my attention a veritable library of related publications, having researched and identified relevant pages for me in advance. I have not done them all justice. His father, Rev. W J Grier, was my own minister for the first 40 years of my life and I remain deeply thankful to God for the high privilege of such an influence throughout my formative years. Through many conversations and observations John has taken me further into his father's heart, mind and sense of calling. In addition he has provided the family biographical information.

David Watson managed the publication project and without his vision and drive it would not have advanced through its stages as it did. It has required a lot of time on the road, in addition to working at his desk, but he gave the project absolute priority and did everything connected with it quickly. He presented the project to Presbytery with the printing options and costs. He applied his skill in graphics to produce an appealing and very fitting cover design, and to the compilation and layout of the photographic sections. With the assistance of Colin Campbell, manager of Evangelical Book Shop, he dealt also with the book-trade necessities.

Many friends have helped and encouraged me during my church history years and have prayed during the final editing and publication phases. In recording my appreciation I acknowledge that it is a wholly inadequate expression of my own and the Church's indebtedness. Rev. Andrew Woolsey acted as my theological consultant over various issues. Rev. Gareth Burke advised me on various matters and responded to all my frequent requests for items of information. Patricia Gibson, Julia Grier and Rev Samuel. Watson read earlier versions of the manuscript and their advice contributed greatly to its development. Julia Grier then undertook the huge, painstaking task of proof-reading the completed manuscript, and Heather Watson followed it with the final back-up read. They also made valuable comments from the perspective of new readers. Some final editing took place after the proofs were read so any residual blemishes in the text are mine.

The Trustees of the Evangelical Book Shop, and manager, Colin Campbell, have readily undertaken publication jointly with the Church, along with distribution and sales. It has been a pleasure to work with our printers, Kingsbridge Press, who have given us very personal service and allowed us to work with them at levels of detail.

Dr Robert Beckett did a great deal of work in the 1970s and 80s with EPC congregations on the first phase of their histories and we look forward to the congregations updating and publishing these in due course.

And my sincere thanks to the contributors: Iain D Campbell (Free Church of Scotland), David McKay (Reformed Presbyterian Church of Ireland), Derek Thomas (Reformed Theological Seminary), John Grier and Andrew Woolsey (EPC) who wrote the articles for Chapter 11 – Theological Review. These superlative articles address the key issues of 1927 – Imputation, Scripture, Christology, Sin and the Trinity – but powerfully apply them to our ongoing Church and Christian lives. Mark Johnston, John MacIntosh, Iain Murray, Derek Thomas and Carl Trueman provided the generous endorsements which appear on the back cover. Stephen Tracey (Rockmount, Maine, Orthodox Presbyterian Church) contributed to Chapter 5 – the Broadening Church; John Grier and David Watson (EPC) respectively to Chapter 14 – Post Mortem and Chapter 26 – Living to the Standard. Quotations from past and present authors express my appreciation of and dependence on their work.

Finally I wish to record my very personal thanks to my wife, Shona, for her patient endurance of this long project and for her unfailing advice, encouragement and support throughout it. It has been a welcome and vital factor for me.

"Now to Him who is able to do exceedingly abundantly above all that we ask or think, according to the power that works in us, to Him be glory in the church by Christ Jesus to all generations, forever and ever. Amen" (Eph 3.20-21)

ECB
Belfast
January 2016

List of Abbreviations

ACTS	Africa Christian Textbooks
AIM	Africa Inland Mission
BEC	British Evangelical Council
BIOLA	Bible Institute of Los Angeles
BTI	Bible Training Institute
CDC	Church Development Committee
CEC	Church Extension Committee
CKGN	Christian Reformed Churches in the Netherlands
CLC	Christian Literature Crusade
CSSM	Children's Special Service Mission
CWI	Christian Witness to Israel
CWU	Christian Workers' Union
EBS	Evangelical Book Shop
EDNT	Exegetical Dictionary of the New Testament
EMF	European Missionary Fellowship
EP	*Evangelical Presbyterian* Magazine
EPC	Evangelical Presbyterian Church
EPCEW	Evangelical Presbyterian Church in England and Wales
ESV	English Standard Version
ETS	Edinburgh Theological Seminary (formerly Free Church College)
EuCRC	European Conference of Reformed Churches
FCC	Finance Consultative Committee
FCOS	Free Church of Scotland
FIEC	Fellowship of Independent Evangelical Churches
FPCU	Free Presbyterian Church of Ulster
GKGN	Christian Reformed Churches in the Netherlands
GKN	Reformed Churches in the Netherlands
GKNV	Reformed Churches in the Netherlands (Liberated)
IACWU	Irish Alliance of Christian Workers' Unions
ICCC	International Council of Christian Churches
ICM	Irish Church Missions
ICP	Inter-Church Process
ICRC	International Conference of Reformed Churches
IE	*Irish Evangelical* Magazine
IEC	Irish Evangelical Church
IMB	International Missions Board
IVP	Inter Varsity Press
KJV	King James Version
LDOS	Lord's Day Observance Society
LC	Larger Catechism

List of Abbreviations

LUMPM	Ladies United Monthly Prayer Meeting
LXX	Septuagint
MERF	Middle East Reformed Fellowship
NAM	North Africa Mission
NASV	New American Standard Version
NIV	New International Version
NKJV	New King James Version
NKJVA	New King James Version - Anglicised
OMF	Overseas Missionary Fellowship
OPC	Orthodox Presbyterian Church, USA
PAC	Presbytery Arrangements Committee
PAE	Presbyterian Association in England
PBSL	Presbyterian Bible Standards League
PCI	Presbyterian Church in Ireland
PCUSA	Presbyterian Church (USA)
PHSI	Presbyterian Historical Society of Ireland
PMC	Public Morals Committee
POCVA	Protection of Children and Vulnerable Adults
QUB	Queen's University, Belfast
RCS	Reformed Churches in Spain
Record	*Record of the Trial of the Rev Prof J E Davey*
RES	Reformed Ecumenical Synod
ROUTE	Reaching Out Unitedly to Europe
RPCI	Reformed Presbyterian Church of Ireland
RTS	Reformed Theological Seminary
RU	Royal University of Ireland
RV	Revised Version
SC	Shorter Catechism
SCM	Student Christian Movement
SIM	Sudan Interior Mission
SPCK	Society for Promoting Christian Knowledge
SUM	Sudan United Mission (now Pioneers UK)
TCD	Trinity College, Dublin
TCNN	Theological College of Northern Nigeria
TOM	Training for the Ministry Committee
TOMA	Training for the Ministry and Admissions Committee
UF	United Free Church of Scotland
UFM	Unevangelised Fields Mission
VALA	Viewers and Listeners Association
WCC	World Council of Churches
WCF	Westminster Confession of Faith
WTS	Westminster Theological Seminary
YPA	Young People's Association

Select Bibliography

Addley, W P, *A Study of the Birth and Development of the Overseas Missions of the Presbyterian Church in Ireland up to 1910*. Unpublished Ph.D. thesis.
Allen, R, *The Presbyterian College, Belfast*, Centenary Volume 1853-1953, William Mullan & Son Ltd, 1954.
Barkley, J M, *The Eldership in Irish Presbyterianism*, 1963.
Barnes, S, *All for Jesus – The Life of W P Nicholson*, Ambassador, 1996.
Boice, J M, *Foundations of the Christian Faith*, IVP, Revised Edition, 1986
Brown, N, *Knock Presbyterian Church 1872-1972*.
Bruce, S, *God Save Ulster*, The Religion and Politics of Paisleyism, Oxford, 1989.
Bruce, S, *Paisley*, Religion and Politics in Northern Ireland, Oxford, 2007.
Buchanan, R, *The Ten Years' Conflict*, Blackie & Son, 1867.
Bunyan, J, *The Pilgrim's Progress*, Banner of Truth, 1977.
Calhoun, D B, *Princeton Seminary, The Majestic Testimony, 1869-1929*, Volume 2, Banner of Truth, 1996.
Calvin, J, *The Institutes of the Christian Religion*. (Battles Edition), Westminster Press, 1960.
Calvin, J, Commentary on Luke (22.37). *A Harmony of the Gospels*, Volume III, St. Andrew Press, 1972.
Campbell, Iain D & Malcolm Maclean, Editors, *The People's Theologian*, Mentor, Christian Focus Publications, 2011
Campbell, J M, *The Nature of the Atonement*, Handsel Press, Carberry/Eerdmans, 1996.
Collins, G N M, *The Heritage of our Fathers*, Knox Press, 1974.
Collins, G N M, *Principal John Macleod, D.D*, The Publications Committee of the Free Church of Scotland, 1951.
Collins, G N M, *Whose Faith Follow*, 1943.
Dabney, R L, *Discussions*, Banner of Truth, 1982.
Dallimore, A, *George Whitefield*, Volume 1, Banner of Truth, Reprinted 1979.
Davey, J E, *The Changing Vesture of the Faith*, James Clarke & Co, 1923.
Davis, D R, *Joshua, No Falling Words*, Christian Focus Publications, 2000.
Denney, J, *The Christian Doctrine of Reconciliation*, James Clarke, 1959.
Duncan, L, Ed, *The Westminster Confession into the 21st Century*, Christian Focus, Mentor, Vol 1 2003, Vol 2 2004, Vol 3 2009.
Edersheim, A, *Old Testament Bible History*, AP&A, Hendrickson, 1995.
Fesko, J V, *The Theology of the Westminster Standards*, Crossway, 2014.
Finlayson, R A, *Reformed Theological Writings*, Christian Focus, 1996
Fulton, J A, *Biography of J Ernest Davey*, PCI, 1970.
Gillespie, J H (Leloumenos), *Faith in an Unchanging Vesture*, Evangelical Book Shop, 1927.
Grier, W J, *The Origin and Witness of the Irish Evangelical Presbyterian Church*, Evangelical Book Shop, Belfast, 1945.

Grier, W J, *The Momentous Event,* Banner of Truth, 1970.
Grier, W J, *The Best Books*, Banner of Truth, 1968.
Grier, W J, *The Life of John Calvin,* Banner of Truth, 2013.
Hamilton, T, *History of Presbyterianism in Ulster*, Mourne Missionary Trust, 1982.
Hart, D G, *Calvinism – A History*, Yale, 2013.
Hart, D G, Ed, *J. Gresham Machen, Selected Shorter Writings*, P & R Publishing, 2004.
Hendriksen, W, *Romans*, Banner of Truth, 1980.
History of Congregations in the Presbyterian Church in Ireland 1610-1982, PHSI.
Hodge, C, *Systematic Theology*, Eerdmans, 1960.
Hodge, C, *The Epistle to the Romans*, Remarks, 4, Banner of Truth, 1972.
Holmes, F, *Our Irish Presbyterian Heritage*, Publications Committee of the Presbyterian Church in Ireland, 1985.
Holmes, F, *Henry Cooke,* Christian Journals Limited, 1981.
Holmes, F, *The Presbyterian Church in Ireland, A Popular History*, Columba Press, 2000.
Hulse, Erroll, *The Story of the Puritans, Who were they? What did they accomplish? Why should we listen to them today?*, Chapel Library, 2000.
Jess, I T, *Ravenhill Presbyterian Church 1898-1998 – Centenary History*, 1997.
Kirkpatrick, L, *Presbyterians in Ireland, An Illustrated History*, Booklink, 2006.
Kistemaker, S J, *1 Corinthians*, Baker, 1996.
Latimer, W T, *A History of the Irish Presbyterians*, Belfast, J Cleeland, 1902.
Lewis, C S, *Surprised by Joy*, Geoffrey Bles, 1955, Harper Collins, 2002.
Livingstone, D N and Wells, R A, *Ulster-American Religion*, Notre Dame, 1999.
Loetscher, L A, *The Broadening Church*, University of Pennsylvania Press, Philadelphia, 1954.
Lucas, S M, *On Being Presbyterian*, P & R, 2007.
Machen, J G, *Christianity and Liberalism*, Victory Press, 1923.
Macleod, D, *Behold your God*, Christian Focus Publications, 1990.
Macleod, D, *The Person of Christ*, IVP, 1998.
Macleod, D, *Christ Crucified, Understanding the Atonement*, IVP, 2014.
MacQuigg, J C, Ed, *The Minnis Mills Tapestry*, 2005.
Maloney, E & Pollak, A, *Paisley*, Poolbeg, 1986.
Marsden, G, 'Understanding J Gresham Machen' in *Understanding Fundamentalism and Evangelicalism,* Eerdmans, 1991.
McCune, R, *Promise Unfulfilled, The Failed Strategy of Modern Evangelicalism*, Ambassador International, 2004.
Muller, R, *The Unaccommodated Calvin*, Oxford University Press, 2000.
Murray, A, *The Two Covenants and the Second Blessing*, 1899, Kessinger Publishing, 2010.
Murray, I H, *D Martyn Lloyd-Jones, The Fight of Faith 1939-1981*, Banner of Truth, 1990.

Murray, I H, *The Forgotten Spurgeon*, Banner of Truth, 1966.
Murray, I H, Ed, Murray, J, *Collected Writings of John Murray*, Vols 1-4, Banner of Truth, 1976-1982.
Murray, J, *The Epistle to the Romans*, Eerdmans, 1968.
Murray, S W, *W P Nicholson, Flame for God and Ulster*, The Presbyterian Fellowship, 1973.
Nicholson, W P, *On Towards the Goal*. Messages given at the Bangor, Co Down, Easter Convention, 1925.
O'Neill, M, *Frederick – The Life of My Missionary Grandfather in Manchuria*, Joint Publishing (H.K.) Co., Ltd, 2012.
Packer, J I, *'Fundamentalism' and the Word of God*, IVP, 1958.
Paton, D K, *The Higher Criticism: the Greatest Apostasy of the Age*, Passmore and Alabaster, 1899.
Piper, J, Taylor, P, Helseth, K, (Eds), *Beyond the Bounds: Open Theism and the Undermining of Biblical Christianity*, Crossway Books, 2003.
Poole-Connor, E J, *The Apostasy of English Non-Conformity*, London, 1933.
Pressing Towards the Mark, OPC, 1986.
Record of the Trial of Rev. Prof. J E Davey, 1927.
Reid, J S, *History of the Presbyterian Church in Ireland*, Vol III, Second Edition, Tentmaker Publications, 1998.
Reilly, Tom, *An Honourable Enemy-the Untold Story of the Cromwellian Invasion of Ireland*, Brandon/Mount Eagle Publications, 1999.
Reymond, R L, *A New Systematic Theology of the Christian Faith*, Nelson, 1998.
Runia, K, *Reformation Today*, Banner of Truth, 1968.
Sproul, R C, *Truths we Confess, A Layman's Guide to the Westminster Confession of Faith*, P&R, 2006.
Stewart, D (Muckamore), *A Short History of The Presbyterian Church in Ireland*, The Sabbath School Society for Ireland, 1936.
Stewart, D (Cregagh), *The Seceders in Ireland*, PHSI, 1950.
Stonehouse, N B, *J Gresham Machen*, Banner of Truth, 3rd edition, 1987.
Van Dixhoorn, Chad, *Confessing the Faith – A reader's guide to the Westminster Confession of Faith*, Banner of Truth, 2014.
Warfield, B B, *The Person and Work of Christ*, Presbyterian and Reformed, 1970.
Warfield, B B, *Works*, (10 vols), Oxford New York, 1927 and following.
Warfield, B B, *Biblical Doctrines*, (2nd vol. of above (1929)) Banner of Truth, 1988.
Warfield, B B, *Critical Reviews*, Oxford University Press, NY, 1932.
Watts, R, *The Newer Criticism and the Analogy of the Faith*, T & T Clark, 1882.
Westminster Confession of Faith, Free Presbyterian Publications, 1976.
Wilson, R D, *Is the Higher Criticism Scholarly?*, Bible Institute Colportage Ass'n, Chicago, 1922.
Witherow, T, *Historical and Literary Memorials of Presbyterianism in Ireland 1731-1800*, 1880.

... most historians would, I believe, both acknowledge the biased nature of the history they write and also maintain that they aspire to be objective in what they do. ... At the heart of the historian's task is this matter of verifiability and accountability by public criteria ... the bottom line is that most historians do acknowledge in their procedures and methods that such public criteria do exist ...

Carl R Trueman, *Histories and fallacies*, Crossway, 2010, pp 27-28

By Honour and Dishonour

Introduction

Conflicts do not usually arise spontaneously. Many feature a longer-term background, key personalities and issues or events that bring it all to a head. The formation of the Irish Evangelical Church followed this pattern. The background was the serious decline in theological orthodoxy in the Presbyterian Church in Ireland during the 18th century and the successful battle for its reform in the 19th. But fresh issues over orthodoxy began to surface towards the end of the 19th century. Battle was re-joined which climaxed in the *Heresy Trial* of 1927 from which the Irish Evangelical Church emerged.

Dramatic events marked the early 20th century in Ulster. There was the sinking of the Titanic in April 1912 and, in September, the signing of the Ulster Covenant as a pledge of resistance to Home Rule in Ireland. On 1 July 1916, the 36th Ulster Division sustained grievous casualties at the Somme. The 1920s opened with serious civil disorder and bloodshed as the Irish Free State and Northern Ireland came into existence. But into this situation, in the mercy and providence of God, came the renowned evangelical missions of W P Nicholson, 1921-23 and 1924-26, which were the means of transforming community life and restoring a large measure of civil peace. Over 12,000 were reported as passing through enquiry rooms during the first mission alone.[1]

For 25 years Rev. James Hunter had identified doctrinal broadening in the Church and opposed the instances in which it came to light. In 1924 he retired to devote himself to this task. But events concurrent with the latter stages of the Nicholson missions in 1925-26 precipitated a crisis: the Church was debating a change to its Formula of Subscription and evidence that questioned the orthodoxy of Professors at its Theological College had recently come into Hunter's hands. He felt an imperative duty to respond, and the evangelical revival through the Nicholson missions persuaded him that the time was "a time to speak" (Eccles 3.7).

In May 1926 he set up the Presbyterian Bible Standards League to organise his public campaign against Liberalism in the College. Then, in December of the same year, he indicted Rev. James Ernest Davey, Professor of Church History at Assembly's College,[2] Belfast, before the Belfast Presbytery "on five several charges of teaching doctrines contrary to the Word of God and the standards of the church." The charges, which Hunter based on the Professor's published writings and notes of his lectures to his students, related to the major doctrines of Imputation (Justification), Christology, Scripture, Sin, and the Trinity. The Presbytery heard the case during February-March 1927 and acquitted Professor Davey on each count by majorities close to 90%. James Hunter appealed to the General Assembly in June 1927 and maintained his public campaign in the interval; but the members, in a "crowded house", upheld the not guilty verdict of Presbytery by a similarly huge majority.

Hunter viewed this verdict by the highest and most representative Court of the Church as a declaration of the Church's institutional unorthodoxy and a considered acceptance of the liberalism he had campaigned against in its College. In addition, the Assembly appointed a Commission to deal with matters including his non-compliance with Belfast Presbytery's direction that there should be no public reference to the case before the hearing of Appeals. Hunter considered that its Terms of Reference, which brought similar future cases within its powers, had unacceptable implications for his freedom to carry on the battle for orthodoxy in the future.

He therefore decided he could not in good conscience remain under "an alien yoke". He resigned his membership of the Presbyterian Church in Ireland in July 1927 and, with others of like mind, notably William James Grier, a licentiate and key divinity student witness at the trial, formed the *Irish Evangelical Church* in October 1927. In 1964, with the unanimous agreement of its congregations, the Church changed its name to the *Evangelical Presbyterian Church* to identify it with the Westminster subordinate standards and form of government that it had progressively espoused.

Part 1

The Background Centuries

1

The Pre-Presbyterian Era

"I, Patrick, a sinner ... did not know the true God ..."

Patrick's Confessions

There is general agreement that invaders from different parts of the European mainland, and particularly Celtic tribes from Great Britain, populated Ireland progressively from the BC era. Early religious practice is associated with the Druids, the polytheistic priesthood and intelligentsia of the Celts. They believed in the immortality of the soul, supposing that it occupied a new body after death. They sacrificed animals and, some consider, human beings as well. The oak tree and the mistletoe plant are examples of plant life they regarded as sacred. However, the Christian faith appears to have come to Ireland early in the Christian era.

Patrick, Columba and Others (400-800 AD)

Patrick arrived in the 5th century AD, describing the circumstances at the beginning of his *Confession*: "I, Patrick, a sinner … did not know the true God, and was taken in captivity to Ireland with many others, in accordance with our deserts, because we were living far from God, and did not observe his commandments." He was converted during the six years of his captivity and, after returning to his parents, he studied in France in preparation for missionary service in Ireland for which he received a Macedonian-type call in a dream. He returned in 432. His programme of evangelisation was instrumental in establishing Christianity throughout the country. One account credits him with setting up 365 churches and another 700, his organisation being one church, one Bishop. His *Confession* is Trinitarian, full of Christ, his glory and his return, and is concerned that every nation would hear the Gospel. He died about 461.

The Christianity of the 400s deteriorated in the following centuries, but there was notable Christian witness. A network of 'monasteries' grew up that served as schools, study-retreats, Bible colleges and centres of missionary activity. Prominent among these missionaries was Columba, the Apostle of the Picts and Scots. In 563, he and his 12 companions sailed to Iona and made it the centre of Bible transcription and missionary outreach that extended to the extremities of Scotland and its isles. Columbanus, who studied at Lough Erne and at Bangor, Co Down, went to France in 580, and others of the same period evangelised elsewhere in Europe and in England. The *Book of Kells* is an outstandingly beautiful 'illuminated' Latin manuscript of the four Gospels, produced by scribes in Columba's monastery in Kells, Co Meath, around 800. It is on permanent display in the library of Trinity College Dublin.

Vikings, Anglo-Normans and Tudors (800-1600 AD)

For two centuries from 795, Norwegian and other northern European Vikings attacked Ireland, mainly along its east and south coasts, but moved inland ransacking monasteries, burning, killing and committing other atrocities. The monks built the famous Round Towers as safe depositories for their treasures. The Norsemen founded coastal towns, for example, Dublin, Waterford, Cork and Limerick, and settled in them. Brian Boru finally defeated them at the Battle of Clontarf, north of Dublin in 1014, but many of them stayed in Ireland.

The ecclesiastical influence of the Roman Catholic Church had grown since the time of Patrick, but successive Popes failed to bring the Celtic Church into full alignment. In 1110 the Synod of Rathbreasil, Co Tipperary, with the Pope's representative at its head, established a system of Diocesan Episcopacy throughout the country, for the first time bringing it under the rule of the Pope. However, when the arrangement had achieved only limited implementation after 40 years, they convened the Synod of Kells in 1152. Kells consolidated the Rathbreasil arrangement with a revised Diocesan structure, but likewise failed to achieve the full compliance intended.

William the Conqueror, Duke of Normandy, established Norman rule in England by victory at the Battle of Hastings in 1066, and his dynasty continued until 1154. In 1155 soon after the Synod of Kells, Adrian IV, an English Pope, issued a Bull giving Henry II, grandson of the Norman monarch, Henry I, and the first of the Plantagenet[3] line, permission to invade Ireland. The Pope urged the Irish to receive him honourably as their lord. The conquest began in the 1160s, and in 1171 Henry arrived himself to complete it. Circa 1180-1190, one of Henry's commanders, John de Courcy, built Carrickfergus Castle to guard the approach to Belfast Lough. It was the first of the Irish castles and is a good example of Norman architecture. Circa 1200 he built another at Dundrum to command the approaches from the south and west. Within 200 years the Anglo-Normans possessed virtually the whole country, but as they intermarried, assimilated Irish culture, or preferred the role of rent-extracting absentees, ownership reverted, and by the early 1400s only an area around Dublin, known as *The Pale*, was in English hands.

From 1534 Henry VIII, second monarch of the House of Tudor, reasserted England's control and, in 1541, he coerced the Irish Parliament into declaring him King. His family successors, Edward VI (1547-1553), Mary I, 'Bloody Mary', (1553-1558) and Elizabeth I (1558-1603) continued the policy, with Mary attempting to consolidate it by the Plantation of Ireland. In England she burned at the stake nearly 300 Protestant martyrs, an episode that helped to inspire the call to William and Mary 130 years later. Elizabeth was successful in restoring stability to Ireland by quelling civil war revolts during the second half of the 16th century and she established Trinity College Dublin in 1592. In the early 17th century James I countered further uprisings by *The Plantation of Ulster* with English and Scottish settlers; and with the *Plantation* begins the history of the Presbyterian Church in Ireland.

During more than a millennium since Patrick, true religious life was often at low ebb, with the church in a deplorable state. The 16th century Reformation had little impact. But God was about to intervene again.

2

The Presbyterian Church Begins

Although I was presented to several charges *in Scotland*, and had an invitation, and a great inclination, to go to *France*, yet the sovereign Lord, who hath determined the bounds of our habitation, thrust me over to *Ireland*, altogether contrary to my inclination; and thus it was.

... an invitation was sent to me from the Lord *Clanniboy*, patron of the kirk of *Bangor*, in the County of *Down* in *Ireland*, to be minister of that parish. ...

Such was my aversion to *Ireland*, that I prayed him [the bearer] to speak no more concerning it, and rashly repelled that motion with a flat denial, telling him that I had an invitation to *France*, which I intended now to embrace.

Yet, notwithstanding this precipitant answer, it was my request in my daily prayer to God, that He would be pleased to dispose of me according to the good pleasure of His will; and one day, being in prayer, I did find myself as sensibly rebuked as if one standing by me had audibly said, *Thou, fool, art thou taking the disposal of thyself, not submitting to Me; thou must either preach the gospel in Ireland, or no where at all.* In this way I was several times rebuked, so that I found myself bound in spirit to set my face towards a voyage to *Ireland*.

Robert Blair of Bangor

The First Ulster Awakening, The Irish Evangelical, February 1933

Since such a wealth of Irish Presbyterian Church histories is available it is needful only to sketch an outline here. Rev. W J Grier in his *Origin and Witness of the Irish Evangelical Church* introduces his overview with Thomas Witherow's summary.[4]

Introducing Presbyterian History

"In the Conclusion to his *Historical and Literary Memorials of Presbyterianism in Ireland* (published in 1879-1880) Prof. Thomas Witherow of Magee College, Londonderry, wrote: 'The history of the Presbyterian Church in Ireland ... may be divided into three periods of nearly a century each. The first of these, covering the 17th century, is the period in which Presbyterianism first appears, and, in spite of persecution and opposition, secures for itself a footing in the country: the second, coinciding with the 18th century, is a time of religious declension—declension in doctrinal purity, in zeal and in usefulness: the third, or 19th century, is a period of revival and recovery, characterised by growth in orthodoxy, in activity, and in every symptom of spiritual life.'"

The *Origin and Witness* proceeds: "In September, 1607, the Earls of Tyrconnell and Tyrone, believing the treasonable designs formed by them to have been discovered, fled to the Continent. Their estates, with those of Sir Cahir O'Dogherty, in the six Counties of Derry, Donegal, Tyrone, Fermanagh, Cavan and Armagh, amounting to half a million acres, were forfeited to the Crown. Shortly afterwards, Con O'Neill, who owned great tracts of Down and Antrim, being rebellious, forfeited a considerable part of his estates. There ensued the plantation of Ulster with English and Scottish settlers."

Early Blessing (1610-1630)

The Plantation settlers began to arrive in 1610, with the English locating mostly in the south and west of Ulster and the more numerous Scots in the northeast. A great influx from Scotland followed and within a few years much of the counties Antrim, Down and Londonderry were populated. Londoners built Londonderry and Coleraine; Sir Arthur Chichester acquired a large estate in Co Antrim. Those who came were generally poor and, like the ministers who accompanied them, had little desire for godliness or its way of life. However, in the good providence of God a group of able and godly ministers arrived from Scotland who became the founding fathers of the Irish Presbyterian Church. The first was Edward Brice who came in 1613 to Broadisland, near Carrickfergus. Others followed, such as Robert Cunningham to Holywood in 1615, Robert Blair to Bangor in 1623 and John Livingstone to Killinchy in 1630.

The *Origin and Witness* takes up the issue of the orthodoxy of these men: "The absurd assertion was long ago made by the biographer of Montgomery, Henry Cooke's 'New Light' opponent, that the founders of Irish Presbyterianism 'entered on their work on the strictest principles of non-subscription'. Irish Presbyterian Modernists have repeated this assertion, but it is utterly unfounded." The *Origin and Witness* goes on: "All the ministers at the first Presbytery formed at Carrickfergus in 1642 had subscribed to the old Scottish Confession of Faith.[3] ... Prof. Witherow declares that 'there was no discernible taint of false doctrine in the teaching of the ministers whom we regard as the fathers and founders of the Church. In Blair of Bangor or John Livingstone of Killinchy, one would have as much difficulty in finding a single speck of heresy as in Andrew Melville or in George Gillespie, in John Calvin or in Martin Luther.'"

God crowned the labours of these first ministers with notable success, giving the Church the first of its two phases of initial advance[6] – phases separated by a decade of hostility and persecution. There was revival along the Sixmilewater valley in Antrim during the years 1625-32, connected initially with the ministry of James Glendinning and then Josias Welch, grandson of John Knox, who resigned his chair at Glasgow University and came to Ireland at the invitation of Robert Blair around the beginning of this period. He ministered at Templepatrick. The renowned Antrim Monthly Meeting for the instruction of new converts began at this time.

Laud, Wentworth and Repression (1630-1642)

The Puritan movement had developed during the reign of Elizabeth I (1558-1603) and was at its height from 1603 to 1662.[7] William Laud came to prominence in the Church of England during the reign of James I (1603-1625), the first Stuart King of England,[8] whose 1605 Hampton Court Conference approved a new translation of Scripture – the King James Version of 1611. Laud was a prelate and chief advisor of James's successor, Charles I. The dominant figure of the period, he was the scourge of Puritan and Presbyterian non-conformity especially when Charles appointed him Archbishop of Canterbury in 1633. From the start of Charles's reign he set about coercing the church in England, Scotland and Ireland to conform to Episcopacy.

Following the famous preaching occasion at the Kirk of Shotts in June 1630 when hundreds were converted under the ministry of Robert Blair and John Livingstone, the Bishop of Glasgow charged both with religious incitement. He involved Dr Echlin, Bishop of Down, already displeased about the progress of the Presbyterian cause in Ulster and in September 1631, under pressure from the crown, Echlin suspended them from their ministry. This turned out to be the first in a progressive series of anti-Presbyterian measures. When Echlin quickly lifted his suspension of Blair and Livingstone, through the good offices of Archbishop Ussher, the Bishop of Glasgow pursued the matter with King Charles, whom Laud induced to re-suspend them for non-conformity in May 1632, along with Josias Welch and George Dunbar.

Wentworth, Earl of Strafford, appointed Lord-Deputy of Ireland in 1632, arrived in Dublin in 1633 and began to implement Laud's repressive anti-nonconformist agenda. He rejected the appeal to reinstate the suspended ministers, although this was granted for six months in 1634. One of his appointees, Dean Leslie of Down, deposed five ministers in 1636 for refusing to subscribe to new conformist Articles of Religion. Consequently, in 1636, the *Eaglewing*, with 140 refugees including Blair and Livingstone, sailed from Groomsport, Co Down, for New England, but returned two months later, battered by wind and wave. During the next two years, 1637-38, the deposed ministers returned to Scotland accompanied by many of their people. Among those who remained, many were punished with fines and imprisonment. The early advance of the Presbyterian Church in Ireland had been checked – but much worse was to come.

The Black Oath came into existence in Ireland in 1639. It required all Presbyterians over 16 to swear on the four Gospels their full submission to the King and his commands, and their repudiation of the National Covenant, under threat of rigorous punishment. Episcopal Clergy were required to read it from their pulpits and to submit a return of all Presbyterians in their parishes so that individual compliance could be tracked. The great majority of the Church stood firm, but fines, imprisonment and ejection from homes produced another evacuation to Scotland. Large numbers of those who remained crossed to Scotland at communion seasons.

Laud's Failure in Scotland

Meanwhile Laud was pursuing similar designs in Scotland. Tensions boiled over in 1637 when Charles ordered 'Laud's Liturgy', the English Prayer Book, to be introduced. There was the near-riot sparked by Jenny Geddes throwing her stool at the Dean of Edinburgh in St Giles Kirk, with the reputed words, *Villain! Dost thou say Mass at ma lug?* In 1638 Scotland expressed its united rejection of Episcopacy by renewing the *National Covenant*, committing themselves to the reformed faith and to the civil, ecclesiastical, and spiritual liberties secured under the Reformation settlement of 1581. They bound themselves to withstanding Episcopal impositions and to supporting the King in upholding religion, liberty and law. The General 'Covenanting' Assembly met in Glasgow in November 1638 and sat for a month. It abolished Episcopacy, re-established the Presbyterian structure, and enacted laws designed to secure the spiritual independence of the Church, and to encourage national godliness. Charles sent his forces north in 1639, but at Dunse Law he encountered a well-organised Covenanter army with the watchword, *For Christ's Crown and Covenant*, and found himself obliged to sue for peace.

Presbyterian Church in Ireland – Phase 2

Wentworth's time in Ireland was one of tyrannical misrule in both civil and ecclesiastical spheres. He alienated the population, bringing the people to breaking point. Charles recalled him in 1641, the Long Parliament impeached him and he was beheaded on 12 May 1641. Laud was impeached at the same time and beheaded in 1645. After Strafford's recall, passions accentuated by his administration boiled over in an outbreak of rebellion on 23 October 1641, led by Sir Phelim O'Neill. It was more successful in its early objectives in Ulster than it was in Dublin, surprising the Protestant settlers and killing many of them. Estimates of the numbers killed vary widely but modern calculations suggest about 12,000 out of a total plantation population of 40,000 died.[9] A Scottish army brought stability to Ulster in 1642 and, with the help of its Church of Scotland Chaplains, phase two of the establishment of the Irish Presbyterian Church began. The first Presbytery met in Carrickfergus on 10 June 1642, its commissioners from Regiment Sessions. The Church of Scotland sent ministers and a new lease of life appeared.

Civil War, Westminster and Cromwell (1642-1690)

Charles's post-Covenant attack on Scotland in 1639, along with the political and economic grievances he had inflicted on England, led to civil war in 1642. In 1643 the General Assembly of the Church of Scotland and the English Parliament, united in their suffering at the hands of the King, signed the *Solemn League and Covenant*. Its pledges included "the preservation of the Reformed religion in Scotland", "the reformation of religion in the kingdoms of England and Ireland" and to bring the three into "the nearest conjunction and conformity in religion". The monumental and lasting result of its implementation was the production of the Westminster Standards by the body of "learned, godly and judicious Divines", who met 1643-1649. 1649 became a significant year in other ways. In England the Parliamentarians had defeated the Royalists in the Civil War by 1645. They were divided into moderately royalist Presbyterians and Independents who were republican. Oliver Cromwell, an Independent, had led the Parliamentary forces, his 'Ironsides', and in December 1648 a unit of them led by Colonel Pride excluded from the Long Parliament Presbyterians and others who were opposed to the trial of King Charles. It became known as *Pride's Purge*. The residual body, the Rump Parliament, tried and executed Charles I in 1649 for "treason to his people", against which the Presbyterians of Ireland protested vehemently.

With the King's death, the decade of Commonwealth and Protectorate began and Cromwell became Lord Protector in 1653. But further significant events took place in 1649. The 1641 Rebellion in Ireland was still in progress and had spread to other areas of the country. The Civil Wars in England and the events of 1648-49 had occupied the English authorities, but that period having ended, Cromwell arrived with his army in Ireland in 1649. In September he attacked Drogheda, killing about 3,500 soldiers and civilians and the following month some 2,000 Irish soldiers were killed in his assault on Wexford. Of the killing in Ireland in the 1640s and 50s, 1641-42 in the north and 1649-50 in the south remain the indelible memories. Other histories say more about the hatred, cruelty, privations and shame that marked the period. Such was a feature of the century in which the Irish Presbyterian Church was established.[10]

Cromwell died in 1658 and, when his son could not maintain effective rule, the Stuart monarchy was restored under Charles II in 1660. The Act of Uniformity in 1662 resulted in *The Great Ejection* of about 2,000 Puritan ministers who would not reject the *Solemn League and Covenant* nor fully assent to the Book of Common Prayer. Charles's younger brother, James, a convert to Roman Catholicism, succeeded him in 1685. James's two adult daughters from his first marriage were Protestants and the eldest, Mary, was next in line to the throne. But the birth of a royal son, James Francis Edward,[11] in 1688, threatened the Anglican establishment.

Meanwhile, in 1677 Mary had married her cousin, William of Orange, a grandson of Charles I. William had already earned Protestant acclaim through clearing the invading Catholic forces of his arch-enemy Louis XIV of France from much of the Dutch Republic in 1673. So Tories and Whigs combined to invite him to England. He landed with his army in Torbay in Devon in 1688 and the English Parliament offered the throne to William and Mary in 1689 in 'The Glorious Revolution'. James II fled to France in 1688, but returned to Ireland with forces of Louis XIV of France. He failed to take Londonderry in 1689 and William's army defeated him at the Battle of the Boyne, near Drogheda, in 1690. William III reigned from 1689-1702, jointly with his wife Mary, 1689-1694.[12] The Church in Scotland had suffered much under Charles II and James II, and Scotland had given its voice to James's overthrow. King William's *Revolution Settlement* for Scotland in 1690 established the Westminster Confession as the Church's standards, abolished patronage, albeit temporarily, and reinstated the General Assembly.

So the 17th century saw the Presbyterian Church established in Ireland through the blessing of God and its faithfulness in the persecutions and civil conflicts it had to endure.

3

Doctrinal Surrender, Counteracting Grace

We believe in one God, the Father almighty, maker of all things visible and invisible; And in one Lord Jesus Christ, the Son of God, begotten of the Father, only-begotten, that is, of the substance of the Father, God of God, light of light, true God of true God, begotten not made, being of one substance with the Father, through Whom all things came into being, things in heaven and things on earth ... And in the Holy Spirit. ...

Extracts from the Nicene Creed, 325 AD

And in the Holy Spirit, the Lord and life-giver, Who proceeds from the Father [and the Son],[13] Who with the Father and the Son together is worshipped and glorified, Who spoke through the prophets ...

The Holy Spirit addition in the Niceno-Constantinopolitan Creed,

381 AD

Non-Subscription and Arianism

The 18th century witnessed heterodoxy, conflict and division in the Synod of Ulster. Subscription of the Westminster Confession of Faith lapsed and with it came the development of Arianism—the non-Trinitarian system that denies the deity of the Lord Jesus Christ and of the Holy Spirit. Irish Presbyterian historians acknowledge the fall from confessional orthodoxy during the 18th century as the proximate cause of the subsequent events, although not all interpret it in the same way. However, in the mercy of God Ireland shared in the blessings of other shores.

Orthodoxy Reigns

Dr James Seaton Reid (1798-1851) published his *History of the Presbyterian Church in Ireland*, in three volumes, 1834, 1837 and 1853. It covered more than the first two centuries of Church life, 1603-1841, taking it forward chronologically in chapters with an average span of less than eight years. His assessment of the Church at the beginning of the 18th century is remarkably uplifting:

> Hitherto the Presbyterian Church in Ulster had peacefully reposed upon the same basis, and under the same standards, as the parent Church in Scotland. Both ministers and people were Presbyterians of the old school, warmly attached to all its principles and usages, and, for the most part, thoroughly instructed in the controversies by which their Church had from time to time been tried. The ministers of the Irish synod, many of whom had been licentiates of the Scottish Church, and nearly all of them educated at her universities, had cordially embraced the same theological doctrines with their Scottish brethren, and in their sessions, presbyteries, and synods, had closely followed the same system of discipline and government. The standard of ministerial attainments since the Revolution[14] had been gradually rising, and stood higher at this period than it did during the remainder of the century. The people were carefully instructed in catechetical doctrine, were well versant in the Scriptures, and heartily approved of the Westminster Confession of Faith, as faithfully embodying the teaching of that infallible standard. At the commencement of the eighteenth century, not the slightest symptom had appeared of any departure from these doctrinal views, or of any alienation from the constitutional principles of Presbyterianism as established and practised in Scotland.[15]

The Belfast Society and 'New Light'

However, in 1702 Rev. Thomas Emlyn of Dublin affirmed his Arian views to an enquiry of his fellow ministers in the city and they forthwith removed him from the ministry. Subscription of the Westminster Confession became mandatory in 1705, replacing the existing practice of verbal assent, but the same year saw the formation of *The Belfast Society*, drawing a change in tone from Seaton Reid:

> It was not long, however, until the same latitudinarian notions on the inferiority of dogmatic belief, and the nature of religious liberty, which had obtained currency on the Continent and in England, appeared in Ireland. ...[16]

> In this society were first promulgated many opinions hitherto new in Ireland, which, being at variance with both the doctrine and constitution of the Presbyterian Church, naturally excited, so soon as they became known, much attention, and gradually created no little disaffection and alarm. These opinions did not directly impugn any of the leading doctrines of the Gospel, as embodied in the Church's confession of faith, but they tended to undermine the entire system of a sinner's acceptance as taught therein, by placing that acceptance mainly on sincerity, by inculcating the innocency of error when not wilful, and by undervaluing all belief in positive doctrines as uncertain, or, at all events, as non-essential. In reference to ecclesiastical discipline, the members of the society taught, among other things, that the Church had no right to require candidates for the ministry to subscribe a confession of faith prepared by any man or body of men, and that such a required subscription was a violation of the right of private judgment, and inconsistent with Christian liberty and true Protestantism.[17]

Rev. Thomas Hamilton in his *History of the Irish Presbyterian Church*, which he prepared as a concise handbook in comparison to Dr Reid's monumental work, presents the same picture of the change that came over the church at the beginning of the 18th century:

> IN the beginning of the eighteenth century a cloud appeared on the Church's sky, which, though apparently no bigger than a man's hand, was destined in the end to breed much mischief. Hitherto the Synod's troubles had all come from without. Her own ministers and people had stood firmly and compactly together, one in doctrine, as in polity and worship. This happy condition of things was now to be changed, and changed in a very simple way.[18]

Hamilton was also referring to the emergence of the *Belfast Society*, the forum of the advocates of non-subscription of the Westminster Confession of Faith, whose views came to be known as 'New Light', and his synopsis of their position closely follows that of Dr Reid.

The Belfast Society rapidly grew in influence, giving rise to a series of conflicts with the orthodox section of the church during the early 1720s. In December 1719 Rev. John Abernethy, Antrim, delivered a sermon at a meeting of the Society, with the title, *Religious Obedience founded on Personal Persuasion*. From this address grew the 'New Light' descriptive title of the movement's views, and it proved to be the catalyst for a controversy of seven years' duration. In June 1720 the Synod passed *The Pacific Act* with the objective of bringing the protagonists to a workable compromise. The Act declared the Synod's loyalty to the Westminster Confession and Catechisms and advocated adherence by all parties. But it also gave liberty to any who objected to phrases in the standards to substitute their own, provided in the Presbytery's judgement the substitute expressions were "consistent with the substance of the doctrine" and the person was considered sound in the faith. Thus a diluted Formula of Subscription undermined the subscription's effect.

Non-Subscribers and the Presbytery of Antrim

There was not long to wait for a test case. The following month Rev. Samuel Halliday, a *Belfast Society* member, was installed in Belfast on the basis of a substitute declaration that the majority of the Presbytery accepted. The disregard of the minority view became a contentious issue and as a result the members of the majority party in Presbytery were censured over the conduct of the Presbytery business. However, Halliday would still not subscribe[19] and the matter was referred to successive Synods. The Synod of 1721 adopted voluntary subscription of the Westminster standards and although the *Belfast Society* objected, the vast majority present subscribed, dividing the house into Subscribers and Non-Subscribers.

The Advance of Arianism

As the battle raged on the Synod of 1725 segregated all Non-Subscribers into the Presbytery of Antrim and, in 1726, separated the Presbytery of Antrim from the Synod altogether, bringing that phase of the conflict to a conclusion. However, the separation related essentially to church courts. 'Antrim' ministers could still preach throughout the church and 'New Light' sympathisers remained in the Synod. But a "little leaven leavens the whole lump." (1 Cor 5.6) Thomas Hamilton noted that the 18th century gave rise to "a time of deadness" all over Europe and that the local scene was marked by the steady advance of 'New Light' views:

> ... and the Church over here in Ireland did not escape the prevalent infection. The Westminster Confession of Faith began to be thrust more and more into the background. The practice of requiring subscription to it from licentiates and ministers fell into abeyance. Most of the Synod's theological students received their education at Glasgow College, and here the prevailing influences were all on the side of moderatism, or something worse. Professor Simson, who occupied the chair of Divinity in Glasgow for several years, was a man deeply imbued with the prevailing spirit. Dr. Leechman, who afterwards filled the same chair, is believed to have been at heart an Arian.
>
> With such professors poisoning, at its fountainhead, the stream of the ministry, it is not to be wondered at that the pulpits of the Synod of Ulster began to give a very uncertain sound on the great verities of the faith, and in some cases to ignore them altogether. Little by little the orthodox band, which had turned a stern face towards non-subscription, waned and dwindled away; and as the old heads disappeared, and a new generation arose trained under Hutcheson and Simson or Leechman, the former majority sank into a minority which was powerless against the rising tide of error, until in the end 'New Light' principles gained a complete ascendancy. Life seemed now to leave the Synod almost entirely. There was none of that 'outward propagation' of the faith which is as essential to the life of a Church as 'inward preservation.'[20]

Rev. David Stewart, Muckamore, in *A Short History of the Presbyterian Church in Ireland*, 1936, accepted the Church's widespread departure from Westminster subscription during the 18th and early 19th centuries, but with an approach characteristic of the broadening church:

SUBSCRIPTION to the Westminster Confession had been the law of the Church since the year 1705, but the law had been generally disregarded. Even after the year 1726, in which the non-subscribing Presbytery of Antrim had been excluded from communion with subscribers in the judicatories of the Church, non-subscription had continued; and in the year 1821, when the Arian controversy began, nine of the fourteen Presbyteries of the Synod were in practice, if not in principle, non-subscribing. For almost one hundred years the brethren, holding firmly their own principles and respecting the principles of those who differed from them, maintained the unity of the Spirit in the bonds of peace. But for better or worse this peace was not destined to last.[21]

Blessings from Without

However, the 18th century was not a time of unrelieved decline in Ireland. It saw powerful evangelical revival in England mainly under the ministries of the Wesleys and of Whitefield, and in the goodness of God people in parts of Ireland shared in its blessings.

Cennick, Wesley and Whitefield

John Cennick was born in December 1718 in Reading. After strong, prolonged conviction of sin he found joy and peace in believing when he was 19. He joined the Methodists, and John Wesley appointed him to a teaching post in Kingswood, Bristol, when he was 20. But after accepting a stand-in preaching engagement he added regular preaching to his duties at the school. When Wesley parted company with him over doctrinal issues, Cennick joined forces with George Whitefield. In 1740 he was invited to Wiltshire to what became the first of the three great missionary assignments of his short life, the other two being in Ireland. He laboured in Wiltshire until 1746, subjected to the opposition and persecution he had tasted in Bristol and which would mark the remaining years of his ministry. When Whitefield went to America in 1744 for four years he left Cennick in charge of the Tabernacle in Moorfields, London, and with the oversight of his network of Societies. But Cennick was not equipped to handle the difficulties that arose and moved away to join the Moravians in 1745.

Two young men from Ireland, who heard him preach in Whitefield's Tabernacle in 1744, invited him to Dublin. The weather turned him back the following year, but he arrived in 1746 and began a ministry in Skinner's Alley Baptist Church. Although threatened by persecution and mob violence he was used by God in a remarkable way and numbers in the church rose from very few in 1746 to 520 in 1747. He records preaching to crowds of over 1000.

In 1746 Joseph Deane, a shopkeeper in Ballymena, heard Cennick in Dublin and invited him north, but he met strong resistance during this initial visit. Two years later, in 1748, Deane again invited him to preach at a series of meetings, an invitation that led to a seven-year Gospel ministry based at Ballymena, the main one of his life. Cennick did not spare himself, preaching, whatever the weather, in barns, mills, cock-pits (enclosed spaces for cock fights) and in the open air, walking from venue to venue when lack of funds made it necessary. The Lord attended his preaching with outstanding blessing and he set up some 40 societies and built 10 churches in Co Antrim and further afield. He also founded the first Moravian settlement at Gracehill, Ballymena in 1749 and in the same year the Moravian Church ordained him as a deacon. Poor health cut short his ministry and he returned to England in 1755 where he died on 4 July, aged 36. He is perhaps best known for his hymns, such as *Lo! He comes with clouds descending* and *Children of the heav'nly King*.

> Cennick became not only one of Whitefield's closest friends and, for some time, his chief assistant, but a preacher of such power as to stand, in that day of great preachers, in the rank of the first four or five. … Cennick later joined the Moravians, under whom he served with great heroism and wondrous success in Ireland. The eighteenth-century Revival produced no more beautiful and holy life than that of John Cennick, and it is a sad loss to the Christian world that his career has been so flagrantly overlooked.[22]

Before the end of Cennick's ministry Wesley and Whitefield also became instruments of revival in Ireland. Wesley visited in 1747, the first of more than 40 visits, and took over the Church in Skinner's Alley, Dublin, making it the first of his Methodist congregations in Ireland. Soon, Whitefield gave support to the persecution-threatened work of the Wesleys and was a means of reviving it. He first came in 1751 and preached about a dozen times in Cork, on one occasion to a congregation of 10,000, before moving north. Like Cennick and Wesley he ran into opposition from violent mobs that sometimes reached life-threatening proportions, particularly on his 1757 visit to Dublin, but great blessing attended his preaching.

The Secession Church

Whilst there were notable outbreaks of revival under the Cennick, Wesley and Whitefield ministries in parts of Ireland in the 18th century, the period was marked by a significant development in the denominational field. While the Synod of Ulster was winning battles but losing the Arian war, another body known as the Secession Church was coming to prominence.

The first Seceder ministers were not men who had left the Irish Presbyterian Church to set up an alternative denomination. They came from Scotland, from a Secession Church that had recently come into existence. Again there was a background. Robert Buchanan, DD, in *The Ten Years' Conflict, being the History of the Disruption of the Church of Scotland*, borrows Dr Chalmers' expression to describe the 18th century in Scotland as "the dark age of the Scottish Church". The Act of Union of 1707, uniting the parliaments of England and Scotland, guaranteed the maintenance of Presbyterian church-government in Scotland. Patronage, a system that gave landowning nobles, backed by the state, the power to nominate candidates for church ministerial vacancies, had been abolished in

1649, "by which this last fetter was struck from the church's neck."[23] But by the Patronage Act of 1712, just five years after the Act of Union, Queen Anne's parliament re-imposed patronage on the Scottish church in violation of its Act of Union pledge to the church's spiritual independence.

Little changed for 20 or 30 years because of the strength of opposition to patronage on the ground, but a 'Moderate' party had been growing in influence in the church courts:

> The party which grew up in the manner now explained came in process of time to be distinguished by the name of "Moderate;" a good name misapplied to designate a very pernicious thing. "A moderate divine," said Sir Richard Hill, who seems to have thoroughly comprehended the practical meaning of the term, "is one who has a very moderate share of zeal for God. Consequently, a moderate divine contents himself with a moderate degree of labour in his Master's vineyard."[24]

But the Scottish church experienced the delayed effect of the 1712 Act when the landowner-state patrons began to find support among the Moderates, and the system gained momentum. Several secessions from the Church of Scotland in the 18th century ensued. Ebenezer Erskine, minister of Stirling, led the first of them and, with three other ministers, formed the Associate Presbytery in 1733, later known as the *Original Secession Church*.[25] But the growing influence of Moderatism, not patronage, was at the root of the 1733 division. Professor R F G Holmes comments, "The issue of lay patronage was the occasion rather than the cause of the secession", but his account of the proceedings shows it to have been no small occasion![26]

The 18th century non-subscription controversy in Ireland had alerted vacant congregations in Scotland to exercise greater care in examining candidates. In 1741 the people of Lylehill, Co Antrim, who belonged to the Templepatrick congregation, applied to the Associate Presbytery in Scotland to be taken under its care as a new congregation. Several reasons are adduced to account for the Lylehill application, such as distance from Templepatrick, but a Lylehill grievance about the lease of a farm to the minister or his son by a Templepatrick elder when a Lylehill man was very keen to have it, is at the heart of the problem. In any event Thomas Hamilton affirms that it was not due to "the prevalence of unsoundness in the faith" in the ministry at Templepatrick. Rev. William Livingstone had strongly opposed the *Belfast Society*. So Rev. Isaac Patton of the Scottish Secession Church was ordained at Lylehill in 1746 and was soon extending his ministry to congregations at Lisburn and Belfast.

As the resources of the Associate Synod in Scotland developed, it sent more ministerial help across the Irish Sea. But in 1747 the Secession Church in Scotland split into two Synods, Burghers and Antiburghers, over the Burgess Oath. The Oath required those elected to serve in some of the Scottish Burghs, such as civil magistrates, to swear their lifelong commitment to the true religion "presently professed within this realm" and authorised by its legislation. The split registered conflicting interpretations as to whether the wording of the oath amounted to swearing of allegiance to the Established Church. The Ulster brethren replicated this breach, with two parallel Synods, even though the Oath had no jurisdiction in Ireland.[27]

Dr David Stewart of Cregagh Presbyterian Church, Belfast, the historian of the Secession Church, regards the hostility of the Synod of Ulster as the prime obstacle the Secession Church had to face. Relationships between ministers of the Presbyterian and Seceder churches were soon strained, producing polemic sermons, public debates and 'pamphlets' that had featured in the non-subscribing controversy in the 1720s. But he also acknowledges that the Seceders made their own contribution to the problem in the formation of two Secession Synods after the Burgess Oath breach of 1747. "For upwards of seventy years the Burghers and Antiburghers stood apart, nursing angry feelings and endeavouring to thwart each other's purposes."[28] Of the triangular dimension he added: "Both stood apart from the Synod of Ulster and from each other. All three Synods were mutually suspicious and judged each other with asperity. Their interests clashed, and for many years they looked upon each other as an oppressive evil."[29] Because it viewed the Secession as damaging to the peace and unity of the church in Scotland, the Synod of Ulster in 1747 even issued a 'Serious Warning' to its people denouncing the Secession Church, evidence perhaps that it had quickly become a force to be reckoned with.

In spite of the hostility and tension, the Secession Church in Ulster grew apace and numbered some 150 congregations within 100 years. Its Burgher and Anitiburgher Synods united in 1818. David Stewart, Cregagh, provided this assessment:

> The numerous adherents who gathered round the Secession preachers, in the fields in summer and in barns in winter, were, for the most part, small farmers, labourers, artisans, and tradesmen of the humbler sort. Very few of that rich and influential class, who would carry the movement to immediate success, entered into fellowship with them. Like their Master, the Secession preachers might have said "unto the poor the gospel is preached," and it might have been said of them, as it was of Him, "The common people heard them gladly."
>
> These poor and common people constituted an ecclesiastical organization which marked the beginning of a new era in the religious life of Ulster. The Seceders revived in the minds of the people those evangelical truths which were fast becoming obscured by the moderate doctrines which prevailed.[30]

Another David Stewart, minister at Muckamore, records a qualified acknowledgement:

> It must be said that if the Seceding preachers who were sent from Scotland did not foment strife, they took full advantage of it to establish preaching stations … The Seceding ministers were not always guided by the wisdom from above,

nor by the love that never faileth; but their labours awakened the consciences of many, and, on the whole, exerted a most salutary influence.[31]

However, William Thomas Latimer is prominent among the Seceder-friendly historians in his sense of indebtedness to the Secession Church:

> The Secession Church became at this period a means of establishing many new congregations where they were required, of leading the more zealous out of the Synod, of keeping them pure from generation to generation, and of bringing back their children's children better Presbyterians than those who had been taken away.[32]

The Reformed Presbyterian Church of Ireland

The 18th century saw the emergence of the Reformed Presbyterian Church.[33] Like Irish Presbyterians generally, it has had a long Scottish connection, starting with the ministers and people who came as part of the Plantation of Ulster in the early 17th century.

Many in the Church of Scotland were satisfied with the 1690 settlement of William III that established the Westminster Confession as the Church's standards, abolished patronage and reinstated the General Assembly. But the Scottish Covenanters were not. They had drawn up and signed the *National Covenant* in 1638 in defiance of Charles I who was attempting to impose a new liturgy and Prayer Book on the Church of Scotland in breach of existing covenants agreed by Church and State. The 1638 Covenant abolished Episcopacy and re-established the Presbyterian system; it enacted laws designed to secure the spiritual independence of the Church and to encourage national godliness. From it dates the Blue Banner with its declaration, *For Christ's Crown and Covenant*. Then in 1643 the General Assembly of the Church of Scotland and the English Parliament signed the *Solemn League and Covenant* pledging the preservation of the reformed faith in Scotland and reformation of the church in England and Ireland. An enduring result was the Westminster Standards produced between 1643 and 1649.

The Scottish Covenanters believed in the continuing obligation of these two Covenants, and the specific recognition of the Kingship of Christ over State as well as Church that they stood for. So they found their omission from the 1690 Settlement unacceptable. Consequently, in 1743, they inaugurated the Reformed Presbyterian Church. Those in Ireland, who shared the same view, developed separately from the Ulster and Secession Synods. They were quite dependent on visiting Scottish ministers from 1696 until 1757, but constituted their own 'Reformed Presbytery' in 1763, followed by a Synod in 1811.

So, to borrow Thomas Witherow's expression again, the 18th century was "a time of religious declension—declension in doctrinal purity, in zeal and in usefulness." But God sustained his work by bringing to the people gracious influences from England and Scotland, a token that better days lay ahead.

4

Counter-Offensive, Returning Life

The church has regarded expressions like "Trinity," "Person," etc., as necessary to unmask false teachers.

However, the novelty of words of this sort (if such it must be called) becomes especially useful when the truth is to be asserted against false accusers, who evade it by their shifts. Of this today we have abundant experience in our great efforts to rout the enemies of pure and wholesome doctrine. With such crooked and sinuous twisting these slippery snakes glide away unless they are boldly pursued, caught, and crushed. Thus men of old, stirred up by various struggles over depraved dogmas, were compelled to set forth with consummate clarity what they felt, lest they leave any devious shift to the impious, who cloaked their errors in layers of verbiage. Because he could not oppose manifest oracles, Arius confessed that Christ was God and the Son of God, and, as if he had done what was right, pretended some agreement with the other men. Yet in the meantime he did not cease to prate that Christ was created and had a beginning, as other creatures.

Calvin: *Institutes of the Christian Religion.* 1.13.4

The Battle Joined with Arianism

The Arian influence that the 'Antrim' segregation, 1725-26, was intended to quarantine continued to spread through large sections of the Church during the course of the century. "Thus it was," says Thomas Witherow, "that for 60 years after the separation of the Presbytery of Antrim, the Church went from bad to worse, until in the end the Presbytery of Antrim was perhaps as orthodox as the Synod which cast it out."[34]

Henry Cooke

Henry Cooke was born near Maghera, Co Londonderry, in 1788[35] into an Irish Presbyterian family. In 1802 he began his studies at Glasgow University where the theology courses bore the marks of "the dark age of the Scottish Church", as Dr Chalmers described the 18th century. However, he had learned the Confession of Faith and Shorter Catechism from his mother and came through university with his commitment to their theology unscathed. After an assistantship in Duneane, near Toomebridge, Co Antrim, from 1808-1810, he was minister of Donegore, Parkgate, Templepatrick from January 1811 until 1818. James Seaton Reid became his successor. Cooke's next charge was Killyleagh, Co Down and his period of ministry here, 1818-29, coincided with the key years of the Arian controversy.

The First Battle

In 1821, about three years after Cooke's induction to Killyleagh, Rev. John Smethurst, of the English Unitarian Fund, came on a preaching tour of Ulster, at the invitation of local Arians, to promote their teachings in the face of renewed evangelical activity in Ulster. Cooke was present at his Killyleagh meeting, and at its conclusion promised those assembled to refute Smethurst's arguments from his own pulpit on the following Sunday. The power and effectiveness of Cooke's rebuttal that Sunday and the popular acclaim with which it was received encouraged him to track Smethurst from venue to venue, delivering the same refutation, and precipitating the conclusion of the Smethurst tour. So in 1821 the decisive battle with Arianism had begun and with it Henry Cooke had come to public prominence. It is difficult to underestimate its significance, not just because the Arians had been caught in their own net but also because for Cooke it was God's crash course that prepared him for the pre-eminent phase of his life's work. In the providence of God it is also true that "Cometh the hour, cometh the man."[36] Finlay Homes suggests that it was the Smethurst encounters that established the essentials of Cooke's creed.[37]

The Belfast Academical Institution

Meanwhile, another battlefront was looming. Irish Presbyterian students had traditionally been trained in Scotland but there was a long-standing desire in the Church for a training facility at home. A section of the Church had hoped for academic training for the students for the ministry in an upgraded Belfast Academy, founded in 1785 in Academy Street, where Rev. William Bruce, minister of Belfast 'First' (New Light) congregation, was Headmaster. But many more welcomed the opening of the Belfast Academical Institution school in 1814, followed by its collegiate department for students for the ministry in 1815. Both the Synod of Ulster and the Burgher Synod had agreed to recognise the General Certificate of Education as equivalent to a university degree, subject to the appointment of Professors whom the College had invited the Synods to appoint.

However, there was political opposition to such an Institution-Synod link. The Act of Union had taken place in 1800 and, although the Institution was non-sectarian, the founders of the Institution were generally not of unionist persuasion.[38] Consequently, representatives of the Crown were concerned about the influence the Institution might have on a major Protestant body, whose direct allegiance they were keen to nurture. This opposition found support within the Synod too, and as the maintenance of the *regium donum* (the royal grant to Presbyterian ministers in Ireland) became involved, the question of independence of church and state widened the debate. But the Synod of Ulster proceeded with the Institution arrangement and from 1815-1853 the Presbyterian Church trained the majority of its students there.

Standing Alone
In October 1821, the Institution had appointed Rev. William Bruce as Professor of Hebrew and Greek. He was from the Arian constituency, son of Rev. William Bruce of the Belfast Academy, and this united the Arians behind the Institution. The Bruce appointment triggered opposition to the Synod-Institution arrangement on theological grounds, with Cooke warning the Newry Synod in 1822 of the heightened influence of Arianism at the Institution. But he found a spring tide of opinion running against him. At that point Cooke stood alone, with the key evangelical figures among his opposition. Cooke was certainly not aligned with the leaders of the Institution politically and, although it would be hazardous to maintain that his own political views had no influence whatever in moulding his opposition to the Synod link, it is certain that his motivation was theological rather than political. Driven by his sense of calling he was determined to see the removal of Arianism from the Synod and from the Institution, should its link with Synod continue. To achieve his goal he brought his campaign to successive Synods from 1822 and at the same time appealed directly to the people. "The strategy which he had learned in his campaign against Smethurst was repeated as he reached out to popular opinion by peripatetic preaching. Friend and foe testify to the ardour with which he travelled throughout Ulster, rousing his church against the dangers of Arianism."[39]

Cooke was of course aware that the divinity chairs at the Institution were Synod appointments and that Arian personnel were currently in the school or academic departments. The fact that the Bruce appointment had brought the Arians on board was significant too. To Cooke there was an important sense in which what was true of a part was true of the identity of the whole. In modern terms it was part of the Institution's brand. Cooke did not want any association with Arianism. He was contending for a training college that would be free from any connection, direct or indirect, with error.

In 1824 Bruce's father, William Bruce Snr, published a book of sermons, asserting in the preface that Arian views were making quiet progress throughout the synod of Ulster. This was a bold move, but it heightened the Arian debate in the public arena, where Cooke was a powerful player. It was also significant that the 1824 Synod refuted Bruce's claim and expressed its opposition to Arianism with unaccustomed conviction. The tide had begun to turn and Cooke was no longer standing alone.

Henry Cooke and Henry Montgomery

Cooke gave evidence to "The Commissioners of Irish Education Inquiry" in 1824 into the state of education in Ireland. His assertions of Arian influence in both Synod and Institution at points of his evidence fuelled huge controversy in church and press when the Report was published early in 1827. At the 1827 Synod at Strabane, Cooke moved that since the number of Arians in the Synod could not be determined at the Commission, which was interested to do so, the Court should do so by applying a test to its members. The test would be the answer to question 6 of the Shorter Catechism: "There are three persons in the Godhead; the Father, the Son, and the Holy Ghost; and these three are one God, the same in substance, equal in power and glory." Henry Montgomery, minister at Dunmurry, Headmaster of the English Department of the Institution school, and leader of the 'New Light' movement opposed Cooke's motion. With brilliant oratory that gripped the attention of the house he argued against the validity of confessions, but after a debate of two days Cooke's motion carried by a massive majority. Only two ministers registered themselves as Arians! The omens for Arianism were not good.

Public controversy over the Arian issue continued throughout the following year, and intensified as the Cookstown Synod of June 1828 approached. There, as the battle moved towards its climax, Cooke presented an eight-part motion requiring in particular that Synod appoint Committees to establish the commitment of students to the Westminster Confession, before and after training. He specified the Trinity, original sin, justification by faith and regeneration by the Holy Spirit for inclusion in the pre-training tests. Other parts of the motion tested future Confessional adherence. Montgomery again opposed with another outstanding performance, but the motion carried with a 70% majority, thus barring to Arians the future path to the ministry. For the Arians, the writing was on the wall and Hamilton captures its tremendous significance with a lovely turn of phrase: "Victory had now unmistakably seated herself on the banners of Cooke."[40]

The Synod met in Lurgan in June 1829 against the background of another controversy at the Institution. Mr John Ferrie of the Church of Scotland had been unexpectedly preferred for a vacant chair to Rev. James Carlisle of Dublin, an able exponent of the Deity of Christ, and Arian influence was suspected of being at the root of it. Cooke brought it to the floor of the Synod and there followed the most famous of the Cooke-Montgomery encounters. Such was Montgomery's eloquence, and the apparent irrefutability of his quality research, as he accused Cooke of statements on the Ferrie case that contradicted his evidence before the Education Commission four years before, that Cooke's supporters feared the worst as he rose to give his unprepared reply. But engaging the house for two hours, Cooke won the day, as in his own famous words he proceeded to "dash to atoms the atrocious calumny with the talisman of truth." Montgomery's accusations lay in ruins and his finest hour had become the death knell for the Arian cause.[41]

Separation

The Synod met again at Cookstown in August to deal with its other business, but only Rev. William Porter of the Unitarian party attended and this was to present their 'Remonstrance' against the relevant decisions of Synod. The Synod refused to repeal them and terms of separation were soon agreed. The Unitarians constituted themselves as the "Remonstrant Synod" which later became a constituent of the Non-Subscribing Presbyterian Church.

David Stewart's version of the famous Cookstown Synod of 1828 when Cooke and Montgomery clashed over Cooke's motion that all ministry candidates holding Arian views and denying certain other key doctrines be excluded, which Cooke won by a majority of 70%, was this:

> The strength of the opposition vote is accounted for by the fact that there was a considerable number of orthodox ministers who saw the danger of the course favoured by the Synod, and dreaded a schism. They felt that the orthodoxy of the Church could be secured, and the congregations of the unorthodox ministers preserved for an orthodox ministry, if these ministers were suffered to die out, and subscription to the Westminster Confession made absolute, and without exception.
>
> It must be a matter of lasting regret that this wise course was not followed, but the extremists had their way, and seventeen congregations and their ministers left the Synod and formed themselves into a separate body, known as the Remonstrant Synod. A great number of the members of these congregations were sound in the faith, but with characteristic Presbyterian loyalty they clung to their ministers; and their children's children are still lost to the Church of their fathers.[42]

This is a shallow assessment. In advocating the 'run-off' of non-subscribing ministers Stewart has failed to recognise that when the 'Non Subscribers' were quarantined in the Antrim Presbytery in 1725 it did not terminate the dissemination of their views. And what was the nature of the soundness in view when congregations who are "sound in the faith" cling to ministers, their teachers, who clearly are not? Compare the verdict of Seaton Reid:

> The annals of the synod of Ulster, for the hundred years prior to the Remonstrant separation, singularly display the spirit and tendency of Unitarianism. It entered "privily" into the Irish Presbyterian Church, like the pestilence that "walketh in darkness," and its virulence soon appeared in the traces of its desolation. Wherever it spread its infection, piety withered and died; and the deserted meeting-house proclaimed that "the glory" had departed. Under the pretence of contending against the imposition of creeds, it contrived to conceal its own creed from the people. According to the statement of one of its advocates, the year 1824 witnessed "the first printed avowal and defence" of its principles among the Presbyterians of the North of Ireland. And experience has demonstrated that it is entirely unsuited to the actual state of man. Other forms of error may captivate the senses and administer a measure of false comfort, but Unitarianism can neither satisfy the reason, nor light up the imagination, nor pacify the conscience. As, with the eye of scepticism, it surveys the glorious truths of revelation, it scarcely ever changes its frigid countenance; and, as it fails to catch the spirit of the holy oracles, no wonder that it cannot impart either the "faith, nothing wavering," or the hope that "maketh not ashamed." It is, in fact, little better than a species of sublimated deism, and it must be peculiarly offensive to Him on whose head are "many crowns," as it at once degrades His character, and makes light of His salvation.[43]

Returning Life

Cooke to Belfast

Cooke moved from Killyleagh to May Street, Belfast, in 1829 to a new church specially erected. In 1829 the Synod of Ulster started a new periodical, *The Orthodox Presbyterian*, which ran until 1940. Dr Cooke was one of its main promoters and a regular contributor. In 1829 a body of non-subscribers in the Clough, Co Down, congregation seceded to the Arian Presbytery of Antrim, taking the building with them. The Presbytery soon placed the congregation back in the Synod of Ulster and the building was recovered by legal process in 1836. Henry Cooke was prominent in the battle. In 1831 the Government's introduced a new system of National Education. The synod of Ulster, led by Cooke, opposed it and achieved a settlement after a decade. Similar battles for truth and Church continued throughout his life.

General Assembly, Foreign Missions and Assembly's College

W J Grier's conclusion concerning the Arian controversy was this:

> In 1835 subscription to the Westminster Confession was made absolute on the part of all licentiates, ministers and elders. After the purge of the Unitarians there was now no obstacle to the Union of the two Synods, and so in 1840 the

Synod of Ulster and the Secession Synod united to form the General Assembly. Almost the first act of the newly-constituted Assembly was the establishment of a Foreign Mission and its first foreign Missionaries were set apart to labour in India. In 1853 the Assembly's College was formally opened by the celebrated Dr. D'Aubigné of Geneva, Dr. Cooke, being appointed its first president.[44] These were the days of returning life—the days of the Evangelical Revival—after the deadness of the eighteenth century."[45]

Cooke was the first Moderator of the General Assembly 1841-42 but withdrew from the Assembly 1843-47 because he was opposed in principle to a church court passing political resolutions – in this case for better representation of Presbyterians in the legislature of the country. He resigned his pastorate in 1848 after his appointment as President of the Church's Divinity Faculty and Professor of Sacred Rhetoric and Catechetics in 1847, but continued as stated pulpit supply, at the congregation's request, until his retirement from Church and College in 1867. The founding of Assembly's College in 1853 was the fulfilment of his 1822 objective of an orthodox seminary.

The Irish Famine and Irish Church Missions
The 1840s which saw such change for good in the church, were also the years of the Irish Famine, one of the great human tragedies of the century and one of the most important events in Irish history. The people of Ireland had become highly dependent on the potato and when the crop failed between 1845 and 1848 the effects were overwhelming. By about mid-century two million people, a quarter of the population, had died from starvation or disease or had emigrated to North America or Great Britain. But in the providence of God the famine was instrumental in the rapid progress of the Anglican (Church of Ireland) Irish Church Missions (ICM), founded in 1849. The western province of Connaught was badly affected by the famine and it was there that the ICM work was first concentrated, preaching, building schools and churches, training ministers, colporteurs and male and female Scripture Readers. Such was God's blessing on the work that it is often called the "Second Reformation".

The 1859 Revival
Revival came 1859 in which 100,000 new members were added in one year to the Presbyterian Church alone. However, it did not arise spontaneously out of the new condition of the church. It followed a campaign of concerted prayer, which in turn arose from recognition that revival was the need of the hour.[46]

The Cooke Legacy
Cooke died on 13 December 1868 aged 80, having completed 60 years in the ministry. In 1876 a statue was erected by public subscription in College Square East looking along Wellington Place towards the city centre. It replaced a bronze statue by Belfast-born Patrick MacDowell of Frederick Richard Chichester, Earl

of Belfast (1827-1853) which was relocated to the Belfast Museum and later to the City Hall. The Cooke statue inherited its predecessor's popular designation, 'The Black Man', and is a well-known Belfast landmark.

But Cooke does not secure unbroken acclaim among historians. On the cover flap of Finlay Holmes' *Henry Cooke,* Cooke is described as "the great architect of modern Irish Presbyterianism and founding father of Ulster Unionism". The blurb also notes that Cooke had polarised some opinions: "The official Victorian biography by his son-in-law is an extended eulogy and, at the other extreme, some modern debunkers have dismissed his great crusade for evangelicalism and orthodoxy in his church rather too easily as a mere front for his political and personal objectives." Holmes also sees what many would regard as a flaw in Cooke's psyche, as he emerged a champion of orthodoxy from the events at Killyleagh in 1821:

> Cooke had now tasted the excitement of public controversy and the heady wine of popular acclaim and he was to remain an addict for the remainder of his life. Almost by accident he had stumbled upon a way of reaching and influencing public opinion, by peripatetic preaching. It was a method he employed repeatedly over the years to win support for the cause he adopted. He found, too, that there was a popular response to the message he proclaimed.[47]

However, 100 years later Henry Cooke became a role model for the founding father of the Irish Evangelical Church, James Hunter. Hunter kept in his papers a student testimonial that Cooke had written for a congregation. Cooke's determined leadership in the battle for orthodoxy and his methodology in taking his message directly to the people from a point when recalcitrance marked church courts and left him standing alone, was persuasive for Hunter who saw himself compelled by a parallel situation. It is likely also that he cherished hopes of a comparable outcome. But opponents saw the Cooke comparison differently. Rev. William Corkey said of Hunter at the Heresy Trial Appeal in June 1927:

> He claims to be the successor of Dr. Cooke, and he has told us that he has accomplished more in rousing the country in twelve months than Dr. Cooke had accomplished in seven years.
>
> But Mr. Hunter is fighting for a principle diametrically opposed to that for which Dr. Cooke contended, for Dr. Cooke's great work was to vindicate the authority of Presbytery against men like Montgomery who refused to be bound, while Mr. Hunter actually makes the claims of the Unitarians and the non-Subscribers, that no court, secular or sacred, ecclesiastical or civil, will bind him (vide speech delivered in Derry Guildhall, 31st March, 1926).[48]

In fact, Hunter fought for a principle that was at one with Cooke's, whose great work was to bring the Synod of Ulster to an unequivocal commitment to confessional truth when it stood on the brink of corporate defection to Arianism.

To borrow from Thomas Hamilton: "... for seven years every annual meeting of the Synod of Ulster saw Cooke determinedly battling for the truth. ... But [at Newry in 1822] he stood almost alone."[49]

Great Expectations?

The encouraging events of the 19th century prompted Thomas Hamilton to offer a vibrant, warning-free assessment of the Irish Presbyterian Church in the 1880s with confident expectations of an even better future:

> The Church was never more heartily united than at present. She has a life and a vigour about her which augur well for her future. The old dead days of dry pulpit routine and pew somnolence are all but extinct. There is a fervour in the prayers of the sanctuary, and a heartiness in its songs of praise, which are at once the evidences of life and a powerful means of further developing life. There are higher ideals of Christianity among us. An earnest evangelistic spirit yearns over the lost sheep, and exhausts every means which a sanctified Christian ingenuity can suggest to bring them into the fold. All over the Church the missionary spirit never rose so high as it has done within the last few years. The evangelization of the world is now seen to be the grand duty of the Bride of Christ. Altogether, the present condition of the Church may well inspire the deepest gratitude and the brightest hope. She has done much not unworthy of such a Church. But there are yet greater things in store for her, if, looking around with a large eye, and recognising the breadth and grandeur of the mission which lies at her door, she braces herself earnestly to her work in the strength of God. 'The isles shall wait for His law,' and among them it may confidently be said of Ireland, in a higher and holier meaning than the words of one of her own poets were intended to convey,—
>
> 'Though slavery's cloud o'er thy morning hath hung,
> The full noon of freedom shall beam round thee yet.'[50]

Whilst Hamilton held out great hope the future, Thomas Witherow had read the recurring lessons of history better. Publishing in 1879 he asked with a backward look at the Arian controversy, "Is there not a still lower depth? May not some reach it even in this nineteenth century?" Events were soon to justify his fears.

Seaton Reid's warning note as he concludes his account of the removal of Arians to the Antrim Presbytery in 1725 is predictive of Witherow's fears, and a classic of church history:

> From that portion of her history which has been detailed in this chapter, let the Presbyterian Church in Ireland learn the important lesson of abiding faithfully by her confession of faith. That confession may, indeed, be enlarged, or abridged, or varied to suit abounding error; but let her ever "hold fast the faithful Word as she hath been taught," in a definite and authorised confession, and let her suffer no latitudinarian pretexts of Christian liberty to absolve those who seek to exercise the ministry in her communion from declaring their concurrence in her recognised standards.[51]

But the last word on future prospects goes to Thomas Latimer. Writing a little later, at the turn of the century, and very much aware of a new downward trend in the pluralism of the "broad church", he felt the need to pray for another Secession church:

> This success of the Secession Church produced three great results:—It prevented Synod of Ulster clergymen from publicly teaching heterodox opinions; it provided Gospel ordinances for many people whose ministers withheld the truth; and it was the means of erecting new congregations in districts where Presbyterians were in danger of being absorbed by other churches. Would that there was now another "Secession" to counteract the "broad church" views so rapidly spreading in our own General Assembly, and to provide a Presbyterian refuge for many who are leaving her communion! [52]

To what extent the emergence of the Irish Evangelical Church in 1927 was an answer to that prayer is one of the questions as the events unfold.

Part 2

The Developing Crisis

5

The Broadening Church

By the last quarter of the nineteenth century the influence of the new Liberalism which had taken possession of the principal German schools began to reveal itself in the Free Church of Scotland, both in Church and classroom. Under pressure from current trends the Church had become less sure of herself and more receptive to the new learning. The Free Church must not be obscurantist! Her ministry must be second to none in intellectual attainment and breadth of scholarship! So, more and more, the custom grew of sending her most promising students to the seats of learning in Germany which had been taken over by the Higher Critical movement.

Now this zeal for scholarship was good up to a point. Obscurantism is not to be equated with orthodoxy, and the Church that fails to keep herself abreast of advances in scholarship is assuming an attitude that is unworthy of her high calling. But her thinking must always be governed by reverence, and she must never permit herself to forget that the "things most surely believed" -- the doctrines committed to her keeping -- were not devised by man's wisdom, but given by revelation from God. The Holy Scriptures are self-authenticating and will bear the test of investigation, but the grasp of Reason will always come short of the reach of Faith.

G N M Collins, *The Heritage of our Fathers*

Lefferts A Loetscher

Dr Lefferts A Loetscher, researcher and prolific author of Presbyterian history, was Instructor-Professor of American Church History at Princeton Seminary 1941-1974. David B Calhoun assessed Loetscher's endorsement of the 1929 Princeton reorganisation, in line with the PCUSA's doctrinal broadening, as "the passing of the rigid theology of the past". And he quotes Loetscher's own view of the change at Princeton: "a new start and a very different perspective. The historical-critical approach is now dominant and assured".[53] In 1954 Loetscher published *The Broadening Church*, a study of theological issues in the Presbyterian Church since 1869.[54] Rev. Stephen J Tracey[55] provides this summary:

> In this book Loetscher argues that, "the American Presbyterian Church has been from the beginning a combination of diverging tendencies, maintained in fairly equal balance."[56] In 1729 the fledgling church tackled the question of subscription to the Westminster Confession of Faith. It came up with an Adopting Act which required ministers to accept the Westminster Confession of Faith and the Larger and Shorter Catechisms by declaring their "agreement in and approbation of" these standards "as being in all the *essential and necessary articles*, good forms of sound words and systems of Christian doctrine." (Italics added). The little phrase "essential and necessary articles" would prove contentious for many years to come. It even merits a place in the Special Commission of 1925. Loetscher argues that this deliberate ambiguity was the central direction for American Presbyterianism. The trend was always to allow for divergent theological views in order to preserve institutional unity.
>
> The William Robertson Smith case brought the issue of Biblical criticism to the surface in America in the 1890s. Professor Charles Briggs, Union Theological Seminary, was in sympathy with Robertson Smith and apparently receiving inside information from prominent Scottish sympathizers. Loetscher traces the rise of broad churchism—as opposed to the extremities of the liberals and conservatives—through various heresy trials, e.g. Prof. H P Smith of Lane Theological Seminary, Cincinnati, in 1892 and C A Briggs of Union Theological Seminary, New York, in 1893, followed by various attempts at revision of WCF, beginning in 1889 and renewed in 1900, and then through the organisation of various Church seminaries, ultimately coming to a head in the reorganisation of Princeton in 1929. The motive of this broad churchism was "the subordination of unresolved theological differences to the necessities of co-operation for the successful promotion of the Church's work."[57] Essentially this was a pragmatic doctrine of the Church. Interestingly Loetscher only briefly touches this point in two places.[58] The tendency was towards a more organic conception of the Church, a communion of saints more to do with teamwork than defining the true religion we profess. Dr William Brenton Greene Jr. clearly perceived the consequences of this changing doctrine of the Church. "The broader a church becomes, the fewer and the less definite must be the truths to which it witnesses."[59]

Irish Presbyterian Colleges and Biblical Criticism

Such broadening in theological perspective began to assert itself in the Irish Presbyterian Church later in the 19th century, following an already established trend in Scotland. The brilliant William Robertson Smith was appointed Professor of Oriental Languages and Old Testament Exegesis at the Free Church College in Aberdeen[60] in 1870, when just 24. It was especially through him that Higher Criticism from the German schools of Wellhausen and others spread through the College. Concern in the Church over the Higher Critical stance of Smith's 'Bible' articles in the *Encyclopaedia Britannica* led to his own demand for a formal trial in the Church Courts in 1880 at which the indictment was dropped. But when complaint was renewed as further *Britannica* articles appeared, he was removed from his chair in 1881. However, his teaching and its influence remained.

In 1888 the General Assembly of the Presbyterian Church in Ireland appointed Thomas Walker as Professor of Hebrew at Assembly's College. W J Grier says this: "Walker was an out-and-out adherent of the German schools of unbelieving Higher Criticism. Many of the students in the College imbibed his notions and looked upon him as the up-to-date man of learning, while they regarded his older colleagues as antiquated. … But though Walker's position was well known, no strong stand was taken against him, and certainly no attempt seems to have been made to root out modernist teaching from the College or to prevent it from being disseminated through the land."[61]

Finlay Holmes, referring to the Fundamentalist-Modernist controversy that had featured in W P Nicholson's American background, speaks similarly:

> The death of Robert Watts in 1895 had marked the end of an era. Tentative questionings of traditional doctrine, centring, as so often in Irish Presbyterianism, on the issue of subscription to the *Westminster Confession of Faith*, had begun to be voiced once more in the inaugural lecture of Watts' successor in the chair of systematic theology, Thomas Hamill. Soon theological students were asking for greater latitude in the terms of ordinands' subscription to the *Confession*. Thomas Walker, who was appointed to the Chair of Hebrew in 1888 as a brilliant young scholar of 26, was known to hold critical views of the bible which had hitherto been anathema in the Belfast College."[62]

Lower or 'Textual' biblical criticism is concerned with the text of Scripture. It seeks to achieve a 'pure' text, that equates as nearly as possible to the original autographs, through the application of established selection principles to variant manuscript readings. 'Higher Criticism' dealt with the broad areas of authorship, sources, date, and historical and cultural background of the books of the Bible, rather than the details of the text. The discipline of biblical criticism is part of the scholarly study of Scripture but the Higher Criticism of 18th century German scholars which flooded into Europe and America in the 19th, rejected the status and authority of Scripture. It treated Scripture as it would any body of secular writings and subjective judgement became the criterion as its adherents pronounced on the authenticity of biblical books. To them, the Bible was a record of human experience and experience became an important standard for the modern church. James Montgomery Boice aptly says: "For the church of the age of rationalism, the Bible became man's word about God and man rather than God's word to man."[63]

Dr Robert Watts of Assembly's College wrote *The Newer Criticism*, a reply to the public lectures of W Robertson Smith, after Smith had been dismissed from his chair at Aberdeen. It was published in 1882 and went to the third edition in under six months. In the preface to the second edition he says this:

> Thus, with every new appearance, "the newer criticism"—octopus-like— reaches out still further its relentless arms, drawing into its deadly embrace priest and sacrifice, prophet and judge. Already the Pentateuch is dismembered; Joshua is assigned to a late date because of its relation to Deuteronomy, and because of its altar of witness, so fatal to the claims of "the New Apologetic"; Samuel is declared to be teeming with interpolations; the Chronicles are unhistorical; Isaiah and Zechariah are each rent asunder; Ecclesiastes proclaims a lie; and now Joel and Judges are discredited. Thus, with a persistency that will brook no repression, this school prosecutes its destructive task, rifling the Bible of pre-exilic times of its chiefest glory, and stripping it of every symbol and type that could signify or foreshadow the redemptive work of Christ.[64]

Various authors such as D K Paton, R L Dabney and Robert Dick Wilson of Princeton also took up the challenge[65], but W J Grier's survey of the subsequent Professorial appointments provides focus on the local trend:

> In June 1907 the General Assembly passed a law abolishing religious tests for Chairs in the Arts Department at Magee College, Londonderry[66], and merely required a colourless declaration not to write or say anything which might tend in any way to subvert the Christian religion. This amounted to throwing the doors wide open to Arians of the type of Hutcheson and Simson and Leechman of Glasgow, who in a past generation had done such damage while professing to hold the *truth*.
>
> In 1909 Rev. David Smith of the United Free Church of Scotland was appointed to the important Chair of Systematic Theology at Magee College. Years before he had written his well-known book, *The Days of His Flesh*, in parts of which he had shown a pronounced radicalism, with the utmost assurance taking upon him the task of separating the reliable from the supposedly unreliable elements of the Gospels. Some eight or nine years after his appointment as professor, he published another book, *The Atonement in the Light of History and the Modern Spirit*. Dr. C. W. Hodge, in reviewing this book, stated, 'This little volume adds another to the many which have been written to construct a modern doctrine of the Atonement, and to prove that Christ did not bear the guilt and punishment of our sins, and that His atoning work was not a satisfaction of the Divine Justice.' Dr. Hodge went on to say that Dr. Smith thinks 'we have now learned that the fundamental ideas of

Christianity are the love and universal Fatherhood of God, and consequently that no Atonement in the old sense is necessary. Christ teaches us the love and Fatherhood of God, and thus reconciles sinners to God.' (Princeton Review, April, 1919).[67]

The broadening that had so clearly become apparent in the Colleges before the close of the 19th century found open expression in various aspects of Church life in the first 25 years of the 20th. Within the Presbyterian Church in Ireland the Liberal advance was registered in a series of landmark events, each a signpost of the new direction the Church was taking and a declaration of the Church's growing openness about its course. But it was not until the mid-1920s that particular circumstances combined to draw opposition to a head under the leadership of Rev. James Hunter whose biographical data appears in the next chapter.

Free Church of Scotland 1900-1905

The first of these 20th century pointers to a broadening church was the reaction to the dramatic events in Scotland at the turn of the century.

One result of the Evangelical Revival that visited Scotland during the first decades of the 19th century was the progressive ascendancy of the Evangelical Party in the Church of Scotland over the moderates, already in decline by the end of the 18th. In 1834 the Evangelicals secured the passing of the Veto Act that revived the right of majority dissent to nominees under the Patronage Act of 1712 that was still in force. But a series of decisions in the Scottish Law Courts between 1834 and 1842 left no doubt about the intention to enforce the provisions of the Act. The Evangelical Party could not accept this renewed challenge to the Church's spiritual independence and, in 1843, withdrew from the Established Church, the Church of Scotland, to form the Church of Scotland, Free, in what has been known as 'The Disruption', a term which refers to the severing of the link between Church and State, not to the division of the Church that was simultaneously involved. Since the Free Church adhered to the Confession of Faith, Constitution, and principles, including the Establishment principle, of the Church she had left, she claimed identity and continuity with it.

Like the concurrent events in Ireland, the ensuing 19th century history of the Disruption Church is a timeless reminder that a corporate commitment to orthodoxy may not endure: "Somehow, we relish the call for heroism but not that for durability".[68] Between 1839 and 1852 various unions of 18th century Secession Churches had taken place, fuelling moves in the second half of the century to advance the process. The Bodies to become involved were the Free Church and the 1847 United Presbyterian Church, made up largely of the New Licht Burghers and New Licht Anti-Burghers, two of the descendants of the Burghers and Anti-Burghers who were connected with the Irish Secession Church. But union was going to be viable only on the basis of doctrinal compromise as the two churches differed radically on the Establishment Principle and the Atonement.

Nevertheless, there was a party in the Free Church who favoured union and succeeded in carrying a motion to that effect at the Assembly of 1867. The need to organise the growing opposition and defend the Church's constitution brought the Free Church Defence Association into being in 1870. A magazine, *The Watchword*, already in existence and edited by Dr James Begg, also a member of the Defence Association, alerted the Church to the issues. As a result of the protests, the proposed union did not proceed.

However, the desire for union survived. In 1879, in sympathy with the mood of their Church, the United Presbyterians passed a Declaratory Act that introduced significant changes to doctrine, formula of subscription and ordination vows. Twelve years later, in 1891, the Free Church Assembly approved a similar Declaratory Act and sent it down to Presbyteries for deliberation. Whilst it met substantial opposition in the lower Church Courts, it was not sufficient to prevent the Act becoming law at the Assembly of 1892. But resistance continued and, when a motion placed before the Assembly of 1893 for the repeal of the Act failed, there was an immediate secession to form the Free Presbyterian Church of Scotland.

Plans for union with the United Presbyterian Church got under way again in 1895. Two years later a Committee was appointed to move the process forward, and in 1898 the Free Church Defence Association was revived to organise opposition. The Association contended that since the Free Church could not change her Constitution, however large the majority of votes in its favour, those adopting change would place themselves outside the Church. Although this minority, known as the 'Constitutionalist' party, continued to oppose the process step by step, the Union was consummated in 1900 under the name of The United Free Church of Scotland. Of the Constitutionalist minority, 26 ministers finally refused to enter the Union, electing instead to continue the Free Church of Scotland. The majority of the United Free Church re-united with the Church of Scotland in 1929.

The Free Church initiated action in the Scottish courts to recover its name, lands, property and funds, arguing that these could not pass to an organisation that did not maintain the fundamental principles embodied in the Constitution of the Free Church. When the case went against the Free Church in the Scottish Court of Session, and again in the Second Division of the Court, they appealed to the House of Lords who found in their favour on 1 August 1904. However, the Free Church was clearly unable to administer the whole of the property, and in response to a campaign of protest by the United Free Church, Parliament divided the funds and properties between the two Bodies under the Churches (Scotland) Act, 1905.[69]

In 1900 Rev. James Hunter was 37 and had been minister of Dundela-Knock, Belfast for 12 years. The Union controversy in Scotland would doubtless have occupied his attention as it developed. The succession of actual or attempted heresy trials involving Professors Marcus Dods 1878, William Robertson Smith

1880, A B Bruce 1890, and George Adam Smith in 1902, could well have alerted him to the path he might yet be obliged to take.

W J Grier provides an account of the response of the Irish Presbyterian Church to the events of 1900-1905 in Scotland:

> The attitude of the Irish Presbyterian Church towards this case was clearly expressed, and thereby her own position was clearly revealed. At the Irish Presbyterian Assembly in 1900 (before the Union was consummated) a motion was passed unanimously congratulating the Free Church on her approaching Union with the United Presbyterians. The Belfast Presbytery, after the judgment of the House of Lords (announced on 1st August, 1904) passed a resolution expressing profound regret at the decision and their deep sympathy with their brethren of the United Free Church. Against the passing of this resolution Rev. James Hunter, M.A., protested and gave notice of an appeal to the Synod. His appeal came before the Assembly in June, 1905, but the Assembly approved 'heartily' of the Belfast Presbytery's resolutions (by a vote of 208 to 62) and took the opportunity of 'expressing its deep sympathy with the United Free Church of Scotland in the great trouble which has come upon it.' ... In his speech before the Assembly Mr. Hunter quoted from United Free professors, showing their Modernism. At this the United Free deputies to the Assembly, who were seated below him, looked rather uncomfortable.
>
> A motion was brought forward by Rev. George Magill (of Cliftonville) to enter into friendly relations with the Free Church—this was defeated by 74 votes to 15.[70]

The *Monthly Record* of the Free Church of Scotland, July 1905, carried comment on the stance of the Belfast Assembly:

> LED by Rev. Samuel Prenter, D.D., Dublin, ex-Moderator, the General Assembly of the Irish Presbyterian Church rejected the appeal of the Rev. James Hunter, of Knock, against the resolution of the Belfast Presbytery to recognise any element of right in the decision of the House of Lords in favour of the Free Church. This attitude of the Irish Church as a whole has not surprised us, because of the ostentatious way in which its Assembly blessed the Union of 1900 ... and there is an element of logic in the position of *The Witness* that the Assembly having blessed the Union in 1900, could not very well ban it in 1905. ... To [Mr. Hunter] and those who took his part in the division on the Belfast appeal the thanks of the Free Church are deeply due, as well as to Rev. George Magill and those who voted with him when at a subsequent stage he moved that the Assembly should resume fraternal relations with the Free Church.
>
> The grounds upon which Mr Magill's proposal was rejected, as set forth by the exponents of that view, were intelligible enough. These men hate the Free Church because she stands for purity of doctrine, worship, government and discipline, according to the standards of 1843 and the formula of 1846. These

men have sat at the feet of the Rationalising teachers of the U.F. Church. The evangel is not to them a matter of life and death. They are attracted by the fetish of culture, progressive theology and the other lying vanities of the semi-Socinian school.

Robert Allen saw Hunter's role in opposing the Church in the Free Church of Scotland case as the beginning of a long road: "These decisions were regarded by Mr Hunter as tantamount to an implicit acceptance of the views of United Free Church scholars such as George Adam Smith and Marcus Dods; and for the next 20 years, he was to hold a watching brief for orthodoxy in the Irish Presbyterian Church."[71] To Hunter, the doctrinal shift that had facilitated the 1900 Union in Scotland and the appointment of Thomas Walker in Assembly's College in 1888, made the Church's acceptance of the United Free views explicit.

The Free Church story is significant since it was the stance of the Presbyterian Church in Ireland in the events of 1900-1905 that first brought James Hunter to prominence in the church as an exponent of orthodoxy and marked the beginning of his public campaign against the growing modernist ascendancy in the Church. It also brought him to the attention of the Free Church of Scotland which was to prove significant in future years.

Code Revision 1904-1911

The 1904 Free Church of Scotland ruling, particularly the absence of provision in the constitution of the Free Church to change it, provided part of the background to the 1911 Code Revision. The General Assembly of 1904 appointed a Committee to revise the Book of Constitution. In 1905, the Presbytery of Dublin petitioned the Assembly asking that, in view of the House of Lords' decision in the Free Church of Scotland case, the Assembly should take steps to safeguard the rights of the Church to shape her testimony to her sense of truth according to the teaching of Holy Scripture as revealed by the Divine Spirit. Chapter 2 - The Rule of Faith, of the new Code, published in 1912, incorporated a clause along the lines advocated in the Dublin overture: "In the Church resides the right to interpret and explain her standards under the guidance of the Spirit."[72] The 1904 ruling in Scotland may have prompted this insertion, but the wording did nothing to counter the church's historic penchant for latitudinarianism or a repetition of its 18th century confessional lapse that had facilitated *New Light*. Whilst the 1911 clause did not specifically offer relief to individuals in relation to the standards, as the *Pacific Act* of 1720 had done, it facilitated potential breadth of opinion.

The desire for doctrinal latitude had again become part of the prevailing ecclesiastical spirit, and the statement in the 1911 Code indicates that the Irish Presbyterian Church was not exempt. A 'Broadening Church' under the influence of Liberalism was emerging. The appeal to "the guidance of the Spirit" in interpreting the standards set aside a vital principle of Spirit guidance—"the Holy Spirit speaking in the Scripture."[73] To the Westminster Divines, the Spirit had inscripturated his guidance and they provided abundant Scripture proofs. The 1928 Assembly resolved: "The Church is fully agreed on the fundamental doctrines of the faith as set forth in the Westminster Confession, and regards the present form of subscription as a declaration of adherence to the said doctrines." This statement became a footnote to paragraph 20 of the 1948 Code.[74] Finlay Holmes assessed its "declaration of adherence" to the "fundamental doctrines" as set forth in the Westminster Confession, as "another indication that a liberalising spirit was in the ascendant".[75]

The Church's attitude to the Union sequence in Scotland, 1900-1905, had brought James Hunter to the attention of the wider Church, and the Code Revision debate that followed it re-engaged him. He was a member of various Assembly committees and in these as well as on the Assembly platform he stood for confessional adherence. During the 1914-18 war, for example, he introduced a motion deploring the absence of the widespread spirit of prayer and repentance that should characterise the church at times of national crisis. His activities were sometimes labelled a heresy hunt, but he did not have to hunt in the period now in view.

Rev. F W S O'Neill, China

Soon, the case of Rev. F W S O'Neill, missionary to China, pressed itself upon him.[76] In 1869 missionaries of the Irish Presbyterian Church began work in Manchuria, a region in northeast China sharing a border with Russia. They co-operated closely with colleagues from the 1847 United Presbyterian Church of Scotland who had started to arrive in 1872, and continued to do so with the Scottish missionaries aligned with the United Free Church after the Union of 1900. While Scots and Irish were not always in complete harmony, they developed evangelical, educational and medical work. The Belfast Presbytery had appointed Rev. F W S O'Neill as a missionary to Manchuria in 1897.

In July 1914 *The Presbyterian Witness* published an address, *The Miracle of the Kingdom*, that Mr O'Neill had given at a mission conference for Scottish and Irish missionaries in Manchuria. In September Rev. James Hunter drew the attention of the Foreign Missions Board to theological issues arising from the article, providing what he regarded as five key extracts, together with his interpretation of their meaning, on the subjects of Pantheism, The Estate of Innocency, Divine Vengeance, The Way of Salvation and Christ's Infallibility (subject headings ours).[77] Hunter met with a Consultative Committee of the Board and arranged to submit to O'Neill, through the Board, two questions that he felt "dealt with vital truths which Mr O'Neill's article called into question." The members of the Foreign Missions Board were greatly concerned about the damage to the Mission that would arise from any suspicion of heresy, so correspondence with O'Neill and Manchuria continued into 1915. Taking account of the views of the Board and of his colleagues O'Neill replied to Hunter's two questions of March 1915:

Hunter: Was the Lord Jesus Christ infallible?

O'Neill: Our Lord Jesus Christ was God manifest in the flesh.

Hunter: Did the Lord Jesus Christ die a substitutionary death as atonement for the sins of his people?
O'Neill: Our Lord Jesus Christ is the propitiation for our sins.

Hunter and those he consulted were of one mind in writing O'Neill's answers off as evasions. On hearing nothing by July 1915 he wrote to one of the Conveners asking "whether the Consultative Committee of the Mission Board does or does not contemplate taking any further step in the matter of the questions upon doctrine forwarded to Mr O'Neill of China?" The reply confirmed that the Committee had no intention of involvement beyond routing the questions and answers. It would have been better had Hunter's questions been framed to elicit O'Neill's personal beliefs, for his laconic answers evaded that key issue. They did nothing to remove the disquiet, being essentially quotations from Scripture – 1 Tim 3.16 (perhaps following the textual position of the English Revised Version of 1881) and 1 John 2.2, 4.10. James Hunter clearly understood the situation in saying to the Committee in his letter of 15 July 1915: "It is for the Committee to judge what respect has been shown it in this deeply important matter."

The sequel was that Hunter withdrew his case against O'Neill at the October 1915 Belfast Presbytery. On a personal level his grounds were entirely compassionate in the light of trials that had recently afflicted the O'Neill family, including the death of their son of 16 months in August 1915.[78] Later that year in a letter to Hunter, O'Neill included thanks for his kindness and courtesy. O'Neill acknowledged that he had done harm, gave an "on reflection" withdrawal of most of the passage on which Hunter had based the first of his five points, asserted his belief in the deity of Christ, calling Him "very God of very God", and emphasised his commitment to evangelism. He asked too that his address be seen as devotional, not a theology statement. His approach bore similarities to his replies to the March 1915 questions.

O'Neill's address raised questions about his orthodoxy which the Missions Board declined to press. His approach was in keeping with the Church's alignment with the Union of 1900 and of its stance in the subsequent Code Revision. The United Free Church, whom the Lord Chancellor in 1904 pronounced as having departed from the Calvinistic doctrines of the Confession of Faith, was one of the Mission partners in Manchuria. Everything in the handling of the case fitted the inclusivism of a broadening church. The Westminster Standards epitomise precision and the need for clarity of theological expression, but O'Neill's statements were of quite a different order, and whether or not they were devotional is irrelevant.

During the 1924-25 session of Assembly's College O'Neill delivered a series of lectures on *Comparative Religion and Christian Missions*, and the substance of them was published as *The Quest for God in China*.[79] W J Grier's review[80] places many of O'Neill's views outside the pale of Scripture, as he adulated a selection of world religions and espoused the language of Arianism. Strong similarity in thought and approach between *The Quest* and the 1915 exchange with Hunter is evident. So the enquiry did not get to the bottom of O'Neill's theology. But the significance of the case lies in the stance of the Church, evidenced in the unwillingness of Missions Board and Presbytery to deal conclusively with evidence of unorthodoxy.

In 2012, Mark O'Neill, grandson of 'FWS', produced a life of his grandfather. On the 'Heresy charge' he quoted Rev. William Addley: "He was less circumspect than the average missionary. ... While other missionaries kept to themselves opinions that would upset people at home, Frederick was willing to express them and risk controversy. ... The China experience changed him, as it changed other missionaries. ... These changes got him into trouble at home. The Foreign Missions Board was embarrassed by Frederick but stood by him."[81] Not that much trouble at home! In 1933 the Faculty conferred a DD degree on O'Neill and the Church appointed him as Moderator in 1936.

Robert Allen assesses the significance of the O'Neill case for Hunter: "He regarded it as his supreme task to stem the tide of theological liberalism, and he now became confirmed in his opinion that the Church was less than loyal to her credal standards."[82] Referring back to Hunter's defeat in the Free Church of Scotland case ten years earlier, Allen notes a similar outcome to his action against O'Neill: "Again he was to suffer disappointment, for, despite all his efforts, neither Mission Board, Presbytery, nor Assembly was prepared to press the case against Mr. O'Neill."[83] However, when Hunter came under attack for operating outside Church Courts during the Heresy Trial proceedings in 1927, he was able to point to the obstruction he encountered in the case of O'Neill where he had followed the strict constitutional processes.[84]

Publications

As part of the picture of the growing confidence of modernism in the church W J Grier gave examples of publications by ministers and professors:

> *Rev. John Waddell* of Fisherwick has for more than twenty years occupied a prominent or even dominating place in the councils of the Irish Presbyterian Church. In 1919, while serving in the English Presbyterian Church, he issued a book, *The Life Here and the Life Hereafter*, in which he states the doctrine of 'the larger hope.' He says, 'We dare not say that God's mercy is limited by the incidence of death and that human probation ends there.' (p 223).
>
> *Rev. W McNeill*, Minister of Rostrevor 1924-1930, in a booklet *Talks on the Bible to Sunday School Teachers*[85], stated, 'it is coming home to us all that there is not and never can be an external infallible authority in religion' (p 27). Again, he stated, 'The story of the wise men and the Star is probably only a story. The physical Ascension is beyond our power to grasp or to understand. The question of the Virgin Birth and the physical Resurrection you must study for yourselves, and form your own conclusions, as I am trying to form mine. The former has little to do with the substance of the message we have to teach, and I find myself interpreting it as poetry, rather than history.' (pages 47-48).

Rev. J. T. Anderson, of Banbridge, who for many years acted as Convener of one of the most important Committees of the Church, delivered three lectures in September, 1926, at a week-end Conference of the Irish Christian Fellowship. These Lectures were issued in pamphlet form by the S.C.M., in March 1927, with the title, *The Cross and Its Meaning*. He repudiates the doctrine of Christ's satisfaction for sin and says, 'It almost seems as if some men clutch at the straws of substitutionary theories because they are afraid to make the venture of trust in God. ... On the theory set forward in these papers justification comes not through resting on Christ's finished work, but follows repentance, a change of heart. The disciples, who followed Jesus in the days of His flesh, were justified not because they had any theory about His death, but because, as Sir John Seeley put it, 'they conquered convention and ranged themselves on His side.'"[86]

James Ernest Davey – The Changing Vesture

The most significant publications were the two by James Ernest Davey, Professor of Church History at Assembly's College (1917-1922), of Biblical Literature and Hellenistic Greek (1922-1930), of Hebrew and Old Testament (1930-33) and of New Testament Language, Literature and Theology (1933-1960). Finlay Holmes described him as "probably the most brilliant scholar ever to hold a chair in an Irish Presbyterian Theological College".[87] In 1921, when just 31, he gave the Carey Lectures, published as  *The Changing Vesture of the Faith*, in 1923. They were endowed by John Carey of Toome, Co Antrim, as lectures "on a religious, moral or social question of general interest and passing importance."[88] In January 1922 Davey delivered four lectures at the Belfast conference of the Student Christian Movement and the Irish Christian Fellowship, published as *Our Faith in God* in 1922. James Hunter Gillespie, nephew of Rev. James Hunter, writing as *Leloumenos* 'having been bathed' John 13.10) reviewed the *Changing Vesture* in *Faith in an Unchanging Vesture* –"an Exposure of Modernistic Principles", 1927.[89]

These publications show Davey's rare breadth of scholarship, his constructive mind, marked gifts of reasoning, anecdotal skill and sincerity. He wrote in a discursive style, at home in the fields of psychology and philosophy. His two main *Changing Vesture* propositions were: "That life creates forms" and "That forms react upon life".[90] But it is essential to understand what he means by forms. He groups them under three heads: "beliefs, or forms of thought; institutions, or forms of social development and agreement; and observances and customs, i.e., forms of conduct and practice."[91] Christian forms of belief included all the Creeds and Confessions – dogma and doctrine; Christian institutions included all forms of Church government and certain bonds of social unity such as the Scriptures, the sacraments and the like – primarily polity. Observances were essentially the means of worship of the Christian Churches. So Davey's 'forms' were all-embracing.

In Chapter 1 of *Changing Vesture* Davey called for the faith to be expressed in the forms of the present, "as a reflex of the life behind it,"[92] and not in hindering forms of the past:

> It is the realities of life which really matter in the sphere of religion; not formulae, but moral values, not the scaffolding, not even the house, but the tenant: and, inasmuch as forms stagnate, while life is ever growing and developing, the value of forms must never blind us to the need of their constant revision, that they may be adequate and helpful so far as possible, and not mere out-of-date hindrances to developing life. Once the necessity of forms is admitted, and also the vital relation which should subsist between present forms and present life, revision will be regarded as an essential of each generation, for it is the only alternative to a tyranny on the one hand which chokes out life, and to a formlessness on the other, which, to exist, must both beget forms of its own, so putting the fool's cap upon itself, and at the same time by its very efforts plunge deeper into the mire of provincialism and sectarianism.[93]

Davey applied his argument to music, the arts, and the church: "In music, as in other spheres of life, the classical period is no doubt greater in permanent value, but the present day must express itself in its own way, or lose its soul … and so in particular with the theology, worship and social activities of the Church."[94] There is little Scripture orientation in the above quotations, and this is significant even when taking account of the terms of the trust: " … these lectures, according to the trust under which they were delivered, were destined for the public at large, I have, in my treatment of the subject, aimed at popular lucidity rather than technical exactitude." The public at large was, first of all, the church: "The studies are meant in the first place for those who belong to the Churches, and aim throughout at challenging thought upon serious matters." They were written, "in the first instance by a Presbyterian for Presbyterians …"[95] Davey's approach to reformations, creeds and confessions is fully consistent. To him, confessions and creeds are part of the hindering forms of the past:

> The implications of former dogmas were gradually seen and expanded, and these orthodox developments, together with the continual rise of new heresies, calling for ever more detailed definition of orthodox belief and refutation of error, have all tended to give the growth of creeds and confessions in the Church the look of an arithmetical progression, the appearance of a wedge of authority driven deeper and deeper into the domain of human thought. … A large creed may serve as a bulwark against error, but it can never be accepted whole-heartedly by any considerable section of the Church which has adopted it.
>
> … lengthy creeds only minister to hypocrisy and unreality, as men and women try to square themselves with the authorised views of their symbols, either by pretending to accept, or suggesting to themselves, views which they do not spontaneously hold; or else, and more frequently, they do violence to the literal

meaning of the symbol. ... The discrepancy between the present life of our Church and the historical symbols of nearly three hundred years ago, in which it is supposed to be expressed, is so manifest that we see the Church reaping the fruit to-day in a religious system which, to the unprejudiced mind, savours of insincerity. ... Even the unity towards which we are consciously feeling our way to-day we can no longer visualise as a uniformity either of thought, organisation or practice. Our greatest need assuredly is that the Spirit who is both Truth and Love shall have free course in us.[96]

The concluding sentence is a plea for an ongoing broadening process and goes beyond the expression in the 1911 Code: "In the Church resides the right to interpret and explain her standards under the guidance of the Spirit." In a letter to W J Grier in April 1927 on the *Changing Vesture*, Dr J Gresham Machen observed: "Professor Davey ... intimates that the things contained in the Creed are 'forms' in which something else is expressed. Of course if that be admitted the whole debate is over. If anything in the Creed is a form for the expression of the Christian life, then it cannot be a fact. ... It is not merely that elements in the Creed are denied, but rather that a skeptical view is held as to what any creed must necessarily be."

Chapters 2-7 dealt with the "psychological foundations of historical Christian forms" – "the search after safety or certainty ... the quest for ideals ... the embodiment of concrete forms of actual experience ... the formal expression of the instinct for sacrifice." *Changing Vesture* extracts featured in the first four of the five charges brought against Davey in 1927.

In Chapter 8, Section 8, Extraneous Influences, Davey engaged Westminster, Chapter 2 – God and the Holy Trinity: "Philosophical prejudice leads to a definition of God in terms of abstraction, i.e., abstracting from the idea those things which belong to concrete human experience, such as feelings, limitations, and in the end personality itself; and of the resultant definition our Westminster Confession gives a typical example in Chapter II". After quoting Section 1 and the first half of Section 2, he goes on:

In part the definition represents an attenuated Christianity; but it is a long way from a description of the God and Father of our Lord Jesus Christ. And it is interesting to note how, as the definition of God by the Westminster Divines diminishes in length from Confession to Larger Catechism, and from Larger to Shorter, it is the philosophical attributes which maintain their place most firmly, and the distinctively Christian which disappear. The first change omits the words 'most loving,' the second omits 'merciful, gracious and long-suffering,' thus showing the abstract and anti-Christian tendencies of a theology founded upon pure philosophy, and acknowledging it as master rather than as servant. ... and the Church has been 'bluffed,' by the philosophical prejudices of theologians, into accepting this negative definition to such an extent that, as shown above, the first words its representatives are willing to drop, in abbreviating a definition of God, are those which have reference to positive moral qualities.[97]

Here he compares his 187 word quotation from Chapter 2 with the 42 words of the Larger Catechism (Q 7) and the 18 of the Shorter (Q 4) and selects what he sees as two omissions in the Catechisms to support his contention that the Confession, at least at this point, is "a theology founded upon pure philosophy". Basically, in proceeding from Confession to Larger to Shorter, he moved in the wrong direction. Thomas Manton said in his Epistle to the Reader: "First, let them read and learn the Shorter Catechism, and next the Larger, and lastly, read the Confession of Faith." Furthermore, the Catechisms are not abbreviations, rather summaries.

John Murray said of the Shorter Catechism: "It is the most perfect document of its kind that the Christian church has produced. ... a catechism, and a small catechism at that; there are numerous needs which the Shorter Catechism does not fulfil and was not intended to supply. ... there is no other document of human composition that packs into so few words such an excellent summary of the truth respecting God and his holy will revealed to us in the Scriptures of the Old and New Testaments."[98] The Shorter Catechism answer to Q 4 is: "God is a spirit, infinite, eternal, and unchangeable, in his being, wisdom, power, holiness, justice, goodness and truth." Even God's so-called 'incommunicable attributes' such as omnipotence and omniscience have "analogies in our own human existence."[99] The transcendence of God is fundamental to the faith and comfort of daily Christian experience, and is neither abstract or negative. What greater positive moral quality could there be than, "Be holy, for I am holy" (1 Pet 1.16)? God requires the holiness of his moral character to engage his people continuously and be re-produced in them.

The philosophy-theology conflict depends on how the two disciplines are defined, how they interact or stand in opposition. Davey's concerns were: "chiefly [philosophical] prejudices as to methods of thought, which emphasised the abstract and logical, as against the concrete and experimental in life ...". The Westminster Confession of Faith is essentially theology since it handles revelation and supports its statements extensively by Scripture quotations. This distinguishes it fundamentally from other systems of thought, their pre-suppositions and authority. Davey's statements that "distinctively Christian" attributes disappear in the Catechisms and his entanglement of the Confession's theology with "anti-Christian" tendencies highlight his basic discomfort with the Westminster forms.

Passages from *Our Faith in God Through Jesus Christ* provided material for charges 2, 3 and 4. The 1922 lectures published under this title dealt with the Christian view of God, in the form of answers to four common questions about the subject: Is it Reasonable? Is it Necessary? Is it Effective? Is it Final? The approach had similarities to that of *The Changing Vesture*:

> The aim of the writer throughout has been practical rather than theoretical, and these addresses are offered to the public, not as a considered statement of systematic apologetics, but as the attempt of an individual to deal positively, and un-theologically, so far as

possible, with some of the more persistent doubts in the general mental atmosphere of our day.

Like *The Changing Vesture*, *Our Faith in God* discourses are of philosophical bent, separated by a great gulf from the language, content, and emphases of the reformed faith. They reason from a human standpoint, marginalise Scripture, and emphasise the life, example and spirit of Christ.[100]

So the first 25 years of the 20th century were replete with evidence of a broadening Church, moving away, with increasing boldness, from the orthodoxy of its Confessional standards. Thomas Latimer's prayer for the refuge of another Secession Church was surely that of a man of vision and understanding.[101] Significantly, the change appeared in the College before the close of the 19th century, but College appointments revealed a shift that had already taken place: when Eve ate the forbidden fruit, something had already happened. So the growing influence of modernism had appeared in the College, General Assembly, Belfast Presbytery, Overseas Missions, and the wider Church, and in the emergence of Rev. J E Davey, Professor, eminent scholar, public lecturer and writer, and foremost advocate of modernism.

The period also saw James Hunter emerging as the defender of Confessional orthodoxy. The longer-term history of the church, particularly the campaign of Henry Cooke in the mid-19th century, motivated him. The events of the first 25 years of the 20th established his sense of calling to take up this "imperative duty", as he would later describe it. At what point Hunter engaged with Davey's two lecture-publications is not clear. The four to five year gap between publication and charges supported by material from them became an issue at the Heresy Trial. However, such publications would not have escaped the attention of a man with Robert Allen's "watching brief for orthodoxy in the Irish Presbyterian Church."[102]

These were the elements that incrementally developed the crisis and brought it to a head.

6

The Founding Fathers

From the Rev. MATTHEW LEITCH, D.D., D.Lit., Professor of Biblical Criticism, Assembly's College, Belfast; Moderator of the General Assembly of the Presbyterian Church in Ireland, 1897-1898.

I HAVE much pleasure in testifying to the character, ability, and ministerial efficiency of the Rev. JAMES HUNTER, M.A. He was a distinguished student of Queen's College, Belfast, obtaining a literary scholarship every year, and graduated in the Royal University with "First Class" in Ancient Classics. He was equally distinguished as a student during the three years of his attendance at our Theological College in Belfast. Since his ordination he has devoted himself with faithfulness and success to the work of the ministry, and is now one of the most scholarly and most promising of the younger ministers of our Church.[103]

MATTHEW LEITCH

17th January, 1897.

Three families, the Hunters, Gillespies and Griers, were to play a significant part in the events that led to the emergence and establishment of the Irish Evangelical Church.

James Hunter

The Hunter Family
In the middle years of the 19th century, Charles and Catherine Hunter owned a large shop in the main street of Newtownstewart, Co Tyrone, and lived above it.[104] The Hunter family were ardent Liberals, and during the pre-Gladstone Home Rule period, while the Abercorns ran the Tory party, the Hunters ran the local constituency of the Liberal party from their shop. They enjoyed considerable prosperity and sent their three sons, Charles, John and James, to Strabane Grammar School and the older of their two daughters Maria to the school that later became Cheltenham College. The family's way of life changed completely, however, following the death of Charles Hunter Senior. They moved to College Gardens, Belfast, where they attended the old Fisherwick Church, on the site of what is now Church House. Maria was brought home from Cheltenham and she and her younger sister, Catherine, went to Mrs Byers' College, later Victoria College. The sons were moved to 'Inst' – the Royal Belfast Academical Institution.

Charles W, the eldest of the family, was minister of Ballyrashane Presbyterian Church near Coleraine, 1880-1928. The second son, John R, was a bachelor. He worked in the Ulster Bank for 40 years, being manager of the Shankill branch for most of his career. James was the third member of the family and will occupy a central role in the unfolding events. Maria (pronounced Ma-rye-ah) did not marry and kept house for James during much of his ministry. The youngest, Catherine Trimble Hunter, married John Gillespie and their three[105] children were the only grandchildren of Charles and Catherine Hunter.

Brilliant Academic
James Hunter, the third son, was born 14 April 1863. He studied at the Royal Belfast Academical Institution and Queen's College, Belfast, and graduated with First Class Honours Degrees in Classics at the Royal University of Ireland, first as a Bachelor of Arts in October 1883 and then as a Master of Arts in October 1886.[106] Both degrees refer to his "Distinguished Answering". The whole of his academic record was exceptional; he was regularly top of his year and won a gold medal for his MA. The scholarships, exhibitions and prizes won by him reached a total of about £250, a considerable sum in the late 19th century. C D Yonge, MA, Regius Professor of Modern History and English Literature, Queen's College, Belfast, and Fellow of the Royal University, gave him this testimonial:

> In the twenty years that I have been a Professor at Queen's College, there has been no student who has distinguished himself more highly, and who has done so in more than one department. The subject to which he chiefly devoted

himself was Classical Literature, in which not only in this College, but in the Royal University also, he obtained the highest Honours attainable by an under-graduate being in the final examination for the BA degree not only in the First Class, but *first in that class* and obtaining *the same distinction* in the examinations for the MA degree. And in this College, in the examinations which take place at the end of each session in the various subjects, he was also on every occasion the best man in the year in my subjects.

Similar testimony was borne to him by President J L Porter and Professors Hastings Crossley and Thomas Dougan of Queen's College.

The story of his call to the Ministry has not been handed down, but he began his theological studies at Assembly's College in 1883. There he was taught by Matthew Leitch, the very conservative, 'old school' Professor of New Testament, 1879-1922, who later became an opponent of Thomas Walker, Professor of Hebrew, 1889-1929.[107] Another of his teachers, in his final year, was Robert Watts of Princeton who served Assembly's College as Professor of Theology, 1886-1895. Both Leitch and Watts bore high testimony to his ability and achievement.

First Newry

Rev James Hunter, MA

After his graduation from Assembly's College, the Belfast Presbytery licensed him on 3 May 1887, and within a year he was called to Sandys Street Presbyterian Church in Newry - First Newry. He set the tone for his ministry at his ordination on 10 April 1888: "Novelty of thought or of diction, commanding power of speech, I cannot promise, but only such attractiveness as comes from the plain statement of the plain truth of God." On that occasion, he pledged himself "to the cause of God and our Saviour Jesus Christ."[108]

Hunter stayed just 19 months in Newry but the unfolding story shows how the short period had lasting significance.

The Dundela-Knock Years

In 1889 Hunter moved to Dundela, Belfast, which reverted to its original name, Knock, in 1921. He succeeded Dr James Heron, the church's first minister, who had become Professor of Church History at Assembly's College. At his installation, 5 December, on being presented with a pulpit gown and Bible, he said that the gown reminded him of the duty of being the same person when attired in the gown that he was when it was off, and he "pledged himself with the help of God to speak from the bottom of his heart what he felt convinced to be the truth as well in the pulpit as out of it." The Bible reminded him of another duty: "They did not expect him to be an original investigator, nor to forge for them a new creed out of the fragments of the old, but rather to present entire the old faith once delivered to the saints. ... It would be for him then to walk in the old paths." He spoke of the necessity of the power of God's Spirit to make the preaching of the truth effective, and expressed his fervent desire that "his speech and his preaching might be, not with enticing words of man's wisdom, but in demonstration of the Spirit and of power." In concluding he declared himself "not averse, should it be the will of God, to the prospect of many years at Dundela, if only he might be owned at the last as a faithful steward of the mysteries of God." He is reputed to have worn a monocle in the pulpit.

In his history of Knock Presbyterian Church, Nelson Brown provides insight into various features of church life in the Hunter years:

> Mr. Hunter was a pioneer of instrumental music and a small American organ was to be found in the Church as early as 1892 and he successfully resisted official pressure to have it removed. Thanks to Mr. Hunter, Church music at Knock became the envy of many other Congregations and we owe to him the practice of having an annual performance of Handel's 'Messiah' the first presentation of which at Knock dates from 1916. It is worth remembering, too, that Mr. Hunter personally paid the salary of a professional singer in the Soprano section of the Choir.
>
> Services were distinguished by a dignity and order—features of public worship amongst us that are noteworthy today—and Mr. Hunter encouraged the recitation of the Nicene Creed as well as the regular use of the Magnificat, Te Deum and other ancient hymns. The evening services had interesting departures from common usage in that a Scottish Mission Hymn Book of the Moody and Sankey type superseded the Church Hymnary and there was a Prose Psalter in which the words were pointed for chanting. Other variations were the singing of a hymn by a seated congregation and another hymn was one in which the verses were sung by Choir and congregation alternately, 'all singing the refrain'.
>
> In general services were longer than they are today and many young worshippers at the evening service became impatient long before the whistle of the 8.21 train from Knock to Donaghadee on the old B.C.D.R. intimated that in another five minutes or so all would be over.
>
> During World War I Mr. Hunter introduced a set form of prayer which he had printed and distributed. This was to be used at twelve noon each day and was always incorporated in the morning service on Sundays. On the Sunday following the Armistice Mr. Hunter preached from a pulpit draped with the Allied flags.[109]

When James Hunter had completed his course at Magee College, Londonderry[110] in the 1880s, Professor J. MacMaster, D. Lit, paid tribute not merely to the thoroughness of his scholarship but also to his "clearness of judgment and aptness of expression which mark cultivation of intellect as distinct from mere accumulation of learning." Robert Allen described him as "an acceptable preacher",[111] but Nelson Brown's account of Hunter's preaching suggests that Allen's comment was indeed economical with praise:

He brought to his new charge the energy of youth and a brilliant academic reputation. He was one of the finest classical scholars of his generation and his intellectual gifts were reflected in his sermons which were masterpieces of evangelical fervour, evincing an uncommon grasp of Biblical exegesis and a deeply moving eloquence which rivetted the attention of his listeners. He had, too, the ability—unusual, perhaps, in a clergyman in those days—to draw illustrations from contemporary events which from their topicality had all the greater appeal. Many older members will recall vividly the dramatic effectiveness of Mr Hunter's pulpit ministry. In fact, concealed from view by the existing organ structure, is the text in richly illuminated Gothic script: 'Christ is all and in all'. A sermon of Mr Hunter's on this theme was the means of changing a man's life.[112]

James Hunter ministered at Dundela-Knock for nearly 35 years. It is some indication of the influence of his ministry through the blessing of God that the church was enlarged twice during those years as Belfast gradually extended its boundaries and housing developed around the church; a new manse was erected, a pipe organ installed, and the stained glass war memorial windows placed in the north wall.[113] At some stage in his career he offered to serve in the Colonial Mission but the Belfast Presbytery advised him to stay because he was doing a useful work. He experienced times of tension with the elders in the Dundela-Knock years, and this may explain why eldership was not instituted in the early years of the Irish Evangelical Church. Nelson Brown summed up James Hunter's Dundela-Knock ministry like this:

> When Mr. Hunter retired he could contemplate a pastorate of thirty-five years during which a Congregation which was small in numbers and semi-rural in location had become a thriving centre of spiritual life, pioneering considerable missionary effort at home and overseas and securing for itself a tradition of work and worship which would endure.[114]

He was keen on travel and in the early 1900s he made the arduous journey to Manchuria to visit his sister Catherine and brother-in-law, via Moscow and the trans-Siberian railway. He visited Palestine in February-March 1899, New York in 1910 and on other occasions Greece, Italy and Germany. He regularly attended the annual Keswick Convention.

James and his elder brother John were generous and, when the Kirkpatrick church was erected in Ballyhackamore between 1914 and 1924, John paid for the tower and substantial charitable donations were attributed to James. James left comparatively little money, but was a supporter of good causes and gave away substantial sums during his life. With the passing years most of the family came to live near one another in the Castlereagh-Knock area of Belfast. James had a house built that he named 'Moyle', on the rural side of the Upper Knockbreda Road, near the Castlereagh junction, off what is now a dual carriageway.

John Richard Gillespie

There seems to have been an Anglican connection in the family history of the Gillespies of Trevor Hill, Newry, but for the years here in view they were Presbyterians. The father of the family was an independent banker before the modern banks were founded. William and Harriet Gillespie had eight children of whom seven lived to adult life. The first, Dr Annie Gillespie, kept house for her parents until the youngest, Ethel, took over. Annie then studied medicine in Edinburgh and went out to Manchuria with the Irish Church's Foreign Mission. In 1897, six months after her arrival, she died of fever in the arms of her eldest brother William who was already serving there as a minister. William was murdered in Manchuria in 1920 by bandits. James, the third member of the Gillespie family, became a High Court judge in India. The next son, Alfred J, was a Presbyterian minister serving first in Waringstown from 1906-1931 and then in Coagh until his retirement in 1947. Harry was a doctor in London. Ethel kept house in Newry and then at Warrenpoint for her father, and lived until 1970.

Marriage and Missionary Service
The middle one of the seven was Dr John Richard Gillespie. He was born 29 December 1871 in Newry where he had his early education and was converted during his boyhood years. He was a talented tennis player. He studied chemistry at Queen's College Belfast, and in common with most of the family paid for it out of scholarships. He later gave up chemistry in which he had two very good degrees, and funded himself to graduation in medicine through another scholarship. During this time he had also joined the Student Volunteer Movement. In 1900 he married Catherine Hunter whom he met when her brother James Hunter had been minister in Newry, 1888-89. The day after their wedding they sailed for Liverpool and the following day to the church's mission in Manchuria. Before her death, John's sister Annie had warned him about theological liberalism in the China Mission and advised him not to go, but with her death on the field, John felt compelled to follow her.

During 1901-1902 the Manchuria Mission Conference established the Machurian Christian College at Moukden, for the higher education of Christian youth, especially those who wished to enter Christian service. The Conference appointed John Gillespie as principal, "because of his scientific knowledge, and not because his medical work was considered unimportant."[115] A son, James Hunter Gillespie, was born to John and Catherine in Manchuria in 1906. Tension existed between the United Free Scots and the Irish Presbyterians and, as an aid to keeping the peace, they agreed to alternate responsibilities. When the Gillespies were leaving on a year's furlough in 1907, the Scots appointed a theological liberal as his substitute and colleague on his return. Gillespie considered that evangelicalism and liberalism could not coexist, so he did not return despite pleas from the mission field over a dozen years, one of which still exists in letter form. He applied to the China Inland Mission and they sent someone to interview him in Belfast, but for some reason the interviewer did not reach him.

Medical Officer of Health

Dr Gillespie became Medical Officer of Health in Hampshire until 1914 when the family returned to Belfast. Their daughter, Catherine, was born just before the move, on 13 July 1913. From 1914 until his retirement in 1947 he was Tuberculosis Medical Officer for County Down. Back in Belfast the Gillespies attended Knock Presbyterian Church and lived about 300 metres from the Manse. When James Hunter retired in 1924 Catherine and the two children left Knock Presbyterian with him, but John remained for a time to teach his Bible Class. In the mornings they worshipped in Ravenhill Presbyterian Church where there was a reformed ministry.

William James Grier

The Griers have rather a different background. They had a smallholding at the Little Ards near Ramelton, Co Donegal. There were three generations with three sons in each. W J Grier's father, John Grier, had two brothers. One of them had died at Magee College, the family said of overwork, but health issues may have played a part. John Grier married Elizabeth Barrett. The first of the three sons, George, ran the farm, the second, John Robert, went to America and the family sacrificed to educate their third son, William James, born 18 November 1902. He was William at home, and elsewhere James, or Jim in later years. The Griers attended Second Ramelton, known locally as the 'Scots' Church, but William James's Certificate of Christian Baptism was issued by Third Ramelton and administered by its minister, Rev. Robert Parke, on 15 January 1903 – a Thursday. Second and Third Ramelton were formally united in 1911, but "came together" in 1903[116]—perhaps to begin the process. The insertion of '(Scots Church)' on the Baptism certificate may point to one such interim arrangement. Francis Makemie who became known as the Father of American Presbyterianism was also born in Ramelton – in 1658.[117]

Although the Griers of Ramelton attended the Presbyterian Church, there are traces of a Reformed Presbyterian influence on the father's side. Even in his own church where everyone else sat to pray he stood and, if there was something on in the church he did not like, he went to Milford Reformed Presbyterian Church to hear Rev. G Blair, father of Hugh J Blair, later Professor of Hebrew and Old Testament in the Reformed Presbyterian Theological Hall, Belfast. A number of family stories have been handed down. On one occasion William's mother sent him for the shopping with a ten-shilling note, but he lost it on the way. He remembered pulling out his handkerchief, so he went back and began to search at the place he thought it was. Another man came along and also started to look, but on the side of the road where William had already searched. While the man was occupied with his fruitless search William found his money. He arrived home late but felt that the outing was a useful lesson in perseverance. In later years he taught his family to be persistent, as he had been from his youth.

Foyle College

When he was 13 he went to Foyle College, Londonderry, and lived with an aunt in the city. During his Derry weekends he by-passed the local Presbyterian Church to attend another where a Bible Class teacher, a praying man, witnessed to him. In the summer of those years Jim worked on the farm and often spoke about a thorn that stuck in his hand for some time and made manual labour difficult. His brothers said that the spade, not the thorn, was the problem, but one day, in the middle of parsing Greek, the thorn came out. He brought the precious evidence home the next weekend!

University, Conversion and Call

In 1920 when still only 17, he came to Belfast and began a three-year period of study at Queen's University.[118] He went into digs and, still in his unconverted days, he found his recreation for a time at the local theatre. But God was soon to change the course of his life.

While at Queen's one of the Assembly's College Professors approached him about going into the Ministry, but recognising he was unconverted Jim knew he must decline. However, Charlie Ross, a friend who was training to be a doctor and later worked with leprosy patients in Africa, often witnessed to him, particularly during long walks together over the Castlereagh Hills. And the witnessing bore fruit, for Jim Grier was converted in a W P Nicholson meeting in Rosemary Street Presbyterian Church in October 1922, at the beginning of his final University year. S W Murray reports of this mission: "Here also there were overflowing crowds and numerous decisions were made by young and old."[119] Frequent references in the course of his ministry to John 6.37: "All that the Father giveth me shall come to me; and him that cometh to me I will in no wise cast out" (KJV), suggest that this was Nicholson's text on the night of his conversion.[120] Soon he met Charlie Ross in University Avenue and told him with joy, "I am the Lord's."

Queen's Bible Union, as it was then known, began in the same year. It was not a recognised University body at that time and the handful of Christian students met in an attic in one of the Lanyon Building towers. The students knelt to pray and anyone who failed to take part had his ankles kicked by someone within range. So he learned to pray publicly! The members were keen on outreach and preached in the open-air in the University area. Such was the outgoing Christian Union and the discipleship ethos in which Jim Grier lived his early Christian life. He graduated with a Second Class, Second Division degree in Classics in 1923. He had worked very hard particularly in his final year; indeed, in the vacation before it, his father had put a plank across the orchard shed to keep the cows out so that William could use it for study throughout the summer. He had always felt he would apply to the Indian Civil Service, but after his conversion his future took on a new perspective and he began to feel a call to the ministry. The turning point came when a local Donegal Christian, Jim Watters, pressed him to take a service the next evening in the Mission Hall in Milford, not far from Ramelton.

Immediately his soul was in conflict. He had agreed to take a meeting while resisting the call of the Lord and it became imperative to him to settle the matter before the next day.

Jim Grier's ministry was characterised by a reticence to discuss himself. Even in over 50 years of editing *The Irish Evangelical/The Evangelical Presbyterian* there are few allusions to himself. As he was to say on the occasion of his retirement, it was the demands of the Gospel ministry that exerted the most influence upon his reluctance to present personal matters. "I have tried during the course of my ministry to speak not of myself but of my Lord and Saviour Jesus Christ." So it is not surprising that it was not until 6 November 1977, when preaching on Romans 10 at the evening service in his own pulpit at Stranmillis Evangelical Presbyterian Church, that he told the story of his call to the ministry in public for the first time.

> Some months after my conversion there was something like an inner voice. This is a very indefinite expression, I know, but the call seemed to keep coming up to my mind again and again - the work of the Ministry. And I put it from me. Again and again I put it from me, even for months. And then there was something happened that brought all that hesitation to an end. It happened away in the county of Donegal where I was brought up. I was there on a Saturday afternoon in the summer. It was a lovely summer's day. And there came a young man who had been at Foyle College in Derry with me. I was there four years in Derry, and he came to me on this Saturday afternoon and said to me: "You're speaking at the meeting at Milford tomorrow night!" "Well", I said to him, "you know, I have given some words of testimony and …" (I don't know whether I told him this or not) I had led one of the study groups at the University just on one occasion. I never forgot that occasion. I was trying to explain and get a message for that little company who were gathered, a message from the eighth chapter of Romans, a great chapter, and just taking some verses from it. He just wouldn't take "no" as an answer.
>
> And so I felt that here I was committed to this meeting the next evening. Well, what could I do? Could I go and face an audience anywhere, and still battling with God? And so I took a book and away out over the fields. And the book, it will interest you to know was a book by Bishop Ryle with a title *Knots Untied*. And the knot was untied for me that afternoon. Well, I remember saying to the Lord I didn't know my own mind, whether I was willing to go on for the ministry, or not willing. But one thing I did know that I was willing to be made willing for whatever His will was. I never had another moment's struggle, never another moment's struggle. And I went the next evening to Milford, four miles away, and the best part of the sermon was the text. It was John 3.3: "Verily I say unto thee". He was speaking to that very respectable man Nicodemus. The Lord said to him: "Verily I say unto thee, Except a man be born again, he cannot see the kingdom of God."
>
> Well I often thanked God and was grateful that I had a battle, a battle for months over this matter, because I could always feel sure that I had been called.

And you know, I can remember, and this is one of the saddest parts of my life, I can remember young men who were more promising, far more promising than I was; and how they made a profession; how they professed conversion at the Nicholson meetings; and how their lamps seemed to go out, seemed to go out, seemed to go out. I went round to one of those men a year or two ago and I talked to him in his own house for an hour or two. Well, I'm talking here about the call: "How can they preach except they be sent …?" Mark you, I'm not saying that I have been as zealous all the way since as I should have been. I haven't been as devoted as I should have been, but I thank God He has kept my face going forward, looking forward, forward, all by grace, all by grace."

Princeton Theological Seminary

Jim Grier informed his own minister in Ramelton of his desire to enter the ministry, and events moved quickly. He received a note to appear at Presbytery the following week to be examined with regard to his call, a meeting at which he was accepted as a student for the ministry. Back at Belfast he sought out the Professor who had approached him before, and brought him up to date. But having seen that a Professor was willing to have unconverted people in training for the ministry and, anxious for training at a college with an established reputation for orthodoxy, he decided, in consultation with the Church, that he should begin his studies at Princeton, New Jersey. The Ravenhill manse was undoubtedly the primary influence in this— Allen Ross, eldest son of Rev. John Ross and brother of Charlie Ross, had already studied at Princeton, 1920-21. So in the summer of 1923, with civil war still raging at home, Jim Grier, not yet 21, set out for America. He lay on the floor of the train in Derry station as IRA gunfire erupted, but as the train pulled out the troops arrived and the IRA departed.

He learned the characters of the Hebrew alphabet as he crossed the Atlantic. But travel arrangements had been hurried and difficult, with the result that he did not have the right visa. So he approached the Ellis Island immigration station[121] with considerable apprehension, uncertain if he would be allowed to stay. However, the American immigration authorities were satisfied that he had sufficient money to get to his aunt in Pittsburgh and cleared him for entry. Jim Grier's two years at Princeton had great significance for events that were to follow in Belfast. Without those two Princeton years, local church history would have been different.

A remarkable providence in 1926, when Jim Grier had returned to Belfast, completes this stage of the story of the families. His mother, Elizabeth, was attending a missionary rally in Belfast. Conscious that her brother-in-law who had died at Magee had been working excessively, she was very concerned that her youngest son was following a similar pattern. During the rally she got into conversation with a woman from Belfast who seemed very friendly, and in her she confided her fears about the work rate that was absorbing her son. The woman was the ex-missionary, Catherine Gillespie, and she promised to have Jim out to her home on Saturdays. So, from mid-1926 he began to visit the Gillespie home in Knockdene Park South

where they had moved in 1919. Catherine Gillespie junior was just about 13 at the time and her first recollection of Jim Grier was of trying to haul him off her brother as they wrestled on the lawn. His comment about this first meeting with his future wife was that she was "only a schoolgirl". There was plenty of fun. Catherine Gillespie's diaries show that he visited for tea most Saturdays from 1926-1943.

So the different branches of the family came together with the Gillespie line providing the links. A Gillespie son married a Hunter daughter in 1900; the Gillespie daughter of that marriage was to marry a Grier son in 1943. Theologically, most of the Gillespies stayed in the Liberal camp, the most notable exception being John Richard Gillespie, husband of Catherine Hunter, whose commitment to the Presbyterian Church had been undermined by Liberalism on the mission field in China. However, it is interesting that at James Hunter Gillespie's funeral in 1934, the father of the Gillespie clan, William Gillespie, who lived to be 94, expressed his support for James Hunter in what he had done in 1927.

But this is not the end of the story of the part the families played, only the end of the beginning.

Part 2 - The Developing Crisis

The Family Trees

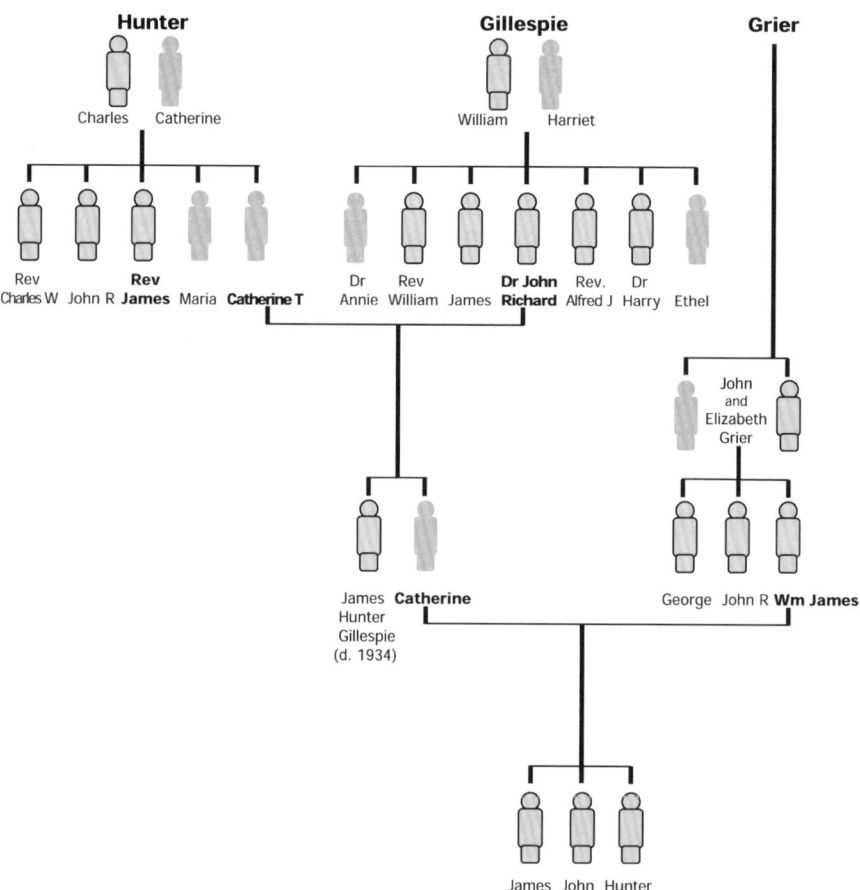

7

The Princeton and Machen Input

The Old School patriarch Archibald Alexander had symbolised the fixed nature of historic orthodoxy on his deathbed [1851] by giving Hodge an ornately carved bone cane, entreating his younger colleague to leave it to his successor [at Princeton] in like manner as "kind of symbol of orthodoxy". ... When Warfield died in 1921, the cane of orthodoxy metaphorically passed once again, this time into the hands of one of Warfield's students, J. Gresham Machen, who had joined the Seminary faculty in 1906 and became its Assistant Professor of the New Testament in 1914. ...

He became one of the nation's leading New Testament scholars and spent much of his career denouncing the insidious influence of modernism on historic Presbyterian orthodoxy. In 1929, his convictions led him to withdraw from Princeton Theological Seminary with a number of other professors to found the more conservative Westminster Theological Seminary in Philadelphia.

Paul C. Gutjahr, *Charles Hodge, Guardian of American Orthodoxy*, Oxford University Press, 2011, pp 379-381

The 19th century expulsion of Arianism, the dynamic of Henry Cooke, and the succession of Confession-challenging developments in the first two decades of the 20th century did not lead directly to the 1927 Heresy Trial, but they had an underlying cumulative effect. What they did was to sustain within the Church a living conviction of the need for a defence of the faith. The crisis came when this conviction was rapidly and powerfully engaged by a group of interacting contemporary events. The first was W J Grier's time at Princeton. Subsequent to his conversion in October 1922, he settled with God his call to the ministry and arrived at Princeton, New Jersey, to begin two years' study, in the autumn of 1923. His room-mate was another student, C H Thomas. Rev. Derek Thomas, editor of *The Evangelical Presbyterian* 1981-1996, devoted the issue of October 1983 to a W J Grier memorial article, and its Princeton section underlies the following paragraphs.

The Princeton Controversy

During the first quarter of the 20th century Princeton Theological Seminary was still regarded as the centre of pure orthodoxy and piety. While other seminaries were shifting their positions and discarding the historic creeds of Christendom, Princeton remained faithful. It was not simply Evangelical; it was unreservedly Calvinistic. Among those of the outstanding Princeton faculty in the mid-1920s were William Park Armstrong, Professor of New Testament, with J Gresham Machen assisting; Caspar Wistar Hodge, Jr, grandson of Charles Hodge, and successor to B B Warfield who died in 1921, Professor of Theology; Geerhardus J Vos, Professor of Biblical Theology; Robert Dick Wilson and Oswald T Allis, Professors of Old Testament. One can only imagine the young Jim Grier browsing through the 118,000 or so volumes in the Seminary library, and handling even the recent acquisition of 1,241 volumes that had once been the property of Benjamin B Warfield. In a personal testimony, W J Grier would later write of his first week at Princeton:

> I had heard of Princeton's reputation for orthodoxy and so I applied in the summer of 1923 and was accepted as a student at the seminary ... I arrived at Princeton a week before the classes were to begin.
>
> That week I attended the midweek service in the Second Presbyterian Church. The speaker was Professor Oswald T. Allis, and his text was, "Give diligence to present thyself approved unto God, a workman that needeth not to be ashamed, handling aright the word of truth" (2 Tim 2.15). I imagine I was the only theological student in the meeting, and that address seemed specially for me, an unforgettable message from God for my soul. So Dr. Allis was the first of the 'men of Princeton' whom I saw and heard. It was a foretaste of things to come.[122]

But an all-important development was taking place in Princeton, namely the attitude it was now taking to the Liberalism then affecting the Presbyterian Church. Princeton was by no means advocating Liberalism, but as Iain Murray points out with respect to John Murray's time there, the distinctive position of the Seminary was being weakened by the views of the Rev. Dr J Ross Stevenson, the Seminary's President, and by Charles R Erdman, Professor of Practical Theology. Jim Grier had been unaware of the growing conflict, and it came to him as a shock, but he was to witness the unfolding of the controversy that would change the entire course of Presbyterianism in the United States. And it was to have a profound effect on his own future.

J Gresham Machen was then 42 and the stated supply at the First Presbyterian Church of Princeton. One notable attack on him came from Henry Van Dyke, Professor of English Literature at Princeton University. He advised his Session, and the press, that he was giving up his pew while Machen preached because he refused to listen to "such a dismal, bilious travesty of the Gospel ... We want to hear about Christ, not about Fundamentalists and Modernists".[123] A year later, Machen was to publish *Christianity and Liberalism*, a book which was to challenge not only men like Harry Emerson Fosdick, a Baptist minister then occupying the pulpit of First Presbyterian Church, New York, but also faculty members like Erdman and Stevenson. It was not that Erdman had himself advocated Liberal views but as Machen was later to write in the columns of *The Presbyterian*:

> Dr Erdman does not indeed reject the doctrinal system of our church, but he is perfectly willing to make common cause with those who reject it, and is perfectly willing on many occasions to keep it in the background. I, on the other hand, can never consent to keep it in the background. Christian doctrine, I hold, is not merely connected with the gospel, but it is identical with the gospel, and if I did not preach it at all times, and especially in those places where it subjects me to personal abuse, I should regard myself as guilty of sheer unfaithfulness to Christ.[124]

These words of Machen were a harbinger of the Heresy Trial to be fought out in Belfast some four years later. Machen separated himself not only from Liberals but from those fellow evangelicals who were prepared to tolerate a breadth of view on the fundamentals of the Gospel. Grier took a similar stance in forming the Irish Evangelical Church in 1927, despite the cost and self-sacrifice it involved. Truth was more important than anything else. Machen's principles are enunciated in sermons that were later printed in *God Transcendent* and presumably Jim Grier heard them. But in any event they became a formative principle with him. The outcome at Princeton was the resignation of Oswald T Allis, Robert Dick Wilson, Cornelius Van Til, who had been appointed to the chair of Apologetics in the spring of 1929, and Machen himself, to form the beginning of Westminster Theological Seminary, Philadelphia, on 25 September 1929.

The Princeton Influence

The impression of Princeton and its teachers on W J Grier's life and ministry was immense and lasting. His life-long friendship with John Murray, later Professor of Systematic Theology at Westminster Seminary, stems from this period, for

Murray's student days at Princeton were 1924-1927. Grier enjoyed life there. There is a photograph in existence of the Scots and Irish, John Murray and Jim Grier, outside Alexander Hall. The culture was different. And the grapefruit were so luscious they used to joke that they should put waterproof coats on at breakfast!

The influences on Jim Grier were not confined to the battle with Liberalism. The effect of the Princeton classrooms was a key one. The Hebrew Professor, Robert Dick Wilson, and his New Testament colleague, J Gresham Machen, were both powerful influences. Dr Wilson proved a profound stimulus to Jim Grier's studies. He had studied Semitic languages at Berlin and at the turn of the century occupied the chair long held by William Henry Green, the mighty champion of the integrity and historical trustworthiness of the Old Testament, and the Mosaic authorship of the Pentateuch. At the time of Dr Wilson's death in 1930, only a year after he had left the faculty of Princeton Seminary to join the staff of Westminster Seminary, Dr Oswald T Allis wrote of him: "With all his brilliancy and fire and all the rich treasures of his accumulated learning, he was remarkably patient as a teacher". He added:

> A great teacher must be a man and a lover of men: an ardent lover of knowledge, tireless in seeking it, skilful in imparting it: a passionate lover of truth and zealous in proclaiming it ... A question or objection from the class would often lead to a digression in which he would pour a wealth of information quite overwhelming to the inquirer or confounding to the caviller.[125]

Wilson wanted Jim Grier to take four cognate languages in his second year, but, convinced that he was called to the pastoral ministry, he only took two. But the conservative position of Wilson on Daniel and other Old Testament critical matters was very decisive. His books such as *The Scientific Investigation of the Old Testament* bear evidence to his position. The other major influence was Gresham Machen, and through his teaching Grier won a New Testament prize for Greek. Professor Edward J Young used to joke that this was what pushed him into Old Testament studies—it was Jim Grier going for Greek. Jim Grier regretted to the end of his days that he had been slow to appreciate Geerhardus Vos, who was elderly by this time. In his first year he didn't go to Vos's lectures at all, but he vastly enjoyed them in the second.

Jim Grier heard a lecture from Caspar Wistar Hodge Jr on *The Glories of the Reformed Faith* at the close of his second year Systematic Theology course, and he recalled it with enthusiasm. The Reformed Faith, he heard, was characterised by three features:

1. Theism come to its rights. It acknowledges God to be God and so gives Him His due. It joins already in the great song ushering in the marriage supper of the Lamb, "as it were the voice of a great multitude, and as the voice of many waters, and as the voice of mighty thunders, saying, Hallelujah; for the Lord our God the Omnipotent reigneth."

2. Pure religion. It is a religion of absolute dependence on God, for it casts men at his feet, as with Moses and Isaiah and Job and Saul of Tarsus on the Damascus Road.
3. It is consistent evangelicalism. It gives all the glory to divine grace, and so bestows the crown where it belongs. Salvation is by grace alone through faith alone.

And so Dr. Hodge sent us forth in that closing lecture to cast men on the mercy of God. We are to hold aloft Christ as Saviour and look for the results to God. We are to preach and pray but God alone can regenerate.[126]

Two months earlier, Jim Grier had heard another sermon, this time preached by Machen in the Miller Chapel of Princeton Seminary, in which Machen brought home to him the cost of defending the Reformed Faith. The sermon closed with these words:

What are you going to do my brothers, in this great time of crisis? … Will you stand with the world, will you shrink from controversy, will you witness for Christ only where witnessing costs nothing, will you pass through these stirring days without coming to any real decision? Or … will you hope, and pray, not for a mere continuance of what is now, but for a re-discovery of the gospel that will make all things new? … God grant that some of you … may come to say, as you go forth into the world: "It is hard in these days to be a Christian; the adversaries are strong; I am weak; but thy Word is true and thy Spirit will be with me; here am I, Lord, send me."[127]

Summers in Canada 1924-25

Another important influence for Jim Grier was his summer supply arrangements. Students were expected to use their vacation months for some form of pastoral work. For Jim Grier the selected venue was Canada. In 1924 he worked in the prairie province of Saskatchewan under the Home Missions Board of the Presbyterian Church in Canada. But a new ecclesiastical situation had developed in Canada by the following year, which John Murray explains:

In that same year, 1925, a great spiritual calamity occurred in the church history of Canada. It was in that year that the union of the Methodist, Congregational and Presbyterian churches was consummated. By this union a large proportion of the Presbyterian Church in Canada abandoned the historic Presbyterian witness and entered into a communion that had as its basis a confession acceptable to the overwhelming majority of Methodists and Congregationalists in that Dominion.[128]

About a third of the laity and 10% of the ministers did not join the Union.
Machen became involved in recruiting students for the continuing Presbyterian Church in Canada from the summer of 1925, and he often saw them off on the

railway platform, with money for their expenses. He arranged for Jim Grier to spend his second holiday assignment in River Denys Station, Inverness Province, Cape Breton Island, Nova Scotia, off the east coast of Canada. The largely forested Cape Breton was three-quarters the size of Northern Ireland, and with no causeway across the Strait of Canso in those days it was truly an island. Jim Grier arrived mid-May and worked there for four months. He wrote to Machen on 26 August 1925 from River Denys, three or four weeks before leaving to pick up his belongings from Princeton: "I have now been about 15 weeks in Cape Breton and am very thankful that I was led into the work. I have been working among 3 substantial 'minority' groups and enjoyed the ministry of the Word very much."

Grier was reluctantly obliged to raise with Machen the issue of his own and his colleagues' travelling expenses. The understanding of the students working in Nova Scotia was that their fares to and from Princeton would be paid, but it appeared that the Nova Scotia Presbytery was expecting to fund the return journey only as far as the Canadian border: "They are cutting us down to the minimum of 15$ a week, but most of us would be quite content with that if our railway fares were paid. I have enjoyed the work here and if I never were paid a cent, it would all have been well worth-while. Yet to me the financial end of the matter is of some importance, as I am crossing the Atlantic in the near future." Machen wrote three very directly worded letters to the Church in Canada, to clear the matter up, adding: " … but if the worst should come to the worst I will pay all the fares myself, so that in any case the students will not be allowed to suffer." And Grier was concerned that the fares issue should not make the students appear 'mercenary': "But you will readily understand that all of these students are carrying on their education on a very close margin, so that the financial question becomes for them a life-and-death matter."

The Nova Scotia correspondence revealed a developing bond between Machen and Grier. Machen replied to Grier on 3 September 1925: "All summer I have been desiring to write to you, but did not know your address. I particularly appreciated your sending me a postcard from New Glasgow on your arrival; especially since you were, if I remember rightly, the very first of the men from whom I heard. … I shall miss you ever so much next year and wish that it were possible for you to stay with us. But wherever you are I shall have a deep personal interest in you, and shall always be appreciative of news about you and about your work."

The Machen-Grier Correspondence

Westminster Theological Seminary, Philadelphia, has archived 50 letters that passed between Machen and Grier between August 1925 and October 1936, of which 22 were Machen's and 28 Grier's.[129] They began when Grier was in Canada in the summer of 1925 and resumed when he returned to Belfast later that year. The correspondence dealt with the growing Church conflict in Ulster in 1926, the Presbyterian Bible Standards League, its bookshop and books, James Hunter's

SOS pamphlets and related public meetings, the Heresy Trial, and Machen's 1927 and 1932 visits to Belfast. Later it moved to *The Irish Evangelical*, the developing *Irish Evangelical Church*, its subordinate standards and name, current ecclesiastical issues on both sides of the Atlantic, and Christian books. Machen was always encouraging and supportive, but cautious over involvement in a situation outside his own domain.

So the influence of mid-1920s Princeton on W J Grier was a key factor in the unfolding events, but there were others, each of them local.

8

The Nicholson Missions

Sydney, 19th October 1926

My Dear Mr Hunter

Your letter to hand. I have had great joy in praying for you in the fight over there and it has been a great joy to me to be able to say "you are a friend of mine." I love a "Bonnie" fighter, as the covenanters called Mr Rutherford. God bless you for the fight you are putting up for the Lord and His word and church. Five minutes in the presence of the Lord and you won't be sorry you fought for Him and suffered as you have for Him. I don't understand these "D.D.s" for some of them used to be out and out for the Lord when I was a boy … to see them out for your scalp because you are fighting for the Lord, is a solemn and strange thing. But you are right, it is not the men who are out and out against the standards of the church and the Lord, but it is the religious pacifists that are the bother. It was the same when Dr Cooke was fighting the fight you have on hands. His bother was with that dirty, mean, middle of the road Merozites.[130] But go on dear Brother, we are sure to win if we weary and faint not in our minds. I have had sent to me all the pamphlets you got out, they are fine and just hit the nail on the head every time. God bless you. …

I hope you keep well and cheery in spite of the devil and knocks. It is fine the way the Bible School is forging ahead. Remember me to them all and tell them to love me and pray for me hard in the fight here. Love to Rev. Ross. I hope he is mending and able to be in the fight again. Keep believing.

Yours restfully busy.

Wm P. Nicholson.

In a wonderful way the influence of mid-1920s Princeton interacted with concurrent events at home to bring matters to a head. But it would be hard to underestimate the huge catalytic effect on the critical sequence of events of the Nicholson evangelistic campaigns in Ulster, 1921-26.

The First W P Nicholson Campaign

The Political Situation

The first phase of the meetings, 1921-23, coincided with a period marked by serious outbreaks of communal violence that threatened full civil war. In 1800 the Act of Union made Ireland part of Great Britain, but to many, independence remained the burning issue. A movement for Home Rule began in Ireland in 1870 by which Ireland would remain part of Britain but have its own Parliament to deal with domestic affairs. Gladstone eventually acceded and introduced a Home Rule Bill in 1886, but it split the Liberal Party and  was defeated. The House of Lords rejected a similar Bill, passed by the House of Commons in 1893. Protestants of Ulster, led by Sir Edward Carson, seeing themselves as a minority under a Home Rule arrangement, formed the *Unionist Party* in 1905 to oppose it, the year that saw the birth of *Sinn Féin* (We Ourselves).

When the Liberal Prime minister, Herbert Asquith, introduced the third Home Rule Bill in 1912, the Unionists formed a provisional government to govern Ulster should the Bill become law, and the Ulster Volunteer Forces came into being. At the same time Nationalists in the south formed the Irish Volunteers. Nevertheless the House of Commons passed the Bill in early 1913, only to have it rejected by the Lords. After Parliamentary debate and conflict the Bill became law in May 1914, but the outbreak of World War I later in the year suspended its implementation. Carson urged the Ulster Volunteers to join up, and many of the Irish Volunteers did the same. Tragically, on 1 July 1916, the first day of the Battle of the Somme in northeast France, the 36th Ulster Division sustained 5,500 casualties near Thiepval Wood, including over 2,000 dead. With more than 57,000 casualties overall and nearly 20,000 fatalities, it was the worst day for losses in the history of the British Army. Opposing forces suffered similarly. Prior to this, on Easter Monday, 24 April 1916 the Easter Rising had taken place in Dublin.

The establishment of Northern Ireland in 1920 under David Lloyd George's Government of Ireland Act, and the Irish Free State, in 1921, was followed by two years of violence and civil unrest of an intensity that exceeded much that had gone before. But in the mercy and providence of God the Nicholson evangelistic campaigns were instrumental in bringing much needed healing to the land. In them God brought to bear a power for good that had defied the best and prolonged efforts of government and political leaders.

Nicholson's Training

William Patteson Nicholson was born in Cottown, Bangor, Co Down, in 1876 and was called after Rev. William Patteson, minister of Bangor Trinity 1829-1875, the church of his maternal grandparents. The Nicholson family moved to Belfast during William's childhood and attended Albert Street Presbyterian Church, Falls Road, where William came under the influence of the strongly reformed and evangelical ministry of Rev. Henry Montgomery.

William went to sea when he was 16, serving as an apprentice on the sailing ship, *Galgorm Castle*. He adopted the rough seafaring life of the day including excessive drinking, but he was never free from conviction of sin. At the end of his four-year apprenticeship he worked on the Cape to Cairo railroad in Africa, continuing the same life of sin that he had followed at sea. But in May 1899, three weeks after arriving home in Bangor, he came to Christ in a sudden conversion, convinced that he faced his final opportunity to accept God's offer of mercy. His new life soon found expression as he began to speak at open-air and cottage meetings. He started studies at the Bible Training Institute (BTI) of Glasgow in 1901 where he was greatly influenced by James Orr, Professor of Systematic Theology and Apologetics at the United Free Church College in Glasgow, and by his colleague, James Denney, Professor of New Testament. He also liked to sit under the preaching of Dr Alexander Whyte, minister of St George's United Free Church in Edinburgh, whose powerful emphasis on sin, including its remnants in the life of the believer, became a prominent feature in Nicholson's own ministry.

After his training in BTI he worked as an evangelist with the Lanarkshire Christian Union from 1903 until 1908 when he crossed to the United States to join the evangelistic partnership of John Wilbur Chapman and Charles McCallon Alexander. Dr Chapman was a minister of the Presbyterian Church in the USA whom the Church had appointed to the wider work of evangelism in 1903. Chapman had had an association with D L Moody and had worked with the evangelist R A Torrey, but teamed up with Alexander to conduct evangelistic campaigns in Australia and America during 1909-1910, with W P Nicholson assisting. Alexander was the song leader, the best known and most influential of his time. He compiled a number of hymnals and with his wife founded the Pocket Testament League. In 1911 Nicholson returned to Glasgow for a one-year temporary pastorate in St George's Cross Tabernacle, before returning to evangelistic work in the United States. He settled with his wife and family in Pennsylvania where in 1914 he was ordained as an evangelist of the Presbyterian Church in the USA. In 1918 the family moved to Los Angeles when Nicholson joined the staff of the Bible Institute there.

Ministry to Main Cities and Towns

The first of Nicholson's two major missions in Ulster took place in the years 1921-1923 and some consider that in it he did his finest work. He had an urban focus - Belfast, Portadown, Lurgan, Newtownards, Lisburn, Londonderry, Ballymena, and Carrickfergus - preaching mostly in Presbyterian churches, but also in

Methodist venues, often with groups of local churches co-operating. Usually he would devote the first part of any mission to speaking to Christians, denouncing sin and naming particular sins in the Christian life.

He preached the love of God, but regularly his subject was the terrors of Hell. Great crowds pressed into these meetings with real desire for the preaching of the Word of God. One such occasion was in February 1922 when Nicholson began a mission in the Albert Hall, home of the Shankill Road Mission, opened in 1898 by the church he had attended in his youth, Albert Street Presbyterian. Rev. Henry Montgomery had resigned from it in 1902 to concentrate on the work in the Albert Hall. The Hall, with a capacity of almost 3,000, was packed each evening of the Nicholson mission, and over 2,000 passed through the enquiry rooms. One of the best-known examples of these meetings took place during the series at the Ravenhill Road Presbyterian Church, 11 February–11 March 1923, when over 100 men professed faith in Christ:

The Donkey is inside the box

> The second mission in East Belfast was held in Ravenhill Presbyterian Church where the scenes of the Newtownards Road area were largely repeated. Here too there was a special "men's only" meeting for the workmen in "The Island" [the Belfast shipyard] who marched to the church straight from the shipyard. So great was the crush at the entrance to the church building that the pillar supporting the gates was moved off its foundation. On a subsequent occasion, the evangelist referred to the event as "the night of the big push." Many men from the factories and workshops of East Belfast date their conversion from the "men's only" meetings held in these campaigns.[131]

Instrument, Strange but not so Strange

It is surprising in many ways that Nicholson was the man that God should choose for such a momentous work. Writing in 1983 about Nicholson's weaknesses, Professor Adam Loughridge, of the Reformed Presbyterian Theological Hall, Belfast, speaks unequivocally:

> W. P. Nicholson was a strange instrument in the work of revival, but God graciously overruled his many weaknesses. He was vulgar and rude and his language at times was ungracious as he indulged in personal abuse, not only of those who had dared to criticise him, but of any who may have interrupted the meetings by late arrival or early departure. He was useless in controversy for he became increasingly hostile towards the Churches. But in spite of all that God was pleased to use him and his zeal for the furtherance of the gospel.[132]

But in other important ways he was not a strange choice at all. He was exceptionally gifted in terms of charismatic personality, with the ability to rivet his hearers. He was the very antithesis of a team player, taking charge of the services personally, leading the singing, and conducting every part of them from beginning to end himself. He was a fervent, passionate preacher, above all sincere, but with a quick, penetrating wit and lively memory from which he illustrated his sermons with anecdotes from his unconverted life and the experiences of his ministry. But the personal features to emphasise are his burning zeal, his life of prayer and his devotion. He loved to pray, spending many intense hours alone and undisturbed in the presence of God. Fellow believers supported his campaigns with whole nights and half nights of prayer. Nicholson later wrote:

> I do not know anyone in the world that I know better than the Lord. I do not know my wife or my mother the way I know the Lord. I do not know the best friends I ever had the way I know the Lord. We walk together, my Lord and I, because we are in fellowship, and there is nothing that I have but is His.[133]

Newness of Life

Livingstone and Wells in *Ulster-American Religion* argue that "Nicholson's unique work among working people, especially men, was of great importance in directing the loyalty of Ulster's working classes towards Unionism. He was successful because he was able to speak from, and to, the populist ethos that makes Ulster Unionism so fascinating (as Aughey says, completely loyal and completely rebellious)."[134] The heading of the chapter, from which this reference is taken, is "*Populist Ideology and Revivalism*, W. P. Nicholson and the Forging of a Unionist Identity".

Populism is a political philosophy that identifies with the needs of common people, and the parallels with God's purposes for the Gospel are unmistakable; but preachers do not select the objects of God's populist outreach: "For you see your calling, brethren, that not many wise according to the flesh, not many mighty, not many noble, are called. But God has chosen the foolish things of the world to put to shame the wise, and God has chosen the weak things of the world to put to shame the things which are mighty; and the base things of the world and the things which are despised God has chosen, and the things which are not, to bring to nothing the things that are, that no flesh should glory in His presence." (1 Cor 1.26-29) The common people heard Christ gladly, whilst the self-appointed role model Pharisees asked: "Have any of the rulers or the Pharisees believed in him?" (John 7.48)

Political influence was not Nicholson's objective. It was not what he wrestled in prayer over, nor what he counselled people in enquiry rooms who were grappling personally with the basic question of all religion, "But how can a man be righteous before God?" (Job 9.2). He operated on a higher level than political direction. He was a man called of God and equipped by Him for a special work in the spiritual realm. He had surrendered his life to God for the greatest calling in the world, the ministry of the Gospel. No doubt the preaching of Protestant theology had a bearing on Protestant consciousness, and for the very best reasons. It certainly was a means of turning back the horror of daily bloodshed, where all else had failed, and it changed social values. Scripture brings its beneficial teaching to bear on every aspect of life, including life in the State. Nicholson's work, like any work of God, cannot be understood or accounted for on the human level, and its deficiencies do not rob it of its true nature as a work of God.

Livingstone and Wells suggest revival problems as they conclude their Populist chapter:

> What William P. Nicholson would have had a difficult time admitting is that "revivals" come and go; they wax and they wane. For one who believes that a revival is "a mighty work of God," the waning of a revival is hard to explain because one has already given the entire agency to God. Has God withdrawn his Spirit? These are questions that historians cannot answer, but they surely vexed the people who had to explain a revised view of the world after the singing stopped.[135]

In fact, Nicholson would have had no difficulty in admitting that revivals come and go for that is their very nature and one of the things that gave him urgency. God grants them rarely and intermittently. They wax and wane precisely because the entire agency is of God. God does indeed withdraw His Spirit, within and outside the context of revival, though never in the sense that the Church is without Him. God appoints His Church the normality of living as a remnant in "the day of small things", when it is all too apparent that "narrow is the gate and difficult is the way which leads to life, and there are few who find it." (Matt 7.14)

In the course of the Nicholson missions more than 12,000 people passed through his enquiry rooms in two years. On occasions the numbers seeking counselling exceeded 1,000. Communicant rolls saw substantial increase and the Christian Endeavour movement expanded its membership and opened new societies. Christian Workers' Union branches opened in areas where his meetings had been held and Nicholson helped to organise them along the lines of the Christian Workers' Society of Bangor, 1878. "At the close of his missions Mr Nicholson advocated the young converts getting together and forming a Christian Workers' Union, a fellowship and Gospel meeting to be held weekly. He did not believe, he said, in 'putting live chickens under a dead hen'".[136] Prayer meetings and Bible classes took on a new lease of life, a new batch of missionary recruits offered for service, and the number of candidates for the Presbyterian ministry doubled in the first half of the 1930s. Evidence of newness of life appeared in society and places of work. For example, early in 1923, following the East Belfast missions the Belfast shipyard found it necessary to allocate a special store to accommodate stolen tools and materials that were being returned—an insight perhaps into the demands of Ephesians 4.28: "Let him who stole steal no longer".

A few months before the first Nicholson mission was beginning to deliver its powerful, transforming impact on the spiritual and community life of Ulster in 1921, Professor J E Davey of Assembly's College had presented his sophisticated, philosophical Carey Lectures. The contrast in content and effectiveness could not have been greater. Nicholson, unswerving in his commitment to the infallibility of Scripture as the Word of God, preached the great doctrines of grace—the cross of Christ and His atoning blood, as the only remedy for sin. Through this message God had given a great measure of peace to the community and revival to the church.

The Second W P Nicholson Campaign

In June 1923 Nicholson had returned to his work with Biola, the Bible Institute of Los Angeles, but resigned a year later to fulfil invitations from Ulster to return. Livingstone and Wells consider that a major factor in the resignation from Biola was the appointment of J M MacInnis to succeed R A Torrey. MacInnis was on the moderate wing of fundamentalism, advocating alliance with mainline churches, and they consider that the militant Nicholson would be unwilling to serve under a leadership that he would see as compromised.[137]

In any event, in July 1924, halfway through Jim Grier's time at Princeton, W P Nicholson commenced his second series of missions that continued until March 1926. For this series, apart from Belfast, he selected smaller localities. August 1925 saw the major mission of the period. Supported by various denominations, it was held in the Assembly Hall in Belfast where the attendance, in a holiday month, so surpassed every expectation that accommodation twice the size could sometimes have been filled. He ministered in locations outside Northern Ireland too. In July 1925 he spoke at the jubilee Keswick Convention, in November he opened a five-week campaign in the Metropolitan Hall YMCA, Dublin, and in January-February 1926 he conducted a mission at Cambridge University.

Attacks on Modernists

Whilst the blessing of God attended the second mission, sometimes very powerfully, overall it did not attain to the exceptional heights of the first. Politically, a measure of peace had returned by 1924, and the sense of need in the community was not as great as it had been in 1921-23; interest in spiritual things is often born of need. There was not the same church unity in organising the missions that had characterised the earlier series, nor the same level of support. Nicholson's heightened criticism of liberal theology and its exponents goes some way to explaining the restraint by sections of the church during the second mission. He denounced individuals by name, including professors of Assembly's College whom he judged as modernists. He could shock and cause offence, as Austin Fulton, biographer of J Ernest Davey indicates:

> If the evangelist restrained himself in his references to Roman Catholics, he more than compensated by the extravagant licence of his attacks upon 'liberals', 'modernists', 'higher critics' and Unitarians. Such attacks gain tremendously in momentum if they can be aimed at a particular target. Professor Davey provided the target.[138]

So the second mission, even more than the first, made orthodoxy a live issue in the Presbyterian Church. Nicholson was an evangelist, but a polemic evangelist who believed that his message incorporated exclusive rights; "Nor is there salvation in any other" (Acts 4.12). To him, the terms of the Gospel demanded an offensive against everything that stood in opposition to it, and so he attacked cults and theological professors alike. He and James Hunter were friends. The chapter preface records that in an October 1926 letter to Hunter from Sydney, Nicholson said: "… it has been a great joy to me to be able to say 'you are a friend of mine.'" Hunter and Rev. Henry Montgomery accompanied Nicholson to the platform at the opening meeting of the Belfast Assembly Hall Mission in August 1925. Livingstone and Wells conjecture about W J Grier's attendance at that meeting: "While there is no record of Grier attending the August 1925 Nicholson Mission at the Assembly Hall, one supposes he would have eagerly attended a meeting in which his two mentors, Nicholson and Hunter, figured so prominently."[139] In fact, Grier did not arrive back in Belfast from the United States until 6 October 1925.

The 'Second Blessing'

The Nicholson picture would be defective without noting that he belonged within the 'second blessing' constituency, a grouping that is not easy to define since its system developed along several distinct lines. In the 18th century Wesley had proposed an experience subsequent to conversion, known by various descriptions such as 'entire sanctification', 'heart purity' or, his favourite, 'perfect love'. He based it on 1 Thessalonians 5.23: "Now may the God of peace himself sanctify you completely; and may your whole spirit, soul, and body be preserved blameless at the coming of our Lord Jesus Christ." The verse in fact expresses Paul's desire for such a separation to God as would progressively permeate every part of every believer. Nevertheless, in the 1770s Wesley's colleague, John Fletcher, equated Wesley's 'heart purity' with the 'baptism of the Spirit', coupling it with the idea of 'spiritual power for service'.

From then, the Holiness Movement developed its 'second blessing' theology with its variations of sinless perfection, and towards the end of the 19th century 'spiritual power for service' became a major distinctive of the Keswick 'Higher Life' movement. Andrew Murray, leader of the South African Dutch Reformed Church, who spoke at Keswick in 1895, writes:

> In the life of the believer there sometimes comes a crisis, as clearly marked as his conversion, in which he passes out of a life of continual feebleness and failure to one of strength, and victory, and abiding rest. The transition has been called the Second Blessing. … Confessing and giving up all that is of self and sin, yielding himself wholly to Christ and His service, he believes and receives a new power to live his life by the faith of the Son of God. The change is in many cases as clear, as marked, as wonderful, as conversion. For lack of a better name, that of A Second Blessing came most naturally.[140]

Stanley Barnes gives an account of Nicholson's 'baptism of the Holy Spirit' that took place about the end of 1899. Nicholson said of himself: "I blundered on in my half-saved condition for seven months", but after attending a Convention in Bangor "for the deepening of the Christian life" addressed by Rev. J Stuart Holden of London, "I made the complete unconditional surrender." He cried out: "Come in. Come in, Holy Spirit. Thy work of great blessing begin. By faith I lay hold of the promise and claim complete victory over sin." He dated the power and effectiveness of his ministry from that occasion. Barnes outlines Nicholson's 'second blessing' views: he believed the baptism of the Spirit to be a separate experience to salvation, but did not link it with speaking in tongues; he did not regard his experience as a once-and-for-all Spirit encounter, but, differentiating between Spirit baptism and Spirit filling, he looked for many fillings subsequent to his one baptism and he did not claim sinless perfection.[141]

Reformed theology has its own divergent positions on the baptism of the Spirit, but contends essentially that it is not to be understood as a work of grace subsequent to conversion, or as the reception of charismatic gifts. The baptism or seal of the Spirit is the universal privilege of *all* believers and comes to them simultaneously with being united to Christ in salvation: "For by one Spirit we were all baptized into one body – whether Jews or Greeks, whether slaves or free – and have all been made to drink into one Spirit" (1 Cor 12.13; cf Eph 4.30). Nowhere in the New Testament is a believer called upon to seek baptism of the Holy Spirit—it has already taken place. Nicholson was wrong to identify his post-conversion experience as a 'baptism' of the Spirit, but he was right to see the 'filling' as a progressive and repeatable aspiration. The 'filling' or 'fullness' of the Spirit refers to a high degree of consecration to God and the manifestation of power or godliness that accompanies it. It characterises some believers more than others and it may appear in particular believers more at some times than at others in association with special providences. But it is available to all believers, because all have been baptised with the Spirit, and all have a duty to seek the Spirit's filling by submitting to the Spirit's ministry, whatever the sacrifice may be. While Christians are not asked to seek baptism with the Spirit they are urged to seek His filling: "And do not be drunk with wine, in which is dissipation; but be [being] filled with the Spirit." (Eph 5.18)[142]

Whilst Austin Fulton may not have been well disposed towards Nicholson's role in the events that were about to unfold, there are elements of truth in his assessment:

> He contributed to the turbulence in the atmosphere which surrounded the heresy trial. Some have conjectured that if it had not been for the Nicholson campaigns the trial would not have got off the ground at all. However this may be, in the event he did kindle much of the inspiration which gave encouragement to the plaintiffs in the case, and, possibly, caused them to think that their backing was more determined than it proved to be.[143]

There is no doubt that the Nicholson phenomenon was a key factor in the final sequence, and that should not be surprising after such a work of God. Such a pedigree can only be encouraging. The book of Acts is full of "turbulence" as the Gospel claimed territory from the powers of darkness. The Gospel never advances without conflict. About his early Lanarkshire days Nicholson said: "When we began a mission in a town or village, we weren't there long before we had either a riot or revival. Sometimes we had more riot than revival but never a revival without a riot."[144] We can be certain too that James Hunter was encouraged by the revival, and that the changes it brought about made him hopeful about his battle for orthodoxy.

Jim Grier was conscious of the Church-Nicholson situation, as early as August 1925, when he was at Cape Breton, and before he had actively engaged with James Hunter: "There is, it seems, a strong and subtle force working in the Presbyterian Church there too, but the Lord is blessing an independent 'mission work' there richly indeed." Writing again to Machen on 4 November 1925, within a month of returning to Belfast, he shows an even clearer awareness of the developing battle lines: "So the issue is joined all over. They would have had things pretty much their own way here, but – praise God for the revival – they're not so confident now."

So, in the providence of God, a crisis was building. Nicholson had been the means of a spiritual awakening in the church and he had attacked theological unorthodoxy. At the same time, Princeton and Machen had been instrumental in preparing W J Grier for his vital role in the unfolding events. For James Hunter's battle for orthodoxy, marked until now by recurring issues, disappointing results and little impact, there was a changed situation, although its final shape would be very different from his rising expectations.

9

The Leaders Engage

"Contend earnestly for the faith which was once for all delivered to the saints."

As the law was kept in the ark, so was truth delivered to the church to be kept: 1 Tim.i.11, 'The glorious gospel committed to my trust.' There is a trust lieth upon us; upon the apostles first to publish the whole counsel of God, and then upon pastors and teachers in all ages to keep it afoot, and upon all believers and members of the church to see that after ages be not defrauded of this privilege ... none of the jewels which Christ hath left with his spouse must be embezzled; that it be not corrupted and sophisticated, for we are not only to transmit to the next age the scriptures, those faithful records of truth, but also the public explications of the church in summaries and confessions must be sound and orthodox, lest we entail a prejudice upon those that are yet unborn. Every one in his place to see that these things be accomplished.

Thomas Manton on Jude 3

Hunter and Grier Join Forces

W P Nicholson had been God's instrument for bringing a great measure of healing to a strife-torn community and especially spiritual life to many in the church. The revival had created the fertile ground that pressed James Hunter to mount his offensive for orthodoxy.

The Formula of Subscription – Proposed Change 1924-25

Before a church applies its confessional standards it must first set them. It may accept a confession such as Westminster as it stands, or it can regulate it by Declaratory and Amending Acts. Declaratory Acts are statements clarifying a church's interpretation of its standards; they do not amend the standards and should not be tantamount to doing it. Amending Acts do change the standards at specified points and consequently produce a church's own version of the standards. Having set its standards a church will then seek to safeguard them by the personal commitment of each of its ministers, licentiates and office bearers to implement them. This is done by a *Formula of Subscription* – a set of questions that these individuals must answer and subscribe to. The *Formula* wording determines the extent of the commitment and implementation that the church requires to its defined standards.

In 1924, a few months before the second Nicholson mission began in July, thirteen students at Assembly's College wrote to the College Committee seeking information about "the precise obligations imposed by signing the formula of subscription."[145] These students were unhappy about the term "Word of God" being applied to the Bible and wished to accept the Westminster Confession of Faith and Catechisms only in a general way. A deputation conferred with them and a Memorial seeking "relief with respect to the formula of subscription", signed by 23 students, was prepared for presentation to the 1925 General Assembly. It was withdrawn when the Students' Committee undertook to bring a proposal that the Assembly appoint a Committee to consider and report. The 1925 Assembly, by 157 votes to 114, accepted the proposal to consider whether change to the Formula was necessary or desirable, taking account of the practice in other churches. Although James Hunter spoke in opposition to it he was one of those appointed to the Committee. But there were concurrent developments.

James Hunter: Retiring to Work

In July 1924, the same month in which Nicholson began his second mission with meetings at Whiteabbey, James Hunter retired from the pastorate of Knock to devote himself to the defence of the Word of God. The pattern of events strongly suggests that the timing was no coincidence. As a member of the College Committee he would have been aware of the student move on the Formula, but his plans to retire are likely to have pre-dated that development. Of far more influence was the fact that the Church was enjoying the fruits of revival from the first Nicholson mission, and invitations to Nicholson to return had already been sent. The circumstances were now more favourable to orthodoxy than for many years and there was every reason to see the time as significant. Nicholson's first mission had begun in 1921 and, exactly 100 years before, in 1821, Henry Cooke had been pursuing Smethurst around Ulster in a movement that led to the purge of the Synod of Ulster of Arianism in 1829.

Jim Grier: Assembly's College and Licensing

In early October 1925, about five months before the close of Nicholson's second mission, and while the Formula Committee was deliberating, Jim Grier returned from Princeton to begin the final phase of his theological studies—the compulsory year at Assembly's College.

After Princeton he was shocked at some of the men going into the ministry, unconverted men that he thought would never have dreamed of it. He described it to Machen in his letter of 4 November 1925 as a "grim reality". In the classroom, after three weeks listening in silence to things he knew were wrong, he challenged Professor Davey's statement that Paul had never said that Jesus Christ is God, by quoting Philippians 2.6: "Who, being in the form of God, thought it not robbery to be equal with God" (KJV). The next day Davey responded, "What you have said is right! Your quotation from Lightfoot[146] is perfectly adequate. It cannot be argued with. But my faith is not in Paul." This was indelibly fixed in Jim Grier's mind and he referred to it regularly throughout his life.

From then Jim Grier had courage to contend for truth. He said to Machen, 4 November 1925: "I am alone too as far as the students are concerned and seek the prayers of those who love the Lord … I pray for more grace and fearlessness to withstand this teaching. … My courses in Systematics, in N T Department, and under Dr Wilson are now more precious than mines of gold, and I am assured above all that Almighty God will keep me." Machen began his reply of 19 November 1925: "I do not know when I have received a letter that has interested me more than your letter of November 4th. You have my very deepest sympathy in your brave witnessing to the gospel in the midst of such a hostile environment." And in January: "I have seldom received more intensely interesting letters than those you have written to me."

In Grier's next letter to Machen, 11 December 1925, he revealed his growing sense of calling to the challenge in Belfast: "I am one of those very much among the τὰ ἀσθενῆ τοῦ κόσμου ["the weak things of the world"], and the τὰ μὴ ὀ ντα ["the things which are not"]", but I feel that this tide of modernism must be stayed and that God may in some measure use the τὰ μὴ ὄντα, ἵνα τὰ ὄντα καταργήσῃ. ["the things which are not, to bring to nothing the things that are." 1 Corinthians 1. 27-28.] Near the end of the letter he added: "They know by this time that I am tainted with orthodoxy pretty thoroughly." Machen replied: "I wish that a larger number of your colleagues and companions could be tainted with you. … I am glad to observe that when you quote Greek you get the breathings and accents right. This is more than Nunn [a then current Greek Grammar] does!"

So throughout the year the end of lectures saw him at the rostrum debating openly with the Professors, in friendly manner, but on substantive issues; it was never a matter of mishearing. He had the inconvenience of living out because he did not arrive back from his summer supply in Canada in time to secure College accommodation, but he was soon to be thankful for the detachment and relief his digs at 12 Hatfield Street[147] afforded him as his disagreement with the teaching of the Professors developed. They provided some free and cultured recreation too – his back room overlooked the grounds of the North of Ireland Cricket Club!

On 26 April 1926 he was one of a number licensed to preach by the Letterkenny Presbytery. For someone in the Presbytery the contrast between Jim Grier and a candidate of Liberal persuasion was an opportunity for wit: "Today we have licensed both Origen and Athanasius!" Athanasius (c298-373) was the great champion of the deity of Christ "against the world", whilst Origen (c185-c254) was seriously defective and damaging at various key points of doctrine.[148] Grier became assistant to Rev. Robert Anderson in Richview Presbyterian Church, Belfast, in April 1926 and, whilst Anderson was not in full agreement with him, he gave him liberty to preach the Gospel. Anecdotes from that period record that on a Richview Sunday School outing to Newcastle he went up Slieve Donard to pray and think about his message for the next day, and the bus went home without him. It was at Richview that he met the Shanks family and some others who became members of the Irish Evangelical Church in 1927-28.

The CWU Bible School

The School was to play an important role in the quickening pace. It was decided during the Nicholson mission at the Belfast Assembly Hall in August 1925 that the Irish Alliance of Christian Workers' Unions, formed in Londonderry in 1923, should start a Bible School to cater for young people who had to cross to England or Scotland for training. The Secretary presented a progress report to the IACWU Council on 10 September 1925 and W P Nicholson, who was present at the meeting, supported it. Nicholson had announced the project at his meetings and the initial meeting of the Bible School, with 300 men present, was held on Monday 31 August 1925 in the Minor Hall of the YMCA. At that meeting the Alliance Secretary, J Allen Ross, made a statement about the nature of the Bible School and Rev. James Hunter gave the address. The series of Friday evening classes began on 11 September with ministers interested in the work providing the teaching. The 'Upper Room' of the Magdalene Schools, Shaftesbury Square, at the apex of Great Victoria Street and Dublin Road, was secured as the venue. It became known as the Alliance Hall, and was to feature in the early history of the Irish Evangelical Church. The Alliance used it for office accommodation and Council meetings, and the South Belfast CWU rented the Hall for its meetings.

The Bible School held its inaugural public meeting on an unrecorded date between two Council meetings, 15 October and 12 November 1925. Nicholson was the main speaker and James Hunter, standing in for representatives of the CWU District Councils who were unable to attend, gave a supplementary address.

Council decided that the Bible School would run as a separate department of the Alliance with its own committee, although under Council's control and supervision. Council provided a small library. On 27 April 1926 the Council appointed a Bible School Committee: Rev. James Hunter, Rev. John Ross, Rev. J Allen Ross, John King and Andrew Graham. James Hunter was one of the teachers. So for Hunter, the Alliance Bible School became one of his regular duties in little over a year from 'retiring to work' in July 1924.

More than 100 regularly attended some of the classes, including W J Grier. In his letter of 4 November 1925 to Machen, Grier spoke of: "… a projected Bible School in Belfast, where systematic instruction is already being given by evangelical ministers on the Bible and its doctrines. … A former pupil of yours (namely myself) is being asked to take some classes in N.T. Greek in the Bible School and was just wondering the other day if Dr. Machen's N.T. Grammar for beginners was procurable from any London bookseller."

Machen replied: "I am greatly interested in the prospect of your teaching New Testament Greek. You are well qualified to do so, as well as to enter into teaching work in general." Grier's next letter noted an attendance of 20-30 at his Greek class, on which Machen commented: "It is most remarkable, I think, that you should have so many as twenty or thirty in such a class, and I congratulate you on this most encouraging number. Also I desire to congratulate the class on its teacher." One of Grier's letters reveals that he was also teaching a Women's Bible class on Monday evenings.

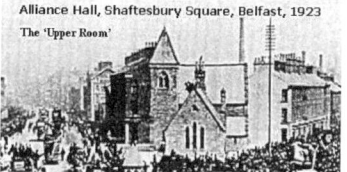
Alliance Hall, Shaftesbury Square, Belfast, 1923
The 'Upper Room'

Grier Informs Hunter

As Jim Grier encountered the teaching in Assembly's College from October 1925 he was unable to remain silent about it. He rejected any idea of speaking to W P Nicholson, fearing it would soon be in the public arena, but decided to consult Rev. James Hunter, who he knew shared his concern, and from whom he was assured of a scholarly approach. Hunter and Grier had become acquainted in Ravenhill Presbyterian Church where they were both members.[149]

When speaking at the opening of the new Somerton Road Church on 18 January 1932, Mr Hunter provided information about his critical meeting with Grier:

> When speaking in the Magdalene School six years ago, a young theological student told me that he had been taught by his professors that the Lord Jesus on the Cross thought He had let God down. I told him that if I could get anybody to corroborate that statement I would prosecute the matter. Another man corroborated the statement.[150]

Writing in July 1932 Hunter began: "It had been known for a long time that things were not right in the Assembly's College." He outlined reports of false teaching, one of them with written examples. Referring to Grier's "thought he had let God down" report he added: "The blasphemy was so shocking that I resolved to do what I could to expose this infidelity.[151]

The quotation from the lecture that Christ "thought he had let God down" is included in Charge 2 of the Heresy Trial with the lecture dated as 5 December 1925. So it is likely that Grier referred it to Hunter soon after that. Grier's record of events in 1925 states that he began making his lecture notes available to Hunter "in the following winter and spring".[152] This would allow for a date in December 1925 subsequent to the Davey lecture of 5 December, or early in 1926. However, in his letter to Machen of 4 November 1925, a month after his return to Belfast, Grier referred to Hunter without having to introduce him, and spoke of Hunter's work on a pamphlet for the next General Assembly that would contain "ex cathedra" statements from the College – "a secret as yet". Clearly, then, Hunter and Grier were at least in communication as early as October 1925, during the first weeks of Grier's studies at Assembly's College. Again, Ravenhill could well have facilitated it, for James Hunter had joined not long after his retirement from Knock in July 1924 and Grier had resumed his attendance in October 1925.

So the CWU Bible School provided the opportunity and the perfect context for Grier to make his approach soon after 5th December 1925. There is no doubt about the significance of this meeting. Jim Grier initiated it, and for Hunter it was the defining moment. For him it was now a bounden duty to proceed towards a formal confrontation with Assembly's College.

The Cape Breton Call

Evidently Jim Grier had been appreciated in Nova Scotia, for he said in a letter to Machen, 11 December 1925: "They offered me a church in Nova Scotia and I promised to 'consider it favourably', but until <u>something is done</u> here, I feel I can hardly leave, and I think I shall tell my Cape Breton friends not to look for me in May at any rate, and after a little when the course becomes clearer, I may have to ask them to let me off." On 3 March 1926 Grier advised Machen that he had received a call "properly made out" from a congregation in the Presbytery of Cape Breton. There is no record of the date he declined the offer but there was probably little delay as he already had an identity with the battle being fought at home and a clear sense of calling to it. No doubt it would have been vastly more pleasant to escape.

10

The Battle is Joined

Lastly, Spurgeon reminds us that piety and devotion to Christ is not a preferable alternative to controversy, but rather that it should – when circumstances demand it – lead to the second. He was careful to maintain that order. The minister who makes controversy his starting point will soon have a blighted ministry and spirituality will wither away. But controversy which is entered into out of love for God and reverence for His Name, will wrap a man's spirit in peace and joy even when he is fighting in the thickest of the battle.

The Forgotten Spurgeon, Iain Murray, p 205.

"The storm broke with the formation of the Presbyterian Bible Standards League, and the addressing by Mr. Hunter and others of large meetings throughout the Province. Excitement rose among the people when, in April and May, 1926, he circulated large numbers of leaflets which described the College as 'a seed-bed of rationalism,' and which denounced the teaching of several members of staff."[153]

SOS to Irish Presbyterians

Following Jim Grier's visit to Hunter events moved purposefully. Hunter's approach was first to gather and assess the evidence, then to proceed to a public awareness campaign. His knowledge of the Henry Cooke experience a century earlier had taught him the importance of Church public opinion in securing the victory for Confessional orthodoxy.

Grier's lecture notes and Hunter's own knowledge of the Formula of Subscription affair as a member of the Committee, prompted him to issue four SOS pamphlets to Irish Presbyterians, No 1 in April 1926, Nos 2 and 3 in May, and No 4, which had only a token circulation, in June. Each was a folded sheet giving four pages approximately 25x19cm. Each had the same front page – top: **"S.O.S. To Irish Presbyterians."**; middle, **"FAITH or INFIDELITY: Which is it to be?"**; bottom, **"The Assembly's College a Seed-Bed of Rationalism."**

SOS No 1: May 1926 – Professor Haire

The subject of the first SOS was a critique of the teaching of James Haire, Professor of Systematic Theology at Assembly's College, 1919-44. Under the title on the left middle page, "Did the Lord Jesus make mistakes in His teaching?" Hunter began: "Professor HAIRE strives to have his students believe that the Bible is not infallible, and that the Lord Jesus Christ was not infallible." The caption on the right middle page read, "About the Holy Spirit" - "In an examination paper at the beginning of last session Professor Haire gave these two questions in print:

> How do you account for the absence from Jesus' own thought of the idea of the Spirit?
> How far is the doctrine of the Trinity implied in the New Testament?

The SOSs caused no small stir among people and Church and College authorities—Grier described their effect to Machen on 10 May 1926 as "causing a sensation". The demand for Issue No 1 was sufficiently encouraging for Hunter to add a footnote in SOS No 2:

> Thanks be to God for the interest, generosity, and enthusiasm manifested through the issue of No. 1. It will be necessary to double or treble the number for circulation. Next issue will (D.V.) appear before the end of the month, and is to contain a setting forth of the views of another professor. Those who feel

led to take some part in the crusade can communicate with (Rev.) JAMES HUNTER, Moyle, Knockbreda Road, Belfast.

SOS No 2: May 1926 – Formula of Subscription and Principal Paul

This sheet focused on the 1925 Formula of Subscription Committee and its Convener, Francis J Paul, Professor of Church History, 1922-41 and Principal of Assembly's College 1924-41.

The Formula Committee appointed James Hunter to a sub-committee of six to consider "necessary and desirable" changes, but he declined to act from February 1926 and did not identify himself with the report that was unanimous on the part of the other five members.[154] He said this about the Committee in SOS No 2:

> The report of this Committee is now ready for the Assembly, and its proceedings throw a flood of light on the revolutionary notions of those who are now attempting to alter our creed. The convener of the Committee (the head of the College, Professor Paul) presented a sheaf of suggestions, and the first surprise was that the question about the Word of God was shunted to third place. When asked why it should not occupy the prominent place it had always held, his answer was that 'experience' came before the Scriptures. This is the Modernist position. ... The next move was to drop the word 'infallible' as applied to the Word of God. 'There is no external infallibility,' he affirmed. This is the slogan of the new teaching. ... There is no mystery about the source whence the students derived their dislike of the name 'Word of God'; it came from the atmosphere of the college.

Dr Machen commented on SOS 2 in a letter to Grier in May 1926, in response to Grier's earlier in the month, which began: "Some more 'small shot'; the canon are being loaded":

> It is very encouraging to learn that the standard of revolt against modernist tyranny has been raised in Ireland. Part of the pamphlet seems to me to be very strong – especially that which concerns the proposed changes in the formula of subscription. Perhaps the difficulty will be that where the evidence is not documented, as may perhaps be the case with part of the evidence that is contained in this pamphlet, the persons criticised may engage in the prevalent prevarication, and so avoid the consequences of what they have said. At any rate I admire Mr. Hunter's courage, and I hope that the great aim that he has in view may by the blessing of God be accomplished.

When the Report came before the 1926 General Assembly in June the question on the Word of God remained as Question 1 and the word "infallible" was retained. Principal Paul proposed that it be received and the Committee reappointed with the same Convener, but a contra motion to pass from the question was carried by 316 votes to 302. A further motion that the Committee be thanked and discharged was defeated by 290 votes to 288,[155] and the house enlarged the Committee by 14 members, six ministers and eight ruling elders. W J Grier concluded his detailed treatment of the subject: "It continued in being for some years, but it was eventually decided for the sake of peace to abandon the project of the proposed change meantime."[156]

SOS No 3: May 1926 – Professor Haire

Again the subject was Professor Haire, and under the heading, "The Supposed Errors of the Bible", provided extracts from the synopses of his lectures that he had given to students in the previous term. The opposite page listed extracts from the Lectures of J Ernest Davey, Professor of Biblical Literature and Hellenistic Greek, 1922-30. Hunter summarised his feelings about the College he was portraying in these SOS sheets like this:

> Would it not be almost as safe to close the Assembly's College, and to send the students to Manchester Unitarian College, where they would be on their guard against what they would hear, instead of having the poor fellows swallow all this horrible stuff? Or, if there is a desire to give the old theology a chance— send them to Princeton, at a fraction of the cost of the present establishment, where very able men defend the old bulwarks.[157]

This Princeton dimension was noted in the *Belfast Telegraph's* report of the League's Formula of Subscription meeting in the Belfast YMCA on 9 June 1926 under a sub-heading, "Inauguration of New Fund": "The Chairman announced a considerable sum of money to inaugurate a fund to be immediately available for assisting students to attend Princeton Theological Seminary in the United States to have them taught in keeping with the principles of the Irish Presbyterian Church." Grier's letter to Machen on 21 June 1926 informed him of the fund and its purposes, adding: "The League is willing to pay their ocean fare. With Princeton's 'grant' ($150) they should be able to get along pretty well."

The College Committee Investigation

The College Committee met on 30 April 1926 to consider the serious reflections brought on the teaching of Professor Haire by SOS No 1, and its deliberations ran concurrently with the issue of SOSs Nos 2 and 3. The Committee summoned Professor Haire and James Hunter to attend a preliminary investigation. Hunter did not attend: "As the Committee had no authority over me, and I knew they were out-and-out Modernist I did not choose to do this."[158]

A sub-committee questioned the students about the professor's teaching. One of them, W J Grier, provides his own account of the meeting, Monday 24 May 1926:[159]

> … Most of the witnesses summoned were before the Committee for but a few minutes each. The present writer was interrogated for some fifty minutes and

he has six pages of a record of what transpired. No small part of the time was spent in attempts to entangle him with ensnaring questions. He quoted before the sub-committee the following questions dictated by Prof. Haire to his class:

1. Is Omniscience necessary to our conception of Christ? Would Christ have been human if He had been omniscient?
2. Is infallibility in everything necessary to God manifest in the flesh?

He told the sub-committee that the Professor's own answers were in the negative. Members of the sub-committee sought to justify the Professor by questioning the writer as to Scripture passages setting forth Christ's subordination.[160] One member of the sub-committee, an ex-Moderator, asked the writer to explain the words 'He emptied Himself' (in Phil 2.7, RV). The writer referred to an article by Dr. B. B. Warfield as giving a good explanation, but was told, 'It doesn't matter what Dr. Warfield said. What do you think?' The writer replied, 'I don't believe in the Kenosis theory.' When he protested that he was present to give evidence about Prof. Haire and not to be questioned on his own faith, the Moderator of the 1925 Assembly, who presided, replied, 'Oh; but you have made very serious allegations with regard to Prof. Haire.' The sub-committee said in their report that Prof. Haire also appeared before them. On 1st June the Sub-committee reported to the full College Committee, which received its report and authorised it to be published.[161] According to this published report Prof. Haire said that 'he did not impress this teaching on his students, but took pains to controvert it.'

Now note this amazing fact—the Committee went on to affirm that Prof. Haire's statement was in their opinion 'fully borne out by the evidence of the students' (of the present writer among others). Mr. Hunter, who was present as a member of the College Committee on June 1st (and in this Committee he stood alone), asked the Convener whether, when the seven students of Prof. Haire's class were being examined eight days previously, a question had been put to one or more of them—if Prof. Haire had taught that the Bible was not infallible and that the Lord Jesus was not infallible? The Convener answered that this question had not been put directly to any of the students. Yet here is the record made by the present writer on May 24th of what took place that day before the sub-committee:

I was asked if it was correct to say that Prof. Haire did strive to have his students believe that the Bible was not infallible, and that the Lord Jesus Christ was not infallible. I replied, 'Yes'. The question was put to me. 'If other students said that Prof. Haire affirmed Dr. Oman to be wrong in saying Christ was fallible, then they would be telling untruths?' I answered, 'Yes.'

At the meeting of the General Assembly on June 8th, 1926, the same assertion was made as in the report of the Committee, namely, that the evidence of all the seven students exonerated Prof. Haire. Mr. Hunter affirmed that this was not so in the case of the evidence of at least one student. There were cries of "Name, Name?" Mr. Hunter was about to give the name, when some, who thought to shield the present writer from the rage of the powers that be, shouted, 'Don't, Don't,' and Mr. Hunter forebore.

115

The Public Meeting 9 June 1926

Grier made a statement at a huge public meeting in the large YMCA Hall, Belfast, on the following evening, 9 June 1926, which meeting he notes was "almost three hours long". He preserved the record of his hand-written speech, of which the following is an extract:

> I do take the opportunity of saying that every reference Mr Hunter has made in his leaflets to the teaching in Assembly's College is true. ... I also take the opportunity of saying that my testimony to-night at this meeting under the auspices of the Bible Standards League is not different from that given before a sub-committee of the College Committee.

"Thus he gave the lie direct to the Committee; and there that matter ended."[162] Grier's conclusion that night revealed an awareness of the cost he knew must be faced: "Do not, I ask of you in closing, be misled by the honied accents of modern preachers into refusing to stand at all times and everywhere for the faith once for all delivered – just because the stand is going to cost."

Grier confided to Machen on 11 June 1926: "It was no light thing for me to take that stand. I felt that it was one of the most tremendous decisions in my life. The Lord indeed stood by me and strengthened me—as I am persuaded He will continue to do." In his next letter he spoke of the personal cost: "… your humble servant is being looked on in some quarters as responsible for the whole 'rumpus'." Grier also confessed to Machen following his experience with the College and its Committee: "My ignorance on some of these questions was perhaps due to a certain kind of 'indifferentism' during my stay in the United States. I did think that perhaps there was something 'in' the complaints against the attitude of those popularly called 'bitter-enders'. The Irish Presbyterian College drove the last remnants of 'indifferentism' away."

Censure of James Hunter

W J Grier ended his *Origin and Witness* account of the College Committee's investigation by noting Belfast Presbytery's censure of James Hunter just before the 1926 Assembly for his SOS attacks on the professors, which the Presbytery regarded as an unconstitutional procedure. Hunter indicates that his decision not to go before the College Committee in April 1926 with his complaints was also a reason for the censure.[163] He appealed to the General Assembly but it was dismissed by 499 votes to 115 on 8 June, two days before the Formula vote.

Unconstitutional procedure raises difficult questions for Hunter's cause, and provides an easy target. Livingstone and Wells in *Ulster-American Religion*, in a line that closely follows that of Robert Allen and Steve Bruce,[164] say this about the SOS attacks on the College: "These were unorthodox methods of attack, especially in view of the existence of the special committee. The Presbytery of Belfast censured James Hunter for using unconstitutional means of attacking the college, since he had constitutional means at hand to advance his grievances."[165] Hunter did indeed favour the constitutionalist process, but his opponents' control of it was part of the total problem he faced. He had been constitutional in the O'Neill case 10 years before but found his path obstructed. Grier was fully constitutional in the current Formula Committee process but his very distinctive evidence was suppressed. So those accusing Hunter of unconstitutional procedure in 1925-26 were hardly in a position to throw the first stone.

SOS No 4: June 1926
The College Committee accepted its Sub-Committee's Report on 1 June 1926 asserting that Professor Haire did teach the infallibility of the Bible and that Hunter's charges were without foundation, and sent it to the press. SOS 4 contained a contrary version of the investigation, much of which appears in Grier's statement above. Hunter also reviewed the six reasons that Professor Haire gave against the inerrancy of the Scriptures in the synopses of his lectures. He concluded: "The Bible is a truthful book. The Modernist will have you believe that this fight is all about trifles, discrepancies, that count for nothing. Leave Modernists to themselves and in a little while the whole body of the sacred book will will lie dismembered limb from limb."

SOS 4 did not reach the public, however, since the General Assembly had prohibited further SOS circulation. Consequently the Committee's press release went unanswered.

Presbyterian Bible Standards League
James Hunter had no wish to act alone. On Wednesday 12 May 1926, just two months after the second Nicholson mission, when the SOSs were making their public impact, the College Committee investigation was under way and the 1926 General Assembly was less than a month away, he founded the Presbyterian Bible Standards League. Its purpose was to give organisational structure to his campaign against doctrinal aberration in church and theological college, and in keeping with this the text on its letter heading was Isaiah 59.19: "When the enemy shall come in like a flood, the Spirit of the Lord shall lift up a standard against him." (KJV) One of its early publications, in April or May 1927, presented *Comparisons between Doctrinal Positions of Professor Davey—and the Bible, and Standards of Irish Presbyterian Church.*[166]

W J Grier sent the League's constitution to Machen, 21 June 1926. Its preamble read:

> THE pressing necessity for some Presbyterian organization, upholding the Divine Authority of the Holy Scriptures as the supreme standard of our Faith, and the existing subordinate standards, the Westminster Confession and Catechisms, has been long felt by many of our people, and the Presbyterian Bible Standards League has been formed to endeavour to meet this need, with its objects as set out in the undernoted Articles of Constitution, which were adopted, unanimously and enthusiastically, at a meeting of Communicants of the Irish Presbyterian Church, called by public advertisement, and held in Belfast on 17 May 1926.

The League's publication also contrasted the Formula that had been in existence for 90 years with the one to be proposed at the 1926 General Assembly:

> *Existing*: I believe the Westminster Confession of Faith, as described in the Code, to be founded on, and agreeable to, the Word of God, and as such I subscribe it as the confession of my faith.
> *New*: I acknowledge the Westminster Confession of Faith, and the Larger and Shorter Catechisms, as the subordinate standards of this Church. I accept these standards as an historic testimony for truth, and against error, and as a continuing bond of union for members of the Church.

The League had few ministers among its members, but the laity identified with it strongly. The Ruling Elders' Union came into being in June 1922 with objects designed to promote fellowship, efficiency, spiritual life and dissemination of information throughout the Church.[167] In a reference to the Union to Machen, 4 November 1925, Grier said: "There are not a great many evangelical ministers in our Church evidently, but the Elders' Union is strongly against Modernism." In March 1926 he re-asserted: "Our strength can only come from 'members of session' … and some of them just look for a leader." It was to the eldership and the laity who followed them that Hunter offered leadership. Under the League's auspices, and following the strategy of Henry Cooke, Hunter toured the country, alerting the people to what was at stake. Fulton says: "The attack was carried up and down the country. Attacks by pamphlet and from a variety of platforms were mounted and the campaign was vigorous and sustained."[168]

Premises, Bookshop, and W J Grier
In March 1926 Jim Grier had told Machen that he was at the "parting of the ways", with three options before him: the Cape Breton call, the organisation of a Bible School in Belfast, or settlement in a congregation under the Presbyterian Church in Ireland; "I trust I am completely in the hands of One who will guide with His eye." By June a new option had appeared: "I have been asked privately to speak on behalf of the conservative cause 'up-and-down' the country, taking it up as my definite work at a fixed salary, but it is a serious step and I must consider it very prayerfully." On 9 August 1926 he wrote, more fully, to Machen again:

> Now, Dr Machen, I come to the part of my letter which will surprise you I'm sure. It still surprises me, while I wonder at the strange providences of God and the wondrous and unexpected ways in which He works. For months, I may say an offer was before me—from Presbyterian Bible Standards League—that I should act as their Deputation Secretary. I have accepted. …
> The chief part of my work will consist in organising and taking charge of a large, new Bookstall of the P.B.S. League with literature in defence of the truth, in dealing with enquirers and organising deputations of speakers. We could fill the largest hall in Belfast … The main part of my duties from October on, will be the sale of <u>defensive</u> and <u>offensive</u> literature. … I feel my inexperience very much and can only lift up my eyes to the hills (Ps 121).

The background was that the Bible Standards League now had its own premises, 15 College Square East, Belfast. The sale of Bibles and Christian literature was to be a core element of its work. Writing in later years Grier said that James Hunter had invited him to become manager of the fledgling bookshop, appealing to him, as the only possible candidate he could envisage, to accept the job. Grier did accept and left Richview at the end of September, but returned for his farewell service on Sunday evening 10 October. So on 1 October 1926 he became manager of the bookshop, and one of his first tasks was to write to Dr Machen on 7 October, on Bible Standards League notepaper: "Am now engaged in superintending new book room. It is thought to be essential to our work. It certainly is a change for me. … The Lord has been prospering us and we look to Him for further blessing. We begin on our knees here each morning." Soon, a young man, Joseph McCracken, who will feature in later chapters, became Jim Grier's assistant, and by April or May 1927 the shop was advertising: "Books and Pamphlets to combat German Rationalism and Modernism, and other literature, can now be obtained at the Book Depot, 15 College Square East, Belfast (near Cooke Statue). Kindly call or write."

League Membership

Grier commented several times to Machen in 1926 about the League's rapid growth. In June, three weeks after its formation, he said: "… has been most enthusiastically supported and the people are joining in large numbers." Later that month he added that the League "is still going strong … and members are 'coming in' constantly." In this early period of the League's existence Grier speaks of the laity being aroused, of intense excitement, and of Cooke being read, "a most 'stimulating' book in view of recent events."

Interestingly, Grier would not join the League himself initially. He told Machen on 11 June 1926: "I have not joined as I think some of its office-bearers while sincere and honest are too liable to run into 'snags'. They are too liable to be tripped up by some of those subtle 'modern intellects'. Yet men who are more capable and who are in sympathy have not the pluck or the conviction (or something—some minus quantity) to take their stand."

So events moved towards a climax. The Nicholson missions had lifted the evangelical cause to its highest profile for half a century, particularly since during his second visit Nicholson had publicly denounced the College professors for unorthodoxy. Into this heightened situation came the emotive 'Formula of Subscription' debate, and the disclosures about the theology of College lectures. Hunter and Grier came together, and there followed the SOS circulation, the formation of the Bible Standards League, and the campaign of public meetings. Machen had said to Grier in his letter of 19 November 1925: "Who knows what may come in the next few decades? Has God in store for us a new Reformation? We cannot tell. But at any rate I think we can say that some of the conditions for such a glorious thing are present." For James Hunter's 25 year campaign for orthodoxy it all seemed like "the sound of marching in the tops of the mulberry trees". (2 Sam 5.24)

But ominously for Hunter, as he proceeded to formal charges of heresy, the appeal of Nicholson and the Bible Standards League was largely to the laity of the Church. Many who attended League meetings were just caught up in the excitement and not theologically engaged. Cooke had certainly held sway in the public arena, but had also achieved a dominant presence in Synod. Unlike Cooke, Hunter did not have the ear of Church courts, or the backing of an evangelical party of ministers. And unlike Cooke he was not to have an opportunity to confront his opponent in Assembly debate. It was a different day.

Rev W J and Mrs Grier, 1974

*The Alliance Hall Men's Bible Class, Shaftesbury Square, Belfast, 1925-26
Rev James Hunter and W J Grier are standing at the right rear*

The Earlier Days

The Republic of Ireland commemorative stamp, 1982

Extracts from W J Grier's notes for his address at a Presbyterian Bible Standards League public meeting, 9 June 1926

> I do take the opportunity of saying that every reference Mr. Hunter has made in his leaflets to the teaching in Assembly's College is true.
>
> I also take the opportunity of saying that my testimony to-night at this meeting under the auspices of the Bible Standards League is not different from that given before a sub-committee of the College Committee
>
> Do not, I ask of you in closing, be misled by the honied accents of modern preachers into refusing to stand at all times & everywhere for the faith once for all delivered — just because the stand is going to cost.

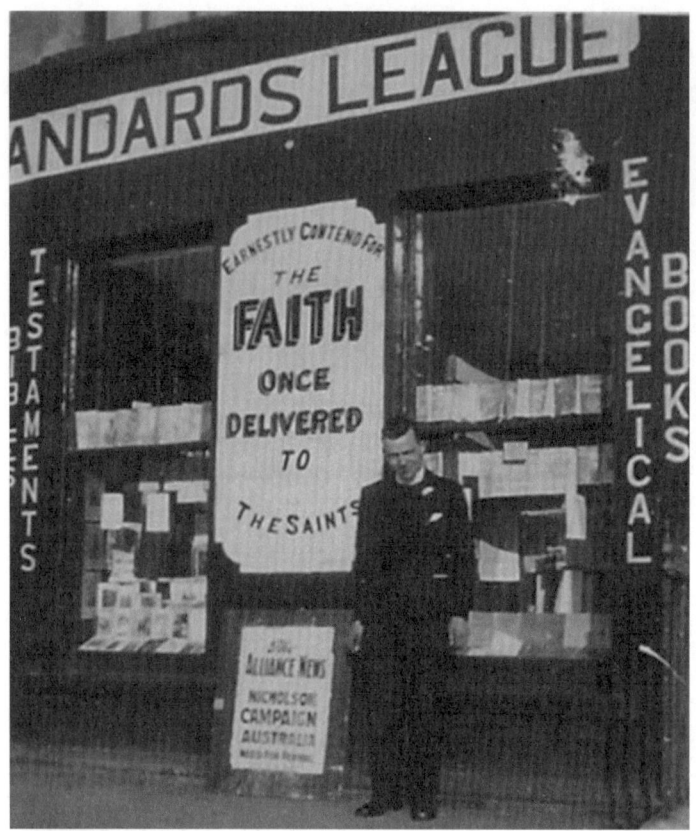

W J Grier, 1926
Presbyterian Bible Standards League Bookshop

15 College Square East, Belfast, October 1931
Tom Swann and S G Shanks are at the first floor window

C E Hunter, S G Shanks, W J Grier, October 1931

Dr James Hunter Gillespie at the River Jordan, opposite Jericho, when he and Jim Grier visited Palestine together in 1931

C E Hunter and W J Grier, July 1934

Ministers, with some men from Knock Irish Evangelical Church, 1928-29
Top L-R: Harold Lindsay, W J Grier, S Molyneaux,
Bottom L-R: Dr J R Gillespie, Mr Kenyon, J J Patterson, Rev J Hunter

Ministers of Irish Evangelical/Evangelical Presbyterian Church, 1935-1969
Arranged chronologically by date of Ordination-Installation

The Earlier Days

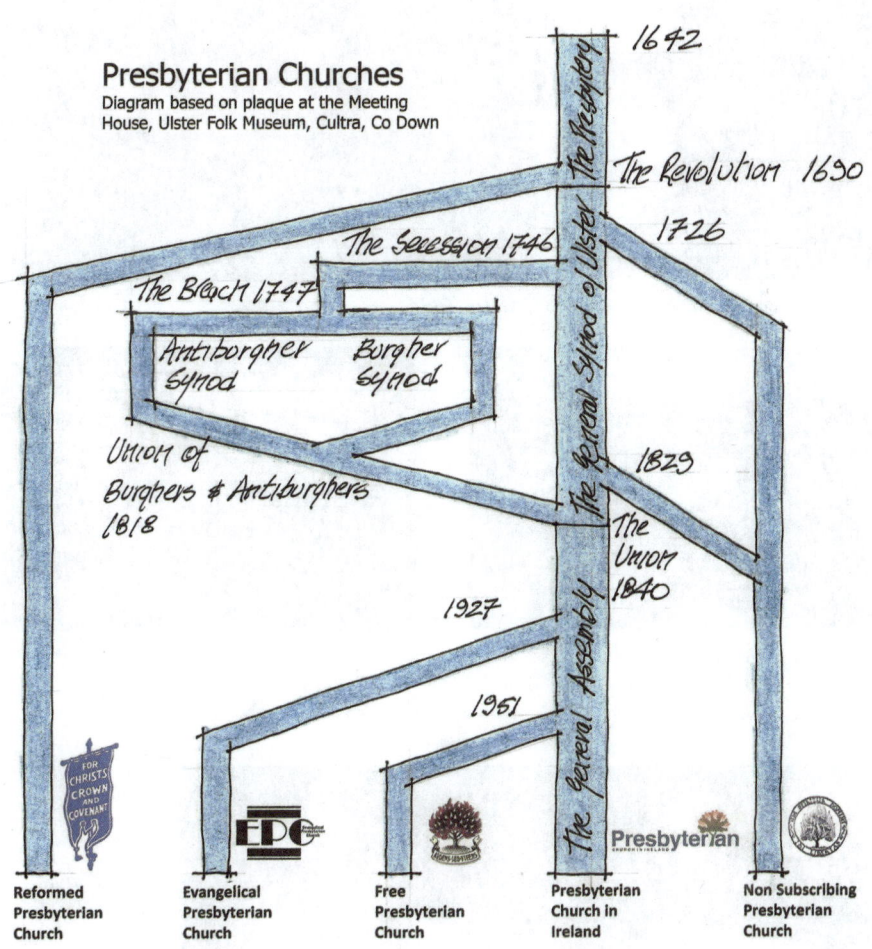

McCrackens and McDowells with W J Grier, 1974

*Rev W J and Mrs McDowell
At the last Harvest Thanksgiving Service
Ballyclare, in the original 1969 building*

*Rev C E and Mrs Hunter
Holiday, 1975*

*Rev C H and
Mrs Garland
Visit to Nigeria
1981 with Sid,
Jean and family
at Theological
College, Northern
Nigeria*

Part 3

The Heresy Trial and Appeal

11

The Heresy Trial

One day just before the meeting of the General Assembly Mrs Stevenson, the wife of the seminary president, met B B Warfield on the street and said, "Dr Warfield, I hear there is going to be trouble at the Assembly. Do let us pray for peace." "I am praying," replied Warfield, "that if they do not do what is right, there may be a mighty battle."

W J Grier, "Benjamin Breckinridge Warfield, DD, LLD, Litt D", *Evangelical Quarterly* 22 (1950)

David B Calhoun, *Princeton Seminary, The Majestic Testimony, 1869-1929*, p 347, Banner of Truth

The 1926 General Assembly upheld Belfast Presbytery's censure of James Hunter for his SOS attacks on the professors. Hunter later recalled his next step: "Like a dutiful son, I then went before the College Committee with charges against another of the professors, and the Committee handed them back to me with the statement that they had no jurisdiction in a matter of that kind!"[169] Robert Allen notes that the College Committee's investigation of Professor Haire after SOS 1 was not in response to formal charges and that only church courts could do so.[170] However, that investigation was scarcely distinguishable from a court. Dr W G Strahan said at the General Assembly in June 1927: "I cannot forget that last year we had Professor Haire at the bar in similar circumstances."[171] Robert Allen, referring to the College Committee's enquiry, said: "… the committee nevertheless proceeded to investigate the charges."[172] So it was the College Committee's investigation of Professor Haire that led Hunter to begin there.

Formal Indictment

James Hunter then formally indicted Professor James Ernest Davey before the Belfast Presbytery on 7 December 1926, on five charges of teaching doctrines contrary to the Word of God and the standards of the Church. The printed version of the charges, circulated as a confidential document to the members of the Presbytery of Belfast, carried the following introductory note: "These charges have already been read to the College Committee by its convener, on the 15 November. They were handed back with the information that the Code made no provision for dealing with any charges made against a Professor before that Committee."

The Charges

The charges ran to over 3,000 words and they are reproduced in full in Appendix 1. At this point the summary in the General Assembly minutes of 9 June 1927 will suffice:

1. That Professor Davey denies that "God pardoneth all our sins and accepteth us as righteous in His sight, only for the righteousness of Christ imputed to us."
2. That Professor Davey taught what is contrary to Holy Scripture concerning the absolute perfection of our Lord's character.
3. That Professor Davey taught what is contrary to the Word of God and the Westminster Confession of Faith regarding the inspiration, infallibility, and Divine authority of the Holy Scriptures.
4. That Professor Davey held and taught what is contrary to the doctrine that "the sinfulness of all sins proceedeth only from the creature and not from God."
5. That Professor Davey held and taught that the doctrine of the Trinity is not taught in the Word of God.

The five charges were based on evidence from the following sources:

Charge 1	*The Changing Vesture of the Faith*	Lecture Notes of one student
Charge 2	*The Changing Vesture of the Faith* *Our Faith in God*	Lecture Notes of two students
Charge 3	*The Changing Vesture of the Faith* *Our Faith in God*	Lecture Notes of two students
Charge 4	*The Changing Vesture of the Faith* *Our Faith in God*	
Charge 5		Lecture Notes of two students

The Accusers

There were originally 44 accusers – 27 from Belfast, four from Londonderry, two from Portadown, Co Armagh, three from Co Antrim, four from Co Down, two from Co Londonderry and two from Co Tyrone. Fermanagh was the only Northern Ireland county not represented. The geographical spread may reflect Hunter's expectation of the later involvement of the wider church. Four were ministers, James Hunter and three others, two of whom had not signed all five charges. The other accusers were elders and members, including six women. Three were Justices of the Peace. Various issues reduced the number to 42.[173]

Trial Overview

The Belfast Presbytery tried the charges over 14 sessions, 15 February-29 March 1927.

The Opening Session

W J Grier captures something of the emotion: "The stirring scenes of the morning of the first session of the Presbytery (February 15th) should have left no doubt in his (Hunter's) mind as to the amount of wrath evoked by his action."[174] And the *Record* supports his description. In this opening session the court appointed a doorkeeper, a journalist to record the proceedings and a King's Counsel for the guidance of the Moderator. Some of the accusers protested about the appointment of a legal assessor, and they all protested about the decision to hear the case in private, but to no avail. Rev. Samuel Hanna objected to the inclusion of the Fisherwick representatives in the court since he alleged that its Kirk Session had adopted a resolution pre-judging the case, but the court overruled his objection. Rev. S Thompson questioned the validity of the indictment because he said that certain quotations from the Bible and Shorter Catechism were inaccurate, and he too was overruled.[175]

One of the two student witnesses for the prosecution wrote to the court stating that he had not given permission for his name to be appended to any of the charges. Professor Davey cited six students as defence witnesses. When he also cited all the accusers eight of them protested. Presbytery allowed the professor's refusal to accept a citation as a witness, arguing that an accused person could not be compelled to give evidence in a charge against himself. James Hunter said near the end of the Charge 1 proceedings: "Although it may seem egotistical and perhaps you will say I have no right to put it so, as God lives if I were accused in a civil or ecclesiastical Court on any charge I would go into the witness box certain of my innocency."[176] Professor Davey pleaded 'not guilty' and after formalities the trial got under way. The total attendance must have been in the region of 120.

Trial Structure
It was a trial of two parts in that the court dealt with the first charge differently from the other four. Only on Charge 1 were witnesses called. Of the 14 sessions, it took up part of 1, the whole of 2-9 and part of 10, and it accounts for about 30% of the total transcription record. For charges 2-5 Professor Davey appealed to section 448 of the church code: "Before witnesses in support of the charge are examined, the accused may, with the consent of the Court, put in a plea of justification, or show he had a perfect warrant to do what he is charged with. Should the Court find the plea sustained the process shall be determined."[177] The court agreed and the professor presented a verbal plea of justification for each of Charges 2-5.

Pleas of Justification
The pleas, including the similar Statement of the Accused on Charge 1, amounted to some 51,500 words, accounted for 55% of the whole transcription record and would have taken around 6-7 hours non-stop speaking to deliver. The indictments were read to the College Committee on 15 November 1926 and tabled at Presbytery on 7 December 1926, and for these substantive pleas to be ready for presentation by mid-March, is in itself evidence of Davey's ability and diligence. The pleas comprised the central defence strategy. They gave Davey a platform which he used to develop his attacks on the competence and integrity of the accusers that ultimately proved a persuasive factor. But whilst questions existed before the pleas, more existed after them.

Evaluation of the Pleas
On Charge 1 the minutes noted that after Professor Davey's statement the Moderator addressed the court, and "Thereafter the Court proceeded to consider the evidence and come to its Finding." Such consideration of the evidence is not recorded for charges 2-5, and apart from this one instance, whatever it amounted to, there was no formal evaluation of the pleas recorded. There was no time to do so. The accused's statement on Charge 1 and his pleas on 2-3 were presented on three separate mornings and the court voted on each in the afternoon of the same day; pleas 4-5 were both presented and voted on in a single session. Yet the court

reached its verdict after "a minute examination of the points at issue".[178] Who could claim that the court assessed the *points* at issue in such a volume of output?

The Record
The Record of the Trial of the Rev. Prof. J. E. Davey runs to over 93,000 words but James Hunter always contended that the *Record* was not complete:

> A Record of the Trial was published, but this record was seriously defective. Of the four last charges all that is published is the four long addresses of Professor Davey ... four addresses of mine were given in reply to those of Professor Davey. Not a single word of these addresses was printed, nor one word of the statements of the Professor in reply to those given by me.[179]

Hunter was right, for the Presbytery minutes noted the fact of these four speeches, adding in each case that he addressed the court "by permission of the Presbytery". Hunter complained to the General Assembly on 9 June 1927 about the missing speeches and was told that *The Record* meant the minutes of Presbytery, and that the speeches made subsequent to the professor's defence were not regarded as part of the minutes.[180] Yet the summary minutes of Assembly, 9 June 1927 read: "The whole record of the proceedings in the Presbytery of Belfast in the case with the evidence of the witnesses, and statements by the accusers and the accused, having been printed and circulated among the members of the Assembly, were taken as read." Hunter made the speeches and the professor replied before each of the four divisions, and the pleas were not sustained until after these speeches. These Hunter-Davey exchanges were the nearest the trial came to having Professor Davey in the witness box. That Hunter protested about their exclusion suggests that he saw them as significant for the prosecution.[181]

Charge 1 – Imputation
The volume of the proceedings on Charge 1 amounted to 27,000 words. The court interacted with six witnesses and the proceedings were often entangled and protracted.

W J Grier: Student Witness for the Prosecution
W J Grier, and later his notebook, were major points of focus for the court. Grier was in the witness box twice during the hearing of the first charge, and again immediately after it to answer charges of discrepancies between his testimony and his notebook.

Starting in session 1, and concluding with the end of session 2, James Hunter examined and Professor Davey cross-examined W J Grier about Davey's teaching, on the evidence of Grier's classroom notes. Hunter's examination would have taken 10-15 minutes and Davey's 45 minutes to an hour, with other members of the court interjecting questions and comments throughout. In answer to Hunter's questions Grier confirmed his assertions in the charge that Davey had taught

Paul's philosophy of sin to be "different to ours."[182] Paul saw sin as a physical taint that can be transferred and lifted off but to Davey this was an impossible thing – to Davey, sin cannot be transferred. This was the only point from Grier's notes included in Charge 1, but Hunter broadened his questioning, and Grier stated as Davey's views:

> *Substitution*: The acceptance of Christ as our ideal being is the equivalent of a doctrine of substitution. We are accepted not for what we are but what we intend to be.
> *Gethsemane/Calvary*: There Christ felt he had made a mistake and let God down. Regarding the deity of Christ, if Christ was omniscient then the suffering on Calvary was only in the nature of an anaesthetic.[183]

In a cross-examination where subjects kept changing, Davey and others questioned him on substitution, justification, Gethsemane-Calvary, the constitution of the Irish Presbyterian Church, the atonement and the deity of Christ, majoring on Paul's philosophy of sin, the deity of Christ and Grier's notes. A substitution issue is treated later in the chapter, under 'W J Grier's Notebook'.

The court probed the reliability of Grier's notes and Grier's grasp of them, while Davey sought to identify differences between Grier's notes and his own. Grier stated that he had very full notes that were in many cases, such as the extract in Charge 1, *ipsissima verba*, and that he thought that no notes were as full and complete as his own. But he also said at some points that he had no statement in his notes, or that he did not remember the point. Professor Haire asked: "Would Mr. Grier admit that there are some things Professor Davey said which either he did not hear or which he has not got in his notes?" Grier replied: "I think everything that was of any importance I have some record of it." "Then your point of view is if Professor Davey made a statement such as he says he made you are bound to have some record of it?" Grier seemed to let this pass. Principal Paul asked: "If three or four other students came in and said it definitely, would he say it was wrong?"

On Grier's Charge 1 extract – "Paul's philosophy of sin is different from ours ..." Davey asserted that his whole lecture was an affirmation of Paul's doctrine of Justification, and that the extract was an end of lecture caution. Grier was definite that the extract had come in the centre of the lecture. Davey pressed Grier to say whether he, Grier, regarded Paul as final as a psychologist and in his forms of expression, and Grier affirmed that he did on the basis of the doctrine of inspiration. In this context Davey asked the cryptic question to which Hunter objected: "... would you recognise in relation to the whole question, that a man's doctrine and a man's statement of his doctrine might be different things?"

The deity of Christ was the major issue of the Davey cross-examination, much of it related to Gethsemane-Calvary. Christ's "moral perplexity" was one aspect and Grier said it appeared in his Davey lecture notes for both Gethsemane and Calvary. Grier affirmed his own belief that Christ suffered as very God on Calvary.

In answer to a question from Principal Paul, "Did Professor Davey teach the deity of Christ?" Grier said that he did not think so: "He said if Christ was omniscient then the agony in Gethsemane was in the nature of an anaesthetic." Under further questioning Grier said that Davey's lectures denied Christ's deity and added: "He said that Paul did not think Jesus to be God. ... He [Davey] said that the suffering and agony were the agony and suffering of a human being ... If he denies the suffering of God it deprives the suffering of all value ... He ought to have taught He suffered as God." The discussion progressed into omniscience and Grier's view was that if Christ was not omniscient he was not God.

Regarding Christ being "in the dark" about his sufferings Grier said: "In Professor Davey's lecture he said Christ at the Cross was simply taking a venture of faith in the darkness and He was going by faith and not by sight. The impression was that He did not know the issue of His sufferings on Calvary. Was it the same in regard to Gethsemane?—Yes, the same in regard to Gethsemane." Davey challenged what he termed as Grier's implication "that Christ was not in the dark or in doubt with regard to His sufferings at all?" He appealed to Matthew 26.39: "If it be possible, let this cup pass from me ..." (KJV). Grier did not agree: "No. He taught elsewhere that He knew what was before Him, and we are told that for the joy that was set before Him He endured the cross, despising the shame." (Heb 12.2 KJV)[184]

Davey also returned to Grier's assertion that he, Davey, had stated that Paul denied the deity of Christ. Davey said that he had spoken in class of the cases where *theos* was used in the New Testament and said that there were two undoubted uses of it in John, but questions existed over the other cases. Grier said that Davey had stated that the *theos* did not mean deity but in some sense divine, but Davey was insistent that he had said "not the Father, but divine". With regard to Paul, Davey went on: "Do you know the word God is not used except in places where the text is doubtful?" Grier replied: "I remember the passage about being "in the form of God". This led to the Philippians 2.6 encounter that is covered later in the chapter under 'W J Grier's Notebook'.

During his time on the stand Grier comes across as a nervous witness, at points disconcerted by the hostile, cluster questioning from the floor. He was 24 years of age and the only witness to experience it. However, he stood up well to Davey's cross-examination, which was intellectually probing. He did not give ground on the theological issues and displayed strong tenacity about things Davey had said. He used the expression "I think" some eight times suggesting, in about half of them, some uncertainty. At five other points he did not answer questions and on some of these the response of members of the court was hostile: "The witness was asked a straight question and we want a straight answer." "I want an answer. Does Mr. Grier refuse to answer? I want an answer—'yes' or 'no.'"

In a probable reference to Nicholson, Rev. Wm Corkey, who targeted Grier throughout the trial[185] and appeal, asked Grier if he had ever heard Davey condemned in public before going into his class. When Grier answered, "I am not sure whether I can give an answer," Corkey went on, "In other words you went into his class on prejudice, believing he was an unsound theologian?" Grier answered: "I went into his class with an open mind, willing to be convinced either way." "Did you ever hear him condemned in public meetings?" "Not that I remember." Certainly Grier could have given a clearer first answer but the court was quick to jump to conclusions.

But it is important to understand Grier's predicament. During this phase eight members of the court, apparently favourable to Davey, made 25 interventions taking up over a third of the cross-examination. This intimidating barrage could have been better controlled from the Chair.

W H Snoddy - Prosecution Witness

In the third and fourth sessions Davey examined two of the accusers on the Charge 1 quotations from W J Grier's lecture notes and Professor Davey's *Changing Vesture of the Faith*. The first was W H Snoddy, secretary of the Bible Standards League. Davey's examination would have lasted at least one hour and Hunter cross-examined. The court's interaction with Snoddy, particularly Davey's, was testy, with Davey categorising him as an unfriendly witness.

The opening exchange concerned Snoddy's knowledge of the charge and its basis. Snoddy affirmed that its basis was *Changing Vesture* which he had read some years before the trial and that he stood over the evidence in the charge. Davey selected the statement, "Sin cannot be transferable" from W J Grier's lecture notes[186] and asked Snoddy, "Do you hold that that is untrue?" Snoddy responded: "The guilt of our sin is transferred to Christ," and the exchange developed into the key issue of whether the penalty of sin and the guilt were both transferred to Christ or just the penalty. Snoddy argued that both were transferred. But when he resumed his evidence at the next session he revised his original statement, saying that what he had wished to convey was that "the guilt of sinners is reckoned to be transferable to our Lord," that "criminality was forensically and legally reckoned to Jesus Christ ...," but not "in the sense that it made Him sinful." Davey claimed this revision as "the whole point", "the very point" he was making in his book. "Do you not recognise," he asked, "that in my book the penalty is transferable but not the criminality?" But Snoddy's revised statement was not at all "the very point" Davey was making in *Changing Vesture* where he had stated that guilt and righteousness "simply represent states of the consciousness, and are in no sense transferable."

To Davey, guilt was "guilt for past sins"; "man's guilt cannot become God's"; "... He may overrule the effects of our sins for good, but He cannot take from our personalities the fact of our having done them, in which consists our guilt; this guilt He may overlook, but He cannot change it. Our sins may be made of no account for present and future, but they cannot be removed from the past as historical events ..."[187] Snoddy's revision was in head-on conflict – the guilt of the sinful human nature and the actual sins of Christ's people were transferred to Christ as their substitute, constituting him guilty, but not sinful. Historical sins, with the inseparable guilt they incur, become historically pardoned sins through their transfer to Christ.[188] When Davey pressed Snoddy to affirm that his statement that "the guilt of sinners is reckoned to be transferable to our Lord" meant that he was now agreeing with him, Snoddy very properly declined.

During the discussion on the transference of sin and guilt Davey complained that "modifying" clauses had been "rather carefully omitted from the charges." In this context he referred to the fourth extract from the *Changing Vesture* and to the opening sentence of the paragraph, shaded below, which comprised the offending omission from the extract:

> In this criticism I am quite aware that every point adversely criticised can be found to have some real value if rightly appreciated. God does actually take responsibility for all things past, present, and to come, but imputation is not only an unsuitable word in virtue of its commercial derivation, but it stands for an absurd theory of what actually happens in experience; and it is an almost exact parallel to the Roman Catholic doctrine of Transubstantiation, each of these two branches of Christendom positing the same irrationality at the very centre of its system of salvation. It is surely, then, not for us to sneer at others, till at least our own house has been set in order.[189]

Davey argued that it was unfair to omit this significant sentence but Snoddy regarded its omission as perfectly fair, "having regard to the whole sense and purpose of the book." He affirmed his approval of the omission from the extracts of what Rev. John Waddell termed "pertinent sentences that might have modified those extracts," because, Snoddy said, he considered them to have no modifying effect. Snoddy was convincing at this point for the sentence at issue is so vague and conditional, both in expression and concept, that the only value in raising it was its omission. It did nothing to modify the very robust assertions of the rest of the paragraph, which in any case needed more than 'modification'—a vague and limited term in itself. The sentence was really a link with the previous paragraphs from which key extracts were already included in the charge.[190] Nevertheless, it is difficult to justify omitting one sentence from a paragraph, albeit to make the substantial quotations in the charge more concise. Moreover, it handed to Davey the obvious counter-charge of prejudicial, deliberate omission.

The session ended with further probing as to whether Snoddy had read Grier's notes, the identity of the person who had made the selection from them for Charge 1 and the omitted 'modifying' sentence from extract 4. Snoddy was again pressed on the date when he had first read *Changing Vesture* and whether he then saw it as inconsistent with the Church's standards. Snoddy stuck to his earlier 'some years ago' position but affirmed that he had noted the Church standards issues when he read it. The apparent delay in raising issues from the book came next:

PRINCIPAL PAUL—The book is out four years and now suddenly you come forward and say the book is unsound?

THE WITNESS—Not suddenly.
PRINCIPAL PAUL—Why didn't you do it sooner? Was that not your duty?
THE WITNESS—Because you did not begin to alter the formula sooner.

At this point the court diverted to the alleged identity between Davey's views on imputation and Calvin's to which Snoddy aptly replied: "The Confession of Faith of the Westminster Assembly is the standard of orthodoxy of the Irish Presbyterian Church." But his quick formula retort was not forgotten. At the appeal in June 1927 Rev. Dr W G Strahan cited this 'delay' exchange as evidence that the accusers dragged Davey and his hitherto unchallenged *Changing Vesture* into the 1926-27 formula of subscription debate to incite the passions of the people towards the rejection of the proposed changes.[191] In fact, it was Davey who had raised the formula question in *Changing Vesture*: "It is the realities of life which really matter in the sphere of religion; not formulae, but moral values ... the value of forms must never blind us to the need of their constant revision ..."[192] SOS 2 dealt with the formula debate and it was Principal Paul who was in focus.

At the following session Davey moved to the question of "quantitative satisfaction".[193] Snoddy asserted that in Westminster forgiveness was conditional upon a quantitative satisfaction being made on the cross. Snoddy at first said that "quantitative" was from the Standards, but later conceded that not the actual word, but to his mind, the equivalent, was in the Standards. In the exchange over the source of the word, Snoddy realised that it was from *Changing Vesture* – part of the second extract dealing with the Protestant theory that "... God cannot forgive by grace upon change of heart. He must have some quantitative satisfaction for sin." Davey quoted from WCF 11.3 - *Justification*: "Christ, by his obedience and death, did fully discharge the debt of all those that are thus justified, and did make a proper, real, and full satisfaction to his Father's justice in their behalf." Snoddy said immediately and correctly, "That is the quantitative." But Davey asked: "Does 'full' not mean that which is accepted by God as satisfactory?" and he pressed Snoddy to agree that the word "satisfactory", rather than "quantitative", was sufficient to explain the Standard. But Snoddy was resolute: "There would be no satisfaction unless it was quantitative."

It is difficult to follow Davey here. He quoted "proper, real and full satisfaction" but then, restricting himself to "full", interpreted it as meaning "satisfactory" to God. Satisfaction and satisfactory have different meanings. God did not regard Christ's work as just satisfactory! He was fully satisfied because it was a quantitative satisfaction. The same WCF section speaks of "the exact justice" of God that was involved in justification.

Davey then returned to an alternative view of imputation, the point that had arisen at the close of the previous session. He argued that both Charles Hodge and James Denney (United Free Church College) denied that a quantitative satisfaction was made – a quite unacceptable claim. When Snoddy asked him to produce what Hodge had said Davey read two extracts from Hodge's *Systematic Theology* Volume 2, Page 471. They are shaded below, and separated by 200 words. Davey placed the words, "and again" between the two parts, indicating a break:

> As the satisfaction of Christ was not pecuniary, but penal or forensic; a satisfaction for sinners, and not for those who owed a certain amount of money, it follows, —
> 1. That it does not consist in an exact *quid pro quo*, so much for so much.

This, as just remarked, is not the case even among men. The penalty for theft is not the restitution of the thing stolen, or its exact pecuniary value. It is generally something of an entirely different nature. It may be stripes or imprisonment. The punishment for an assault is not the infliction of the same degree of injury on the person of the offender. So of slander, breach of trust, treason, and all other criminal offences. The punishment for the offence is something different from the evil which the offender himself inflicted. All that justice demands in penal satisfaction is that it should be a real satisfaction, and not merely something graciously accepted as such. It must bear an adequate proportion to the crime committed. It may be different in kind, but it must have inherent value. To fine a man a few pence for wanton homicide would be a mockery; but death or imprisonment for life would be a real satisfaction to justice. All, therefore, that the Church teaches when it says that Christ satisfied divine justice for the sins of men, is that what He did and suffered was a real adequate compensation for the penalty remitted and the benefits conferred.

> His sufferings and death were adequate to accomplish all the ends designed by the punishment of the sins of men. He satisfied justice. He rendered it consistent with the justice of God that the sinner should be justified. But He did not suffer either in kind or degree what sinners would have suffered.

In value, his sufferings infinitely transcended theirs. The death of an eminently good man would outweigh the annihilation of a universe of insects. So the humiliation, sufferings, and death of the eternal Son of God immeasurably transcended in worth and power the penalty which a world of sinners would have endured.[194]

Had Davey taken the quotation up to the end of the paragraph, it would have made it clear that Hodge was not denying a quantitative satisfaction, but only the exact *quid pro quo* version of it. Hodge's declaration here was that Christ's sacrifice was so quantitative that it infinitely exceeded what a world of sinners would have endured.

The Snoddy examination was an engaging, testing encounter that drew out several significant points that Davey took up again in his Statement of the Accused on Charge 1. However, there is little doubt that Snoddy was an effective witness for the prosecution. He was always in control and a match for Davey throughout the exchanges.

John Shiels, Magherafelt - Prosecution Witness

In the course of his examination, probably around 90 minutes, John Shiels described himself as "a plain man" and stated openly that he had never read Dr Hodge and that he knew nothing about Dr Denney or about Mr Grier's notes. Nevertheless he demonstrated an able grasp of the theology of the Shorter Catechism that he had learned as a boy, and, throughout his life, W J Grier spoke with great appreciation of John Shiels's testimony. In the initial encounter with Davey he showed his insight in his assessment of the *Changing Vesture*: "In reading the book I feel there is a vein running through it that cuts right against what I believe to be the doctrine of our Church as contained in the Larger and Shorter Catechisms."

It was difficult for Shiels as he coped with questions from a dozen different sources. Professor Davey opened and closed the examination, taking up about one third of the whole. Between the Davey sections, Hunter, Snoddy and Hanna intervened for the prosecution and Principal Paul and Professor Haire were the major contributors for the defence. Some of the questions were related to Shiels himself. In the central section the Defence returned to the issue of when he signed the charge and he confirmed that it was after reading the whole chapter from which the extracts were taken. Rev. Wm Corkey returned to the omitted sentence and Shiels answered with impressive clarity: "... I read the whole of the charge, and in connection with those sentences that went before, and to my mind they were qualifying sentences; but they do not affect the truth, or what Professor Davey was trying to bring out. Not to my mind." Rev. Waddell argued that just as claiming 'Word of God' status for Bible texts taken out of context would be unfair and ineffective, so the *Changing Vesture* extracts were unfair and ineffective, being taken out of context. But he did not specify.

The dominant theological themes in the examination were "God forgiving by grace on change of heart", the significance of Christ's life, and 'pre-forgiveness' (God atoning for our future sins as well as those past and present) coupled with antinomianism ("Let us go on sinning that grace may increase.")[195]

God Forgiving by Grace on Change of Heart. Although he had signed the charge in full Shiels was adamant that he was sustaining it on the basis of part of the second of the four *Changing Vesture* quotations. Replying to Principal Paul he said that whilst the other extracts may contain unsound teaching, the one he had selected was for him "bottom rock" where he knew he was standing and "the principal thing". The key sentence he found irreconcilable with his own faith and the Church's standards was: "Perhaps the weakest spot in the Protestant theory was the specific doctrine of imputation which underlay its theory of Justification. The theory in question rested on the assumption that God cannot forgive by grace upon change of heart. He must have some quantitative satisfaction ...".

When Davey asked him to specify how the statement was defective, Shiels revealed that he had understood Davey's "God forgiving by grace, on change of heart" as the new heart of regeneration, leading to salvation by grace and that Davey disagreed with it. He seemed to think that Davey was advocating the alternative or addition of quantitative satisfaction. Davey replied that it was others, not he, who had said that God must have some quantitative satisfaction! But Davey did not say what he meant by "change of heart" or how it could arise. Hunter, Snoddy and Hanna intervened to clarify the situation. They established that Shiels believed in the great satisfaction Christ had achieved by his death on Calvary as the central doctrine of Protestantism, and that it dealt with his sins, past, present and future. In addition they elicited that, to Shiels, Davey's book criticised this central doctrine, and appeared to give him licence to go on sinning if his future sins were already atoned for.

In his appeal speech on Friday 10 June 1927 Rev. William Corkey said with reference to John Shiels and the above "change of heart" encounter: "The same accuser told the Presbytery that he only took exception to the doctrine taught in one paragraph in Charge 1, and when he was questioned upon that paragraph, as you will see on page 40 of the Record, he showed that he had misunderstood its meaning, and was in absolute agreement with Professor Davey's doctrine."[196] Shiels did not limit his disagreements to a single Charge 1 paragraph. He selected the paragraph as his basis but widened his objections into other areas. It is true that he originally misunderstood Davey's undefined "change of heart" but quickly clarified his thinking. He was never in agreement with Davey – their whole exchange was a battle.

The Significance of Christ's Life. As the discussion proceeded, Shiels told Principal Paul that he also took exception to the extract 1 statement, that salvation is usually connected with Christ's death. The Principal pressed him to explain how this showed that Davey held a view inconsistent with the Church's standards and Shiels replied that the standards placed the emphasis on Christ's death, that it is "altogether connected with Christ's death". Shiels brought in another extract 1 quotation - Davey's "notorious reply of an orthodox Protestant to a supposed legalist – 'Your religion is all doing, mine is all done.'" Shiels insisted that it was clear that Davey took exception to the historic fact of Christ's death "by the way he mentions it" and said that he, Shiels, took his stand "on the fact that my salvation is all done." It may be that someone who says, "Your religion is all doing, mine is all done" has an inadequate view of sanctification, but the truth of "mine is all done" is unassailable as a statement of Christ's finished work.

Davey later returned to Shiels's stance that "our forgiveness was bound up with Christ's death alone" and that "His life had nothing to do with His Atonement", arguing that it was bound up with Christ's life *and* death. He quoted from the Westminster Confession 8.5: "The Lord Jesus, by his perfect obedience and sacrifice of himself." Shiels agreed that Christ's life was involved but "If it had not been for the death there would not have been any forgiveness." Davey remarked: "Therefore you admit that my view is right?" Davey gave no chance for Shiels to respond but kept talking and passed immediately to the issue of antinomianism. But Shiels was right to lay the weight on the death of Christ, where Scripture lays it, for the cross was the climactic commitment of his life, and made his obedience perfect. There was no issue that his sinless character and his fulfilment of all righteousness uniquely qualified him to die as the substitute of his people. But, the "perfect obedience and sacrifice of himself" argument was a shift in the Davey position, for that is not what he had said in the *Changing Vesture*. There he moved the focus in salvation away from the historic fact of Christ's death to the divine-human character which it reveals.

Pre-Forgiveness and Antinomianism. As further evidence Shiels raised Davey's apparent difficulty with the view that Christ bore both the guilt and punishment of future sins on Calvary and that Paul was troubled by its ethical implications. Shiels argued that Paul was not troubled about it concerning our salvation. When Principal Paul contended that Davey could hold imputation as a view although it had a "weak spot", Shiels insisted that "there is no weak spot in this view" and that Davey "makes weaknesses where there is nothing but strength." Furthermore, Davey did not say that imputation was a "weak spot" but "perhaps the weakest spot" which indicates that he saw it as possibly the weakest point of its weaknesses – in "the specific doctrine of imputation which underlay its theory of Justification". Principal Paul's purpose in this examination was to convince the court that the extracts from *Changing Vesture* did not reflect Davey's personal view, but were quoted by him as those commonly held. His efforts demonstrated the need to do so.

Professor Haire took up the pre-forgiveness issue and Shiels affirmed that he did not object to the statement: "My sins past, present and future were laid upon Christ." Professor Haire asked Shiels if that was the best way of putting it, quoting from Charles Hodge in support of his contention that it was not. The words, which Haire presented as a single continuous extract, are shaded:

> The sins which are pardoned in justification include all sins, past, present, and future. It does indeed seem to be an error [Haire 'solecism'] that sins should be forgiven before they are committed. Forgiveness involves remission of penalty. But how can a penalty be remitted before it is incurred? This is only an apparent difficulty arising out of the inadequacy of human language. The righteousness of Christ is a perpetual donation. It is a robe which hides, or as the Bible expresses it, covers from the eye of justice the sins of the believer. They are sins; they deserve the wrath and curse of God, but the necessity for the infliction of that curse no longer exists. The believer feels the constant necessity for confession and prayer for pardon, but the ground of pardon is ever present for him to offer and plead. So that it would perhaps be a more correct statement to say that in justification the believer receives the promise that God will not deal with him according to his transgressions, rather than to say that sins are forgiven before they are committed.[197]

Haire went on: "Dr. Hodge thinks that is the better way to put it than to say our sins past, present and future are forgiven." Rev. Dr Irwin pressed Shiels for a 'yes' or 'no' answer on the "simple question": "Would you condemn Professor Davey for putting it in Charles Hodge's way, instead of in the way that is in inverted commas there?" In the first place, it was another appalling misuse of Hodge who was asserting that sins, past, present and future were pardoned in justification – that is how he began this quotation. Hodge was still upholding pre-forgiveness, which Davey was not. In *Changing Vesture* Davey had not been attempting to uphold Charles Hodge's position. He had not referred to Hodge or to better ways of putting it. His point was to express his unhappiness with the concept of the guilt and punishment of future sins being "expiated and borne by Christ on Calvary", however it was expressed, and the line that Hodge and Davey were distinguished only by "two ways of putting it" was a red herring.

Davey had also said "The apostle Paul was greatly troubled about the ethical deductions from such a theory, and whatever its values in the past or present, no one at any rate could accuse it of a primary regard for Christian morality." He quoted James Denney in support: "It cannot be denied that this perversion of the truth that Christ died for our sins has actually emerged in human experience. Even in the apostolic age the thought came to the surface—'let us continue in sin that grace may abound.'" It was preposterous for Davey to suggest that Denney was agreeing with him. Denney was saying that antinomianism was a *perversion* of the truth—the fact that Christ died for our sins was the truth! John Shiels said: "I believe that when the work of atonement was done all my sins were in the future and, of course, they were all borne by Christ." Earlier he had said: "… after that great fact had come into my life [the acceptance of Christ as his Saviour] my whole being came under a change, a new life came into me which made me hate sin." And at the end: "he [Paul] asks the question in order to present it in a ludicrous light; that the thing was impossible."

Throughout this exchange the accomplishment of redemption and its application were confused: "My sins past, present and future were laid upon Christ" (the concept that Davey was unhappy with) relates to the once-for-all accomplishment of redemption. Its application is not once for all. WCF 11.4-5: "… they are not justified until the Holy Spirit doth, in due time, actually apply Christ unto them. … God doth continue to forgive the sins of those that are justified." Davey, in concluding the Shiels examination, again argued that Hodge disagreed with the concept of sin being remitted before it is incurred. Hodge did not and Shiels ably replied, "I know if all my sins were not atoned for on Calvary I have no other Saviour."

Near the conclusion of the Shiels examination Davey argued that in *Changing Vesture* he was not supporting licence for ongoing sin – the exact opposite. But the point at issue in the charge was whether Paul was troubled that the 'theory', "My sins past, present, and to come, were laid upon Christ" had implications for Christian morality. In Romans 6 Paul declared that only the perversion – antinomianism – had such implications. But he rejoiced in triumphant grace in the life of the believer. It produced a walk in "newness of life" and its implications were transforming. "How shall we who died to sin live any longer in it?" (Rom

6.2) God sets up the conflict with sin. "And why not say, 'Let us do evil that good may come'?—as we are slanderously reported and as some affirm that we say. Their condemnation is just." (Rom 3.8) "There is no better evidence against the truth of any doctrine, than that its tendency is immoral. And there is no greater proof that a man is wicked, that his condemnation is just, than that he does evil that good may come. There is commonly, in such cases, not only the evil of the act committed, but that of hypocrisy and duplicity also".[198] (Charles Hodge, Rom 3.8)

Divinity Students - Defence Witnesses
In Sessions 5, 6 and part of 7 Davey and others examined three Divinity student defence witnesses. Hunter and Rev. Samuel Hanna cross-examined. The focus was Grier's lecture notes but other subjects were introduced - the deity of Christ, the divine-human character of Christ, Paul's philosophy of sin, justification, transferability of sin and guilt, the atonement, the standards of the Irish Presbyterian Church. All were questioned on the *ipsissima verba* quality of student notes. But Grier's only specific *ipsissima verba* claim for his notes was the Charge 1 extract. Whilst none of the other students would confirm this precisely, none challenged it with an alternative version. The court took in all four notebooks and had the opportunity to examine its witnesses on any comparative evidence on the point, but did not do so.

So what did the examination of the student witnesses for the defence establish? They agreed that Davey believed and taught the deity of Christ, but none touched on Grier's deity of Christ evidence on the opening day. The three agreed with Grier that Davey saw Paul's view of sin as a physical taint, and they had nothing definite from Davey about its moral and spiritual implications. Two of them interpreted the remarks about physical taint as a warning against the wrong interpretation of Paul by early heresies. The question of sin as an impersonal thing arose with only one witness, who confirmed Grier's extract to be substantially correct. On transferability of sin and guilt, the witnesses also agreed that Grier's extract was substantially correct. And all three agreed that Davey had taught that Paul's philosophy of sin was "different from ours". The three agreed on Davey's definition of justification - identification or mystical union with Christ as a risen, exalted, omnipotent Saviour – a definition which omits the key confessional element of pardon of sin through imputation, the point at issue in Charge 1. One student said he could not remember Davey mentioning the word imputation in his lectures.

Closing Speeches
The proceedings on Charge 1 were concluded with speeches from W H Snoddy, Rev. James Hunter, and Professor Davey. Davey's defence speech, the 'Statement of the Accused' on Charge 1, consisting of 9865 words and taking around 65-75 minutes to deliver, is addressed, along with his pleas on the other four charges, in Chapter 15 – Theological Review.

Snoddy spoke first, probably for about 15 minutes. He assessed the evidence as inconclusive, a quicksand, which might establish Professor Davey guilty at one court and innocent in another. To him it identified two distinct types of theology in the Presbyterian Church in Ireland, with the Calvinistic system "now challenged and challenged openly and challenged squarely, within our borders." He felt that the general evidence had revealed that there was not unity with regard to the Atonement, "that great central doctrine of our faith" set forth in Scripture and the Westminster Standards. He contrasted this with the modernistic and rationalistic theory of the Atonement which he described as "shifting as a quicksand because it changes ever with the changing mind of the person who holds it."

He said in an exchange with Rev. William Corkey that the evidence showed the theological differentiation in the Church to be deeper than some in the court believed, and that it did not provide a strong enough bridge "on which to rest confidently the view either that all is right with Professor Davey, or that all is right with Assembly's College." He questioned the value of student witnesses who had been "specially coached by either party to give certain evidence beforehand, with one definite object in view to exculpate or convict an individual." Snoddy noted: "It cannot finish here. It is bound to go to a higher place, and it may not even finish there."

James Hunter took a different line, speaking for about half an hour. He began with "a very clear statement" of the doctrine of imputation, quoting from Spurgeon, Calvin and Charles Hodge, and then moved to what he saw as Davey's repudiation of it—"because he characterises it as an absurd theory, as an irrationality, and he compares it at length to transubstantiation." Hunter quoted from the Westminster Confession of Faith 11 - *Justification*, and Chapter 8 – *Christ the Mediator*, and extensively from Scripture. He denounced Davey's comparison of imputation with transubstantiation as a travesty, "a gross misrepresentation of the Protestant doctrine" because "the righteousness of the Saviour does not leave him, and that the sinfulness of the sinner does not leave him. It is not a transference of holiness and sinfulness—so that there is absolutely no parallel between transubstantiation and imputation."

Hunter argued that Davey's *Changing Vesture* arguments were the same as those of the Remonstrants,[199] 300 years before. He said that he would like to have seen in Davey's book some statement of the orthodox position on the Atonement, but that Davey had suppressed it. He summarised Davey's position as three main propositions—God forgives by grace without atonement, guilt and righteousness cannot be transferred, and the evangelical doctrine encourages sin. Hunter contended that these were identical to the Arian/Socinian[200] position on the Atonement. He declared that Davey's three tenets were almost indistinguishable from those of the Arian Henry Montgomery in *The Creed of an Arian*. Hunter dealt with the three, saying of the first: "He does forgive by grace and by costly grace. He does forgive on change of heart, but it is the costly grace of Christ that changes the heart, a very, very quantitative satisfaction this."

He moved to the centrality of the doctrine of imputation: "If you allow this doctrine to be a matter of uncertainty there is not a doctrine of the faith that does not become an uncertainty." "The doctrine of the Holy Trinity leans upon the doctrine of the Atonement as set out in the Word of God and in the standards of our Church." "When you swerve in the doctrine of Atonement you swerve in every other doctrine." Hunter gave this opinion of *The Changing Vesture of the Faith*: "—it is not the vesture that is changed ... it is the soul and not the vesture that is being changed. It is not the substitution of one figure for another, it is the substitution of a wax model in the window—pardon me if it is a vulgar illustration—for a living throbbing being who fights the battle of the day."
And turning to the teaching of Professor Davey:

Is this Church going to become a Socinian Church? Is the doctrine not only of the Atonement but the doctrine of the Trinity becoming an uncertainty? Are men going to teach what they like? ... This matter has been taught by Professor Davey not for a year or two, because these lectures were delivered in 1921, and published in 1923. He was accepted as an elder in December, 1922. The lectures from which quotations have been given by the witnesses in most cases, if not in all, were delivered in the session 1925-1926, so that it is not merely that something has come out on one occasion, but it is a conviction, a teaching he has held for years.

James Hunter brought his speech to a close on a strong personal note:

I have, if you will pardon my saying it, for my knowledge of Professor Davey is not an intimacy, I have a great admiration for his scholarship and his ability, and I know that those intimately related to him, if I may say so and rightly so, are the very darlings of our Church. God knows I wish him no wrong. I wish that the mercy and blessing of God may be upon him, but I feel in my own inmost soul that spiritual darkness will come over our Church if the doctrine that he has been teaching becomes the doctrine of our young ministers. As I said before, I occupy a most painful position. I know motives have been attributed to me. I leave it with God the searcher of all hearts, the Lord Jesus Christ, who on the great White Throne shall judge me, what are the motives that impel me to take up this task, a very painful, sacred and imperative duty.

Why the Debate?
Different assessments of the Charge 1 witness examinations may exist, but the debates did have the content described. Why was it necessary for these arguments over words and expressions and their meanings? Why not the clarity and precision of the church standards? To quote John Murray and R C Sproul:

The Westminster Confession and Catechisms are, therefore, the mature fruit of the whole movement of creed-formation throughout fifteen centuries of Christian history, and, in particular, they are the crown of the greatest age of confessional exposition, the Protestant Reformation. No other similar documents have concentrated in them, and formulated with such precision, so much of the truth embodied in the Christian revelation.[201]

I would argue that the Westminster Standards are the most precise and accurate summaries of the content of biblical Christianity ever set forth in a creedal form. … in my judgement, no historic confession surpasses in eloquence, grandeur, and theological accuracy the Westminster Confession of Faith.[202]

The Verdict

On Friday morning, 4 March 1927, two days after Snoddy and Hunter presented their closing speeches, Professor Davey addressed the court, with his 'Statement of the Accused'. The court gave its verdict on charge 1 on the afternoon of the same day – "not guilty", on the basis of the following decisive vote in favour of Professor Davey:

			For	Against	%
Charge 1	Imputation	4 March 1927	60	5	92.3

The Clerk was directed to communicate the result of the trial to the press. James Hunter registered the intentions of the prosecution to appeal. On the motion of Rev. Wm Corkey the court resolved that W J Grier be cited to appear at the next meeting of the court to explain discrepancies between his evidence and his notebook.

W J Grier's Notebook

The most emotive, painful and aggressive phases of the trial concerned W J Grier's notebook, extracts from which appeared in four of the five charges. The first of the two issues concerned Grier's extraction of a section of notes before handing in his notebook and the court took it up before the Charge 1 closing speeches. The Moderator took the lead, although there were 14 other participants, excluding Grier. The pages Grier had extracted contained Old Testament lecture notes, which did not relate to the charge. Professor Davey tried in vain to come to his rescue: "Might I say I am not sure there is not a misunderstanding. I think Mr. Grier stated that he had only withdrawn the Old Testament notes which did not belong to this charge." It reads as a harrowing episode to this day.[203]

The notebook was returned to Grier to put back his OT notes and he eventually handed it back, after the court had clarified the terms of its use and return. Grier's silence at points when questioned heightened the tension but he had already answered the point at issue. In addition there were exchanges going on between the Moderator and other members over the court's rights and intentions regarding the notebook and it is likely that Grier was looking for guidance from his team. Sixteen members of the court made 74 interventions, 30 of them by the Moderator!

At the beginning of Session 10 the court addressed a set of issues concerning the content of Grier's notes. It began with a tense argument as to whether the court had jurisdiction over Grier between two charges and could require him to take the stand. Rev. William Corkey questioned Grier on four matters. The first two concerned points that Grier had said in giving evidence that he could not remember, but which Corkey claimed to have discovered in his notes. The third probed the identity of the person who had chosen the extract from Grier's notes for Charge 1. The fourth questioned whether a word in Grier's notes had been tampered with.

Corkey began by asking Grier to confirm his statement about the fullness of his notes and that the evidence he gave for Charge 1 was taken *ipsissima verba* on 9 January 1926 and Grier did so. Corkey then turned to an exchange between Davey and Grier on Philippians 2.6-9 on 15 February 1927, the opening day of the trial, and stated:

> You were then referred to a passage in Paul's epistle—"Wherefore God also hath highly exalted Him and given Him a name above every name," and I asked you the question—you would not deny that Professor Davey said that?—"Did Professor Davey affirm that Paul in using the words about Christ: 'Wherefore God also hath highly exalted Him and given Him a name above every name' refer to Christ as God in the highest and fullest sense." Then the Moderator asked "Do you not remember that point?" and you said "No."
> I have looked up your notes on the point, and I find in your notes this passage "Wherefore also God highly exalted Him and given Him name Yahweh, sacred name Yahweh—not pronounced; Kurios, LXX.—Confess. Ἰησοῦς Χριστός. Jehovah (in Hebrew); name used= Nature." Do you acknowledge that as a correct statement?
> MR. GRIER—Yes, that is in my notes.
> Your notes say name equals nature?—Yes.
> And the name used to describe Jesus was Jehovah? Yes, the name used in that passage.
> REV. WM. CORKEY—That is all I want in regard to that.[204]

Corkey avoided Grier's emphasis that Jehovah was the name *used in that passage* of Scripture (italics ours). Grier was not saying that he did not remember the exchange or the quotation from Philippians 2! The charge related to what Davey held and taught. What Grier was not confirming was that Davey had taught it as his own belief. In answer to Davey's question, "Which name was it that I said it was?" Grier had replied, "You said it was the name of Jehovah and you also said it was a piece of mythology on the part of Paul." Corkey also avoided this part of Grier's answer.

Corkey then took up an issue that arose earlier in the Davey cross-examination concerning Grier's lecture notes of 9 January 1926:

> When Professor Davey asked you in your evidence: "Would it be a correct statement to say that I said at the beginning of my lecture that Paul's doctrine of justification was justification by an act of acceptance of Christ and identification with Christ and consequential salvation?" you replied "I have no recollection of that," and then Professor Davey asked you "You have not got that in your notes?" and you answered "Not that I can see." Now, at the opening of those lectures that Professor Davey referred you to—on that occasion—I find these words "An act of identification—salvation is through death to sin, identification with Christ's death to sin—the death in which we share." Do you agree that is in your notes?
> MR. GRIER—Yes, that is in them. Perhaps you should finish that quotation.
> REV. WM. CORKEY—Salvation through (1) death to sin. Identification with Christ—death to sin, a death in which we share. Paul had the idea that physical death is the wages of human sin. Christ died and so broke that law." Those are the words of your notes.[205]

On 15 February 1927 Grier could neither recall nor locate the passage but on 15 March he was so familiar with it that he knew Corkey's quotation from it was incomplete. No doubt he had refreshed his memory in the meantime but the explanation for the earlier lapse is not clear. It would have been advantageous to Grier's argument to remember it. The tension of the moment can cause such things. The other student witnesses said some 15 times between them that they did not remember. And Grier did not deny that the passage was in his notes, just that he could not see it at a particular point. Corkey's split quotation did not match Grier's notes in any case.[206] Corkey passed very quickly from the point when Grier asked him to finish the quotation, for the statement "Paul had the idea that physical death is the wages of human sin" is significant. And he did not finish the quotation either. Corkey should have been more concerned about Davey's content than about Grier's recall.

Corkey returned to the point at the Assembly appeal:

> Mr. Hunter did indeed produce one student who swore he had no recollection of Prof. Davey teaching Paul's doctrine of justification, and stated that he could not see it mentioned in his notes, but when this student's notes, which were very reluctantly given to the Court, were examined they were found to confirm word for word, what the other students testified as to Prof. Davey's teaching —namely—and these are the words out of his notes—"Salvation is through death to sin, identification with Christ's death to sin—the death in which we share," and yet that is the sole witness on whose evidence the Assembly is asked to condemn Professor Davey on this charge No. 1.

Why did he say that Grier "swore"? All witnesses were under oath. Everything they said was sworn. Corkey did not tell the General Assembly of Grier's challenge to him to complete the quotation. He did not say what Davey had taught about

Paul's doctrine of Justification. And Grier was not the sole witness for Charge 1 – Charge 1 was very much wider than this exchange with Grier. There were other witnesses and the evidence of Davey's own statement.

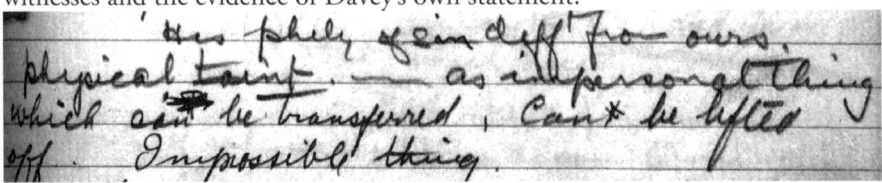

Corkey's third issue was to establish if Grier himself had selected the "physical taint" quotation for Charge 1 and Grier confirmed that he had not. Corkey's fourth attack concerned tampering with a word in a Charge 1 quotation. The word at issue was "can" in "can be lifted off".[207] The word was "can" and there was no issue over it. The Defence accepted the quotation as substantially correct. Paul's 'philosophy' was said to be that sin can be transferred, can be lifted off. The mark at issue was a false stroke of the pencil in rapid note-taking, and it was this that Grier later crossed out. In four other cases of 'can't' that a scan of his notes has detected the 't' is perpendicular, crossed, and with an apostrophe between the 'n' and 't'. There are five other examples of Grier's 't' in the exhibit. Grier was right not to accept that the word was ever changed from "can't" to "can".[208] It was not.

The notebook issues related only to an element of Charge 1 and had not the slightest bearing on the content of the trial. To proceed as the court did suggests a felt need to discredit Grier as a witness. His restraint throughout was greatly to his credit.

Charges 2-5

Professor Davey also pleaded 'not guilty' to Charge 2. The Court then agreed to his application to answer the charge by a 'plea of justification'. The concluding sentence of his request read: "Therefore I would ask the Court to allow me to make a statement of justification, explaining what I said and what I meant, what is the essential context of each quotation, and what is the essential background of them all in my own faith and theology." The professor's opening sentences of his Charge 1 statement was typical of his stance on all the charges:

> I do not deny and never have denied the statements quoted at the head of this charge from our standards by the accusers, statements which they allege that I have contravened in my teaching. I believe, as our Shorter Catechism teaches, that God freely pardoneth our sins in virtue of "the righteousness of Christ imputed to us and received by faith alone." However imperfect my teaching may be, or may have been, these are my views. I believe in the Atonement both as an eternal work and as an act in time; I believe in satisfaction, in imputation, in justification and sanctification as separate in thought but in common with most theologians, as never really separable in experience. I believe that through

Christ's atoning work we have pardon, peace and power, and that chiefly, not through a legal fiction or external act of God but through actual living identification with Jesus Christ, the God man of our faith.

		Words	Approx Time in Mins
Charge 1	Imputation	9,865	70
Charge 2	Christology	11,571	80
Charge 3	Scripture	19,981	150
Charge 4	Sin	3,446	30
Charge 5	The Trinity	6,599	50

Charges 2-5: The Verdicts
After Davey's statement, Hunter's extemporary assessment, and Davey's reply, the Court sustained the plea of justification and voted, using the same procedure for Charges 3-5. The Court returned a "not guilty" verdict on each, on the basis of the pleas of justification:

			For	Against	%
Charge 1	Imputation	4 March 1927	60	5	92.3
Charge 2	Christology	15 March 1927	63	7	90.0
Charge 3	Scripture	23 March 1927	65	11	85.5
Charge 4	Sin	29 March 1927	69	10	87.3
Charge 5	Trinity	29 March 1927	69	11	86.3

Notice of Appeal

Appeal was inevitable from the outset, for Hunter knew the prevailing Belfast Presbytery view. But the issues at stake warranted it and he would have been confident of greater support in the wider church. So he gave notice of appeal as each "not guilty" verdict was declared.

The Presbytery Inhibition
The Court had decided in its first session to hear the case in private, and in the fourth session had prohibited public discussion. The Court's final decision extended this restriction until the conclusion of the appeal: "That the Presbytery inhibits all who are under its jurisdiction from every kind of public reference to this case, until the appeals have been heard by the Assembly," and the press was notified. Presbytery made this decision knowing that the Bible Standards League was opening its public campaign with rallies in Belfast and Londonderry on the following three evenings. The inhibition would be a major issue during the following two months and it greatly influenced the outcome of the appeal to the General Assembly in June 1927.

Machen's letter of 22 February 1927 would have done Jim Grier good: "I was simply delighted by an article of yours which Mr Fulton showed me. It certainly displayed a clear grasp of the real issues of the day, and was, I thought, very finely expressed." This is likely to have been *Controversy*, published in *The Alliance News*, April 1927. It dealt with Scripture, Higher Criticism, Christ's attitude to false teaching, modernism and contending for the faith. It had some lovely expressions:

> 'Heresy-hunting' is decried, and those who are contending for the faith are spoken of as if they were chasing butterflies which would do no one's fields any harm, and those who catch them little good."
>
> One of the most despicable features of Modernism is its prevarication and 'word jugglery'.
>
> Many are sitting to-day on the top rail of the fence, like sleeping fowls, and from their theological roost they insist on peace. And from the other side—from the modernist camp—the cry is re-echoed: "Let us have peace." Yes, the Modernist does love peace—peace to propagate his own views— for "there shall be false teachers among you, who *privily* shall bring in destructive heresies." (2 Pet 2.1, KJV)

12

From Trial to Appeal

His [Henry Cooke's] fame as a pulpit orator of rare power soon spread far and wide, and in 1818 he accepted a call to Killyleagh. He had been about three years here when a Rev. J. Smethurst was brought over from England to the North of Ireland by the New Light party to infuse life into their cause ... In the course of an itinerant preaching tour he made his appearance in Killyleagh. Cooke attended his meeting, and, when he had done, invited the whole assemblage, Smethurst included, to his church the following Sunday, where he pledged himself to refute every dogma which the commissioned advocate of Arianism had propounded. Sunday came, and a tremendous crowd thronged the edifice. Cooke, according to promise, took up the Arian arguments, and tore them to shreds.

He then announced his intention of following Smethurst from town to town, and from village to village, wherever he should go, and refuting his unscriptural heresies as soon as they were uttered. A chase more exciting than any fox-hunt ensued. From district to district Cooke pursued the apostle of Arianism, until the leaders of the party perceived that his mission was doing their cause far more harm than good, and he fled back to England.

Rev. Thomas Hamilton, *History of Presbyterianism in Ulster*

The ten weeks between the end of the trial and the appeal before the General Assembly in June 1927 were an intensely busy time for James Hunter. In April and May of the previous year, 1926, he had toured Ulster under the auspices of the *Presbyterian Bible Standards League*, addressing large public meetings and issuing SOSs to inform the wider church about teaching in Assembly's College. In this he was following Henry Cooke's strategy of 100 years before. Now, in post-trial 1927, convinced of the critical nature of the issues at stake, the need to inform the wider church and of his own compliance with the Church Code, Hunter set aside the Presbytery injunction and resumed his public campaign in the weeks between the trial and appeal. He did so confident of substantial success in the wider arena. Grier had written to Dr Machen on 24 March 1927 after the votes on the first three charges had been cast: "The figures certainly do not indicate quite the real state of affairs in Belfast Presbytery and certainly not in the Irish Presbyterian Church as a whole."

The Public Meetings

Hunter re-launched his campaign. He began with three meetings on successive evenings, the first on the day after the trial ended: Wednesday, 30 March 1927 at Belfast YMCA, Thursday 31 March 1927 at Londonderry YMCA, and Friday 1 April 1927 at Belfast YMCA. The *Belfast Telegraph* of 31 March carried the following account of the opening meeting:

RECENT HERESY TRIAL

ALLUSIONS AT BELFAST MEETING.
MARCHING HYMN SINGERS
HAVE TROUBLE GETTING SEATS.

Scenes of the greatest enthusiasm marked the meeting held under the auspices of the Bible Standards League in the large hall of the Y.M.C.A., Wellington Place, Belfast, on Wednesday evening. Every seat on the floor, platform, and balcony was occupied, and prior to 7.30, the scheduled time for commencing the meeting, the huge audience indulged in community singing of favourite hymns.

The opening devotions had scarcely been concluded when a big contingent of supporters marched in from one of the corridors singing "I Know the Book is True" and continued the hymn as they were compelled to break up into groups of two and three and endeavour to find seats in an already crowded hall.

DELEGATION FROM TYRONE

There was another outburst of enthusiasm later when the Chairman, Mr J. C. Graham announced that Rev. James Edgar of the Dungannon Presbytery, together with nine of his elders, had come up from the country to sign their pledge. There was a cry of "Good old Tyrone!" from the body of the hall, and Mr Graham said: "It is not a city movement; it is all over. Ulster and the country is with us." (Applause)

The first speaker at the Belfast YMCA Rally on 30 March 1927 was Rev. John Macleod, no stranger to Belfast. He became Principal of the Free Church College in Edinburgh in 1927, but during 1895-96 he had been a student for the ministry of the Free Presbyterian Church of Scotland, finishing his studies at Assembly's College, Belfast, when Dr Robert Watts of Princeton was Principal. Rev. G N M Collins fills in some of the background:

> In the student body, however, there were others who gave evidence, even then, of a changing attitude to Confessional teaching, and it caused him no surprise to find some of these men openly on the side of Modernism in the heresy trial which disturbed the peace of the Irish Presbyterian Church some thirty years later. It was indicative of his continued interest in Irish Presbyterianism that when the minority who were contending for the old faith, during that bitter controversy, appealed to him for assistance he unhesitatingly responded and appeared in platforms in various parts of Northern Ireland to speak in support and exposition of the conservative position in theology. [209]

At the rally he described believers as "legatees of the past" who owed a duty to those who would come after them, and dealt with the responsibilities of signing the Westminster Standards. Rev. James Edgar spoke on getting back to the deep things of the Word. Rev. James Hunter "was received with prolonged applause" and "delivered a powerful speech dealing chiefly with the heresy trial." Rev. W M Robertson of Liverpool spoke on the conflict between modernism and Christianity. The meeting protested against secrecy at the trial and unanimously passed a resolution demanding the publication of the report of the trial.

On the following evening, 31 March 1927, Londonderry YMCA was the venue. Rev. W M Robertson of Liverpool spoke on "The Authority of the Bible" and Rev. John MacLeod, then minister of the Free North Church, Inverness, on "Shall we keep our Creed?" but the report in the *Derry Standard*, 1 April 1927, registered a note of tension:

> There was a certain liveliness at the meeting held under the auspices of the Presbyterian Bible Standards League last evening and the Y.M.C.A. Hall was well filled, considerable interest being evinced in a subject which has of late attracted a great deal of public attention. Although, however, divergent views were held on matters connected with the League, and a section of the audience was not always in agreement with the expressions of the speakers, there were no interruptions.

The Chairman, the Lord Mayor, considered it his duty "in the interests of justice", "to advise the various speakers not to refer to the brother whose case has been before the public so much lately, seeing that that case was still *sub judice* and will be heard in the General Assembly." After stating his own position on the case, James Hunter submitted himself to the ruling of the chairman as to whether he should proceed, but offered amidst laughter and applause not to state the individual's name if he would be allowed to proceed on that basis!

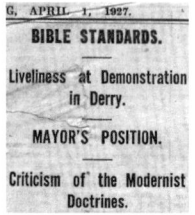

J C Graham, Chairman of the Bible Standards League, protested against the secrecy the Belfast Presbytery had imposed on the trial, its prohibition of public comment until after the appeal and its refusal to make the Record of the Trial available to the Church. However, he did say: "In consequence of this decision of the Presbytery for a private trial, we regret that just at this moment we are precluded from making any exhaustive public statement, even though it is your legitimate right to have such." This appeared effectively to accept Presbytery's ruling, and to be at some variance with what Hunter had said earlier in the meeting: "In any matter theological that concerns my Lord I will speak while there is breath in my body. There is no decision in all the courts of the earth, civil or ecclesiastical, that will ever cause me for one day to keep silent in regard to the infallibility of my Lord and the final morality of His character."

Graham's speech led to a resolution, proposed by A T Goligher and seconded by R D Gordon: "As the interests of every Presbyterian in Ireland are vitally affected in this present controversy, this large meeting demands that at the earliest possible moment the fullest publicity should be given to the entire proceedings at the recent trial of Professor Davey for holding and teaching doctrines contrary to the Standards of the Church." Another speaker queried entitlement to vote on the resolution: "... if everyone was allowed to vote the resolution would have no effect, because it would be passed at a meeting that was, so far as he could see, packed with Baptists, Methodists, Plymouth Brethren, and he did not know who else." After discussion all Presbyterians who wished to vote for the resolution were asked to vote by a show of hands and the result was "decidedly in favour of its adoption."

The *Belfast Telegraph* of 2 April 1927 headed its report of the second Belfast meeting, held the previous evening, as follows: **"CHALLENGE TO DEBATE. MINISTER'S VIEW OF MODERNIST. 'BOLSHEVIST MORE HONEST'"** Dr John Thompson, Killowen, Lisburn presided and spoke about "this terrible fight for the Bible, the whole Bible, and nothing but the Bible." Rev. W M Robertson of Liverpool spoke on 'The Authority of the Bible', his subject of the previous evening in Londonderry. W H Snoddy appealed for recruits to the League and again demanded publication of the trial proceedings. Rev. Samuel Hanna asked: "What is the difference between a Bolshevist[210] and a Modernist?" He said: "It was only a difference in degree, and the Bolshevist was the more honest of the two. The Bolshevist trampled openly on the Bible; the Modernist held it up to ridicule. The Bolshevist openly blasphemed the Saviour; the Modernist clouded

His glory."²¹¹ James Hunter gave details of questions he had put to Professor Davey along with Davey's answers, presumably referring to their non-recorded speeches. After meetings in Coleraine and other towns Grier wrote to Machen, 6 April 1927: "The enthusiasm is growing and we are having a great deal of additional members to our League."

Ulster Pamphlets

The Bible Standards League supported the campaign of public meetings with a series of nine *Ulster Pamphlets*. These were booklets measuring, with one exception, 8 x 5¼. Numbers 8 and 9 were post-appeal:

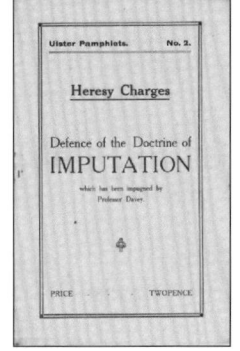

Charges of Heresy
Made against Professor Davey - 8 pages.
Defence of the Doctrine of Imputation
which has been impugned by Professor Davey - 8 pages.
Defence of Divine Character of the Lord Jesus
against the representations of Professor Davey - 8 pages.
Who is Infallible—God or Man?
A Plea for the Holy Scriptures - 8 pages.
Full-Text of *Reasons of Appeal*
against the decision of the Belfast Presbytery - 10 pages
Shall we Abandon our Heritage of Presbyterian Doctrine? - 7 pages.
Modernism What does it Stand for? Is it Heresy?²¹² - 12 pages.
Was Dr Henry Cooke on the Wrong Side? - 12 pages.
Was our Saviour Deluded when on the Cross? - 13 pages.

The Bible Standards League also issued two broadsheets:

Some Extracts from Professor Davey's Defence
Which he put forward at the Trial on Charges of holding and teaching Heresy.
This was a single sheet, 12¾" x 8", with quotations dealing with Scripture, Christology, the Trinity and Sin. Key quotations were underlined.
Comparisons between Doctrinal Positions of Professor Davey,—and the Bible, and Standards of Irish Presbyterian Church.
This was a four-page broadsheet of the same size. The first three pages compared quotations in three columns—'Professor Davey', 'Bible', 'Westminster Confession of Faith, and Larger and Shorter Catechism'.
The back page carried a **Comparison of "The Faith once for all delivered to the Saints," WITH German Rationalism and Modernism. NO MIDDLE GROUND: Only a Bridgeless Chasm!**²¹³
There was a back page appeal to join and support the Bible Standards League.

The nine Pamphlets, of which Hunter wrote seven (1-5; 8-9), amounted to some 80 pages and over 30,000 words. Indicative of his strongly polemic approach, he prefaced No 5: "Full-Text of **Reasons of Appeal**" as follows:

> These are not the Reasons of Appeal which have been forwarded to the General Assembly; they are the Reasons as presented to the Presbytery of Belfast. This court saw good to eviscerate them, leaving practically the bare bones of what the accusers had presented to the Presbytery. After this process of mutilation, they then by resolution agreed to hand the Reasons in their original form to Professor Davey. The favour thus shewn to Professor Davey is now offered to the general public, but not by the Belfast Presbytery.

Also in No 5, *Full-Text of Reasons of Appeal*, Hunter cited as a reason for appeal against the verdict on Charge 2, the plea of justification procedure itself:

> Because it was irregular and unconstitutional to hear a Plea of Justification, seeing that Professor Davey did not accept as true and correct all the evidence advanced against him in the charge. The Legal Assessor pointed this out and advised the Presbytery against receiving the Plea. The first thing which Professor Davey set out to do was to criticise the evidence against him, when the witnesses as a matter of fact had never given their evidence, and when under examination and cross-examination the truth might have been elicited.

However, the accused's pleas of justification provided James Hunter with much more evidence of unorthodoxy than he had when he framed his charges.

The Days Before...

Dr Machen, on a tour of the UK, arrived in Belfast on the ferry from Liverpool on Friday 3 June 1927.[214] Jim Grier met him. His four meetings in Belfast and one in Londonderry a week before the 1927 Assembly were the greatest possible boost for Hunter's campaign. Grier's prediction, in his letter to Machen on 24 March 1927, turned out to be well judged: "If enthusiasm grows at the present rate, you will have 'some' audience". On the Friday evening of his arrival Machen spoke to a well-attended meeting at the Guildhall in Londonderry on the subject *What is Christianity?* On Saturday afternoon he gave the same address to "a very great crowd" at the Wellington Hall, Belfast. On Sunday morning he preached to a Belfast congregation sympathetic to the evangelical cause.[215] On Sunday afternoon he spoke again to a "packed and jammed" Wellington Hall, and in the evening at the larger Ulster Hall, "similarly crowded", where he estimated that almost 1,600 or 1,700 persons were present. At the meetings on Sunday afternoon and evening Machen summarised the differences between modernism and the historic Christian faith. He referred to the current ecclesiastical situation in Belfast but made it clear that he did not become involved publicly in the controversy: "The interest is intense. The meetings at which I have spoken are of course connected with the ecclesiastical situation, though naturally I have not referred to the personal details in my addresses." He did comment quite specifically, however, in his own account, describing Davey as "whitewashed" by the Presbytery:

> The curious situation prevails that the ministers (with few exceptions) are standing on the Modernist side in the ecclesiastical fight; but there is a tremendous tide of evangelical and polemically anti-modernist sentiment among the laity. In the last five years a real revival of religion has been going on. It has been discouraged in every possible way by the great mass of the ministers.

Machen also spoke warmly of W J Grier:

> Heroic work has been done by Mr Grier our Seminary graduate of whom I have already spoken. He has thrown away all his ecclesiastical prospects for the sake of the cause. His work now is in the conduct of the Bookshop of the Bible Standards League. Most of the pulpits, of course, are closed to him.

The General Assembly convened on Monday 6 June 1927. The Assembly was due to consider the appeals on Thursday 9 June, and on the evening before, the Bible Standards League held a huge rally in the Wellington Hall, Belfast. The report in *The Northern Whig and Belfast Post* the next morning with the headers "**BIBLE STANDARDS LEAGUE RESOLUTIONS ON THE 'HERESY' CASE Crowded Belfast Meeting**" recorded an occasion of enthusiasm and great expectation. One speaker described the forthcoming vote as "The most tremendous moment in the history of the Presbyterian Church." J C Graham raised applause in saying that: "One could not fail to be encouraged by the tide of fervour flowing over Ulster in connection with their campaign for a whole Bible." Enthusiastic applause greeted James Hunter when he rose to deal with charges against Professor Davey. W H Snoddy spoke like a man certain of success as he moved a resolution "that the meeting affirm the complete and final authority and infallible truth of the whole Bible": "…they were not going to be satisfied with the Bible which Professor Davey had cut to pieces and they said to the General Assembly 'Neither are you to accept it'". Dr John Thompson, Lisburn, seconding the resolution, got loud applause from a question aimed at the Belfast Presbytery: "Were they going to be ruled by Popes in the North of Ireland?" Another supporting speaker (in language not seasoned with salt!) hoped that "God would help them to kick this crowd out." Only two dissented from the passing of the resolution. The meeting passed another resolution, proposed by Rev. James Edgar, "that the meeting affirmed the absolute necessity and supremacy for a sinner's salvation of the Deity of Christ and atonement by His blood." Rev. Dr Samuel Hanna's speech aroused considerable enthusiasm. He moved that:

> the meeting empowered their leaders to refuse all compromise on these vital issues, and called upon the General Assembly to maintain the existing formula

of subscription to the standards, and called for the complete reformation of Assembly's College, and the overthrow of the rationalism and modernism in their midst.

According to Dr Hanna…

> the question was far too big and important to be finished at a single sitting of the Assembly. A suggested change in their creed was being proposed this year, and the specific purpose of the proposed revision was to alter their interpretation of the Word of God. Their opponents said that they were only proposing to alter the form or expression of their creed, and that the meaning would remain substantially the same. He would like to put this question to their opponents. Was it not true that a principle stood or fell by the form of its expression? A lawyer would tell them that the alteration of a single word in a will would make all the difference in the world whether they would receive their legacy or not. (Applause) Some people to-day, he declared, dealt with the Word of God as though it were merely the fiction of a modern writer. God would deal very strongly with those men (or that Church) who laid impious hands upon His Word. (Applause)
>
> He declared that the elders would be called upon to vote without a single fraction of evidence before them. … "They have tried this case in secret," said the speaker in conclusion, "and they are going to try it in secret in the Assembly. If I know my Presbyterian brethren over the Six Counties, I can say this—if they carry this game of theirs a little further the people will rise and say: 'The Church is not the clergy's, it belongs to the people.' (Applause)

James Brady, Portglenone, seconded the proposal and the meeting carried the resolution with acclamation.

So the imminent climax promised much for the Bible Standards League, now leading the campaign. But the enthusiastic audiences at public meetings were not those who would be voting. The floor of the General Assembly would be a different forum from the provincial venues or the YMCA Wellington Hall in Belfast.

13

The Appeal

By the time that Constantine brought the Roman Empire into the Christian church around AD 325 you could say that Christianity had become Hellenised. It was very difficult to recognise it as the same thing that had started in the first century, the church of the New Testament. It had become Hellenised, so permeated with the influence of Greek philosophy that it had almost become the exact opposite of what it was originally.

Now there were certain people who saw this danger clearly. There was a great man in the Christian church round about AD 200, a little before and a little after, called Tertullian. He focused this problem, this danger, by putting what became a very famous question. It was this: What has Athens to do with Jerusalem? What has the academy to do with the church? That is the great question: What has Athens, the centre and home of philosophy, to do with Jerusalem, the home of the church? What have the academy and the porch, the places where the philosophers taught, to do with the Christian church? If only the church in those days had paid attention to that question! But are we paying attention to that question today? What is happening today, as I see it, is that 'Athens' is coming back into evangelicalism, the academy is coming back into the church and Christian organisations. It is always one of the most dangerous things that can happen, if not indeed the most dangerous of all.

Dr D Martyn Lloyd-Jones, *Knowing the Times*

Part 3 - The Heresy Trial and Appeal

The Appeal Structure

The Assembly began the hearing of the appeals in private at its sixth session on 9 June 1927. The *Belfast Telegraph* of 9 June 1927 displayed the headers, "Davey Heresy Trial", "Appeal Launched at Assembly", "The Charges and Defences" with a photograph of the professor, who was then aged 37. The text catches the excitement: "In a tense atmosphere the eagerly anticipated hearing of the appeal ... was entered upon this afternoon ...". Then a contrasting picture of the parties:

> The appeal is from the findings of the Belfast Presbytery in dismissing (by large majorities) an indictment against Rev. Professor J. Ernest Davey, M.A., B.D., the brilliant young occupant of the Chair of Church History in the Assembly's Theological Faculty in Belfast. ... The indictment consisting of five separate charges of teaching doctrines contrary to the Word of God and the standards of the church was brought by Rev. James Hunter B.A., former minister of Knock congregation, and a number of clergy and laymen identified with the militant organisation known as the Bible Standards League.

Only parties to the case, official delegates from churches in fraternal relations, ministerial assistants, licentiates and theological students of the Presbyterian Church in Ireland were permitted to attend. It was unanimously agreed that all the appeals be taken together. The decisions appealed against, and *The Record* of the whole Presbytery already circulated to Assembly members, were taken as read. The reasons of appeal were read. Assembly members had a mass of intricate and discursive material before them. Clarity had drowned in verbosity and semantics - the charges amounted to 3,500 words, the evidence of witnesses on Charge 1, to about 21,000, the Statements of the Accused, to 51,500. The sequential appeal speeches assessed the trial evidence with the speakers focusing the court's attention on what each considered to be the key evidence and the proper interpretation.

There were ten speeches, four each from Prosecution and Defence, and one proposing and one seconding the motion that the appeal be dismissed. With intervals and interruptions such as applause, they would have taken much longer than the times suggested below:

9 June 1927

Representatives of the Appellants	Times in minutes estimated
S G Montgomery	25
Joseph Goligher	7
W H Snoddy	50
Rev. James Hunter	25

10 June 1927

The Accused, Rev. Prof. J Ernest Davey	40
Representatives of Belfast Presbytery	
Rev. George Thompson	10
Rev. Wm Corkey	40

Saxon J Payne	15
Proposer and Seconder of Motion	
Rev. Dr W G Strahan	20
W J Leeburn	2

The Case for the Prosecution

Charge 1: Imputation – Mr S G Montgomery

He began deferentially, including praise for Ernest Davey the man, and explaining that he spoke on behalf of the laity, encouraged that Christ chose and equipped common men as the founders of Christianity. He aptly described the matters before the court as "the most awfully serious crisis we have had to face in this generation." He denounced modernism as "another gospel entirely", applying the curse of Galatians 1.8. Of its advocates he said: "They will allow us to hold our 'old' views if we will let them hold their new views and remain in good standing in our Churches." He dealt effectively with imputation and Higher Criticism and brought a range of Scripture passages, supported by the *Shorter Catechism*, to show the necessity of "quantitative satisfaction". About the accused he did not mince his words:

> I freely acknowledge that Professor Davey has made a wonderful defence. His pleas of justification are so manipulated that he actually makes himself out the orthodox man, the upholder of the doctrines of the standards of our Presbyterian Church, the innocent one, and we, his accusers, are the unorthodox, and guilty of heresy. I said to a friend the other day, there is not a K.C. or Q.C. or M.P., from the great Dan O'Connell to Sir Edward Carson, K.C., who could hold a candle to Professor Davey. But what after all is it? Just a great, clever, elaborate and intricate piece of human reasoning for which he gives us no Scripture whatever.[216]

He concluded his candid, engaging address with a prayer that God would abundantly bless the accused and deliver him, and himself, from all that was contrary to the Word.

Charge 2: Christology – Mr Joseph Goligher

This speech was brief, alternating between Christology and Scripture. Goligher had read *The Changing Vesture* and *Our Faith in God* and he put his feelings strongly: "It seems to me that Professor Davey would leave us no Bible at all - either Old Testament or New - and no reliable Saviour at all, and no good news to proclaim to sinners …".[217] There is no doubting Goligher's love for the Saviour and the Bible but he did not engage with many of the Christology issues.

Charge 3: Scripture – Mr W H Snoddy

This lengthy speech, based substantially on Davey's plea of justification, was well-structured and supported with references and quotations from Charge 2, the plea, the Confession and Church Fathers. Snoddy got to the point: "Professor Davey's attitude towards Scripture was shown to be Rationalistic, and wholly inconsistent with the standards of the church, because Professor Davey based all Authority and Infallibility finally on human experience, resting upon inward light in the heart, and denied External Authority and Infallibility in the Scriptures."[218] He listed 11 texts as evidence that Davey's views were "contrary to Scripture" and quoted from WCF 1 on Scripture to show that they were "contrary to Standards". "The root difference then between Professor Davey and our Confession is, that while he makes Experience (the character of which he has not defined) the test of the reality and genuineness of God speaking in Scripture, our Confession makes Scripture—or God speaking in it—the test of the reality and genuineness of Experience."[219] Snoddy quoted a dozen of Davey's trial statements on Scripture, eg: "My view of the story at crossing of Jordan is, that it grew up in imitation of the Red Sea crossing ... and there was no miracle here at all." "Christ's theories of Deuteronomy and the Psalms ... of angels and demons, I do not personally think are final for us."[220] He concluded that Davey's views were incompatible with the historic stance of the Presbyterian Church in Ireland, Calvin and Hodge.

Snoddy spent time on WCF 1.5 - the church may induce esteem of Scripture from its abundant internal evidence, but our full persuasion and assurance is from the inward witness of the Holy Spirit "bearing witness by and with the word in our hearts.". He concluded, with reference to WCF 1.5: " ... it is just here that Professor Davey first goes wrong ... from his cardinal error here flow all his other errors; here is the trunk of the tree of his errors, the rest are merely branches and twigs."[221] Snoddy overworked his material, but it was a competent performance which brought the Assembly face to face with many issues concerning Davey's doctrine of Scripture. It earned this sneer from Rev. Wm Corkey the next day: "to whose profound and exhaustive theological exposition we listened yesterday ..."[222]

Charge 4: Sin and Charge 5: The Trinity – Rev. James Hunter
This concluded the appellants' case taking Charges 4 and 5 in reverse. On the Trinity he made it clear that Professor Davey was not being charged with denying the doctrine, but of teaching that it was not taught in Scripture: "In his Plea of Justification Professor Davey affirmed these very positions [in the Charge], insisting that the doctrine of the Trinity is not clearly stated in the New Testament, so that it seems unaccountable that any court could decide that he is not guilty of teaching the very opinions which he fearlessly asserts."[223] He engaged Davey's views of the history of the doctrine, the testimony of Scripture, and the personality of the Holy Spirit. He quoted from ancient and modern participants demonstrating that even among the opponents of the Trinity there was acknowledgement that the doctrine was taught in Scripture.

He appealed to the Church's adherence to its Standards: "The whole subject of this fifth charge, with the proofs adduced, brings into prominence the question: What may this Church teach or refrain from teaching, and retain its identity?" He concluded: "The question is a vital one for us to-day, whether we are to be simply Presbyterians, or are also to have some fixed and permanent creed."[224]

On Charge 4: Sin, Hunter quoted the extracts from the *Changing Vesture* and *Our Faith in God* that constituted the Charge, and declared:

> The root of the error in these strange statements is that the author has ignored two great truths of revelation, namely, the stupendous transcendence of God and the atonement. While God is in and through all, He is transcendently above and separate from all, and the essence of this thought is His unapproachable holiness. Professor Davey speaks in the same sentence of the responsibility of man and the responsibility of God, and according to his teaching the only way of peace is to roll one of these over upon the other. This is in point of fact only a form of pantheism.[225]

He concluded: "And the only teaching which is consistent with a full acknowledgment of the holiness of God is what all the Christian Fathers maintained, that sin is the product of the freewill of man alone, and that God is not responsible for our sins. To give any countenance to doctrine which imperils the holiness of God is destructive of all vital religion."[226]

The appellants had presented strong evidence from the charges and the defendant's statements that seriously questioned the professor's biblical-confessional orthodoxy, but there is nothing to suggest they were ahead at this stage, after their 'day in court'.

The Defence: Discrediting the Accusers

Whilst Professor Davey's long statements dominated the trial, five closely linked defence strategies prevailed at the appeal, four attacking the plaintiffs and one commending the accused. Professor Davey had used the four anti-accuser strategies very effectively at the trial and, supported by the Presbytery representatives, he re-employed them at the appeal.

Contextual Manipulation

The first was to attack the validity of the quotations from Professor Davey's books and lectures on which the accusers had built their case. Repeatedly the defendants asserted that the quotations had been isolated from their contexts and otherwise manipulated. There was no substance to this; none of these claims threatened the accusers' position on the core theological issues, covered in chapters 11 and 15. In his trial statement on Charge 1 Davey set out the theme that he and others developed: "Many of the quotations from my books and lectures, let me say at this point, are seriously out of their context, and one reading the whole books or hearing the whole course of lectures would form quite a different impression of my view from that which would be formed by one reading only the parts quoted in the charges."[227] In fact, someone reading the whole books would only have the impression made by the charge quotations confirmed. Davey was even more pointed in dealing with a quotation from student notes in his plea of justification on Charge 2: "… but by suppressing the context the passage has been twisted to mean the exact opposite of what I meant."[228] Here he asserts an intentional creating of a false impression. But not content with "suppressing" by itself, he suggested, as his argument developed, that it was carefully premeditated.[229]

In his plea on Charge 5, in dealing with his accusers' use of an extract from a student's notes, Davey referred to it as "culled" from the student's notes.[230] This extract consisted of three separate sentences and therefore opens itself to the obvious criticism. But whilst Davey used "culled" in a specific reference, and this is the only instance of its use during trial and appeal, both Dr Robert Allen[231] and Dr A A Fulton[232] later used it unjustifiably to describe the whole process by which the accusers selected the extracts for the charges.

Davey was very pointed about manipulation: "My accusers are fond of omitting words and clauses and sentences; it is so much easier to prove a bad case so; and I shall give you other examples."[233] " … but in any case they once more omit certain words, and so alter the sense of what I say."[234] Rev. Wm Corkey stated: "It required great manipulation to so twist and distort Professor Davey's statements as to make them appear heretical."[235] And on two Charge 2 phrases: "they have been wrested from their context for propaganda purposes, and made to mean the very opposite of the meaning attached to them in their true setting." He added: "In quoting that half sentence in what they knew to be such an unfair way these accusers should have remembered—'That a lie that is half a truth is ever the blackest of lies.'"[236]

Theological Incompetence

A second strategy portrayed the leading accusers as not masters of their subject, and in conflict with prominent reformed theologians like Calvin and Hodge. Chapters 11 and 15 and comment even from within PCI recorded in chapter 12, dismiss this high-sounding assertion. But Davey pressed the point: "… nearly all my opponents seem to make this mistake";[237] "But I know, too, what may surprise my opponents, that on many of the charges made in this indictment John Calvin is in the dock with me."[238] "The amazing thing in this connection is, unless I am greatly mistaken, that my opponents hold this very point as definitely as I do.";[239] "Again I have been accused of denying the perfection of Christ. I doubt if my opponents have even seriously tried to define the word 'perfection' in relation to personality as a social thing …"[240] "But to many of my opponents I believe the doctrine of the Spirit is simply a shibboleth, a form of words for which they would persecute without understanding it, a formula which enables or requires them to call the Spirit 'He,' but means little else."[241] "As regards Charge 4, I have good reason to believe that I am nearer to the confessional doctrine of the eternal decrees than my opponents."[242]

The defendants even attributed heresy to the accusers! In his statement on charge 1 Davey said: "Judging, however, by statements made in the course of the trial, I am inclined to think that if there be heresy in this case it is not in me but in my opponents".²⁴³ And in similar vein: "I believe that my opponents are in a heretical position, so far as I can judge either from their quotations or their remarks in the course of this trial."²⁴⁴ Later, in defending his views on Christology he spoke at greater length²⁴⁵ and then more plainly: "I am afraid my opponents here are heretics, and do not believe in the true humanity of Jesus, but in some more docetic or unreal view of His human nature."²⁴⁶ On charge 4, the professor made the point again: "It is not I but my opponents who are the heretics here with their suggestion that God's eternal decrees, through their provision for our sin, involve Him in unholiness. Whether they, or I, am right, I am at least nearer to the standards of our Church (see Confession, 5.1-4, 6.1)."²⁴⁷

Austin Fulton's description of the accusers' approach as "intransigent fundamentalism" was not used during the trial and appeal, but association of the accusers with the fundamentalist position and disagreement with that position were prominent enough. Professor Davey took issue directly with "fundamentalism" or "fundamentalists" at least a dozen times.²⁴⁸ In one of them he suggested that statements from his fundamentalist opponents made him look more fundamental than they: "They call themselves fundamentalists, well, I was once a fundamentalist; but I think I am now more fundamental than fundamentalist so far as I can judge from a comparison of their words with the words of Christ and the Scriptures."²⁴⁹

Rev. William Corkey again targeted W J Grier saying that there was no reference to his evidence in any of the four appellant speeches, implying that his own side had distanced themselves from him. But the defence had accepted Grier's statements in the charges as substantially correct and his evidence had been tested only in Charge 1 where he proved a tenacious witness. Since that point Davey's pleas of justification had dominated the trial and, consolidating all the evidence that had gone before, they now provided the focus. Dr W G Strahan, another of the Presbytery representatives, attacked the accusers: " … Each charge has appended to it a formidable list of accusers. … As to those from the books … possibly some of them did not read much more (if any more) than the quotations … as to those based upon students' notes, what knowledge of the teaching represented by those notes could the majority of the signatories to the charges possess?"²⁵⁰ The defence also attacked the accusers for errors. In quoting from page 76 of *The Changing Vesture* for Charge 1, the accusers had "definitive" instead of "definite".²⁵¹ This was not a material issue, but it provided an obvious target.

Unworthy Motives
Comments of Professor Davey on Charge 1 suggest that his accusers had some relish for their actions: "… but a section of our Church has been spoiling for a fight, and they have had no past heresy hunt to deter them since the distinctively modern study of religion and its forms began with the scientific revival of last century."²⁵² Dr Strahan revived an early issue at the trial – the 4-5 year delay between the publication of *The Changing Vesture* and the Charges:

What does that mean, Moderator? ... that what he had written was counted by his accusers so innocuous that it was being ignored, and would have continued to be ignored, only that a question in which Professor Davey was not implicated was up for debate in the Church, and something must be found to incite the passions of the people? Where will you find anything so lacking in fairness? anything more indefensible in principle?[253]

But, during the trial, Hunter had committed his motives to the great white throne judgement!

Discreditable Tactics and Conduct
This was the fourth and greatly worked element. Central to it was James Hunter's decision to campaign outside the church courts between trial and appeal, for which he claimed constitutional right. Rev. Wm Corkey took this up:

> In the first place, the constitution of our Church declares that this General Assembly is the only proper tribunal before which such an appeal should be heard (v. Code, par. 111). And in the second place, we were honourably bound by a unanimous resolution of the Presbytery, which directed the members of Presbytery not to enter into public discussion on this case as long as it was sub judice (v. Record, page 16).[254]

Corkey hit out at 'washing the dirty linen in public': "It may be popular for Mr. Hunter and his associates at gatherings composed of all denominations to attack one of our professors because he is a true Presbyterian, and a staunch, uncompromising Calvinist, but the Belfast Presbytery needs no defence for refusing to join in that condemnation."[255] Nearing the end of his speech, he commended Professor Davey to the Assembly: "... against whom his accusers have absolutely failed to substantiate any charge, but whose condemnation they have sought to bring about by appealing to the prejudice, the ignorance, and the passions of the people in such a way as to remind us of the persecuting spirit of Rome in her worst days."[256] Professor Davey had earlier set the tone:

> ... my accusers have pursued a campaign against me, marked by bitterness and misrepresentation, in an attempt to influence the public and my judges in the Courts of the Church. ... But I wish to deal briefly with a few of the statements assiduously circulated about me which are lies, or that kind of half truth which is almost worse than any lie. These frequent misrepresentations so carefully spread abroad, must, I imagine, have influenced some minds in this Court, and, therefore, I wish to take some examples to make clear the kind of spirit with which I have to contend, not so much among the rank and file of my opponents, whose chief defect is lack of information, but among leaders in whose complete sincerity I was at one time ready to believe.[257]

Dr Strahan, in proposing the motion that the appeal be dismissed, returned to the theme: "To-day we have another Professor before us, another reputation up for massacre on the sworn explanation of the man who is probably most competent to explain that it is because of the discussion about the formula. Could venom be more poisonous?"[258]

The Defence: Vindicating the Accused

Professor Davey, the first defence speaker, attacked the procedures and competence of his accusers. On the charges he said: "Some of our Presbyterian Churches, who have had this battle already over, would hardly even investigate them seriously ...".[259] He concluded:

> The times are critical for our Christianity. I do not ask you to choose what will suit me, but to choose with your face to the future, not the past, and as those who own allegiance to the Person and Spirit of Jesus and to the rule of that God Who is Omnipotence and Wisdom and Love. If you think me worthy of your continued confidence I shall be glad, as this is my own Church but with your decision, whatever it is, I shall be content as making clear at least God's will for my own life. ... God guide you to do that which is best and to stand for His truth.[260]

Rev. Dr George Thompson

Thompson touched on each of the five charges but avoided key issues. "The attempt in the fourth charge to father upon the accused that he taught God to be the author of sin is too absurd to merit any notice." But the professor did say that God must take responsibility for whatever happened as a result of his eternal decrees, including human sin. "... on the fifth charge one of our elders asked Professor Davey did he accept the answer given in the Catechism to the question, 'How many persons are there in the Godhead?' and the reply was 'Yes.' But this was not the point at issue in Charge 5. Thompson liked the 'changing vesture' approach: "Definite as are the main lines of our evangelical belief, are we bound to use exactly and always the same worn phrases, or guided by the Holy Spirit into a fuller understanding, are we not to apply these words in terms suitable to the needs of our own generation?"

Rev. William Corkey

Rev. William Corkey was the most powerful of Davey's speakers. The *Irish Evangelical* of March 1933 quoted the *Scots Observer* of 18 February describing him, then Moderator-Designate: "In the critical year of 1920 he was sent to the United States as a member of the Ulster delegation to explain the attitude of the Protestant Churches in Ireland. After he had addressed a great gathering in Fifth Avenue Church, New York, the famous preacher, Dr. Kelman, declared that Mr. Corkey's address was the finest oratory he had ever listened to. This remarkable gift was conspicuously demonstrated at the famous 'heresy trial' in 1927."

Corkey attacked the prosecution witnesses Grier, Snoddy and Shiels. Of Grier he said: "Mr. Hunter did indeed produce one student who swore he had no recollection of Prof. Davey teaching Paul's doctrine of justification, and stated that he could not see it mentioned in his notes ..." Grier had clear recollection of the professor teaching Paul's doctrine of justification as a subject, but what he could not recall or locate in his notes were statements confirming the professor's agreement with Paul. Corkey concluded: "and yet that is the sole witness on whose evidence the Assembly is asked to condemn Professor Davey on this Charge No. 1." Sole *student* witness, but not sole evidence!

Corkey represented Snoddy's statement: "the guilt of sinners is transferable to our Lord" as heresy, adding that someone must have pointed this out to him since he later said that the transfer did not make Christ sinful. Corkey argued that this brought Snoddy into agreement with Davey's *Changing Vesture*. "Mr. Snoddy also stated that 'before any forgiveness could be granted a quantitative satisfaction had to be made upon the Cross' (Record, page 36), which is the Roman Catholic doctrine of a quid pro quo, and is repudiated by Charles Hodge and orthodox theologians." This was an utter distortion of the "quantitative satisfaction" debate.

Turning to John Shiels: "he stated that 'Christ's life had nothing to do with His atonement.'" But this was just half of what Shiels said: "The Atonement only took effect on His death. His life had nothing to do with His Atonement." To Shiels, who was not a trained theologian, the cross was the vital element of the atonement, and both Scripture and Confession (8.4-5) accord fully with that emphasis. Corkey went on: "The same accuser told the Presbytery that he only took exception to the doctrine taught in one paragraph in Charge 1...". He did not! He said that he was confining himself to one issue as "the principal thing to my mind". Corkey continued: "... when he was questioned on that paragraph ... he showed that he had misunderstood its meaning, and was in absolute agreement with Professor Davey's doctrine." Indeed, Shiels had not fully grasped the "quantitative satisfaction" issue, but his views were in sharp conflict with Davey's throughout the exchange.

Corkey surveyed the charges in turn, giving most attention to the first three and stressing Davey's personal affirmations. On the first he asserted that: "Professor Davey was clear and sound in his affirmation and interpretation of this great evangelical doctrine ..." "While stating that Imputation was his own faith, Professor Davey ventured to suggest that we needed a bigger and grander word than Imputation to describe fully the wondrous fact of salvation." On the second, Christology, he repeated Davey's affirmation: "I believe in the Divinity of Christ in the full sense of Deity as set forth in the Trinitarian Doctrine. I believe in Christ as very God of very God ... in His humanity as consubstantial with ours. I believe in the reality of the Incarnation."

Corkey dealt with two phrases from the charge: on the first, that Jesus on the cross "*felt He had let God down*", Corkey told the Assembly: "... and this is what Prof. Davey did say, 'Assuredly Christ did not let God down.' But what Davey actually said was: "The history of Christianity alone is sufficient to prove that God did not fail Christ, and assuredly Christ did not let God down or fail Him; and I know no one who seriously believes that I taught that He did." But the issue was whether Davey taught that Christ *felt* he had let God down. At least one student, supported by a full note, testified that he had, and it was not denied.

About the phrase "*It is not the Galilean Jew that is final ...*" Corkey followed Davey in complaining of instances that the second half of the sentence had been omitted - "*... but something which tabernacled in Him*". But that omission did not misrepresent Davey's position on the personality of Christ: "Whatever finality there may be about the revelation given us in Christ, it is not a finality of personality or of truth *in toto*; on the aesthetic and intellectual sides of His life, at least, no finality is to be found ... and even on the moral side finality must be sought in the spirit, not always or necessarily in the historical forms, of Christ's teaching and life."[261] Davey had said at the trial: "That which we worship in Him is not the Galilean Jew, the man, but the Divine, or, as I say on page 116 (*Our Faith in God*), 'that Spirit which is none other than the eternal God manifest in the flesh.'" Scripture does not portray Christ as this "Galilean Jew" – the unbelieving Jews did! The incarnate Christ was the God-Man, a single, indivisible Personality.

On Charge 3 Corkey was dramatic: "The third charge deals with 'the Holy Scriptures,' and called forth from Prof. Davey that lucid, masterly and scriptural exposition of the teaching of the Confession on the authority of Scripture which you find in the Record—a statement that is worthy to become one of the great classics of our Church." And he ended: "The doctrine of Inspiration set forth in the Confession of Faith, and which Prof. Davey signed, is not a doctrine of the inerrancy of Scripture—our Church never held that—but of the sufficiency of Scripture as a guide, under the Spirit of God, which is trustworthy in matters of faith and life, and there was no evidence brought forward in any extracts in the charges that Prof. Davey had written or taught anything contrary to the standards of the Church." Between these statements he said:

> Our Church has never held the doctrine of verbal infallibility. ... And in his doctrine in regard to this Prof. Davey is absolutely sound, and stands with the Reformers and the Westminster standards. They never once held that the Bible was an infallible guide in geology or botany, or astronomy, or such things. For them the Bible was an infallible guide in faith and morals. ... But infallibility in this sense, in the sense of the Bible being an external infallible authority, apart from the inward witness of the Spirit, was never taught by the Reformers, and is not taught in the Confession of Faith, and is not the doctrine of this Church.

Corkey also approved Davey's statement: "throughout all the search for external infallibility the heavens are as brass," and that "the quest of infallibility (meaning as the context shows external infallibility) ... is the pursuit of the *ignis fatuus*, the will-o'-the-wisp of theology." But here is what Davey said in his Statement of the Accused on Charge 3:

> The whole question of the New Testament is in measure a question of variable and uncertain evidence, giving us probability but not certainty. There is no way of getting a rigid doctrine of inspiration so long as text and canon are

uncertain, and there is no way of getting rid of that uncertainty. We have enough to go on with in all these matters, so long as we confine ourselves to the experimental doctrine of the authority and sufficiency of Scripture in general for the life of the soul, but not if we desire to hold a doctrine of external infallibility and inerrancy. God has denied us that kind of certainty, and for very good reasons, lest we should put the creature in the place of the Creator, the Book in the place of the invisible God.[262]

By contrast, the teaching of the Confession is "The Old Testament in Hebrew ... and the New Testament in Greek ... being immediately inspired by God, and by his singular care and providence kept pure in all ages, are therefore authentical". Corkey is utterly wrong too. The Confession does not say that Scripture is not infallible apart from the inward witness of the Spirit. It says a completely different thing: "*our full persuasion and assurance* (italics ours) of the infallible truth, and divine authority thereof, is from the inward work of the Holy Spirit, bearing witness by and with the word in our hearts."[263] Corkey was just repeating Davey's trial plea:

... the only **infallible** guide is the living Spirit of God—which is the teaching of the Confession—an inward infallibility found in the corroboration of the historical record of revelation by the illumination of the Spirit in the heart. **That** infallibility I have not denied but affirmed. But the way of faith must be maintained, and external infallibilities are a denial of that way of faith.[264]

Corkey's support on Charge 4, Sin, was just a brief evasion: "The fourth charge simply accuses Prof. Davey of maintaining the Calvinistic position of the sovereignty of God." "The fifth charge is ridiculous on the face of it. ... and it is an insult to the intelligence of this Assembly to ask it to investigate such a charge." The Charge read: "WHEREAS it is in accordance with the Word of God that 'the Son and the Holy Ghost are God equal with the Father, ascribing unto them such names, attributes, works, and worship, as are proper to God only' (The Larger Catechism) ... we (the Accusers) charge the Rev. Professor Davey with holding and teaching that this doctrine is not thus taught in the Word of God." Corkey argued: "How could it (the doctrine of the Trinity) be thus taught in Scripture when the words ('attributes' and 'equal') used in the Larger Catechism are not found in Scripture?" The use of non-biblical words, including *Trinity* itself, to describe biblical truth is confessional. The Charge specified Davey to have said: "No clear Trinitarian conception in the New Testament. Only later that Trinitarian doctrine evolved." "In the Fourth Gospel there is a conception of Binity not Trinity. The Fourth Gospel is not Trinitarian at all."

One strange thing about Charge 5 is Hunter's own omission! He began his quotation from the Larger Catechism: "the Son and the Holy Ghost are equal with the Father ..." Why did he not begin four crucial words earlier: "*The Scriptures manifest that* the Son and the Holy Ghost are equal with the Father..." (italics ours)? He could also have quoted WCF 2 – *God and of the Holy Trinity*, that abounds with Scripture references, including the Gospel of John.

Whilst William Corkey identified with Davey and brought his doctrinal errors into sharp relief, his speech had the quality of powerful oratory. At points it brought on his own head the Tennyson line he quoted against his opponents: "That a lie that is half a truth is ever the blackest of lies."[265] There is little doubt that his performance was a significant factor in how the house divided.

Mr J Saxton Payne

An elder, Mr Payne, was the third Presbytery representative. He detested division and desired unity above all: "After yesterday's discussion I feel all the more that we are fighting over mere words." He thought Hunter's trial statement on the atonement eloquent and excellent, but that such lose their impressiveness when delivered in a spirit of controversy. And he thought that Davey, who delighted Presbytery with his incomparable defence, was more in harmony with the Church and Calvinism than his accusers. He spoke only on Charges 1 and 3 "round which the fiercest controversy raged". And his concept of truth: "The Ark of God needs no support from any League; truth will prevail, and you cannot keep it back; it will assert itself. You may defy it, like Canute is said to have defied the waves, but it will overwhelm you."[266]

Defence Tributes to J E Davey

The defence speeches included tributes to Professor Davey. Rev. Dr George Thompson spoke of his "great scholarship and beautiful spirit." Rev. Wm Corkey spoke of "his great gifts and his saintly spirit, a brilliant scholar, whom God has given to us," and concluded his address: "I would ask you to turn your thoughts in the quietness of your own heart to Christ, and seek His guidance before you cast your vote to break and silence this gifted man of God, who has been given to our Church that he might guide the youth of the Church into light and truth, and establish them in the faith once delivered to the saints." J Saxton Payne: "… on hearing the Professor's incomparable defence I now feel that the Rev. Charles Davey's greatest service to the Church was to rear and educate and train for the ministry and the Professor's Chair, his gifted son, for whom I predict a distinguished career amongst the scholars and theologians of the age."

Put to the House

Rev. Dr W G Strahan proposed the motion that the appeal should be dismissed. He began: "I do not identify myself with every interpretation of Scripture contained in Prof. Davey's books or in his speeches and pleas before the Presbytery of Belfast. … In judging one another in this matter of Scripture interpretation we must be charitable." He said that the Assembly had to do with the case, the culprit, and the church. Summarising the charges, he said: "The man not sound upon these doctrines must be the personification of perfidy—touch him anywhere and falsity must be exuding from him." He said that there were four things to be done:

1. We must be strict to see that justice is done.
2. We must prove our allegiance to the historic faith of our Church.
3. We must make it plain that we possess liberty.
4. We must honour the Holy Spirit.

Of point four he said: "Our doctrines are carefully fashioned. They belong to a system almost as closely articulated as the parts of a skeleton. By fitting them together there can be produced a show of life that has intense fascination. But it is all a futility if they are not alive. Life is from the Spirit of God." And he concluded his proposal for the dismissal of the appeal:

> Now, here is a man at your bar to-day who honours your ancient creed, and believes in the Holy Spirit. As I read his words before the Belfast Presbytery I was amazed. There was a reverence, a profundity, shall I say a depth of fellowship with the Holy Spirit, and a consciousness of how essential is His power that filled me with wonder. And this man we are asked to declare a heretic to-day. Moderator, I think we will not do it. We are here for justice, for justice to him, justice to the college, and justice to the Church. We will do our duty.[267]

Verdict

On Friday 10 June 1927, following Dr Strahan's proposal, the motion to dismiss the appeal on Charge 1 was put to the General Assembly which voted as follows:

For the Motion: 707 **Against the Motion: 82**
(89.6% in favour)

The same motion was put to the General Assembly on each of the other charges in turn and declared to be carried by a show of hands.

The Assembly authorised the Publications Committee to publish for general circulation the *Record of the Trial of the Rev. Professor Davey* by the Presbytery of Belfast and, on the following day, authorised the Committee to publish the 10 appeal speeches under the same cover.

14

'Post-Mortem'

Some men fall away under opposition; others only become clearer in their insight and braver in their service. It is cause for the greatest rejoicing that you belong in the latter category.

J Gresham Machen to W J Grier, 24 August 1926

The Combination of Factors

The implications of a Davey conviction were awesome for the Presbyterian Church in Ireland as Livingstone and Wells comment: "J. Ernest Davey was a 'child' of Irish Presbyterianism in all affective senses of the word. ... Moreover, Davey was later described by Professor J. M. Barkley, a prominent scholar, as 'the most brilliant and versatile scholar Irish Presbyterianism had produced' up to that time. Thus, for James Hunter to accuse J. E. Davey was to bring accusation to the very heart of Irish Presbyterianism."[268] Dr Austin Fulton also highlighted the significance of the trial: "This trial, as famous in the story of Irish Presbyterianism as the Robertson Smith case in Scotland, and for us more decisive, ..."[269] James Hunter, for his part, knew there was never any realistic chance of outright victory at the June 1927 Assembly in the prevailing theological climate in the Church. Perhaps, with 1829 in mind, the centenary year of Cooke's victory over Arianism, he was hoping for a new 'Evangelical Party' to mount a progressive challenge in church courts. Would history repeat itself? It would not! But why did the appellants lose the vote so heavily? With the perspective of the passing years it was seen to be for a combination of reasons.

Timing

The timing of Hunter's campaign was influenced by the evangelical revival under W P Nicholson and the conflict in the American Presbyterian Church. More immediately, it was driven by the need to defend the Formula of Subscription and by the concurrent evidence from College lectures. Against this, the Nicholson revival had its greatest impact on the laity, and the SOS campaign of 1926 had demonstrated effective resistance in church courts. However, although 1927 offered no guarantees, the providential pointers in its favour were stronger than they had been for years, and James Hunter had by then retired. When contending for the truth, likelihood of victory in a particular battle may not be the deciding factor. So it was 1927 or not at all. Could he not have moved earlier, when the church retained something more of the influence of the 19th century awakenings? In fact, he did. He campaigned on the Free Church of Scotland case in 1900 and on the Code Revision and Rev. F W S O'Neill cases in the opening two decades of the 20th century, but saw no encouragement.

James Hunter

When Hunter instigated the Heresy Trial, he was 63 and retired. He was academically brilliant, but his attainments were in the previous century. For all his gifts and his service in the cause of orthodoxy, he was not a charismatic figure and, in the eyes of many, did not represent the future. Ernest Davey was 37, from a highly respected church family, exceptionally gifted intellectually, and seen to be on the threshold of a distinguished scholarly career in a new millennium when the Church's consciousness was awakening towards innovations in theological disciplines.[270] There was no comparison between their respective appeals. In addition, James Hunter himself had not proved to be an influential figure in church courts. In June 1905, when he appealed against the Belfast Presbytery's attitude to the Free Church of Scotland, the Assembly upheld the Presbytery's resolutions by 208 votes to 62 (77% of the vote). In 1926, exactly one year before the trial appeal and immediately after phase 1 of his public campaign, he appealed to the General Assembly against his censure by the Belfast Presbytery for his SOS attacks on the professors. But the Assembly dismissed his appeal by 499 votes to 115 (81% of the vote). He had not become associated with success.

Henry Cooke Role Model
Hunter had studied the approach of Henry Cooke and cherished the expectation that the use of his methods 100 years on would again triumph. But there were critical differences. Cooke originally stood alone, but he consolidated his public opinion gains in church courts from 1822 through the growing strength of the Evangelical Party. Hunter did generate public support, but he was unable to achieve it in church courts. Cooke also had a popular political element that was not an option for Hunter with his Liberal political background. Furthermore, Cooke had the clear target of a well-defined heresy, Arianism, and he had conspicuous opponents in Smethurst and Montgomery. Hunter did not enjoy such well-defined battle lines, for the very nature of modernism is breadth and inclusiveness and its recourse to much of traditional Christian terminology. Arians were non-subscribers of the Westminster Confession, but Hunter had to challenge claims of confessional orthodoxy—William Corkey at the appeal called Davey "a staunch, uncompromising Calvinist"!

Weak Support Base
Another problem was the weakness of Hunter's support base. Out of 610 ministers only four were willing to be signatories of charges. The Church had an educated ministry and, if there is any truth in the view that the Presbyterian Church is loyal to its ministers, Hunter faced an uphill struggle. The composition of the accusers reflected this. Certainly they possessed the key qualities of concern for the truth, conviction, and ability, but they were not what the church sees as its leadership, and the geographical spread of their representation did not compensate for this. They were vulnerable to charges that they did not understand the theological issues, that they had not read the books, that they did not know Greek, that they were in no position to assess the calibre of lecture notes on theology.

Students and Student Notes
Hunter committed to the trial with two student witnesses, and he knew he needed at least two, not just as a code requirement, but to substantiate a case against a professor's teaching. But one effectively withdrew at the door of the court, leaving the other isolated, an obvious target, and facing six of his colleagues as witnesses for the other side. Reliance on student notes is by its very nature problematic since

they are recorded quickly in the momentum of a lecture. This was particularly true of Charge 5, The Trinity, where one student's notes were the only evidence.

Nature of the Trial

Even when code procedures are followed, a trial consisting of the testimony of inexpert witnesses dealing extemporarily with major theological issues, untrained witness examiners, prepared defence statements and sequential, unchallengeable appeal speeches is surely not suitable to decide, by more or less immediate vote by members of the house, such major issues as those which arose at the Heresy Trial of 1927. Is it not preferable for a panel of theologically trained judges to pronounce its findings in detailed written judgements, after lengthy deliberation in which all aspects have been carefully weighed? Reserving judgement pending full consideration is a safer basis on which a church may safeguard its standards.

Charge Quotations

If each one of the defence's much-vaunted omissions from the charge quotations had been included it would not have altered the case, but, branded as deliberate, they provided emotive ammunition. Davey attacked the point again and again, and every defence speaker at the appeal took up the refrain. The defence argued contextual manipulation to the same effect, speaking of material "torn" from its context, "twisted" and "manipulated" to make the case sound credible. But its speakers, especially at the appeal, did not always give supporting evidence. People challenged about what they have said often appeal to context, but a glance at the volume of quotations in the charges (Appendix 1) shows that they were not isolated extracts. It is worth noting that the defence made no specific reference to *Changing Vesture* at the appeal.

Presbytery Injunction

One key factor in the size of Hunter's defeat was his decision not to comply with Presbytery's injunction with regard to public reference until after the appeal. It was not that Hunter had no grounds to act as he did. He considered that procedural manoeuvres had blocked his case in his constitutional attempts against Rev. F W S O'Neill more than ten years earlier. He explained the immediate context at a public meeting in Londonderry on 31 March 1927:

> At the conclusion of that trial a member of the court asked a King's Counsel—the legal assessor he was called—if he would say whether or not it was against the law of the Church to have anything said about a matter in regard to which there was an appeal to a higher court, and the King's Counsel said he had searched the code and could find no direction that nothing should be said betwixt the determination of a case in the inferior court and its appearance at the superior court. (Applause.) That answer was unsatisfactory to the brother who had put the question, and there was a further question asked as to what would be the position in civil law. The Counsel answered that in civil law

when a matter was sub-judice one could not open his mouth. Not content with having the answer that there was nothing in the code against referring to the case, the Presbytery imposed a law where the General Assembly had no law and tried to determine a matter that was outside their province to determine.[271]

Civil trials and ecclesiastical trials are different and those applying the *sub judice* norms of the civil case to the ecclesiastical should recognise that the content of civil trials is normally in the public domain and that there is often no embargo on reporting the trial. And what was at stake for Presbytery in informing the public by issuing the *Record*? Presbytery's ban on pre-appeal public reference is of questionable validity, but that is what it did, and did with the knowledge that meetings had already been arranged for the following three evenings. Hunter's non-compliance made it easy for his opponents to portray him as a man who was not subject to the authority of church courts and willing to prejudice court proceedings by disdaining *sub judice* norms. Hunter may have done better to reserve his statements about the Presbytery's prohibition for the appeal as one which was invalid but to which he had nevertheless submitted. Some have even argued that the vote at the appeal was more a censure of Hunter's breach of the injunction than a measure of the theological views of the house. But whatever the strength of feeling generated at the appeal over that issue, there were theology-based motions before the house and on them the votes were cast.

The *Belfast News-Letter* of Monday June 13, 1927, page 9, reported under the headings: "The General Assembly. Right of Inhibition. Suggested Legislation To Confer Explicit Powers. Commission Nominated." Under 'Cases Sub Judice', the article reported Rev. Dr McMillan as saying "there was a need for something in the Code to give a Church Court explicit power to inhibit one of its members or anyone under its jurisdiction from discussing a matter that was sub judice." The Clerk confirmed that there was not a paragraph of that kind in the Code. Whilst the mood of the Assembly appeared to favour explicit legislation there was doubt about the timing being right, and some did not want to introduce a "jarring note" into what they had been grateful for and proud of the previous day. Consequently the legislation did not proceed.

Appeal Speeches
These were a crucial factor, integrating all the others and delivered on a momentous church occasion in a tense and packed house. The focus must fall on those from the defence, which, coming last, concluded the trial process as they climaxed in the motion that the appeal be dismissed. There was no David-Goliath, Cooke-Montgomery type encounter. These defence speeches, particularly William Corkey's, were, at points, powerful and effective performances that read well to this day. Their content is critiqued in the previous chapter.

The defence advocates attacked the accusers, their motives, behaviour, competence and integrity, particularly their activity outside church courts. For these attacks they reserved their most emotive language, labelling the accusers guilty of abuse and vilification of the accused and the church court, appealing to the prejudices, ignorance and passions of the people, seeking to influence the judges, wanting in fairness, chivalry and moral quality, being dull to moral value, marked by bitterness, misrepresentation and propaganda. This is emotive rhetoric from men who were respected, prominent leaders of the Church and they exercised a powerful influence on the outcome. Hunter's case lacked freshness at the General Assembly.

Davey's own speech was composed and convincing and there was general agreement about his commendable spirit and his appealing demeanour. As he neared its end he spoke about his family upbringing as a son of the manse, his own conversion, his second blessing experience at Keswick, and his consequent, but victorious struggles:

> Three years after my conversion I received the so-called Keswick blessing, and the first thing which God sent to meet me in that new attitude of a deeper consecration was the challenge of Old Testament criticism. I fought the battle alone, as my parents were in Australia, and for weeks I struggled, but truth was stronger than prejudice in the end, because even in the darkness and pain of it I knew that if there was a God He must be a God of truth; and from discrepancy to discrepancy I passed, and from conflicting account to conflicting account, till, in spite of all the strength I had spent fighting for the old view, I came to know that the modern views were not only truer but also more helpful. I kept for a good while a note-book in which I jotted down every argument I could find for the traditional view as I came across or conceived it, but in the end I had to admit defeat as an honest man—or one trying to be so—and I have never regretted my tribulation or its results in a new freedom, a new message, a new faith, a new power to help others, and a better love for God and the things of God. I believe in miracle—that God's resources are always greater than our knowledge of them—but I believe also firmly in sincerity as an essential of a true faith and life. This crisis and its all important issues have been forced upon me. The final outcome I cannot foresee, but this I should like to say: my roots are in the Irish Presbyterian Church on both sides for centuries, and there is no Church I would rather serve than my own, so long as she permits it and trusts me to do so.

Davey was open about some of his experiences here and how he had let go his lines to his earlier theological moorings. There was plenty in this extract alone to alarm the General Assembly, but the great majority of the house supported him.

Socio-Political Conditions
Steve Bruce considers that a socio-political aspect in the 1920s was not in Hunter's favour. Comparing 1927 with 1951 when the Free Presbyterian Church was formed, Bruce says:

But by far the most important difference between 1927 and 1951 was the general social climate of the times. I have already mentioned the tenor of the early Nicholson crusades with their appeal to social cohesion and the way in which that harmonized with a very general desire of Ulster Protestants to pull together after the crises which accompanied the formation of the Ulster state. The 1920s were a period of consolidation. The Unionist Party was firmly established as the political voice of the Ulster Protestants and there was little desire to create other divisions in a society which felt that it had just survived a major crisis.[272]

If consolidation was the mood of the hour there was nothing in the timing for Hunter, but whether this made the timing neutral or negative is more difficult to say. There appears to have been no awareness of this factor, for each side saw substantial division as a potential reality. There were many in the Nicholson following who were ready to identify with him in criticising the professors of Assembly's College, and Hunter found the same in his campaign within the church and outside it. And there were different political views within the Presbyterian Church. So the socio-political situation was, at its greatest, a sub-conscious factor.

Broad Church

'Broadening' had taken place in the Presbyterian Church in Ireland in the late 19th and early 20th centuries and the Heresy Trial provided evidence of its extent. Speakers for the defence urged the Assembly to be 'broad' in its approach and not to be governed by the theological issues. Rev. Dr W G Strahan said in proposing that the appeal be dismissed: " ... I am not distressed when I cannot agree with Professor Davey in all he says about deep and difficult Scriptures. In judging one another in this matter of Scripture interpretation we must be charitable." Mr Saxton J Payne, for the Belfast Presbytery, appealed: "as one who cherishes the evangelical, Apostolic faith in all its simplicity, grandeur and fullness, ascribing to Christ all glory and power in the Church throughout all ages ... May I appeal I say, to our friends to let this agitation drop, to accept Professor Davey's frank and full statement, his confession of faith, and to refrain from crippling his usefulness in the important office he fills? Let them be satisfied with having raised the issue as watchdogs of the Church".[273] Hunter said to W J Grier in his post-resignation letter of 27 July 1927: "Surely it is not the will of the Lord that people should remain banded together who have so little in common as the Modernists have with those of the old faith."[274] It was his final rejection of the broad church.

A Miserable Farce!

Dr Samuel Hanna, one of the minister-accusers, for a time remained an outspoken critic of his church over its conduct of the Heresy Trial. He referred to it in a Berry Street sermon, 29 October 1933, with the title, "The McKenzie Heresy. One of the 'Shock-Troops' Exposed."[275]

The stage was set in favour of the accused even to the extent of enlisting the co-operation of a King's Councillor, while every effort was made to prevent a clear presentation of the evidence against the accused. The composition of the court—the Presbytery, which first heard the case was illegal, at least two members of that court, and one of them a leading advocate on behalf of the accused, had already prejudged the issue in favour of the accused, and had therefore no right to sit as members of the Presbytery which was supposed to judge the case with unbiased minds. This was a clear case of prejudice from the beginning. Then this Presbytery, which had declared itself in favour of the accused actually had the effrontery to form a part of the General Assembly—the final court of appeal. Such a procedure turned the whole trial into a miserable farce. There was only one intention from the beginning, and that intention became clear when the accused was given every facility to justify himself, that is to say the accused was allowed to become his own judge; and acquitted himself manfully while the court applauded him. This has been referred to as the overwhelming decision of the Church. It was no such thing, it was the decision of a number of ecclesiastical tyrants, and a still greater number of spineless sycophants, who, in order to better exploit their tyranny turned the property of the Church into a prison by locking the doors. I am sorry to have to put it so bluntly; but you know it's true; and yet we have ministers who have the nerve to still refer to this ecclesiastical farce as a sweeping victory. It was a victory engineered by a certain sect who have used it ever since to advance their schemes of Church Reform.

'Unfair Character' of the Trial
In July 1932 James Hunter's usual leader article for the *Irish Evangelical* bore the title, "Five Years Ago and Today". In it he records his enduring sense of injustice:

> … To put a fair face on the trial, the Presbytery paid a lawyer to act as an assessor to the Moderator. When the lawyer's decision did not suit them, however, they refused to be guided by him. The first charge was entered into at length, but the other four charges were not entered into. The Professor claimed in these to enter a plea of justification. The lawyer gave it as his decision that the circumstances did not allow of such a plea, but the Moderator and the Presbytery ignored this decision; fear drove them to this injustice. … When the first of these addresses was finished the Moderator turned to me and said that I could reply if I chose, and when I answered that I thought it very unfair to call upon me at a moment's notice to answer the long statement that had been made, he simply said that there was no need to speak if I did not like. Not wishing the matter to go by default I took the opportunity that was offered and addresses of mine were given in reply to those of Professor Davey. Not a single word of these addresses was printed, nor one word of the statements of the Professor in reply to those given by me.
>
> … The course of the trial before the higher court was of the same unfair character. … The Rev. Wm. Corkey … charged me with going about the

country and telling what was untrue, that Professor Davey had taught his students that Jesus let God down on the cross. The falsehood was Mr Corkey's and not mine.

Diversion
James Hunter's efforts in the cause of truth were of epic proportions and, helped by the pleas of justification, he emerged from the trial with a powerful theological case. But by some of his tactical decisions he facilitated the diversion of this case into related issues that his opponents manipulated so persuasively to the detriment of the calibre and integrity of the accusers. Had these aspects been marginal factors it is worth pondering the outcome. Undoubtedly, in a purely theological encounter, the percentages would have been different and Hunter could well have emerged with a viable level of support on which to build his reform. James Hunter was a model of watchfulness, unwavering commitment to the reformed faith, courage and sacrifice. He did what he could with the resources at his disposal. He might have done some things differently, but in everything he did he contended earnestly for the faith. In the depths of defeat he "strengthened himself in the LORD his God." (1 Sam 30.6)

Whatever the combined influence of the various factors, it is apparent that there would be only one outcome to the Heresy Trial, however the prosecution ran its case. The court's focus on matters other than the accused's theology speaks for itself.

Davey Theology – Irish Presbyterian Comment
Rev. Dr John Knowles
In the July 1955 *Irish Evangelical* leader, *Dr Knowles on "Schism"*, W J Grier drew attention to extracts from the address of the outgoing Moderator, Dr John Knowles, who had followed Principal J E Davey (1953-54), taking his quotations from reports in *The Northern Whig* and *The News-Letter*):

> Dr. Knowles ... stated that a "schism" existed in their Colleges (Belfast and Derry) on the interpretation of the doctrine of the atonement. The "schism" was between the members of the Student Christian Movement and the members of the Evangelical Union. Dr. Knowles declared: "We know that this division in the College is carried into the ministry of the Church, and that already we have the beginning of a divided Church." He went on to say that "to cure this schism is a matter of life and death."
>
> Dr. Knowles said that when he asked the cause of this "schism," both parties gave the same answer, namely, that the S.C.M. does not "consider the atoning blood of Christ as the central point in their message."
>
> "We are in the happy position," Dr. Knowles claimed, "that the doctrine of the atonement ... was interpreted and explained by our Church not long ago. In 1927 there was a heresy trial in which the doctrine of the atonement was a main issue. In that trial the interpretation put forward by the Rev. James

Hunter and others was not explicitly rejected, but the interpretation given by Principal Davey was accepted by 707 votes to 82."

Dr. Knowles went on to say that the least the decision then taken could mean was that "Principal Davey's interpretation of the atonement was in agreement with the Word of God and the subordinate Standards of our Church and was not heretical." ...

... On Friday, June 10, the General Assembly unanimously adopted a resolution proposed by Dr. Wm. Corkey that "membership of the Student Christian Movement or the Evangelical Union is not incompatible with the Standards of the Church, provided neither body claims that their statements alone are infallibly or exclusively correct." ...

Grier commented in concluding:

> ... The Irish Presbyterian Church is now more clearly than ever an inclusive Church ... Rev. James Hunter was referring particularly to Irish Presbyterian leaders over a quarter of a century ago when he said: "No one is afraid of heresy; all are afraid of 'schism'. That is to say, Believe and teach what you please, but stand shoulder to shoulder. But the Word of God teaches us that it is the Truth which gives and guarantees our unity – and that error ought and must make division."

Very Rev. T A B Smyth

In the January 1971 issue of *Biblical Theology*,[276] Very Rev. T A B Smyth favourably reviewed Dr Austin Fulton's *Biography of J. Ernest Davey* (PCI 1970). In it he said:

> Many were surprised, on hearing the Professor's defence and pleas of justification, to find how closely he adhered to the Church's standards and his illuminating exposition of doctrines he was accused of denying gave many members of Assembly a clearer understanding of them.
>
> With the conclusion of the Heresy Trial it seemed that the victory over theological obscurantism had been won and that the Church would move forward to more constructive thinking and into a new day of freedom. The Assembly acquitted Professor Davey by an incredibly large majority and then failed to follow up the advantages he won for it. How has it happened that a Church that expressed its attitude so convincingly in 1927 appeared later to abandon it – if one is to judge by the revival of fundamentalism and the opposition to ecumenism in certain quarters.

There is wide interpretive latitude in the expression, "surprised ... how closely he adhered to the Church's standards". Is 'close' acceptable in any case? And did many members voting in the house lack clear doctrinal understanding until the Professor's defence? Apart from that, it is difficult to make the 'close to standards' claim compatible with those of "the victory over theological obscurantism" and "a new day of freedom" or with Smyth's chagrin over the reversal of the Davey gains within the church.

Rev. John Thompson

In the same publication Rev. John Thompson[277] expressed a more analytical view:

> To evaluate Davey's theology even in a small way has its own problems. Dr. Fulton's estimate seems near the truth—that he was a radical with a conservative element in his make-up and thinking. ...
>
> Davey's was not a full-blown Hegelianism but he did nonetheless clearly apply the philosophic frame-work of the great German thinker to the understanding and interpretation of the faith. It is clear that Davey made ample use of this schemata as well as of the new science of psychology, particularly in his attempts to understand the Person of Christ. Davey emphasises an honest search for truth but his radical criticism — though this is not always recognised — brought its own preconceptions to the interpretation of the Biblical witness. The truth is always so conditioned and biased.
>
> This has certain unfortunate results. It takes away from theology its autonomy and seeks to squeeze it into the mould of a current philosophy. ... The result invariably is a constriction leading to an undermining of certain aspects of the faith. That these general patterns and results emerge in Davey's thought seems clear. ...
>
> ... his defence at the heresy trial both surprised his supporters in the Assembly and nonplussed his critics. How can one reconcile the two? My suggestion is that Davey tried to do so with the help of his Hegelian dialectic which made it possible for him to say "I accept these — the radical and the conservative — as two 'moments', each of which in its own way is true but neither of which can claim to be the whole of the truth and which when seen together form a whole." ...
>
> These conservative views could only be held as a "moment" or aspect of the faith but not as its essential content and nature—which the Church has normally held it to be. To this extent his plea at the trial which gave the impression of being his full and considered theology was not completely fair either to the Assembly or to himself.
>
> ... his contribution to the social and political thinking of the Church was great and for it we are grateful. His theology is a much more dubious affair and taken as a whole can scarcely be a guide to the present or the future. That it is little read or quoted to-day is adequate commentary upon it.

These extracts outline Thompson's startling assessment of how he saw Davey's defence at the General Assembly of 1927. His defence was essentially predictable, in line with his pleas of justification at the trial. This would not have thrown those who were informed, although his reference to his family, conversion, and Keswick were probably surprising elements. And his defence was hardly 'conservative', hardly in line with the standards of the church. But for Thompson to assess his testimony as not the whole truth, as he does here, and then to declare it "not completely fair" is to evade the only proper verdict.

Denial

John Grier, EPC elder, provides a more comprehensive view:

> We live in a world of spin doctors and so it is natural that we want to believe that things were what we would like them to have been. Holocaust deniers have to be answered and their local equivalent corrected. We all have to be careful to watch that we do not retell the story to suit our current views and feelings. In recent years a number of friends have said to me that the PCI was always basically an evangelical Church.
>
> There is much irrefutable evidence that the teaching of the Assembly's College in the first two thirds of the last century was not conservative or consistently evangelical. For many years the IE magazine highlighted the radical nature of the reading lists of Assembly's College and it is also observable that library accessions in this period give the same picture. Indeed it was only as late as about 1980 when a then college student representative stated that he had suggested to the faculty that the college reading list include a selection of evangelical titles like John Stott's *I Believe in Preaching* to redress the balance, and that they had been glad to agree. A great many of the moderators and key Church House appointments reflect the same trend in this period.
>
> As to Davey's theology, again there is hard evidence. After many years of absence from the realms of book authorship, about which his friends complained and for which they blamed the 1927 accusers, he published *The Jesus of St John* in 1958. It reflected the mature result of "a process of development" which had lasted 40 years and in part rested on work done "more than a third of a century ago" (pre-Heresy Trial). His leading position in the Church's teaching and intellectual life is shown by his 42 years as professor, his 16 as college principal and the massive support he received as moderator of the General Assembly (1953) as well as in the Heresy Trial.
>
> What were the tenets of his faith finally and frankly disclosed to the public? On the sources of the doctrine of Christ in John's Gospel his belief that "other considerations of historical probability and improbability are needed at times to determine whether certain material is human and mystical in significance or divine and ontological, belonging to a life of Jesus of Nazareth, or to a theological construction and perhaps to a Christ myth".[278] This leaves his text littered with the words "probably" and "possibly" and the like (no less than eight such on p 61). This is very different from the "certainty" of Luke 1.4, "so that you may know the certainty of the things you have been taught", or the equivalent affirmation in 1 John 5.
>
> The Biblical record was only evidence to him when he chose to select it as such. The selection was controlled by his lifelong desire to maintain a dominant emphasis on the humanity of Jesus during his life on earth. This led to the removal of elements which he clearly saw in John's Gospel and parts of Matthew's as "belonging to a theological construction and perhaps to a Christ myth." He concluded that "it is true that much of John's Gospel is not history". If the intended conclusion thus guided the selection of material as evidence, a

flawed methodology, open to the charge of circularity of argument, has been followed. He heartily affirmed Christ's two natures: "Thus the divinity of Christ and His humanity i.e. His perfect love and His perfect dependence Godward are found in a real natural harmony".[279] Davey's redefinition of Christ's natures thus vitiated his affirmation of them.

He considered the latter as an eternal feature of His Sonship: "The Son is eternally dependent for being and all else upon the Father."[280] He was openly critical of the classic formulations of the person of Christ promulgated by the councils of Chalcedon: "the solution of the problem as given was psychologically a piece of nonsense". There appears to be a closer relationship between the two books of the 1920s, quoted by the accusers, and Grier's lecture notes to *The Jesus of St John* than to his statement of justification in 1927.

15

Theological Review

What of the considerations mentioned at the beginning of this chapter, that every creed is historically complexioned in language and content, that the progressive understanding of the truth of which the Confession is a conspicuous example did not terminate with 1646, that the Confession is fallible and shows the marks of human infirmity? When the Confession is examined carefully in the light of Scripture and in relation to the demands of confessional witness in the church today, the amazing fact is that there is so little need for emendation, revision, or supplementation. And of greater importance is the fact that justifiable or necessary amendments do not affect the system of truth set forth in the Confession. In other words, the doctrine of the Confession is the doctrine which the church needs to confess and hold aloft today as much as in the 17th century.

John Murray, *Collected Writings of John Murray*,
Vol 4, p 260-1, Banner of Truth 1982

In this chapter there is a short break from the sequence of the story of the Evangelical Presbyterian Church. In it, a panel of reviewers address the main theological issues that arose from Professor Davey's Heresy Trial statement on Charge 1 and his pleas of justification on Charges 2-5. These issues are very much alive today and will continue to have vital significance for the church in the future. The reviewers' terms of reference were to assess, in approximately 2,000 words, one of Professor Davey's statements, as a stand-alone document, in the light of Scripture and the theology of the Westminster standards. Each reviewer has written in a personal capacity, without reference to this publication, and is not otherwise identified with formulating its arguments. The story of the church resumes in the next chapter.

Charge 1: Imputation
Prof. Derek W H Thomas, BSc, MDiv, PhD *(EPC Minister, 1979-1996)*
Robert Strong Professor of Systematic and Pastoral Theology - Theology and Philosophy, Atlanta Campus, Reformed Theological Seminary

Charge 2: Christology
John Grier, MA, Elder of Evangelical Presbyterian Church and Manager of Evangelical Book Shop, 1974-2012.

Charge 3: Scripture
Prof. W D J McKay, BA, BD, MTh, PhD, *Reformed Theological College, Belfast,* minister of Shaftesbury Square Reformed Presbyterian Church, Belfast

Charge 4: Sin
Rev. Dr Iain D Campbell, MA, BD, MTh, PhD
Minister of Free Church of Scotland, Point, Isle of Lewis,
Adjunct Professor of Church History, Westminster Theological Seminary London.

Charge 5: The Trinity
Rev. Dr Andrew A Woolsey, MA, BD, PhD
Minister of Evangelical Presbyterian Church, Crumlin 1989-2008

Charge 1 Plea – Imputation – Derek Thomas Review

The Charge in summary: "That Professor Davey denies that 'God pardoneth all our sins and accepteth us as righteous in His sight, only for the righteousness of Christ imputed to us.'"[281]

Centrality of Imputation
No more central charge could be lodged against any teacher of theology than one made against what Luther called *articulus stantis aut cadentis ecclesiae*—the point of belief which determines (theologically and spiritually) whether the Church stands or falls. And what was this article? The doctrine of justification by faith alone in Jesus Christ alone, 'an act of God's free grace, wherein he pardoneth all our sins, and accepteth us as righteous in his sight, only for the righteousness of Christ *imputed* to us, and received by faith alone.'[282] The Genevan Reformer, John Calvin, expressed it this way:

Therefore, we explain justification simply as the acceptance with which God receives us into his favour as righteous men. And we say that it consists in the remission of sins and the *imputation* of Christ's righteousness.[283]

The key word in both of these definitions is 'imputation'—a concept which Professor Davey finds particularly offensive, not least because of its (for him) inherently unethical basis. How can someone *else* be legally considered liable for something that is mine? In his book, *The Changing Vesture of the Faith*, he wrote:

> Perhaps the weakest spot in the Protestant theory was the specific doctrine of imputation which underlay its theory of Justification. The theory in question rested on the assumption that God cannot forgive by grace upon change of heart. He must have some quantitative satisfaction for sin, and this was found in the positive righteousness of Christ, and in a definite transference of man's guilt from his own shoulders to other shoulders, i.e., Christ's, which could bear it and bear it away.[284]

A few pages later he adds:

> The centre of [Protestantism's] orthodox system is a doctrine of atonement resting upon a theory of imputation which is only another form of transubstantiation. Guilt and righteousness are relative terms, which refer to the personal will and cannot be dissociated from it by any mental jugglery. Guilt is our obligation to have done otherwise than we did, righteousness is our voluntary acceptance of, and abiding in, the will of God. These words simply represent states of the consciousness, and are in no sense transferable. The effects of sin may, or might, be cancelled, but a man's guilt is merely a fact of the past which is as certain and inalienable as his birth; and again, no righteousness is of any real moral value which is not personal, appropriated, and voluntary.[285]

Imputation and Antinomianism

One of Davey's concerns is a perennial one: the possibility of antinomianism if all responsibility for atonement lies in another. If all responsibility is taken away on the part of the sinner, "let us continue in sin that grace may abound." The fact that this deduction was possible in Paul's own defence of justification (cf Rom 6.1) implies that any view of justification which does not raise this antinomian inference *as a possibility* must be rendered deeply suspect!

Imputation and Union with Christ

What precisely did Davey claim? What every reformed theologian claims—that he agrees with John Calvin, whom Davey calls, 'the father of our Presbyterian theology'! As if anticipating what would later develop in Calvin studies in the 20th century, Davey has recourse to Calvin's doctrine of union with Christ as the missing factor in the Westminsterian understanding of faith. "I plead for the addition of a conception of identification or union with Christ," he adds. It is unclear as to what this assertion of affinity with Calvin is meant to achieve for Davey—probably little except to create the smokescreen that somehow Westminsterian theology moved beyond Calvin (or didn't fully understand him). Such claims have been legion in the years since Davey's trial, but have proven false purveyors of either Calvin or Westminster![286] Whatever else was true of subtleties of Calvin's doctrine of union with Christ, he was not the least shy of using the federal language of imputation with its associated ideas of substitution and satisfaction, as a few (and only a few) quotations will show:

> When he [Paul] afterwards states that we are made righteous by the obedience of Christ, we deduce from this that Christ, in satisfying the Father, has procured righteousness for us. It follows from this that righteousness exists in Christ as a property, but that that which belongs properly to Christ is imputed to us. At the same time he explains the character of the righteousness of Christ by referring to it as obedience.[287]
>
> How can we become righteous before God? In the same way as Christ became a sinner. For He took, as it were, our person, that He might be the offender in our name and thus might be reckoned a sinner, not because of His own offences but because of those of others, since He Himself was pure and free from every fault and bore the penalty that was our due and not His own.[288]

Imputation and Penal Substitution

At the heart of Professor Davey's rejection of the traditional doctrine of imputation, and its related ideas of *substitution* and *satisfaction*, is the notion that "sin cannot be transferable." It regards the notion of an innocent party bearing the punishment due to another as inherently unjust and contrary to acceptable laws of jurisprudence. Evidently the apostle Paul did not see it that way. He asks Philemon to have Onesimus's debts transferred to him: "If he has wronged you at all, or owes you anything, charge that to my account" (Philem 18, ESV).

The objection to imputation had arisen long before Davey's own criticisms of it. In an address delivered in 1902 at Princeton Theological Seminary and published 1903 in the *Princeton Theological Review*, Benjamin Breckenridge Warfield had examined in detail federal views of the atonement which some (mainly 19th century writers) had regarded as "unethical."[289] Warfield draws the conclusion that apart from satisfaction for guilt through substitution (Anselm's formula) all views of the atonement must conclude that we are responsible for atoning ourselves. And this, as Warfield concludes, can only be done through a diminishment of the seriousness of sin. "Nothing indeed," he writes, "is more startling in the structure of recent theories of the atonement, than the apparently vanishing sense of sin that underlies them."[290]

At the heart of Davey's objection is that imputation implies dealing with the innocent as though they were guilty (or *vice versa*), a situation that is inherently contrary to the laws of jurisprudence. Tempting as it is to ask, "whose laws of jurisprudence?" It will suffice to state instead that this is not the Bible's way of presenting substitution and imputation. As R A Finlayson put it:

> Imputation involves for us the moral problem of how a blameless person can stand for the blameworthy. But this is not the biblical way of presenting it. Rather is it that His people's sins were so set to Christ's account that He became a sin-bearer, and that He so remained to the end, "bearing [His] sins in His body right up to the tree" (1 Pet 2.24). This was undoubtedly the principle underlying all the blood-sacrifices of the Old Testament. By the laying on of the hands of the offerer, or vicariously of the priest, there was a symbolic transference of guilt from the sinner to the sin-bearer.[291]

When the God-man is judged on the cross, that is when the cross is viewed as penal (Christ offering satisfaction for covenant violation of law and suffering the curse as a consequence—2 Cor 5.21; Gal 3.13), Christ is not being judged "as an innocent" but as one who *is guilty*! Substitution renders him guilty and the judgement that results is in accord with divine standards of penal rectitude. As Calvin put it:

> For the apostles, the cross was a place of penal suffering. Christ endured the agonies of Calvary because in the profoundest possible sense, God orchestrated it. It was "by the determinate counsel and foreknowledge of God" (Acts 2.23 KJV; cf 4.27-28). God himself has a hand in the death of Jesus. In some sense at least, there is a necessity for Calvary arising within the character of God himself if sinners are to be reconciled to him.[292] The cross is therefore 'penal' (Lat. *poena*). A penalty was inflicted upon Christ. In priestly fashion, God the Father offers his Son (cf John 3.16). This understands the suffering of Jesus on the cross as an act of divine malediction: the hand of God in judgment descends upon Jesus. "Christ was put under the condemnation which we had all merited, and reckoned among the godless."[293]

This does not solve every issue relating to imputation. As R A Finlayson wrote:

> We are faced with a mystery we cannot fully penetrate, since there is no proper analogy to it in human relationships: it is the mystery of how the implication of guilt can morally be transferred from the sinner to the sin-bearer, even when the sin-bearer voluntarily accepts this position.[294]

Federal Imputation Today
The issue raised by Professor Davey nearly 90 years ago has reappeared in a different guise. The church continues to face opposition to the doctrine of federal imputation from many sources. On the side of what we might call Presbyterian neo-orthodoxy there is the significance of the re-publication of J. McLeod Campbell's *The Nature of the Atonement*[295] in 1996 which signalled an important

milestone in evangelical discussions on the theology of the atonement, questioning as it does the very idea of penal substitution. Like Professor Davey, Campbell too fell foul of ecclesiastical trial and in his case was found guilty of heresy. From the side of what at first appeared to be evangelical Anglicanism, but has since moved in a more radical direction, there is the *New Perspective on Paul* as championed of late by the Bishop of Durham, N T Wright. Wright's output is too considerable to include here, but the gist of this theology can be accessed in his books, *What St. Paul Really Said* and *Climax of the Covenant*.[296] He too dislikes the notion of federal imputation, calling into question our understanding of Inter-testamental Pharisaism and its allegiance to a works-based view of salvation.[297]

Davey Methodology
Typical of Professor Davey's defence, not only as to this charge but of all the others, is his way of denying something in one place whilst affirming it in another. Thus, in his official defence on March 4, 1927, he said, "I believe in satisfaction, in imputation, in justification and sanctification..." adding, "imputation, for example, is my own faith even when I criticise the use of the term." It is "satisfactory up to a point" but "too external and legal in its meaning," "the atmosphere of the true Christian is that of the Father's house, not that of the law court."

It is difficult to know how to reason with those (neo-orthodox) theologians who relish the dialectical language of contradiction as essentially expressive of truth. One thing is certain, whilst Davey will use the language of imputation and its forensic categories in his defence, he means something entirely different from that which the Westminster tradition intended this term to mean.

Charge 2 Plea – Christology – John Grier Review
The Charge in summary: "That Professor Davey taught what is contrary to Holy Scripture concerning the absolute perfection of our Lord's character."[298]

Davey produced a plea of justification of 11,500 words, about the same length as this entire chapter. Space does not permit a point-by-point analysis of his statement, just the identity of key issues with examples. The witness examination sections of Chapter 11, The Heresy Trial, have already provided sufficient insight into the issues. These issues will be the focus here, and not the many conflicting heresies which Davey imputed to his accusers, nor the straw men – views not held by them - which he set up and demolished.

Evaluating the Christology of his books on the one hand, and his plea of justification on the other, reveals the presence of a dichotomy. The nuances, or as his critics thought inconsistencies, of Davey's Christology leave an impression of a brilliant mind that at times fluctuated through mutually irreconcilable positions. On the one hand Davey could agree that John 1.14 "And the Word was made flesh, and dwelt among us (and we beheld his glory, the glory as of the only begotten of the Father), full of grace and truth" applied to the time of Christ's earthly ministry, but on the other he denied the historicity of much of John's evidence of the glory of the unique Son full of grace and truth.[299]

Exegesis

At the outset he declared his interpretation of Colossians 2.9, "in Him dwelleth all the fulness of the Godhead bodily": "I would point out that the quotation from Col. 2.9 is a reference to the risen and exalted, not the earthly, life of Christ, the verb 'dwelleth' is in the present tense." This text however, with its reference to Christ's body, has a primary reference to the incarnation, and Paul uses the present tense to affirm that the "fulness" dwells in Christ eternally. J D G Dunn confirms this: σωματικῶς (bodily) "can hardly refer to anything other than Jesus' life on earth"; "At the same time the present tense indicates this function of Jesus is ongoing."[300] F F Bruce and Douglas Moo hold essentially the same view and all three refer to the parallel text at chapter one verse 19 where there is a past tense.[301]

To Davey, "He could there do no mighty work because of their unbelief" (Mark 6.5-6) demonstrated the limitation of Christ's power.[302] However D A Carson gives the sense "The 'could not' is related to Jesus' mission: just as Jesus could not turn stones into bread without violating his mission (Matt. 4.1-4), so he could not do miracles indiscriminately without turning his mission into a sideshow. The 'lack of faith' of the people was doubtless a source of profound grief and frustration for Jesus rather than something that stripped him of power."[303]

To Davey, "But of that day and that hour knoweth no man, no, not the angels which are in heaven, neither the Son, but the Father" (Mark 13:32) demonstrated the limitation of his knowledge. The specific instance does not prove the rule. Macleod comments: "It is virtually certain that the reason why it was not revealed was that this was not something that his people needed to know." And again, "If he knew that he did not know the day and the hour of the parousia, could he not also have known that he did not know the speed of light; and even that many questions relevant to the environment and to cosmic origins had not even been posed in the first century?"[304]

In these cases Davey's exegesis of the New Testament text does not sustain the case he was seeking to build.

Kenosis

Davey's *kenosis* (self-emptying) theory governed his Christology. He placed his emphasis on "the human Jesus": this is shown when he says "I believe Incarnation as taught in Scripture implies a voluntary self-limitation of God." "The Kenosis line of thought solves the problem ... What is true of Divine nature *in itself* is not necessarily true of Christ's personality if Incarnation demands limitation."

Philippians 2.7 does teach Christ did not insist upon his rights, but to Davey it meant that Christ on earth was deficient in attributes of deity, rather than the orthodox view that Christ fully retained them, although he veiled and restricted them in his capacity of a servant. Donald Macleod[305] points out that this sort of kenotic theory left a figure with almost total disconnection with his previous existence in terms of knowledge, power and divine consciousness. The New Testament shows the God-man who knew undeclared motives and thoughts, controlled nature and repeatedly taught his disciples of his impending death. Again when Davey said: "our final faith cannot be in the transient forms which show humanity at a particular stage of development, but in the abiding reality and spirit which used these forms in default of better",[306] he opens up a second discontinuity, this time between the Jesus of history and the Christ of worship. The latter was to him an uncertain figure founded on experience. This Kenosis also sits uneasily with the Christology of Chalcedon which Davey was later openly to call "one of the least satisfactory of the great Catholic dogma of the early councils"[307] His criticism of the Chalcedon formula was clear when he stated that its "solution to the problem was psychologically a piece of nonsense".[308]

Subsequent research has shown the credibility of the accuracy of oral transmission of material in largely non-literate communities[309] and of the eyewitness character of the gospel records.[310] The latest possible date for the composition of John's gospel was made much earlier by the discovery of the Bodmer papyrus (dated 125 AD) in 1952, and there is now the possibility of evidence that fragments of Mark from about 90 AD have been found in a death mask. These also limit the possibility of the development of doctrine in a time gap between the Jesus of history and the Christ of faith which Davey often postulated.

Davey laid great stress on Calvin's treatment of the emotions of Christ in Gethsemane and Calvary to justify his statements in his books and lectures. However it is important to note what Calvin actually said: "This was no rehearsed prayer of Christ's, but the force and onset of grief wrung a cry from Him on the instant, which He at once went on to correct," and again, "We should give God's Son all honour, and not reckon Him by our standards. In us, all the emotions of the flesh seethe and leap up boldly - or at least drag up some dirt with them. Yet Christ's passion of grief and fear was such that He held Himself in limits."[311]

Concerning the cry of dereliction from the cross, Calvin says: "Before uttering the temptation, He first says He takes refuge in God as His God ["My God, My God"], and so with the shield of faith bravely repulses the sort of dereliction that shot at Him from the other side ["why have You forsaken Me?"]. In this fearful torment His faith was unscathed. Though He laments that He is forsaken, He takes confidence in the close assistance of God."[312] It is true that the whole gamut of human emotions consistent with His perfect holiness was present in Christ's life. He was fiercely tempted to succumb to doubt, which is a sin, but did not give in. Davey loses the balance between both the terrors of Gethsemane and the dereliction on the Cross on the one hand, and Christ's perfect response on the other.

To Davey Christ was the "moral hero" of the world with "moral glory". B B Warfield's critique of William Sanday's Christology is apposite here:[313]

> The principle of the Chalcedonian formulation (of the Two Natures of Christ) does full justice to the entire body of the Biblical data, but men are no longer

seeking to do full justice to the entire body of the Biblical data. The Bible has fallen to pieces in their hands and they are impatient of an effort to synthesise all its points of view…What each successive investigator is endeavouring to accomplish is to discover… the lost truth which has been covered up and hidden under all the Biblical ideas and can be recovered only by tearing them away and laying bare the forgotten reality beneath. The Bible having been lost, the Christ of the Bible has naturally been lost also; and each thinker is left very much to his own imagination to picture how it were fitting that God should become man.

Charge 3 Plea – Scripture – David McKay Review
The Charge in summary: this is quoted in the next paragraph "[314]

What we believe about Scripture shapes our entire theology. Do we have a revelation from God? Is it contained in a single book? Can human language adequately convey divine truth? How we answer such questions will determine our understanding of God, man, Christ, salvation, Christian living and hope. It is therefore no surprise that again and again in the course of history the orthodox Christian doctrine of Scripture has come under attack. This is exemplified in the case of Professor Davey. To quote from the General Assembly Minutes, "The third charge alleges that Professor Davey taught what is contrary to the Word of God and the Westminster Confession of Faith regarding the inspiration, infallibility and Divine authority of the Holy Scriptures" (9 June 1927).

In his defence Davey dealt at length with his understanding of the Confession of Faith, the views of the Princeton theologians and the opinions of contemporary biblical scholars. Space does not permit extended critique of Davey's position, although his claims regarding the views of the Confession's authors are clearly open to challenge. More fruitful for a short study will be an examination of the Bible's witness to itself, set in stark contrast to Davey's statements.

The Inspiration of Scripture
Fundamental to Davey's position is a distinction between the Word of God and the written Scriptures, a distinction which he erroneously attributes to the Reformers. For Davey the Word of God is the original revelation of God to his spokesmen, whilst the Scriptures are a record by fallible men of that revelation. "Scripture is not the revelation itself but its record".[315] Hence he can say, "There are human and divine elements in the Bible, only the latter is the Word of God".[316] It is a view which later came to be associated with the German theologian Karl Barth.

Consequently, for Davey "inspiration" is detached from the written Scriptures and becomes an activity of God, initially in those who received his revelation and now in those who read the Bible. "Thus inspiration means the direct speech of God in Scripture *to our hearts*" (emphasis added).[317] In essence, inspiration for Davey is located in the reader's interaction with the text of Scripture rather than in the text itself. Again there is a marked similarity to Barth's idea of the

Bible "becoming" the Word of God to particular readers at particular times. What should our response to Davey's view be? The clearest biblical testimony to the nature of inspiration is undoubtedly to be found in 2 Timothy 3.16, which could be most helpfully and accurately translated as "All Scripture is God-breathed". A proper understanding of this text will yield an understanding of inspiration very different from that of Davey, but one accurately expressed by the Westminster Divines and the Princeton theologians.

Note first that the whole Bible is included here. Paul was of course referring in the first instance to the Old Testament, the Scriptures given by God up to that point. Very significantly, however, we see from 1 Timothy 5.18 and from 2 Peter 3.16 that the New Testament Gospels and the Epistles were being recognised as belonging among the "sacred writings" of God's people. The crucial term used by Paul is the Greek word *theopneustos*, translated in the Authorised Version as "given by inspiration of God", but more accurately as "God-breathed" (New International Version) or "breathed out by God" (English Standard Version). It was the great Princeton theologian B B Warfield who demonstrated in an exhaustive study entitled "God-inspired Scripture"[318] that *theopneustos* does not indicate that something was breathed into the words, but that the words themselves were breathed out by God himself. As Warfield rightly states, Scripture is "the product of Divine spiration, the creation of that Spirit who is in all spheres of the divine activity the executive of the Godhead."

Strictly speaking, therefore, it is the written Scriptures that are said to be inspired, rather than the writers. Of course the Holy Spirit did work in the writers, guiding and superintending even their choice of words. As Peter says, "men spoke from God as they were carried along by the Holy Spirit" (2 Peter 1.21, ESV). Nevertheless we must maintain the testimony of 2 Timothy 3.16 that the written Scriptures are in the fullest sense "God-breathed". The Bible is "inspired" apart from any response in its readers.

Since it is a miraculous work of the Holy Spirit, inspiration has in it an element of mystery that we cannot fully unravel. We do not know how precisely the Spirit "carried along" the writers, but it is clear that he made use of their background, education, personality, writing style and historical research. The writers were not used like inanimate machines but rather with their whole being engaged. This view of inspiration has been termed *organic* and is well summed up by J I Packer as "God's *concursive operation* in, with and through the free working of man's own mind".[319] It is futile even to think of untangling man's words from God's words, and indeed arrogant to presume to be able to do so. The whole Bible is man's word and God's Word.

The Infallibility of Scripture
Once we have established that the Bible is God-breathed Scripture, its infallibility follows logically. It is the Scriptures - the written Word - that are God-breathed. Inspiration does not merely apply to the ideas contained in Scripture, but to the

words that express them. Indeed we have no access to the ideas except through the words. The text before us is God-breathed. Textual scholars have given us access to a text of the Bible which is in all significant respects that penned by the original writers. Despite what Davey and others claim, the textual variants among existing copies of the Hebrew and Greek Scriptures are tiny and affect no doctrine of the faith. Warfield's ascription of infallibility to the original text of the Bible poses no problems for us: we have that text.

According to Davey, "Infallibility has not to do with intellectual truth but with spiritual understanding".[320] This assertion allows him to claim "infallibility" for a book that, on his own admission, contains errors in matters of history and science, to name only two areas. Infallibility thus applies only to the "spiritual truth" contained in the Bible: on other issues this book is to be examined like any human book and, in the light of human reasoning, its historical and scientific content may be accepted or rejected. In response to Davey's position, we must reply with the words of John 17.17 "Your word is truth." God's Word is truth and, as we have seen, it cannot be separated from other parts of Scripture which are merely man's word. The whole Bible, in all that it teaches, is the very truth of God. It is all infallible.

We cannot accept any view which seeks to distinguish infallible "spiritual" teaching from fallible statements on other subjects such as historical events or scientific issues. Many have sought to make such a distinction, including the modern Dutch theologian G C Berkouwer, but such a distinction is in fact impossible to sustain. Consider the statement "Christ died for our sins according to the Scriptures" (1 Cor 15.3). Undoubtedly this is "spiritual" truth, but it is also "historical" truth. Indeed if the statement is not true historically, if Christ did not in fact die as the Gospels tell us, it cannot be spiritual truth either. This is but one example of how theology and history are intertwined throughout the Bible. If the Scriptures cannot be relied on when they make historical statements, they are unreliable as far as their spiritual content is concerned. The same is true when scientific matters are addressed. When the text of Scripture is rightly interpreted, whether about creation or any other scientific issue, if it is shown to speak falsely, its reliability on spiritual issues is likewise fatally compromised.

The Inerrancy of Scripture

It is impossible to deny infallibility to part of what the Bible teaches, yet assert it of other elements of its teaching. The attempts of theologians to make this artificial distinction, which allows them still to speak of "biblical infallibility", has led many orthodox theologians, holding a high view of inspiration, to speak of the "inerrancy" of the Bible. The ambiguities that some have introduced into the term "infallibility" have unfortunately made such a step necessary.

To be consistent with the Bible's own testimony to itself, we must assert that the entire book is infallible and inerrant in *all* that it teaches on *whatever* subject. Careful exegesis is certainly needed to determine what the Bible teaches, but, with the help of the Holy Spirit, that is what godly scholars (and non-scholars!) do all the time. We must bear in mind that Scripture reflects the standards of its time regarding historical and semantic precision: any history is a selective record, for example. Verbal exactness is not required when the New Testament cites the Old: modern ideas of "quotation" should not be imposed on ancient writings. The literary genre of books and passages of Scripture must be kept in mind. None of this undermines biblical infallibility. It is simply to say that good exegetical methods must be used in biblical interpretation, and the higher our view of Scripture, the more careful we will be to interpret it correctly.

It should also be noted that Davey's claims to share the views of the Reformers should not be accepted. Significant work has been done by Evangelical and Reformed scholars since Davey's day, especially in the 1980s when the so-called "inerrancy debate" was raging in the United States, that demonstrates conclusively that the assertions of Davey and others like him are simply wrong.

The Authority of Scripture

If the Scriptures are indeed "God-breathed", as we have argued, then they must be *absolutely authoritative* in all matters that they treat. Whether addressing science, history or theology, the Scriptures are supremely authoritative. Just as it is impossible to limit their inspiration or infallibility to so-called "spiritual" matters, so with regard to their authority, we must submit to them in every area they address. It is important to assert that the Scriptures are "self-attesting". In other words, they cannot be proved to be God's Word by appeal to some higher authority such as scientific or archaeological discoveries. That higher authority would then be replacing Scripture as our supreme authority and would be treated as more trustworthy than the Bible. The Reformers, in opposition to Rome, emphasised that the Bible has authority in and of itself. No external authority, such as the Church, need be invoked to ratify the Scriptures as our rule of faith and practice. Ultimately the Bible is to be believed for its own sake: the Church should *acknowledge* the Bible for what it is, but it cannot *make* the Bible what it is.

We have to recognise that there is a circularity in this argument: we believe Scripture is God's Word because it claims to be and we believe its claims because Scripture is God's Word. That, however, is the case with any final authority, whether it is human reason, sense experience, the Bible, or anything else. In the case of the Bible we have the working of the Holy Spirit who increasingly confirms our belief that this is God's Word as we study and submit to it. Rather than a circle, our acceptance of Scripture is more like a spiral of increasing evidence and conviction.

i. For the Christian, therefore, the Bible has absolute authority. For the sake of clarity we can distinguish two senses in which it is authoritative:*Historical authority*: Scripture is a true and absolutely reliable *record* of all the events and words that are found in it. There are no errors of history, geography or science in Scripture. Davey and many like him have denied that the Bible has any such authority.

ii. *Normative authority*: Scripture is the *rule* of faith and life which demands complete obedience on the part of all men.

A difficulty arises at this point as to how far normative value may be ascribed to the separate parts of the Bible. It is evident that not every statement and command contained in Scripture can be binding on us. Scripture records, for example, the words of Satan and of false teachers, which we must not believe. Thus Satan's words in Genesis 3.4, "You shall not surely die", do not have normative authority. (They *do* have historical authority: the verse accurately records what Satan said). Another example would be some of the statements of Job's comforters. We must also recognise that some commands bind only the specific individuals who received them. Thus Jesus' command to the rich young ruler, "Go, sell everything you have and give to the poor" (Mark 10.21, NIV), does not have normative authority for us, at least in that specific form.

How are we to decide what in Scripture does have normative authority? Some cases are straightforward: many commands are obviously meant for all ages. Examples would be moral and ethical commands that are not tied to one specific situation, and dogmatic statements directly from the mouth of God or through authorised spokesmen speaking in his name. Other statements by individuals can be tested against the standard of God's moral law, as can actions on which the Bible does not directly comment, as for example in the historical books of the Old Testament. Clearly no normative authority attaches to the statements of Satan, or of evil men, or of godly men if they conflict with God's moral law. Sometimes we may not be sure about the normative authority of particular passages. This is reflected in debates among equally Reformed, Bible-believing scholars about the details of the Mosaic civil legislation. Careful study of what Scripture actually says is essential, and yet sometimes a degree of uncertainty may remain even among those equally committed to Scripture's normative authority. The areas of disagreement, however, are small in comparison to the overwhelming majority of biblical passages whose normative authority is clear. Our problem is less one of determining what has normative authority and more one of accepting and obeying.

Present Challenges

The trial of Professor Davey took place many years ago and theological debate about the doctrine of Scripture has in several respects moved on. At the same time, we can see in contemporary debates positions that have their roots in issues that arose in the Davey case and, indeed, that are developments of views he expressed. We may note several present challenges to the orthodox view of Scripture which the Church of today and tomorrow must address:

1. The Bible is viewed by many, especially in the academic world, as nothing more than a human document. Davey argued that the Bible contained both human and divine elements: almost inevitably the divine has gradually been minimised and eventually abolished.

2. An increasing number of biblical scholars take the view that the meaning of any passage of Scripture is to be determined not by the intent of the original author (which, it is claimed, cannot be discovered anyway), but by its significance for the reader. Such a "reader-response" approach is but a development of Davey's locating inspiration in the reader rather than in the text. The fruit growing from such a root is destructive of spiritual life since the Bible no longer has any objective meaning. Such an approach is helpless if a reader "finds" a meaning in the text that is diametrically opposed to what the words say.
3. Many "postmodernist" theorists argue that all human language is opaque and incapable of conveying objective truth statements about anything. Without delving into the complexities of such a philosophy, it can be said that it destroys any concept of the Bible being a revelation from or of God.

In the face of these ever-changing challenges, it is essential that God's people hold firmly to the Bible's own teaching about its nature as God-breathed Scripture, infallible and authoritative in all that it says on any subject. Not only must they hold to such a position: they must live it out in humble and joyful submission to the Word of God.

Charge 4 Plea – Sin – Iain D Campbell Review

The Charge in summary: "That Professor Davey held and taught what is contrary to the doctrine that "the sinfulness of all sins proceedeth only from the creature and not from God."[321]

I am grateful for the invitation to contribute to this history of the Evangelical Presbyterian Church of Ireland, a denomination which has enjoyed cordial relations with my own, the Free Church of Scotland, from its inception in 1927. A continuing acceptance of the final authority of the Scriptures and a continuing loyalty to the Reformed doctrine of the Westminster Confession of Faith still characterises these twin branches of Christ's church, and it is our prayer and fervent desire that the Evangelical Presbyterian Church will go from strength to strength in its proclamation of biblical Christianity.

The historical context which saw the formation of the EPC is recounted elsewhere in this volume, and I have been asked to comment on the fourth charge which was raised against Professor J. Ernest Davey in his trial for heresy. This charge indicted Professor Davey on the grounds that he had taught what was contrary to the doctrine that "the sinfulness of all sins proceedeth only from the creature and not from God."[322] Those who so charged him did so largely on the basis of Davey's two works *The Changing Vesture of the Faith* and *Our Faith in God*. In the former of these, Davey appeared to undermine the doctrine of imputation, and in the latter to describe faith in God as the only "sure escape … from the burden of responsibility", by which the burden of our sin is rolled "upon God".

In his plea before the Belfast Presbytery in 1927, Professor Davey acknowledged that he did regard God as being 'responsible' for sin in a primary sense. He argued that "When one could prevent a thing and does not, because He has a purpose which can be fulfilled even through it, then in some real sense he takes responsibility for what happens."[323] Davey argued that, far from undermining the confessional position, he was actually arguing in defence of it. How can God NOT be, in some sense, 'responsible' for our sins if he has a purpose to fulfil in them? However, Rev. James Hunter counter-argued that if the sense of 'responsibility' is the same when applied to God and man, then the result is merely a form of pantheism, and went on to argue cogently that Davey's case fell in his failure to distinguish between *liability* and *responsibility*. If God is responsible for our sin, even in Davey's nuanced sense, is he liable for it? And is atonement necessary if he is?

Those who framed the charges did so because they understood Davey to be teaching that in his dealings with sin, God does not lay them to Christ's charge but actually bears the transgression himself. This undermined, in their view, the confessional doctrine of the seriousness of sin, with its emphasis on personal accountability. In the Reformed view, the glory of the cross is that the Mediator, Jesus Christ, stands answerable and accountable for the sins of his people, since, by a sovereign judicial act on the part of God, these sins have been laid to Christ's charge. Davey's insistence on the inadequacy of 'imputation' as a theological construct seemed, as far as his opponents were concerned, to detract from the personal nature and biblical definition of sin. Davey also insisted that permission of something implies responsibility for it, and that the cross is a declaration to us of how God permitted wickedness in order to overcome it. What is not clear is Davey's insistence that "Christ bears our human sin but not its guilt".[324] Where is the righteousness of the cross if Christ is not being punished as one who is declared guilty?

My purpose in this short paper is neither to assess Davey's theology nor to assess the merits or otherwise of the trial against him. As with many trials for heresy at the end of the 19th and the beginning of the 20th centuries (in the Scottish churches as well as in the PCI), claims and counter-claims of orthodoxy were rife. That was hardly surprising, given the doctrinal changes which had come into the churches over the course of the 19th century. Changes in biblical scholarship as well as the relaxation of credal subscription in many churches led to a bifurcation in the understanding of the nature of evangelicalism. Those who moved away from confessional positions often argued that *contemporary* evangelicalism demanded it; while those who raised charges of heresy counter-argued that *radical* evangelicalism demanded it. The legacy in many instances was polarisation leading to the fracturing of the church itself.

Of course, however much we know and learn about the historical influences which have shaped our past, it will be of little use or benefit to us unless we are prepared to learn from them. Therefore my paper will focus on the cause of the contention at the heart of the fourth charge, and will simply ask two questions:

1. Why does the Westminster Confession of Faith labour the point that the sinfulness of sin proceeds from the creature, rather than from God, and

2. How does a correct understanding of this point of doctrine influence and shape our presentation of the Gospel?

Sinfulness Proceeds from Man

To turn to the first of these questions: what does the Confession mean in its insistence that the sinfulness of sin proceeds from man rather than from God? It is important to note that the statement is to be found not in a discussion of sin (or of anthropology) but in a discussion of providence (that is, of theology proper). The doctrine of the fifth chapter of the Westminster Confession of Faith is that God exercises universal, sovereign control over everything that takes place in the world. This control is absolute, extending to both the greatest and the least of events in the world. The statements of the Confession regarding this providential control are magisterial: we are reminded, for example, that God is the ultimate cause of all things, yet, within the ambit of providence, events take place 'according to the nature of second causes'. That is to say that some events occur within a necessary sequence, while other events take place freely, while yet others happen by what we might call 'chance', or contingency. Every event is woven within a tapestry of sovereign design, so that God remains timelessly in control of every time-bound event.

This doctrine has important implications, not least in the Reformed polemic against open theism, an old heresy which is enjoying a considerable and remarkable comeback. It is the view that events in the future remain entirely 'open', with not even God able to tell which of countless possible futures we may plot out for ourselves. While God knows every possible permutation of choices and actions, open theism argues that he respects our freedom of choice to such a degree that he co-operates with us, sometimes changing his plans to accommodate our choices.[325] In spite of appeals to biblical passages, open theism undermines the clear biblical teaching regarding God's sovereign control over history, and his foreordination of every event within history. The Westminster Confession's view of providence, therefore, is very much under the spotlight at this time.

The fourth charge laid against Professor Davey focussed particularly on the relation between sovereign providence and human sin. If every event is ordained by God within a providential scheme aimed ultimately at his own glory, what is the relation between that ordination and the fall? The Confession of Faith had no difficulty in asserting that providence extended to the fall both of angels and of men, but found it necessary to insert the disclaimer that this was "not by a bare permission, but ... a most wise and powerful bounding, and otherwise ordering and governing of them, in a manifold dispensation, to his own holy ends" (WCF 5.4). The language, as always, is careful; but it is incontrovertible: God's providence both orders and governs the sinful acts of men for God's holy purposes.

The words "not by a bare permission" are an attack on the Council of Trent, which bequeathed to the Roman Catholic Church the view that 'God permits evil in order to draw forth some greater good'.[326] However, although the Confession does employ the language of permission (for example in 6.1), it also "commendably avoids expressions that might appear to relieve God's decree of its immutable and predetermining efficiency".[327] In relation to sin, God's providential decree is such that God so guides men "in the exercise of their wickedness that the particular forms of its manifestation are determined by his will".[328] This is true from Genesis, where Joseph says that in all his brothers had done to him "it was not you that sent me here, but God" (45.8, ESV), to Revelation, where we read that "God has put in their hearts to fulfil his will, and to agree, and give their kingdom unto the beast, until the words of God shall be fulfilled" (17.17, KJV).

The Confession, however, recognises that a further nuancing of the doctrine is required. The fact that God guides men in their sinful actions does not mean that the sinfulness of the action is from him, nor that he is its cause, nor that he is in any sense an approver of sin. There is no contradiction between the fact that sin is both forbidden by God *and* decreed by God. God's law, which highlights the nature of sin, and is intended to restrain sin, is the revelation of his own holy nature; and that holiness is not compromised by his decree to ordain and permit acts of wickedness. While God's revealed will forbids sin, his decretive will ordains it, and brings even the rebellion against what he has revealed within the ambit of his overarching purpose. There are not two wills in God, only one, "most holy and righteous" will, which at one and the same time shows us that sin *ought not to be*, and that the fact that it *is* falls within God's sovereign plan for the universe. To quote John Murray:

> ...when the Confession says that God was pleased to permit sin, it is not for the purpose of toning down the decree or providence of God to the notion of mere permission, but to conserve the responsibility of the human agents and to maintain that the decree and providence of God, though all-inclusive and immutably certain, do not operate so as to deprive moral agents of their liberty and responsibility.[329]

In other words, God's foreordination of sin, which includes his permitting it, his guiding the events of men in the execution of it, his restraining it, his overruling it and his delimiting of it, do not detract one bit from the responsibility that is ours in sinning against God. The sinfulness of the action is entirely ours; the sin originates with us; and in committing sin, we approve that of which God disapproves.

When the fathers of the Evangelical Presbyterian Church raised the charge against Professor Davey that he was teaching something contrary to this doctrine of the Confession, they were not dealing with a peripheral doctrine. Davey taught that God takes the responsibility for sin both in permitting it, and in dealing with it. The response of the EPC Fathers to this was to return to the first principles of biblical and Reformed doctrine: God's relationship to sin may be defined in many ways, but the one thing that a sovereign, holy God cannot do is take responsibility for sin.

Our Presentation of the Gospel
Which brings us, at last, to the second question: how does the Confession's doctrine shape our presentation of the Gospel? What is the evangelical content of a scriptural view of God's relation to sin? What, indeed, did the EPC stand for at the outset, and what does she continue to proclaim now?

Let me answer this question in three ways. First, the Confessional position of the Reformed churches requires us to proclaim *man's personal responsibility and accountability before God*. We cannot appeal to God's sovereign providence, or to his election, or to his foreordination as a reason for, or as an excuse for, our own sin. Sin remains objective fact: it is a breach of God's law. All our actions are culpable, simply because they are free actions. Bound as we are by nature in sin's bondage, all our movements within that cage heap guilt upon our heads. The God of the Bible remains holy and righteous, who can in no way clear the guilty (Num 14.18). Unless our evangelism begins at this point, it will be truncated and unbalanced. We begin with man's ruin and need.

Second, the Confessional position requires us to proclaim *God's gracious provision for our sin*. That provision is only found at Calvary, where sin is condemned in the flesh (Rom 8.3), destroyed on its own battlefield and in its own territory. God does not take responsibility for our sin at Calvary. But he does deal with it, finally and definitively, through the Mediator, the Lord Jesus Christ. He carries our sins in his body to the tree (1 Pet 2.24); and on the cross Jesus Christ is made sin for us (2 Cor 5.21) in a sovereign act of imputation which renders him exposed to the wrath of God in our place. The debt is ours, for which we are wholly responsible. The payment of it is his, on which we wholly depend. Imputation does not mean that our agency and responsibility are diminished; but it does mean that our inability to pay the debt is met by Christ's willingness to give his life as a ransom (Mark 10.45). At Calvary, the demands of God's law are met, and the death of Christ becomes the ground of our peace with God.

Third, the Confessional position requires us to proclaim *a warrant of faith for all who will trust in Christ*. The Gospel proclamation is as wide as the problem of sin itself. We are mandated to go into all the world and declare that the issue which causes estrangement between man and God has been removed, and that there is a ground on which reconciliation is possible. By faith in a crucified Saviour, men and women everywhere may know that peace for themselves. We are warranted to say to sinners without exception, 'Believe on the Lord Jesus Christ, AND YOU WILL BE SAVED' (Acts 16.31).

It was for that Gospel that the EPC fathers contended. We wish their sons every blessing and encouragement in the Lord as they continue to proclaim Christ as the only remedy for sinners.

Charge 5 Plea - The Trinity – Andrew A Woolsey Review
The Charge in summary: "That Professor Davey held and taught that the doctrine of the Trinity is not taught in the Word of God."[330]

To evaluate Professor Davey's statement on the Trinity several questions need to be asked: he affirms his belief in the doctrine as expressed in the Confession of Faith,[331] but does he strictly adhere to this? Are his statements and comments always consistent with Confessional theology? When Davey says, "That is my faith", what does he mean? Does he have the traditional view of the confessional standards in mind, or is he speaking through the grid of philosophical presuppositions which are far removed from those of the Confession, and inevitably change the meaning, at least in Davey's mind, of the Westminster statements? Again, does Davey deal adequately and conclusively with the evidence adduced in the students' notes?

When we read through Davey's plea and appeal, to say nothing of his other writings, there are so many nebulous statements that repeatedly we have to ask, 'What is he actually saying here?' This leaves us wondering what he really means when he says of the Confessional statement, "That is my faith." The general impression we get is of someone who has left behind Aristotle's maxim: "There is no mean between two opposites." It is the impression of someone trying to find a mean between divergent views, or trying to hold on to diverging views at the same time, and say of both, "That is my faith." His writings are like some of the impressionist paintings. The detail is vague and hazy; you can take it this way, or you can take it that way. The crucial thing seems to be the impression that is created at any given moment. In most of Davey's writings the impression is of a radical, frontier theologian wanting to distance himself from out-dated traditional teaching, but in the Heresy Trial documents the aim is to promote a conservative image. He affirms his faith in the Confession. He quotes James Denny at length, claiming to be more conservative than he on the doctrine of the Spirit.

What is the Trinity?

In the opening words of the plea, Davey does three things: he immediately declares himself to be a staunch upholder of Confessional orthodoxy: "Let me begin by making clear that I myself hold the doctrine of the Trinity as set forth in our Confession." And, after quoting Chapter 2.3, he says, "That is my faith." Secondly, he describes how he views this doctrine. It is not to him "a mystery and a great perplexity". Rather, he views it "as a Christian philosophy of life and experience". There is no real explanation here or elsewhere as to what Davey means by defining the Trinity in this way. A further definition follows - "the Christian Trinitarian philosophy of the Godhead".[332] Later, he brings these definitions together, telling us that the Trinity is more of a rational concept that is "a key to the mystery of God and life",[333] although at times it does shade "into the infinite mystery of God".[334] And thirdly, he insists that this doctrine "was not reached all at once". It was "a slow and painful development"[335] during the early centuries of the Church's life. Davey's approach to the doctrine of the Trinity is invariably from a philosophical perspective. This is more obvious in his other writings, but it shows here also.

Two Sources or One?

As Davey proceeds he makes much of a principle from elsewhere in the Confession (1.6) to contend that the doctrine of the Trinity was not "expressly set down in Scripture", but "deduced" from it. He then says that Trinitarianism rather than Unitarianism explains the complexity of the world in which we live. Is this what he meant by defining the Trinity as a "philosophy of life and experience"? We are not told. But it does pose the question: is the complexity of the world Trinitarian in nature? There follows a brief, fairly traditional exposition of the doctrine, apart from limiting the Holy Spirit to being an experience of unity in the Church, until he hastens to add that the Spirit is more than that, and is "a personal or superpersonal entity" who existed in other forms from the beginning. This view of the Trinity, Davey says, is pictured in the New Testament: "Here then in the New Testament story we have the revelation of the three persons of the Godhead".[336] But then he maintains that this view was only deduced from material which Scripture provided, and "that in Scripture there is no actual statement of the Trinity". It is important to note that when Davey speaks of the doctrine being deduced from Scripture he usually adds a qualifier: "The Trinity ... was a doctrine deduced from the Holy Spirit's word in Scripture *and the hearts of men* by a long process of discussion in the early Church". Again, "the Christian revelation in Scripture *and in the life of the Church* ... has given us the doctrine of the Trinity". And again, "the doctrine was formulated in the early Church writings and councils ... being deduced from Scripture *and experience*".[337]

When Davey looks at "the actual position of Scripture" he mentions only three texts as relevant. In critical mode, he plays down the significance of these, and other general passages, especially from the Johannine material, which have reference to the Trinity. He stresses that many of the words used in the early Church creeds, including the word "Trinity" itself, are not to be found in Scripture. Therefore, he concludes, "men had to go beyond Scripture to define the Trinity; and Scripture therefore gives us no definite Trinitarian doctrine".[338] Davey makes much of the early Church writings and councils in relation to the formulation of the doctrine of the Trinity, but the role that these played is left ambiguous. Sometimes he gives the impression that the early Church writers merely rephrased and defined the doctrine, but he also gives the distinct impression that the hearts, lives, experience and thought of these men contributed to the doctrine itself. There is a tendency to confuse the teaching of the doctrine as we find it in the Scriptures and the more systematic statement of the doctrine by the Church Councils. Davey certainly seems to be saying that the Councils were not merely stating the doctrine in a more systematic way, but were actually creating the doctrine out of some material that Scripture provided plus what came from their own thought and experience.

When the Westminster theologians set out their articles of faith they had a firm basis for what they believed. They received the Scriptures of the Old and New Testaments as the Word of God revealed and the only rule for faith and life. And when they penned Chapter 2.3 they were affirming that this is what Scripture taught concerning the divine Trinity. This is what God had revealed to be true of himself. Scripture may not put it in these precise words or phrases, but this is the truth of what God in his Word has revealed concerning his triunity, and consequently they believed it. The same can be said concerning the position of the Church fathers in council at Nicea, Chalcedon, or elsewhere. They were not formulating a doctrine out of their own hearts and experience plus some scriptural material. Scripture alone was their source and authority. Davey rejects such a basis. Nowhere does he appeal to Scripture alone as the basis for his doctrine of the Trinity, and his treatment of the material from Scripture is both highly selective and critical. A comparison of Davey's treatment of the biblical material with that of B B Warfield is very illuminating, especially on the Johannine writings.[339]

Scripture does not in any one place give a fully formulated definition of the doctrine of the Trinity. The same is true of other doctrines. But the teaching is clearly alluded to in numerous places, which together give an overwhelming consciousness of the doctrine. As Warfield has said, "It is not in a text here and there that the New Testament bears its testimony to the doctrine of the Trinity. The whole book is Trinitarian to the core; all its teaching is built on the assumption of the Trinity; and its allusions to the Trinity are frequent, cursory, easy and confident". This is a different picture from that which Davey paints of "dreadful conflicts", of "slow and painful business" in the early Church Councils in order to produce a doctrine of the Trinity. The "dreadful conflicts" were not efforts to complete something that was still in the process of being revealed. They were efforts to defend and define more concisely what Scripture taught in the face of those who had departed, or were threatening to depart, from the apostolic testimony. The early Church Councils were heresy trials. The inevitable and more precise definitions did not change or add anything to the doctrine as revealed in the teachings of Christ and the apostles. The Councils simply taught what Scripture taught, which contradicts what Davey says, "The long fight over the points in question shows clearly that Scripture gave no certain teaching on the matter." We can only conclude that Davey maintained, as the charge says, that "the doctrine of the Trinity is not taught in the Word of God."[340]

A Philosophy of Development?
With the help of an extended quotation from Denney, Davey deals with the statements from the students' lecture notes. Here he expounds the thesis that there is a movement in Scripture from Jewish Monotheism, through Greek Binitarianism towards the Christian Trinity, but this is not finally reached until the eighth century. Indeed, he is of the opinion that this Trinitarianism has not yet reached its full expression, and he has "great hopes" that we will arrive at a much deeper comprehension of it in modern times. Davey maintains that the disciples of Jesus were adoptionists, beginning with Christ as a man, and it was only in Paul's writings that "the beginnings of an incarnational theology" are to be found. Paul thus provided a bridge for further "Incarnation development" in John, who adopted from Philo of Alexandria the "Hellenistic Logos philosophy

of a Binity".[341] This binitarian view, Davey maintains, persisted in Christian orthodoxy for a long time, and then in turn provided a bridge for later "clear Trinitarian development"[342] after the days of Irenaeus, Tertullian and Origen who paved the way for it.

This liberal theory of religious development may have been popular in Davey's day, but many of the presuppositions upon which it is built have long since been found wanting. The gospel writings, the Synoptics included, are awash with evidence of Christ's deity; this was grasped in some measure by the disciples from the beginning, and was a solid conviction by the time of the resurrection. Again, because John once described Jesus as the divine Logos it cannot be taken as proof that John's concept of the Logos was the same as Philo's. Also, John's gospel is saturated with evidence of the divine personality of the Spirit. We conclude with Warfield that "The doctrine of the Trinity does not appear in the New Testament in the making, but as already made." We would also contend that Davey's thesis of the development of Trinitarian doctrine does not conclusively refute the statements from the students' notes. Even his cursory dismissal of the reference to "two elements", saying it is "a reference not to two persons in the Godhead but to two natures in Christ" is still suspect, for the simple reason that Davey did refer to the persons in the Godhead as "elements" as well as "hypostases".[343]

The Leap of Faith

Davey eventually gives us a clue as to the real explanation for his theological position. He acknowledges that "Hegel has given us some help philosophically" with the doctrine, although he denies holding Hegel's "abstract and superficial view" of the Trinity.[344] Davey's method of presentation is very typical of theologians who were influenced by Hegelian philosophy and the higher critical schools of biblical interpretation. Hegel's shifting view of truth-in-synthesis effectively removed any base for saying, "this view is right and therefore that view is wrong; this is true and that is false." This relative view of truth infiltrated theology and accommodated "the leap of faith" mentality. Consequently, because he feels it still gives some sort of undefined meaning to his life and experience, a man may continue to say he believes in something even though he has long since rejected any rational basis for what he says he believes. There can be no doubt that this is what helped Davey to say of the confessional standards of the church, as he could also say of concepts that were at variance with those standards, "That is my faith." For Davey, Christian theology, including the doctrine of the Trinity, was an ongoing philosophical development, not confined to divine revelation in the Scriptures, and consequently not to the subordinate statements of the Confession.

The story of the Irish Evangelical-Evangelical Presbyterian Church now resumes. What happened after the appeal to the General Assembly in June 1927 failed?

Ministers since 1970

S J Tracey · W C J Ballantine · G N Burke · S J Garland · M P Hobson

N Green · A A Woolsey · N E Reid · M G Johnston · S Watson

R C Beckett · D W H Thomas · S G T Atkinson · J S Ross · W L Elliott

R J Johnston · A M Hambleton · J S Roger · A J Lucas · N Whitla

Presbytery Day Conference, 2015

Photographs in the book have largely been restricted to the denominational level. We recognise with gratitude the many members and friends, male and female, past and present, who have served their Lord sacrificially and faithfully, in and from each congregation. They are not viewed here, but are known to God. Psalm 115.1

Elders of the Church who have been Chair of Council or Moderator of Presbytery

Dr J R Gillespie

W A Sampson

J D P Blair

E C Brown

D Watson

J Grier

M Langtry

T Gilliland

K McDonald

H Gibson

Dr James Hunter Gillespie, member of Council, who was tragically killed in a road accident in February 1934, when just 27.

'Transitional years'
Some ministers and elders at the Annual Presentation of Presbytery Reports, Crumlin, May 1982

Congregations by chronology.
Dates indicate the commencement/completion of the location witness.

Knock, 1927
New building, 2015

Crosscollyer Street, 1927

Botanic Avenue, 1930-1971

Stranmillis, 1971

Botanic Avenue (formerly Shaftesbury Square and South Belfast) was vested by the Government in 1971 to accommodate a proposed ring road. This led to the move to Stranmillis in 1971 although plans for this section of the ring road were afterwards cancelled.

Lisburn Road, 1928-2008. Building destroyed by bomb, 1986. Rebuilt, 1988
After closure, acquired by Stranmillis congregation for outreach

Somerton Road, 1928
Hope Fellowship Church Plant 2013

Ballyclare, 1928
New building, 1970

Crumlin, Co Antrim, 1929
New building, 1999

Clintyfallow, Co Tyrone
1931-1985

Finaghy, 1946
Several re-furbishments

Dublin, Perrystown Community Centre, 1979-2007,

Omagh, 1982
New Building, 2015

Richhill, Co Armagh, 1984. New building, 1990

Bangor, Co Down, 1994
New Building, at Groomsport, 2004

Church and Evangelical Book Shop

Outgoing and incoming Trustees of Evangelical Book shop, with wives and staff, Belfast, June 1985

Colin M Campbell Manager, 2012-

Successive Book Shop Managers: Rev Samuel Watson, Sam Shanks, John Grier

With the Compliments of the Council of the Royal Ulster Agricultural Society.

This limited edition medallion was commissioned in 1996 to celebrate the Centenary of the opening of Balmoral Showgrounds.

The Book Shop exhibited at the Balmoral Show for 70 years, 1939-2008. In 1996 the Manager was presented with one of the Centenary medals

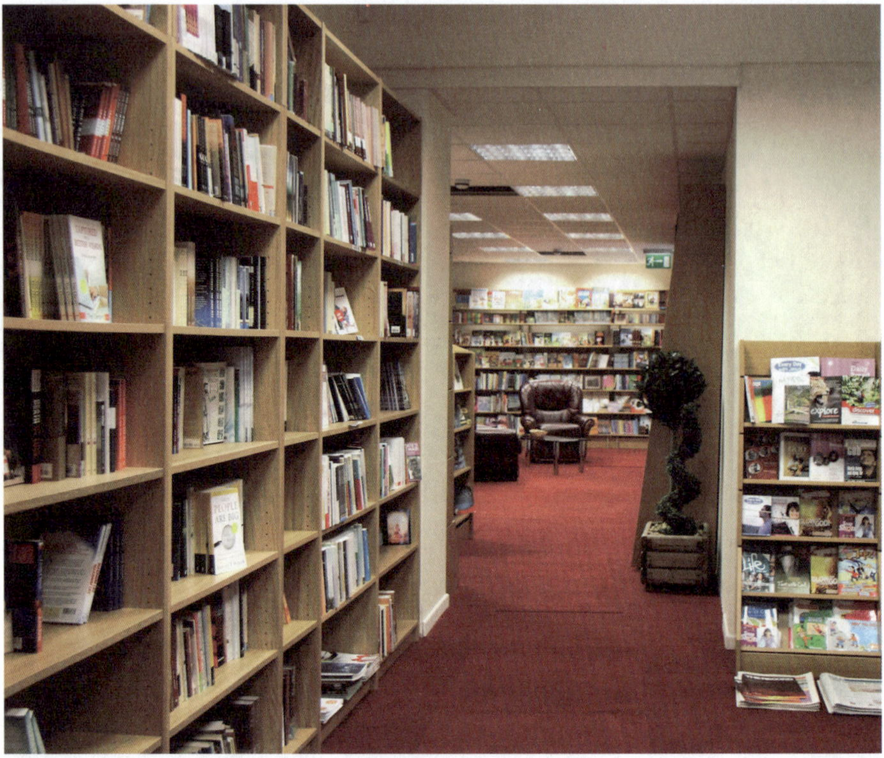

Official Opening of the re-furbished shop, August, 2011

Part 4

The Evangelical Presbyterian Church

16

Severing the Bonds

On the appointment of John Macleod as Professor of New Testament, Free Church College, 1906:

Professor Macleod came to his teaching post at a time when the old principles of Biblical interpretation were being strongly challenged by the exponents of the "new learning," who were speaking with such confidence that even men who were evangelical at heart were showing them a timorous deference.

But the new Free Church Professor was not of this order. His inaugural address, delivered in the Free Church College on 18th October 1906, was the manifesto of an evangelical of the old school. The Bible was to him "an historical organism."

"The progress of Revelation," he averred, "resembles the path of the just, that shines more and more unto the perfect day. ... With the advent of the great Prophet of the church the great day came. The sun then arose. All supernatural revelation is summed up in His Person, word and work."

G N M Collins, *Principal John Macleod, DD*
Free Church Publications Committee, p 98

After a campaign that had raised high expectations, James Hunter emerged from the General Assembly of 1927 with an overwhelming vote against him, and it was from such a base that he set out to consider the way ahead. Only a handful of those who had joined closely with him in his campaign saw the need to leave the Church, and among those who did there were no ministers, just one licentiate, William J Grier. Livingstone and Wells saw the Heresy Trial as a matter of great significance for the Presbyterian Church in Ireland: "With historical hindsight, we can now see that this trial was the turning point in the struggle for the soul and mind of the Presbyterian Church in Ireland."[345] It generated emotion, an enormous amount of work, and opened the Church to public and ecclesiastical gaze.

The Local Press

The main Belfast newspapers, the *Belfast Telegraph*, the *Belfast News-Letter* and *The Northern Whig and Belfast Post*, reported the events and the speeches of both sides extensively.

Completely Vindicated

The Northern Whig and Belfast Post, Saturday, June 11, 1927 headed its report, "Professor Davey Vindicated", "Heresy Appeals Dismissed by Overwhelming Majority", "Mutilated Statements", "Campaign of Bitterness and Misrepresentation".

> The Announcement, (of the vote) which completely vindicates Professor Davey, was received with enthusiasm, which was only restrained by the Court rule of "no applause". The Assembly adjourned immediately, and as the members left the hall the Doxology was sung with befitting solemnity and thanksgiving.
>
> The whole attitude of the members showed distinct relief that the ordeal was over, and one heard the whispered comment, "Surely this will end all this nonsense."

The *Belfast News-Letter* was less hostile to the accusers in its headlines, but on 11 June 1927, under "Assembly Notes", "By a Member", recorded a similar triumphant note:

> Professor Davey, immediately after the court had opened, proceeded to deliver his defence to the charges made against him. It was given in a speech which displayed the marvellous scholarship of the professor and in a spirit characteristic of the man, and made a profound impression upon the Court. He pointed out that his accusers were very fond of omitting words and taking clauses out of the context, and in that way, he said, they had attempted to prove the charges they had brought against him. These tactics, he contended, were not worthy of men who profess to be so concerned about the faith of the Church.

He then proceeded to deal in detail with the various charges, and let it be said at once that he completely turned the tables on his accusers, and showed that there was no evidence whatever to justify the attacks that had been made upon him. ... How any individual could entertain a charge of heresy against Professor Davey after listening to his defence and final utterances it would be difficult to understand, and few were surprised at the result of the vote. ... The excitement in the House when the vote was being taken was intense, and the atmosphere can only be described as electric. When the result was declared, 707 for Professor Davey and 82 against, it was with difficulty that the members were restrained from breaking into applause. No one, we believe, expected the majority to be so great. Professor Davey was the recipient of congratulations on every hand when the result was announced.

The Gallery 'Mob'

The *Belfast News-Letter,* Friday, June 10, 1927, noted in the introduction to its report on the opening of the Appeals: "The public were rigidly excluded from the proceedings yesterday, but the body of the hall was packed to overflowing with members of the Assembly..." The weekly *Presbyterian Witness*, Friday, June 17, 1927, confirms the assertion:

> The body of the hall was packed to its utmost capacity by ministers and elders, while in accordance with the arrangements previously made by the Assembly, seats for corresponding members, delegates, and theological students were reserved in the first balcony. The general public were excluded.[346]

Press coverage in June 1927 also indicates that there was controversy over interruptions from the gallery. There is agreement in the various accounts that Assembly members occupied a very crowded ground floor, that delegates, licentiates and theological students had seats in the first balcony, and that a particular sequence of interruption did emanate from some part of the balcony. The point at issue is not the fact of the interruptions but the identity of those responsible. A letter to the editor of the *Northern Whig* from A M Purce, JP, appeared 10 June 1927, in answer to a letter to the paper from a 'Committee Man', alleging that the interruptions were caused by "ministers and students":

> I cannot allow this to pass without emphatically contradicting same. I sat in the middle of the gallery during the whole time the question was being discussed, and could easily see who the interrupters were. Although I noticed quite a number of clergymen in the gallery not in a single instance did I see any interruption from them; like myself they seemed to look on in "silent contempt."

So Purce is concerned to exonerate ministers but does not come to the defence of the students jointly accused in the letter that produced his response. However, with members of the public excluded, any reference to the presence of a "mob"[347] is regrettable. The identity of those responsible is not now known but unqualified disapproval of any such behaviour is appropriate. But the *Witness* makes it clear that the noise problem was not confined to the gallery, noting that at times the Assembly members were noisy and emotional too. Examples of participation from the floor are recorded as: "There were immediate cries from all over the house of "Withdraw" and 'Shame'", "Laughter", "Loud Laughter", "There were loud and insistent cries of "withdraw"" "When the uproar subsided", "Loud cheers".[348] "Before the vote was taken the Rev. Charles Hunter, the brother of James, endeavoured to make his voice heard, but in vain. He was howled down and could not even be heard at the press table beneath the platform where he stood."[349]

Transience
There is no doubt that the drama of the occasion had excited public interest. The prominent advertisement near the top of the title page of the Belfast Telegraph of Friday 10 June 1927 used it as an eye-catcher, but said much about how transient interest would prove to be, especially in the issues that lay at the heart of the whole affair!

The Heresy Trial

has aroused great interest, but MORRISON'S amazing Trunk, Bag and Suit Case Holiday Bargains merit the attention of all who desire to exercise economy.   Largest selection in Ulster.   Initials free.

Open all day Saturday 72/74 North St. only.

Branch—82 HIGH STREET.

Severance

Immediately after the adjournment that followed the voting on 10 June 1927, the Assembly turned to a reference from the Belfast Presbytery:

> On resuming the Assembly proceeded to consider a reference from the Presbytery of Belfast in relation to the cases of the Rev. James Hunter and the Rev. Samuel Hanna who failed to obey a direction of the Presbytery, and the case of Mr. William Dunn who, having been cited to attend as a witness, refused to give evidence in the trial of the Rev. Professor Davey. ... Moved by the Rev. A. F. Moody, seconded by Mr. John Williamson, J.P., and resolved— That the reference be received, and that the Assembly appoint a Commission of Assembly, with Assembly power, to deal with, and issue these cases and any similar cases that may arise.[350]

The "direction of the Presbytery" relating to Hunter and Hanna was their non-compliance with the injunction that the case should not be referred to in public until after the appeal. The *Belfast News-Letter*, Monday 13 June 1927, listed the names of the 31-man Commission: the Moderator, 15 ministers and 15 laymen. The ministers included 6 Rev. Doctors and the laymen, 2 Senators, 5 JPs and 2 MPs. To Rev. James Hunter it was the deciding act. He judged that the issue of his case would effectively inhibit any further action in the cause of Confessional orthodoxy. Consequently, he sent to the Belfast Presbytery his resignation of membership of the Presbyterian Church in Ireland and his position as one of its ministers in July 1927. Of this he said: "… I received from them no acknowledgement, good, bad, or indifferent."

He wrote to W J Grier on 27 July 1927:

> I do not see, however, what hope there is for the organised church if the preparation of its ministers is left in the hands of men who are half sceptical. Surely it is not the will of the Lord that people should remain banded together who have so little in common as the Modernists have with those of the old faith.

The Commission reported at the 1928 General Assembly:

> The Commission on Reference from the Belfast Presbytery (Minutes, 1927, pp. 45, 46) report that they held three meetings and arrived at the following decisions:
> 1. That as the Rev. James Hunter has by his resignation severed his connection with this Church, his name be now removed from every roll of the General Assembly; that the Belfast Presbytery be directed to remove his name from its roll, and that the Session of the congregation with which he was connected be directed to remove his name from its roll of membership.
> 2. That in view of the decisions arrived at by the General Assembly in the Appeals against the decisions of the Belfast Presbytery in the Heresy Trial against Rev. Professor Davey, no further action be taken in the case of Mr. Wm. Dunn.
> 3. The Rev. S. Hanna having admitted (1) that he disregarded the injunction of the Belfast Presbytery in relation to the Heresy case; (2) that he had made serious charges against Co-Presbyters at a meeting at Portadown, the Commission decides that the Rev. S. Hanna has in these matters acted in a way unbecoming to a Minister of Christ, and prejudicial to the work of the Church, and it rebukes him for these offences which he admitted and admonishes him to refrain altogether from such conduct in the future, and it decides that Rev. S. Hanna shall continue under the jurisdiction of the Commission in this matter.
>
> The Moderator conveyed to Rev. S. Hanna the decision of the Commission and addressed him thereon.[351]

James Hunter afterwards made this comment on Section 1 of the Report which appeared in the press: "My brother asked me what I thought was the meaning of this strangely worded resolution, and I said I believed they wished the public to think that I had been guilty of some grave immorality. He replied that that was his opinion also."[352] The statement was certainly not drafted to prevent any misconceptions! However, Machen kindly acknowledged, in his correspondence with Grier: " … I know the step was taken because of an unselfish and whole hearted devotion to Christ, which is a rebuke to many of us in these sad days."

Ivan T Jess in his *Centenary History of Ravenhill Presbyterian Church* reveals that Jim Grier was nominated for the eldership at Ravenhill when the Heresy Trial was in hearing:

> However, Ravenhill Kirk Session's sympathies continued to lie with the instigators of the trial for, on 21st March 1927, a week before the trial ended, Mr Ross proposed at a meeting of Session that *'two members of the congregation should be nominated for eldership namely J. A. Ross and W. J. Grier'* a proposal which was unanimously agreed. Three weeks later however, on the 10th April, at a meeting specially convened to reconsider this nomination, some members expressed the opinion that it was *'inadvisable to proceed with the election of Messrs. Ross and Grier'* and the matter was left *'in the meantime.'* On 8th May, at the next stated meeting, the elders demonstrated their opposition to modernism by agreeing *"to memorialise the General Assembly to have its office bearers, ministers and elders re-sign the subscription to its standards as contained in the Confession of Faith and Catechisms."*[353]

However, the Heresy Trial had brought Jim Grier to a decisive point in his life. He was now certain that he must separate from the Church that had so decisively upheld the teaching he had heard and sought to oppose. So he submitted his resignation soon after James Hunter, advising Machen on 11 August 1927 that he was at the point of doing it. It was a huge step for him and he never minimised the momentous effect it had on him. He often referred to Polycarp of Smyrna's story about the Apostle John arriving at the baths in Ephesus, and realising that Cerinthus the heretic was inside, he hastened out immediately, exclaiming: "Let us fly, lest even the bath-house fall down, because Cerinthus, the enemy of the truth, is within." To Jim Grier in 1927, the situation had a critical parallel with that.

17

Constituting the Trust (1927-1928)

Ours is a goodly heritage—the heritage of Reformers and Puritans, of Covenanters like Samuel Rutherford, of the founders of Irish Presbyterianism like Robert Blair and John Livingstone, and of the champions of orthodoxy like Henry Cooke, J. G. Machen, and James Hunter.

W J Grier, *The Origin and Witness of the Irish Evangelical Church*, p 57

The *Chat Noir* 'General Meetings'

James Hunter remained busy in the weeks following the Appeal. He concluded the series of *Ulster Pamphlets* with the issue of numbers 8 and 9 and took stock. Then he organised six 'General Meetings' between September 1927 and February 1928 at *Le Chat Noir*, a café in Fountain Street, Belfast.[354] Twenty men and women attended the first of these *Chat Noir* meetings on 17 September 1927, called to ascertain the mind of "those summoned" about future practical steps.

A Union Church?

The mind of the first 'General' meeting was firmly towards "a new church organisation" with the suggestion of launching it through the Irish Alliance of Christian Workers' Unions (IACWU), a cross-denominational federation of evangelicals.[355] The ministers among them would occasionally dispense the sacraments. The administration of the sacraments to such bodies was not exceptional—the Bible Standards League held a Communion service in the Ulster Hall about this time,[356] and it was also a practice at the Keswick Convention. So the meeting appointed a delegation of seven men and two women to attend the IACWU Council where Dr J R Gillespie presented the overture. The IACWU Council Minute, 28 September 1927, makes the *Chat Noir* strategy clear:

> At this stage in the meeting a deputation representing the new Evangelical Church appeared before the Council to enquire if it were possible for the CW Unions to become a nucleus for a Union Church.[357] ... Dr James [J R] Gillespie who headed the deputation urged the Council that liberty be given to members of the Unions who might join the new movement to still retain CWU membership and that the time of meetings in CWU halls, might be re-arranged, which previously have been held at other than church hours. ... After the deputation withdrew, a discussion ensued and the general opinion was that it would be disastrous to the work of the Unions as they at present stand in relation to the churches to change the hour of the meetings.

W J Grier, in his first letter to Machen from Belfast, 4 November 1925, had spoken of "leading laymen throwing themselves into the Christian Workers' Union disgusted with the Modernism of the pulpit". James Hunter was already active within the IACWU as a lecturer in its Bible School since August 1925, and at its AGM, 8 April 1926, he strengthened his involvement by becoming a member of Council – just at the time when he was setting up the Bible Standards League in the Presbyterian Church. Eight of his fellow accusers, including Rev. John Ross, were either Vice-Presidents or members of Council in April 1927. Rev. J A Ross was Editor of the IACWU Magazine, *The Alliance News*, that carried an article, "The Activities of the Bible Standards League" and a full-page advertisement for its Book Depot. James Hunter was also a contributor to *The Alliance News*. The minutes of the AGM, 21 April 1927, three weeks after the conclusion of the Heresy Trial, note: "In the closing address Rev. James Hunter mentioned the present day apostasy, and said he believed God had raised up the IACWU to meet the need."

So the initial desire at *Chat Noir* was to identify with an existing structure of like-minded believers, and the CWU-Church concept looked ideal. Its close connection with Nicholson and the continuing evangelical cause, its inter-denominational membership, and a functioning Bible School, probably looked to Hunter like the emergent Church structure which would exchange denominational affiliation for the greater biblical principle of evangelical unity on the fundamental doctrines of the faith. It was bold thinking for that day and in some key respects in line with the principles of Dr Lloyd-Jones' famous appeal for evangelical unity in 1966.[358] Lloyd-Jones did not advocate that evangelicals leave existing denominations and form a new one—he did not specify the machinery for his concept of evangelical unity. Nor did Hunter, but his 1927 concept was definitely for a new denomination that would develop its own constitution.

But it should not have been surprising that the IACWU would not change its structure from a union of Christian workers to a church, for there were strong denominational identities, including Presbyterian, within it. In April 1926 J Allen Ross, IACWU Organising Secretary and Editor of *Alliance News* explained the Alliance position:

> Many there are who assert that the Alliance is against the churches. I would show you that it is not essentially so. It would not interfere with your doing your duty to the church with which you are connected. It would rather seek to assist you to do so. This is evident when we remember that membership in some evangelical church is a condition of membership in the Alliance. The same spiritual weapons are used by it as the churches use, or at least ought to use, and great fundamental truths, common to all denominations, have been accepted as its basis. Consequently, where a church is true to itself, the Alliance is true to it: but on the other hand where a church is not true to itself, the Alliance is not true to it.[359]

He distanced the Alliance from those in the churches who employed worldly methods, were lazy, or taught the traditions of men. Separation was not on the agenda in 1926, but when the issue arose through the *Chat Noir* overture in September 1927 the Alliance identified with evangelicals working within or alongside existing denominations. The events of 1926-27 never featured explicitly in its minutes. There is no minute that the Alliance Council answered the Irish Evangelical Church's query about the eligibility of its people for IACWU membership. Since membership was open to those belonging to evangelical churches the request seems strange. Perhaps it was to clarify that resignation from the Presbyterian Church would not disqualify from the strongly Presbyterian CWU.[360]

At the Alliance AGM in May 1929 the meeting noted that the work had been "hampered and injured" during the year by changes of teachers. The services of Revs S Hanna, James Lyons, R Nevin Lyons, John Ross, and J Allen Ross were acknowledged. James Hunter was no longer involved. The minutes show that Hunter's Council participation lapsed about the time of the IEC overture in 1927, and the May 1929 AGM's note of staff changes at the Bible School referred to his withdrawal. There was no mention of the Bible School at the AGM in May 1930, but in March 1931 votes of thanks were passed to the honorary lecturers of the Alliance Hall Bible School "who in the past few years had given so much help." Thanks went to the five listed in 1929 with the addition of Rev. S Simms and Mr S G Montgomery. Other sources record the temporary services of W J Grier and of Mr James Scott of the Brethren Assemblies. It is not clear when the Bible School closed, but the Alliance received notice to quit the Alliance Hall from 31 July 1931, and it appears that the school did not survive this loss of premises.[361] So the difficulties inherent in a Church of evangelical unity asserted themselves, but it was instrumental in the adoption of a better course.

A New Denomination

On Saturday, 8 October 1927, James Hunter addressed a conference in Cregagh Mission Hall, reported in the *Belfast Telegraph* on 10 October: "The Might of Faith. Witness for Truth." In welcoming him the chairman said: "They wanted more men of his type in these days when nine-tenths of the people who should be preaching the Gospel did not know what it was. They attempted to teach the truth, but in the way a donkey ate thistles; they were very shy about it." Hunter spoke about the five instances of Christ's expression, "be of good cheer" or "be courageous". The last was to Paul: "Be of good cheer, Paul: for as thou hast testified of me in Jerusalem, so must thou bear witness also at Rome." Hunter referred to Luther's memorable declaration: "Here I stand, and I can not do otherwise, God helping me." He spoke about the courage to separate: "There were people who never saw any need for separation from those who cast discredit upon God and His word; but let them remember the necessity for separation from every kind of sin and particularly when dishonour was done to the great 'I'."[362]

This is what he and those of like mind did one week later, on 15 October 1927, at the next *Chat Noir* meeting. The proposed development of IACWU having come to nothing the meeting decided to proceed independently and to form "a new organisation". The following arrangements indicated something of the early strategy:

1. The new organisation was designated *The Evangelical Church*.
2. Each meeting place was left free regarding the use of this name for the present.
3. James Hunter was appointed to prepare documents setting out the basis, reason and purpose of existence of the new organisation for the next meeting.

4 On 29 October 1927, a committee of 7 was appointed to act as a central body to deal with immediate matters, and to consult with Mr Hunter on the 'basis and purpose'.
5 A committee member was delegated to find out if Botanic Avenue Reformed Presbyterian Church would be available for meetings.
6 All were asked to advise about Halls whose leaders might be willing to associate.
7 All were asked to provide names of any Christian workers so inclined.

Presbyterian histories tend to focus on 'heritage', emphasising inheritance and continuity with it. G N M Collins called his history of the Free Church of Scotland, *The Heritage of our Fathers*, Finlay Holmes, Presbyterian Church in Ireland, *Our Irish Presbyterian Heritage*, and Philip Kyle, Free Presbyterian Church of Ulster, *Our Own Heritage*. The quotation on the title page of this chapter records W J Grier's claim for his Church of a heritage with defenders of the faith. He entitled his leader of the January 1955 *Irish Evangelical* "Our Precious Reformed Heritage" and used the sub-headings "The High Doctrines of the High-Flyers" (the high doctrines of 18th century Calvinistic evangelicals), "The Peril of Losing our Heritage" and "The duty of Preserving this Heritage". But the founders of the Irish Evangelical Church in 1927 declared discontinuity with their immediate denominational past.

The Purpose and Basis of Existence
At the following Fountain Street meeting, 12 November 1927, the Committee presented the *raison d'être* and basis of the new "spiritual organisation" in the Preamble:

> On this twelfth (12th) day of November 1927 we the undersigned recognising that the highest court of the Irish Presbyterian Church has put its seal upon false teaching in a case where full and conclusive proof of such teaching was presented—and being convinced that however wise and useful it may be to remain in a church in the first stages of declension, after that a church has become corrupt there remains no other course in accord with the plain teaching of the Word of God than to 'come out of her'.
>
> In loyalty to the Head of the church and for the maintenance of a testimony to His truth (we) do hereby unite in the purpose of forming a new spiritual organisation—and we accept as articles of Faith of the Evangelical Church the following:

There followed eight *Articles of Faith*, and these appear in Appendix 2. They are a brief statement of each of the following doctrines:

1 Holy Scripture
2 The Trinity
3 The Lord Jesus Christ
4 The Holy Spirit
5 Imputation
6 Salvation from the Fall by free grace alone
7 The Sacraments
8 The Lord's Day

[Signatures: John R. Gillespie, [illegible], W. J. Millar, Mrs Wm. J. Millar, Helen Calhoun, Isabella Douglas, Ruby J. Tait, M. Rea, Wena Rea, Sara Crowe, Rachel Patterson, Mary J. Hooke, Kay Patterson, Catherine J. Gillespie, Anna M. Kell, Andrew Graham, Wm. J. Grier, I. M. Wilson, Dot. Wilson, Jean Fleming, James Hunter, James Dixon, John Britton, John King, Alexander McFadden, William O'Neill, David Kelly, Alfred Carson, Samuel G. Shanks, Harry Magill, James A. Kell]

The meeting accepted this 'basis' or Declaration of Faith. Of the 35 who attended on 12 November 1927, 27 signed the Articles, and a further 4 at the meeting of 10 December 1927.

The Eight Articles

The first six articles identified cardinal doctrines of the faith—Scripture, the Trinity, the Lord Jesus Christ, the Holy Spirit, Justification (Imputation), and Sin. They enshrined the issues thrown up by the Heresy Trial in a creed. Article 7 incorporated the Sacraments: it was paedobaptist which would have limited the new church's constituency; on the Lord's Supper, in another reference to the Heresy Trial, it noted the error of transubstantiation. Article 8 was a commitment to keep the Lord's Day holy as a perpetual command of God, to which attached special national blessings.

Articles 1-3 expressed Westminster theology and often reflected its language.[363] Article 4 used less of the Confession's wording but related clearly to six of its Chapters and to four answers of the Larger Catechism.[364] Article 5 leaned heavily on the Shorter Catechism - 33, *What is Justification?* Number 6 conveyed the teaching of Chapters 6-7 of the Confession on the Fall and the Covenant of Grace. Articles 7 and 8, on the Sacraments and the Lord's Day, incorporated areas to which the Westminster Catechisms give particular emphasis. The *Larger Catechism* is extensive in its treatment of the Confession on the Sacraments, especially the Lord's Supper. On the commandments, the *Shorter Catechism* deals most extensively with the fourth, and in the *Larger* only the fifth receives fuller treatment. So the Articles had a strong Westminster ethos.

The original subscribed Articles were handwritten, but were soon circulated as a single printed page. Subscription, often of just the first six, was a condition of membership. A typical formula read: "I believe in Jesus Christ as God the Son and my personal Saviour and accept the Articles on the opposite page." As a one-page statement of key doctrines, they were readily accessible to all. In its favour, the full title of Calvin's 1536 Geneva Confession was: *Confession of Faith which all the citizens and inhabitants of Geneva and the subjects of the country must promise to keep and hold*. J R Payton points out that the Scots were willing to sign the National Covenants, but that the increasing detail of the late-Reformation confessions produced a distinction between the subscription required from ministers and from members.[365]

The Articles constituted the Church's doctrinal standards until 1933 and remained a component of them until 1964, but for succeeding generations in the Church they have regrettably dropped from view. Whilst they have given way to the far superior Westminster Standards they deserve permanent recognition for their historical value.

The Council

The first signatories of the *Articles of Faith* appointed Dr J R Gillespie as Church Treasurer, an appointment he held until his death in 1960. They also asked the ordained office bearers among them to constitute themselves as a court to arrange the administration of the Sacraments and similar matters of central government. The 11 men who comprised the first meeting of this court on Saturday 26 November 1927 at 15 College Square East were:

John Britton	Rev James Hunter	Harry Magill
Alfred Carson	James A Kell	Alexander McFadden
Dr John R Gillespie	John King	William O'Neill
William J Grier	Samuel P Luke	

They took the following decisions:

1. They appointed W J Grier as Interim Clerk.
2. In addition to Rev. James Hunter, they appointed John Britton, Alexander McFadden and W J Grier to administer the Sacraments, with others authorised "as occasion offered".
3. The Court designated itself "The Council of the Irish Evangelical Church".

The court suggested two possible meeting places for a congregation, one of which was the Alliance Hall in Great Victoria Street, and, looking ahead, discussed application for marriage licences when buildings became available. From this meeting, almost unnoticed, dates the change of name to *Irish Evangelical Church*, replacing the short-lived *Evangelical Church*, the name agreed on 15 October

1927 and under which the *Articles of Faith* had been drawn up and adopted on 12 November 1927. The governing body designated itself "the Council", taking the title from the "Council of Jerusalem", the name commonly given to the meeting of Acts 15 between the apostles and elders of the Jerusalem church, and the Antioch representatives.

In January 1932 Council decided that all new members of Council should sign the *Articles of Faith*, and during 1932 and 1933, they placed their signatures after the original 31. Among them were the names of those who were to become well known in the work of the Church in future years: Joseph Craig, C H Garland, Thomas Swann, C E Hunter, Houston Todd, George Bellew, R Shannon, John Shanks and J H Gillespie.

Initial Strategy

In addition to establishing the basis of faith, setting up a central governing body and appointing a treasurer, the meeting of 12 November 1927 made two other strategy decisions:

1. People in the districts should meet in one of the homes of the district taking steps to secure halls where possible.
2. Conferences to be arranged to explain why the action taken was necessary.

The Latter Chat Noir Meetings

The General Meetings at *Chat Noir* had achieved their objectives in constituting a new church with a central governing body. But three of the six 'General Meetings' took place after the formation of Council. They were transitional as responsibilities transferred to Council and congregations. There was evident respect by Council for the Fountain Street forum. The General Meeting of 10 December 1927 appointed a committee to inspect the Alliance Hall following the suggestion of the first Council meeting on 26 November. Council appointed the General Meeting of 21 January 1928. The last General Meeting, 25 February 1928, approved the conferences that Council had recommended on 17 February 1928, and appointed a Conference Committee. The final *Chat Noir* function was to receive "a list of sound missions and organisations" from James Hunter, again in response to a Council discussion. There were regularly seasons of prayer at Fountain Street, but the penultimate meeting of 21 January 1928 stands out for its testimony to dependence on prayer: "a considerable portion of the time was spent in prayer" and the meeting was brought to a close with the singing of "ALL HAIL THE POWER OF JESUS' NAME" and prayer.

Apostasy?

The preamble to the *Articles of Faith* stated, as the grounds for their departure, that the Church they had left had moved beyond the early stages of declension and had become 'corrupt'. W J Grier described those who had left the Presbyterian Church in Ireland as "free from connection with a church that had become apostate".³⁶⁶ Finlay Holmes noted: "James Hunter and others of Davey's accusers felt bound in conscience to leave the Irish Presbyterian Church which they believed to be now apostate." Holmes goes on to defend his Church: "The Irish Presbyterian Church had not apostatised, there was no departure from essential orthodoxy on the part of theological professors, ministers or church members ..." He does however accept that a "liberalising spirit" was in the ascendant."³⁶⁷

In declaring a church apostate it is important to define how the term was used. 'Apostasy' may refer to the complete and wilful, fatal abandonment of the faith. But there is another sense that Grier's friend, E J Poole-Connor, so aptly expressed in his little book, *The Apostasy of English Non-Conformity*: "Apostasy is departure from a faith originally held. To speak of the apostasy of Nonconformity, therefore, is to allege a retreat from a position formerly occupied."³⁶⁸ In his conclusion Poole-Connor distinguished between two senses of apostasy: "SUFFICIENT has been adduced in the preceding pages, it is believed, to demonstrate the departure of organised Nonconformity from its original doctrinal position. The far more serious question as to whether it is also a departure from 'the faith once for all delivered to the saints', a surrender of the sacred deposit entrusted to their charge, each man must decide for himself."³⁶⁹ It is in the former sense that Grier used 'apostasy' in reference to the Church of 1927, but this is not to minimise its seriousness. Grier said in the concluding paragraph of his *Origin and Witness*: "The Irish Presbyterian Church has given herself over to Modernism."³⁷⁰ But he looked forward to the day when doctrinal reform would make separation no longer necessary.

Early Restraints

The young Church faced significant internal and external forces interacting against it, arising mostly from its pre-development state.

The Non-Secession Alternative

The great external factor was rejection of secession. Strangely, those members of the Bible Standards League who had left the Presbyterian Church or were contemplating it, wanted to extend the basis of League membership to include them. But at a meeting in the YMCA Minor Hall the League decided against it, effectively declaring that whilst an ongoing campaign was necessary, it was an internal matter for the Presbyterian Church. So, ironically, it was the Bible Standards League, that Hunter founded in 1926 and in which he had vested his campaign, that became the focus for pursuing the campaign within the Church. The December 1931 issue of the League's magazine, *The Standard-Bearer*, carried an account of the resignation of its secretary, William Snoddy, a prominent accuser, Trial witness and speaker at the Appeal. He had declared himself satisfied that with one exception the professors at Assembly's College were now teaching the doctrines of the Church as set forth in the Westminster Confession of Faith and Catechisms, and had urged the Council to abandon the campaign of intense propaganda that it had carried on during the preceding five years. The Council did not agree.[371]

The IACWU took the same non-secession line in September 1927 as did the three other minister-accusers who each remained in the Church. One of them, Rev. Dr Samuel Hanna of Berry Street, claimed that his congregation had become a rallying ground in the post-Trial period, and had received a new lease of life. On 2nd November 1927 it was reported to the Session that 45 new members had been added to the roll by certificate, and that some 53 others were to be received into membership on their making a public profession of their faith for the first time.[372] In his Annual Report for 1927, he looked back on "a remarkable year." Of the Heresy Trial and its outcome, he wrote:

> Berry Street has always stood for a pure gospel and a simple worship and we believe that recent events fully justify her position. She has now become the rallying ground for what is left of real religious life ... The Prayer Meeting has been largely attended throughout the year by an average attendance of close on 200 ... Berry Street has taken on a new lease of life ... our members are able to conduct the service in other congregations where the minister has been laid aside. I do not think there is another congregation in the Presbyterian Church where there is such a host of men able and willing to help in the service of the Sanctuary.

However Dr Hanna's tone changed. The March 1936 issue of *The Irish Evangelical* carried a terse article by the editor, *Of What does Rev. Samuel Hanna Approve?* It began:

> In the January issue of the *Standard-Bearer* (issued, we believe, in February), Rev. Samuel Hanna writes of a recent series of articles by Professor Davey in the *Missionary Herald* as follows:—"We gladly welcome these articles not only because they reveal afresh the profound simplicity and dignity and Divinity of our church's doctrine, but, etc." ... Dr. Hanna proceeds to give Professor Davey's statement on the atonement which makes him (Dr. Hanna) "unfeignedly glad." The statement is quite similar to one which filled Dr. Hanna with wrath in 1927.

Grier then quoted Davey's statement in full, adding seven more examples from Davey's *Missionary Herald* series on which to base his conclusion:

> We could give other quotations equally bad, but we have given sufficient to show the sort of thing which now gives satisfaction to Dr. Samuel Hanna. Here are Dr. Hanna's own words in the January Standard-Bearer: "We are now satisfied that views once held contrary to the teachings of our Church have been abandoned, and that the doctrinal position of our Church remains unaltered." Our readers can judge for themselves which of the two—Professor Davey or Rev. Samuel Hanna—has changed.

Credibility

The new Church's leaders emerged from the Heresy Trial with a heavy voting defeat and strong negative criticism from both church and local press. The Church began with the teaching ministry of one retired minister and one licentiate, with no buildings, no funds, no sister relations with other churches, and little by way of recognised denominational ethos. With such desperately inadequate resources it did not look like satisfying normal expectations of church life and many questioned its viability. This enhanced the non-secession alternative. The *Origin and Witness* captures the mood of the early years:

> They had now to put their hands to the task of rebuilding the walls which were broken down. They had their difficulties as Nehemiah's builders had long ago. They had to endure, as those builders, taunts and jeers. "They laughed us to scorn and despised us. ... Sanballat said, What do these feeble Jews? Even that which they build, if a fox go up, he shall even break down their stone wall" (Neh 2.19; 4. 2-3, KJV). There were those who said that the whole movement would come to nothing inside a very few years; some who were especially generous gave us a ten years' lease of life; many who even professed a certain amount of friendly interest were openly dubious as to our church surviving the death of our leader, Rev. James Hunter.[373]

Limitations of the Articles of Faith

The Articles were an internal factor. Excellent as they were, two critical defects must be acknowledged. The first was the condensed nature of their statements. This made them vulnerable, and so it proved in an attack from dispensationalists prepared to manipulate the stance of the articles on a single return of Christ. So it became necessary to buttress them with the Westminster Catechisms as soon as 1933. When writing to Machen on 31 May 1933 Grier revealed:

> You may remember speaking to me of the standards of the Irish Evangelical Church. In January last I gave motion to adopt the Westminster Confession. Mr Hunter at first held strongly that our 8 Articles were sufficient. Later he came to see the necessity of a Reformation Standard. ... Mr Hunter said in fact, after his mind had changed, he wouldn't continue in a Church which did not hold Reformation Standards. Still he thought the Westminster Confession difficult in parts for some ordinary people to understand. I did not agree with him in this altogether.

Then, Article 4 contained a drafting error which appears to be at the heart of a query raised in Council in 1954, probably about clause 2: "[The Holy Spirit] is He through whom the soul is born again which repents and believes savingly in the Lord Jesus Christ." Rev. Dr A A Woolsey points out in a note on the matter:

> Repentance and faith are the activity of conversion which is of course also the work of the Holy Spirit as the Confession says. But regeneration or new

birth precedes that. Conversion is the first fruit of new birth. Regeneration is not conditioned by repentance and faith. Regeneration is the gracious, sovereign, quickening work of God's Spirit in the soul without which we are dead in sins and incapable of repenting or believing. The clause in Article 4 as it stands gives the impression that new birth is conditioned by repenting and believing. If the word 'which' was replaced with the word 'and' it would read differently and indicate the continuity of the Holy Spirit's work in the soul, which undoubtedly was the intention of those who framed the Article.

The other defect was also related to the area of credibility. How could this new Church, born out of detailed confessional controversy, set aside all that the church had learned over two millenniums as to the absolute necessity of a comprehensive Confession of Faith? Dr Martyn Lloyd-Jones, in speaking to the Westminster Fellowship in July 1967 about the dangers of over-precision in trying to safeguard orthodoxy, said: "Even the detailed statements of the 16th and 17th centuries have not been able to safeguard the faith. You can never safeguard the truth by statements on paper or guarantee continuing orthodoxy by paper declarations."[374] This will certainly be true whenever the statements on paper are not constitutionally and personally binding, but it is the confessional standards which demonstrate the lapses.

Much can be said for a well-expressed, quick-reference, summary of doctrine, provided it is recognised as introductory. Machen said to Grier on 16 January 1926, in a point of criticism of James Denney's *Jesus and the Gospel*, "It is extremely faulty in some particulars, and I think that the proposal that it makes at the end for a brief creed is very bad." Grier asserted in 1955: "We are not of those who desire a reduced creed – a minimum creed. We want the finest and most full-orbed expression of Christianity. We feel that we have such an expression in the Subordinate Standards of the Church – the Westminster Confession of Faith and the Catechisms, Larger and Shorter."[375]

Non-Standard Government
Another questionable area was the early form of government. James Hunter had not found his experience with elders an entirely happy one. In addition, he had depended on their support at the General Assembly of 1927. He therefore appeared reluctant to set up the office in the new Church. So men who had already been ordained and installed to that office and who had been significant recruits to the new Church because of it, effectively relinquished this asset by joining it. To their great credit they were willing to do this and to use their gifts to the benefit of their new Church. Some of them later became deacons! With one exception, in 1932, the diaconate did not feature in the first five years either. Committees, usually consisting of men and women elected annually, ran the congregations in consultation with the Council to which the congregations sent male representatives. This was an unusual church government feature.

Lack of Inter-Church Relations

The new Church also lacked formal ecclesiastical ties. The absence of minutes on the subject would suggest that the founders did not give sufficient priority to this important aspect of their standing. Perhaps too, its irregular structure made potential church allies tentative at the beginning. In his correspondence with Machen during 1927-28, Grier spoke about organising small groups of people who had left the Presbyterian Church in Ireland, about the erection of modest buildings, and about the *Irish Evangelical*, but not about the constitution of the Church or its name. No doubt he was sensitive to what he knew would be Machen's view about its structure and doctrinal standards. It came up later.

At home, neither *The Covenanter* nor the *Reformed Presbyterian Witness* covered the events of 1927. One Free Church of Scotland minister identified with James Hunter's public campaign between Trial and Appeal, and another with the conferences to launch the new Church. But the first reference in the Free Church of Scotland *Monthly Record* to the June 1927 Appeal was not until April 1928 when Dr John Macleod, Free North Inverness and Principal of the Free Church College since 1927, wrote under the heading, *Dragging the Anchor in Ulster*:

> One of the most ominous things in this connection is the line taken by last Assembly in Belfast with regard to a serious doctrinal issue that was raised by the published teaching of one of the theological professors. In his work entitled, "The Changing Vesture of the Faith," Professor Davey challenged the old orthodoxy of Ulster; and if it still exists to any great extent among the ministry of his Church they must have been sunk in a deep sleep when they failed to see the meaning of the vote that acquitted the accused professor. The movement to change the subscription to the Confession is still at work; and if it should succeed it will do incalculable harm in the days to come. Indeed the work of the fathers and founders of the Irish Presbyterian Church will be overturned. As yet the Constitution of the Church defends its defenders. However much the personnel of the majority in the Church Courts may be disloyal, the upholders of orthodoxy have the shelter of their Church's Constitution. An unfaithful majority may go out of their way to introduce a tyrannous gag into the procedure of the Church. They may seek to throttle discussion and to stifle the voice of witness. But if they should dare to act on the bluff policy which they hang as a threatening sword over the head of faithful witness-bearing, they may find out that what is a perversion of Presbyterian Church power will land them in difficulties from which they will not soon work their way out. *Proximus ardet Ucalegon*.[376] (Pages 87-88)

This comment was essentially a warning to the Presbyterian Church in Ireland regarding the doctrinal significance of the 1927 Assembly vote, the current campaign to change the Formula of Subscription and the stifling of faithful witness. It supports the position of the defenders of orthodoxy who had remained within the Church on the grounds that the Church's constitution was sound and still intact. This may all seem very strange in the light of John MacLeod's identity with James Hunter's campaign, and with the Irish Evangelical Church now six months old and five congregations strong. But the objective at the time of MacLeod's involvement was the ongoing reform of the Church, which was very much in line with the Free Church's own history and ecclesiology. It came into being at the Disruption of 1843 when the Evangelical Party in the Church of Scotland severed the links that bound the Church to the State over the issue of State interference in the Church's realm. However, although the Church of Scotland did split over the issue along the evangelical divide, the evangelical party never intended this to happen.

Whereas personal links had been established, the relationship between the Irish Evangelical Church and the Free Church of Scotland had not developed in 1928. With the training of Irish Evangelical ministers about to begin, it very soon would.

"Let Israel now say"

So there is the picture of a new denomination, at one level small, isolated, critically short of resources, something of an ecclesiastical mismatch, and with low credibility. But at another level it was a church with the consciousness of right on its side and of acting in obedience to the Word of God. James Hunter later said, "The Irish Evangelical Church has abundant reason for its existence and for its testimony, if any denomination ever had." The tenacity, sacrifice, enthusiasm, prayer, faith and vision of the men and women who were its first members bore witness to this assertion. Steve Bruce's comment in *Paisley*, 2007, is so wide of the mark: "…the dissidents did not work hard to recruit a following. They set out their stall and waited for customers to turn up. Having been members of a large organization of congregations, they were not prepared for the arduous task of selling their product."[377] The testimony of history is quite otherwise.

The Church would readily acknowledge that in the face of so many weaknesses and difficulties it could never have come into existence without the particular favour and blessing of God. Psalm 124.1 aptly expresses this lasting recognition: "If it had not been the LORD who was on our side, Let Israel now say …" But many difficulties and trials lay ahead.

18

Gaining a Foothold ... (1928-1939)

The Lord is indeed blessing our work here. New buildings are being erected and though the outward glory is not as great as in the former houses—there is the undoubted presence of the Lord of Hosts. Souls are being added to the church. We have much more contentment – feeling that we are doing a positive work – than in our previous situation where we were fighting a hopeless battle as far as numerical strength was concerned.

W J Grier to J G Machen, 16 October 1928

Industrialisation and Depression

These were generally hard times for the people of Britain and Ireland. Belfast had enjoyed some 80 years of prosperity, but this was drawing to a close at the end of the 1920s. It was the only city in Ireland to experience the mid-19th century Industrial Revolution which applied powered machinery to manufacturing, and it was a factor in drawing "the north" towards the mainland with its similar economic developments. The revolution locally focused on the dominant linen business that had developed as a cottage industry during the 17th century between the rivers Bann and Lagan – the Linen Homelands. Industrialisation transferred it to factories concentrated in Belfast. An immediate effect was urbanisation as people flocked from the countryside to work in the Belfast linen mills, and the human tragedy of the Irish Famine, 1845-1848, added to the migration. It was largely instrumental in the rapid growth of the population from 20,000 in 1800 to 350,000 in 1900, and 438,000 in 1939. There were over 70,000 Belfast linen employees at the end of the 19th century, many of them the women and girls among whom Amy Carmichael[378] worked in the 1880s. These were the 'shawlies', mill girls who wore shawls rather than hats.

Shipbuilding began in 1853 and developed quickly into a golden era, with Harland and Wolff boasting the largest shipyard in the world by the early 20th century. The launch of the luxurious, technically advanced Titanic in 1912 symbolised its prestige. Rope making also flourished during the 19th century and the Belfast Ropeworks became the biggest in the world, at one point employing 4,500 people. However, Belfast did not escape the post-World War I industrial decline nor the impact of the global *Great Depression* (1929-1941) following the Wall Street crash of 1929. High unemployment marked the period in many parts of the world, earning it the epithet, the *Hungry Thirties*. Belfast was one of the places badly affected. Harland and Wolff's workforce, for example, fell from 20,000 in 1924 to 2,000 in 1933. Added to this was a resurgence of political tension, with weeks of serious violence in Belfast in 1935.

This was the period in which the Irish Evangelical Church began and made its early progress.

Announcing IEC

The Conferences
The *Chat Noir* decision of 12 November 1927 to use conferences to spread awareness of the new Church was implemented by Council with a series beginning on 31 March 1928 in the YMCA Minor Hall. "The Hall was filled, some being present from the counties of Down, Antrim, Tyrone and Derry."[379] The handwritten programme showed a busy two hours, 3.30 pm – 5.30 pm. Andrew Graham, Lisburn Road, presided and some will still remember the others who took part. The programme shows that five congregations or groups were already in existence:

Hymn 355: Alexander's Hymns No 3 - Psalm 121
Prayer: Mr C E Hunter, Ballyclare
Scripture Reading: Galatians 1 and Chairman's Remarks

1   Dr Gillespie, Knock
    Chorus: *God of Elijah, send the fire*
2   Mr Samuel Shanks, Lisburn Road
    Announcements: W J Grier
    Address: W J Grier
    Prayer: Mr J A Kell, Knock
    Hymn 367 with Chorus: Alexander's Hymns No 3 – At the Cross
3   Mr Willie Kinghan, Crosscollyer Street
    Chorus: *He did not come to judge the world*
4   Mr Reynolds, Dundonald
    Prayer: Mr Magill
5   Mr Houston Todd, Ballyclare
    Chorus: *I know HE is wonderful*
    Rev. James Hunter MA
    Hymn 241: The Church's One Foundation
    Benediction

At that time Lisburn Road was part of the South Belfast congregation and 'Dundonald' referred to an emerging group that became Jocelyn Avenue in 1930.

In April 1928 Council decided to alternate Council meetings and conferences month about, but the pressures of Council business allowed only partial adherence to this pattern during the conference phase. The conferences continued in the following sequence, some of the earlier ones incorporating progress reports from the churches.

31 May 1928	Thursday	7.45 pm	YMCA Minor Hall
1 September 1928	Saturday	3.30 pm	Ballyclare, CWU Hall
29 December 1928	Saturday	3.30 pm	Knock Evangelical Church
27 April 1929	Saturday	3.30 pm	Lisburn Road Evangelical Church
20 July 1929	Saturday	3.30 pm	Lisburn Road Evangelical Church
26 October 1929	Saturday	3.30 pm	YMCA Minor Hall
25 January 1930	Saturday	3.30 pm	YMCA Minor Hall
22 February 1930	Saturday	3.30 pm	Crumlin, Memorial Hall
12 April 1930	Saturday	3.30 pm	Knock Evangelical Church
28 June 1930	Saturday	3.30 pm	YMCA Large Hall
27 September 1930	Saturday	3.30 pm	Botanic Avenue R P Church
3 January 1931	Saturday	3.30 pm	YMCA Minor Hall
21 March 1931	Saturday	3.30 pm	Lisburn Road Evangelical Church

The YMCA Minor Hall, and on one occasion the Large Hall, still featured as conference venues, but more often district locations were chosen. The first was

Ballyclare on 1 September 1928. The chairman was Mr Robert Shannon and the speakers James Hunter and Mr Jack Currie, Portadown. The conference moved on to an open-air meeting which formed 'a large ring in Market Square'. A 'Special Bus' took the Belfast contingent.[380]

At the May 1928 conference, Charles E Hunter of Ballyclare gave his testimony and his reasons for separation from the Presbyterian Church in Ireland. W J McDowell, who became the Church's colporteur in February 1929, addressed the April 1929 conference. There were some notable speakers at these conferences too: Dr E J Pace,[381] director of the Field Extension Department of the Moody Bible Institute in Florida, spoke in October 1929, and Rev. R Wright Hay, secretary of the Bible League, in January 1930. Rev. Angus Mackay, Free Church of Scotland, Kingussie, was the speaker in April 1930, and Dr Basil C Atkinson, Under-Librarian of Cambridge University, in January 1931. Missionaries addressed two of the conferences. Of special significance was the ordination of Rev. W J Grier at the Lisburn Road conference, 20 July 1929.

A highlight was the visit of Dr Lewis Sperry Chafer, President of Evangelical College, Dallas, Texas, on 28 June 1930. Chafer was a Presbyterian and a strong defender of fundamental Christian doctrine. S G Montgomery, who spoke in James Hunter's support at the appeal, quoted from Chafer's *Major Bible Themes*: "Imputation is one of the most profound doctrines in the Scriptures." However, Chafer was the foremost dispensationalist[382] theologian of his day, and one of his Dallas graduates who came to IEC in 1930 plunged the young Church into crisis in 1933 through his introduction of dispensational teaching. And the Church's first two students for the ministry were initially accepted for training at Dallas!

Dr Machen had visited Belfast in 1927 as Assistant Professor of New Testament at Princeton. Since then he had become President and Professor of New Testament, Westminster Theological Seminary (formed in 1929), and in that capacity he visited Belfast in June 1932. He addressed a conference in the Botanic Avenue Church, acquired in 1930, on Saturday afternoon, 25 June 1932, and another in the Wellington Hall of Belfast YMCA on the following afternoon. On the Sunday morning he preached at Knock IEC and in the evening at Crosscollyer Street. There is no report of the June 1932 visit to Belfast in either minutes or magazine. In the Banner of Truth series in 1983, *J Gresham Machen in the United Kingdom*, Geoffrey Thomas records a similar scarcity of information: "Dr Machen's return visit to Britain in 1932 has no vivid documentation like the 1927 visit … For the 1932 visit we only have a few business-like letters, arranging the meetings, and some memories from a few people of this, his last visit to the U.K."[383]

One interesting feature of the visit appeared in a Western Union cablegram from Machen to Grier in June. It revealed that Machen would be addressing the Presbyterian Bible Standards League and he felt it necessary to put Grier in the picture: "Will my speaking before Belfast Bible League hinder your movement? I shall of course speak strongly against any peace based on compromise with forces now generally dominant in Protestant churches of world. Has Irish Evangelical church maintained distinctively Presbyterian doctrine? ... Cable just received from Mr McConnell [Secretary of PBSL] says League has not compromised with position of Professor Davey. I desire to serve League just in order to combat whatever compromise movement there may be in Belfast." There is no copy of the cable that Machen asked Grier to send him in reply but in a related note to Robert Wright-Hay, Secretary of the Bible League, on 16 June 1932, Grier indicated that the PBSL had invited Machen.

Dr Cornelius Van Til, Westminster Theological Seminary, addressed a Botanic Avenue conference on 10 September 1938. He spoke on 1 Corinthians 1.20-21: "Where is the wise? where is the scribe? where is the disputer of this world? Hath not God made foolish the wisdom of this world? For after that in the wisdom of God the world by wisdom knew not God, it pleased God by the foolishness of preaching to save them that believe." (KJV) He said that it was plain that the schools of Philosophy of Paul's day had no answer to Paul's challenge, and that likewise the modern thinkers had no answer to the Christian challenge, no solution to offer for the real problems of life, its origin and destiny. He appealed to his audience to hold fast manfully and consistently to that which was "the wisdom of God".

The first decade saw the conferences become a regular feature of denominational life with most congregations hosting, and some establishing it as an annual event. During the period its purpose evolved from external advertising to internal bonding.

The Irish Evangelical

In 1987, Rev. Joseph McCracken, then a retired missionary in South Africa, wrote a 60th anniversary article on the Evangelical Book Shop. In it he looked back on his own early days as an employee in the shop: "I can recall the day when I said to Mr Grier, 'We need a magazine', and he heartily agreed, and so was born *The Irish Evangelical*". Whilst Council appointed Dr J R Gillespie and W J Grier as joint editors it was Grier who undertook the work, although his name did not appear as editor until April 1936. Dr Gillespie provided the initial support. Council also agreed that Thomas Johnstone of Great Victoria Street, Belfast, would be the printer, a role the firm retained until 1981, with a break from 1931-42.

The Logo

The *Irish Evangelical* title at the top of the cover page was plain until February 1933 when it became more ornate and superimposed on a sketch of the seven-branch golden lampstand of the Tabernacle – the *Menorah*. The lampstand symbolised the church's calling to be the light of the world, fuelled by the oil of the Holy Spirit and energised by the power of Christ (Ex 25.31-40; Zech 4; Rev 1.12, 20). To the left was the *Chi Rho* monogram of the first two letters of the Greek word for Christ, and on the right, the Alpha and Omega, signifying that the Lord Jesus Christ is the beginning and the end of all things. (Rev 1.8) The

text in the lower left box changed with each issue. A plain white title on a black background took over in August 1956 and in June 1963 it was superseded by a larger font *Irish Evangelical* on white background – some had considered the former white on black to be 'too sombre'! The 1963 title font continued until the end of Rev. W J Grier's editorship in 1981.

The Gillespie Children's Page
Dr James Gillespie began his November 1932 Children's Page: "How do you like our new heading? The little verse explains what it stands for. The picture on the right stands for the fighting against sin which we all must do if Jesus has saved us from its punishment. The girl on the left stands for the peaceable part of the Christian's life – praying and reading the Bible, and enjoying having God with us."

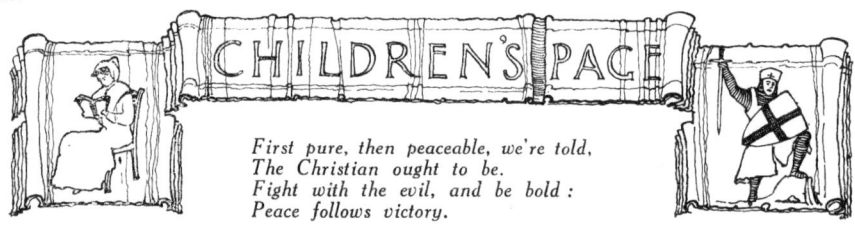

The Ethos
The first issue, June 1928, set a lasting pattern. It was a 16-page publication measuring 9½" x 7" (24x18 cm), with about 12,500 words. It carried substantive articles—exegetical, devotional, evangelistic and missionary, W J Grier writing two of the articles himself. It included reprints from magazines in UK, USA and Canada. It had an evangelistic address from Mr Houston Todd, a founder member of Ballyclare congregation, and an IEC news section emphasising the need for prayer. There were 'Gleanings'—brief quotations from well-known Christian writers. And its strong polemical note was a feature of Grier's 50-year editorship, presenting a global picture of Higher Criticism, evolution, modernism, ecumenism, heresy in theological colleges, opposition of the professing church and the suffering of the church in parts of the world. The back page began its

lasting Evangelical Book Shop advertisement, with offers of devotional, doctrinal and teachers' books by Machen, Andrew Murray, Andrew Bonar and others, as "Companions for a Summer Holiday". There were also Bibles, Revised Psalters, the Pilgrim's Progress, Nicholson's Sermons, Hymn Books, and Children's Books.

James Hunter started his long series of leading articles with *The Surety*. It was almost 3,000 words in length, but had just four paragraphs and no sub-headings! Its topics were: Surety of the Covenant of Grace, Surety of the Covenant of Works, Surety of a Third Covenant (Scripture), and the Surety of a Fourth Covenant (Creation). His concluding comment focused on the Lord Jesus Christ as Mediator and Surety of all the heavenly covenants – "To Him be glory for ever and ever. Amen." (Gal 1.5, KJV)

The First Congregations

The IEC did not affiliate any existing congregations, but the strategy of meeting in homes, with supporting conferences, produced 10 congregations in the first five years, 1927-1932. Grier described it to Machen in February 1928 as "the re-organisation of those who for the sake of the truth have been driven to separate themselves from the Irish Presbyterian Church". This was to be the most concerted of the Church's three phases of congregational growth.

1927
Knock
Crosscollyer Street
Shaftesbury Square*
(South Belfast)

1928
Lisburn Road*
Ballyclare, Co Antrim

1929
Crumlin, Co Antrim
Somerton Road

1930
Jocelyn Avenue
Botanic Avenue*

1931
Clintyfallow, Co Tyrone

1932
Slatehill, Co Antrim

*Shaftesbury Square became *South Belfast* when its Lisburn Road group opened their own church in 1928. *South Belfast* then became *Botanic Avenue* in 1930.

Knock and Crosscollyer Street opened in October 1927, meeting at first as house churches. Shaftesbury Square began in November 1927 with evening services in a Lisburn Road home, before starting morning worship on 11 December 1927 in the Alliance Hall, Shaftesbury Square, where Rev. James Hunter had conducted Bible Classes in 1925-26. Ballyclare, Jocelyn Avenue and Clintyfallow also began in members' houses. Somerton Road started in the local Unionist Hall, and Slatehill[384] was a Mission Hall.

The September 1929 story of the beginning of the Church in Crumlin, a small town 18 miles west of Belfast, is an interesting example. A group of people from the Presbyterian Church there, concerned by events within the denomination as a whole and also by some local issues, had invited Jim Grier to discuss their situation. After his round of duties in Belfast he set off by bicycle. He thought that Crumlin was at the terminus of Belfast's Crumlin Road, not far from the city boundary, but it was three times that distance. The journey was also more difficult for a cyclist than he realised: for the first seven miles the road climbs to about 300 metres through the locally well known 'horseshoe bend', and then falls through a dozen miles to Crumlin. He became aware of his miscalculation when he got to the top of the hill and, to make matters worse, a headwind from the west made his progress downhill little better than it had been on the way up. He had planned to be in Crumlin in time to spend an hour with the leaders before the public meeting, but when he arrived the people had already gathered. However, one of the men who met him, seeing him drenched in perspiration from his journey, postponed the meeting for 20 minutes and in the interval took him to his house for refreshment. The Crumlin Church began the following Sunday.

There was tremendous fervour in those early days. There were nights of prayer in the Alliance Hall until the man in the house next door started hammering the wall when the prayer and praise continued into the middle of the night. After that it was 'half nights' that stopped at midnight. They preached in the open air. They used every means that they could. This was a time of encouraging progress but it outstripped the limited manpower resources and produced its own difficulties, as will later become apparent.

Early Congregational Life

One of the characteristics of those early days was strict observance of the Lord's Day. A 'Gleaning' in the *Irish Evangelical*, April 1934, "20 Miles Through Fourth Commandment", captured the spirit of many:

> When Moody held his first great campaign in Edinburgh, the committee responsible for arrangements, said to him: "We have hired a carriage to take you to the various meetings on Sunday." Moody replied: "I will not drive on Sunday. I will walk." They ejaculated: "Impossible! The distance to cover during the day will be at least twenty miles." The great evangelist answered: "And so you ask me to drive through twenty miles of the fourth commandment? No, I shall walk." At the end of the day he was very tired, but gloriously happy, because he had not caused others to work on the day of rest.

There was caution over engagement with culture, required by their view of being "strangers and pilgrims on the earth" (Heb 11.13 KJV). There was great awareness of Bunyan's Pilgrim who walked through "the wilderness of this world". The picture of the godly Pastor in the House of the Interpreter portrayed him with "the best of Books in his hand" and "the World was behind his back".[385] People came to church dressed in their 'Sunday best', regarding the worship of God as a special occasion. Singing, accompanied by a pedal organ, was from the Psalter and *Golden Bells* or, in some cases, from *Redemption Songs*. Two Psalms and two hymns was the regular pattern. The call to prayer at the weekly or pre-service prayer meetings produced general movement as those who were able, men and women too, turned round and knelt at their chairs. Prolonged silences between prayers sometimes prompted someone to start singing a verse of a hymn, the most frequent being "Spirit of the living God fall afresh on me." There was a great deal of door-to-door visiting and 'open-airs' with tract distribution around the local streets in the summer. Many people would open doors and windows or gather in front of their houses to watch and listen.

Annual meetings were big occasions, with people from the different congregations visiting one another's annual meetings. There was 'tea' either before or after the meeting, often supported by a 'workers' tea' first. The Annual Reports were formally adopted by proposal and seconding from the floor. Annual conferences were an additional means of bonding. At Ballyclare they continued into the 1990s and at Clintyfallow they ran from 1932-1968. 'Watchnight' services, beginning at 11.00 pm on the last night of the old year and ending shortly after midnight, were common practices. The Sunday School Social was another annual event. Individual children, or groups, practised 'party pieces' for weeks in advance and turned out in their finest on the night. Sunday School excursions, in days when trips to the seaside were quite rare, produced big turnouts. The whole congregation was involved. Transport was by double-decker bus and the catering might arrive in the form of white paper bags of sandwiches and cakes – one bag each.

The First Ministers

Ordination of Rev. W J Grier

Jim Grier was ordained to the work of the IEC ministry at the Conference held in Lisburn Road Irish Evangelical Church on Saturday 20 July 1929. The Minute read:

> A Conference was held in Lisburn Road Evangelical Church on July 20th at 3.30 pm.
>
> Mr Hunter presided. Rev. W A Nisbet BA of St John's Evangelical Church, Toronto, gave the opening address. Mr Jack Currie gave a message in song. After Mr Hunter's address, the ordination of Mr Grier took place. The Council and Mr Nisbet took part—Mr Hunter offering the ordination prayer.[386]
>
> There was a large attendance, many coming from a distance. There was a fine spirit in the meeting and much blessing.
>
> Council minutes, 13 August 1929, noted those taking part in the laying on of hands:

Rev James Hunter, MA	W Beggs	J A Kell
H Reynolds	Rev W A Nisbet, BA	E Chism
W J Millar	W Shaw	J A Harvey
J J Patterson	R Shannon	

Rev. Joseph McCracken recorded his assessment of Mr Grier's preaching during the time that he was assistant minister at Richview, April-September 1926:

> One night at the Bible School it was announced that an all-night prayer meeting was to be held in Richview Presbyterian Church. I sent word to my folks at home that I was going to that meeting. It was here that I first personally met Jim Grier. He was in charge of Richview Presbyterian Church while the minister was on prolonged leave. I was so impressed by the earnestness and sincerity of this young minister that the next day I walked the four or five miles through the City to hear him preach. I found the Church packed, with seats in the aisles. Mr Grier preached with great power and I was not surprised to hear of conversions taking place.

This agrees with Grier's own comments to Machen on 9 August 1926 that he was "continuing to work in a congregation where the senior minister is opposed to the Bible League, but where, praise God, He is blessing and using me in the conversion of souls."

For some years after the Heresy Trial Jim Grier suffered from a facial twitch, and Helen McCracken, South Africa, recalled that it could become quite pronounced. It seems to have affected his preaching too for she considered his delivery to be indifferent and a poor indicator of the pulpit gifts he would afterwards display. But she viewed the content of his messages as always excellent—"his heart was so in his message, his anxiety for sinners so great." She reflected also on the part he played in her own conversion and her coming to assurance of faith.

The First Admissions

With the ordination of W J Grier in July 1929 the Irish Evangelical Church had two ministers, but the rate of growth made further ministerial resource an urgent need and one that could be met only through recruitment from outside. In response to that pressing need Council appointed Rev. H Andrew Morrison, a graduate of Dallas Evangelical Seminary, in March 1930. The wording of the Council minute does not suggest a long-term appointment, but when the Crosscollyer Street Committee requested, in August, that Mr Morrison be associated with Crosscollyer Street as its minister Council agreed – on the understanding that he might also be associated with other congregations, particularly with nearby Somerton Road, and that he "continue to preach and visit in other branches as before." In October 1930 Somerton Road congregation did ask that Mr Morrison be with associated them on the same basis as with Crosscollyer Street and this appears to have been granted. In January 1931, Crosscollyer Street requested permission to install Mr Morrison but Council deferred the matter for another six months, probably in view of the Somerton Road dimension.

Herbert H Murphy applied to Council in October 1930. He grew up in Newtownards and had done missionary work in Queensland, Australia for several years before coming to Westbourne Presbyterian Church, Belfast, as assistant minister. Council prescribed a two-year course in theology, church history, english, and Greek New Testament, but agreed to use Mr Murphy's services during his training. In January 1931 Council approved requests from the Crumlin and Jocelyn Avenue congregations that Mr Murphy be associated with them.

First Students and the Free Church College

Member-students have come in distinct phases. The first was 1932-1940 when Council sent for training to the Free Church of Scotland, C E Hunter, Ballyclare (1932), J McCracken, Crosscollyer Street (1932), W J McDowell, Crosscollyer Street (1935), and C H Garland, Botanic Avenue (1936). Such was the shortage of preaching and pastoral resource that Council placed these men in congregational charges from the beginning of their training! The Council minute of 20 May 1932 read: "Rev. W J Grier asked for the direction of Council in the matter of students preparing for the ministry, and suggested that their studies be with a view to entrance to the Free Church College, Edinburgh. Rev. Mr Hunter spoke commending this course and the Council adopted the recommendation." C E Hunter, who had announced his acceptance for training in Dallas at the same meeting, switched to the Free Church. Joseph McCracken spoke of his own decision in his *Reminiscences of a Veteran Missionary*, 1985:

> Then came one of those crises in my life. I had been accepted as a student for the Evangelical Theological College, Dallas. At the same time Mr Grier obtained permission for students of the IEC to study at the Free Church College. For two weeks I wrestled in prayer, going through a very anxious time. Finally I decided that the Free Church College was the place for my studies.

In his *Student Days* article, April 1935, Joseph McCracken reflected on his three years at the Free Church College: "If I went to Edinburgh a professed Calvinist, I have returned a convinced Calvinist ... The College staff are uncompromising in their opposition to modernism ... I am sure that not only the Council of our Church, but also the members feel grateful to God that such a door has been opened at such a time." The arrangement bonded the developing inter-church relationship with the Free Church.

Charles E Hunter and Joseph McCracken were ordained to the ministry in the Botanic Avenue Church on 30 June 1935. Rev. G N M Collins, Free Church of Scotland, preached on Jude 20-21, KJV: "But ye, beloved, building up yourselves on your most holy faith, praying in the Holy Ghost, keep yourselves in the love of God, looking for the mercy of our Lord Jesus Christ unto eternal life." Writing in 1977, after more than 40 years in the ministry and more than 30 as a missionary in South Africa, Joseph McCracken recalled this ordination sermon, saying, "I felt at the time the sermon was very appropriate and suited to my needs." Council appointed McCracken to the work in Crosscollyer Street and Hunter to Ballyclare, Slatehill, and Somerton Road. W J McDowell was ordained on 8 June 1939 in Ballyclare and appointed to the work at Ballyclare and Slatehill. Rev. W

J Grier preached his ordination sermon. C H Garland's ordination followed on 28 September 1940 when Rev. W J McDowell preached from Genesis 5.24, KJV – "And Enoch walked with God …". Garland began his ministry in Crosscollyer Street. These four men were the first students for the ministry in the Irish Evangelical Church to be ordained. They spent the whole of their ministries in the Church, one becoming an overseas missionary.

Steve Bruce, concluding his review of the beginnings of the Irish Evangelical Church, had this to say about training students in the Free Church:

Finally, there is a small point with profound implications. Hunter and Grier decided to have their students for the ministry trained by the Free Church of Scotland in Edinburgh. In many ways this was sensible as the two churches were extremely close in doctrine and practice and the Free Church College was well staffed with extremely able teachers. But this decision made it very difficult for a clear 'Irish Evangelical Church' identity to develop among the ministers, who instead saw themselves as being simply 'evangelical' Presbyterians. A dynamic movement needs a strong sense of identity and purpose and while the decision to work with the Free Church of Scotland was superficially rational it was sociologically unsound.[387]

The implications of training in Edinburgh were not at all detrimental. A Church may be unable to resource its own training establishment, but this need not dilute the denominational identity of its students. Presumably it did not in the case of the Presbyterian Church in Ireland which trained students in Scotland for over two centuries.[388] And it did not in the case of the IEC ministers who trained in Edinburgh. Developing connections with the Free Church of Scotland had made it the obvious choice and it gave these students a Confessional Presbyterian training that played such a vital part in the Presbyterian journey that the IEC would make. Dallas influence at this stage would have made this history altogether different.

Rev. W A Nisbet

Rev. W A Nisbet,[389] who took part, as a visiting conference speaker, in the ordination of Rev. W J Grier in July 1929, served in the ministry of the IEC for a short time from December 1932. Council received his application in September 1932 through a letter to Rev. James Hunter suggesting "that a building capable of seating about 600 people be erected in a populous district of Belfast to serve as a centre of work." Council decided that Nisbet should initially conduct one Lord's Day service in Botanic Avenue and the other in Crosscollyer Street until his settlement was decided, and in January 1933 agreed to Nisbet's desire to concentrate on Somerton Road. But Nisbet's stay was to be short-lived. In February 1933 James Hunter advised Council of Nisbet's resignation on the grounds that he was unable to agree with IEC's system of Church government, and that he was not content with being located in any of the existing congregations. He returned to St John's Toronto in 1934 and retired in 1941.

Temporary Help

J Campbell Andrews, a student of the Free Presbyterian Church of Australia studying at the Free Church College in Edinburgh, who became an ordained missionary doctor in South Africa in 1948, visited IEC during the summers of 1934 and 1937. In January 1935 he offered this kind appraisal of his 1934 visit:

> Two things about the Irish Evangelical Church must impress a stranger. One is the spiritual fervour of the members with whom one comes in contact. They are zealous for the glory of God in the salvation of souls. The other is the great volume of earnest and definite prayer rising from the church to the throne above. It must be prevailing prayer because it is offered in faith, in Christ's name, to the end His glory and the good of men's souls. Such zeal and prayer must have results, and for this reason one feels that, under God, the Irish Evangelical Church is to be a means of great blessing to many.

The editor commented: "May we be more worthy of the word of praise!"

Speakers List

The shortage of ministers made pulpit supply an ongoing responsibility for Council. There was the need to approve speakers and to book them for the vacant pulpits. Dr J R Gillespie produced a "schedule of speakers" in November 1932 which became Council's 'pool' of preachers and S G Shanks administered it from the Book Shop. Names were added to the list over the next 15 years and the system continued until 1960 when each minister took over the responsibility for the supply of his own pulpit(s).

Home Missions – Mainly Colportage

Pre-1937, when the Church had no overseas missionaries, it applied its efforts to outreach at home. In January 1929 Council advised the congregations of the financial needs of two potential projects, one being: "the desirability of sending a colporteur into those districts of Ireland where the word of God is not being proclaimed." In February, *The Irish Evangelical* took it up:

> The proposal took the substantial form of the offer of the sum of £100 for the purchase of a suitable motor. The Council, after consulting the members of the Church, was led to undertake this work in the name of the Lord, and hopes in a brief time to appoint a colporteur. Prayer is requested for guidance in the whole matter, and in particular that the Lord may prepare the person to be sent forth and that a wise decision may be arrived at in respect to the sphere of his work.

William J McDowell

Council appointed Mr William J McDowell to this work on 14 February 1929 as a probationer for the first year, and ordained him as a missionary of the Church at a meeting in Crosscollyer Street on Thursday 6 June 1929 when the convener of the Colportage Committee, W J Grier, gave the address. A colporteur is a travelling seller of Bibles and devotional literature, but this title did not do Mr McDowell or his work justice for he was in every sense a missionary, fulfilling that office to the full. From July 1929 Mr R J Hanna of Shaftesbury Square was appointed to work with him in a tent campaign for one month. Council, keen on sending forth "two-by-two", maintained his employment as Mr McDowell's assistant until March 1930, but owing to a lack of funds the arrangement regrettably came to an end.

Colportage, Year 1 – 1929-30: Ulster Counties
During the first year McDowell and Hanna worked in the province of Ulster in the counties furthest from Belfast: Tyrone, Fermanagh, Londonderry, Donegal, Cavan and Monaghan, as far as Malin Head in the northwest. Their regular reports to the *Irish Evangelical* were immensely encouraging. They recounted conversations, including those with Roman Catholics, visits to homes, speaking at local evangelistic meetings, prayer meetings and a two-week mission, as well as professions of faith. They sold Bibles, New Testaments, Gospels and Christian books, among them *Pardon and Assurance, Grace and Truth, Traveller's Guide, Pilgrim's Progress,* the *Douay New Testament, His Unspeakable Gift, How to Pray,* and *Pleasure and Profit in Bible Study.* Their sales amounted to £110 in the first year, a significant sum in 1930. The CWU in Magherafelt gave them opportunities to speak and advertised their literature. Their contacts in Tyrone helped in the establishment of the Clintyfallow congregation of Tyrone in 1931.

But there were difficulties too. They encountered opposition from Russellites (Jehovah's Witnesses), who had sometimes covered the ground before them with their literature. They had problems in finding lodgings at times, on one occasion searching two or three days before they found a place. The car had not materialised at this stage, and their luggage weighing 3½ cwt (180kg) was awkward to move from base to base. But the men worked on, calling for prayer for the work, their guidance as to locations, and for themselves that they would be 'fit' physically, and 'keen' spiritually. In August 1929 they reported in *A Call to Prayer*: "Pray that every day we may be 'full of faith and of the Holy Ghost' (Acts 6.5, KJV). In 1 Samuel 12 the people asked Samuel to pray for them. His reply was, 'God forbid that I should sin against the Lord in ceasing to pray for you.' (12.23, KJV) Do we realise the sin of not praying? If so, do not let us commit it."

Colportage, Year 2 – 1930-31: Co Tyrone and Co Antrim
During April-August 1930 Mr McDowell continued his labours in Fermanagh and Tyrone, mostly in Tyrone, and from September 1930 to March 1931 in a succession of locations in Co Antrim. As well as extensive visitation and literature sales he held a few meetings in an old school and had the opportunity of conducting a weekly cottage meeting. In requesting prayer, he developed an expression he had used in June 1929: "A colporteur needs three G's—Grace, Grit,

and 'Gumption'; also two P's—Prayerfulness and Patience. Ask the Lord to give me these." As his time in Antrim drew to a close he requested prayer for guidance as to the sphere of his future labours.

Colportage, Year 3 – 1931-32: The Irish Free State and Co Down
McDowell commenced his third year further afield, with work in Laois (Queen's County) and Kilkenny in the spring of 1931. The May 1931 report by the editor described the work as "… difficult, at times very discouraging, and not without danger. Our brother needs prayer-support more than ever. For the few days in this district the sales have been very small, but among other things a few Douay Gospels and two Douay Testaments have been disposed of." The 1931 magazine reports were brief and non-specific about locations. In July-August the work moved to Co Kerry, described in the public reports of the magazine as "much further south than before"; "in a south-west district of the Irish Free State". The approach was to leave the Word of God in homes rather than to become involved in discussion that could lead to controversy. In September "two western counties", Clare and Limerick, were the new locations. There he found a mixed reception, with New Testaments and Scripture portions being purchased readily in some areas, and declined in others. Again, Russellites were there before him.

At this time Lady Hayes of Co Donegal,[390] who took an interest in the work of IEC and assisted the colporteurs when they were in her neighbourhood, invited Mr McDowell to conduct a mission in Ballybofey in October, and Council approved a change of plan to accommodate this opening. The meetings were well attended, particularly by men, and led to other opportunities to speak in Donegal.

The next locations were the Downpatrick and Ballynahinch areas of Co Down in the first months of 1932. He addressed meetings for three weeks in a country schoolhouse "where the people are not very willing to attend any Gospel services outside their own Church." Nevertheless he found in it a ready sale for Christian literature. This brought his third year to a conclusion, an annual landmark he was always careful to note.

Colportage, Year 4 – 1932-33: Co Antrim, Co Leitrim, Co Down
McDowell went to Co Antrim on 14 April 1932 for 10 weeks, beginning in Ballyclare. While there he had the opportunity of being present at two of the services of the recently opened Slatehill congregation and also worked in that district. He concluded his Co Antrim tour in Muckamore. He recorded that in the 10 weeks he sold 90 Bibles, 120 New Testaments, 360 booklets, and 26 *Traveller's Guide*. He interrupted his time in Co Antrim to work in support of the Jock Troup mission in Crumlin in June and returned in September for the mission that followed the opening of the new Crumlin Church in August. During October and November 1932 he helped out in the Evangelical Book Shop.

Towards the end of 1932 he worked for a short time in "a western district of the Irish Free State", Co Leitrim. One of the few Protestants he met described spiritual conversation as "only dry talk", adding, "Your job is to make sixpence on a book." It was his final colportage visit beyond Ulster. January to March 1933 in Rathfriland and Banbridge, Co Down, concluded the fourth year and there was a note that in one 12-day period he visited 269 Protestant homes and 23 Roman Catholic. Mr McDowell's end of year report noted that up to that time he had worked in 13 different counties.

Colportage, Year 5 – 1933-34: Co Armagh, Church Duties, and Co Antrim
A change of direction had become apparent in the fourth year, as Council required Mr McDowell to divert a part of his resource to the growing demands of the Church. He had had direct involvement with the work in Slatehill, Crumlin, and the Evangelical Book Shop, and with the exception of his brief time in Leitrim, he had kept fairly close to Belfast to help with preaching. In year five the need for his services in the Church became more pressing as cover was required for Charles Hunter and Joseph McCracken who were studying in Edinburgh. In addition, the Dispensationalist controversy of 1933, covered in the next chapter, reduced the already short supply of ministers.

However, April and May 1933 saw the colporteur at Newtownhamilton, Co Armagh, and elsewhere in the same county in early June. With Joseph McCracken he conducted a three-week mission at Slatehill, Co Antrim, from 18 June to 9 July. That was the occasion when someone called after Joseph McCracken as he left on his bicycle, "You have no light!" and he called back, "The Lord is my Light!" (Ps 27.1) From August 1933 until April 1934, as a direct result of the Dispensationalist controversy, he worked in the congregations, with Jocelyn Avenue and to a lesser extent Crosscollyer Street as his main assignments. Records show that in a seven-week period in September-October 1933 he visited 561 Protestant families and 87 Roman Catholic.

Colportage, Year 6 – 1934-35: Co Antrim, Church Duties, Co Armagh
During May and June 1934 McDowell returned to Armoy, in the north of Co Antrim. He visited 629 Protestant homes and 68 Roman Catholic. In August and September he moved location to Craigs, Ballymena, where he called on 412 Protestant and 19 Roman Catholic homes. In his September 1934 report he summed up the difficulty of regular reporting and noted a recurring feature of his work, now drawing to a close: "It is not an easy matter to have entirely fresh incidents for every report. Human nature is much the same in every district. One meets Obstinates, Pliables, and Talkatives very often in the course of this work."

A request to Council from Somerton Road and Jocelyn Avenue that W J McDowell take up the work during the absence of C E Hunter and Joseph McCracken was granted, and he was co-opted as a member of both congregations during his period of service, September 1934 to April 1935. Clearly he had a heart for outreach for he distributed *The Evangel*, a small Gospel magazine the church had produced, to 640 homes round Jocelyn Avenue and 578 round Somerton.

From May to July 1935 Charles Garland joined William McDowell in his final colportage tour. They based themselves in Keady, Co Armagh and did some work also in neighbouring Tyrone, and during this outreach visited 471 Protestant and 335 Roman Catholic homes.

W J McDowell – Call to the Ministry
The direction of William McDowell into work in the congregations was all in the good providence of God, and preparatory for his life's work in the Christian ministry. In May 1934 the Jocelyn Avenue representative spoke of the congregation's regret over losing his services, "and he suggested that if the way were clear to put him forward as a student it would be of great benefit to the Church." There was enthusiasm for this course from members of Council, but at that time severe financial constraint made it impossible. However, in March 1935, just as McDowell's sixth year as colporteur was coming to a close, James Hunter drew Council's attention to the continuing desire in congregations that McDowell be given the opportunity to train for the ministry. Council agreed, but since it was about to finance the two new ministers who had completed training, it would not be possible to guarantee Mr McDowell's future support beyond his salary level as a colporteur. At the second March meeting McDowell sent his acceptance of the terms and started to study in Edinburgh in the autumn.

A new colporteur, James Jones, was appointed to the work in July 1935. The whole story of his 20-year involvement is deferred until the next chapter.

The Evangel
In May 1934, W J Grier advised Council that 500 copies of an outreach magazine, the *Gospel Trumpet*, overprinted with Church name and details of services, had been purchased for each of the Crosscollyer Street, Jocelyn Avenue and Lisburn Road congregations. Each congregational Committee would decide how to use them. Only a few months later, Grier advised Council that some of the *Gospel Trumpet* content was unsuitable, and Council appointed an editorial committee to consider publishing its own quarterly outreach magazine. This resulted in the quarterly *Evangel* in April 1937. In May 1946, just after the war, Council decided to re-issue it provided supplies of paper were available, appointing W J Grier and W J McDowell, members of the 1934 Committee, as the new editorial committee. Apparently only one copy of one *Evangel* has survived. Strangely, it never had a mention in the *Irish Evangelical* nor in its back page Evangelical Book Shop advertisements. However, it was widely used and is a testimony to the Church's early desire to evangelise.

The Gospel Tent
Alongside the work of colportage, door-to-door outreach and missions in the various churches, there was a tent that made a tenacious contribution to the work of home missions. Its life began with a mission in Ballyclare in the summer of 1934. For the next five years Council made several attempts to dispose of it, with various outside bodies expressing interest, but none came to fruition. The tent

saw another phase of service in 1939 and 1940 in accommodating a mission in Edlingham Street, north Belfast, when many strangers attended and three professed faith in Christ. It returned to storage in Botanic Avenue and became a great boon to the Boys' Camps in the mid-1950s. An overnight storm at Tyrella, Co Down, in 1957 drew its story to a close!

Foreign Missions – First Steps

Commitment to work overseas was present in the IEC from the beginning.

Initial Direction

The fourth Council meeting, 17 February 1928, recorded: "It was recommended that the question of missionary support be thought over and that advice be given to our members in this matter." The response was James Hunter's list of 'sound Missions' presented at the last *Chat Noir* meeting, 25 February 1928, and these comprised the Church's initial missionary interest:

Scripture Gift Mission, London	Nile Missions Press
Worldwide Evangelisation Crusade	Japan Evangelistic Band
China Inland Mission	Japan Rescue Mission
North Africa Mission	Inland South America Mission Union
Africa Inland Mission	Spanish Gospel Mission
Soudan Interior Mission (Mr Bingham)	Barbican Mission to Jews
Regions Beyond Mission (Dr Meyer)	Russian Missionary Society

A deleted note to the side mentions the Belgian Gospel Mission, French Bible Mission, and the Ceylon and India General Mission (Russell Howden), each of which would soon feature.

The next Council meeting, 27 April 1928, strongly encouraged support for missions: "It was thought right that each body of people in connection with the IEC while doing their utmost to further the work of the Lord in their own district, should not neglect His work in the foreign field but should begin contributing to foreign missionary work. The Council expressed itself in favour of having a definite missionary interest." In August 1930 it was agreed as a general rule to have missionary speakers at Lord's Day services at intervals of not less than three months.

At the first Conference, 31 May 1928, one of the speakers was Rev. John Hay, General Director of Inland South America Mission Union, and in March 1931, Rev. W Arnold Bennett, Home Director of the European Christian Mission gave the missions address. In January 1938 Council appointed its first Foreign Missions Committee, consisting of four ministers, to deal with requests for deputation from missionary societies. In September of the same year Council recommended that congregations hold an annual Foreign Missions Day and it became an established practice in some of them until the 1960s.

The Irish Evangelical Coverage
In this early period, congregations developed their own missions contacts following Council guidelines. However, the *Irish Evangelical* expressed the denominational consciousness of the Great Commission (Matt 28.19-20) and from April 1929 periodically offered the Church's facilities to forward contributions to missions loyal to the Word of God. During its first year it carried regular articles on the Belgian Gospel Mission, China Inland Mission, Inland South America Mission Union, Indian Village Mission, Sudan Interior Mission, and the French Bible Mission whose Deputation Secretary, Pastor Emile Guedj, began his annual visits to IEC in September 1929. Work in Africa, Manchuria, Spain, and 'unoccupied fields' also featured. In the early 1930s readers were informed about the Egypt General Mission, the Ceylon and India General Mission, and work in Palestine and Mexico. Missionary biography added to missions interest. In August 1932 Dr James Gillespie wrote on the work of the Belgian Gospel Mission after a visit to Belgium. So a comprehensive but diverse foreign missions agenda marked the first phase.

Free Church of Scotland
Council reviewed the claims of several missions in November 1932 and approved the Free Church of Scotland's mission in India and its work among Jewish people. Both were added to the list of recommended missions for congregations to consider supporting financially. This was the beginning of an enduring participation in Free Church Missions and it coincided with the sending of the first two IEC students for the ministry to the Free Church College. In October 1937 Council decided to obtain Free Church mission boxes and appointed Rev. Joseph McCracken as 'Box Secretary'. The boxes were opened twice a year, and by 1940 most congregations had their own Box Secretary. In December 1937, the Church's first missionary, Dr Harold Lindsay, a deacon of the Knock congregation, set sail for the Free Church Mission in Peru. Council appointed a Foreign Missions Committee in 1938.

In 1939 the Free Church Students' Missionary Society published *The Macedonian Cry*, a compilation of articles from missionaries in Peru, India and South Africa, and from other contributors, including *Calvinism is not an Excuse for Carelessness*, by Rev. W J McDowell, *A Bulwark of God*, by Harold C Lindsay, and *With the Bible in Ireland*, by James Jones. It was a superb introduction to the new fields of missionary endeavour.

Council and Constitution
The 1930 Form of Government (Code)
The single page *Form of Government of the Irish Evangelical Church*, 1930, had 14 numbered sections (Appendix 3) and reflected the Church's early stage of development. It covered the government of congregations, Council representation, Council responsibilities, annual reporting, the appointment, roles, ordination and subscription of office bearers.

It is clear that the objective of the 1930 Code was to have a congregational oversight structure of minister and deacons. There was no mention of ruling elders. But Section 1 requires some explanation: "That this Church be under the government of such members as have been baptised and are regular partakers of the Lord's Supper, and have subscribed to the first six articles of the Creed." At first sight this Section is approving government by *members* after the congregational model, but it was simply saying that the system of government was to be effected through a qualified membership who would elect its overseer and deacons. Subsequent versions of the Code expressed this more clearly.

It was already the practice in congregations to have committees. Council minutes were acknowledging congregational committees as early as August 1930 and references to them continued until they were progressively replaced by diaconates from 1932. But there was never a decision to govern by committees. Perhaps the first congregations took their cue from the composition of the *Chat Noir* meetings and, although men and women comprised the Committees, they appointed men as representatives to Council. In June 1930 Council decided to appoint its own committees only "as occasion demanded".

The matter of ordination, Section 14 in the 1930 Code, also requires comment. It did not specify the offices to which ordination applied, but the context and subsequent practice indicates that those specified in Section 13 were in view: deacons, colporteurs, theological teachers, evangelists, missionaries and pastors. Ordination incorporated subscription to all eight *Articles of Faith* and became a requirement for all Council members from January 1932. The reference to the gift of the Holy Spirit for the fruitful exercise of office and the power of the Spirit for daily Christian life was an important emphasis.

Overseer's and Visitation Reports

The 1930 *Form of Government* required the 'Overseer' to present an annual report to congregation and Council - the Overseer's Report. It usually came to Council in February or March, combined with a financial report. In November 1932 James Hunter drew Council's attention to the fact that no arrangements had yet been made for the supervision of the congregations and he gave Notice of Motion, which the January 1933 meeting adopted unanimously, that each minister be asked to furnish the following particulars to Council, every four months:

1. The number of services on the Lord's Day which he has personally conducted in the Church or Churches given to his care
2. The number of families professing connection with them
3. The number of visits he has paid to these families
4. The number of visits paid to the sick
5. The number of visits paid to the non-churchgoing

The first 'Visitation Report', May 1933, produced the following statistics:

W J Grier		Services	Families	Visitation		
				Family	Sick	Other
	Botanic Avenue	14	40	160 including 37 sick		
	Lisburn Road	14	49	Included in row above		
A McFadden	Employed for full-time visitation, Jan 1932			307 including 65 sick		
H A Morrison	Crosscollyer Street	19	40	104	87	38
H H Murphy	Crumlin	16	24	106	28	25
	Jocelyn Avenue	14	31	Included in row above		
C E Hunter	Somerton Road	Part of period		All ex 1		20
W J McDowell	Returns began to appear in his colportage reports.					

But James Hunter was clearly not happy. After saying that allowance must be made for Mr Grier whose work in the Book Shop and editing *The Irish Evangelical* "accounted for a considerable part of his time", the minute recorded that:

> He stressed the importance of efforts being made to reach the non-churchgoing community, and said that, the membership of the various churches being small, the reports submitted were not, in his opinion, satisfactory as regards district visiting, and he urged upon those in charge of the various congregations to devote more time and effort to reach the careless and indifferent ....

Evidently there was a felt need to introduce some form of accountability. But there is also an indication here of the sense of responsibility towards home mission. It was not seen as discharged by colportage alone. Congregations held missions and there were constant efforts to reach the unsaved through open-air meetings and door-to-door visitation. By 1939 visitation statistics were included in the Overseers' Reports. The revised Form of Government of 1952 required the same information but twice annually. This was replaced by annual "state of the congregation" Pastoral Reports in 1957, and in 1961 they became Congregational Reports and included the returns, later expressed in the Annual Statistical Returns.

Central Fund
Although there is no minute of the setting up of the Central Fund, the accountant's report of the Fund's first two years in December 1929 gives the inauguration date of the Fund as 12 December 1927. In February 1928 Council expressed its first funding strategy: "It was thought advisable that the amount which each centre should contribute to the central funds should be decided upon by the local members." There was a similar message in January 1929 when Council, after discussing the state of the Central Fund, decided to remind each local

treasurer that it was the prerogative of each congregation to fix the amount of its contribution. Central targets were not yet in vogue! In July 1932, Council was sympathetic to the suggestion that congregations allocate 20% of their income to the Central Fund, but referred it back for prayer and consultation. It appears that it did not proceed.

In April 1928 Council appointed a committee to define the purposes of the Central Fund, and to act under control of the Council in distributing the funds. Council accepted the committee's recommendations as to the purposes of the Central Funds in June:

1. To make advances to centres requiring assistance.
2. To meet the expenses of General Conferences, the offering at such Conferences to be paid into the Central Funds.

There was no mention of salaries, but in June 1929, Council approved the payment of half of W J Grier's salary from the Central Fund, and the December 1929 report showed that the Fund was taking up salaries, colporteur's expenses, and the *Irish Evangelical* deficit. The treasurer made a Central Fund appeal in the *Irish Evangelical* of November 1931, mainly for the support of ministers, but also for the Colporteur and magazine.

The Church received its first bequests, both of £1,000, in 1932 and 1934 - significant sums in those days. The treasurer placed £950.00 on deposit which Council agreed should be used as loans to congregations with large debts. However, by September 1937 the amount on deposit had been all but absorbed by the monthly shortfall in Central Fund income. This produced an immediate Council decision to place a quarterly statement in the *Irish Evangelical*, highlighting the needs of the Central Fund. The first of these statements from the Treasurer appeared in October 1938, under the title *Gift Days*, which he commended as an effective existing practice on the part of two congregations:

> As we do not think it right to exceed our income, an increase in the givings to the Central Fund is required, if the work of our Church is to be consolidated and extended. ... Out of the Central Fund are paid the salaries of ministers and of our colporteur, allowances to students for the ministry, and the loss which there still is on our magazine, THE IRISH EVANGELICAL. ... Pray that the Central Fund may grow in proportion as the Lord would have the work of our Church to grow; and that those of our congregations which are burdened with debt may soon be delivered from that burden. Till they are, they cannot contribute much to the Central Fund. ... A considerable number of our members realise their responsibility, and are of the habit of contributing from time to time to the Central Fund. It is not desired that such members should give their whole annual contribution on the Gift Day. It is very useful having gifts coming in at different times of the year.

It is notable that the Central Fund Gift Day practice has continued among congregations to this day, and that much of Dr Gillespie's statement has been relevant in every decade.

The Lord's Table – Early Administration

During these early years Council appointed ordained officebearers to administer the Lord's Table. John Britton, Alexander McFadden and W J Grier were appointed in 1927, with others to be authorised "as occasion offered". Council added Dr J R Gillespie and W J McDowell in 1933, followed by C H Garland and W A Sampson in 1937. James Hunter was clearly unhappy with the developing practice in the early years, for in November 1932 he spoke at Council on the advisability of ministers officiating at the Communion services in the churches under their care.

Inter-Church Greetings and Correspondence

In the 1930s and 40s inter-church activity was mostly in the form of letters of greeting and the appointment of inter-church correspondents. Dr J R Gillespie drafted the greeting from Council in September 1936 to the General Assembly of the newly formed Presbyterian Church of America (later renamed Orthodox Presbyterian Church), of which Dr Machen was the first moderator. In addition to the connection with Machen, the greeting had historic value as the first that the Church sent to another body, whose beginnings had parallels with its own. The greeting made reference to the Westminster Larger and Shorter Catechisms which IEC had added to its standards in 1933:

> …We are your brothers, and companions in tribulation, and in the kingdom and patience of Jesus Christ …
>
> Though we have not the word Presbyterian in the name of our denomination, all our ordained office-bearers are required to sign once a year, without equivocation, a declaration of their belief in the doctrines of the Larger and Shorter Catechisms of the Westminster Divines.
>
> Previous to June, 1927, we were nearly all members of The Presbyterian Church in Ireland, maintaining the truth of the Bible against unbelievers, euphemistically called Modernists. In June, 1927, the General Assembly of that church having voted by an overwhelming majority (707 to 82) in favour of Modernism, we felt that we ought not to remain any longer under its authority.
>
> A number of persons who were with us in protesting against Modernism while we were in the Presbyterian Church, did not come out with us. They said they would continue to fight for the truth inside that church. But their testimony has dwindled away till it is now negligible. So, we fear, will it be with those who were with you, and remain behind in the Presbyterian Church in the USA. …

The Second General Assembly of the Presbyterian Church in America responded through its clerk, Leslie W Sloat, 13 November 1936:

> ... It is indeed wonderful to know that there are so many Churches throughout the world who are interested in and praying for our work. And we rejoice in the Christian fellowship which we have with those who, though separated from us on this earth, are united with us in Christ before the Throne of Grace. We do pray that the Irish Evangelical Church may be abundantly blessed of Almighty God, and that its testimony may be used to His glory, for the saving of souls and the edification of the saints. ...

It was noted earlier that the Free Church of Scotland case, 1900-1905, provided a basis for future relationship with the Free Church. When the Belfast Presbytery of the Presbyterian Church in Ireland sent a message of sympathy to the United Free Church in 1904, James Hunter protested and appealed to the General Assembly of 1905, although unsuccessfully. The potential strengthened in 1927 when Rev. John MacLeod of Inverness, later Principal of the Free Church College, spoke in support of Rev. James Hunter in his public campaign. When the Free Church began to train IEC students in the 1930s, the relationship took on a corporate dimension. However, it would be in the field of overseas missions that co-operation between the two churches would be most pronounced.

Psalter and Hymnbooks

Council gave early consideration to a denominational hymnbook which would reflect the Church's reformed theological stance. It first appeared on the agenda in April 1928, but there was no decision. Rev. W J Grier raised it again in October 1933 when it was referred back to the congregational committees with the suggestion that the old Presbyterian Church Hymnary (1898) and Psalter might be a suitable book of praise. In December Council agreed to recommend the Psalter[391] and *Golden Bells* to the local committees, the timing of the change to be at local discretion. Then, in February 1934, Grier drew Council's attention to alterations to the wording in some of the hymns in *Golden Bells*, which he suggested may lessen the book's value as a praise book.[392] There is no record of the specific issues he raised, but he did express concern, from time to time, over Arminian elements in *Golden Bells*, and he always took exception to the line, "Emptied himself of all but love" in verse 3 of Charles Wesley's *And can it be that I should gain*, as expressive of the Kenotic Theory.[393] However, in May 1934 Council confirmed its decision to use *Golden Bells* and the Revised Psalter. Most congregations accepted *Golden Bells* which remained in general use until 1983 when the 1961 *Trinity Hymnal* of the Orthodox Presbyterian Church (USA) was adopted.

However, whilst *Golden Bells* came to be loved by many during its 50 years of use, it was never regarded as distinctly reformed. Writing in February 1937 about the Presbyterian Church of America's (later OPC) discussion of hymnology, the *IE*

Editor said: "The Irish Evangelical Church has felt the need of a suitable hymnal of its own, but in the meantime we must be content with selecting Scriptural hymns from the books at present in use."

Youth Work – In Embryo

A Young People's Association?
Youth work operated at congregational level from the beginning. It engaged Council's attention from the 1930s but it was not denominationally organised until the 1960s. In February 1932 Rev. W J Grier asked Council's direction in responding to a group of young people who had asked him to guide them in a theological study course. He was appointed to provide one for them! In September 1935, Rev. Joseph McCracken submitted the following motion: "That a Young People's Association be formed in the Church, for the purpose of promoting fellowship and strengthening faith of young believers." Council decided not to proceed with a YPA at that time, but deferred the matter to the meeting of January 1936 for re-consideration. However, it did not re-appear on the agenda, perhaps due to pressure on leadership resources at the time.

Sunday School
Council began its participation in Sunday School development in the mid-1930s, always paying attention to lesson material. In September 1934 it called a meeting of two Sunday School teachers from each Sunday School, to discuss the advisability of adopting a common lesson programme. There is no note of the outcome but the Council minute of August 1939 referred to the lesson books of the Children's Special Service Mission (CSSM) as having been in use. Change was considered desirable but neither of the two options which a Sunday School Committee examined proved suitable.

The Boys' Camp
There are no written records of camp history until notices and reports began to feature in the *Irish Evangelical* from July 1951. These references were very brief and usually just advertised a particular camp. The fuller report of August 1952 noted: "The Boys' Camp began in 1939 with a few boys camping in a single bell-tent – two ministers of the church shared in the experiment!" This is the only official record of the formal beginning, but conversations with participants from more informal camping activities pre-1939, notably Rev. W J McDowell and Mr George Bellew and a few of their friends, have established the outline.

William McDowell, George Bellew, Joe McCracken, Tommy Spears, Bob Magee, George Stewart and George Keith were young friends associated with Newington Presbyterian Church. On Monday evenings they shared activities in Currie Primary School, north Belfast, where Joe McCracken's mother was caretaker. Around 1925 these friends bought a bell-tent and straw mattresses for use at week-ends. For some years they set out on bicycles on chosen Saturday afternoons, and started home at 5.00 am the following Monday morning. They camped on sites around Carrickfergus – Kilroot House, Hart's Loney and Boneybefore to the north of Carrickfergus. They cooked on oil stoves and over open fires and took turns at the chores. George Bellew remembered Willie McDowell and Joe McCracken rolling through grass, nettles and bushes as they wrestled. They attended the Methodist Church on Sunday mornings and the Wilson Hall in Eden in the evenings. George Bellew was the treasurer and Bob Magee, later Haypark Baptist Church, Belfast, and a joiner by trade, enlarged a brown wooden storage box which served the Boys' Camps until 1978 when canvas gave way to buildings.

These early activities did not have a direct link to the Church or its camps, but they had planted the idea, provided the experience, the first tent and the brown box. When the Church held the mission at Slatehill in 1933, Willie McDowell and Joe McCracken slept in the same bell-tent.

Ladies' United Monthly Prayer Meeting

This prayer meeting began before the Church! During the sessions of the Heresy Trial in February-March 1927 a group of ladies met in a room at the back of the Bible Standards League Book Shop to pray for the men who had left for the Assembly Buildings. In an early reference W J Grier wrote to Dr Machen on Wednesday 6 April 1927, just two months before Machen's first visit to Belfast: "We had a prayer meeting this afternoon attended by some twenty or thirty ladies at which I spoke a word—but would not venture to ask you to pass through such a dangerous ordeal!" *The Irish Evangelical* began advertising the meetings from October 1928: "Ladies' Monthly Prayer Meeting – First Wednesday of each month at 3.30 pm at 15 College Square East, Belfast." Wednesday was chosen because it was half-day closing in Belfast and more could come on that day. Catherine Grier's diary noted: "The ladies knelt at LUMPM on the tiled floor at the back of the shop." The Book Shop was the venue until April 1938 when it became the Botanic Avenue Church.

Miss Kathleen Speers was the first leader, followed by Mrs Grier with Mrs McDowell as assistant and deputy. It is impossible to estimate the Church's indebtedness to this group of praying women, not just for what their prayers achieved during the first critical decade, but in the years to follow. The story is resumed in a later chapter.

The Emergent W J Grier

In the first decade, with few resources and hard work by all concerned, Jim Grier played a key personal role. As a bachelor, he lived in digs off the Lisburn Road with a bicycle for transport. With James Hunter devoting most of his energies to the congregation at Knock, Grier had a nigh impossible schedule, that made him look back from near the end of his ministry with misgivings about the amount of time he had been able to spend on preparation. He was manager of the Evangelical Book Shop. He had charge of two congregations which filled most evenings -

the Lisburn Road prayer meeting on Wednesday, Botanic Avenue on Thursday, a young people's Bible Class on Monday, along with open-air meetings in the summer months. In addition, he edited the monthly *Irish Evangelical*, writing articles and reading proofs. He was Interim Clerk of Council until April 1931 and co-ordinated pulpit supply for some years from 1932. He wrote to Machen on 28 May 1928 about his "exceedingly busy" programme with the shop, the emerging groups and the magazine: "A great portion of the burden of this work has fallen to my lot. I lack experience and many gifts that would seem to be necessary for such a work, but my eyes are upon Him."

In January 1929 Council decided to advise the congregations of the financial needs of two projects - colportage and W J Grier: "that Mr Grier be set free to devote a portion of his time to congregational work in the various centres." This enabled him to restrict his work as Book Shop manager to the mornings so that he could visit and prepare in the afternoons.

The early thirties were often a time of intense loneliness for him and a feeling of isolation would sometimes threaten. One day two ladies came into the shop and said: "Did you hear what those two ministers outside were saying?" He replied: "I was meant to hear!" They had been saying that he had no future and was facing potential ruin. Such things gave him a fellow-feeling with Athanasius, 4th century Bishop of Alexandria, whose lifelong and triumphant battle with Arianism earned him the epithet, 'Athanasius *contra mundum*'. Grier's family life in Donegal entered a difficult phase too. He went regularly to help his brother with the haymaking or the harvest and on one occasion came back distraught because his mother's memory had very quickly failed and she had not recognised him.

He had important times of relaxation such as his visits to the Gillespie home at Knockdene Park South most Saturdays, and the occasional round of golf with James Gillespie. But the outstanding event of this period was the trip to Palestine in 1931 with James Gillespie. They went to Venice and then by train and boat to Egypt where a long-term missionary, Miss Ella Murdoch (later Mrs Ardill), was their acting tour guide. They took the train up through Palestine, then under British mandate. The trip was formative to Grier's whole ministry and for over 20 years afterwards he showed his slides of Palestine.

Whilst these first years had many difficulties for Jim Grier, it was a period of immense usefulness. The new congregations and buildings and the training of people who went on to notable Christian service, were matters for particular thankfulness. Joseph McCracken had left school at 14 but Jim Grier took him as a trainee in the Evangelical Book Shop where he learned the rudiments of reformed theology. Charles Haddon Garland, a member of the South Belfast-Botanic Avenue congregation, he also influenced towards the Christian ministry.

So the early years were marked by enthusiasm and measurable progress but they were not free from the pain of major trials.

19

... and Experiencing Pain (1933-34)

The clouds that shut out the sunshine from the inner world are dispersed by faith. The sorrows and perplexities of this life are innumerable, and we all stand in need of a more than human comforter. We are told that the blueness of the sky is due to innumerable motes that reflect the sunshine. All the trials and troubles of this life are like those motes. "We glory in tribulations also, knowing that tribulation worketh patience, and patience experience, and experience hope. ... In all these things we are more than conquerors through Him that loved us." (Rom 5.3, 8.37, KJV)

Gleanings from Rev. James Hunter

There were two events in this first period of progress that inflicted immense pain and considerable disruption on the young Church.

The Dispensationalist Controversy

The first was the Dispensationalist controversy, 1930-1933. Weaknesses in government, doctrinal standards and in the teaching ministry had made the Church vulnerable. The main exponent was Rev. Andrew Morrison, the Dallas graduate, supported by Rev. H H Murphy.

Dispensational Premillennialism
Morrison and Murphy described themselves as Premillennialists, but there are critical differences between historic premillennialism and the system with which the two men were aligned—*dispensational* premillennialism. There is no record of the particular strands they espoused, but the context of the period suggests that it was close to that of C I Scofield (1843-1921), of which L S Chafer of Dallas was representative. The system can be outlined under three headings, Israel and the Church, the Seven Dispensations, and the Millennium sequence.

Israel and the church: Scofield's system, like J N Darby's, makes a fundamental distinction between them, seeing them as two distinct peoples of God. God operates his purposes for both in parallel, Israel being the people of God's programme for the earth, and the church the people of his programme for heaven. Prophecy relates directly to Israel and, if at all to the church, only by application.

Seven dispensations: Scofield divided history into distinct ages of unequal length, each being a new test of the natural man, each ending in failure and consequent judgement. Five of them are past and the present time is the sixth, probably near its end.

1	Innocence	Creation to Ejection from Eden
2	Conscience	Eden to the Flood
3	Human Government	Noah to the Tower of Babel
4	Promise	Abraham to Egyptian Bondage
5	Law	Moses to the Death of Christ
6	Grace	The Death of Christ to the Rapture
7	Kingdom	Millennium reign of Christ

Millennium Sequence: For the duration of the Dispensation of Grace, while the church is being gathered, God suspends his programme relating to the people of Israel. The church is therefore a 'parenthesis', or interlude. At the end of the Dispensation of 'Grace' there is a two-stage Second Coming of Christ. The first is the *Rapture* when Christ descends to the air above the earth to take the church to heaven. After a seven-year period of tribulation Christ descends to the earth to fight the Battle of Armageddon, judge the nations and purify the earth. Christ then inaugurates His 'Kingdom' - his millennial reign in Jerusalem over a restored Israel. It is the culmination of the Dispensations. The church 'parenthesis' is over, and the suspended programme for Israel is resumed. After the Millennium, Satan is "loosed for a little season" (Rev 20.3, KJV) and gathers his forces for the battle of Gog and Magog. The final events follow—the raising of the wicked dead, the Great White Throne Judgement, and the eternal New Heavens and Earth.

Adoption of the Westminster Catechisms
Matters came to a head when Rev. W J Grier gave notice of motion to Council on 13 January 1933 that the Church should adopt the Westminster Standards and include the word 'Presbyterian' in its name. The proposed name change was dropped at the meeting of 24 February, but on 17 March Rev. W J Grier duly proposed the adoption of the Westminster Standards as the subordinate standards of IEC. After a process of consultation with congregational committees and Council debate, Council decided on 29 May 1933, by 17 votes to 7, to adopt Westminster's Larger and Shorter Catechisms. Council then adopted a new Formula of Subscription:

> I believe the Catechisms compiled by the Assembly of Divines at Westminster to be founded on, and agreeable to, the Word of God, and as such I subscribe them as the confession of my faith, and this I do without any reservations.

It was further resolved: "That every ordained person, and every salaried office bearer, and every member of Council subscribe to the above formula, and that such subscription be required annually after the first subscription." A book for formula subscription was made available at the August 1933 meeting, and from then subscription of Council members was recorded in it rather than appended to the original *Articles of Faith* as they had been since January 1932. Before proceeding with the subscription of the new formula, Council agreed to amend it to include the declaration: "I also affirm my belief in the 8 *Articles of Faith* of the IEC as set out on the first page of this book."

Five members, including Rev. H H Murphy, expressed their dissent and refused to sign. Rev. H A Morrison had decided not to be present at the meeting although James Hunter had gone to see him in an unsuccessful attempt to resolve the matter. After debating Mr Morrison's situation at its meeting of 4 August 1933, Council decided to terminate his employment. Mr Murphy agreed to spend two months studying eschatology more widely, but wrote to Council on 12 August 1933 declaring that he could not conscientiously accept the teaching of the Larger and Shorter Catechisms on the subject.

Dispensational premillennialism regards the covenant of grace as not being one in all ages and to this the Westminster Standards present uncompromising opposition. This is why the introduction of Westminster was the key factor that brought the issue to a head. Dr Robert L Reymond argues in his *Systematic Theology* that there are two "tragic implications" of the dispensational interpretation of Scripture: "Dispensationalism's unwitting justification of the Crucifixion" and "Dispensationalism's implicit suggestion that the Cross was not absolutely essential to the sinner's salvation."[394] The wording of Morrison's written question to Council on 29 May 1933, "Will subscription to the Larger and Shorter Catechisms be expected to preclude the teaching by ministers of the IEC, of the doctrine of our Lord's personal return to inaugurate His kingdom?" masked the vital issues at stake. There is latitude in the Westminster Standards regarding millennial views.

Countering False Rumours
So the effect of Dispensationalist teaching was significant, involving unrest within a number of congregations, particularly those whose ministers were its advocates, and the severance of the Crumlin congregation in August 1933. When rumours about IEC beliefs began to circulate, Council decided to use the magazine to define the Church's position. So in September 1933 *The Irish Evangelical* leader, usually written by Rev. James Hunter, was titled, "Editorial Notes and Comments", and the first of these bore the subtitle, *The Second Coming of Christ*:

> False rumours have been persistently circulated that the leaders of the Irish Evangelical Church do not believe in the second coming of the Lord Jesus Christ. Lest any of our readers should be misled by these rumours, we emphatically deny them. ... Most of us were members of the Presbyterian Church; and we came out of that church, not because we objected to the system of doctrine taught in the catechisms which are nominally the subordinate standards of that church, but because that church had in reality abandoned those standards.
>
> The Council of the Irish Evangelical Church was, therefore, not introducing any new doctrine when it enacted recently that all ministers and other ordained office-bearers of the church, all paid agents of the church, and all members of Council, should be required periodically to affirm their belief in the doctrines set forth in the Larger and Shorter Catechisms of the Westminster Assembly of Divines, as well as in the existing eight *Articles of Faith*. ... In refutation of the rumour ... we quote the answer to the question, "What do we pray for in the second petition?" as given in the Larger Catechism: ... "that Christ would rule in our hearts here, and hasten the time of His second coming, and our reigning with Him for ever; and that He would be pleased so to exercise the kingdom of His power in all the world, as may best conduce to these ends."

In 1945 the Evangelical Book Shop published *The Momentous Event*, by W J Grier, "A Discussion of Scripture Teaching on the Second Advent and Questions Relating Thereto". The chapters were originally written as articles for *The Irish Evangelical* between March 1944 and June 1945 and, although pressures of work delayed them until 10 years after the conflict with Dispensationalism, his motivation to write on the subject stemmed from that period. In the introduction to the first edition the author said: "Extreme and fanciful views as to the Lord's second advent and the accompanying events are common to-day. There is undoubtedly need of a sane and balanced statement in accord with the time-honoured views expressed in the great creeds of the Church in all ages. Such a statement the author has attempted in these pages." By the end of 2002 the book had sold 49,650 copies excluding those published in German, Portuguese, French, Italian and Japanese.[395]

God Meant it for Good

So IEC had an early encounter with heresy! It now seems strange that Council accepted a student from Dallas Theological Seminary, the leading Dispensationalist school of the day. Dr T T Shields of Toronto said this of C I Scofield:

> We rejoice in much of the teaching of Dr. Scofield's notes, which are printed together with the Holy Scriptures, and called "The Scofield Bible." Respecting the essentials of evangelical faith, Dr. Scofield is generally sound enough; but we know of few books that contain more eschatological error than the Scofield Bible.[396]

But sympathy with these early leaders is in order. The growth in the first few years had outstripped resources and they were desperately stretched to keep it going. Council and people were praying for urgent help in the ministry, but there had been no time to develop Training for the Ministry and Admissions and Church Government procedures. Dispensationalism was relatively new and, whilst the clause in No 3 of the Church's Eight Articles: "… and He will come again in glory to judge the living and the dead" (Nicene Creed), gave no mandate for Dispensationalism's two-stage Second Coming, it was capable of manipulation. The Catechisms, particularly the Larger, were specific in their teaching one Covenant of Grace administered differently and with greater fullness in the New Testament than it was in the Old, one return of Christ, one general resurrection, and one general judgement. Given an unwillingness to adopt Westminster in full at this stage, the Catechisms were a fairly conspicuous signpost, and they sat comfortably with the *Articles of Faith*.

Looking back on it W J Grier said that if the situation had not been put right, he would have left the IEC and started all over again. Doctrinal standards do not in themselves guarantee freedom from error, or from difficulty in applying them, but genuine subscription engenders the unified commitment to the truth they are designed to promote. To the very great credit of the Church's early leaders they quickly identified the problem, applied themselves to it and learned the appropriate lesson. And in doing so they took an important early step towards a more distinctive, reformed, Presbyterian position.

James Hunter Gillespie

The other painful event, following hard on the heels of the Dispensationalist controversy, was the death of Dr James Hunter Gillespie in 1934 when he was just 27. Rev. James Hunter had suffered the loss of his sister Maria, who kept house for him, on 7 June 1929 when she was 71, and on 8 March 1930 of his other sister,

Catherine Gillespie, just 59, who lived adjacent. But the death of his nephew, James, Catherine's son, was a colossal blow both to James Hunter personally and to the whole Church.

Memorial Minute

The Council Memorial Minute of 16 March 1934, re-produced in the *Irish Evangelical*, April, 1934, recorded the circumstances of his death and reviewed his short life:

> The death of Dr James H Gillespie, a member of this Council, at the age of 27 took place in London on Sabbath, 25 February 1934. He was returning from a morning meeting at the close of which the Lord's Supper had been observed. A fast car going at a great speed crashed into the car which he was driving. Dr Gillespie was taken in an ambulance but breathed his last shortly after reaching the hospital.
>
> Dr J H Gillespie was one of the very first to realise the duty of separation from the Irish Presbyterian Church after the decision of the General Assembly in 1927. Shortly after that Assembly he felt constrained to put the position clearly before the people in print. This he did in a very able manner under the pen-name of *Leloumenos* in *Faith in an Unchanging Vesture*—an exposure of Modernistic Principles based on *The Changing Vesture of the Faith* by Professor J E Davey. This book, written when he was 21 years of age, will long be treasured—if the Lord tarry—in the homes of members of our church. He took a deep interest in our monthly magazine and contributed articles for its pages. In May 1929, when a Children's Page became a feature in the magazine, he willingly undertook to provide this page. All the prizes were provided by him. Only a few months ago he expressed his willingness to give additional help with material for the magazine.
>
> From the opening of the Knock church—of which he was a member—he acted as Superintendent of the Sabbath School. A fine Sabbath School and Bible Class grew up under his leadership. When Deacons were elected in Knock Church he was one of six chosen and ordained to this office. He acted as organist in Knock Church and at many of our Conferences. He spoke occasionally from the pulpit and platforms of our churches; he was a zealous and faithful member of this Council; quick in his discernment of issues at stake; wise and far-seeing in judgement.
>
> At Queen's University he was President of the Bible Union in 1929-30, and in University and Hospital—indeed wherever he went, at work or on vacation—he sought to witness for Christ, to strengthen the weak, and lead the unconverted to the Saviour. He loved God's Holy Word and sought to give Christ the pre-eminence in all things. Tender, zealous and skilful in his ministrations to the bodies, he was used as an instrument also to the salvation of the souls of his patients.
>
> A brilliant career in his own profession lay before him, but on this he looked with the eyes of a humble disciple of Christ who sought first the Kingdom of God and his Righteousness.

Although he is thus early cut off, we believe that God has given him his twelve hours in the day. ... Dr James Hunter Gillespie now enjoys sweet converse in the presence of the Lamb.

We praise God for the Christian graces manifest in his life. We praise God for giving him to us in this Church to which he so unselfishly devoted himself, and in which his heart was so set. We are confident that this work, for which we may say that Dr Gillespie lived, will go on under the blessing of God. His going to be with the Saviour is a strong call to us who remain to glorify God in our bodies and in our spirits, which are His; and to live for Christ and eternity.

Our love and prayers and sympathy are with those who are bound to him by close ties of kinship and affection.

The *Irish Evangelical* of July 1935 carried "A TRIBUTE" from a patient:

... his life still speaks to those who had the privilege of knowing him. Every one who came in contact with him felt the power of his wonderful personality. He radiated the love of Christ and the peace of God, and not only did he minister to the bodies of those who were sick, but he also was a blessing to them spiritually. He always 'sought first the Kingdom of God and His righteousness,' and never lost an opportunity of speaking a word for the Lord Jesus, whom he loved and served so faithfully. At the mention of his name, faces brighten, and we each can recall something helpful which he said to us, and we thank God for every remembrance of him. Truly the memory of the just is blessed.

Reflection of an Eye Witness

It would be impossible to overestimate the impact of James Gillespie's death on Church and family. Helen McCracken, retired missionary in South Africa, remembered him as a keen, highly-strung young man and an engaging preacher. On one occasion when the breeze from an open window was disturbing his notes he left the pulpit, crossed the church, and shut it! In November 2002, her 93rd year, she could vividly recall the day he was killed. She related how 'Dr James' had gone to London to do a three-month course on chest therapy. He was staying with the family of James Scott, who before moving to London had taught Greek in the Alliance Bible School, preached regularly for the Irish Evangelical Church and contributed frequently to the *Irish Evangelical*.

The way the news of his death broke to the family in Belfast could not have been more devastating. John R Gillespie, James' father, was receiving medical treatment at the time, and his daughter Catherine was at home alone when reporters called for an account of her brother's life. When Jim Grier came to see her later that day he was in tears, but she said to him, "Don't cry, Mr Grier, 'The Lord gave, the Lord has taken away.'" John Gillespie reacted to the news similarly, with another quotation from Scripture. James Hunter crossed to London to make the arrangements. That night Jim Grier was preaching in the Somerton Road Church in north Belfast and Mrs McCracken, the organist in those days, remembered him making "an awful noise" as he came into the prayer meeting before the service. He stood with his arm on a little shelf and his head resting on his arm. When the others moved into the service she hung back a moment and asked him, "Is anything wrong?" Through tears he told her the news. He had great difficulty getting through the service and had to cut it short. On pronouncing the benediction he went straight into the back room, unable to face the customary shaking of hands with the members of the congregation, who were unaware why he was so clearly distressed.

An Inscrutable Providence
James Gillespie had been President of the Queen's University Bible Union[397] and at the time of his death had just equipped his consulting rooms in Queen's Elms Belfast to work as a Consultant Radiologist. His outstanding leadership gifts made him the heir apparent of his uncle, after whom he was called. His death was a stunning setback for the Church. For Jim Grier it was the loss of his only personal companion with whom he had become bonded in the work of the Church and had enjoyed his times of recreation. In June 1927 Jim Grier had confided in Dr Machen something of James Gillespie's longer term plans "as he looks forward to some day being one of your students if the Lord will." It was not the Lord's will, and that is the only explanation of this inscrutable providence.

Stories of Christian Heroes
This is a little book containing cameos of 56 Christian Heroes, published in 1937. The Preface is addressed: "To Boys and Girls who Read this Book". Here are two extracts:

> Perhaps you wonder why some of these heroes have been chosen, while others about whom you would like to read have been left out. The reason is this—the young man who wrote them died. James Hunter Gillespie was suddenly taken home to Heaven by a motor accident on 25th February 1934. He was then just twenty-seven years old. For about four years he had written one of these stories of Christian Heroes each month for the Children's Page of a monthly magazine (Irish Evangelical). A few which he left already written were added to the others after his death. ...
>
> If you look at the end of the last story in the book, you will see what Dr. Gillespie thought was the best thing any one could say about you. ... if you trust in the Lord Jesus Christ as your Saviour, and try to please Him every day, it does not matter a bit whether the life you live be short or long.

The last story, on the Frenchman, John Frederick Oberlin, ended:

> He made many enemies, of course, but he also found many staunch friends, and when he died they put a lovely text upon his grave. It was: "They that turn many to righteousness shall shine as the stars for ever and ever." (Dan 12.3.

KJV) Would it not be worth more than anything else in the world to have that said of YOU?

James Gillespie had written the Children's Page in the *Irish Evangelical* since May 1929. On his death, his sister, Catherine, took over the Children's Page.

So the Irish Evangelical Church had gained a foothold during its first 10 years. There were the more visible landmarks of 11 new congregations, three member-students for the ministry ordained and one in training, the launch of the *Irish Evangelical*, and the establishment of home and overseas missions. Alongside them were important constitutional developments in doctrinal standards, church government and administration, and in inter-church relations. So whilst there was excessively hard work, an acute lack of resources, opposition, disparagement and some very great pain, the dominant message of the first decade was progress. There was abundant reason for thankfulness and encouragement. However, difficult decades lay ahead, overshadowed by the threatening international scene.

20

Forging the Identity (1940-1967)

Now, why have I gone on at length about this issue of identity? And what does it have to do with "Presbyterian identity"? Those are fair questions. First, I wanted to describe "identity," because it is one of those words that we use frequently without pausing to think about what we mean. This is particularly true when we talk about "religious identity." But I also want us to begin to see how a particular type of identity is formed, as the confluence of ***beliefs***, ***practices***, *and* ***stories***. *And I needed to alert you to how, in our contemporary situation, this issue of identity is quite conflicted due to the "postmodern turn" of our society.*

Above all, I want to suggest in the rest of this book that Presbyterian identity is formed through shared beliefs, practices and stories. These three things work together to forge what one nineteenth-century Presbyterian theologian[398] *called the Presbyterian idiosyncrasies of mind.*

Sean Michael Lucas, On Being Presbyterian[399]

Adolf Hitler became Chancellor of Germany in 1933 and within a few years tension was escalating in Europe. The annexation of Austria by the German Reich (the *Anschluss*), came in March 1938 and a rapid succession of menacing developments followed in 1939. Germany occupied Czechoslovakia in March, Italy seized Albania in April, Germany and Italy signed a military alliance in May, and the German non-aggression pact with the Soviet Union followed in August. The scene thus set, Germany invaded Poland on 1 September 1939 (the *Blitzkrieg* or lightning war), starting World War II. Two days later Britain and France declared war on Nazi Germany, joined quickly by most members of the Commonwealth of Nations.

The International Scene

Northern Ireland played a full part in the Second World War. With Eire's neutrality, it provided vital air and sea bases for the anti-U-boat war in the Atlantic in the early years of the war. Churchill expressed his gratitude to Mr John Miller Andrews[400] on his resignation from the Premiership of Northern Ireland in May 1943:

> We were alone and had to face single-handed the full fury of the German attack, raining down death and destruction on our cities, and, still more deadly, seeking to strangle our life by cutting off the entry to our ports of the ships which brought us our food and the weapons we so sorely needed.
>
> Only one great channel of entry remained open. That channel remained open because loyal Ulster gave us the full use of the Northern Irish ports and waters, and thus ensured the free working of the Clyde and the Mersey. But for the loyalty of Northern Ireland, and its devotion to what has now become the cause of 30 Governments or nations, we should have been confronted with slavery and death, and the light which now shines so strongly throughout the world would have been quenched.[401]

35,000-40,000 of Northern Ireland people joined up. When the Japanese surprise attack on Pearl Harbour, Hawaii, in December 1941 brought America into the war, the Government stationed US troops in Northern Ireland and the numbers grew to more than 100,000 ahead of 'D-Day' in June 1944. The Church welcomed the American forces, and the Orthodox Presbyterian Church made an announcement to this effect at their General Assembly in June 1942.

Local industry experienced a temporary boom during World War II as it geared up for the national war effort. It produced a wide range of war commodities, including the strategic manufacture of fighter aircraft, aircraft carriers, warships and munitions. It also majored in naval repairs. The 'Short and Harland' aircraft factory, founded in 1936, built Short Stirling bombers for the RAF. Many war components were made from linen products in both world wars. But Belfast, like many other UK cities, paid a price. Its shipyards and aero engineering industries were the prime targets in the Luftwaffe's blitz of Belfast in April and May 1941 which killed 1,000 people and destroyed or damaged tens of thousands of homes. The city, originally judged to be out of effective range for German aerodromes, was no longer so when Germany occupied France, and local anti-aircraft defences proved seriously inadequate.

One interesting consequence of the war was its effect upon the celebration of the Lord's Supper. In January 1942 Rev. W J Grier drew Council's attention to the shortage of Communion Wine, suggesting that it may be necessary to hold Communion Services quarterly rather than monthly. It was left to each congregation to decide. However, in June 1942, Council did recommend that congregations switch to a quarterly Communion because of the shortage of the branded non-alcoholic wine in use.

Interceding for the Nation

Like other church bodies, the Irish Evangelical Church committed itself to prayer for the nation throughout the Second World War and beyond. Council sent a letter to the King in September 1939 assuring him of the Church's loyalty, interest and prayerful support. The Council meeting in February 1942 provides the standard arrangement: "It was unanimously agreed that Wednesday, March 25 be set apart throughout our churches as a Day of Prayer for the nation and that a United Service be held in Botanic Avenue Church at 3.30 pm conducted by Rev. James Hunter MA; special prayer meetings to be held in all the branches at 8 pm and that posters be placed at all the churches announcing these meetings." When the King appointed 3 September 1942, and 3 September 1943, as Days of National Prayer, Council repeated its March 1942 arrangements. In August 1944 Council arranged a special Day of Prayer and Thanksgiving "in connection with the allied victories" – a reference to the success of the Normandy landings and the subsequent advances. It also appointed Thanksgiving Services throughout the churches on VE Day (Victory in Europe) and VJ Day (Victory over Japan), allocating the VE offerings to the Dutch Reformed Church at Oosterbeek[402], near Arnhem, where the main airborne landings were made, and the VJ gifts to the China Inland Mission Relief Fund.

There was good reason for Days of Prayer to remain a feature of Church life after the war. In March 1947, Council, conscious of its role and responsibility to intercede for the nation in times of peace as well as war, called the Church to prayer:

> Inasmuch as evidences abound on every hand that our own nation has forgotten God and broken His Holy Law, that our Government refuses to recognise Him and that our Churches have to a great extent trampled His Word under foot, we call upon our people and others who may join with us, to humble ourselves, to confess our national sins and shortcomings and seek God's face, that He may have mercy upon us, that He may forgive our sins and heal our land; and we set aside Wednesday April 9 as a Day of Humiliation and Prayer.

Another followed in March 1948, the wording demonstrating awareness of deepening crisis:

> Inasmuch as our nation is in a serious plight – in our national economy we face bankruptcy; in spiritual things our affairs are at a low ebb; moral evils abound; the professing church is weak and has largely lost her message; many of our national leaders are utterly irreligious men and no voice sounds from high quarters in church and state to call the people back to the Book of God and to the Redeemer's blood – in view of these things, we should humble ourselves before God and seek his face on behalf of our land.
>
> We therefore appoint Wednesday 17 March as a Day of Humiliation and Prayer and call upon our people and all friends willing to associate themselves with us to observe this day.

Council called Days of Prayer for the nation and for the international situation throughout the 1940s, 50s and 60s. From 1945, the Cold War between the United States and the Soviet Union, and the arms race that was part of it, was an underlying source of tension.[403] 1948 saw the war between Israel and the Arab States over Palestine. In the 1950s there was the Korean War and the Suez Crisis. International conflict or the threat of it was prevalent in the 1960s, with the Vietnam War, later spreading to Cambodia, dominating the decade. In 1960, the Russians shot down the U-2 spy plane and President Khrushchev slammed the table with his shoe at the United Nations. The construction of the Berlin Wall took place in 1961 and the Cuban missile crisis in 1962. President Kennedy was assassinated in 1963, and in 1974, Turkey attacked Cyprus. The Six Day War in the Middle East was in 1967. The Northern Ireland 'Troubles' came very forcibly onto the prayer agenda at the end of the 60s. All these things engaged the mind of Council and drew the response that only the church is equipped to give.

The Ladies' United Monthly Prayer Meeting continued faithfully throughout the period.

The Presbyterian Journey

In the 1940s, 50s, and 60s the *Irish Evangelical Church* was still in its early years, in a phase of very basic development, and having to re-plot its course. Most of its people had a Presbyterian background, but they found their new Church divergent at several points from the Presbyterian system. The purpose of this chapter is to show how the Church's early leaders progressively adopted the historic Presbyterian creeds, developed Presbyterian structures, terminology and ethos, and integrated with the international Presbyterian and Reformed constituency.

The Westminster Standards
From 1927-1933 the doctrinal standards were the eight *Articles of Faith*. In 1933, in the immediate context of the Dispensationalist controversy, the Church's standards became the Westminster Larger and Shorter Catechisms and the *Articles*

of Faith. This was the first step. Then, more than 10 years later, on 24 March 1944, Council took the major decision to add the Westminster Confession of Faith. It was proposed by Rev. Joseph McCracken, seconded by Rev. W J McDowell, and passed unanimously, that:

> We, the Council of the Irish Evangelical Church, hereby adopt the Confession of Faith of the Westminster Assembly, in addition to the Larger and Shorter Catechisms and the Eight Articles of the Irish Evangelical Church previously adopted, as the standard of faith, and rule of faith and practice for all office-bearers of our church; except that in the passages relating to the civil magistrate we do not receive them in any such sense as to suppose that the civil magistrate has a controlling power over synods or councils with respect to the exercise of their ministerial authority, or power to persecute any for their religion.

It is appropriate to note in recording the adoption of the Westminster Confession in 1944 that the Catechisms and the Confession do not always cover the same subject matters or cover them with similar emphasis. The two are complementary. Good Works, Christian Liberty, Lawful Oaths and Vows, the Civil Magistrate, Marriage and Divorce, Church Censures, Synods and Councils appear only in the Confession. The Catechisms, on the other hand, expound the Ten Commandments and the Lord's Prayer, neither of which is found in the Confession. In dealing with subject matter common to both documents, the Larger Catechism in particular develops some of the Confession's doctrines, such as Christology, Sanctification and the Sacraments. By contrast, the Confession deals at length with the doctrine of Scripture and the Decrees of God, while the Catechisms only touch on them briefly.[404]

So, a major advance in the Presbyterian journey! The adoption of the full doctrinal standard was qualified by the retention of the *Articles of Faith* and by the Declaratory (explanatory) Act with regard to the Civil Magistrate, WCF Chapter 23. The Formula of Subscription was revised at the same meeting to incorporate the new standards, taking account of the Declaratory Act by the expression, "I believe the Westminster Confession of Faith and Catechisms, *as accepted by this Church*, …". This little expression "as accepted by this Church" has rarely caused any difficulty, although it is open to the interpretation *"which this Church accepts"*. Two Amending Acts (by which the text of the Confession is revised) followed in 1968, giving the following three qualifying statements:

1. Chapter XXIII - Of the Civil Magistrate (1944)
   We do not receive this Chapter in any sense as to mean that the Civil Magistrate has a controlling power over Synods or Councils with respect to the exercise of their Ministerial authority, or power to persecute any for their religion.
2. Chapter XXIV - Of Marriage and Divorce (1968)
   We accept all the statements of this chapter except the last sentence of

paragraph IV, which we omit entirely. The omitted words are: "The man may not marry any of his wife's kindred, nearer in blood than he may of his own, nor the woman of her husband's kindred, nearer in blood than of her own."
3   Chapter XXV - Of the Church (1968)
We omit from Paragraph VI in this chapter the following words: "but is that antichrist, that man of sin, and son of perdition, that exalteth himself in the church against Christ, and all that is called God."
The revised paragraph VI now reads:
"There is no other head of the church, but the Lord Jesus Christ: nor can the Pope of Rome in any sense be head thereof. The claim of any man to be the Vicar of Christ, the head of the church, is unscriptural, without warrant in fact, and is a usurpation, dishonouring to the Lord Jesus Christ."

The original requirement for members to subscribe to the first six of the eight Articles was discontinued in September 1952. The *Articles of Faith* were finally dropped from the standards in 1964, although not unanimously. The adoption of the Westminster Confession of Faith and Catechisms made the Articles redundant as a doctrinal standard, but they were a creedal testimony to the theological issues of the Heresy Trial and a special piece of early IEC history.

Developing Forms of Government
The Form of Government of the Irish Evangelical Church, 1930, the single page, 14-point document, which became known as the Code, was developed over the next 20 years. Then, on 21 March 1952 notice of motion was given: "That the Council set forth in writing, for the use of all office bearers, a detailed form of Church Government embodying all the essential decisions of Council." In September 1952, Council unanimously approved a series of Code resolutions grouped in categories, along with several other amendments shortly afterwards. No copies of the printed version of 1952 have been preserved, but a comparison of the minutes of September 1952 - July 1953 with the 'Red Book' of 1964 shows that the 'Red Book' was based substantially on the 1952-53 structure. The additional categories in the 1964 version reflected important changes and developments since 1953. These were the setting up of a new pension fund for ministers and their widows in 1962, and the Training for the Ministry Committee in 1963. In October 1959 Council decided to license students, basing the Formula of Subscription on that for ministers.

The current Form of Government, *The Code of the Evangelical Presbyterian Church*, was adopted in 1982-83 and is a major expansion of the 1964 version. Like any system of law, it requires regular update to reflect new situations and the findings in operation. Ongoing changes were incorporated in revisions of the Code in 1993, 2001 and 2014.[405]

From Committees to Diaconates
Although the 1930 *Form of Government* conceived of government by minister and

deacons, Council accepted that the phasing out of congregational committees would be a process. In fact, it took 30 years. The years in which committees were replaced by Diaconates were:

Knock	1932	Finaghy	1956
Jocelyn Avenue	1936	Somerton Road	1956
Lisburn Road	1937	Ballyclare	1957
Botanic Avenue	1947	Clintyfallow	1960
Crosscollyer Street	1956	Crumlin	1960

The following congregations joined or were established by EPC and appointed their first deacons in the post-committee period:

Omagh	1982	Bangor-Groomsport	2002
Richhill	1989		

Eldership

On 21 November 1952, as part of the Form of Government discussions of 1952-53, Council adopted the principle of a plurality of elders, thereby taking one of the final steps in making IEC a fully-fledged Presbyterian Church. On 17 April 1953 Council agreed that election and ordination would be for life and drew up a formula of subscription based on that for ministers. The years when congregations first elected elders are:

Jocelyn Avenue	1954	Lisburn Road	1961
Crosscollyer Street	1957	Ballyclare	1975
Finaghy	1957	Crumlin	1976
Botanic Avenue	1957	Knock	1979
Clintyfallow	1960	Somerton Road	1989

The dates below reflect a later affiliation of the congregations with EPC:

Richhill	1988	Omagh	1992
Dublin	1990	Bangor-Groomsport	2001

With the gradual establishment of Presbyterian church government through the appointment of local sessions, the strongly centralised form of government that Council exercised in the earlier years progressively devolved to congregations.

Annual General Meeting

The practice of denominational Annual General Meetings began in 1961 – the nearest equivalent of a General Assembly for a small church based substantially in one area. The first was held on 1 June 1961 at Lisburn Road, the church of the new chairman of Council, Rev. A A Campbell. There were reports on finance, Council business, and foreign missions and a panel discussed questions submitted in advance. Rev. A A Campbell gave a closing address.

The pattern of Annual Reports and the Chairman's address became a permanent feature of AGMs and the panel discussions continued until 1970. In 1976 began the practice of inviting delegates to bring fraternal greetings from other churches, the first of these being Dr Hugh J Blair from the Reformed Presbyterian Church of Ireland and Rev. W J Thompson from the Congregational Union of Ireland. The Free Church of Scotland was first represented in 1980, the delegate being the moderator of the 1979 Assembly, Rev. Murdo MacRitchie. In 1979 the AGM switched from a week night to a Saturday with afternoon and evening sessions.

Change of Name
Council, at its meeting 18 October 1963, resolved to change the name of the Church to *Evangelical Presbyterian Church*. This was felt desirable to assert its Presbyterian roots, the adoption of the full Westminster Standards and Presbyterian church government, its membership of a Presbyterian inter-church organisation, and also to express its identify much more specifically than the name *Irish Evangelical Church* could do. On 28 February 1964, after receiving a report from a committee appointed to "examine all the problems and consequences of making such a change", Council drafted a change of name resolution to be put to the Church membership at a meeting in Botanic Avenue, 26 March 1964. Council met after this meeting and inserted the following record in its minutes:

> A meeting of members representing all our congregations was held in Botanic Avenue Church on Thursday, 26 March at 8.00 pm, Rev. W J Grier presiding.
> After devotional exercises and Chairman's remarks, Rev. W J McDowell proposed that "this general meeting of the Irish Evangelical Church, held on 26 March 1964 in Botanic Avenue Church, approve of the change of name of this Church, known since its formation in 1927 as Irish Evangelical Church, from Irish Evangelical Church to Evangelical Presbyterian Church, as from this 26th day of March 1964."
> Rev. A A Campbell seconded the proposal. No other person taking advantage of the opportunity to speak, the proposal was then put to the vote, Messrs Sampson and Blair acting as tellers. 105 affirmative votes were counted – a unanimous verdict.

Presbytery
When Council was re-designated *Presbytery* in November 1980, the Presbyterian journey was complete.

Inter-Church Relations – First Affiliations

The Church re-built its identity not just internally but by integrating with the international Presbyterian, reformed constituency. Inter-Church Relations has been the subject that Council and Presbytery has turned to most often although development was initially slow. In the 1920s and 30s, activity was mostly in the form of letters of greeting and the appointment of inter-church correspondents.

The exception was the Free Church of Scotland with whom the Church had developed close ties in the 1930s through overseas missions and their training of IEC students for the ministry. In April 1943 Council sent greetings to the Free Church to mark its centenary Assembly. In 1945 Council appointed W J Grier as correspondent with the Dutch Reformed Church of the Netherlands.

The International Council of Christian Churches

The World Council of Churches was constituted in Amsterdam in August 1948. While its arrangements were in progress, the American Council of Christian Churches announced:

> The time has come in the providence of our gracious God when a Council of Christian Churches to bear testimony to "the faith once delivered unto the saints," (Jude 3, KJV) and to represent Bible-believing Churches throughout the world should be established.
>
> The projection of the proposed World Council of Churches has given ample evidence that those who believe in an infallible, inerrant Bible and the whole counsel of God revealed therein cannot be a party to that body. Its use in its leadership of prominent Christ-rejecting and Bible-contradicting ministers, its championship of the inclusivist Church displaying complete doctrinal indifferentism with believers and unbelievers partaking of the communion, its union with the Greek Orthodox Churches with their idolatrous mass, superstitious intercession to the Virgin and the Saints, its open invitation to the Roman Catholic Church to join, and its deceptive use of traditional Christian phrases while denying the historic meaning thereof — all combine to project an organisation which will be expressive of apostasy and filled with abomination. The untold harm which such a body will do in misleading the nations, in opposing the pure Gospel, in closing doors to faithful missions and in advancing socialism and political intrigue with the State can hardly be overstated. This situation challenges every Bible-believer throughout the world who desires to lift high the banner of the Cross, and to glory in the precious blood of the Lamb.
>
> ... We ask that Bible-believing Church bodies in true Protestant succession throughout the world send at least one duly authorised representative (more if desired) to a convocation for the purpose of organising and establishing an international council of Christian Churches. The purpose ... would be to adopt a name, to establish a doctrinal standard expressive of the common evangelical doctrines, and to set up a representative democratic body to give a constructive testimony for the Lord Jesus Christ and to stand against the World Council of Churches. Looking to the Lord to provide and to lead, and committing this whole matter into His hands, we name the City of Amsterdam, Holland, August 12-19, 1948, as the place and time of our first assembly.

Dr Carl McIntire,[406] who had helped to form the American Council of Christian Churches in 1941, Dr T T Shields, Toronto, Dr G Ch Aalders, Free University of Amsterdam, and Dr N B Stonehouse, successor to Dr Machen in the New Testament chair at Westminster Theological Seminary, Philadelphia, were among those who attended the inaugural meeting in Amsterdam in 1948. The ICCC strategy was to meet at the same time and in close proximity to the WCC to provide a simultaneous alternative to the latter's profile, agenda, and policy statements. In April 1949 Council decided that the IEC should join the ICCC, and its membership was confirmed in October. Rev. W J Grier, Mr W M Oliver and Mr W A Sampson were appointed as delegates to the second Congress at Geneva in August 1950, at which over 400 delegates from 43 countries were present. Prof. R B Kuiper of Westminster and Rev. F A Schaeffer, since 1948 a missionary in Switzerland of the Independent Board for Presbyterian Foreign Missions, were among those who gave papers. Dr Edwin Kerr represented IEC at the third plenary Congress, 1954, held in a large tent in the grounds of Faith Theological Seminary, Philadelphia, where the theme was "The Historic Christian Faith". Dr Carl McIntire was elected President, W J Grier, a Vice-President, and Mr Norman Porter[407] a member of the Executive Committee.

When the ICCC communicated with Council about its fourth Congress to be held in South America in 1958, Council deferred a response whilst it considered its ICCC membership. The committee that reported to Council on 22 February 1957 stated it was "perturbed and profoundly dissatisfied" with recent developments within the ICCC in America. When ICCC set up a European Alliance in September 1957 W J Grier and W J McDowell were appointed members of its provisional Council, but Council re-stated its dissatisfaction with events in America. However, as ICCC pressed for the names of delegates for the Rio de Janeiro Congress in August 1958 Council replied that financial and manpower constraints prevented participation. ICCC then proposed a meeting in Belfast in December 1958 but Council was only prepared to recognise and announce it, not to give it official organised support. Finally, in March 1959, Council severed its links with ICCC chiefly because of "the dictatorial manner in which its policy was formulated and administered".[408] However it stressed to its members that the Church was not opposing ICCC and that it wished ICCC well. Dr Carl McIntire appealed for reconsideration, but Council felt this to be pointless. So IEC's first international affiliation terminated after 10 years.

Reformed Ecumenical Synod
RES was formed before ICCC, in 1946, at Grand Rapids, USA, when Dr Louis Berkhof was the speaker at the opening service of worship. The founding members were De Gereformeerde Kerken in Nederland (GKN), the Reformed Church in South Africa, and the Christian Reformed Church of America. The following is an extract from the original basis of the Synod:

> The foundation for the Reformed Ecumenical Synod of Reformed Churches shall be the Holy Scriptures of the Old and New Testaments as interpreted by

the Confessions of the Reformed faith, namely, the Westminster Confession, the Thirty-nine Articles, etc. It should be understood that these Scriptures in their entirety, as well as in every part thereof, are the infallible and ever-abiding Word of the living Triune God, absolutely authoritative in all matters of creed and conduct. It has to be emphasised that only a wholehearted and consistent return to this Scriptural truth, of which the Gospel of Jesus Christ is the core and apex, can bring salvation to mankind and effectuate the so sorely needed renewal of the world.[409]

While IEC membership of ICCC was confirmed in October 1949, its involvement with RES pre-dated it, as Council decided in May 1949 to send W J Grier as a delegate to the second Synod in Amsterdam in August 1949. The visit of Dr N B Stonehouse to the IEC in May 1949 is likely to have prompted this. He had attended the first meeting of RES in 1946 as an observer of the Orthodox Presbyterian Church and his favourable report led to the admission of the OPC in 1949. Council records do not give the date of joining but it appears that IEC was one of the churches admitted at the 1949 Synod. There were 25 delegates from churches in four continents in 1949. Dr G C Berkouwer of Kampen preached from Psalm 25.4 at the opening service and Prof. G Ch Aalders was elected president. Although, like others, IEC had an affiliation with both ICCC and RES, the Confessional basis of RES made it a better fit than ICCC. But there was to be disappointment with RES too.

Council nominated three delegates for the third meeting of the Synod in August 1953 in Edinburgh—Revs W J Grier, C E Hunter, and W J McDowell, with Dr Edwin Kerr deputising should this be required. The Free Church of Scotland was the host church and the Synod elected Rev. G N M Collins of the Free Church as its President, Professor N B Stonehouse of Westminster as Vice-President and W J Grier as Second Clerk. Among the items of Synod business were the World Council of Churches, Marriage and Divorce, Racial Relationships, Creation and Evolution, and the 'Post War Migration Movement'. There was a broadcast service from the Synod on the evening of Sunday 9 August 1953 when Grier preached on the Transfiguration. Some, of more mature years, will remember that Grier's congregation in Botanic Avenue, Belfast, listened to the broadcast as part of their own evening service.

Rev. Joseph McCracken represented the Church at the fourth Synod at Potchefstroom, South Africa, in August 1958, and Rev. W J Grier in Grand Rapids in 1963. At the latter, some well-known names were among the officials or 'Moderamen': Prof. G N M Collins, Prof. Fred Klooster and Prof. Herman Ridderbos. Rev. W J McDowell, on the recommendation of his fellow ministers, compiled a statement on 'Inspiration' consisting of quotations from the 1958 RES report, and Council agreed to send copies of *Inspiration* to the 1963 Synod and to some of its constituent members. Regrettably, a copy of the statement has not survived. Grier also attended in 1968 at Lunteren in the Netherlands where Dr Klaas Runia of the Reformed Theological College, Geelong, Australia, was appointed Moderator. Grier's report revealed for the first time developing tensions in the Synod, particularly around the ordination of women and dual membership with the World Council of Churches. The RES story concludes in a later chapter.

British Evangelical Council Organised

The 1940s saw the emergence of ecclesiastical Councils and the 1950s their consolidation. The RES began in 1946, and the ICCC and the WCC in 1948. The British Council of Churches, later affiliated to the World Council, was formed in 1942 with Archbishop Temple as its president. Then, in 1952, as the meeting of the Reformed Ecumenical Synod in Edinburgh in August 1953 approached, the BEC was organised. David Ford, General Secretary in 2002, reflects on its beginnings:

> Was it because of a bad year - the foundation of the World Council of Churches in 1948, or because of God's providence that the BEC started in 1952? Really it was because of both. At the time there was no one who was properly responding to the WCC: the Evangelical Alliance took a benevolently neutral attitude and the militant International Council of Christian Churches led by Carl McIntire was unsuited to the UK situation.
>
> The organisation Prof. Collins, W J Grier and E J Poole Conner initially founded had a cumbersomely descriptive title: 'The British Committee for Common Evangelical Action'. Within about 6 months the stronger title of the British Evangelical Council was adopted. Of this incipient organisation Professor Collins wrote: "The aim would not be to rival existing evangelical organisations but to carry out a task not now being done by any," Still today, the church-based structure of the BEC gives it a unique role.

On 16 January 1953 Grier advised the Council of his own Church of the formation of the new body, of which he was treasurer, and in which ministers of the Free Church of Scotland and of the Fellowship of Independent Evangelical Churches were involved. After a short period of assessment, Council decided, on 31 July 1953, that the IEC should join.

The early years of the BEC were a struggle, financially and in terms of profile and appeal. David Ford notes that its first magazine edited by R A Finlayson survived only six issues. However, an assembly of evangelicals on 18 October 1966 in Westminster Central Hall, organised by the Evangelical Alliance, led to quite a dramatic change in the profile of BEC. That was the occasion when Dr Martyn Lloyd-Jones made his renowned appeal for evangelical unity. The principle he had in mind, as the first stage in a developing process, was a bonding of evangelical churches that would not only oppose ecumenism, but unite in standing for the essentials of the evangelical faith. He considered that the church-based BEC, open to all church bodies that accepted its doctrinal basis and aims, could provide the potential framework. He identified with BEC as a speaker at a large protest meeting in March 1967, and by Westminster Chapel joining the Fellowship of

Independent Evangelical Churches, which in turn belonged to the BEC. So the Lloyd-Jones participation had a massive influence on the standing of BEC in the UK evangelical community.

EPC Council minutes record that at a meeting in London, 2 January 1967, the BEC Council had agreed to start an emergency fund to help ministers and congregations who felt they must secede from their denominations owing to the increasing departure from evangelical truth. It also noted the decision to appoint a full-time secretary, implemented on the appointment of Rev. Roland Lamb, initially on a part-time basis from 5 June 1967, and becoming full-time from the summer of 1968. Reporting on the BEC meeting at Port Talbot 3-5 January 1968, W J Grier spoke of a great increase in support. However, within a few years BEC was finding that the momentum of a heightened period like 1966-67 was difficult to consolidate, as, no doubt, in-house demands absorbed the energies of member churches. The story continues in the context of a later chapter.

Fellowship of Independent Evangelical Churches
The beginning of the FIEC pre-dates the BEC and the international church organisations and, whereas these others emerged in the context of the ecumenical movement, the motivation for the FIEC was inter-church association for independent churches on the basis of the historic evangelical faith. Its founder was Edward J Poole-Connor. As a boy he had met C H Spurgeon and came powerfully under the influence of his writings and of his stand in the 'Downgrade Controversy' within the Baptist Union, 1887-89. After several Baptist pastorates beginning in 1893, Poole-Connor became Deputation Secretary of the North Africa Mission in 1921. As he toured churches in various parts of the country in that capacity he became strongly conscious that they were completely unconnected, and he began to consider the benefits of some form of mutual association. With the help and advice of some friends he formed the Fellowship of Undenominational and Unattached Churches and Missions in November 1922. Within a few years, the title changed to The Fellowship of Independent Evangelical Churches (FIEC) in response to the composition of the developing membership.

IEC invited Rev. John Yuile of FIEC to address meetings, including the Annual Conference at the Clintyfallow congregation, during his visit to Belfast in May-June 1954. When Rev. E J Poole-Connor addressed meetings in Belfast on behalf of BEC in November 1958, it is possible that there was an informal FIEC dimension, for Council appointed Rev. W J McDowell as a delegate to the FIEC Annual Assembly in April 1959 in Glasgow, and again in 1961.

Commemorations
In keeping with its integration with the reformed international constituency, Council was keen on celebrating anniversaries and commemorations and took an important public stance in doing so. On 1 July 1943 in the Botanic Avenue church it held a tercentenary commemoration of the first meeting of the Westminster

Divines. Rev. J McCracken, Rev. W J Grier, and Rev. W J McDowell gave 15 minute addresses on the Puritan Revival, the Divines and their work. Two of these addresses, the Divines and what they believed, were published in the August and September magazines. Another tercentenary service followed on 14 April 1948 – this time to mark the presentation of the Shorter Catechism complete with proofs to Parliament. Rev. W J Grier gave the address in Botanic Avenue and published it as the leader, *Irish Evangelical*, May 1948.

On 13 September 1960, Council organised a Reformation rally in the Wellington Hall, Belfast, to commemorate the establishment by law of the Protestant religion in Scotland 17 August 1560. Rev. Prof. A M Renwick spoke on "John Knox, the Hero of the Scottish Reformation", and Rev. Duncan Leitch, also Free Church of Scotland, on the Word of Authority, the Way of Salvation, and the World Beyond This.

So the Presbyterian journey was complete. It had involved a change of direction and it took time to manage. However, it gave the Evangelical Presbyterian Church the recognised identity that was embedded in its core from the very beginning, and it had taught the Church much. Regarding IEC's own performance during its first twenty years, W J Grier commented:[410]

> We are not saying that in the past twenty years we as a Church have done all we ought to have done. We have not carried the flag to the top of the hill. Yet God has blessed us and prospered us. And we continue to stand for the whole book of God and the whole counsel of God, and for the crown and covenant rights of the God-man, Christ Jesus, the Lord our righteousness.

The next chapter considers other areas of development that were simultaneously in progress.

21

Consolidating the Progress (1940-1967)

Belonging to a church is different from being part of a movement. ... To form a church was to do something different from opposition. A Reformed church would, of course, oppose error and so part of the church's task is to preserve its purity. But a church also has positive work to do, much of it involving the nurture of members, and much of this including tasks that are arduous, not immediately rewarding, and sometimes downright unglamorous.

D. G. Hart, *Between the Times*[411]

Concurrent with the journey to full Presbyterian identity, 1940-67 was a period of progress. Yet in terms of congregations, membership and ministry, there would be much in those three decades in the category of consolidation and maintenance as the Church struggled with too few resources. But quantifiable measures, like numbers, may not be indicators of the faithfulness and spiritual progress that is the church's calling.

As he left for another period of service in South Africa, Rev. Joseph McCracken wrote to the editor of the *Irish Evangelical* on 22 March 1957. His letter gives an important eye-witness assessment of the difficulties of the period, but from the perspective of faith in God:

> The Church is passing through a very difficult period but I believe that God has not raised up this testimony in vain. Let us not be down-hearted but go in and possess the land. May the Head and King of the Church guide the Council. May there be fresh consecration and wider vision, with new approaches to a new situation. Let us not be continually harping on the shortage of man power but try attempting more with what is available. I believe this is the way to blessing. God will raise up other helpers as we attempt new things for Him. Another thing that has warmed my heart is the fact that the Church is fast approaching what she professed to be from the beginning, namely a truly Presbyterian Church.
>
> The Irish Evangelical Church is truly missionary-hearted; this should be encouraged and expanded, *not curtailed*. Herein is another secret of blessing.

In November 1960, a Council discussion indicated ongoing awareness of the difficulties and disappointments of the work: "The general feeling, although not so expressed, was: 'Except the Lord build the house, they labour in vain that build it.'" (Ps 127.1, KJV)

Church Extension: Phase 2

Those looking forward in the 1920s and 30s may have hoped that the initial progress in establishing new congregations would be a future pattern. It was not! The opening of new congregations proved difficult, with years between each of the three phases. The case for separation from ecclesiastical pluralism had little impact on the 'evangelical wing' of mixed denominations.

The first phase was the group of 11 that emerged between 1927 and 1932. The second consisted first in welcoming back the Crumlin congregation in September 1942, after nine years of independence subsequent to the Dispensationalist controversy of 1933. The Finaghy congregation in Belfast began in 1946, as an extension of Lisburn Road, and Finaghy's nearby daughter church, Seymour Hill, in 1965. Phase two was not nearly as distinct as phase one had been, or that phase three would prove to be in terms of new congregations, but the opening of the two congregations did mark the desire to advance and to establish work in suburban communities. On the minus side, there was the closure of Slatehill in 1942 and

Jocelyn Avenue in 1966. It was not until the close of the 1970s that the upturn began.

Ministry Pressures and Progress

An Overextended Ministry

The shortage of ministers was a difficulty throughout the Church's first 50 years and throws light on the consolidating mind-set that has characterised it for considerable periods of its history. The problem was acute for the first 10 years, but eased a little during the next 30. Two ministers served in the 1920s, four in the 1930s and between five and seven in the 1940s, 50s and 60s. Appendix 6 charts the eight additions and eight exits during these three decades, which, with related movements, produced 20 installations. Thirteen ministers served during the three decades and there were 14 sets of double charges (not joint charges, where two congregations are formally linked). Some of them were prolonged, with eight of the 13 ministers involved. C H Garland and W J McDowell had two charges for the duration of the three decades. On top of the two charges situation there were 22 Interim Moderator appointments producing an average of nearly three in each of the 30 years. See Appendix 8. The development of every congregation, with the exception of Botanic Avenue, was limited by these changes or shared ministries.

The Lord's Table – Established Administration

Council appointed ordained officebearers to administer the Lord's Table during the first decade and there was another one-off occasion in 1953. In March 1956, Rev. W W Porter proposed that in future, in accordance with the Westminster Confession of Faith, 27.4, only ordained ministers of the Word should dispense the sacraments. Discussion established that the Confessional requirement was adhered to except in emergency situations, and in the light of this assurance the motion was withdrawn. There is no further record of administration of the sacraments other than by a minister.

The Practical Side

Council also made practical provision for its ministers as far as limited resources permitted. In May 1962, after work by a Pension Committee led by the Honorary General Treasurer, J D P Blair, Council agreed an in-house scheme, *The Irish Evangelical Church Pensions Fund*, and the Church solicitors approved it in June 1962. The question of ministers' salaries was an almost annual item of agenda during the 40s, 50s and 60s. Few today realise how low the salaries were. Until the 1960s they were expressed in monthly terms. The monthly amount was £20.00 in 1947, £40.00 in 1956, and £45.00 in 1958. The annual figure was £700.00 in 1965 and £1,000.00 in 1969. Car and mileage expenses arrangements also developed in the 1960s.

Speakers' Training

The acute shortage of ministers enabled the church to develop the gifts of laymen.

Council had a list of approved speakers from 1933 which it maintained until the late 1940s and, as a mark of Council's commitment to providing the best possible ministry, it set up a fortnightly Speakers' Training Class, also referred to as the Preachers' and Teachers' Training Class. It began in 1947 and ran until 1952 in the Botanic Avenue church. In 1951 Rev. W J McDowell drew up a nine-month course of 18 lectures with focus on the Westminster Confession, and Council appointed Revs C E Hunter, W J McDowell and E H Titcombe to deliver six lectures each. The first six lectures of the 1951 session, which Rev. C E Hunter delivered, were:

'Law' in Scripture
Introduction to Exodus and Leviticus
The Sermon on the Mount
Christ, the end of the Law
The Christian and the Law
Christian Liberty

In February 1952 the subjects were Marriage and Divorce, and the Church, and in March, The Communion of Saints and the Sacraments. The two May topics were "Sheol, Hades and Gehenna" (Dr Edwin Kerr), and "The Resurrection of the Body" (Rev. W J McDowell). This is one of the few instances in EPC history of officebearer and lay training.

Outside Help
The Church received outside help during its early years and in periods of particular difficulty. Ministers of the Free Church of Scotland visited regularly to preach at conferences, missions, and missionary occasions. Revs Hector MacRury (Gairloch), Duncan Leitch (Aberdeen, Kingussie and Dingwall), George Collins (Greenock and Free St Columba's, Edinburgh), were prominent among them. Rev. Peter Jackson (Glasgow-Milton), ministered annually in IEC churches in the summer for seven years from 1953 and contributed articles for the magazine in 1955. Rev. Hugh M Ferrier (Golspie), came in 1956, Rev. Archibald MacDougall (Glasgow-Hope Street) and Rev. Donald Gibson of Glasgow-Govanhill) in 1957, Rev. George C Dunnett in 1958 and Rev. David Paterson in 1962.

Home Missions – Old and New

Though the vast majority of the Church's outreach takes place at congregational level through the ministry of the Word on the Lord's Day, mid-week Bible Studies and Prayer Meetings, special missions, open-air meetings, door-to-door visitation, Sunday Schools, youth and children's work and the distribution of literature, the focus here is on denominational outreach.

Colportage Continues
W J McDowell served as the first Church colporteur from 1929 until he began his studies for the ministry in 1935. R J Hanna assisted him for the first year and Charles H Garland worked with him during his final three months in the summer

of 1935. Mr James Jones became W J McDowell's successor on 15 July 1935. He had been a Presbyterian, but had worked for 5-6 years with Methodist Colportage covering most of the south of Ireland. He resigned that position in 1935 and, with his wife, came to Belfast with the intention of starting up in business. However, he decided to carry on with colportage and so accepted the IEC appointment in which he continued for almost 20 years. His starting salary in 1935 was £2-10-0 per week to cover board, plus "sales at the rate of ⅛ on Bibles and ¹⁄₁₀ on other literature." There were additional allowances for travel. For three months in 1936 Mr Jones worked in Donegal, after paying up to 30% duty on his books. Apart from this, he worked in Northern Ireland, covering all the counties, but concentrating on Antrim and Down during the war years.[412]

For almost 20 years Mr Jones reported on his work to Council at four-week intervals, and extracts from his reports appeared in *The Irish Evangelical*, under the title *From our Colporteur's Chronicles*. These extracts demonstrated well-constructed, detailed reports, statistics of visits, sales, and dates. They majored on accounts of door-to-door conversations, encounters, and his tenacious attempts to get Christian literature into homes. He went to all ages and classes of people and all religious groupings, with a direct evangelistic approach. Sometimes his sales were "exceedingly good", and when all else failed he tried to sell a text card.

As he began, he commented about the value of his work: 'Colportage Work—of what use?'

> When I presented my books to a lady she remarked that, if she wished, she could get these things when she was in town. I told her she would hardly get books in town so good as those I was showing to her. In reply she told me that when she went to town she was not thinking of buying books such as mine. She bought two of the Shilling Series. It came to my mind that there are many like her who wouldn't think of buying a religious book except someone came to their very doors with them.

He visited huge numbers of homes, sometimes up to 1,000 per month. He worked a lot among Roman Catholics and sold many Douay Bibles and New Testaments. He met a Spiritist minister, Russellites, Seventh Day Adventists, members of the Society of Friends, Cooneyites, British Israelites and disciples of Tom Paine. Doors closed to him in Londonderry in 1937 when the local priest warned against him from 'the altar', but he just moved to Tyrone for a time. He met indifference, but noted in May 1941 in Co Down that the air raid evacuees from Belfast were seldom indifferent. In it all he saw professions of faith. He noted 'A Good Opportunity' in August 1935:

> It was at the Royal Black Preceptory demonstration at B——. With the assistance of three Christian friends carrying parcels on their bicycles I was able to show a nice variety of Bibles, etc. During the afternoon we had an open-air meeting. There were five speakers. A hymn was sung between each message,

a solo was also sung and a portion of Scripture read. For over an hour we had an attentive audience, and just before singing the doxology an invitation was given to those who wished to come forward and accept a copy of "Safety, Certainty and Enjoyment" or "God's Way of Salvation." Thirty-two copies were given out in this way. We waited on God before going out and with grateful hearts we thanked Him when we came home for all the way He led.

He coped with all kinds of weather and moved from district to district within counties. In October 1941 the chimney of the house where he was staying in Co Down caught fire, but he escaped with his wife and children and possessions. They lived as 'nomads' until they secured another house. He was not always well, and there were references to his health in the summer of 1937, in 1949, and again in 1950. In October 1950 he had an operation for recurring stomach trouble and was off for a couple of months. In 1938 his wife spent some time in hospital.

In December 1939 he paid a visit to Rathlin Island, off the north Antrim coast:

Forty-four of the homes were Roman Catholic. In them he sold Testaments and Gospel portions, also Calendars with Scripture texts, and copies of Uncle Tom's Cabin. In the few Protestant homes (there are only about 25 Protestant inhabitants) he sold the Pilgrim's Progress, Scripture Motto Cards, and W. J. Patton's "Pardon and Assurance" and "How to Live the Christian Life." In his report he writes, "Some of the Roman Catholics were very suspicious. This, I take it, was due to the visit of two women a few years ago selling Russellite literature to Protestants and Roman Catholics. Very seldom do they visit Roman Catholics on the mainland." If the people had no money, he presented them with their 2d. booklets.[413]

When Mr Jones resigned in March 1954, Council expressed its thanks and good wishes.

From 1 February 1959 Council appointed Mervyn Oliver, a Botanic Avenue deacon, as temporary colporteur. During his year in the work before going to the Indian mission field in April 1960, he provided five reports to *The Irish Evangelical* on his home visits, conversations, battles with the cults, and literature sales. His first, *At Work in Co Antrim*, recounted his ministry in the Crumlin area where he cycled 300 miles. The other two had no location references, but he remained largely in Counties Antrim and Down.

This concluded the Church's 26 year effort in the field of colportage, between 1929 and 1960. The magazine carried two advertisements for a colporteur in 1962, but they did not lead to a new appointment.

Home Missionaries
Miss Eileen Miller, Finaghy, grew up wanting to be a missionary nurse in Africa. But during her nursing training in London (1956-59) and theological studies at

the South Wales Bible College (1962-64) God, by various providences, directed her to the Republic of Ireland. She spent her two years with the European Missionary Fellowship (1965-67) in Dublin doing door-to-door work, speaking at open-air meetings, visiting convents and a home for single mothers. She also did relief at the EMF Bookshop. In 1967 she married James Anderson of the Reformed Presbyterian Church and, aware of their burden for the west of Ireland, the RP Church sent them to Galway to begin colportage work. They developed their role into friendship evangelism through home Bible studies, Sunday School, talks at the Brownies, annual campaigns, outreach to the Galway races, and introducing CEF materials to many convent schools. They formed a group of varying numerical strength which continued to grow after their return home in 1987.

In 1958 Miss Amy Watson, Ballyclare, became Child Evangelism Fellowship's first full-time member of staff in Belfast. In April 1969 she moved with CEF to London where she served for a further five years, first in Wimbledon, then in Hounslow and, for her final few months in 1974, in Shrewsbury. She worked to develop CEF's literature programme – selecting, ordering and distributing books and materials and managing a stand at the annual Keswick Convention. While at Hounslow she helped to run a Good News Club to which mostly Sikh children came with the support of their parents. Some of them even accepted the invitation to attend Children's Day at the local FIEC church. The Lord blessed her work with CEF and she saw significant growth in its literature resource during her service. She returned to Ballyclare in 1975.

Provincial Open-Airs
In May 1956 Council gave permission to Rev. Warren Porter to engage in 'itinerant' Saturday afternoon preaching and literature distribution in provincial towns. Newry was an early venue: "Viewed by a wondering crowd we preached the gospel and distributed quite a number of tracts before proceeding to do house-to-house work in a nearby village. At the Newry meeting there were about 120 people standing to listen." Rathfriland, Donaghadee, Groomsport, Carrickfergus, Rathcoole and Hilltown followed in the summer of 1956. The small team found it "both disappointing and satisfying – disappointing because various circumstances prevented our getting as far afield as we had wished, and satisfying because we found open-air preaching to be appreciated by many of the hearers and stimulating to the preachers."

The Evangelical Book Shop
The Evangelical Book Shop is another aspect of local involvement and outreach. It opened in 1926 under the auspices of the Bible Standards League. Following the Heresy Trial three of the six Trustees resigned from the Presbyterian Church and after discussion it was agreed that the three who had left the church, Dr John R Gillespie, Rev. James Hunter and John J Patterson, should take over control of the shop, and responsibility for its liabilities. Through them the Shop became

closely linked to the IEC. The trust deed stipulates that only members of the Irish Evangelical Church are eligible to become trustees.

The trustees worked closely with Council, informing of trustee appointments and other significant matters. Rev. W J Grier was Superintendent of the shop until 1958, although with reduced involvement after the appointment of Mr S G Shanks as Manager in 1951. The shop operated with a deficit in its early years and in 1948 Council made a £500.00 bequest available to the shop at a favourable rate of interest. By the 1960s Council was thanking the shop for its generous contributions to the Central Fund. In 1939 the Book Shop took its first stand at the annual Royal Ulster Agricultural Show, "The Balmoral Show", and continued the practice until 2008.

From the beginning, Church and Shop, although separate entities, have complemented one another's spheres of witness. The Church's 40th anniversary booklet expressed the bond: "The Church has a Book Shop at 15 College Square East …" The bookshop provided an orthodox alternative to the prevailing liberalism of the 1930s and 40s and has developed this position since, reflecting the Church's reformed position. It has acquired significant influence throughout the British Isles and in other parts of the world. In addition, the shop has been the Church's corporate address, it has provided a forum for communication and has supplied various categories of practical support such as the distribution of the magazine. W J Grier wrote in October 1930: "Not only does the Book Shop exist for the sale of a particular kind of literature – it forms a 'rallying ground' for members of our church … In this way the Book Shop has acted as a connecting link in the work of the Church and as an information bureau."[414]

Foreign Missions – Free Church of Scotland

Work overseas was a distinctive element in the development in this period. A comprehensive but diverse overseas missions policy marked the initial phase, but during the second half of the 1930s co-operation with the Free Church of Scotland began. The Church sent its first missionary, Dr Harold Lindsay, to the Free Church mission in Peru in 1937 and introduced Free Church Mission Boxes in the same year. Congregations maintained their breadth of worldwide missionary participation, and during the 1940s they regularly consulted Council about meetings and conferences. Council supported appeals for refugees and the victims of poverty. Pastor Émile Guedj, French Bible Mission, spoke and sang in IEC-EPC churches almost annually until 1969,[415] and Reformation Translation Fellowship[416] representatives visited in the 1950s and 60s.

However, the growing involvement with the Free Church dominated the overseas missions agenda in the period. The missionaries contributed to church planting and evangelism, and to medical, educational, orphanage, construction and social programmes.

Dr Harold and Mrs Flora Lindsay	1937-1954	Peru
Rev. Joseph and Mrs Helen McCracken	1944-1974	South Africa

Miss Annie J Dunlop	1944-1974	India
Miss Annie Wilkinson	1948-1953	Peru
Miss Florence I Donaldson	1951-1985	Peru
W M Oliver	1960-1963	India

Missionary conferences and magazine articles of the period focused on the work of these missionaries and there was regular Free Church representation at the missionary meetings. In 1944 Rev. W J McDowell was appointed Free Church Foreign Missions Representative in succession to Rev. Joseph McCracken. Rev. C E Hunter took over the role in 1958 and Mr W A Sampson succeeded him in 1965. In 1945 Rev. W J McDowell went as a Foreign Missions delegate to the Free Church General Assembly, the first IEC delegate to the Assembly, and later that year he and Mr S G Shanks joined the Foreign Missions Committee. For some years from 1959 the *Irish Evangelical* printed a Foreign Missions Financial Statement of contributions to the Free Church Missions by congregation, sometimes categorised to Mission Boxes, Collections, Donations, Sunday Schools, and Prayer Meetings – the amount in 1959 was £918. In 1963 the first 'Feed the Hungry' (re-named 'Help the Needy' in 1983) offering took place and it was directed to the need in South Africa. In 1966-67 a project of the Young People's Association raised £1,700 to purchase a Land Rover ambulance for the Indian Mission.

In 1949 the Free Church published *Missionary Enterprise*, an outline of the work in its three mission fields and, in 1962, its young people produced the first edition of *Labourers Together*, a prayer manual for the missions in the three continents and the work among the Jews, along with details of missionaries and their national colleagues. It was re-published as a larger and more comprehensive edition in 1970.

Youth Work - Becoming Established

Youth work operated at congregational level from the beginning. Although it engaged Council's attention from the 1930s it was not until the 1960s that it came to fruition denominationally.

Boys' and Girls' Camps 1939-1968

Camping was an integral part of the denominational youth history. The account of the early years has appeared in Chapter 18, *Gaining a Foothold*. Boys' camps began in 1939, girls in 1953, and they remained separate camps until 1978. The boys were usually under canvas, and the girls in church or community halls. Jim Grier and Willie McDowell were the ministers who put up the first tent and were the first leaders, 1939-1941. In the following years Bertie Howard replaced Willie McDowell. The first sites were at Brown's Bay, a small sheltered beach at the north of Islandmagee. The names of other camp sites were written on the inside top of the original 'week-end' brown box – Kilkeel, Ballywalter, Carnlough, Tyrella. Miss Elsie Gale led the Girls' Camps, 1953-1966.

During 1949-50 Jim Grier was off for 10 months with pleurisy and the break suspended his camp leadership. Edwin Kerr, Finaghy, took over, assisted by "a number of capable lieutenants", among them George Dunn and John Stafford, Crosscollyer Street. The *Pathfinders* for boys began in September 1950 and became a good camp recruitment ground. In 1952 a large marquee with tables and chairs provided a real upgrade. It had been the Church's Gospel outreach tent, 1934-1940, but perished at Tyrella during a storm in 1957. Much else remained the same – paraffin primus stoves went on immediately after breakfast to boil the large quantities of potatoes for lunch. Records of camp development phases and locations are in Appendix 18.

Conferences and Bible Class
Rev. W J Grier started a Young People's Meeting in 1941 for the school leavers age group and during the 1940s it met alternately in Lisburn Road and Botanic Avenue. From 1942 they held 'Annual Anniversary' services in June each year which the young people of other congregations attended. Missionary speakers were prominent on these occasions – Rev. Max Orr of the China Inland Mission spoke in 1947 and Dr Harold Lindsay in 1948. In October 1950 Council approved its re-designation as a Young People's Bible Class and advertised it for the Belfast congregations with an age group of 17-35, meeting in Botanic Avenue on Monday evenings. In 1950 they studied Galatians, in 1951-52, the Second Coming, and in 1952-53, the Doctrines of the Church of Rome. By 1950 the class was already an effective means of spiritual development. In its earlier days the young people took turns in reading papers and received training in leading the meeting. It continued until the late 1950s. Miss Florence Donaldson, who attended from September 1944 until she went to Peru in 1951, regarded it as a vital part of her training.

The young people of Crosscollyer Street organised a series of annual conferences from 1944 to 1955, usually with a missionary as one of the two speakers. At the opening one in October 1944, the first of its kind in the history of the Church, Miss Murdoch, for many years a missionary in Egypt, surveyed the work among Muslims. Miss Christina Mackay, Colegio Anglo-Puerano, Lima, was the missionary speaker in October 1950.

Sunday School Lessons
Council applied itself to Sunday School lesson material during the 1930s, and in October 1940 Grier addressed a Sunday School Teachers' Conference on "The Preparing and Imparting of the Lesson". Another benchmark followed in September 1941 when Council appointed a committee, consisting of one representative from each Sunday School and Rev. W J McDowell as Convener, to select lessons for the coming year. The choice was the *Church Sunday School Lesson Book*, No 1, with lessons selected by the committee. The four in the series were used in sequence 1942-47.

In April 1947, Grier drew up a course of 37 'lesson helps' for the 1948 Sunday School year – 28 from the Old Testament and 9 from the New. He selected lessons, mostly from the Books of Moses and the Gospels, that had not featured recently or at all. A panel of five ministers and Mr W A Sampson enhanced it with supplementary notes. Having used Grier's lesson material in 1948 the Committee reverted to Church Sunday School Lesson Book (No 3) for 1949. In August 1949 the Committee advised Council that the Sunday School Lessons had been completed and 72 sets were ordered for the Sunday Schools for 1950. It appears that this was phase 2 of the in-house programme and consisted of 34 lessons covering Joshua to 1 Samuel and the Gospels. 200 bound copies were produced. Grier's illness may have affected the preparation of material for 1951, so selected lessons from CSSLB No 4 became the syllabus that year.

With just two exceptions, Council appointed the four-year *Church Sunday School Lesson* series from 1952 until the introduction of *Go Teach* and the *Child's Story Bible* in 1976. One exception was 1955-56, when Council selected lessons from "the two sets previously used". The second was in 1966-67 when the syllabus was the "34 lessons prepared by our ministers some years ago" (later referred to as the *Evangelical Lesson Book*). With Rev. W J McDowell as editor, the committee prepared 102 sets with revised notes or 'helps' for them. In 1956 Council approved the formation of a Sunday School Teacher's Association, but it did not develop.

Youth Organisations

The 1950s also saw moves to develop youth organisations. In August 1950 Council approved the commencement of an organisation for boys over 12 – 'The Pathfinders'. It was held in the Lecture Hall of Botanic Avenue, its first meeting on Wednesday 13 September 1950. The format was a series of games concluding with an epilogue. Edwin Kerr, Finaghy, was the first leader and, when he moved to England in 1953, George Dunn, Crosscollyer Street, took over. 'The Young Pathfinders' for boys 8-11 began in September 1951. In October 1950 Council also approved 'The Girls' Own' for teenagers, led by Mrs Catherine Grier, which met in Botanic Avenue on Tuesday evenings. On 14 August 1952 Mrs Helen McCracken sent grateful thanks to the 'Girls' Own' for a parcel of knitted garments, telling of the appreciation that the people of the church in South Africa had expressed. These youth organisations operated at least until 1956.

Dr Kerr addressed the Tuesday evening Youth Rally at the General Assembly of the Free Church of Scotland in May 1956 about IEC youth work. He outlined the Church's difficulties with its youth work, acknowledging that it had not yet found a solution that was acceptable across its membership. Seeking progress towards the solution, Council in January 1957 tackled the question of uniformed youth organisations and commissioned Rev. Warren Porter, who had raised the matter, to investigate. His report expressed a preference for the Boys' Brigade, but Council decided to leave the decision to individual congregations. Following this, *Campaigners* began in Crosscollyer Street and Finaghy in 1960, and in Somerton Road in 1961, and continued through most of the decade.

Young People's Association
Joseph McCracken's 1935 motion to commence a Young People's Association (YPA) did not fail permanently. The subject returned to the agenda 30 years later in May 1965: "The possibility was discussed of organising some kind of Young People's Fellowship which would allow young people from all congregations to meet from time to time. The idea received unanimous hearty approval." In April 1966 Rev. W J McDowell outlined a basis for a YPA and Council appointed a committee of young people from several congregations, with Rev. W J Grier as Council Representative. Perhaps the youth conferences in Crumlin in October 1963 and 1964, at which most congregations were represented, demonstrated the need for development. They certainly built on the joint youth conferences and meetings in Crosscollyer Street and Botanic Avenue-Lisburn Road in the 1940s and 50s. Rev. W J McDowell wrote in November 1965 on *Biblical Teenagers* – on such teenage 'squares' as Joseph, Daniel and his friends!

The Irish Evangelical – Tributes and Change
Council's Tribute
From mid-1949 Rev. W J Grier was off work for 10 months with pleurisy. In September 1949, Council passed a unanimous resolution, proposed by Rev. E H Titcombe, regarding the *Irish Evangelical*. It is a commentary on the magazine's contribution to the building of IEC identity:

> WE, the members of Council, desire to record thanks to Almighty God for the witness of our monthly magazine, The Irish Evangelical, the first number of which appeared in June 1928, and which has completed twenty one years of service.
>
> IN this we have to record our indebtedness to the Rev. W J Grier BA and our appreciation of his able editorship, who has kept the testimony of the magazine since its inception true to the Reformed Faith.
>
> THE great Christian truths, from the foundational fact of the Divine Inspiration of the Holy Scriptures, have constantly been reiterated, and the trumpet sounded in Zion against doctrinal error and heresy.
>
> NOT only have our own congregations benefited, but also readers in England, Scotland and abroad. Thus the witness of the Irish Evangelical Church has become known and has been blessed through the influence of our periodical.
>
> OUR prayer is that Rev. W J Grier may be strengthened by the Spirit to continue by his pen to exalt the Lord Jesus, to the blessing of His church.
>
> WE link herewith the able services of Mrs W J Grier, who since 1934 (then Miss Gillespie) has conducted the Children's Page of the magazine on the same high level.

30 Years of Circulation
The magazine celebrated 30 years of circulation with a special issue in May 1958 which included the text of 13 messages of greeting from various parts of the world:

Rev G N M Collins	Free Church of Scotland
Rev R Strang Millar	Editor, 'Evangelical Presbyterian', New Zealand
Prof Dr W Stanford Reid	McGill University, Montreal
Dr D Martyn Lloyd-Jones	Westminster Chapel, London
Rev Timothy Tow	Bible Presbyterian Church, Singapore
Rev W R McEwan	Bible Union of Australia
Dr David Hedegard	Mjölby, Sweden
Prof Dr G Ch Aalders	Heemstede, Holland
Rev Joseph McCracken	Free Church, South Africa
Dr N B Stonehouse	Westminster Theological Seminary, Philadelphia
Prof Martin Monsma	Calvin Seminary, Grand Rapids, Michigan
Bishop D A Thompson	Bognor Regis, Sussex
Rev E J Poole-Connor	Editor, Bible League Quarterly

These messages spoke of the magazine with warm appreciation and thankfulness, noting its faithfulness to Scripture, devotional spirit, commitment to the reformed faith, and its awareness of ecclesiastical developments throughout the world. Dr David Hedegard's comment was representative: "We need very much such Christian journals as *The Irish Evangelical*. The Lord bless its esteemed Editor and all its readers." Space does not permit the insertion of each of these appreciative greetings, but the contribution from Dr Lloyd-Jones is of special value:

> I am happy to send a word of very warm greeting on the occasion of the 30th anniversary number of the Irish Evangelical. I look forward to its coming month by month with great pleasure. It always seems to me to have the ideal blend as regards matter — theology, devotional element, first-class book reviews, pungent comments on current affairs, biographical material, and choice extracts from the writings of the masters. The industry and versatility of the Editor astound me more and more. May he and the magazine continue under the blessing of God to help us and enrich our lives, and stimulate us to continue in the good fight of faith without wavering for many years to come.

The Evangelical Presbyterian

The *Irish Evangelical* became the *Evangelical Presbyterian* in June 1964, the beginning of its 37th year, to reflect the Church's name change in March 1964 and to take account of feedback from mainland readers that the old name suggested local interest. There were 12 issues a year until June-July 1976 when it reduced to 10. A browse through a bound volume shows the colossal work involved. The Grier family life was built around its schedule. The magazine continued its themes—exegetical, devotional, evangelistic, historical and missionary, and applied a rigorous polemic to world ecclesiastical affairs. There were regular items of IEC news. Book reviews always featured, with the back page allocated to the Evangelical Book Shop advertisement. One of its enduring qualities was the wide variety of contributors, local and international.

The Children's Page Stories
Mrs Grier wrote the Children's Page from her brother's death in 1934 until the final issue of her husband's editorship in May 1981. The page carried stories from church history, overseas mission work, competitions, acrostics and superb 'parables'. *The Red Candles,* April 1956, is an example. These two special candles were chosen for the candle-lit Christmas supper. They were proud of their role and disappointed when it was over. They were then forgotten about until an electricity strike brought them to the homework table. After it they were about burnt out, which made one of them very unhappy. But the other assured his companion that they had really been indispensable – a candle is only useful as it burns itself out! John the Baptist, the "burning and shining lamp" was the application. (John 5.35) Real shining for Jesus means burning out as well. "Are you willing to give up anything for him?"

Council Committees Begin

In comparison with Presbytery agendas from the mid-1970s onward, Council activity in the 40s, 50s, and 60s was often light and, whilst they were difficult decades, the substantial preparatory work that took place in them laid the basis for the advances in later years. Council had decided in June 1930 not to have permanent committees. However, the need for continuity in issues like finance, pulpit supply and student training, nudged Council towards standing committees almost as soon as it decided not to have them, and a committee trend soon became apparent. A Foreign Missions Committee was appointed in 1938 with evidence of some continuity, and the Annual Minute Book Inspection Committees began in 1944. However, the first Standing Committee was the Training for the Ministry in 1963, followed by Public Questions in 1964 (renamed Public Morals in 1977).

Training for the Ministry Committee and Fund
Council/Presbytery has engaged with great frequency with Training for the Ministry. The first reference to it was in October 1930 in relation to the application from H H Murphy. During the next 33 years the references were mostly in connection with the first group of member-students during the 1930s, followed by one in the 1940s and another in the 1950s. Trial Sermons and early forms of Council examinations for students in training were in force from the 1930s and Council set up a Board of Examiners for Students in January 1939. There were 12 years in which there was no mention of training. However, on 13 September 1963, Council made a significant decision regarding the Church's future ministry in setting up the Training for the Ministry Committee:

> On the proposal of Rev. A A Campbell, seconded by Rev. C H Garland, it was agreed (1) that the Council institute a Training of the Ministry Committee, (2) that a fund for the training of young men for the ministry be inaugurated, (3) that the Church should keep before it the necessity of encouraging young men of our membership to enter the ministry.

Rev. W J McDowell proposed that the Training for the Ministry Committee consist of Messrs Campbell, Hunter and Garland, with Mr Campbell as Convener. This was passed unanimously, Mr Sampson seconding.

The Committee's procedures, including an annual gift day, were approved in October 1963 and the resultant increase in prayer and financial support soon bore fruit in the third and largest phase of students for the ministry. The Training for the Ministry Fund set up in 1963 received annual support from most congregations, although Council felt obliged to urge increased giving from time to time.

Public Morals
Council was active in this field before the appointment of the Public Questions Committee in 1964. For example, it sent a resolution to the Chancellor of the Exchequer with copies to the press in April 1956, opposing the introduction of Premium Bonds:

> We, the Council of the Irish Evangelical Church, deplore and protest against the proposal of Her Majesty's government in the recent Budget, to issue Premium Bonds in which an element of profit by chance is involved. We believe that such action would be contrary to the principles of honesty, industry and generosity set forth for us in the words of Scripture – "Let him that stole steal no more, but rather let him labour with his hands that he may have to give him that needeth." (From Eph 4.28, KJV) We believe, too, that the issue of these Bonds by Her Majesty's Government would discourage true thrift, and promote the idea that rewards can be obtained without effort. This proposal, if carried out, would, when taken in conjunction with the Small Lotteries and Gaming Bill, constitute a retrograde step in the life of our nation.

On the related subject of Betting and Lotteries, Council passed the following strongly worded resolution in May of the following year:

> We deplore the proposal to amend the Laws on Betting and Lotteries in a way which would have the effect of legalising gambling. We regard this as a very serious social and moral menace to the life of our Province. We regret the utter failure of the authorities to implement the present laws against gambling, and we regard the amendments proposed as a condoning of, and legalising of what should be stamped out. We feel it is our duty to our whole membership to make our attitude and theirs plain on this important matter.

The resolution was sent to the Press and to interested MPs. In October 1961 Council passed a resolution urging the Government of Northern Ireland to retain the death penalty for murder, and its just administration. In the national arena, Council took note in January 1967 of the good work being done by the Viewers and Listeners Association (VALA) in seeking to check the growing tendency towards indecency and irreverence in television and radio. Council agreed to distribute the organisation's literature. This faithfulness and courage played its part in inhibiting decay and in bringing the light of Scripture to bear on local and national life for its benefit. "You are the salt of the earth; ... You are the light of the world" (Matt 5.13-14)

The Lord's Day
The commitment of Church and magazine to the sanctity of the Lord's Day gives the subject a special place in the field of Public Questions and Morals. From the beginning, Article No 8 of the *Articles of Faith* had made the Day of specific doctrinal standing – "The Lord's Day is hallowed by a perpetual command of God … and a special blessing attaches to the land which keeps holy the Lord's Day." Until the 1950s the Church's teaching and support came largely through regular articles in the *Irish Evangelical*. A change came in October 1951, however, when the Secretary-elect of the Lord's Day Observance Society (founded in 1831), H J W Legerton, came to Belfast and organised a local branch of the LDOS. Since then Council adopted a more prominent public role, working with successive local secretaries, Alistair MacKenzie (1951-55), Samuel McCrea (1955-57), and particularly with Mr John A Fullerton who held the position from 1957 until 1980 when ill health necessitated his retirement.

In 1952 Council wrote to the Ulster Automobile Club protesting against the decision to hold the *Circuit of Ireland* rally over Easter week-end. However, in May 1957 the letter from Council was one of appreciation of the Irish Football Association's stand against Sunday football. It requested the Association to reject a resolution tabled for its AGM that would permit World Cup Sunday football matches to be played outside Northern Ireland, and permit individual players to play on Sundays outside Northern Ireland. The IFA decided by a huge majority to maintain its total ban on Sunday fixtures, but later agreed that the Northern Ireland team could play Sunday fixtures in the World Cup Finals in Sweden in 1958. The IFA maintained the ban on Sunday football for almost another 50 years, until 28 November 2007.[417]

In 1958 Council wrote to the Parks Committee of Belfast City Council protesting against the proposal to have Sunday band recitals in public parks, and appointed two representatives to the Belfast Sunday Observance Vigilance Committee. The Sunday band recitals did not proceed. The following month Council protested to the Belfast Town Clerk against the opening of children's play centres on Sundays. The letter received good publicity in the press and through the BBC. In September 1964, when the Belfast *News Letter* announced the publication of *Sunday News* early in 1965, Council sent a letter of complaint. In July 1966 the EP editor gave examples of "serious inroads" into the Lord's Day, concluding: "So the old landmarks disappear."

One of the magazine quotes during the period was from Dr John 'Rabbi' Duncan: "Never since our Lord honoured this day by His resurrection do I believe has the day passed without some absolute gain to His kingdom." The June 1937 issue noted the two *Rules for the Sabbath* from Dr Charles Hodge's *Systematic Theology* – the design of the commandment, and the precepts and example of the Lord and of his apostles. In October 1947 the editor wrote under the title, *Did St Paul Abolish the Sabbath?*, in response to correspondence in the local press arguing that Colossians 2.16-17 abolished the Sabbath. Grier contended, among other things, that the Lord's Day or Christian Sabbath was not 'the sabbaths' in view in this text because, unlike the Jewish ceremonials Paul was discussing, *it* was not "a shadow of things to come."

Finance

By 1941 the level of the Central Fund income was still a concern. For the first time on record, the treasurer, Dr Gillespie, listed the contribution from each congregation; Knock, Rev. James Hunter's congregation, produced 55% of the total at that time. So Council decided that each treasurer should submit a quarterly Central Fund statement, that Committees and Deacons' Courts should discuss the situation, and that congregations should pray over it.

Throughout the 1940s Central Fund contributions showed a general pattern of increase although expenditure regularly exceeded income. In January 1948 Council decided to use the 1947 contributions from each congregation as a base, and asked each to aim at increasing by 25%. This was a departure from the previous principle of congregations deciding their own level of contribution, and the first attempt at the target system which became a standard feature of Church financial strategy from the 1980s. Council's concern over the Central Fund continued throughout the 1950s and 60s. A modest credit balance was usually maintained, but the level of income suppressed ministers' salaries unacceptably. There is no doubt that this financial constraint was a major factor in the all too frequent loss of the services of ministers. In 1954 Council decided to distribute a summary of Council's Financial Statement throughout the membership. The first denominational Annual General Meeting was in June 1961 and following it Council circulated 500 copies of the Financial Report. General circulation of this report became a standard practice from then.

Widows and Orphans Fund

In August 1940 the Treasurer reported that a lady had given £8.0.0 to start a Widows and Orphans Fund, and Council decided to establish the Fund. The *Irish Evangelical* made it known and by the end of the year receipts totalled £13.0.0. Income tended to be low, so that at the end of 1943 the Fund stood at £23.5.0, and at the end of 1945, £40.0.0. This Fund, and the Ministers' Pension Scheme, were administered as part of the Central Fund under separate headings, but in May 1959 Council decided to open separate bank accounts for them.

The 'Hunter Trust'

In April 1941 James Hunter set up the John Robinson Hunter Trust Fund to supplement the salaries of Church employees. The Fund consisted of stocks and shares he had acquired from the estate of his brother John Robinson Hunter who died in August 1939. The Fund has grown through wise investment by succeeding trustees and their professional advisors and has achieved, to the present day, James Hunter's salary-supplement objective.

Church Extension Fund
On 19 April 1957, the editor of *The Irish Evangelical* received a letter from a correspondent, under the name *Presbuteros*, offering to contribute £50.00 to a Church Extension Fund if 20 others would do the same within two months. Council accepted the proposal and published the letter in the magazine. When *Presbuteros* stated in August that his offer would stand even if the total contributors fell below his stipulated number of 20, Council decided to set up a Church Extension Fund with separate banking arrangements. This is how the Fund began.

The Grammar School Syllabus

The Church's major local involvement, 1940-1969, was its leading role in the protest against the Grammar School Syllabus in Religious Instruction of 1948. Council passed a resolution, 19 November 1948 and copied it to the Prime Minister, the Minister of Education NI and the Press:

> We protest emphatically against the type of religious instruction for secondary schools appearing in the new syllabus and in the textbooks and handbooks recommended therein. We desire to express our unqualified rejection of such teaching which regards the Bible as an unreliable book containing contradictions, myths and "layers of folk tales". Realising our responsibility to our children, we are determined to expose the soul-destroying character of this teaching to the people of Ulster and are resolved to use all legitimate means to secure its withdrawal.

The Irish Evangelical Lead
Under the title *A Terrible Menace*, the *Irish Evangelical* of November 1948 drew up the battle lines. The Syllabus had been "prepared under the direction of a Conference representing the Church Boards of Education (Church of Ireland, Presbyterian, Methodist) and the Secondary Teachers' Associations, and published by the Conference with the approval of the Joint Board of the Churches." The article attacked this Syllabus for its espousal of the Wellhausen school of Higher Criticism and as a menace far more serious than attacks from Romanism or Communism. It said that it would be infinitely preferable to ban religious instruction in schools.

The subject dominated the December issue with seven separate articles. The leader, "Christians, Awake!", used the SOS terminology of 1926 to ask in its bold sub-heading: "Are our Secondary Schools to be the seed-beds of Rationalism?" The articles quoted from the Syllabus and recommended textbooks, demonstrating a sceptical view of Scripture, with regard to matters such as the Mosaic authorship of the Pentateuch, and the authorship of Isaiah, Zechariah, and Daniel. The accounts of creation and the flood were said to be contradictory. The records of the serpent of Genesis 3, Cain and Abel, the crossing of the Red Sea, the stories of Samson, Balaam's ass, and Jonah were presented as folklore, parables, symbols, or fables. Adam and Eve and Noah were not even historical figures. The leader of the January 1949 issue continued the exposure under the title *An Entirely Different Bible*, dealing with a further range of Syllabus recommended textbooks. The article concluded: "May God save the youth of our Province from this tide of unbelief." The February and March 1949 issues also carried major articles.

Widespread Public Protest

The Syllabus's attack on the authority and infallibility of Scripture and on the historic Christian faith, generated powerful protest within Northern Ireland. The December *Irish Evangelical* drew the attention of parents to their rights, under Section 21 of the Education Act (Northern Ireland) 1947, to have their children excused from religious instruction. On 15 November 1948 a protest meeting, with Rev. W J Grier as chairman, filled the Lisburn Road Irish Evangelical Church. The meeting passed a unanimous resolution similar to that of the IEC Council on 19 November and appointed a committee to carry on the campaign. A *Great Protest Meeting* followed on 19 December, after church, in the main YMCA Building. The advertising leaflet, *Danger Ahead!*, asked: *Do you wish the Children and Youth of Ulster taught as follows?* What followed was a digest of the unbelief of the Syllabus and its textbooks. About 3,000 people attended, necessitating overflow meetings in the YMCA Minor Hall and in the open air, in front of Belfast City Hall. Mr Harry Brown of the China Inland Mission presided over the Minor Hall meeting, and among the speakers at the City Hall were Mr Norman Porter and Rev. Ian Paisley. All three meetings passed the following resolution, with only one dissenting voice:

> That this meeting of citizens filling the Wellington Hall, Y.M.C.A., Belfast, begs to inform the Minister of Education of their determination – so far as it may lie within their power – not to suffer their children and youth of this Province to receive the type of religious instruction in the Grammar School Syllabus and books recommended therein.
>
> This meeting is not impressed with the argument that the use of this Syllabus is not compulsory – the Syllabus is issued with the approval of certain representatives of the three largest Protestant bodies and with the assistance of the Local Education Authorities, and will no doubt on that account be adopted by most Grammar Schools.
>
> This meeting repudiates the right of the clerical and lay representatives of the Conference which prepared the Syllabus to prescribe for the Protestant children of Ulster a type of teaching which impugns the authority of the Word of God and is altogether out of line with the belief and testimony of the historic Christian Church.

This meeting recommends parents to withdraw their children from religious instruction in the schools wherever such text-books as those quoted in accompanying leaflet are used—unless and until sound religious instruction is assured.

This meeting of citizens requests that this Syllabus be withdrawn.

By January 1949, public meetings were held in Bangor, Donaghadee, Lisburn and Omagh, and later in Coleraine, Lurgan, Armagh, Antrim and Banbridge. On 30 November 1948 a local Senator described the Syllabus as: "a most damning piece of work to have been produced and handed over for the instruction of children in Protestant Grammar Schools in Northern Ireland, especially during what one might describe as the four most important years in the life of a boy or girl." An article, *Turning the Bible Topsy-Turvy*, appeared in several Provincial newspapers.

Syllabus 'Revision'
The Minister of Education, since 1944, was Lieutenant-Colonel Samuel Hall-Thompson. He had introduced a major Education Bill in 1945 which applied the essential features of the English Education Act, 1944 (the Butler Act), to Northern Ireland when it became law in 1947. This Act generated 10 years of argument with both Protestant and Catholic constituencies, neither of whom approved it. However, the Minister of Education agreed to receive a deputation from the Protest Committee on 28 January 1949. The deputation of 20 represented 12 churches or societies, and a petition with 23,000 signatures requesting the withdrawal of the Syllabus, was handed over. However, the Protest Committee could only report on the very unsatisfactory nature of the Minister's written response. They received an undertaking to revise the Syllabus; however, the Committee feared that the revisions would not amount to more than the addition of some conservative textbooks to the recommended list. Still, on the strength of the commitment to the revision, the Protest Committee ceased its public protests.

The *IE* article of March 1949 was entitled, *The Battle Goes On*, but the meeting with the Minister largely concludes the Grammar School Syllabus story. The *Battle* article urged tenacity: "If this protest is going to carry weight, it can do so only with the wholehearted, prayerful, intelligent support of Christian people throughout the length and breadth of this province." Folded inside W J Grier's own annotated copy of the Syllabus there are seven pages of typed notes, addressed as a letter to Mr F Jeffrey, the Syllabus Editor, which began: "Knowing that the Syllabus Conference is engaged in revising the Syllabus we feel it our duty to point out the parts of the Syllabus to which we take exception. You have stated that helpful criticism would be welcomed. Our desire is to be helpful." In December 1949, Rev. W J McDowell, acting editor of the *Irish Evangelical* during Grier's illness, finished his review of the situation, saying: "Let us be watchful. The Old Syllabus may be published again with a new cover."

From this point the Syllabus topic disappeared. Perhaps the Christian community felt that whatever the revision would bring, it was the best they could achieve. No doubt, also, events in the political sphere intervened. In January 1950, Lieut-Col. Hall-Thompson resigned as Minister of Education, owing to a disagreement with the Prime Minister, Lord Brookeborough, over an education policy. In October 1953 he lost his Belfast, Clifton seat which he had held since 1929, to the Independent Unionist, Mr Norman Porter, who had campaigned against the Syllabus.

Rev. W J McDowell addressed the questions on Scripture that arose in the Syllabus controversy in a booklet, *Have we a Reliable Bible?*, published April 1949. Such questions were:

Are there discrepancies in the Scriptures?
If it is for the inspiration of the original autographs we contend, what of translations like the Authorised Version?
Are the Scriptures inspired in matters of fact and history as well as in spiritual truth?
Can we believe in verbal inspiration?

McDowell also wrote the similar booklet, *The Incomparable Book*, published in 1988.[418]

The Free Presbyterian Church of Ulster

This new body began its witness in March 1951 in Crossgar, Co Down. The Presbyterian Church of Ireland withdrew its grant of the local Presbyterian Church hall for a Gospel mission in February 1951 and suspended the elders who did not accept the ruling. These elders and others seceded from the Presbyterian Church of Ireland and, working with Rev. Ian R K Paisley, the mission evangelist, they set up the Presbytery of the Free Presbyterian Church. The Church had four congregations in its first year and by 2012 had grown to more than 100 congregations and extensions in various parts of the world. It trains its ministers, missionaries and workers at its *Whitefield College of the Bible* in Belfast. The Church has a world-wide radio ministry, *Let the Bible Speak*. Articles of Faith, together with the Westminster Confession of Faith and the Larger and Shorter Catechisms, form its subordinate standards. On the mode and subjects of baptism "each member of the Free Presbyterian Church shall have liberty to decide for himself which course to adopt on these controverted issues ...".[419]

Free Presbyterian Forefathers, the opening chapter of *Our Own Heritage*,[420] which, with acknowledgement, leans heavily on W J Grier's *Origin and Witness*, outlines the background to the Heresy Trial of 1927. Rev. James Hunter and W J Grier are included with the 'Forefathers'. The Bible Standards League and the founding of the Irish Evangelical Church "outside the camp" (Heb 13.13, KJV) also feature prominently in the story. *Our Own Heritage* claims a direct link with 1927: "During that period people made a complete break from the Apostasy,

315

while others dithered and remained within. ... It pleased God to move in 1951 and start this new witness outside the camp of apostasy. Many of those who failed to separate during the days of Rev. James Hunter came out in 1951 to join the Free Presbyterian Church."[421]

Visiting Speakers

Rev. W P Nicholson, whose campaigns in the 1920s influenced the founding of the Irish Evangelical Church in 1927, conducted two weeks of meetings in the Wellington Hall, Belfast, 2-16 March 1947. The Hall was not available for his final week and Botanic Avenue IEC was willingly granted. The church was packed to capacity each evening, as was an overflow in the Lecture Hall from the third evening. On Sunday morning, 23 March, Nicholson spoke on "The Unequal Yoke" (cf 2 Cor 6.14), dealing with compromising relationships in business, social life or marriage, with a word on divorce. One IEC member, then a boy of six, has a vivid recollection of people sitting on the pulpit steps and benches lined along the aisles. Over 1,000 people were packed into the Church and Lecture Hall an hour before the evening service and hundreds were turned away. Substantial numbers of seekers waited for spiritual help each evening and a number of Botanic Avenue and Lisburn Road adherents professed faith in the Saviour.

Dr N B Stonehouse, Westminster Seminary, Philadelphia, visited in May 1949 and spoke at a conference, the Lord's Day services, and at a meeting of the Graduates' Fellowship. Other Faculty members came too – Edward J Young in June 1958 and Leslie Sloat in July 1962.

Early Anniversaries

Council led the Church in celebrating a series of the Church's anniversaries. At the 20th, 11 October 1947, Rev. G N M Collins, Free Church of Scotland, was guest speaker and Rev. W J Grier spoke on the Church's origin. At the 25th, in Botanic Avenue Church, 11 October 1952, Rev. A R Fraser (Dumbarton Free Church) spoke on Proverbs 23.23 – "Buy the truth and sell it not". Grier recalled the *Chat Noir* meeting, 25 years before, and the decision to form the IEC. Some present in 1927 were also present in 1952. The Church published a semi-jubilee booklet, *The Irish Evangelical Church – WHY?*, by Rev. W J Grier. It reviewed church history from the 17th to the 20th centuries and summarised the charges of heresy brought in 1927.

The visiting speaker, as at the 20th anniversary celebration, was Rev. Prof. G N M Collins, Free Church College in Edinburgh, with whom W J Grier had developed a strong friendship. "Prof. Collins expressed the privilege he felt in being invited. There were those who, no doubt, expected the cause to die out quickly, but 'having reached your fortieth birthday you can use the words of Charles II, and apologise for being such a long time in dying.'" He spoke on Psalm 60.4, KJV, "Thou hast given a banner to them that fear thee, that it may be displayed because of the truth." There was a *Conflict* raging that began in Eden when the Devil insinuated that God's word might not be true, and then openly denied it. In the Conflict there was a *Commitment* – the Banner was given to those that feared God. There is the certainty of a *Coming Conquest*.

At the 30th anniversary, Botanic Avenue, 3 October 1957, there were three speakers: Rev. W J Grier – Our Beginnings in the Past, Rev. W J McDowell – Our Witness in the Present, Rev. C E Hunter – Our Hopes for the Future. Mr McDowell declared that the Church had 10 congregations and buildings compared with none in 1927. However, he said, more regular attendance at all the means of grace, greater enthusiasm, and more zeal for the Lord's cause were pressing necessities. At the meeting, Council presented Dr Gillespie with an easy chair in appreciation of his 30 years' service as Treasurer. In thanking Council later, he included a word of disavowal, but Rev. Stuart Law, Knock, commented that "they would have all been deprived of very real pleasure had the presentation not been made." The 30th anniversary booklet was, *WHAT IS The Irish Evangelical Church? What does it Believe and Practise? Why does it exist?*

The 40th anniversary took place in Botanic Avenue on Tuesday 10 October 1967.[422] The chairman Rev. W J McDowell said that the Church "had endeavoured during the past forty years to maintain and proclaim the Christian Faith in its purity, and at the same time act graciously toward all men." Rev. W J Grier recalled the decision of 15 October 1927 to form the Irish Evangelical Church and its early house churches. He spoke of Rev. James Hunter, "an able man, scholarly and devout," the decisive Heresy Trial vote at the General Assembly, June 1927, and about "some of the few" who had left the Presbyterian Church and formed the new body. The Presbyterian Church in Ireland kindly sent a letter of greeting and good wishes.

The 40th Anniversary Booklet was *The Evangelical Presbyterian Church – Why does it exist? For what does it stand?* The Booklet's three sections were: Its Origin, Its Witness, and Its Aims. The Witness section was closely aligned with the original Eight Articles but was more specific in the areas of Divine sovereignty in election, the perseverance of the saints, the resurrection and the spiritual unity of all believers. The Aims covered calling the nation back to the Bible and the need for Christian principles in its life, true ecumenical unity, missionary activity and the work of the Evangelical Book Shop. There were also warnings against the dangers of departure from the historic Christian faith, and the desecration of the Lord's Day.

"These Forty Years"

The 40th anniversary report by Rev. W J McDowell appeared in the *Evangelical Presbyterian* of November 1967. He took his title, *These Forty Years*, from Deuteronomy 2.7, KJV: "For the Lord thy God hath blessed thee in all the works of thy hand: he knoweth thy walking through this great wilderness: these forty years the Lord thy God hath been with thee; thou hast lacked nothing." Mr McDowell was a precise theological thinker and he would not have taken his title from this text just because it contained the words "forty years". For him, the passage would have to be exegetically appropriate. In it Moses reviewed the 40 years of desert history and applied its lessons to the future in Canaan. The Lord had blessed them in the day to day responsibilities and practicalities of life. He had watched over their difficult, wearisome journey through that vast wilderness so that they had lacked nothing.

So the text was an apt summary of the Church's first 40 years. They had been extremely difficult years, with limited numerical advance and resources, but always with the Lord's presence, provision, and preservation. But the passage was appropriate for the Church's future too, for Moses in his addresses essentially looked forward. To him, history prompted this, for it demonstrated the unchanging, covenant love and power of God alongside the demands of human responsibility. Just as the people of Israel were on the threshold of new potential for service, so was the Evangelical Presbyterian Church as it moved into the 1970s.

22

Paying Tribute (1940-1967)

The Wings of Prayer

A prayer written by Rev. James Hunter and believed to have been offered by him at an IEC Ordination Service

We praise Thee, O God, for the Life Eternal given to us in Thy Son, Christ Jesus our Lord. We praise Thee, O Son of God, who didst empty Thyself that we might be filled unto all the fulness of God. We praise Thee, O Holy Spirit, Inspirer of prophets and apostles, that Thine anointing is upon us to tell the glory of our Redeemer.

O God of our salvation, let the good news of this salvation be proclaimed with the fire that has come down from heaven. Thou, O Christ, who dost baptise with fire, and who didst send at Pentecost the heavenly flame, when thousands were converted—convert thousands and tens of thousands through us.

Bring us near the Cross, that we may see the gore, and behold the darkness, and hear the cry of anguish, and listen to the word of triumph—"It is finished." (John 19.30, KJV)

Come Thou into our presence ever, O Risen and Enthroned One, breathe on us and say, Receive ye the Holy Spirit: whose soever sins ye remit, they are remitted unto them; and whose soever sins ye retain, they are retained. Say unto us: As My Father sent Me into the world, even so send I you into the world.

Thou, tenderest Jesus, who didst warn of the terrors of the world to come, and who dost give an elated heart in prospect of the joys of heaven, let the goodness and severity of God be set forth in all the love and power of the Holy Spirit.

Spirit of the Lord God, be upon us, and upon these, because Jehovah hath anointed us to preach good tidings to the meek, He hath sent us to bind up the broken-hearted, to proclaim deliverance to the captives, the opening of the prison to them that are bound.

Saviour, because Thou art gone to the Father, the works Thou didst do, and greater than those, are done now by Thine own who believe in Thee. All power in heaven and earth is Thine, and Thou every day art with those sent by Thee.

Give us times of refreshing from Thy presence greater than ever Thou hast vouchsafed. And fill Thy holy Church with a longing for Thine appearing. While we are yet speaking, do Thou hear us—in the name of Jesus.

Rev. James Hunter (1863-1942)

James Hunter died on Lord's Day 20 September 1942, in his 80th year. Pastor Minnis Millis recorded in his diary on 22 September: "Rev. Hunter laid to rest to await the resurrection morn. I would like to have attended but the funeral was strictly private. Rev. W. J. Grier, McCracken, McDowell, C. E. Hunter and C. H. Garland took part."[423] He was buried in Dundonald cemetery in the grave where his sister Maria and brother John R had been laid to rest, and not far from where his sister Catherine Trimble Gillespie and his nephew James Hunter Gillespie had been buried. So in death, as in life, they were a closely united family. His last Council meeting was 24 November 1939, and the joint National Day of Prayer meeting of 3 September 1942 is likely to have been his last denominational engagement. In the gracious providence of God he had the pleasure of seeing Council welcoming the Crumlin congregation back into IEC membership two weeks before his death. The arrangements for the meeting between Crumlin and Council representatives were made with him by telephone.

Some 170 written examples of his sermons appeared in the *Irish Evangelical*, 1928-1942. Structurally they were not often characterised by a distinct demarcation of headings, for he tended to move almost imperceptibly from one point to another. In terms of content they were doctrinal, devotional and encouraging, increasingly mellow in his closing years. They were marked with applications from history, his own experience and, from time to time, from the wonders of insect life in which he clearly had an interest. The leading article of the October 1942 issue carried an account of his life and witness under the title, "Whose Faith Follow" (Heb 13.7).[424] Its conclusion summarised the period since the formation of the Irish Evangelical Church:

> From that day he was among us in this Church a wise counsellor and leader, a faithful friend, an able minister of the new covenant, an unflinching defender of the faith. From 1928 until his death he acted as minister of our Knock congregation.

The Council Memorial Minute included the following:

> We, the Council of the Irish Evangelical Church … desire to express our sorrow and sense of loss that we feel, because of the death of our beloved leader the Rev. James Hunter MA … We wish to put on record our thankfulness to God for the grace given to Mr Hunter to "earnestly contend for the faith which was once for all delivered unto the saints" (Jude 3, KJV) in a scholarly and courteous manner. … We wish also to praise God for the generous heart which He gave to Mr Hunter. He subscribed largely to many evangelical causes, being deeply interested in the work of Foreign Missions, which field of labour he considered in his youth, only turning from it on medical advice. His generous subscriptions to all our congregations, and the Central Fund of our Church were always hidden under anonymity. We are today the poorer, and so also is the Church of Christ on earth, because of his absence.

Dr John Richard Gillespie

The contribution of Dr Gillespie and his family to the beginning and building of the Irish Evangelical Church has been traced in the preceding chapters. When he suffered the massive blow of the death of his son James Hunter Gillespie in 1934, his response was spiritual. His special role in the Church was as Honorary General Treasurer from 1927 until his death on 29 July 1960, aged 88. The Council Memorial Minute recalled his conversion in his youth, his brilliant academic and medical career, his missionary service in China, his part as a foundation member of the Irish Evangelical Church and his generosity in the service of Christ's Kingdom.

Mr James A Kell

Mr Kell fulfilled the demanding role of Clerk of Council from May 1931 until March 1935, taking over from Rev. W J Grier, the first Clerk. Mr Kell died suddenly on 2 March 1952 after a period of poor health. He had been an elder in Knock Presbyterian Church when Rev. James Hunter was minister, and one of the members of the Belfast Presbytery in 1927 who supported Mr Hunter. He was a foundation member of Knock IEC and became a deacon in 1932.

Mr John J Patterson

Apart from Rev. James Hunter, John Patterson was the only 1927 accuser to hold office in IEC. He was an elder in the Knock congregation of the Presbyterian Church during James Hunter's ministry. He attended the Fountain Street meetings with his wife Rachel and daughter Ruth (Ray) in 1927-28 and all three were signatories of the original Articles of Faith. He served as a member of Council from the beginning until his death in January 1940, and was one of the three laymen appointed in 1937 to ordain deacons. He was a foundation member of the Knock congregation and was elected to the diaconate in 1932. In April 1939 Ruth married Rev. Murdo Nicolson who had been serving with the Free Church of Scotland in Cajamarca, Peru since 1935. They transferred to Colegio san Andrés in Lima in 1940-41 but resigned from the mission in 1944 and moved to Canada.[425]

The First Four Ministers

Earlier chapters have recorded the training and ordination of the first four men who were called to the ministry from within the membership.[426] They each served the whole of their ministries in IEC-EPC, with the exception of Joseph McCracken who became a missionary but retained his Church bonds.

Charles E Hunter ministered in seven churches. Only in 11 of his 38 years did he have a single congregation. There was one year when he had four churches, there were six in which he had three, and 20 when he had two. In addition he was Interim Moderator on seven occasions, one of them seven years. He was Foreign Missions Representative 1958-1965 and Chairman of Council five times. He had a strong devotional spirit, spending much time in prayer in his study, always on his knees. He was a faithful teacher and diligent pastor. From 1983 until his death in 1986 he lived in London with his daughter, Elrose.

Joseph McCracken had two early overlapping ministries. He had had the work of missions increasingly on his heart and when Rev. Gregor Macleod and his wife were lost at sea through enemy action on the way to the mission field in South Africa in 1943, he felt the call to take his place. He arrived with his wife Helen, née Stewart, and daughter Anne in December 1944 and served the Xhosa Church in the Eastern Cape for 30 years with another 13 in retirement, ministering successively in various 'District' groups of churches. He constructed or renovated 13 church buildings and was manager of 12 mission schools. He died in 1987 in East London.

William McDowell spent over 52 years in the ministry after six years as a colporteur. He was minister of five congregations and it was only during his last three years that he had a single charge. He played a vital role in the 'hard' years. In mission, youth-development, administration, writing, teaching and preaching, his contribution to the Church was massive. In particular he was a prolific writer, producing magazine articles and booklets. He was Chairman of Council seven times, Clerk of Council for 15 years in three spells, and Correspondence Clerk for five years. With W A Sampson he drafted and produced the 1964 Form of Government - the 'Red Book'. He also served as a Trustee of the Evangelical Book Shop for 24 years. He was a meek, self-effacing man, ready to bestow honour on others. He died after a short illness in 1991.

Charles H Garland served for 39 years in the ministry and was minister of three congregations. He always served two congregations simultaneously with substantial spells as Interim Moderator. He was Chairman of Council 5 times. He marked the month of his ordination, September 1940, with a Magazine article on *The Prodigal Son*, describing it as "the crowning parable of all Scripture". It declared the great love for the Gospel and for people which so strongly characterised his life's ministry. He was greatly gifted in the whole field of pastoral work, such as visitation, correspondence and giving encouragement, and many profited from his diligent, gracious contact. He maintained a ministry-long interest in missions. He died in 2003, aged 95, after a long, very Church-related retirement.

W J Grier

It is also a suitable point to update the W J Grier story.

The Person

His personal qualities came to life in a gracious personality and bearing, making him eminently approachable. He was commonly referred to as 'a Christian gentleman'. He had read widely and conversed easily on many subjects, particularly theology and the text of Scripture – during walks at camp in the 50s and 60s it was a privilege to attach to him and ask him questions. He read the Hebrew Psalter annually, and campers can remember him reading his Greek New Testament every morning after breakfast.

His own public prayers identified him as a man of prayer. Again and again he used the expression from Solomon's temple dedication prayer: "Hear thou from heaven thy dwelling place" (1 Kings 8. 30, 39, 43, 49; 2 Chron 6.21,30, KJV). He supported those who took part in the prayer meeting, semi-audibly praying with them and for them – and how they felt that help! He was not musical – to the extent that he was tone deaf. Still, he said that he felt he put more into praise than some who were musical – an important insight into engaging in the praise of God. He was nevertheless interested in music, always, for example, concerned to choose Psalm tunes from the right classification. If the set tune was unfamiliar, he requested an alternative from the same or closely similar group, such as Plaintive, Prayerful, Cheerful or Jubilant. He published in the magazine short articles on congregational singing from Calvin, Whitefield and Spurgeon.

He was undoubtedly Unionist in his personal political convictions. His father and brothers signed the 1912 Ulster Covenant, but he was too young. Dr J R Gillespie also signed it in Rathfriland in 1914 on his return from Hampshire. As a graduate Mrs Catherine Grier was a member of Queen's University Unionist Association and their eldest son James was later prominent in student Unionist politics at Queen's too. However, on principle, Jim Grier never became a member of any political party. He worked closely with the leader of the Independent Unionist Party, Norman Porter, but while some church members worked in Mr Porter's political campaigns, Jim Grier's support was limited to the ballot box.

He did not encourage membership of the Loyal Orders (Orange or Black) as he felt that the Orange Order had a dubious beginning after the Battle of the Diamond, near Loughgal, Co Armagh, in September 1795.[427] However, he was not averse to taking the family to watch the annual 12th demonstration on the Lisburn Road, near the Church there. He was always keen to accept the opportunity to preach the Gospel to large crowds such as Orange services. He was essentially a theological Protestant, speaking and writing on occasions for the Protestant Truth Society.

Marriage

During 1943 the long-term friendship between Jim Grier and Catherine Gillespie developed into courtship. She went by train to visit him on holiday on the north coast and when they were walking on the Shepherd's Path above the Giant's Causeway she accepted his proposal of marriage. So after many years' acquaintance but only a few months' courtship they were married by Rev. Joseph McCracken in the Knock Church on 12 October 1943. Catherine's bridesmaid was Bea Shaw (later Mrs Anderson) and the best man was Bertie Howard. The bride's father gave her away and she commented afterwards that he was the only one left of the whole circle in which she had been brought up and which had been so precious to her. Indeed, she would have found it difficult to marry someone who had not known her brother so well. Jim and Catherine were both Classics graduates of Queen's University, Belfast but the centre of their deep unity was their strong commitment to the *Irish Evangelical Church*, arising out of their mutual devotion to God. They honeymooned in Dublin as wartime restrictions precluded travel further afield and, as their train moved out, church members in an adjacent garden waved them off with a tablecloth!

Knockdene Park South

Jim and Catherine lived with Dr Gillespie at 28 Knockdene Park South in the Knock area of east Belfast. There was some initial difficulty in living four miles from the Church in Botanic Avenue but as the congregation began to spread out after the war, the four miles ceased to be a factor. And as the Grier boys settled into local schools Knockdene Park became established as the family home. It also became a focal point of denominational hospitality. The Gillespies had entertained Dr Machen there in 1932, and the Griers his successor, Ned B Stonehouse, in 1949. Other Westminster members of faculty followed, Edward J Young in 1958, Leslie Sloat in 1962 and John Murray in 1967. Visitors came regularly from the UK mainland, the United States, France, and from several other countries of the world. The family Visitors' Book has preserved an interesting record. From 1943, for the 35 years that remained of his ministry, Jim Grier was able to give freely of his services to the Church.

Jim Grier enjoyed family life and the whole of his ministry profited from it. One of its early products was the publication of two books, *The Momentous Event* in 1945 and *The Origin and Witness of the Irish Evangelical Church* in 1948. Family prayers were at breakfast in the earlier years, but later moved to after tea. Within his demanding church and magazine schedule there was proper recreation in the form of participating in sons' games, holiday golf, swimming in the sea. He liked walking – he was slim and wiry and walked at the speed of most other people's trot – and Saturday afternoons brought family walks along the Lagan or across Dunlady with a visit to the sweet shop thrown in. In the garden, he cut grass, made bonfires, mixed compost, grew some fruit, and built walls. There were family outings to Donegal, the Antrim Coast, Ward Park in Bangor, and Tollymore Park in Newcastle. *Carrig Eden*, the Christian Endeavour holiday home in Greystones, Co Wicklow, was a favourite post-Easter venue for some years. The *Daily Telegraph* crossword and Scrabble were regular indoor pursuits and he was always patient with the noise of his boys outside his study on wet or winter days.

He enjoyed very good health except in 1949-1950 when he was off work for 10 months with pleurisy. In the late winter/spring of 1950 he and Mrs Grier went to North Africa, as the doctor would not allow him to resume work without a substantial stay in a warmer climate to recuperate. They toured Morocco for 3 weeks seeing much of local culture, and then stayed in Hope House in Tangiers, living with missionaries of the North Africa Mission such as Dr Harold St John and Misses Higbid and Harmon. They both formed a very high opinion of the dedication and outstanding perseverance of these NAM staff in their difficult work. Indeed they continued to take an interest in the work and kept in contact after the ladies retired to Edgware.[428]

The Leader-Elect

The period 1927-39 had been one of unrelenting pressure for him. He was Superintendent of the *Evangelical Book Shop*, minister of two congregations, and Editor of the *Irish Evangelical* monthly. In addition, the emerging congregations of those years made strong demands upon his time and energy. He had very good fellowship with a group that included the Speers, the Shanks, the Gales and Thomas Swann, and his visits to the Gillespie home were a welcome weekly event. Nevertheless, he lived in digs, and was practically without like-minded colleagues until the first students for the ministry returned from Edinburgh in 1935. But intense as these years were, under God they were outstandingly fruitful. The bookshop staff shared the nightly duties of fire-watching during the war. One night when the air raid warning sounded Jim Grier jumped on his bicycle at his digs on the Lisburn Road and headed into town. He felt he was labouring at the pedals more than usual but it was only when he reached the half-way point of Shaftesbury Square that he realised his landlady had stretched a tablecloth over his bike to dry!

The Leader

The 1920s and 30s were his training and development years but the 1940s, 50s and 60s were in a special way his decades. When James Hunter died in 1942 a key leadership role in the still very young denomination devolved more fully on Grier, and God equipped him for it. The battles of the 1920s had taught him to strengthen himself in the Lord, and he developed courage, alertness, and a commanding presence. He was indefatigable, he worked quickly and achieved objectives. The addition of a ready mind and powerful memory-recall made him formidable in debate. His leadership extended into the field of inter-church relations, reformed organisations, and particularly the Banner of Truth in which he became an advisor in 1957 and later a trustee. He was involved in setting up the Leicester Ministers' Conference in 1962, was its co-chair with Professor John Murray 1967-71 and principal chair 1972-79. He gave the opening address 1969-79. He was treasurer of the Belfast branch of the Evangelical Library that opened in January 1955. He was also a busy correspondent with missionaries, Dr Martyn Lloyd-Jones, Free Church and Orthodox Presbyterian Church colleagues, and magazine contacts. Regrettably, he kept virtually none of his voluminous correspondence, which means we are very thankful to Dr Machen for his retention of the Machen-Grier set. Through the magazine and inter-church relations he was well known and enormously respected throughout the international reformed constituency.

There is no record that he received a call other than the one from Cape Breton Island in 1926 that he declined in the interests of the battle at home. He was appointed in 1929 as minister of the congregation that became Botanic Avenue where he ministered throughout his life. In spite of his leadership and other gifts he was free from the desire for pre-eminence. He loved and admired his colleagues, his attitude towards them a living commentary on Paul's great injunction of Romans 12.10: " ... in honour giving preference to one another". His early colleagues Joseph McCracken, Charles Hunter, William McDowell and Charles Garland had perhaps a special place with him. He encouraged articles for the magazine from all his fellow ministers, some of whom became regular and greatly appreciated contributors.

The Preacher and Teacher

At the early Lisburn Road-Botanic Avenue Young People's Bible Class he delivered vital training to the ladies who served the Lord as missionaries abroad without a Bible College training – Nan Dunlop, Florence I Donaldson and Annie Wilkinson (Mrs Blair). Miss Ella Ball, also a member of the class, served in the Evangelical Book Shop from 1942-1975. Dr Edwin Kerr came to the reformed faith through the teaching of the class and went on to have a major influence throughout his academic career in a number of parts of Britain.

Grier was an earnest, serious, expository preacher and teacher. He always knew his subject, delivering substantial sections of his sermons without reference to his notes and engaging powerfully with the congregation. His facility in quoting Scripture from memory as he preached was remarkable. His passion for souls was vigorously evident in the pulpit and it characterised the whole of his life. Whenever he saw large crowds such as those at a sporting occasion, he would long for them to hear the Gospel. He loved open-air preaching and regarded funerals as a particular Gospel opportunity. The same desire fuelled his organisation of the Church camps and the Book Shop stand at the Balmoral Show from 1939. When he visited he gathered the family for reading and prayer – prayer that was full of the Gospel. Whenever he tested his open-air amplifier he did it with Gospel texts.

He preached on selected texts, sermons which often featured as the leader in the magazine, but also preached series and addressed topical questions.[429] He was fond of quoting Question and Answer 1 of the Heidelberg Catechism[430]: *What is your only comfort in life and death?*

> That I am not my own, but belong—body and soul, in life and in death—to my faithful saviour Jesus Christ. He has fully paid for all my sins with His precious blood, and has set me free from the tyranny of the devil. He also watches over me in such a way that not a hair can fall from my head without the will of my Father in heaven; in fact, all things must work together for my salvation. Because I belong to Him, Christ, by His Holy Spirit, assures me of eternal life and makes me whole-heartedly willing and ready from now on to live for Him.

He could narrate the *Pilgrim's Progress* from memory. He preached and spoke regularly away from home, at Free Church of Scotland Communions, the Strathpeffer Convention, the Cotswold Fellowship at Lancaster and at

Westminster Chapel. He attended Inter-Church conferences and took his turn as a delegate to Foreign Missions night at the Free Church General Assembly. He conducted a series of meetings in Free St Columba's, Edinburgh, in 1946. Inter Varsity Fellowship meetings were a regular part of his agenda.

The Author and Reviewer

His work as an author of books, booklets, articles, tracts, Daily Readings and Calendar Notes is listed in Appendix 13. In addition to his publications he wrote articles for the *Christian Graduate* and *The Banner of Truth*.[431] In his years as superintendent of the Evangelical Book Shop (1926-1958) he developed an extensive knowledge of Christian books, importing publications from Eerdmans, Presbyterian and Reformed, and Baker in the United States to supplement the works of British publishers. He was a prolific reviewer and a regular contributor of book reviews to the magazine. He said in the introduction to *The Best Books* – A Guide to Christian Literature[432]: "What a privileged position we occupy! The ages lay their tribute at our feet. ... An effort is made in this little volume to set the 'goodly land' before students of the Word today and to lead them to the choice of the best pastures." He was Editor of *The Irish Evangelical/Evangelical Presbyterian* 1928-1981, producing 625 issues including several series of articles.[433] At intervals throughout those years he kept alive the themes of the Church's founding and of separation, by articles, re-prints and references. He looked forward to writing a life of Calvin during his retirement, but declining mental powers during those years prevented this.[434]

Part 4 - The Evangelical Presbyterian Church

23

Developing in Troubled Times (1968-1989)

Therefore, my beloved brethren, be steadfast, immovable, always abounding in the work of the Lord, knowing that your labour is not in vain in the Lord. (1 Cor 15.58)

Paul commends the believers for their steadfastness and exhorts them to continue their dedication to the Lord (compare Col. 1:23). Amid the onslaught of diverse teaching in a pagan culture, he urges them to remain firm in the Lord and not to waver. Paul tells the Corinthians to be immovable. This last word is a compound that signifies an inability to move from their spiritual moorings. Paul is not talking about retaining the status quo in the church. He wants the people to grow in their love for the Lord and to communicate this in their deeds. ...

*Paul encourages them to excel in the Lord's work. To express constancy and emphasis he adds the word **always** which, in the original, he places last in the clause for emphasis. ... As his love extends to us without measure, so our selfless deeds are done for him without measure. ...*

*The faithful Corinthians have a sure knowledge that the deeds done out of love and thankfulness to God will not be forgotten (see Heb 6:10). The word **labor** is often used by Paul in a missionary setting and means working with his own hands for his own support (4:12) "and for activity in the Christian community as a whole." (Herbert Fendrich, EDNT, vol. 2, p.307.) Such labor given freely in the service of the Lord is never in vain because the Lord himself blesses his servants (Matt. 19:29).*

Simon J Kistemaker, *1 Corinthians*[435]

The local everyday life of the period, 1968-1989, has been dominated by what has become known as the *Northern Ireland Troubles* (1969-1998), and the related subsequent political tensions. During the *Troubles* of the 1920s God graciously used the ministry of Rev. W P Nicholson to bring a great measure of community healing. There was the IRA's *Northern Campaign* 1942-44 and its *Border Campaign* 1956-62, neither of which achieved its overall objectives. But during 1969-98, communal violence claimed the lives of about 3,500 of the people of Northern Ireland in 'combat' situations. 60% of them were killed in the 1970s, 25% in the 1980s and 15% in the 1990s. More than half of those who died are listed as civilians, about one third members of the security forces, and about 15% paramilitaries. But the tragic, harrowing deaths do not tell anything like the whole story – the bombs, the wreckage, the fires, the bomb-scares, the hoax telephone calls, the check points, the traffic chaos, the security measures, the searching, the disruption, the fear and the propaganda. This is an ecclesiastical history, and it is not the purpose to enter the already well-worked field of political analysis except to note the terror and strain that all local communities lived through in varying degrees for 30 years as the local background to EPC's more recent history. The two north Belfast congregations, Somerton Road and Crosscollyer Street, were most severely affected with about 600 deaths in the three mile radius in which they are located.

Yet, in the providence of God, the 1970s and 80s were arguably EPC's most encouraging decades, with five new congregations, eight member-students for the ministry and the development of administrative structures. And in 1968 the Church was just 40 years old.

Old Attacks Renewed

The death of Professor J Ernest Davey in 1970 revived some dormant issues.

'Intransigent Fundamentalism'
In his *Biography of J. Ernest Davey* (1970), Dr Austin Fulton presented this picture of the Heresy Trial leaders and those who identified with them:

> Those were the days of the Scopes trial in Dayton, Tennessee. This warfare in Ireland was carried on from the same background of intransigent fundamentalism. The people whose antipathy to Professor Davey was aroused had, for the most part, little qualification, if any, for forming theological opinions and less for pronouncing theological judgments. But this did not discourage them from fighting what they took to be for them the good fight of faith.
>
> Some, more sophisticated theologically than those just described, or than Nicholson himself, judged that the time had come to expose the 'rationalism' of the Presbyterian College and the 'errors' of the professors. Doubtless the principal movers were sincere enough men who believed themselves thus called to be defenders of the faith. It may well be that it was unfortunate for them that

many of their followers were not concerned about the proprieties of procedure or careful to observe the rules once judicial machinery had been set in motion. But with the best will in the world to be fair to Professor Davey's opponents it does not seem possible to exonerate them completely from responsibility for the regrettable aspects of the controversy which they precipitated. The ignorance of the rank and file of many of the followers cannot be made to bear all the blame.[436]

Dr Robert Allen resonated the theme: "… apart from the merits of the case he who institutes a trial for heresy undertakes a solemn responsibility. Such a trial is necessarily accompanied by events greatly to be deplored. Not only are bitter feelings aroused, when there are deep and strong convictions on both sides, but the interests of truth often suffer, at least temporarily."[437]

So more than 40 years after the events Dr Fulton gave his considered assessment of those who included IEC's founding fathers. To him they were men who were sincere enough but the product of intransigent fundamentalism, whose theological competence was only more "sophisticated" than their followers who had none or very little. And whilst they may have been unfortunate in attracting such a following they could not escape responsibility for the "regrettable aspects" of their followers' activities. He did not support his assertions with evidence, offering only generalisations. What "regrettable aspects"? What was the blame that the followers alone could not be made to bear? Did his reference to "judicial machinery" point to Belfast Presbytery's prohibition of all under its jurisdiction from every kind of public reference to the case until the appeals were heard by the Assembly? He did not deal with the issue of whether this prohibition was constitutional or whether the rank and file of followers were under the jurisdiction of Belfast Presbytery. Who were these followers, in any case? Why such emphasis on people so lacking in knowledge? This was a theological trial. Part 3 of this book has presented evidence that the leading figures of the prosecution were themselves subjected to regrettable aspects of a more insidious nature than the alleged behaviour of their unidentified followers.

In accounting for their fundamentalist motivation, Fulton points to the impact on Ulster of the *fundamentalist-modernist* controversy in the United States and argues that it was heightened by the arrival in the early 1920s of Rev. W P Nicholson. Whilst warmly commending features of Nicholson's ministry and the changes it brought for the better, he describes him as a "convinced militant fundamentalist" who "contributed to the turbulence in the atmosphere which surrounded the heresy trial", particularly by his extravagant attacks on 'modernist' groupings, and his targeting of Professor Davey.[438] Fulton brought the 1925 Scopes Evolution Trial in Tennessee into his argument. It was a battle for the repeal of legislation forbidding the teaching of evolution rather than biblical creation in publicly funded schools,[439] but Fulton appears to regard it as part of the background to this "intransigent fundamentalism" that arrived on the Ulster church scene.

Since definitions of fundamentalism have lacked consensus since the emergence of the term in the early 20th century, it is a pity that Fulton did not provide one. It is not clear why he labels it with intransigence, and whether this property should be understood as generic, or attaching only to the strain that came from America to Ulster in the 1920s. Ned B Stonehouse, in his discussion of the early history of fundamentalism, sees it otherwise: "'Fundamentalists' thus was the designation that came to be given to those who, singling out certain great facts and doctrines that had come under particular attack, were concerned to emphasise their truth and to defend them."[440] Rolland McCune supports this view, drawing in the element of separation: "Fundamentalism has always been defined by its beliefs on biblical doctrine. Historically, fundamentalists have held core biblical truths, principally those concerning Christ and the Scriptures, as well as the doctrine of ecclesiastical separation. Together with the practical distinctive of militancy, these common biblical convictions have formed the essence of the fundamentalist movement."[441]

'Bigots, Marked by Bitterness'

On Friday 13 November, 1970 the *Newsletter* carried a review of Fulton's *Biography of J. Ernest Davey* under the banner: "Accusers in heresy trial marked by bitterness …":

> 'Tried for treason' is a phrase that calls up nightmare visions of inquisitors and witchfinders, of the rack, the thumbscrew and the stake. Many readers may find it hard to believe that a celebrated heresy trial took place in Belfast less than 50 years ago. …
>
> Bigots were much the same in those days as they are now. Dr Austin Fulton tells us that during the trial a series of interruptions was kept up by a mob in the gallery. A Belfast journalist who produced a daily commentary on the proceedings wrote: 'I had read of the tyranny of King James the Second who decreed the expulsion of the Fellows of Magdalen College, Oxford, because their views were not his. But on that gallery of the Assembly every man appeared to be a James the Second . . . If this campaign goes on it will disgust many with religion altogether. There is no advantage in adhering to a religion that has overthrown not merely the principles but the spirit of its Founder.'

Rev. W J Grier's response to the *Newsletter* review of the Fulton publication appeared on Thursday 19 November 1970. Regarding the alleged "mob" in the gallery he said this:

> But the trial—in Presbytery and Assembly—was held behind closed doors. The public was shut out—by the decision of Presbytery and Assembly (See *Record of the Trial*, pages 11,13 and 159). How could the 'mob' shout in the gallery when it was excluded?
>
> I write as one who was present in 1927 at both Presbytery and Assembly.

Here Grier effectively challenged this allegation of 'mob' shouting. And why single out this 'mob' in any case? There were times during the appeal that the whole house was in uproar with noise that was not sympathetic to the prosecution. When Rev. Charles Hunter, James Hunter's elder brother, rose to speak after the vote in the General Assembly he was howled down and could barely be heard at the press table below him – see Chapter 16, "Gallery 'Mob'." If this gallery problem was so great and persistent why did the Church court not deal with it? All present were under its jurisdiction.

It was Davey, in his speech to the General Assembly, 10 June 1927, who first charged the accusers with pursuing a campaign marked by "bitterness and misrepresentation". He failed to establish how bitterness in particular marked the campaign, but others, including the press, took it up. Bitterness was not characteristic of the leading accusers. The James Hunter of this story withdrew his charge against Rev. F W S O'Neill in October 1915 on compassionate grounds following the death of O'Neill's child – see Chapter 5, Rev. F W S O'Neill, China. Many are still alive today who knew Grier well and would gladly testify that any trace of bitterness was foreign to his personality. The robust pursuit of Church discipline did not preclude mannerly personal contact and Grier continued in courteous, if infrequent contact with Davey in the decades following the Heresy Trial.

Ministry Changes and Development

The ministerial change of the 1940s, 50s and 60s continued into the 70s and 80s, affecting every congregation. These two decades produced 22 ordinations and/or installations of ministers and 21 appointments of interim moderators. The licensing of students for the ministry was a major factor.

Flow of Students for the Ministry

There are obvious reasons for thankfulness for the supply of ministers. The supply through admission from other denominations has featured in every decade of the history, but member-students have come in four phases. The first was 1932-1936: Charles E Hunter, Joseph McCracken, William J McDowell and Charles H Garland. These were followed by F S Leahy in 1945 and W W Porter in 1952 – phase 2. The third phase of member-students, 1967-1987, was the largest in the Church's history and there is no doubt that it was the fruit of the increase in prayer and financial support after the setting up of the Training for the Ministry Committee in 1963. This period of 20 years saw the ordination of eight member-students, listed with the year when training commenced:

N E Reid	1967	G N Burke	1981
S J Garland	1974	M G Johnston	1981
S Watson	1974	W C J Ballantine	1987
R C Beckett	1978	S J Tracey	1987

Development Training

Presbytery has also recognised the development needs of men in the ministry. It has never felt the Church to be in a position to offer sabbaticals until 2014, but there have been limited alternatives. From 1983 Presbytery has arranged an annual two-day Ministers' and Office Bearers' Conference, with the first day specifically for ministers. In addition, the Training for the Ministry and Admissions Committee funds the attendance of the ministers at one theological conference within the British Isles, each year.

Ministers' Pensions and Funding

In November 1983 Presbytery approved an insurance company scheme, administered by Council-appointed Trustees, and replaced it by the *EPC Group Personal Pension Scheme* in October 1995.

Church Extension – Phase 3

One of the great encouragements of 1970s and 80s was the application to church extension. The re-location of Botanic Avenue to Stranmillis in 1971 did not count as a new congregation but this strategic development made it so, *de facto*. In numeric terms the closure of Seymour Hill in 1972 produced a net reduction in the number of congregations for the early 70s.

Church Extension Committee

The Church Extension Committee's brief, when it was set up in 1979, was "to investigate possible openings for our witness". But why did Council set up the CEC when it did? Why was it so far behind the other Committees? Council had considered a number of potential openings, including Donegal in 1933 and Derriaghy in 1962. However, a significant event occurred in January 1978 when Rev. Norman Reid, minister of both Finaghy and Crosscollyer Street congregations, asked Council to send him to Dublin to open a new work there. Council agreed, Mr Reid resigned his charges with effect from 28 February, and began his Dublin outreach on 1 March 1978. This brought church extension to Presbytery's agenda as a new and regular item. Also in January 1978, the Finaghy session advised Presbytery of the offer of a hall at Ballycoan, Shaw's Bridge, Belfast, to begin services there. Presbytery took over the project in November 1978 and, until the following September, this also featured on its church extension agenda. So the 1978-79 activity prompted Council to appoint a Church Extension Committee.

The Committee, Rev. S Watson, Rev. J S Ross and Rev. S J Garland, decided to meet six times a year. Its first project was to design and publish 10,000 copies of a brochure setting out the principles and aims of EPC. The Committee also asked for information about possible openings for Church extension, undertaking to follow them up. As the formation of the Training for the Ministry Committee in 1963 linked with the third phase of EPC students that began in 1967, the appointment of the Church Extension Committee in 1979 linked with the third phase of congregations, 1978-1994. 1984 became a busy year for CEC, with four different locations on its agenda.

In January 1984 CEC presented an interim report to Presbytery which included policy guidelines for church extension, namely, Belfast containment and provincial expansion. They suggested that the north Belfast churches, Crosscollyer Street and Somerton Road, should combine, and that the three on the opposite side of the city, Stranmillis, Lisburn Road and Finaghy, should share two ministers for the present. Provincially, the Committee's thinking was that Clintyfallow should re-locate to an area of greater population such as Granville, and that there should be a re-assessment of the work in Dublin. For places like Richhill or Co Fermanagh they advocated the full-time placement of experienced, suitably gifted men, not necessarily ministers, rather than one of the students for the ministry, then nearing completion of their studies. They also made the point that Presbytery should take steps to enlarge the vision of existing congregations and encourage prayer for new ministers. "Extension work," they said, "is most demanding and requires maximum dedication and effort on the part of all concerned."

Their formulation was predictive in certain respects, in that the north Belfast churches did become a joint charge in 1996, the three on the south had two ministers, 2002-2008, but not as a team for the three. However, Presbytery did not adopt the CEC view that a finishing student should not be appointed to Richhill.

Dublin

When Rev. Norman Reid moved to Dublin in March 1978 the family settled in Templeogue near Tallaght, an extensive stretch of Dublin to the south-west. Lord's Day services began in the annex of their home on 17 October 1979. The early years had real encouragements, including visits from Young People's Association teams, but accompanying problems led the Committee to ask the whole church for daily prayer support. During 1983 the Committee began to meet with Norman Reid monthly for prayer and consultation. By 1984 there was more encouragement with regard to Lord's Day attendance and Tuesday evening door-to-door, although the Thursday Bible Study presented a less positive picture. The 1984 membership was six. The upward trend continued in 1985 with Lord's Day increases and the introduction of a Saturday evening prayer meeting – prayer was clearly the key factor in the upturn. Tuesday evening outreach became more consistent with some homes visited regularly, and membership grew to nine. From 9 April 1985 the Bible Study arrangements were revised and moved to Wednesday.

Norman Reid said at the end of 1985 that the great need was the consolidation of the gains they had made, and for the first time the Dublin Mission Church began to consider full congregational status. By mid-1986 the congregation, with a morning attendance of 25-30, had outgrown the Reids' annex and began to meet in the Perrystown Community Centre. In October 1987, evening classes on Bible Introduction in the Centre resulted in three new recruits for the Wednesday

Bible Study, and membership rose to 11 by the end of the year. 1987 also recorded 15 pupils at the Sunday School. 1988, by contrast, was a difficult year, registering a drop in membership to nine, but there were home Bible Studies for two new families, and the Sunday School grew. The Church took a new step in opening Bible and book stalls in local shopping centres and in presenting a monthly film in the Community Centre. This gave the young church a three-fold outreach strategy – Tuesday home visits, Christian literature stalls, and the monthly film. The goal of full congregational status drew nearer.

On 14 February 1990 the church drew up a petition to Presbytery: "We the undersigned being regular attenders of the EPC Mission Church in Dublin, respectfully request the Presbytery to change the status of the Dublin Mission Church to that of a congregation in regular standing. We are either members of the Church already or are willing to become members. We promise to do all in our power to financially support a full-time ministry among us." 18 people signed the petition, indicating that all in regular attendance were at the point of becoming members. On 26 May 1990 at a meeting in the large hall of the Community Centre, Presbytery conferred full congregational status on Dublin, installed Rev. Norman Reid as minister and ordained and installed two elders. This great occasion brought the 12-year period of the involvement of the Church Extension Committee to a highly satisfying conclusion. In June 1991 the Dublin church became known as Perrystown Evangelical Church.

Omagh
Early in 1981 the Church Extension Committee sent greetings through a mutual contact to a recently formed *Omagh Reformed Evangelical Church*. There was no initial plan to develop the contact, but on 7 September 1981, Rev. A A Campbell advised Presbytery of an approach from the Omagh church about the possibility of linkage. Presbytery appointed a commission consisting of the Church Extension Committee and other Presbytery members, and the outcome was that the Omagh church applied for membership of EPC, and on 5 October 1981 Presbytery instructed the Commission to advance the integration process. Guided by a further report of the Commission on 4 January 1982, Presbytery accepted the Omagh application. At a special meeting of Presbytery in the Omagh church on 3 April 1982 Presbytery received the Omagh Reformed Evangelical Church into the fellowship of EPC as a fully accredited congregation, installed Rev. Norman Green, and ordained and installed three deacons.

Richhill
Close behind the Omagh integration of April 1982, a new opportunity arose in Richhill, Co Armagh. On 11 April 1983 Rev. J S Ross advised Presbytery of an approach to begin Sunday afternoon services in Richhill from May, with a view to establishing an EPC witness there. Presbytery decided that the Church Extension Committee should work with John Ross on the development of this opportunity,

and in November the Committee took ownership of the project. Progress was encouraging and in March 1984, after a meeting with the local people, Presbytery decided to proceed with the Richhill extension. It was noted as an occasion for praise and joy, and of answered prayer. On 14 May 1984 at a special meeting of Presbytery to deal with Church strategy, there was the key decision: "That Presbytery seeks to place a minister in Richhill to further the work." On 1 October 1984 Presbytery decided to invite Mark Johnston, a licentiate, to begin full-time work at Richhill, and on 10 November ordained and installed him to the work there for a period of three years. The Committee continued its involvement until the congregation achieved full congregational status on 13 December 1988.

Fermanagh
In November 1983 the Committee considered an approach from friends in County Fermanagh for an evangelical and reformed ministry in their area. In February 1984 Presbytery authorised ongoing investigation of the potential, but it did not develop.

Granville
By the early 1980s the rural congregation at Clintyfallow was in numerical decline, largely through the waning population of the area. In 1984 the Committee began to work with the congregation in exploring the possibility of a move to Granville, 6 miles away, where a more concentrated population might offer better scope for the work. However, the Clintyfallow people did not feel drawn in this direction and the congregation closed in June 1985.

Bangor
In April 1985 CEC presented a "Report of Enquiry into possible Church Extension in Bangor, Co Down" with a recommendation that EPC begin a new work in Bangor from 1 September 1985. Presbytery discussed it in May and June 1985, the Committee made several visits to Bangor, and together came to the view that the circumstances did not point to proceeding at that time.

Accrington
In May 1988 CEC had a request from a group in Accrington, Lancashire, for help. Discussions involved the Presbyterian Association in England (PAE) and the Reformed Churches of the Netherlands, Liberated, who were already taking an interest. Rev. Norman Green, Omagh, spent time with the group during a home visit to Lancashire in August 1988. The situation solidified in April 1989 as Presbytery learned that the group was keen on a full-time EPC ministry with likely financial support from the Dutch Church. At the meeting Norman Green confirmed his growing sense of calling to Accrington. In May 1989 Presbytery set up a package including permission for Norman Green to take up the ministry of the Accrington Fellowship as an EPC Mission Church. The terms stipulated that the group was to involve fully with the PAE with a view to joining it. In June 1989

Norman Green formally accepted the proposals, and resigned his Omagh charge from 31 July 1989. He was installed to East Lancashire Presbyterian Fellowship as a Mission Church of EPC on 1 September 1989, and Presbytery appointed CEC as the Accrington Interim Session.

Church Extension Fund
During the 1970s and 80s there was debate as to whether the Fund should be available for renovation work, but a decision in May 1986 restricted it to the establishment of new and mission status congregations. Currently the Fund supports building work and evangelistic activity connected with new outreach work, and not normally to existing congregations.

Developing Committee Structures

The functions of Presbyterian church courts are often classified as judicial or administrative. The court acts judicially in matters of discipline or judgement; administratively in co-ordinating church life. EPC's highest court, the Presbytery, deals with matters affecting more than one congregation or the whole denomination. Effective administration is vitally important for every organisation and during this period Presbytery formalised its use of committees in exercising its administrative responsibility. They advise Presbytery through reports and recommendations. The Annual Reports of the standing committees have been included in Presbytery's Annual Report since 1982 and provide useful reference documents.

Council took its first major steps towards working through standing committees in the 1960s with the appointment of the Training for the Ministry Committee in 1963. It became the Training for the Ministry and Admissions Committee (TOMA) in April 1980 to take account of the Committee's role in considering applications from ministers and students outside EPC. It was followed by Public Questions in 1964 (renamed Public Morals in 1977). In 1979 and 1980 Council developed the committee system significantly – the Church Extension Committee came in February 1979, and Code Revision in June. In May 1980 Council 'reconstituted' its existing committees, and the principles of continuity, change, and breadth of representation within committee membership, have remained the basis for the modern committees, although streamlining has since made more efficient use of resources. As part of the May 1980 reconstitution, Council set up two new committees – Inter-Church Relations and Missionary. The Presbytery Arrangements Committee took its first steps in 1982 and the Finance Consultative Committee was appointed in 1987.

Since the 1970s Council and Presbytery have also set up special committees or appointed individuals for particular tasks such as Trust Deeds in 1977, Church History in November 1977, Praise in May 1980, Sunday School Project in March 1984 and Autumn Evening Lectures in 1994. Today they are known as Special

Committees and Appointments and cover Youth, International Missions Board and Affinity representatives, Editor of *The Evangelical Presbyterian*, Church Historian, Presbytery Clerk, and Press Officer. Coming under the general heading of Special Committees was the organisation of Church Holidays in the 1980s – Isle of Man, 1980, Grange-over-Sands, Lake District, 1983 and Tywyn, west Wales, 1985.

Treasurers and Finance Consultative Committee
Just three Honorary General Treasurers have served the Church from its beginning: Dr J R Gillespie (1927-1960), Mr J D P Blair, FCA, (1960-1987), and Mr J R McCormick, BSc, FCA, (1987-2004). Mr J D P Blair, FCA, consulted extensively with the churches and successfully motivated them to increasing financial performance, and he urged greater use of free will offering envelopes and the Covenant Scheme (later Gift Aid). He formally introduced congregational targets in April 1982 to finance the salary and related increases required that year, and the Presbytery Annual Reports for 1983 captured the new level of commitment expected: "It was resolved that once targets had been agreed with individual congregations any failure to realise the target should be the subject of Presbytery enquiry" In line with the Standing Committee approach, Presbytery provided committee support for the General Treasurer in 1985. Mr Blair, who succeeded Dr J R Gillespie in 1960 served until his death in 1987, and the following tribute appeared in the Annual Reports for that year:

> Not only Presbytery but the whole of the E.P.C. experienced a deep sense of grief and loss upon the death of Mr J D P Blair, FCA, on Tuesday 22nd September 1987. He had been given the grace to live for many years a consistent Christian life and the gifts to rule well as an elder in the Stranmillis congregation. In August 1960, following the death of Dr J R Gillespie, Mr Blair very willingly answered the call of the Church to take up the burdensome post of Honorary General Treasurer. He applied his wide financial knowledge and unique commercial ability to the Church's finances, giving unstintingly of his time and attention for the succeeding 27 years without any thought of earthly reward. We miss his kindly presence and wise counsel in our deliberations, but rejoice in the knowledge that for him it is now far better. He adorned the doctrine of God our Saviour, doing justly, loving mercy and walking humbly with his God.

Council began circulating its annual financial statement throughout the membership at the first Annual General Meeting in 1961. From 1988 the statement was combined with the Treasurer's report and a budget for the coming year as part of Presbytery's Annual Reports. They covered the Central, Overseas Missions, Training for the Ministry, Church Extension, and Central Investment funds and maintained the vital emphasis on encouraging congregations to progress towards the level of a minister's full support through annual targets.

They highlighted the desire to raise the level of ministers' salaries, they advocated "using the congregation's accounts as a prayer list", and particular prayer for a specified number of congregations to reach the minister support level within a certain period of years. The reports stressed the need for congregational growth as an important basic means of increasing financial capability. They pointed up the need for awareness throughout congregations of the Church's financial state. Frequently they set out the claims of overseas missions, when necessary expressing disappointment over the shortfall in the Central Fund element of missions support. 1993 saw the setting of longer term financial objectives.

During the years 1988-2005, there was regularly a surplus of income over expenditure. Sometimes this was produced or augmented by a reduction of ministers on the payroll, or by one-off items of income such as bequests, but the overall picture confirmed that the Lord was providing for the Church's needs as it progressively raised the standards. The Finance Consultative Committee that Presbytery appointed in November 1987 was strengthened in 2004 and assumed responsibility for the Church's finance.

Presbytery Arrangements Committee
The PAC developed in connection with the arrangements for the Annual Presentation of Presbytery Reports. The first step was in March 1982 when Presbytery appointed a committee, consisting of "Clerk (Convener), the retiring Moderator, his predecessor and Moderator elect" to organise the Annual Presentation. In June 1982 and in April 1983, in the same context, reference was to the 'Presbytery Procedures Committee'. May 1983 brought the first reference to the 'Presbytery Arrangements Committee', but still in relation to the Annual Meeting.

Public Morals
The Public Questions Committee (1956), renamed Public Morals in 1977, directs much of its work to situations that exist outside the Church. In 1983 the Committee began its Annual Report: "It is the aim of the Public Morals Committee to assist the Church in expounding the law of God and applying it to modern issues, and in issuing a call of repentance to all who will listen, including those in authority over us. This is a necessary, though often unpopular task as John the Baptist found out." It developed the theme in the following year: "The Psalmist asks the question 'When the foundations are being destroyed, what can the righteous do?' (Ps 11.3, NIV) ... There is much that we can do proclaiming God's righteousness and grace, praying earnestly in the confidence that one day the cause of Christ will triumph."

"The Committee is concerned to promote the recognition of God's rule in every area of life. ... Our work may be somewhat negative in emphasis, but our concern is at all times to make known the positive blessings of Salvation and the restoring power of the Gospel." And in 1985: "'You are the salt of the earth ... You are the light of the world.' (Matt 5.13-14) These words of the Lord Jesus Christ from the Sermon on the Mount could be regarded as the Motto Text of the

Public Morals Committee. We have the two-fold responsibility of endeavouring to preserve biblical standards in an increasingly permissive society, as well as positively applying biblical truth to different problem situations in our world." Examples were the Divorce Reform and Sunday Entertainments Bills which came before the House of Commons early in 1968. Council sent a protest to the 12 Northern Ireland MPs at Westminster asking them to vote against these Bills. Seven of the 12 replied and Council recorded their names.[442]

The sanctity of human life in its earliest stages – test-tube babies, human fertilisation, and embryo research and abortion were also prominent in the 1980s, as was the sanctity of the marriage bond and divorce. The best known of the Committee's publications were Rev. Sidney Garland's booklets on *Abortion* and *Alcoholism*, published in May 1981, and *The Beginnings of Life* in 1986 co-authored with Dr N McCune. The Committee also sought meetings with Government bodies and representatives, issued press releases, organised letters to MPs, distributed literature in Belfast City centre, and worked with other Christian bodies in doing so.

The Committee's reports regularly acknowledged further lost ground for Christian standards and could point only to limited or isolated elements of success. Often their press releases did not appear in the media; government ministers and spokespersons were unsympathetic or even unwilling to meet. 1987 noted a further decline in moral standards throughout society and tempted the Committee to see itself as "a voice crying in the wilderness" (Is 40.3, cf Matt 3.3) and to ask in 1988, "What is the good of it all?" The following year was little different: "Nothing shocks us anymore. The seemingly endless cycle of violence in our Province, the spiral of visible and audible filth on our screens, the persistent attempts by the Government to legislate against Christian values leaves us all battle-hardened and weary in our struggle against moral decay. We are tempted to feel like an insignificant minority trying to resist a tidal wave of public complacency." Towards the end of the 1980s the Committee, clearly feeling the need to stimulate the Church's prayer support, began to use the *Evangelical Presbyterian* to put across its message.

Annual Presentation of Presbytery Reports

When Council was re-designated Presbytery in November 1980, the Annual General Meeting which had run since 1961 became the *Annual Presentation of Presbytery Reports*. Most of the AGM features carried over, but there was always the awareness of the General Assembly in larger Churches, and Presbytery took steps to upgrade the significance of the occasion as the EPC's annual denominational event. From 1981 there was better advertising, a printed programme and the publication of committee reports in addition to the General Treasurer's, which had been circulated since 1961. The Sunday School Project prizes were also presented at one of the sessions. From 1981 also, the Chairman of Council became Moderator of Presbytery and the installation of the new Moderator and the Moderator's Address, became features. Variations to the programme were introduced over the next 20 years in an attempt to increase effectiveness. In 1989 the two Saturday sessions were merged in a single Saturday afternoon session and the verbal reports replaced with a review of the previous year from the written reports by the outgoing Moderator. Congregations were invited to attend the debate of the annual reports at the April meeting of Presbytery, but the experiment did not continue.

Developments in Praise

Little had changed since 1934 when Council had confirmed its recommendation of *Golden Bells* and the Revised Psalter of 1880, until 1974 when the possibility of a words only edition of *Trinity Hymnal* (Orthodox Presbyterian Church, USA) was considered, but it did not progress.

Psalter and Trinity Hymnal
There was an important development in June 1979 when Council accepted a proposal from Rev. J S Ross: "The Council of the Evangelical Presbyterian Church recognising the unique place held by the Psalter, as the only divinely inspired collection of Christian praise, stipulates that the singing of Psalms from the Scottish Metrical Version (Revised Edition) be a permanent aspect of Public Worship in all congregations of the EPC."

Underlying dissatisfaction with Golden Bells, and the question of its future availability, led to Council appointing a committee in May 1980 to consider church praise. The committee focused its considerations on the *Trinity Hymnal* and *Christian Hymns* and recommended that Sessions consider *Christian Hymns*. The session reports in February 1980 raised various objections, particularly that the time for change was not considered opportune. In February 1983 the Committee revised its recommendation, having come to the view that the contents of the *Trinity Hymnal* made it the confessional choice. Sessions considered the recommendation and it was passed in March 1983. Most congregations had adopted it by December 1985.

Foreign Missions – An Era Concludes

The original Foreign Missions Committee came into being in 1938 to deal with speaking requests from missionary societies, and there is reference to additional personnel for that Committee in 1945. A Free Church of Scotland Mission Box Secretary and Foreign Missions Representative were appointed in 1937, and succeeding Representatives/Correspondents held office until May 1980 when the new Committee came into being. The outgoing Correspondent, W A Sampson, was one of its first members. However, in less than three years a new arrangement had taken its place: in May 1981 the General Assembly of the Free Church of Scotland welcomed an offer from the EPC to make a more active contribution to overseas work through representation on its Foreign Missions Board (International Missions Board from 2002). Rev. J S Ross, Convener of the Foreign Missions Committee, was the first representative. The result was that from 1982-83 Presbytery began transacting its Foreign Missions business through this *Missionary Representative* whom it appointed in place of a Committee.

Retiring Missionaries
Rev. Joseph McCracken and his wife Helen, missionaries in South Africa since 1944, retired in 1974, but stayed in South Africa and continued to serve the Xhosa Church. Miss Nan Dunlop, who had served in India since 1944, also retired in 1974, and Miss Florence I Donaldson who went to Peru in 1951 retired in 1985. These missionaries were seconded to the Free Church of Scotland, and Florrie Donaldson's retirement in 1985 suspended a service link with the Free Church which had run continuously from 1937 when Dr Harold Lindsay went to Peru.

Inter-Church Relations – The Changing Scene
Council had been involved in Inter-Church Relations since the 1930s through Correspondents, representatives and delegates, but in 1980 it appointed an Inter-Church Relations Committee.

Leaving Reformed Ecumenical Synod
Earlier chapters have taken involvement with RES up to 1968 when a report from W J Grier revealed developing tensions in the Synod, particularly around the ordination of women and dual membership with the World Council of Churches. In March 1970 Council expressed its World Council of Churches position to the RES in the proposal: "that the prohibition of dual membership of the Reformed Ecumenical Synod and the World Council of Churches be written into the constitution of the Reformed Ecumenical Synod, and that a time limit be set for the withdrawal from the World Council of Churches of those member churches already in its membership." The following October, Council considered a letter from OPC to RES about dual membership and wrote to RES and the Dutch Church, GKN in support of the OPC position.

Council arranged for local men to represent EPC at the 1972 Synod in Australia, briefing them on the EPC position on Scripture, ordination of women, and dual membership, and asking them to act in union with OPC. In anticipation of the August 1976 Synod in Cape Town, Council contacted the Free Church of Scotland, the OPC, and the Reformed Presbyterian Church of Ireland about a mutual policy - "grave concern" over the dual membership of GKN, agreement to protest to RES, and a determination to withdraw from RES if there was no action. W J Grier and Joseph McCracken were the EPC representatives to the Synod and Grier visited the South African mission on the same visit. RES agreed by a substantial majority at Cape Town to reject dual membership and urged the churches concerned to review their position. A majority also agreed that GKN take disciplinary action against heretical professors. Council pressed RES for action on these resolutions and in June 1977 received an undertaking that the two matters would be dealt with 'aggressively' at the 1980 Synod.

Matters drew to a head in May 1979 when Council asked the RES Secretary, "by whose authority he attended the World Confessional Families and WCC meetings on 23-25 October 1978, what was his role there, and what line he took." RES did not reply and on 10 October 1979 Council terminated its membership "until such times as we are satisfied that the Synod is fulfilling properly its original purpose as stated in its constitution 'to promote the unity of the churches which profess and maintain the Reformed Faith'." Council informed the Reformed Presbyterian Church, the Free Church of Scotland, and the Orthodox Presbyterian Church. In November 1979 Council read a letter from RES expressing regret, along with letters of EPC support from the Reformed Presbyterian Church and the Free Church of Scotland. The OPC finally withdrew in 1988 because of a refusal on the part of RES to remove GKN from its membership.

International Conference of Reformed Churches
So the first two international affiliations (ICCC and RES) had run for 10 and 30 years respectively, but the foundations for a new reformed international body were laid during the latter RES years. In August 1976 delegates of de Gereformeerde Kerken in Nederland (Vrijgemaakt) (GKNV) – the Reformed Churches in the Netherlands (Liberated) – visited EPC. It produced an expectation of 'further fellowship' and it took place in a follow-up visit by GKNV delegates to Belfast in September 1979. The delegates met Council and afterwards addressed a larger meeting on 21 September. On withdrawal from RES in October, GKNV sent a letter of congratulations. Following the 1979 contact in Belfast, Council appointed Rev. D W H Thomas and Rev. A A Campbell as delegates to GKNV in May 1980. As a result of these exchange visits, Presbytery agreed to enter into 'Correspondence' with GKNV in May 1982.

GKNV had been making similar contacts with other reformed bodies and had developed relationships sufficiently to host a preliminary International Conference of Reformed Churches in October-November 1982, the Free Church of Scotland sharing the leading role. Rev. D W H Thomas represented EPC. That Conference drew up a draft constitution for the ICRC, and Presbytery's Inter-Church Relations Committee proposed amendments to it in October. The organisation of the new body proceeded, and in January 1983 Presbytery appointed Derek Thomas as the EPC representative on the Provisional Committee of ICRC. Subsequently, on 2 April 1984 Presbytery accepted the recommendation of its Inter-Church Relations Committee to join ICRC, noting that the Free Church of Scotland was already a member.

1. The purposes of ICRC are: to express and promote the unity of faith that member churches have in Christ;
2. to encourage the fullest ecclesiastical fellowship among the member churches;
3. to encourage cooperation among the member churches in the fulfilment of the missionary and other mandates;

4   to study the common problems and issues that confront the member churches and to aim for recommendations with respect to these matters;
5   to present a Reformed testimony to the world.

Part of the ICRC strategy is to hold Regional Conferences. A Regional Consultation Conference in Edinburgh in February 1987 led to the first UK Regional Conference in Queen's University Belfast on 24 September 1987, where Youth, Public Morals, and Missions were the major items of agenda. It was an encouraging occasion and led to an agreement among the UK member churches in 1989 to hold an ICRC Regional Conference every four years.

Simultaneous with its international alignments the Church participated in a UK body, the British Evangelical Council. It became Affinity in 2004.

British Evangelical Council – The Middle Years
The participation of Dr Martyn Lloyd-Jones in the later 1960s had a massive influence on BEC support. But within a few years BEC was finding that the 1966-67 momentum was difficult to consolidate, and by the early 1970s was appealing for funds to support its Secretariat. During the 1970s EPC had three representatives on the BEC Council appointed at yearly intervals and each serving for three years. They attended Council meetings and Conferences, usually twice a year. There were BEC public meetings in Belfast in November 1958, January 1961, October 1966, and February 1976.

In the Autumn 1999 issue of BEC magazine, *In Step*, Neil Richards looked back on the early 1980s: "The evangelical scene was confused and, certainly among the free churches, there was a lack of direction and a lingering disillusionment. The secession issue had gained little ground, and the hoped-for quickening in the churches had not come. The BEC itself seemed to falter; numbers at the annual Conference had declined and were to continue to do so. No-one had realised at the time the extent to which the presence and support of Dr Lloyd-Jones had accounted for the large attendances in the '70s." However, the 1980s saw increased EPC interest due mainly to two factors. The first was the appointment of the Inter-Church Relations Committee in May 1980. The other major factor was the appointment of the new BEC General Secretary, Rev. Alan F Gibson in 1982 along with the acquisition of BEC's own premises in St Albans. Rev. Stephen Roger, minister of Ballyclare EPC, writing in 1999 about Gibson's imminent retirement summed up his significance: "Mr Gibson held the different bodies of the BEC together with great skill and empathy and perhaps uniquely entered into the thinking and direction of each body whilst maintaining an overall course for the Council. His knowledge of the British Evangelical scene was great and his attention to detail phenomenal."

In 1982 Presbytery decided to send a delegate to the annual two-day residential meeting of the Executive and appended a letter from Alan Gibson to the 1984 and 1985 Annual Reports. In the first of these he highlighted the significance of BEC for "evangelical church groups disenchanted with the opposite dangers of evangelical involvement and separatist isolation." He explained: "A Committee of the Executive Council is engaged in a long-term study of the rationale in Scripture and Christian doctrine for the planning of future BEC policy." In his 1985 greeting Gibson spoke of the re-launch of the *Foundations* magazine, started in 1976, with its *FOCUS* series of articles on doctrines under threat. The first was on Eternal Punishment. In October 1985 BEC held its first conference in Belfast since the 1960s. However, a comment in the 1985 Annual Report defined the BEC relationship: "Whilst the terms of our relationship with the BEC are much looser and more tenuous than our relations with Reformed and Presbyterian churches, they nevertheless provide us with the basis for an important tier of fellowship with BEC's constituent churches."

There were several issues in the 1980s. The first was the Inter-Church Process (ICP) with its slogan *Not Strangers but Pilgrims*, designed to involve churches, including the Roman Catholic Church, at grass roots. It began in 1984 and culminated in the 1987 Swanwick Declaration with Cardinal Hume's contribution: "It is our conviction that, as a matter of policy and at all levels and in all places, our Churches must now move from co-operation to clear commitment to each other, in search of the unity for which Christ prayed, and in common evangelism and service of the world." BEC led the response, and as part of its campaign published Alan Gibson's booklet, *Holding Hands in the Dark*, 1988. ICP led to the *Council of Churches for Britain and Ireland* replacing the British Council of Churches in 1990. It became *Churches Together in Britain and Ireland* in 1999.

Another key issue of the 1980s was the consideration of a third tier of BEC membership, the 'Guest Status', to cater for evangelical groups within pluralist churches. The other two levels were 'Constituent Member' for denominations, and 'Associate Member', for independent churches. BEC decided against 'Guest Status' since the potential applicants were not church groupings, and a facility for such groupings to have their desired contact was already in place.

The BEC agenda, outlined in the 1986 EPC Annual Report, summarised the beneficial activities: "The BEC, rejecting false ecumenism, and working for a truly Biblical ecumenism encourages evangelical churches to come together to stand for truth against error, for Christian moral standards and against the tide of evil in our society." There has been the regular presentation of theological papers, the provision of information to member churches, engagement with government to represent evangelical opinion on social and moral issues, organisation of local rallies and conferences, youth-work support, a European Bible teaching ministry, and reviews of BEC's long-term goals. In May 1980 Council confirmed its potential interest in candidates for the ministry who approach BEC. On 24 September 1971, at the height of the Northern Ireland 'troubles', the EPC Council read BEC's letter to all its constituent and associate churches. Its prayer was "that God would so intervene in Ulster that even yet true righteousness and peace might prevail and that He might guide and uphold all those who are truly His own in these dark and uncertain days." But there were other areas of church life not directly within the remit of standing committees.

Youth Work - Developing

Young People's Association
1968-1989 was a good period for the YPA, just formed in 1966. It was administratively sound and self-developing with regular committee meetings, elections of officers, revisions of the original YPA constitution, Annual General Meetings until 1980, a Directory of YPA members, and a chronological summary of Minutes 1966-1985! From 1982 there was a YPA section in the annual Presbytery Reports. The Missionary Project was a major activity – see Appendix 17. YPA organised summer and winter programmes of outings and sports, teach-ins, training, Inter-Branch Silver Cup Quiz, a Mastermind series, week-end conferences and house parties, YPA Choir, carol services and social occasions. Joint rallies of the Branches featured strongly, although they decided in 1979 to reduce the frequency in favour of more focus at local level. They engaged in outreach to Crosscollyer Street, Dublin, Glasgow and Sligo, and in various painting and clean-up parties. They attended Lord's Day Observance Society rallies in the later 1960s, arranged a mission at Somerton Road in October 1970 and led summer open-air meetings at Seymour Hill until 1973. There was a YPA magazine, news sheets and events calendars from time to time, and from February-May 1981 *The Evangelical Presbyterian* ran a Youth Focus series on the cults with the articles written by YPA members. There was growing involvement with camps and a YPA holiday to Holland. And they supported it all with prayer.

Of note is a courteous, supportive letter from YPA to Council in November 1972 about lack of support for the YPA and EPC stagnation. Half the congregations were vacant in 1972!

> ... We confess that it seems to us that humanly speaking the EPC is neither progressing nor even consolidating its present position but has come to a standstill. ... We therefore respectfully request Council to give consideration to the following questions:
>
> 1   Can a Church progress without a settled ministry?
> 2   Is sufficient being done to obtain a settled ministry in the EPC?
> 3   Has thought been given to streamlining Belfast work with advance in other areas?
> 4   Does Council attach any importance to the work of the YPA and have they any directions to give it?

Council's reply has not been preserved but the YPA minutes contain a transcript of Council's holding letter: "... The Council was concerned that any idea of lack of interest in YPA activities should have arisen. This is not so. ... The Council appreciates the heartfelt concern of the YPA in present and future prosperity of the Church and we covet your prayers and all the help you can give. We wish you the Lord's favour and guidance in all your purposes. We hope that the promised longer reply will remove many, if not all, of your difficulties." Council discussed the YPA reply in March 1973 including how best to use the YPA in visitation and open-air meetings.

Developing Camps
The camps continued to grow and develop in progressive phases. See Appendix 18.

Phase 1	1939-1952	Boys' Camps
Phase 2	1953-1968	Separate Boys' and Girls' Camps
Phase 3	1969-1978	Separate Boys' and Girls' Camps with Inter-Camps Visits
Phase 4	1979-1985	Joint Mixed Camps
Phase 5	1986-1990	Junior and Senior Mixed Camps
Phase 6	1991-	Junior, Inters and Senior Mixed Camps

The camps have been a bonding force among the young people, a powerful means of strengthening spiritual lives and of conversions. The leaders have applied an outstanding amount of application to this work since it began. Many have seen it as a definite calling.

Sunday Schools
The Church Sunday School Lesson Book – Evangelical Lesson Book arrangement continued from the 1940s until January 1976 when Council adopted new Committee recommendations:

1. *Go Teach* materials to be used for ages 8-13.
2. A selection of 100 lessons from Catherine Vos's *Child's Story Bible* as a two-year course for younger children.
3. The Sabbath School year to be the calendar year
4. A review board to be set up to monitor the standards of the lesson materials

In January 1977 further Committee recommendations were implemented:

1. Summer vacations to be at the discretion of local Sunday Schools with the recommendation that such vacations be as short as possible
2. Lawson's Shorter Catechism recommended
3. AV to be used in class but teachers could use the NIV or the NASV in preparation
4. The 100 texts suggested by the Committee for memory work adopted along with portions of Scripture—Psalm or Bible chapter
5. Examinations to be arranged by the local Sunday School
6. Teacher training to be arranged at discretion of the Committee

The special lessons on Church History and Missionary Endeavour, which began in 1967, laid the basis for the Sunday School Projects of later years - See Appendix 16.

Commitment to Prayer

The previous chapter, under *Interceding for the Nation*, surveyed the Council's programme of prayer for the national and international situation in the 1940s, 50s and 60s and noted the new demands for prayer that the onset of the Northern Ireland 'Troubles' were bringing at the end of the 1960s.

The Days of Prayer

Council appointed Thursday 6 February 1969 as a special Day of Prayer for the local situation. There were prayer meetings at 8.00 am and 3.00 pm in the congregations and a joint meeting in the evening. In addition there was a lunch-time session in the YMCA building in Belfast. Similar programmes took place in the Churches on 11 June 1970, 2 October 1971, 1 January 1974, 2 October 1974 (A Day of Repentance and Prayer), 1 January 1976, 17 March 1977. On 19 May 1978 a Council discussion on "the deplorable moral and spiritual state of Northern Ireland" led to a request to congregations to offer special prayers for the Province on Lord's Day 28 May 1978 and at prayer meetings that week.

In June 1981 Council wrote to the Prime Minister, the Rt Hon Margaret Thatcher, MP, thanking her for her stand on law and order and assuring her of the Church's prayers for her government. The letter also drew her attention to the state of the nation which the Church attributed to a departure from the principles of the Word of God, and it requested her to consider calling the nation to a day of repentance and prayer. The letter informed her of the Church's plans to hold such a day on 6 September 1981 in conjunction with the Reformed Presbyterian Church. The Public Morals Committee produced a leaflet to guide the prayer of the day. The Northern Ireland Office wrote in thanks and extending its good wishes for the Day of Prayer.

Ministers' and Office Bearers' Half Day of Prayer

During the 1980s these general days of prayer gave way to the Ministers' and Office Bearers' annual half day of prayer which began 1 December 1984. From then they have featured in the annual calendar. The first two had morning and afternoon sessions, but since 1986 it has been a Saturday morning event, held usually in the Moderator's church. There have been notable times of prayer during these occasions, such as the one in 1988:

> On Saturday, February 6th, 1988, the Presbytery arranged for a morning of prayer to be held in the Stranmillis Church. All office-bearers were invited to attend and spend some four hours in prayer for the church. It was good to see the response with almost every church well represented.
>
> Of even greater significance was the liberty and volume of prayer that was offered; there were none of those long pauses which sometimes characterise prayer meetings. It was evident that the Lord was drawing us together in a spirit of unity and brotherly concern.
>
> Opportunity was given for each congregation to raise points for prayer and praise and this facility was used to the full. Also present were two delegates

from the Free Reformed Churches of Australia who brought greetings from the Antipodes.

It is on occasions such as these that one can see that there yet remains a bright future for the Evangelical Presbyterian Church; we shall find the strength we need for the future on our knees before God.

In November 1985, when recommending the continuation of the Half Day of Prayer, the Presbytery Arrangements Committee also recommended that all congregations hold a springtime Day of Prayer, on a date fixed by Presbytery. 23 February 1986 was the first of these, but it appears to have been the last and to have concluded the general days of prayer. Faithfulness in prayer was a commendable characteristic of former generations.

Ministers' and Office Bearers' Conferences

In June 1983 the Moderator, Dr R C Beckett, asked that members give thought to the possibility of a Ministers' and Elders' conference. The discussions in September indicated strong support for the suggestion and the Presbytery Arrangements Committee (PAC) was asked to bring proposals in November. The Committee's outline plan was that a Friday afternoon session would be for ministers with ruling elders invited to join the Friday evening and all day Saturday sessions. Arrangements proceeded and the first conference took place at Crumlin on 9-10 March 1984. Rev. Douglas MacMillan, Professor of Church History, Free Church College, was unavailable but Rev. David Paterson, Free Church, Perth, took his place and spoke on 'Togetherness' which he presented under the following headings:

The Development of Fellowship
The Pastoral Duties of Elders and Ministers
The Need for and Development of the Vision within Congregations for Outreach

The report in the *Evangelical Presbyterian* of May 1984 contains pure gold. Here is a rare insight into the demands of shepherding the flock, something that ministers and office bearers can truly "place above the door":

Taking as his theme 'togetherness', something which Mr Paterson felt was lacking generally in evangelical circles, he gave a penetrating analysis of the state of the EP church today as compared with fifty years ago. The analysis was unusually specific, humbling and accurate. The problem we face today – as ministers, elders, deacons, and individual congregations is a lack of love for one another. In what proved to be most convicting he outlined a catalogue of pastoral failures: unredeemed time, untaken opportunities, an unloved flock, unadmitted guilt, unwept tears, unattained consistency, unkept promises, unsanctified service, unaccepted challenges, unsought help, undeveloped graces, unreceived impressions of the Holy Spirit.

... Mr Paterson exhorted ministers to place above the door of their studies the text: "Satan hath desired to have thee" (Luke 22.31).

In three more addresses, Mr Paterson spoke directly to the elders, 'those in whom rule of the church resides'. Elders must be examples of faith, zeal, evangelistic endeavour and an ongoing Christian experience. "It is possible for Elders to live on past experiences," he reminded us. The vision of God which enraptured and humbled Ezekiel (Ezek 1-2) must be our ongoing experience. When Elders become stale they must be evangelised!

Subsequent discussions revealed the desire to make the conference an annual event. 1984 was an eminently worthy and memorable beginning to the series that would follow with little change in the format. The conferences have continued each Moderator-year since, with the exception of 1986-87, 1987-88 and 2003-04. See Appendix 14.

50th-60th Anniversaries

50th Anniversary

The 50th Anniversary services were held on 14-15 October 1977 in the Wellington Hall, Belfast, the scene of some significant meetings of the past. The Bible Standards League held protest meetings in it in 1926-1927, and Rev. James Hunter in March-April 1927 after the Heresy Trial at the Belfast Presbytery. Dr Machen spoke in it twice in 1927, one address being, *What is Christianity?*, and again in 1932. Dr L S Chafer, Dallas, addressed an early Irish Evangelical Church Conference in it in 1930. Rev. W P Nicholson held a week of his 1947 mission in it, and it was the venue of one of the Grammar School Syllabus protests in 1948. Council organised a Reformation Rally in it in 1960 to commemorate the establishment by law in 1560 of the Protestant religion in Scotland. Rev. W J Grier was the Chairman for the 50th Anniversary services. Professor E P Clowney, President of Westminster Seminary, Philadelphia, gave the Friday evening address, *The Worship God Seeks*. There were two addresses on the Saturday afternoon: Professor G N M Collins, Free Church College, Edinburgh, spoke on *Holding the Faith*, and Professor Clowney's subject was *In Search of a City*.

Greetings and good wishes, many of them expressing solidarity in the reformed faith, came from far and near. Among them were Professor Collins, Free Church of Scotland, Rev. Joseph McCracken, South Africa, the Congregational Union of Ireland, Rev. Iain Murray, Banner of Truth, Rev. Roland Lamb, British Evangelical Council, Rev. Norman Porter, South Australia, Bishop D A Thompson, Rev. John D Johnston, Missionary in Taiwan, Rev. Robert Rodgers, Mr Seamus Milligan, Evangelical Protestant Society, Rev. Stuart Law, London, and Mr John C Roberts, LDOS.

Sixty Years of Evangelical Witness

There was no 60th Anniversary celebration but Rev. W J McDowell produced the October 1988 Evangelical Presbyterian as a special issue – Sixty Years of Evangelical Witness. There were four sections, Sixty Years of Evangelical Witness (Origins and Development, The Reasons we Exist, We Must Continue our Witness), Our Leaders, Our Missionaries, The Uplook and the Outlook. Mr McDowell said this:

> The beginnings of the Evangelical Presbyterian Church were small and despised. Our ministerial staff consisted of Rev. James Hunter, who had retired from the oversight of Knock Irish Presbyterian Church after a pastorate of 35 years, and Rev. W J Grier who was at the commencement of his ministerial career. We had no organised congregations, no church buildings, and no finances. Most of our congregations began as "the church in so and so's house". ...
>
> The gloomy prophecies of complete failure have not been fulfilled. The Lord has been favourable unto us. He has given us the grace of perseverance. ...
>
> The Heresy Trial of 1927 is a lifetime away. Those who can remember it now are now "senior citizens". As their number grows smaller should the memory of those days be forgotten? We think not. We owe a debt to those who contended for the faith, and have now gone to their eternal reward.

24

Engaging with Strategy and Change (1990-2014)

Cast your bread upon the waters,
for you will find it after many days ...

He who observes the wind will not sow,
and he who regards the clouds will not reap.
                                        Eccles 11.1,4

"... for if there are risks in everything, it is better to fail in launching out than in hugging one's resources to oneself."

Derek Kidner, The Message of Ecclesiastes, IVP, p 97

This period, which brings the history up to 2014, sees the Church well established in the Presbyterian, Reformed constituency and operating with increased efficiency through its developing structures. From another perspective, historical identity had generally faded from the Church's self-consciousness. The *Origin and Witness* had passed out of regular use, and historical reference came mostly in the context of anniversaries and their information leaflets. So to many in succeeding generations, increasingly removed from the life and times of the early leaders, the founding of the church became remote, not well-known, if known at all.

Strategy and *Vision for the Nineties*

Until the 1990s a forward-planning, strategic approach had not featured prominently in EPC. Scarcity of resources had made the Church focus on consolidation and fire-fighting and it contributed to a corresponding mind-set. It is doubtful if awareness of the Lord's goodness in terms of human resources and new congregations during the 1960s and 70s prompted the strategy approach of the 1990s.[443] But it certainly made it possible and there was a new desire to keep up the momentum.

Vision for the Nineties

In June 1988 Presbytery granted permission to the Church Extension Committee to produce a 'green paper' on church strategy. In October a CEC sub-committee was appointed to help, and it co-opted one elder from each congregation. The Committee report, *Vision for the Nineties*, came to Presbytery in March 1990, who accepted its recommendations in May:

1. That each Session familiarise itself with the summary of the position of the Church as a whole, past and present, found in the first part of the report; and that the information it contains be used to stimulate mutual prayerful concern in the congregations.
2. That Sessions and congregations take the Great Commission to heart and seek God for times of revival.
3. That each Session considers Church-planting and 'tests the waters' by holding services in new locations at appropriate times, eg on Sunday afternoons.
4. That the CEC/Strategy committee report to the September 1990 meeting with recommendations on guidelines for a 'tentmaker' church-planting and evangelistic ministry.
5. That the CEC actively look for openings to establish new EPC congregations.
6. That strong churches be prepared to help needy ones, eg through secondment of members to help in Sunday school work - under the oversight of both Sessions.

7   That congregations explore means of establishing evangelistic contacts, eg by means of Mother-and-Toddler Groups, or Ministers gaining access to local schools.
8   That a Tape Library of sermons preached in the EPC be set up and Ministers encouraged to contribute at least two sermons a year; and that an advertisement be inserted in the Magazine inviting response from anyone willing to undertake the work.
9   That the Church Extension Fund be given the support to finance new ventures.
10 That the possibility of some kind of joint arrangement between small churches be kept under review.
11 That a Missions Committee be appointed to serve for as long as is necessary, having in mind concrete proposals to develop missionary interest-participation.
12 That Presbytery meet at least twice a year for times of prayer and conference.
13 That steps be taken in each congregation to encourage hospitality.
14 That fellowship between congregations be fostered by means of joint Prayer Meetings and support of Special Meetings that are organised.
15 That a regular Church News page be established in the Magazine and that each Session appoint an individual to act as congregational correspondent to the Magazine; and that the Editor be requested to draw up a brief on the requirements.
16 That the design for a denominational logo be pursued by Messrs Harper and D Watson and that Rev. M G Johnston, in consultation with Dr Woolsey, bring to October Presbytery the draft of a new leaflet introducing the denomination.

The booklet *The Way Ahead*, a popular version of *Vision for the Nineties*, was published in May 1991 with the major sections, Past and Present and Vision for the Future.[444]

Bangor-Groomsport

Vision for the Nineties soon bore fruit in a particular way. Bangor had been on CEC's extension agenda in 1985 but the proposal did not proceed at that time. However, in February 1993, as an outcome of *Vision*, Richhill Session tabled a motion: "that Presbytery discusses the possibility and feasibility of starting a new work by 1995." Initially there was concern over the old problem of financial and manpower resources and CEC's capacity for the task, given its current commitments. However, the Richhill men were concerned to establish whether the vision, enthusiasm and faith necessary to go forward with church extension existed, and they argued for the place of faith. Their stance was persuasive and, in June, Presbytery gave its support to starting a new work, urging sessions to re-examine their commitment to what was necessary for effective church extension, and increasing the CEC membership to five for the new task.

In October 1993 CEC provided outline procedures for planning extensions in consultation with sessions and requested prayer for the way ahead. In December,

Presbytery resolved: "that the Evangelical Presbyterian Church commence a new work in Bangor on the first Sunday in March 1994, initially holding afternoon services and at an appropriate time thereafter moving to morning and evening services." Over the next 10 years the work developed steadily in rented accommodation for the Lord's Day services, and after a number of disappointments with regard to a permanent home, a new building was opened in the nearby town of Groomsport on 8 May 2004. The congregation was raised to full status in 2006. The development of Bangor-Groomsport was the major item of CEC agenda for more than 10 years but it did not lead to a phase four of Church extension.[445]

Radio Broadcasts
In June 1981 Presbytery accepted a CEC recommendation to apply to the BBC for a broadcast. The BBC declined it and again in September 1982. The church re-applied in May 1991, but on 26 October 1997 the applications came to fruition and Rev. Gareth Burke, Knock, preached on the Parable of the Rich Farmer, Luke 12.13-21. Other opportunities have followed:

13/05/2001	Rev G N Burke	Stranmillis	Luke 23.33-49	*The Dying Thief*
29/10/2006	Rev G N Burke	Stranmillis	Rom 8.19-22	*The Groaning Creation*
30/01/2011	Rev J S Roger	Ballyclare	Luke 7.36-50	*A Sinful Woman Forgiven*
23/11/2014	Rev G N Burke	Stranmillis	Matt 13.24-30	*Parable of the Weeds*

In addition to the broadcast of Lord's Day services Rev. Gareth Burke has participated in Radio Ulster's *Thought for the Day* about six times annually since 1997.

Balmoral Show
The Evangelical Book Shop held a stand at the Royal Ulster Agricultural Show at Balmoral, from 1939 to 2008. As part of its early phase of activities CEC began taking part of the stand for a Church advertising display on selected years, the first in May 1982. The Committee prepared publications for launch at the Show, such as *The Way Ahead* and *The Anatomy of a Church* in 1991. The Committee's report for 1993 commented on the value of its presence on the stand: "The rationale behind this venture has been to raise the profile of the denomination and to publicise the link between the Evangelical Book Shop and the Evangelical Presbyterian Church. In both these respects the display proved successful. A significant number of people, many of whom had never heard of the Church, stopped and talked with EPC representatives on the stand." 2002, the 75th anniversary year, saw a significant appearance on the stand and the Committee

encouraged others to participate in this important outreach in future. In June 2002 Presbytery agreed that CEC would share the Book Shop stand annually. 2008 was the last year the Book Shop exhibited at the Balmoral Show, concluding a 70 year presence.

Accrington-Blackburn

By 1990 it had become apparent to the Accrington congregation that Blackburn would be a better location for the development of the work. The premises of Fecitt Brow Evangelical Church, on the outskirts of Blackburn, just two and a half miles from Accrington, became available, and services commenced in them in June 1993. The congregation was enabled to purchase the building by a donation from the Alphen-on-the-Rhine congregation of GKNV for the full amount of £25,000. The opening services took place on 28 August 1993. CEC had close involvement with the Accrington project from 1988 but its remit was transferred to the Inter Church Relations Committee in 1993 to coincide with the move to Blackburn.

A full Presbytery of the Evangelical Presbyterian Church in England and Wales was formed from the Interim Presbytery of the Presbyterian Association in England on 20 April 1996. Accrington-Blackburn had already been working with PAE and in May 1996 Blackburn and EPC Presbytery agreed that Blackburn seek dual EPC-EPCEW membership. On 21 February 2001 Blackburn EPC became a full Congregation in regular standing, and on 2 April 2001 became fully integrated members of EPCEW.

In Summary ...

So the full third phase of new congregations covered the years 1978-1994 and in some ways has been the most encouraging, for five new congregations were opened or acquired in 16 years—an average of one every 3-4 years. It would have been difficult to sustain a faster rate of growth. It is encouraging also because it belongs to recent years and to a period of mature Presbyterian structure. The congregations were:

1978	Dublin	1989	Accrington-Blackburn
1982	Omagh	1994	Groomsport (Bangor)
1984	Richhill		

Again, the net growth alters the picture. The small rural Church at Clintyfallow, Co Tyrone, closed in 1985, Blackburn transferred to the Evangelical Presbyterian Church of England and Wales in 2001, Dublin closed in 2007, and Lisburn Road merged with Finaghy in 2008. So there were 10 congregations in 1932 and 10 in 2014 (5 Belfast, 5 provincial). The last new congregation was opened in 1994 so it is difficult to avoid the question about vision to expand into areas of need. Financial and human resources have been strong constraining factors for the Church during its first 50 years, but they have applied to a much lesser extent since 1980. Most 'sister' churches have new-plant programmes.

Further Church Development

New Church Buildings
The Omagh congregation opened a new building in May 1990, Richhill in October 1990, Crumlin in March 1999 and Groomsport in May 2004. Knock opened its new building and Omagh its major extension-refurbishment in 2015. The trustees of the Crumlin Mackey bequest have been generous in substantial funding of these building projects. Looking forward, Stranmillis has drawn up plans for on-site redevelopment.

In 2006 the Church Extension Committee brought the question of planting new congregations back to its agenda. The Committee considered the principles of church-planting, the financial and manpower implications, the relationship of new congregations with those existing, and their possible location - north and south of the border, east and west of the River Bann. The discussions continued into 2007 with increased focus on limiting the impact of new work on the Church's resources. The Committee sought advice from outside bodies and held meetings with the Free Church of Scotland and the Presbyterian Church of America's *Mission to the World*. The CEC developed its church-planting discussions along the same lines in 2008.

Church Development Committee
In October 2007 Presbytery had appointed a Strategy Committee to consider the EPC's long-term strategy, and the CEC began collaboration with it. During 2009 the two committees held joint meetings, concentrating on three broad areas: consolidation of existing congregations, new church-plants, and manpower. The two committees presented a joint report to the Presbytery meeting of 7 December 2009 and the meeting agreed that Presbytery:

1. Combine the Church Extension and Church Strategy Committees under the name of "Church Development Committee".
2. Sanction the Committee to visit all congregations to discuss future development.
3. Sanction the Committee to tentatively explore the possibility of a church plant in the Lisburn, Dungannon and Cookstown areas.
4. Sanction TOMA-CDC to establish a "Ministry Training Day".

The Committee proceeded with its visits to congregations and its exploration of potential church-plants. In October 2011 it proposed to Presbytery that CDC should lead a special meeting of Presbytery to discuss Church Strategy. Presbytery accepted and EPC's long-term strategy project of October 2007 was back on course. The 25 February 2012 meeting discussed:

1. Is there a need for the EPC?
2. Where are we today?
3. Where do we want to be by 2027, our centenary year?
4. How do we get there?

Following the CDC report in March 2012, Presbytery appointed 14 May 2012 as another special meeting to consider the CDC report and session responses. It was unanimously agreed on 14 May 2012 that each Session should spend time considering its own needs for growth, taking account of restraining factors; that each should submit a written report to the Church Development Committee in October 2012; and that CDC should produce a consolidated report for a special meeting of Presbytery in November 2012. Each session and congregation was encouraged to pray throughout the process. In November 2012 Presbytery noted "the sense of agreement reached by the Church Development Committee during the discussions on its document, and mandates CDC and other relevant committees to take these forward." So the main emphasis was on growth at congregational level. One of its blessings is the potential increase in resources needed for the extension of witness into new areas.

Strategy projects should always highlight the interaction of divine sovereignty and human responsibility. In the 1970s and 80s EPC experienced notable growth in its number of congregations and in member-students for the ministry but it was not the result of a strategy project, rather of prayer and the Lord's intervention. Then began a strategy project in 1989 for the 90s. Acknowledging the limitations of human judgement it did not accomplish as much as what the Lord did in the two preceding decades without such a formal project, although the 70s and 80s were not without strategic thinking. So was *Vision for the Nineties* ill-conceived? By no means. It achieved excellent things. Understanding of the times, planning and vision have strong biblical endorsement.

North Belfast – A New Start
In 2012 one of the North Belfast congregations, Somerton Road, received a substantial bequest and the North Belfast Session decided to use it strategically to fund new efforts to revive the work of the Church, which had suffered a downturn through the demographic changes that accompanied the Northern Ireland 'Troubles'. For Somerton Road the session appointed a Youth Outreach Worker, David Burke, in September 2013 and a Church Planter, Pablo Mandresa, in November 2013, and launched the new work officially on 15 January 2014. For Crosscollyer Street the session appointed an Outreach Worker Evangelist, Greg Thompson. To help with the increased demands a member of the Church Development Committee joined the North Belfast Session as an assessor elder in December 2012.

Ministry Growth and Standards
36 ministers in all have served or are serving the Church; the Church has ordained 24 of them. Of the total 36, 16 have left the service for different reasons, eight have retired or died in service, three retired as serving missionaries and nine were serving congregations in 2014. By the end of 2014 only six ministers had served the whole of their pastoral ministry in the Church. Appendices 6 and 8 set out

the succession of ministers and the relation between the numbers of ministers and congregations. The post-1977 years show a much better ratio than the pre-1977. Ministers often served two churches, and the movement through recruitment, resignations, and inter-congregational calls produced considerable traffic in Interim Moderators as well as ministers, as shown in the table below.

	New Installations/Appointments			
	Ministers	Interim Moderators	Average Ministers	Congregations
1920s	3		2	4-7
1930s	15		2-5	8-10
1940s	7	5	5-6	9-10
1950s	8	13	5-6	10
1960s	5	4	5-7	9-10
1970s	8	8	5-9	9-10
1980s	13	13	7-11	10-12
1990s	8	9	10-11	12
2000s	7	13	8-11	10-12
2010s	2	1	7-9	9-10
Totals	**76**	**66**		

It has been encouraging to have a more regular pattern of single congregation ministries since the mid-1970s. There were 20 new ministers since 1970, when the third phase of member-students began to take effect - an average of one about every 2 years, but the pattern of movement in and out has remained, for since 1970, 16 have ceased through retirement, death or calls to other areas of service. There is little doubt that economic factors have played some part in the turnover.[446] The filling of the Finaghy vacancy in May 2014 meant that, for the first time in its history, the Church had no vacant congregations.

17 EPC students have trained at the following colleges:

Free Church of Scotland, Edinburgh   11
Reformed Presbyterian College, Belfast   4
Westminster Theological Seminary, Philadelphia   2

There has also been the training of others whom the Lord has called to serve him in various other capacities. In March to June, 2012, TOMA ran a series of Preaching Workshops which about 40 men from within and outside EPC attended.

In November 1993, arising out of a Training for the Ministry and Admissions Committee report, Presbytery reiterated its commitment to ground the training of students upon Scripture and the subordinate standards of the Westminster Confession of Faith and Catechisms, to avail itself of the colleges of other churches for the purpose, and to prepare a student training curriculum. Presbytery also instructed Sessions to consider their responsibility to encourage potentially suitable men to consider prayerfully the Gospel Ministry. God answered this prayer in a number of important ways including the training from the membership of Robert Johnston, Stranmillis, who completed his studies in 2008, Trevor Kane, Stranmillis, scheduled to complete in 2015 and John Roger, Ballyclare, scheduled to begin in the autumn of 2015.

Training for the Ministry Fund Bequest
In 1995 Mrs Doris McFetrich, a member of the Stranmillis congregation, bequeathed the whole of her residual estate to the Church, an amount exceeding £190,000, "for the purposes of training male Ministers for the Evangelical Presbyterian Church". Presbytery recorded its gratefulness to God for this significant provision for a priority need.

Sermon Recordings
This ministry was a component of *Vision for the Nineties* but it did not develop beyond the early 90s. Local arrangements have continued to exist with varied use of developing options.

A Busy Presbytery

Committee Efficiency
In 2004 PAC produced a paper on the workings of Presbytery which addressed the need for more efficient use of manpower. One major change resulted in that of operating several committees with a single representative. Its own annual report summarises matters such as the composition of Presbytery and its meetings, Presbytery commissions, personnel and appointments, significant events of the Moderatorial year and Membership-Attendance statistics – Appendix 10. PAC also acts as a Commission of Presbytery during recesses, administers the lists of standing committee members whom Presbytery appoints, submits nominations for the Moderator-elect and provides guidance for the Moderator in situations requiring immediate attention. The Committee added the "previous immediate past Moderator" to its personnel from October 2006.

Presbytery Visitations
Presbytery has continued to superintend and provide care and advice to the congregations with regard to their spiritual and temporal affairs by assessment or 'visitation' of each congregation every seven years.

A New Annual Presentation of Presbytery Reports
In 1996 Presbytery expressed concern over declining interest in the Annual Presentation and appointed a committee to consider the issues. Its recommendations to transact all business at the April meeting of Presbytery which all congregations would be encouraged to attend, and to replace the Annual Presentation with a

'Family Fellowship Day', were not implemented at that time, but it did sow the seed.

In 2002 the necessity of an Annual Presentation was queried and resulted in the meeting reverting to a week night as it had been 1961-1978. Since 2002 was the 75th Anniversary year other church delegates were invited to the celebrations in October 2002 rather than to the Annual Presentation in April. Rev. Bill McCully addressed the April meeting as a guest speaker on his work at Hull EPCEW. This led to the practice of inviting just one or two church delegates each year.[447] From 2005 the Annual Presentation reverted to Saturday afternoon-evening and began to incorporate the 1996 recommendation of a 'Family Fellowship Day'. From 2009 it has been known as the Presbytery Day Conference. At these gatherings the new Moderator is installed, key Presbytery Reports presented and the printed Annual Reports published. The Conference speaker has been a major element since 2009 – Appendix 14.

The YPA Family Day
In 1991, its 25th Anniversary year, the Young People's Association began an annual Family Day event for the denomination, usually on the May Day Bank Holiday. Its programme included a range of sports and a barbecue and it often raised funds for the YPA Missions Project of the year. The name evolved from *YPA Family Day* to *EPC Family Day* and the event continued until 2008. Some of its features were incorporated into the new format *Presbytery Day* from 2009.

Finance Consultative Committee
The Finance Consultative Committee was appointed in November 1987 and assumed responsibility for the Church's finance in 2004. The Committee has been able to provide encouraging annual reports. In particular, increasing congregational targets have very largely been met. The Funds reported are Central Fund, Home and Foreign Missions, General, Young People's Association, Capital Investment. The Committee has taken the lead in the huge task of preparing the Church and its congregations for registration with the Northern Ireland Charities Commission and in implementing its Charity Law.

Public Morals
Coming forward from the 1980s the Committee has tackled a wide range of issues: alcoholism, TV and media standards, freemasonry, Christian education, nuclear war, blasphemy and obscenity, euthanasia, the national lottery, gambling, drug abuse, human rights legislation, re-classification of cannabis, medical ethics, parental discipline, the Protection of Children Act, the Adoption of Children Act, *Jerry Springer the Opera*.

In the 1980s and into the 1990s the attack on the sanctity of the Lord's Day in the form of Sunday sport and Sunday trading was prominent, and the Committee worked closely with the Lord's Day Observance Society. In 1995 the Committee put out a statement on the Sunday Trading legislation of that year: "The Evangelical Presbyterian Church feels an immense sense of sadness and dismay at today's government announcement concerning Sunday trading and Sunday sport. Despite many representations being made to the Government by those opposed to these changes the Government has decided to trample the Law of God underfoot and pursue a course of action that is anti-Christian." In 1997 the annual report included the recommendation: "We note and commend the idea of observing an annual 'Sabbath Awareness Day'". Later in the 1990s the issues had become, gay proselytism, same-sex couples, civil partnerships, the redefining of marriage, adoption rights and internet pornography. Continuing up to the present time has been the Lord's Day, human trafficking, organ donation, lowering of the age of consent, gambling and the wide field of sex-related issues – abortion, homosexuality, pornography, video 'nasties', transvestite services, AIDS and marriage.

In the 1990s the Committee felt relentless pressure. In 1989 it spoke of the problem of prioritising "as the battle rages on so many fronts". In 1992 Presbytery's "watchdog on current affairs" reported that "the number of issues requiring our attention is staggering". In 1993: "Our nation has plunged further into wickedness and sin and the Law of God has been trampled underfoot". In 1997: "We are perturbed that the decline appears to be accelerating." The Committee identifies with the *Christian Institute*, a national body which came into existence in 1990. The work of Public Morals has always been exceedingly difficult but successive Committees have been tenacious.

Protection of Children and Vulnerable Adults
In 2005 Presbytery began to implement the new legislation. Dr A A Woolsey drew up the draft policy proposals and in 1996 Presbytery published its policy under the title, *Committed to Care*. It appointed a denominational POCVA committee, which reported to Presbytery. Presbytery majored on policy, the Committee on monitoring compliance and sessions on implementation - checks for leaders and helpers, appointments, training, regulated procedures, document display, recording, and risk assessments. It has added to the work, mainly in connection with youth activities, but the Church acknowledges the need for such regulatory standards. Presbytery carried out a review of its policy in 2013, updated *Committed to Care* and appointed a POCVA Board through which it implements its policy.

Youth Work – New Activities
Assisting congregations – Crumlin, Finaghy, Knock and Somerton Road – with summer outreach became a marked feature of YPA activity from 2008. Annual residential weekends have been continuous since 1976 and combined with the Senior Camp Reunion since 1998. In addition, a YPA outreach team visited Andrew and Eunice Moody in Uganda in 2011 and Almuñécar on the south-east coast of Spain, 2012-2014. The Senior YPA changed its name to *Ignite* in 2013.

Autumn Evening Lectures

Outreach is primarily and most commonly the work of local congregations, but Presbytery saw a denominational opportunity through public lectures. In March 1994 the Training for the Ministry and Admissions Committee asked Presbytery to consider a series of evening classes. On receiving its Evening Class Committee report in June 1994 Presbytery approved an eight-week series beginning 10 October 1994 at Lisburn Road EPC on the subject: *Revival: Principles of Scripture, Lessons from History.* The Committee's report in December was highly encouraging. Around 70 had attended each evening, most of whom came from outside Belfast, and course appraisal forms indicated that the choice of venue, day of the week and time of year had been right. The lectures had substantial appeal outside EPC too. As a result Presbytery requested that the Committee run a similar programme in 1995, and again in 1996.

There were no lectures in 1997 but at Presbytery's request Stranmillis Session organised the 1998 and 1999 series under the new title *Autumn Evening Lectures.* Presbytery resumed direct ownership through a Committee in 2000 and ran the series annually until 2003. The emphasis on history and its applications, along with the issues facing the church in the modern world, were appropriate at the turn of a new millennium. Lecture subjects are in Appendix 15.

The Book *of* Praise

The issue of a suitable hymnbook had exercised the Church from its very inception. Previous chapters have traced the story of the Psalter, *Golden Bells* and the *Trinity Hymnal.*

In May 1994 Presbytery appointed a new Praise Committee to examine the matter of praise. A variety of books had come into use, along with supplements to the Trinity Hymnal. Furthermore, Psalm singing appeared to be declining and the Trinity Hymnal edition in use was out of print. Work proceeded on the feasibility of an EPC book, particularly to do with costs, copyright, and content, but when the consultation process with congregations was inconclusive in September 1998, Presbytery took the matter off the agenda for 12 months.

A Committee resumed work in 2000. After consultations with congregations the Committee issued a discussion paper in May 2002. Presbytery began the debate in June and in October decided in principle to produce its own Praise Book and the Committee proceeded to work towards publication. *The Book of Praise,*[448] incorporating the Free Church of Scotland's new *Sing Psalms* and Rev. Dr Rowland Ward's modern version of the Westminster Confession of Faith and Shorter Catechism, was published in August 2003 - 70 years after Rev. W J Grier raised the matter of "a universal book of praise" in October 1933. Rev. Stephen Roger, Convener of the 2000 Praise Committee, outlined the history, principles, and processes of the project in the *Evangelical Presbyterian,* Sep-Oct 2003:

In essence [the committee's criteria] were that, in considering items to be included in a book to include psalms, hymns and spiritual songs, consideration would be given, in the first instance, to *Trinity Hymnal*, *Christian Hymns*, *Hymns of Faith* and the recently arrived *Praise!* hymnbook. The reasoning was important. *Trinity* was the book approved by Presbytery. *Christian Hymns* was the book in use by a number of the non-*Trinity* congregations. *Hymns of Faith* was the hymnbook follow-on to *Golden Bells*, in wide use across the denomination until the mid-1980s ... *Praise!* had no automatic figuring in this equation ... The committee viewed its inclusion as important in terms of where 'modern', but steady and Reformed items of praise might be going.

The goal of the Praise Committee was to produce a book that could marry the use of psalms, paraphrases, hymns and spiritual songs, and sustain this bond across the breadth of the EPC in terms of praise, and with the prospect of doing so over many years. ... The aim was balance. The issues of gravity, doctrinal content and substance, "understandability", the balance between the declaration of objective truth and its subjective appreciation, and the likely durability of more contemporary items were paramount. Different strains had to be represented whilst holding to the basic tenet of producing a book suitable for a Presbyterian, Reformed, paedo-baptist and conservative, but forward-thinking, church. ...

Change is often uncomfortable, but the change that The Book of Praise is aimed at is that we might, as a denomination, together, across our breadth, hold to a steady course. There are some modernisations that will hopefully go some way to recognising a range of age and taste amongst us, but the overall picture is defiantly conservative.

Sadly worship in so many circles has become an agenda of 'trendy-ism' and man-pleasing. The merest glance at The Book of Praise will demonstrate that this is not what it's about! The desire is, recognising there has to be some movement with time, to remain steady.

Ladies' United Monthly Prayer Meeting – Its 70 Years

This story began in Chapter 20 - *Gaining a Foothold*. The women from the churches in the Belfast area met in Botanic Avenue from 1938 and relocated to Stranmillis in October 1971. Mrs Garland succeeded Mrs Grier as leader in the first half of the 1980s and after more than 10 years she handed over to Helen Houston to begin the new session in September 1996 with Irene Brown's assistance. The speakers were usually ministers, missionaries and the ladies themselves, but the men who visited as speakers left before the time of prayer began. The Leader brought prayer points and they prayed for 'everything'—for the ministers, the Church, the congregations, missions, the Book Shop, and the sick. God blessed them with great liberty in prayer so that it was seldom that everyone present did not take part. Periods of silence were not a feature of these meetings. If there was an attendance register it has not been preserved, but the following would have been among the names it would regularly have recorded:

Annie Blair	Julia Grier	Jessie Reid
Irene Brown	Mary Hamilton	Kathleen Speers
Helen Colhoun	Helen Houston	Madge Speers
Nan Dunlop	Anna Jess	Anna Speers
Roberta Flack	Jean Lemon	Ruby Tait
Agnes Gale	Sadie McDowell	Hilda Thompson
Etta Gale	Sealy McKee	Anne Tollerton
Maisie Garland	S Miller	Irene Totten
Catherine Grier	Agnes Newell	

Attendance post 1930s continued to be about 12, but the numbers reduced in the 1990s. Changing patterns of daily life suggested a change of time, and so a new phase began with Tuesday morning meetings from 3 March 1997. However, the experiment did not succeed and by 1999 the attendance was sometimes as low as three. After further deliberation it became clear that the meeting was no longer sustainable, and in consultation with Presbytery, 5 October 1999 was the closing meeting. Another factor in the closure decision was the increase of Ladies' Fellowships throughout the congregations which had collectively become the prayer successors of LUMPM. The Church cannot calculate its debt to the women who were faithful to this meeting "where prayer was customarily made" (Acts 16.13), for over 72 years. It has been the only denominational meeting outside Presbytery with such an enduring contribution. The Foreign Missions Committee Annual Report for 1999 acknowledged its cessation in the context for prayer for missions.

The Evangelical Presbyterian – A New Chapter

Since 1928 the magazine has been the standard denominational means of presenting its witness. Appendix 12 lists the six Editors and their years of diligent editorial service with details of the changing Magazine formats. With the change to A5 format in 1981 the advent of desk-top publishing facilitated the progressive use of colour and photographs. Post-W J Grier there was less emphasis on polemic with regard to modernism, ecumenism and the state of the professing church but no change in the fields of theology, evangelism, devotional material, children, missions, range of contributors, Church news and books. It has been an exponent for the reformed faith extending the influence of the church far beyond its immediate location. It has also proved an invaluable contributor to historical research.

Inter-Church Relations - Expanding

During the 1990s and 2000s the major items of agenda were the closing years of the British Evangelical Council and its re-launch as Affinity in 2004, the Free Church of Scotland, ICRC's European Conference and the Evangelical Presbyterian Church of England and Wales. In addition, links were formalised with another ICRC member Church in the Netherlands and in this context, in December 2007, Presbytery noted the need to define what EPC means by ICR.

British Evangelical Council – Varying Levels of Engagement

The BEC developed locally in the later 1980s and formed a Regional Committee in 1990. The Committee created local interest and organised conferences, particularly 1988-1991. But this this level of interest did not continue. Annual reports became briefer, noting "quiet encouragements" in 1992. In 1993 the level of interest in the local 40th anniversary rallies in 1992 was "lamentable". The 1994 Annual Report noted that interest in the BEC in Northern Ireland appeared to be lacking, that there was failure of a perceived need, and that denominational work was being given priority. The 1994 Report also acknowledged that: "we have not always shown the knowledge of and interest in the work and rationale of the BEC that we ought." Rev. Mark Johnston had put his finger on a key issue in his 1991 Report: "Then again it is frustrating because it is largely the domain of but one member of Presbytery and it is never easy to generate the degree of interest and enthusiasm that this work deserves. We must consider ways of making BEC membership more meaningful for the whole Church…"

EPC activity with BEC shot up again in 1995-96 with 'Toronto Blessing' issues and discussions with Rev. Ken Morey who had had a Bible teaching ministry in Romania known as *Stream* since 1993 with BEC direction and support. The 1997 comment was: "Our active involvement with BEC during 1997 was not at the fever-pitch level of 1996."! After a review of structures in the mid-1990s the BEC decision in 1997 was largely to maintain the 'as is' with a smaller management Committee. As Alan Gibson's retirement in 1999 approached some of the old difficulties resurfaced—uncertainty over BEC's future course, the shortage of finance, and disparity between member subscriptions. David Ford succeeded him as General Secretary and set about consultation with member Churches about BEC's future.

It has been a privilege for the EPC to maintain its participation throughout the changing phases of BEC since it began in 1952. W J Grier was the first treasurer and Chairman 1957-58. The BEC Secretary Alan Gibson, said of him: "He was present at the first meeting of the Council and his spirit was reflected in the principles which brought Presbyterian and Independent Church bodies from Scotland, Northern Ireland, England (and later Wales) into fraternal association." Rev. A A Campbell was Chairman 1965-66 and served for 10 years as a Council representative. W J McDowell's service was of similar duration. Dr Edwin Kerr was Secretary for some years in the 1950s.

Fellowship of Independent Evangelical Churches

Activity with FIEC had increased in the 1950s and 60s. Rev. A A Campbell was the delegate in 1974 at Bolton and in 1977 at London. On several other occasions in the 1960s, 70s, and early 80s Presbytery sent letters of greeting to the FIEC Assembly. The Inter-Church relations report in 1982 noted that FIEC was one of the bodies with whom the Church enjoyed fraternal relations within BEC. The 2001 report spoke of a visit to Presbytery from the General Secretary of FIEC in October 2000, and noted that: "Our informal discussions earlier that day were useful in renewing a recently dormant relationship." In many ways this sums up the history of EPC relationship with FIEC. It has always been supportive and fraternal, but often dormant. BEC-Affinity has continued to be the forum where FIEC and EPC inter-relate.

Affinity
Affinity, a church-centred partnership for Bible-centred Christianity,

> "was unveiled in March, 2004, the result of a decision by the British Evangelical Council to re-invent itself in the light of the new challenges posed by a post-Christian culture. For over 50 years, the BEC stood for robust evangelical orthodoxy, separate from the contaminating influences of false ecumenism. Affinity is building on this same, firm foundation, amid the swirling waters of what currently passes for mainstream evangelicalism. Nevertheless, both its mission and its methods have been the subject of radical review. Affinity claims to be 'a new approach to the expression of biblical church unity for the 21st century'."[449]

The subject of Affinity has appeared on Presbytery's agenda regularly, often revealing an uneasy participation, especially in the early years. During 2008-09 there was concern over observable New Covenant Theology trends within Affinity and there was a felt need to bolster the Westminster position. In June 2009 Presbytery expressed its disquiet over Affinity's ineffectiveness for the EPC situation and its considerable agenda-demands. Presbytery agreed to remain in membership but to attend only one meeting per year, with EPCEW representation at the others. In September 2009 Presbytery discussed the issue of Affinity's doctrinal basis particularly the definition of the church and covenant children, issues EPC shared with EPCEW. In February 2010 it was confirmed to Presbytery that *Affinity* had accepted EPCEW's proposed amendment of Paragraph 8 of the Basis: "Some churches within Affinity believe that the visible church comprises baptised believers along with their baptised covenant children."[450] After lengthy discussion, which again highlighted time-demand, Presbytery agreed to maintain membership with a review in 2011.

At its Annual Meeting in April 2010 *Affinity* addressed some of the issues facing it and in September it was confirmed to Presbytery that both the finances and administration had been stabilized. In 2011 EPCEW did raise with *Affinity* the issue of Baptism in connection with its Basis of Faith, but favourable delegate reports about the generally improving situation and the desire to be in corporate relationship with evangelical brethren throughout the country, encouraged annual membership renewal and, in 2012, to fix the next review for 2015. In addition, UK member Churches of ICRC had remained in *Affinity* membership.

Aontas

In the 1990s Rev. Norman Reid played a role in formation of Aontas (formerly known as the Association of Irish Evangelical Churches) which is a partnership of Bible-centred churches, organizations, and individuals who have come together to co-operate in advancing the Gospel of Christ in Ireland.

The Free Church of Scotland Split

A division took place in the Free Church of Scotland in January 2000 over a high profile case of church discipline, running since the mid-1990s.[451] From the beginning, Presbytery stressed its concern to remain "non-partisan", to "hold on to our own unity", to "avoid the issue bringing division". There was also the recognition that the differing views of members are held "deeply, honestly and sincerely". In addition, there was regular prayer for the church in Scotland and thankfulness over any steps towards improving relations between both bodies such as settling property disputes amicably. In particular there was the Free Church of Scotland's termination in 2008 of the Sentences of Suspension imposed upon ministers of the FCC since the latter had become distinct from the FCoS and were no longer subject to the jurisdiction of its Courts. Annual Reports referred to "cordial relations", "warm fellowship" and "sister" relationships with both Churches. The 2011 Annual Report noted the prospect of EPC students again being trained at the Free Church College which became Edinburgh Theological Seminary (ETS) in 2014.[452]

Presbyterian Church in Ireland

PCI made an approach in 2005 to explore the possibility of a formal inter-church relationship. Presbytery briefed two delegates to meet with the PCI Committee and advise that in view of PCI's inherently pluralist composition it was not possible for EPC to enter a formal relationship. The delegation declined the offer of further talks but thanked the PCI Committee for the offer. The Presbytery brief acknowledged that some of EPC ministers and elders are happy to work with those in PCI who consistently adhere to the Westminster standards and that some co-operate with PCI personnel on moral and ethical issues. The brief also affirmed the stand of 1927 and encouraged others to secede today and in the future.

ICRC- EuCRC

EPC became members of the International Conference of Reformed Churches in 1984. ICRC decided in 1989 to hold Regional Conferences every four years, after a successful trial in Belfast in 1987. The Steering Committee met in Edinburgh in May 1990 and the first Conference under the new arrangements took place in Edinburgh in 1991. The subjects were Evangelism in Eastern Europe, Evangelism in France and Ireland, National Righteousness, and Reflections on Canada 1989. EPC hosted the second in the series, at Ballyclare, on 13 September 1995. 27 delegates including representatives from the Christian Reformed Church of the

Netherlands, attended and discussed Missions, Gambling, Medical Ethics, and the Family. The Conference merited a very positive report. The Reformed Presbyterian Church organised the next Conference in Lisburn on 1 November 1999. GKNV and CRC Netherlands delegates joined those from the UK Churches. There were papers on Justification, Church Growth, Virtual Morality, and Mission in a Roman Catholic Culture. As in 1995 the Conference fuelled expectation.

The ICRC's Regional Conference in Europe now goes under the title 'European Conference of Reformed Churches'. The first meeting was held in the Netherlands in 2007. The seven ICRC member churches comprised the core group who invited associated churches or groups. The second EuCRC was in Soest, Netherlands, in 2008 which established the desire among the member bodies to co-operate and harness resources for the proclamation of the Gospel in Europe with special emphasis on major cities and areas where the reformed faith is absent or in decline. As a strand distinct from the 'church-planting' objectives Theological Institutions were brought within the scope of the vision, being called on to look for and develop opportunities for cooperation in their work. The third conference took place in Edinburgh in 2010 with the theme ROUTE - Reaching Out Unitedly to Europe - through co-operation between reformed churches in evangelism and theological education. The theme of the fourth gathering, held in Kiev, Ukraine, 2012, was 'Marginal and Missional'. In the context of Europe EPC sent a delegate to the Synod of Reformed Churches in Spain in November 2006 and reciprocated the invitation in 2007 for an RCS delegate to visit the EPC annual meeting in 2008.

In 2011 Presbytery recorded the Church's concerns over views within one ICRC member Church on Divorce, Ordination of Women as deacons and Homosexuality and undertook to monitor the situation in co-operation with other Reformed Churches.

CRCN (CKGN)

In 2005 the Christian Reformed Churches in the Netherlands asked EPC to revive and enhance inter-church relationships. Full corresponding relations were achieved in 2007 following exchange visits in 2006-07. The CKGN is a separate denomination from the Reformed Churches in the Netherlands (Liberated) (GKNV) with whom EPC also has been in 'correspondence' since 1982. Both Churches are members of ICRC.[453]

EPCEW

The Presbyterian Association in England (PAE) emerged from the London Presbyterian Conference in 1986. From 1987, a group of ministers and other men formed a London based Council and three small congregations started Sunday meetings. In 1991, an interim Presbytery was formed consisting of elders from five congregations; Blackburn, Cambridge, Chelmsford, Durham and East Hull. In 1996 these churches declared themselves a Presbytery, taking the name *Evangelical Presbyterian Church in England and Wales*.

EPC welcomed the formation of PAE, conveying its prayerful good wishes in 1987. In May 1988 Presbytery sent a delegation to Accrington in response to a request for help from a group there and during the visit the delegates held discussions with PAE and attended its Annual Conference in London. The formation of Accrington Mission Church in 1989 facilitated growing contact with PAE, especially by the Church Extension Committee and Presbytery recorded its pleasure over the intended establishment of an Interim Presbytery. During the 1990s the progress of PAE/EPCEW featured in EPC Annual Reports. The Church Relations Committee took over the lead contact from Church Extension in 1993 and in December 1993 Presbytery responded favourably to the request from PAE in September for closer links with the future possibility of a Synodical relationship, encouraging PAE to progress towards full Presbytery status. 1996 saw the formation of the Presbytery of EPCEW. It adopted Evangelical Presbyterian Church as part of its name, and entered into Sister-Church relations with EPC. In 1997 EPC supported EPCEW's application to become members of ICRC.

The early 2000s were marked by progress towards the more formal EPC-EPCEW relations, first mooted in 1993 and in 2001 there were positive proposals in this direction which included the mutual eligibility of ministers and the acceptance of members along with the exchange of information. Representatives of the two Churches met in 2002 to consider proposals for mutual relations. In 2006 EPCEW proposed the renewal of the talks which led to a meeting in Ballyclare in February 2007. Exchange Presbytery visits followed and both Presbyteries made a commitment to proceed towards Synodical relations, recognising that issues such as structures and responsibilities would need to be worked out.

Four EPC delegates visited Chelmsford 24 September 2008 for talks on joint Synod procedure. The view of the meeting was that a joint meeting of both Presbyteries should precede such a major step. It took place in Cambridge 9 May 2009 with an agenda of key issues including whether the Synod would be a higher or a wider court. EPC sent a delegation of 10 Presbytery members. A committee from each body met at Chelmsford 17 June 2009 and issued a joint paper for each Presbytery to consider. The EPC Presbytery of October 2009 approved the paper and authorised its Committee to continue discussions in line with its framework. The EPCEW Presbytery of November 2009 agreed to begin co-operation with EPC at committee level in the spheres of training for the ministry, inter-church relations, public ethics, missions and publications. It further proposed another round of joint talks to monitor progress, work at definitions and set up a framework in which on-the-ground co-operation could work.

So efforts towards Synodical relationship shifted to co-operation in defined fields. Relationships continue to be enhanced through Committee and Conference. Two EPC ministers took part in EPCEW theological conference in 2010 and in 2011 EPC expressed its pleasure over the ongoing expansion of EPCEW.[454]

Orthodox Presbyterian Church, USA
EPC and OPC have enjoyed cordial relationships since OPC's founding in 1936.

Dr J Gresham Machen, its founding Leader, had significant background influence in the founding of EPC. Rev. Jack Peterson addressed the Annual Meeting in 2005. Rev. Gareth Burke, Moderator, attended OPC's 75th Anniversary celebrations in 2011. Rev. John P Galbraith visited Belfast in 2004. Jack Sawyer and Mark Bube came in 2013 and had discussions with the ICR Committee.

Reformed Presbyterian Church in Ireland
Local and personal contacts prove beneficial as both bodies support one another in the various ways that provide such opportunities. In particular, the RPCI Theological College has trained four Students for the EPC Ministry with the prospect of another. The RPCI College also regularly hosts theological conferences with guest speakers.

International Missions – A New Phase

The story in the last chapter noted that from 1982-83 Presbytery began transacting its Foreign Missions business through its Representative to the Foreign Missions Board of the Free Church of Scotland, rather than though a Committee. It turned full circle again in June 1990 when Presbytery re-appointed a Foreign Missions Committee arising out of the *Vision for the Nineties* Report, although the FMB Representative continued generally as Convener of the Committee. The Foreign Missions Board became the International Missions Board in 2002. Appendix 11A provides a summary of long-term member missionary service.

Engendering Mission Awareness
There was considerable work in stimulating interest in work overseas through the *Evangelical Presbyterian* and Annual Reports. The Foreign Missions Annual Reports for 1990 incorporated recommendations that Presbytery had adopted in October to keep missionary vision before the young people since there were now no serving missionaries in the historical fields:
1. That consideration be given to appointing a missions' secretary in each congregation, ie someone who would promote missionary vision among young people.
2. That individual young people in each congregation be specifically invited to write to a particular missionary.
3. That young people at secondary school be encouraged to take Spanish with a view to possible voluntary service in Peru, and that they be made aware that opportunities exist for voluntary work on all the fields.
4. That a young people's-YPA missionary weekend be organised for Spring 1991.

In 1995 the Foreign Missions Committee issued a Missionary Pack of seven A5 coloured brochures: *From the Frontiers, Setting the Missionary Agenda, Know India, Know South Africa, Know CWI, Know Peru,* and *Know Qua Iboe.* They gave suggestions for missionary involvement, the Church's mission strategy, and key historical and current information on each field. The *Setting the Missionary Agenda* brochure had a section dealing with the implementation of strategy, 'Making it all Work', at Presbytery, Local Church and Personal levels. It still needs to work in this structured, co-ordinated way right down to the personal level. Sunday Schools, Ladies Fellowships, Prayer meetings and the youth organisations have responded to mission projects, maintaining the EPC tradition of a sending and supporting Church – Appendix 11.

Sidney and Jean Garland
A new phase of missions began on 2 July 1987 when Rev. Sidney Garland and his wife Jean with their three children left for Nigeria as missionaries of Qua Iboe Fellowship, then celebrating its centenary. Dr Harvie M Conn, Professor of Missions, Westminster Theological Seminary, was the guest speaker at their Farewell. They began with two years' service in Abak, in south-east Nigeria, at the Samuel Bill Theological College. On return from furlough in 1990 they were seconded through *Action Partners* to the Theological College of Northern Nigeria at Bukuru, 10 miles south of Jos, in the north-central region. Sidney became Vice-Principal in 1991 and taught mainly in the area of Practical Theology as well as serving with the (SUM-related) Church of Christ in Nigeria. In 1997 Sidney gained a *Doctor of Ministry in Urban Mission* degree, through Westminster Theological Seminary, Philadelphia, where he had studied for the ministry.

Sidney Garland had the key role in the establishment of ACTS (Africa Christian Textbooks) in 1993, in Jos, with the support of several agencies. Its aim, expressed as its Mission Statement is "to strengthen the church in Africa by providing evangelical, relevant and affordable literature and literature-related services for Christian leaders and institutions in order to advance the cause of Christ". The work grew and by 2000 the increasing demands of ACTS and his Associate Pastor role in a local Church led to Mr Garland's re-assignment by Mission Africa (formerly Qua Iboe Fellowship) to ACTS with a part-time appointment at the College. The new phase of service gave him a three-fold function:

1 Ministry of the Word through part-time teaching at TCNN, mostly in the Masters' programme, and a wider speaking ministry.
2 ACTS – directing this growing work of book distribution and publishing.
3 Curriculum Consultancy – offering guidance, training and textbook recommendations to a growing number of Bible Colleges and Schools of Mission.

ACTS acquired a permanent 3 acre site near Jos in 2001 and after planning, fund-raising and building, the Grand Opening of the new Warehouse took place on 26 August 2006. Work has begun to provide a centre alongside the HQ Warehouse for training, conference and study facilities along with editorial assistance for

African writers and editors. By 2006, in addition to the Nigerian network, there were three ACTS branches in Kenya which supply a further four bookshops.

Jean supported the work of TCNN in the College Dispensary and Clinic but in 1997 a new door of opportunity for service opened for her – the training of those involved in AIDS education. By 1999 there were training workshops all over Nigeria as the Aid for AIDS programme rapidly developed. Since then the AIDS awareness project has operated in collaboration with student organisations, churches and government and has involved extensive travelling. Prominent among Jean's writings on the subject is *AIDS is Real and it's in Our Church*, first published in 2003, which she co-authored with Dr Mike Blyth. The Garlands were faithful also in producing regular prayer letters throughout their years in Nigeria and since returning in April 2010 to continue the work from their home in Belfast.[455]

Norman and Angela Reid
When Rev. Norman Reid and his wife Angela went to Dumisani Theological Institute, King William's Town, South Africa in 1999 it revived the missionary service link with the Free Church of Scotland. Presbytery seconded him to the Free Church and commissioned him to missionary service in Dumisani on 12 December 1998. He had previously lectured in Dumisani from July to December 1997 in response to a Foreign Missions Board advertisement for furlough cover.

During his Dumisani years he taught subjects from basic to degree level: Ministry and Leadership Studies, Theology – Historical and Practical, Basic English, Basic Computing, Church History, Systematic Theology, Christian Service Studies, Old Testament Introduction, New Testament Introduction, Systematic Theology and History. He graduated with an MA in Dogmatics at North West University, Potchefstroom, in September 2004, on the basis of his thesis, *The Unity of the Doctrine of Justification by Faith in Holy Scripture*. His Dumisani responsibilities incorporated prison outreach and the marking and administration of correspondence courses with people all over of South Africa, including prisons. He also served the Free Church in Southern Africa through preaching, training of office bearers and preachers, and in Church Courts. He used his considerable practical skills in supervising new building work and the maintenance of existing buildings at Dumisani and the Churches. Foremost in Angela's related work was her devoted care of Mrs Helen McCracken, retired missionary, who died on 2 March 2007. She also worked with the Bible Women of the Free Church and at the King William's Town Orphanage.

Andrew and Eunice Moody
Andrew Moody, Richhill, served with Africa Inland Mission to Kuluva, NW Uganda as a Pharmacist, 1995-1998. He trained pharmacy staff and engaged in Bible teaching and evangelism. To prepare for a wider ministry in Uganda, he began studies at the Irish Baptist College in 2000 and graduated with a Divinity degree in May 2002. In December 2001 Andrew married Eun Hee (Eunice)

Kim, a South Korean nurse he met in Kuluva. In April 2004 they returned to Goli, NW Uganda, as Missionaries of the Korean World Mission, where Andrew began work with the Church of Uganda and Bible Colleges across the country. Through the Goli Christian Resource Centre he provided affordable reformed, evangelical books, and facilitated Bible commentary translation into Alur. Eunice applied her nursing skills to village health and pregnancy care and dispensed and maintained pharmacy supplies. They returned to the UK in August 2006 for one year for Andrew to complete his Master's in theology with a view to teaching in the Church's Leadership Training Centre, Udende. Their next tour of duty was 2007-2011 in Goli and they resumed in September 2014.

Pamela Gaiya née Johnston
On 2 January 2003 Pamela Johnston, a Stranmillis member, left with *Mission Africa* (Qua Iboe Fellowship until 2002) to serve with ACTS in Jos, Nigeria as Administrative Secretary. One of her first tasks was the preparation of an updated ACTS Catalogue. Pamela kept the Church up to date with a series of *Jos Journal*, in which she covered her work in administration, publishing, stocktaking, re-printing, the developing Warehouse Project, language study, and in the local Church. She married Musa Gaiya, a Nigerian University Lecturer, on 4 September 2008.

Ed and Kate Underwood
Members at Stranmillis, Ed has worked home-based with Wycliffe Bible Translators (2008-12) and since then with UFM OneHundredFold Digital Technology, a ministry of UFM Worldwide. OneHundredFold is a group of technology specialists who believe that mobile technology has a key role to play in bringing the Gospel of Christ to every individual on Earth.

Jennifer Ray née Campbell
Jennifer Campbell, member at Stranmillis, went to Ethiopia with SIM to serve as a Teacher in Bingham Academy, Addis Ababa in January 2013. She married Samuel Ray in July 2014.

Overseas Students in Belfast
In June 1996 the Foreign Missions Committee gave notice of motion: "In the light of the growing Overseas Student population and the fact that we have 2 churches [Lisburn Road and Stranmillis] on [near] Queen's University Campus, the Foreign Missions Committee request that Presbytery consider the establishment of a formal work among Overseas Students, based in Belfast, and that Presbytery consider directing a share of our existing resources to it." Presbytery responded with the appointment of Rev. W L Elliott as Co-ordinator of Overseas Student Work on a part-time basis from 1 August 1997. Presbytery retained overall control of the work through its Committee who involved the Session of Stranmillis, the main Campus church, in the day to day oversight. Mr Elliott became an EPC minister

in July 1999 but maintained his concurrent part-time Student Co-ordinator role until June 2001 when he was called to EPC Richhill. The features of this first phase of this work were Bible studies, Scripture distribution, personal evangelism, lunch-time meetings, counselling and social activity. The personal contact side was fruitful in conversions and building up students in the faith. A number of them became effective in Christian work in their home lands.

The Stranmillis Session then took over responsibility and focused on the whole student body. Robert Johnston was the Student Worker 2004-2005 when he became a student for the ministry. Trevor Kane succeeded him in 2009 and in 2012 he also began studies for the ministry. The student lunch on Tuesdays has provided opportunities for spiritual contact with large numbers of students. One-to-one and group Bible studies, friendship, outings, involvement in the welcoming programme of the International Friendship Association were key elements.

Other Mission Activity
However, the Home and Overseas missions picture is much wider than that of EPC long-term member missionaries. A succession of members and former members, particularly those who grew up in the Church, have served or are serving in various missionary callings at home and abroad. The Church remains thankful for the privilege of this association. In addition, since the early 1980s, short-term service at home and overseas along with visits to mission fields by EPC members and adherents has amounted to close on 125 visits to about 30 different countries. See Appendix 11B.

Overseas Mission Legislation
In 2010 Presbytery defined two categories of EPC Missionaries as:

> Missionary: Minister or Elder who God has called to preach the Gospel and teach the word in a cross-cultural context and whom the Church has ordained/installed to this work. (Acts 13)
> Diaconal Missionary: Elder/Deacon/Member engaged in diaconal work, eg, education, medicine, construction, social (Matt 10.5-8, 25.34-46) with the approval of the Presbytery or local Session. The wives of missionaries, who carry out this role, can be recognised as support missionaries.

The Evangelical Book Shop - Changes
John Grier, Manager for 38 years, 1974-2012, retired on 30 June 2012.[456] Trustees, past and present staff, and Church representatives attended a function in the Knockdene Room of the Stormont Hotel, Belfast and paid tribute to his long service, consummate knowledge of Christian books and the immense influence of his life's work at home and farther afield. His successor, Colin Campbell, was commissioned on 7 November 2012 at Stranmillis EPC. Rev. Geoff Thomas, Aberystwyth, was the Guest Speaker. The shop was extensively refurbished in 2011.

Recurrent Censure

The passing of time did not stop attempts to censure the EPC over its beginnings and smallness.

Totally Outclassed!

Strangely the Heresy Trial surfaced again in BBC Radio Ulster's *Thought for the Day* on Sunday 13 June 1999 when Father Michael Collins used it as an example of the need for professionalism. He saw Professor Davey as the professional who totally outclassed and demolished his amateur, bungling accusers:

> The last trial for heresy in Ireland took place not, as you might imagine, in the 17th or even the 18th century but in 1927 in Belfast. A very learned and respected Professor of theology at Assembly's College, Belfast, was charged before the Belfast Presbytery on five counts of teaching doctrines contrary to the Word of God and the standards of the Church.
>
> His forty-three accusers ranged from Bangor to Ballymena and from Coleraine to Castlecaulfield, and displayed an impressive array of qualifications from JPs to DDs. When it came to the trial, however, it was soon brutally clear that his accusers, with the innocence and the impetuosity of all armchair athletes, had entered an arena where they were totally outclassed.
>
> They found themselves up against a professional, whose entire life had been dedicated to theological argument and historical interpretation. It would be fair to say that he demolished them. They lost the thread of their arguments, sometimes contradicted themselves, stumbled over their facts and fears, to such an extent that one accuser was led to regret that he had ever allowed himself to be talked into pursuing such a futile cause.
>
> It finished with the judges themselves expressing their regret that the trial had ever taken place and hoping that they would never live to see the like of it again. Sadly, they probably will see the like again, because amateurs continue to fool themselves into believing that they can play better football, be a better comedian, present a better programme, or provide a better commentary on the Grand National, than the professionals, and they never do.
>
> To be a professional in any aspect of life requires steadfast application, rehearsal and study. In short, professionalism in any sphere is a lifetime's work. As the Book of Proverbs says, "my son if you take my words to heart and treasure my commandments deep within you, giving your attention to wisdom and your mind to understanding, if you cry out for discernment and invoke understanding, if you seek for her as for silver and dig for her as for buried treasure, then you will understand the fear of the Lord and attain to knowledge of God". (Prov 2.1-5, Oxford Study Bible)

The accused and his accusers were all members of the Presbyterian Church in Ireland and the great majority of the accusers continued to be so. But with its permanent identity with the leading accusers, the Evangelical Presbyterian Church felt a duty to respond. Consequently, the Church's Public Morals Committee wrote in protest to the Head of BBC Department for Religious Affairs.[457]

The 1927 Heresy Trial example was a strange, contrived choice for the broadcast. Taking place over 70 years previously, it was hardly a fit for the modern concept of 'professionalism' with which Collins's analogy-mix of athletics, football, comedy and the Grand National was more in line. Perhaps the 1999 listeners could have identified more readily with a contemporary issue. The trial was a strange choice too because the speaker's knowledge of it was limited. The accusers did have three JPs but as a body were not known for their "impressive array of qualifications". There is no record of DDs among them. The accuser who regretted his involvement exited before the Trial began, not because of how it was going. There were no 'judges' in the usual sense – the votes of members, the great majority of whom were laymen, constituted the verdict. The Church controlled the Trial and provided little opportunity for the accusers to engage the Professor directly; he refused to take the witness stand himself. In the single phase when accusers and Davey did engage he did not outclass or demolish them. He did not even outclass a 'plain man' lay witness. (See Chapter 11). More fundamentally, the test at the Heresy Trial was not 'professionalism' but obedience to God in contending for his truth. The accusers had the faithfulness and courage to do it and they identified major theological issues. Proverbs 2.1-5 (quoted from the Oxford Study Bible in the broadcast) is not about 'professionalism' but the diligent search for wisdom that results in understanding the fear of the Lord and in finding the knowledge of God. It was this fear of the Lord that motivated the accusers and their stand still speaks as a persistent witness.

The Failure of the Schism
Steve Bruce in *Paisley*, 2007, presents a section on the Irish Evangelical Church under the heading "The Failure of the Schism". In one-and-a-half-pages he refers three times to "schism" and once each to "dissidents", "Hunter's revolt" and "the schismatics of the 1920s".[458] In the following chapter he refers to "Grier's schismatic Presbyterians".[459] The terminology is similar to that in *Presbyterians in Ireland*, 2006: "Following their rebuff by the General Assembly, James Hunter, who was by then retired from active ministry, and others who had mounted the campaign against Ernest Davey felt they had no option but to leave the Irish Presbyterian Church. As is usual in such circumstances, the schismatic group labelled the majority as 'apostates,' claiming that the false teaching in the Presbyterian College was permitted to continue unpunished."[460] Regrettably, neither party defines "schism", justifies its use or deals with its essential theological genre. Biblically it is one of the most serious charges that can be brought against a church and churches should not do it without due diligence and self-examination. The Evangelical Presbyterian Church rejects the schism charge with full assurance based on the demands of Scripture. The issue is addressed in Part 5 – The Lessons of History.

Post Heresy Trial historians of the Presbyterian Church in Ireland offer varied approaches. Rev. David Stewart, Muckamore,[461] produced *A Short History of the Presbyterian Church in Ireland* in 1936, "for the use of youth groups throughout the church".[462] His penultimate chapter deals with 'Progress from the Union of the Synods' 1840-1936, and although he was publishing in 1936 he omits reference to the 1927 Heresy Trial and to the related events. This is strange in the light of his interest in controversy shown by his treatment of the Arian dispute in the first half of the 19th century, and of the assessment of other Irish Presbyterian writers of the importance of the trial, for example, Dr Austin Fulton, "This trial, as famous in the story of Irish Presbyterianism as the Robertson Smith case in Scotland, and for us more decisive …"[463]

Smallness
Two publications from the 1980s, neither ecclesiastical, continue the breakaway, schismatic theme and highlight the ongoing focus on EPC's relative smallness. The journalists, Ed Moloney and Andy Pollak in *Paisley*, relating to mid-1940s events, describe Rev. W J Grier as: "… a leading figure in the small Irish Evangelical Church, which grouped together a couple of hundred hard-line evangelicals who had broken away from the Irish Presbyterian Church after the Davey heresy trial of 1927."[464] Steve Bruce, in *God Save Ulster - The Religion & Politics of Paisleyism*, under 'The Failure of the Schism', observes:

> Twenty seven years after he had first protested against the lack of doctrinal orthodoxy in the Irish Presbyterian Church, James Hunter felt driven to leave it. In July 1927 he resigned from the Belfast Presbytery. Very few others resigned with him. Most of the supporters of the Bible Standards League remained in the church, arguing that they could best defend orthodoxy from within. Over that summer small groups met in the Belfast area and in the autumn the Irish Evangelical Church was formed. If success is to be measured in numbers, the schism was a dismal failure. William J Grier, the student who had approached Hunter to complain about Davy's teaching, came out but many others who had been vocal in their support for Hunter's campaign preferred to stay within the Presbyterian Church and the great public interest in the controversy evaporated. Slowly congregations were established but by the 1930's there were only nine; six in the Belfast area, two in County Antrim, and one in County Tyrone. Although these congregations became well established, the Irish Evangelical Church made no further inroads into Irish Presbyterianism and there was no further church extension.[465]

David N Livingstone and Ronald A Wells in *Ulster-American Religion* add their voice to the smallness theme: "Grier later became editor of the small church's magazine, *The Irish Evangelical* …"[466] Finlay Holmes, the Irish Presbyterian historian, also notes that the Evangelical Presbyterian Church is small, but acknowledges that it "has maintained its unequivocal witness to traditional confessional orthodoxy …"[467]

Bruce's 1989 assertion of "no further church extension" should not be taken at face value. The story of EPC's three main phases of church extension appears in Chapters 18, 21 and 23 with a visual summary in Appendices 7 and 8. But why has EPC not experienced more numerical growth? Its constituency of 600, including 350 members and covenant children after nearly 90 years prompts that question. Does this suggest that the Lord has withheld his blessing at a very basic level? Churches look for growth and interpret it as evidence of God's favour. Other local evangelical churches have grown much more within the same period. But care is needed in assessing smallness in the work of God's kingdom. Although God's purposes are known in their entirety only to himself, it is within human compass to analyse situations in the light of Scripture and historical perspective.

For EPC, such analysis identifies various growth inhibiting factors which have interacted throughout the Church's history. There was the marginalised beginning and the uncertain initial direction. For the first 50 years there was financial constraint and the related low minister-to-congregation ratio in a society of much bigger churches. In an age in which churches are assessed by what they offer and by the level of comfort they provide, small confessional churches lose out in public perception because of their demands for a high level of commitment and shortage of facilities. More than anything else, the Church has always borne the cost of separation, confessional adherence and the biblical administration of the sacraments. These factors together have deficit popular appeal but the Church must recognise that they have not been wholly outside the area of its human responsibility.

The True Focus

Size is the wrong focus. There is nothing wrong with being small,[468] provided the reason for it is faithfulness in its full biblical scope and demand. Enduring corporate integrity in the faith is what is important. The church at Ephesus was threatened with the removal of its candlestick after about 40 years for losing its first love! The difficulties EPC experienced in its early and middle years are no longer the constraints that they were, but those years were important; a strong sense of calling sustained the work "by the good hand" of God upon it. (Ezra 8.18) Successive generations have built on this foundation, establishing all aspects of the work at denominational and congregational levels. EPC has maintained the practice of corporate prayer, set standards for a trained ministry, proclaimed the whole counsel of God and sent missionaries into the major continents of the world. It has seen successive generations of covenant children coming to and holding the faith and has built up its youth work around them. It has advanced greatly in the important sphere of church government and administration. Above all, EPC has maintained its doctrinal integrity and become established in the national and international reformed community. God has favoured it with a role of challenge and influence far out of proportion to its size and it appears to be in a stronger position today to do greater things for the Kingdom of Heaven than at any point in its history. But much remains to be done. It must identify and apply the lessons of history as it moves forward.

Whatever the Church does and however well, it will be in vain without the Lord's blessing. (Ps 127) He is sovereign in dispensing his blessing but he commonly bestows it on those who desire it most, to those who live near to him. The church on earth will never be free from difficulty and disappointment, never free from the effects of its own sin and failure. There will be providential trials of which there will be limited understanding. Some of God's purposes will be to make the Church aware of its own weaknesses, to humble its people under his mighty hand, to make them feel their need of him, to make them cast themselves upon him with increased trust.

Paul experienced difficulties in his ministry but he endured and triumphed over them: "by purity, by knowledge, by longsuffering, by kindness, by the Holy Spirit, by sincere love, by the word of truth, by the power of God, by the armour of righteousness on the right hand and on the left, by honour and dishonour, by evil report and good report." (2 Cor 6.6-8) Equipped with weapons that are the product of the righteousness of God in the life, he coped with attacks from whatever quarter they came, with bad times as well as good. His devotion and energy in the Lord's service meant that he was never ignored. He was in the middle of controversy—some esteemed him highly and others lived to discredit him. Reports reminded him that the whispering campaigns went on too, even in his absence. But whatever the attitude to his ministry, he did not flinch from the great necessity that was laid upon him to preach the Gospel. (1 Cor 9.16)

75th Anniversary

Its time interval makes a 75th a standard anniversary. Its theme, *Looking Back – Looking Forward*, was built around a Presbytery Family Day on 26 October 2002 at Stranmillis College, Belfast, and a series of lectures. Appropriately the Moderator was Mr John Grier, son of W J Grier, elder in North Belfast and Manager of the Evangelical Book Shop. The lectures were:

21 October 2002	The Atonement	Dr Derek Thomas
25 October 2002	Youth Extra	Rev Paul Levy
26 October 2002	An Historical Narrative (Powerpoint)	David Watson
26 October 2002	The Person Of Christ	Rev Ian Hamilton
28 October 2002	Principled Secession	John Grier

The Family Day was "a day for reflection, thanksgiving, worship and fellowship, particularly among our Church Family". In addition to the two Saturday lectures the Moderator addressed the question, *Why are we here today?*, with an outline of the Heresy Trial events, delegates brought greetings from other Churches, and the YPA Choir participated twice. Sunday 27 October was *Thanksgiving Sunday* and the visiting delegates participated in the pulpit exchanges. *The Evangelical Presbyterian*, Jan-Feb 2003, provided a full report with photographs.

During 2002 the *Evangelical Presbyterian* bore the logo *EPC, 75 years, 1927-2002*, and ran a series of six articles entitled *Remembering Former Days*. They were all from issues of the *Irish Evangelical* between 1928 and 1942, and with one exception were written by Rev. James Hunter or Rev. W J Grier. They had both devotional and EPC historical content. The cover of the Sep-Oct issue presented photographs of Rev. James Hunter, Rev. W J Grier and John R Gillespie, under the title *Contenders for the Faith*. *Declaring our Distinctives* followed, in the first four issues of 2003 – Evangelical, Presbyterian, Seccessionist, and Consistently Confessional.

The Church has celebrated six Anniversaries in all – 20th, 25th, 30th, 40th, 50th, and 75th. Such frequency is more usual in the first century of existence. They were a means of thankfulness and motivation to successive generations as they looked back and looked forward.

The Legacy of J G Machen

EPC marked its 85th Anniversary with a lecture, *Principled Presbyterianism*, by the historian, Dr Darryl G Hart,[469] an elder of the Orthodox Presbyterian Church, USA. It was particularly appropriate for this occasion to have a representative from the Church that J G Machen took the lead in founding in 1936. During his comprehensive lecture, Hart, himself a strong supporter of Machen, turned to his legacy:

> J Gresham Machen may not be the gold standard for 20th century or 21st century reformed orthodoxy but he does stand out not only in every account of American Presbyterianism but in most accounts of religion in the United States as arguably the most important defender of historic Christianity. … Yet for all of Machen's accomplishments the verdict on his legacy has been mixed even among conservative Presbyterians and Evangelicals, at least in America. Much of the discomfort with Machen surrounds his flair for controversy. … But when scholars with ecclesiastical ties to Machen voice similar objections, perhaps Machen's critics have a point.

In his lecture Hart referred to a John Piper article on Machen:[470]

> On New Year's Eve, 1936, in a Roman Catholic hospital in Bismarck, North Dakota, J. Gresham Machen was one day away from death at the age of 55. It was Christmas break at Westminster Seminary in Philadelphia, where he taught New Testament. His colleagues said he looked "deadly tired." But instead of resting, he took the train from Philadelphia to the 20-below-zero winds of North Dakota to preach in a few Presbyterian churches at the request of Pastor Samuel Allen.
>
> Ned Stonehouse, his New Testament assistant said, "There was no one of sufficient influence to constrain him to curtail his program to any significant degree." He was the acknowledged leader of the conservative movement in Presbyterianism with no one to watch over him. His heroes and mentors,

Warfield and Patton, were dead. He had never married, and so had no wife to restrain him with reality. His mother and father, who gave him so much wise counsel over the years, were dead. His two brothers lived 1500 miles to the east. "He had a personality that only his good friends found appealing."[471]

And so he was remarkably alone and isolated for a man of international stature. He had pneumonia and could scarcely breathe. Pastor Allen came to pray for him that last day of 1936, and Machen told him of a vision that he had had of being in heaven: "Sam, it was glorious, it was glorious," he said. And a little later he added, "Sam, isn't the Reformed faith grand?" The following day – New Year's Day, 1937 – he mustered the strength to send a telegram to John Murray, his friend and colleague at Westminster. It was his last recorded word: "I'm so thankful for [the] active obedience of Christ. No hope without it." He died about 7:30 P.M.

So much of the man is here in this tragic scene. The stubbornness of going his own way when friends urged him not to take this extra preaching trip. His isolation far from the mainline centers of church life and thought. His suffering for the cause he believed in. His utter allegiance to and exaltation of the Reformed faith of the Westminster Confession. And his taking comfort not just from a general truth about Christ, but from a doctrinally precise understanding of the active obedience of Christ – which he believed was his own obedience in Christ and would make him a suitable heir of eternal life, for Christ's sake.

So Gresham Machen's personality and willingness for combat have earned him disapprobation even in his own constituency. Personalities do need progressive sanctification but sometimes the Lord brings such personal characteristics as Machen's, flawed though they may possibly be, to his Kingdom for "such a time as this" (Esth 4.14). Those who have had the vision and resolution to take the battle for the faith to the professing church, like Gresham Machen and James Hunter, are unlikely to emerge with accolades. The focus must be on the calling, courage, faithfulness and the lasting achievements of these men, both primary and secondary. No Machen, no OPC. No Machen, no Westminster Seminary. No Machen, no EPC?

W J Grier, who knew him personally, said this:[472]

And he was like Calvin – in his wide correspondence, in his battles for the faith and his loyalty to the truth, and in the warm affection which his character and stand won for him in the hearts of so many of his colleagues and students. He being dead yet speaketh. His works live on and still bear witness. ... May we feel the call to devotion to the Saviour he loved and the truth he maintained! May we each one say in the words of his favourite hymn:

> *Were the whole realm of nature mine,*
> *That were a present far too small;*
> *Love so amazing, so divine,*
> *Demands my soul, my life, my all.*

Looking Back – And Forward – And Upward

The 75th Anniversary borrowed its looking back and forward theme from the *Evangelical Presbyterian* leader in November 1977 reporting on the 50th Anniversary: *Looking Back – And Forward – And Upward*. Its first section, *Back!*, had an important historical perspective:

> In the meetings celebrating our 50th anniversary we were frequently called upon to look back over the past half-century. A letter from one of our well-wishers said: "For half a century the Evangelical Presbyterian Church has bravely and uncompromisingly held aloft the banner of the Reformed faith". It is also true to say that we came to a fuller realisation of our precious heritage as time passed. We began with eight *Articles of Faith*, but after a time we felt the need of a fuller and more complete setting forth of Scripture truths. So it was that we adopted—and adopted unanimously—the time-honoured Standards of the Westminster Divines—the Confession of Faith and Catechisms. This—by the good hand of God—strengthened our position. As we look back we can say with John Knox: "In how great purity God did establish among us His true religion". Thanks be to God for the sense of appreciation of the rich heritage of truth!
>
> As we look back, we can also think of the godly and faithful people who threw in their lot with us. We think of those who have "crossed the flood" and are now worshipping where the angels bow. Thank God for the fellowship we enjoyed with the saints now in glory.
>
> God blessed us in things material also. When our Church began in 1927 we had not a single building of our own to use solely as a place of worship. But the Lord provided in due time. Thank God for the blessings, spiritual and material, which we enjoyed—in the past fifty years. He led and provided. To Him all the glory belongs.

The final section *Upward!* remains an eminently suitable prayer for the future:

> Yes, seek the Lord, look upward. And then it may well be as in 1628 and the following years in Ulster when there was, as Prof. Seaton Reid tells us, a bright and hot sun-blink of the gospel, one of the largest manifestations of the Spirit since the days of the apostles. May God grant it!

Missions and Youth

*Missionaries seconded to the Free Church of Scotland
1937-1985*

*Harold and
Flora Lindsay
Moyobamba, Peru
1937-1951*

*Joseph and Helen
McCracken
with Anne
Eastern Cape,
South Africa
1944-1974*

*Nan Dunlop
Chhapara,
Central India
1944-1974*

*Annie Wilkinson
(Mrs Blair)
Moyobamba, Peru
1948-1953*

*Florence Donaldson
Colegio san Andrés,
Peru
1951-1985*

*W Mervyn Oliver
Chhapara,
Central India
1960-1963*

Missionaries of the Church from 1987

Sid and Jean Garland, Mission Africa/ACTS 1987-
Home-based since 2010

Andrew and Eunice Moody, Joy,
Uganda 1995-98, 2004-06,
2007-11, 2014-

Norman and Angela Reid
Dumisani theological
Institute, King William's
Town, South Africa
1999-2011

Pamela Gaiya, Mission Africa, Nigeria, 2003-
With Musa and Gracie

Ed and Kate Underwood, Ezra, Elijah, Joseph, Moses and
Selah. Wycliffe Bible Translators, 2008-12
UFM/Onehundredfold Digital Technology, 2012-

Jenni Ray, Bingham Academy
Addis Ababa, Ethiopa
2013-

Missions and Youth

Particularly since the early 1980s, EPC members and adherents have carried out close on 125 visits to about 30 different countries to do short-term service of varying lengths. Those below are the longest serving of the large short-term contingent.

  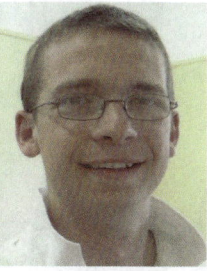 

Ricky and Angie Fitzsimmons, Noah Mission Africa, Nigeria 2010-12

Lousie Higgins Blythswood, Cluj, Romania 2002-05

Peter Grier IFES Staff Worker, Munster 2012-

Jonathan Reid IFES, Crimea, 1996-1999 IFES, Dublin, 1999-2004

Rachel Stevenson (née Reid), OM, Spain, 1997-1999

Overseas Missions Team, Goli, Uganda, 2011

Overseas Missions Team, Almuñécar, Spain, 2012. Team members with football club.

Camps

Boys' Camp, Tyrella, Co Down, 1961, with three future Ministers – Reid, Watson, Beckett

Boys' Camp, Castlerock, Co Londonderry, 1969

Missions and Youth

Girls' Camp, Ballyvester, Co Down, 1955

Girls' Camp, Rathmullan, Tyrella, Co Down, 1956

Girls' Camp
Brown's Bay, Co Antrim, 1963
Miss Elsie Gale (later Mrs Archer) is front right

Mixed Camp, Sligo, 1981

Senior Camp, Suffolk, 2005

YPA Weekend 2010

Inters Camp Moyallen, Portadown 2015

Junior Camp, Bushmills, Co Antrim, 2015

Youth Organisations: Botanic Avenue adopted Pathfinders in 1950s, Crosscollyer Street, Finaghy, Somerton Road, Campaigners in 1960s

Mrs Garland, Somerton Road Campaigner Chief marches her clan to Crosscollyer Street for a united evening service

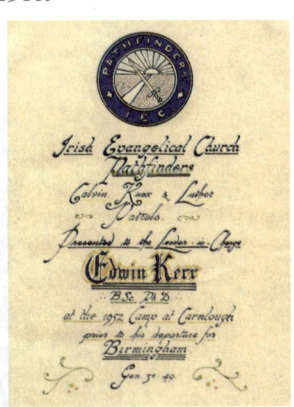

Pathfinders presentation to Dr Edwin Kerr at Carnlough, Co Antrim, Camp 1952

Part 5

Learning from History

25

Identifying the Issues

Human minds are imperfect instruments of thought, and their opinions naturally tend to variety and diversity. Again, the religious world teems with competing clashing doctrines, each striving for recognition and pressing itself on others with its utmost ingenuity of argument.

R L Dabney[473]

The maxim, "The only thing we learn from history is that we learn nothing from history", is attributed to the German philosopher, Friedrich Hegel (1770-1831). Whatever its appeal as a quotation and a general principle, failures to identify, learn and apply the lessons of history will always endorse its validity. In similar vein, the adage "Those who fail to learn from history are doomed to repeat it" is credited to Churchill and others.[474] The historical books of the Bible, and many of its historical references, carry strong elements of exhortation and warning. Forgetfulness of the past and its consequences for the church are prominent biblical themes (eg Ps 106, Zech 1.1-6). This urges EPC to learn from its own history and implement its lessons.

The EPC founding fathers and their contemporaries have died and few now remain who knew them. Succeeding generations will not work as they might without the motivation and sense of identity that the history of the Church provides. G N M Collins said: "... but the Church which allows herself to forget the lessons of her history, and the hand of God in the shaping of her destiny is both unworthy of her high calling and regardless of her own safety. 'Thou shalt remember all the way which the Lord thy God led thee' is as needful a caution for the people of God in this modern world as it was for Israel in the dawn of her history."[475] There is the need to re-capture the early sense of calling and boldness.

So what lessons have emerged from this 18th, 19th and 20th century branch of Presbyterian history? Basically there was 'drift'—the complacency or negligence that results in drifting away from the mooring unawares, or the ring slipping off the finger undetected: "Therefore we must give the more earnest heed to the things we have heard, lest we drift away." (Heb 2.1) The drift facilitated non-subscription and doctrinal latitude,[476] justified by appeal to the principle of *semper reformanda*, the right of private judgement and the power of change.

Drift

Thomas Hamilton described the birth of the Belfast Society in the early 18th century as a cloud apparently no bigger than a man's hand[477]—a negative application of one of Scripture's great heralds of good. But its influence permeated the church. How could something so small and advocating "strange views"[478] gain such momentum in a church commended for its soundness in the immediately preceding 17th century? Seaton Reid commented on confessional adherence: "not the slightest symptom had appeared of any departure from these doctrinal views" at the beginning of the 18th century.[479] But ministry students in Ireland received their theological training in Scotland under men like Simson, Hutcheson, and later in the century, Leechman. In this context Hamilton spoke of professors "poisoning, at its fountainhead, the stream of the ministry." This was of the greatest significance, for "the pulpits of the Synod of Ulster began to give a very uncertain sound on the great verities of the faith, and in some cases to ignore them altogether."[480] Seaton Reid notes: "The two leading members of the Belfast Society, Mr Abernethy and Mr Kirkpatrick, had been fellow-students with

Professor Simson in the Divinity Hall in Glasgow, and were afterwards regular correspondents of his, while most of the ministers who subsequently joined that society had studied theology under him as professor."[481]

But unsound training for the ministry cannot be the whole explanation. How could these men who were the products of an orthodox church be so susceptible to the influence of error? Surely it was because change was already at work, like an infection in incubation before the symptoms appear. That the church continued to send its students to Glasgow was in itself evidence of drift. To the students, the teaching would presumably have the imprimatur of their church. The 'Belfast Society' did not facilitate the creation of new views so much as the organisation, development, and dissemination of views that were already being espoused. The church had been gradually conditioned for the entrance of unbelief as in Jude 4: "For certain men have crept in unnoticed …" The drift lay undetected. When the Church had insisted on more rigorous Westminster commitment in the form of subscription in 1705, it was because evidence of the need was already apparent.

Hamilton also noted that the Confession of Faith began to be thrust more and more into the background as the 18th century ran its course.[482] How does this happen to Confessional standards? Clearly they are not thrust away in a definite act of rejection. The ground is prepared by a type of "ease in Zion" (Amos 6.1) that lulls the church into thinking that everything is safely the same—as happened with the godless, corrupt and affluent of the 8th century BC northern kingdom of Israel. It is already happening when the Confession falls into relative disuse, when reference to it declines, when other starting points and influences are substituted and when adherence to it is assumed. When what the people like in the church, what is fashionable, what other bodies are doing, or the felt need to be compatible with the times become the criteria and prevailing spirit, then there are grounds for concern about drift.

Non-subscription of a subordinate standard may be a pointer to discomfort with its principle or content, but the act of subscription in itself may not be an expression of total commitment, even to the extent that the particular Formula of Subscription demands. Witherow described subscription as a "mischievous farce"[483] in the 18th century. Even annual subscription of the standards, strengthened by an accompanying affirmation of re-familiarisation with their contents, could become a procedural exercise.[484] Church history warns about quiet drift that is the precursor of unbelief, controversy and division until the cycle begins again, sometimes with quite changed bodies re-uniting. But history also warns that it is unlikely to be seen by its advocates as unbelief or drift. They will label it as 'new light', latitude, flexibility, contemporary thought, Spirit-led interpretation, scholarship, the right of private judgement, or even reformation. And so applies the situation: "If therefore the light that is in you is darkness, how great is that darkness!" (Matt 6.23) When Paul urged the leaders of the church at Ephesus to "take heed to yourselves and to all the flock" (Acts 20.28) he gave priority to the most diligent vigilance of themselves.

Scripture approves "understanding of the times" (1 Chron 12.32; Esth 1.13), Ezekiel "came to the captives ... and I sat where they sat" (Ezek 3.15), Christ came "eating and drinking" ... "a friend of the tax collectors and sinners" (Matt 11.19). For the sake of the Gospel Paul said: "I have become all things to all men, that I might by all means save some." (1 Cor 9.22; cf 10.33). But Scripture is concerned that the church avoids conformity to the spirit of the age, and it emphasises the church's and the Christian's incompatibility with the world (Rom 12.2, 1 John 3.1) The doctrine of an unchanging Christ is a call to adhere to an unchanging faith. (Heb 13.8) The Athenian love for "some new thing" (Acts 17.21) is a perennial threat. So is drift.

Semper Reformanda

Finlay Holmes in *Our Irish Presbyterian Heritage*, offers the outworking of *semper reformanda* as one possible explanation for inherent ecclesiastical division: "Protestantism in general, and Presbyterianism in particular, have earned an unenviable reputation for division. It may be that the great Reformation principle of continuing reformation in the church - *ecclesia reformata, semper reformanda* - is essentially divisive."[485]

No Alternative

There is no successful alternative to continuous reformation in any walk of life. Ongoing improvement may be difficult and expensive, but failure to reform continuously is also costly and ultimately divisive. The Reformation was a historical event but reformation is a process. Westminster is concerned to record that: "The purest churches under heaven are subject both to mixture and error" (WCF 25.5). This is not a loophole for laxity, inclusivism, or an acceptable level of error, but a solemn reminder that when the church is as pure as its leaders and people can make it through the diligent knowledge and application of Scripture, it is still imperfect and in need of reform.

"What I Choose it to Mean"

"When I use a word," Humpty Dumpty said in rather a scornful tone, "it means just what I choose it to mean – neither more nor less." "The question is," said Alice, "whether you can make words mean so many different things." "The question is," said Humpty Dumpty, "which is to be master - that's all."[486] This is a fitting commentary on current uses of the expression, *Ecclesia reformata semper reformanda est*— the church reformed and always reforming, or always needing to be reformed.[487] Today it is a popular motif, particularly its *semper reformanda* element, and is used by a range of churches and para-church organisations. It is widely applied to such aspects of church reformation as its preaching, its practices, the lives of its people, its cultural relevance, its strategies and perspectives. Updated interaction with culture is a common emphasis.

Reformation and Biblical Origins

It is important to go back to its strong Reformation associations. To the Synod of Dordt (1618-19) reformation of doctrine had been achieved, but the moral life of the church must continue to be reformed, and future ministers be trained in "the practice of godliness". G N M Collins asserted its primary reference to be to doctrine and creeds:

> The phrase *ecclesia reformata semper reformanda est*, which formerly expressed the Church's concern that her doctrine should be, at all times, truly Reformed, and that the unfinished work of the Reformation should continue to be faithfully prosecuted, has been taken over by leaders of ecumenical movements who use it to urge the virtual pulping of all the historic formularies of the Faith as a necessary part of the process of producing a minimal symbol on which all branches of the Christian Church, and, eventually, perhaps some of other faiths, may be brought into agreement.[488]

However, the *semper reformanda* principle was not a Reformation invention, just a notable statement of an existing biblical one. In one of its early creeds Scripture itself explains the amazing basis of the unity the church is to achieve: "There is one body and one Spirit, just as you were called in one hope of your calling; one Lord, one faith, one baptism; one God and Father of all, who is above all, and through all, and in you all." (Eph 4.4-6) Seven times one! The church is not to think in terms of choices, alternatives, or co-existence. Every aspect of the church has a common, dominant characteristic – "one". Only the Reformation principle is compatible with this. Its purpose is to maintain the state of oneness on the basis of objective criteria. It advises the church that it will always be necessary, that it must work to achieve it. The pluralism of the broad church is by definition a contradiction. The church's 'ism' is one-ism. Among the things that are one there is one faith. Machen said in 1923: "we shall be interested in showing that despite the liberal use of traditional phraseology modern liberalism not only is a different religion from Christianity but belongs in a totally different class of religions."[489] *Semper reformanda*, in achieving increasing conformity to the Word of God in doctrine and practice, is the best unifying principle that can exist.

The Right of Private Judgement

Finlay Holmes suggests that two other factors, inseparably related to the outworking of *semper reformanda*, contributed to the divisions of the 18th and 19th centuries—the right of private judgement and conflicting reaction to change. First, private judgement:

> Division, however, has not always been because the old bottles of institutional religion have been unable to contain the new wine of a fresh movement of the Spirit. A. T. Q. Stewart has suggested that 'the inherent tension of Presbyterianism' is 'between traditional ecclesiastical orthodoxy and the right

of private judgment' and, although this tension is found in all churches 'the democratic nature of Presbyterian church government makes it more sharply apparent'. Certainly the tension between ecclesiastical authority and the liberty of individual conscience was central to the chronic controversy which divided Irish Presbyterianism in the 18th and early 19th centuries.[490]

The Reformation Principle

The Right of Private Judgement, has various applications today but it is best known as a fundamental principle of the Reformation, not in isolation, but alongside the "exclusive authority of the written Word as the rule of faith".[491] The principle declared simply that no person or human authority has the right to decide or impose what anyone should believe. The Reformers contended that the authority of Scripture did not depend on the testimony of the church but entirely on God, its author. Faith must therefore rest on the testimony of Scripture, on Scripture alone—*sola scriptura*. Whilst everything in Scripture was not uniformly plain yet Scripture was *perspicuous*—it clearly revealed all that was essential to faith and practice. The Scriptures, furthermore, are addressed to believers who are commanded to search them and to test all teaching by them, not with unaided human wisdom but with the help of the Holy Spirit. "The supreme Judge, by which all controversies of religion are to be determined, and all decrees of councils, opinions of ancient writers, doctrines of men, and *private spirits*, are to be examined, and in whose sentence we are to rest, can be no other but the Holy Spirit speaking in the Scripture." (WCF 1.10. Italics added).

The Roman Catholic Church has argued[492] that the right of private judgement is demonstrably flawed in the proliferation of sects, heresies and conflict. It is easy to exaggerate this and to ignore the core unity that exists among many Protestant denominations on the fundamentals of the faith; convenient also to disregard the conflict within the Roman Catholic Church through the centuries. But these arguments culpably fail to distinguish between the principle and its abuse – the perversion and misapplication of it that inevitably occurs in human life. The principle itself is biblical, inalienable, self-evident and pervades the whole of life.

So "private judgement" refers to what an individual believes. A person's greatest act of private judgement is to come to Christ, persuaded and enabled by the Holy Spirit to do so, and, with the same right of private judgement, to accept a church's teaching authority. The church does not seek acceptance of its teaching on the basis of its own authority. It requires its people personally to search the Scriptures daily to find out whether these things [are] so (cf Acts 17.11) and to exercise their private judgement. The Liberty of Conscience of WCF 20 is what Christ has purchased for individual *believers* under the Gospel, securing for them freedom from the guilt and consequence of sin, freedom from the burden of the ceremonial law, along with increased free access to God and fuller communications with the free Spirit in the New Testament. Its purpose is that believers may serve the Lord in holiness of life and mutually uphold and preserve one another.

Private Judgement and Confessional Subscription

The right of private judgement is a right, but an accountable right. In upholding liberty of conscience WCF 20 makes it clear that conscience is not the final or independent authority. "God alone is lord of the conscience". It is also a *private* right – the personal right of each individual to choose what to believe. But it is not the right to operate within the teaching structure of a church at variance with its constitutional standards. Doctrinal unity is the essential reason for subscription. All organisations recognise the need for common purpose and the danger of a "house divided against itself." (Mark 3.25)

So how do issues arise over the implementation of subordinate standards? Usually from the subscription side, although subscribers constitute the Church's legislature in the Presbyterian system. Some object to the subscription of subordinate standards in principle; others wish the standards or their application to accommodate plurality of beliefs. In certain circumstances they realise that it is not even necessary for this to be formally defined for, if the prevailing mood is broad and inclusive, subscription is interpreted accordingly. It becomes a hollow procedural formality. Indeed, an open request to change the standards or their application demonstrates a greater degree of integrity.

History bears out the difficulty that the Church has had in relating to its standards. Recalcitrance over subscribing to Westminster is about as old as the standards themselves. Whether the Divines intended the Confession for subscription is beside the point if a church stipulates subscription. The Westminster Confession of Faith culminated a series of Confessions and was the most detailed and precise. Did the amount of detail in itself inevitably make unqualified subscription more difficult? Charles Hodge thought it did. He said: "Such a rule of interpretation can never be practically carried out, without dividing the Church into innumerable fragments. It is impossible that a body of several thousand ministers and elders should think alike on all the topics embraced in such an extended and minute formula of belief." But was Hodge going too far here? The Westminster Confession is just about 1.5% of the Bible in length. The addition of the Larger and Shorter Catechisms makes it about 4%. And the percentage reduces significantly when discounting the overlap between the Confession and its Catechisms. When the requirement is to know the whole of Scripture, is a systematic summary of its teaching amounting to perhaps 3% of its size really an "extended and minute formula of belief"? Moreover, WCF incorporates latitude on a range of doctrinal issues.

The Evangelical Presbyterian Church does not identify with Hodge's misgivings about full subscription: "… we believe these subordinate standards … (as amended by the Amending and Declaratory Acts) … accurately summarise, interpret and apply the teaching of the Scriptures on *important points* of doctrine and worship."[493]

The American Presbyterian Experience

The question of Westminster subscription was a particular battle for early American Presbyterians. Their first Synod, the Synod of Philadelphia, compromised between subscribing and non-subscribing parties with the Adopting Act of 1729[494] – that ministers "shall declare their agreement ... as being in all the essential and necessary articles, good forms of sound words and systems of Christian doctrine, and do also adopt the said Confession and Catechisms as the confession of our faith." A minister could identify and exclude any statement or article in the standards which he considered not of the essence of the system of doctrine (his 'exceptions' or 'scruples') and submit them to his Presbytery for approval. It was subscription of the *system of doctrine*.

There have been differing interpretations in the United States of the Adopting Act's "System of Doctrine". Charles Hodge strongly favoured the "system of doctrine" approach, that is, the "known and admitted scheme" of doctrine of the Reformed Churches, not the "essential doctrines of religion or of Christianity". He calls the latter "this latitudinarian principle of subscription". Rejecting it utterly he says:

> The Old School have always protested against this Broad Church principle—
>
> Because, in their view, it is immoral. For a man to assert that he adopts a Calvinistic confession when he rejects the distinctive features of the Calvinistic system, and receives only the essential principles of Christianity, is to say what is not true in the legitimate and accepted meaning of the terms. It would be universally recognized as a falsehood should a Protestant declare that he adopted the canons of the Council of Trent, or the Romish Catechism, when he intended that he received them only so far as they contained the substance of the Apostles' Creed. If the Church is prepared to make the Apostles' Creed the standard of ministerial communion, let the constitution be altered; but do not let us adopt the demoralizing principle of professing ourselves, and requiring others to profess, what we do not believe. ...
>
> This lax principle must work the relaxation of all discipline, destroy the purity of the Church, and introduce either perpetual conflict or death-like indifference.[495]

This latitudinarian principle of interpretation spread through many of the Presbyteries of the Presbyterian Church in the United States (PCUS) over a period with the resultant decrease of Confessional influence. It was concern over theological standards that resulted in the well-known 'five-point' deliverance of essential articles from the General Assembly in 1910, reaffirmed in 1916 and again in 1923. These articles were: the inerrancy of Scripture, the virgin birth, Christ's propitiatory sacrifice, Christ's bodily resurrection and ascension and Christ's miracles. Challenges to the five points culminated in the *Auburn Affirmation* of 1924 which more than 1,200 Presbyterian ministers signed:

> It declared that the five-point doctrinal statement of 1910, 1916, and 1923 "attempts to commit our church to certain theories concerning the inspiration of the Bible, and the Incarnation, the Atonement, the Resurrection, and the

Continuing Life and Supernatural Power of our Lord Jesus Christ." "We are opposed to any attempt to elevate these five doctrinal statements, or any of them, to the position of tests for ordination or for good standing in our church," the document continued. It explained that "some of us regard the particular theories contained in the deliverance of the General Assembly of 1923 as satisfactory explanations of these facts and doctrines. But we are united in believing that these are not the only theories allowed by the Scriptures and our standards as explanations of these facts and doctrines of our religion, and that all who hold to these facts and doctrines, whatever theories they may employ to explain them, are worthy of all confidence and fellowship.'" ... Gresham Machen stated that the doctrines that the Auburn Affirmation called "theories" were "facts upon which Christianity is based and without which Christianity would fall." The affirmation really advocates "the destruction of the confessional witness of the Church," he wrote. "To allow interpretations which reverse the meaning of a confession is exactly the same thing as to have no confession at all."

... "the assembly ... took no action in response to the Auburn Affirmation or its signers and declared the five-point doctrinal statement of 1923 unconstitutional."[496]

The Westminster Warning

Another effect of Confessional laxity is the silencing of its warnings. WCF 20 warns that the doctrine of Christian Liberty, by its very nature, is open to abuses which are destructive of faith, worship and peace. To believe or publish doctrines or opinions that are in any way contrary to the Word, or beside it in matters of faith and worship, or to use liberty of conscience as a cloak for sin, or to oppose lawful civil or ecclesiastical power, is a betrayal of this liberty. So this liberty is not a constant, invariable possession; it can be misused, betrayed or destroyed. And its abuse can warrant civil or ecclesiastical discipline. (WCF 20.4) So the church is not to be credulous towards the claims of Christian liberty or its associates, the right of private judgement and latitudinarianism, but to be on its guard against their deception and threat. Archibald Bruce aptly noted: "The sound of Christian liberty, to which the enemies of the truth have had recourse, was more engaging, and readier to fascinate and draw others to their side, than a plain declaration of their particular tenets; in consequence of which, no doubt, a number sound in the faith have been involved with them in this cause."[497]

Church members have personal responsibility too in the proper use of the right of private judgement. The Lord made people responsible for their choice of teachers: "Either make the tree good and its fruit good, or else make the tree bad and its fruit bad; for a tree is known by its fruit." (Matt 12.33) He had developed the point powerfully in the Sermon on the Mount. (Matt 7.15-23) Healthy trees produce good fruit and diseased trees bad fruit. People must decide which tree they wish to eat from. They must assess their teachers and make a choice about the teaching they accept. Teachers influence decisions about which gate to enter but, vital as it is, being on the right road is not the only issue. People have a responsibility to watch the influences they allow to bear upon their lives. And it is not easy, for false prophets disguise themselves in sheep's clothing, deceiving and leading people astray.

Defending the Standards
So how can a church defend itself against latitudinarian dilution of its confessional standards? Ecclesiastical history suggests that it is very difficult. R L Dabney said: "We are aware that there is no patent infallible process, in fallible men's hands, for transmitting a doctrinal homogeneity from age to age. But the means which comes nearest, the only means of any tolerable efficiency is, under the grace and light of God's Spirit, the thorough education of ministers in an orthodox theology, and that by similar methods for all."[498] The church must be active, forthright and constant in proclaiming its constitutional standards as a *sine qua non* of its identity and witness. Adherence to its standards must be what that church is known for within and without. At least five things are necessary:

1. An unambiguous statement of its confessional standards.
2. A formula of subscription that requires a sincere commitment to those standards as each signatory's personal faith.
3. A vigilant determination to maintain the standards and the formula whatever the cost.
4. A programme of training, particularly for its ministers, that is wholly committed to its confessional standards.
5. A living dependence on God who is able to keep it from falling.

A church's standards are *subordinate*. They must be open to revision when the church is persuaded that Scripture requires it. The Evangelical Presbyterian Church revised its standards by a Declaratory Act in 1944 and by two Amending Acts in 1968. Revision of its standards publicly re-defines a church's creed. Its creed and faith then agree. The emergence of new theological issues can require the refinement of standards at particular points. But changing the formula of subscription is another matter. Wordings may be improved but a formula should never allow subscribers unspecified latitude in the acceptance or application of the standards. The standards may be revised, but acceptance of them must always be full and unqualified.

The Implications of Full Subscription
A full and unqualified subscription of its standards does not free a church from difficulty in relating to them. A key issue is the subscribers' knowledge of the documents they subscribe. One would expect that the responsible signing of a statement such as: "I subscribe them as the confession of my faith; and this I do without any reservations", requires a signatory to have in-depth personal knowledge. It assumes prior study. Are subscribers familiar with the issues that gave

rise to the contents originally? Can they link the standards to current theological issues? How does a church deal with the issue of knowledge?

This is not latitudinarianism by another name. There is a world of difference between a procedural or sceptical subscriber and one who is wholly committed, albeit with the developing knowledge that is a characteristic of every walk of life. Elders require a level of knowledge that makes them able to teach and defend sound doctrine (1 Tim 3.2; Tit 1.9) and deacons must hold the mystery of the faith with a clear conscience (1 Tim 3.9). From that they develop their knowledge of the faith and their subscription commits them to such a progressive programme. When subscription to standards is an expression of personal faith without any reservation, there is voluntary submission to the discipline of whatever their theological demands may be, even though understanding may be deficient.

So a 'jot and tittle' subscription of its standards does not free a church from problems. But it is the right set of problems to have, for it concerns standards of knowledge. The church gives priority to the knowledge and application of its subordinate standards as they express systematically the teaching of Scripture. The church and its subscribers commit to teaching and learning. The subscribers submit to the standards and discipline of the church.

Reaction to Change

In addition to the right of private judgement Finlay Holmes put forward conflicting reaction to change as a contributory factor in the Irish Presbyterian divisions of the 18th and 19th centuries:

> Another aspect of that chronic controversy was the perennial conflict between conservatives and radicals in the church. In the lives of all organisms and institutions there is tension between the forces of continuity and change. In the Synod of Ulster there was tension between conservatives, who held to the traditional doctrines of Presbyterianism, which were believed to have been given definitive statement in the Westminster formularies, and radicals who, under the influence of contemporary currents of thought, sought wider latitude and greater flexibility in the interpretation of their faith.[499]

Holmes's expression, "contemporary currents of thought"[500] is akin to C S Lewis's 'chronological snobbery': "… the uncritical acceptance of the intellectual climate common to our own age and the assumption that whatever has gone out of date is on that account discredited."[501]

American Presbyterians also experienced it in the Old Side-New Side controversy, 1741-1758, and the Old School-New School, 1837-1869. Both were occasioned by revivals, the 'Sides' by 'The First Great Awakening' led by Jonathan Edwards and George Whitefield, although they differed in their views of revival, and the 'Schools' by 'The Second Great Awakening' of which Charles Grandison Finney was the most prominent leader. The particular issues in the 'Sides' were Whitefield's independent, itinerant preaching as opposed to a church-based ministry and the standing of William Tennant's independent Log College. But underlying it all was existing tension over confessional subscription, with two sides already in the making. However, the 'New' forged ahead of the Old, numerically and in popularity and a reunion substantially on 'New' terms took place in 1758. The issues in the 'Schools' controversy, a century later, were much wider. They included Finney's Arminianism, his elevation of human agency, new methodology, including the famous 'anxious bench', and the place of voluntary societies in the Church's ministry. Conversion through the church's nurture as opposed to the 'crisis' conversion of revivalism featured in both controversies.

John Muether, OPC, comments about the Old-New Sides split:

> ... one doesn't fully understand the Old Side - New Side debate unless one sees what is happening here in sociological terms. The New Siders were "Americanizing" colonial Presbyterianism, reorienting it from the attitudes and practices of Scotland and redefining it according to its American environment. The stress was shifting away from correct belief, adherence to creedal standards and proper observance of traditional forms, to the emphasis on individual religious experience. In this sense, it would prove to be enormously successful. The New Siders may not have understood the Confession better than the Old Side, but they certainly accommodated better to American culture. As the frontier was opening up, as American religion was, in Nathan Hatch's term, "Democratizing", the New Siders were offering populist forms of piety that were much more in tune with the values of the New World. ("Democratizing" - Nathan O. Hatch, *The Democratization of American Christianity* (New Haven: Yale University Press, 1989).[502]

Looking back on a career in Princeton that spanned 50 years, Charles Hodge, himself in the Old School camp, famously said at its celebration: "I am not afraid to say that a new idea never originated in this Seminary."

Change is embedded in the eternal councils of God and he puts it into effect through creation and providence. The world experiences it continuously, from gradual development, to events of global significance. The creation of the universe was the epoch-making change that marked the beginning. Change continued dramatically throughout the days of Genesis 1-2 and culminated in the creation of Adam and Eve, in the image of God. The Fall brought fundamental retrograde change to the human race and to creation itself as it became subject to the curse of sin. The Flood, the diversification of languages and the dispersal of nations followed. Change has been continuous with the succeeding ages or time periods of world history. 'Common grace' continues to bring changes to all aspects of life that are beneficial.

God's plan of redemption selected a people for himself and his dealings with them brought national and international change – Egypt, slavery, the Exodus, the wilderness years, Canaan, kingdom, division, apostasy, exile and return. These changes featured both the blessing and the judgement of God. The coming of

Jesus Christ and the accomplishment of redemption are seminal. They introduced the global changes of the Great Commission, the ingathering of the Gentile nations, and the New Testament church with its formalising structures. And they brought into sharp relief the climactic change of the future – the termination of the present age by the second coming of Jesus Christ and the two eternal destinies of the human race. Personal transformational change comes in conversion to Jesus Christ and in the progressive sanctification that accompanies it. The *semper reformanda* principle commits the church to continuous reformatory change with primary concern for response to the teaching of Scripture and the godliness of its people.

Change is a powerful element in 'the spirit of the age'. It is not just that change is affecting all aspects of life or even that the change is more rapid and radical than ever before. Change is a way of life, producing expectation of it and 'tiredness' with even the recent past and many today feel the need for a 'changing vesture' for their faith. So how should the church respond to the expectation of change? How can it assess the values and influences of the prevailing cultures and guard against general syncretism with them? The church must always relate to the world of its own day and communicate effectively with it but conformity to its ways is a different matter. Holiness has the basic idea of separation. "The whole world lies under the sway of the wicked one" (1 John 5.19), and there is the danger of its subtle input to minds and tastes. "Do not love the world or the things in the world ... For all that is in the world—the lust of the flesh, the lust of the eyes, and the pride of life—is not of the Father but is of the world." (1 John 2.15-16) In sharp distinction, "we are of God". (1 John 5.19) God commissioned Adam and Eve to change the earth but they allowed outside influence to change themselves. Change is never satisfied with confines. Step by step it seeks pervasion of root and branch. Managing it requires assessment, discernment and great wisdom from God in applying the Word. R Kent Hughes noted: "The *Zeitgeist*, the spirit of the age, is a tyrant to be resisted, not embraced."[503]

Secession

Those who have obeyed what they believe is the biblical obligation to separate from pluralist denominations have generally not found sympathy with those of reformed persuasion within such bodies. This 'separation over separation' is arguably a major factor in restricting the unified effectiveness of the reformed constituency. But secession faces its own set of counter-issues. The inter-church debate relates mainly to five intersecting areas: schism, unity and peace, mixture and error, internal reformation and opportunity.[504]

Schism and Separatism

Schism appears in noun and verb form nearly 20 times in the New Testament (*schisma* and *schizo*). Matt 9.16 puts across the sense of rending quite graphically: "No one puts a piece of unshrunk cloth on to an old garment; for the patch pulls away from the garment, and the tear (*schisma*) is made worse." (cf Mark 2.21;

Luke 5.36). "And behold, the veil of the temple was torn (*schizo*) in two from top to bottom; and the earth quaked, and the rocks were split (*schizo*)" (Matt 27.51). Three times the Gospel of John records a split among the people over the Person and work of Jesus Christ: "And there was a division (*schisma*) among them." (9.16; cf 7.43, 10.19; Acts 23.7) Paul uses the word three times in 1 Corinthians to describe and reprove disunity among believers: "… I hear that there are divisions (*schismata*) among you …" (11.18, cf 1.10, 12.25). So although the cause and outcome of *schisma* in the NT are not exclusively bad the word itself conveys division, often strong and violent.

It is these negative connotations that have governed the etymology of the word *schism* – a culpable and damaging division. Sadly the word has a primary association with the church and there is no shortage of case studies. These cases can be complex and emotive, with the influences of history, personality conflict, break-down of relationships, responsibility and denominational loyalty bearing upon them. One of the questions is: Has the separating body been forced out by the parent or placed in a 'constructive dismissal' situation – when an employee is forced to resign because of the employer's conduct?

All separation is not schism, but faced with the pervasive New Testament emphasis on the visible unity of the church, the onus is on those who would take the step to demonstrate that they do so solely in obedience to biblical demand, established by biblical exegesis. Dr Klaas Runia said: "When a church refuses to listen to our protest in the name of the Gospel and declines to submit itself to the clear Word of God, then, I believe, we must *separate ourselves from our church*. Of course this is the *very last thing* we should ever do. It may be done only after we have tried all possible means to reform the church." He goes on:

> By this term (Separatism) we mean the ecclesiology (theological aspect) and the attitude (practical aspect) of those who leave their church without any previous attempt at reformation from within. … The separatist has the mentality of the schismatic. He does not really care for his church. He simply writes her off as apostate because of her shortcomings and leaves her in order that he may find a new spiritual home elsewhere … we have no appreciation whatsoever of any form of separatism, even if we share its concern for the purity of the church.[505]

Lloyd-Jones had another perspective on schism which Runia quotes: "We are already in a schismatic condition by being scattered throughout apostate denominations. To break our unholy association and to join fellowship on a church level with all those who confess the historic Christian faith would not mean an act of schism. It would mean leaving our present schisms in order to enter into true visible unity as the Church of Christ."[506]

The Unity and Peace of the Church
Unity: There is tremendous New Testament emphasis on the unity of the church.[507] This unity is not just the mystical union that all believers have in Christ, but the outward visible unity of the members of the organised church. The force of

prominent passages like John 17.20-23, 1 Corinthians 12.12-31 and Ephesians 4.1-6, 13, 16 cannot be avoided.

It may seem strange that the word *unity* appears just twice in the New Testament: "... endeavouring to keep the unity of the Spirit in the bond of peace." (Eph 4.3); "... till we all come to the unity of the faith" (Eph 4.13). But other expressions have similar effect: Believers are to be *joined* together "in the same mind and in the same judgement." (1 Cor 1.10); the whole body is "joined and knit together" (Eph 4.16, Col 2.19); believers are "joint heirs with Christ" (Rom 8.17). Believers are to be *one*. Some passages root oneness in the divine nature – "that they may be one, just as we are one" (John 17.22); the oneness is Trinitarian, derived from "one Spirit ... one Lord ... one Father of all." (Eph 4.4-6). "Now the multitude of those who believed were of one heart and one soul" (Acts 4.32); there are many members in one body (Rom 12.4-5; 1 Cor 10.17); "the body is one" (1 Cor 12.12-13); Paul hoped to hear that the Philippians were standing fast "in one spirit, with one mind striving together for the faith of the Gospel" (Phil 1.27); his joy would be fulfilled through their being "of one accord, of one mind" (Phil 2.2). Some 50 *one another* passages urge the interaction of believers in unity. Believers are *in Christ*, united with him through his saving work. One purpose of unity is internal development: "till we all come to the unity of the faith ... to a perfect man, to the measure of the stature of the fullness of Christ" (Eph 4.13). Another is external witness: "that the world may know that you have sent me, and have loved them as you have loved me." (John 17.23).

Unity cannot be taken for granted. It was necessary for the Saviour to pray earnestly for it, for the early church to deal with tensions over the daily distribution of food, for Paul to plead with the Corinthians for unity and to urge the Ephesians to work for it. Alongside the positive pleas for unity there are warnings and censures about its failures: "Where do wars and fights come from among you? Do they not come from your desires for pleasure that war in your members?" (Jas 4.1; cf Jude 19). Paul confronts the divisive party spirit at Corinth with the reproving, silencing question: "Is Christ divided?" (1 Cor 1.13)

Peace: Scripture also makes much of peace. God is the God of peace – the creator and dispenser of peace and its benefits: "Be of good comfort, be of one mind, live in peace; and the God of peace will be with you." (2 Cor 13.1; cf Rom 15.33, 16.20; Phil 4.9; 1 Thess 5.23; Heb 13.20). Jerusalem was the city of peace. The coming Messiah would have the name, "Prince of Peace" (Is 9.6) and he would "speak peace to the nations." (Zech 9.10). Forgiveness of sin brings "peace with God" and is the basis of personal peace (Rom 5.1). It is a gift of Christ: "Peace I leave with you, my peace I give to you." (John 14.27) "Peace" is one of the fruits of the Spirit (Gal 5.22) which are to mark church life (Ps 122.6; Rom 14.19; Eph 2.14-18; 1 Cor 14.33). Believers are called upon to promote it: "Blessed are the peacemakers" (Matt 5.9; cf Rom 12.18; Eph 4.3). The development of associated graces is constantly pressed upon believers too – humility, gentleness, longsuffering, bearing with one another in love.

So often, the desire for outward peace is the controlling factor. Iain H Murray summarises the reasons Spurgeon gave in the *Sword and Trowel*, November 1887, for withdrawing from the Baptist Union in the Down-Grade Controversy: "The Union was preferring denominational peace to the duty of dealing with error and thus, by tolerating sin, they made the withdrawal of Christians unavoidable".[508] David B Calhoun highlights the problem in the case of Princeton Seminary as the battle moved towards its decisive phase in 1924: "But Stevenson and Erdman placed the unity of the church above strict doctrinal orthodoxy and promoted peace and tolerance in the interest of the church's mission."[509] Mr J Saxton Payne, speaking at the General Assembly on 10 June 1927 as one of the appointed representatives of the Presbytery of Belfast, said: "I detest division in the Church and desire unity above all things and nothing but a strong sense of duty and a desire to promote peace and reconciliation has led me to take part in the present controversy."

Truth: There is powerful biblical emphasis on visible unity and peace and on the obligation to promote them. But the church must begin with the nature and basis of the visible unity that the New Testament sets out. Johannes G Vos[510] gives essential background to true biblical unity with his focus on the nature of the visible church:

> A low view of the Visible Church is extremely common to-day. According to this view, the Visible Church is regarded as a means to an end, as something which exists for practical purposes only. It is a missionary and evangelistic agency; it is sometimes even asserted that the only purpose of the Church is missions and evangelism. In this point of view, the importance of the Visible Church is discounted. ...
>
> According to the "high" view of the Visible Church, on the other hand, the Visible Church is more than a means to an end, or just a means for missions and evangelism. According to this "high" view, the Church is an end in itself (subordinate, of course, to the supreme end of the glory of God). The Visible Church is important, not only because of what it can do, but much more because of what it is. ... The "high" view of the Visible Church is certainly the view set forth in the Westminster Confession of Faith. According to this view, the Visible Church is the house of God (1 Tim 3.15). It is the visible embodiment of the Covenant of Grace on earth. Therefore it is holy, and its holiness and purity are to be safeguarded at any cost. Unbelief may never be tolerated in the Visible Church. Always separation from it is called for, if the evil cannot be corrected by the normal processes of church government and discipline.[511]

Prof. Klaas Runia brings into focus the essential fusion of unity with objective truth:

> Because believers are one in Christ ... they must always strive to manifest this unity in the world. ... The New Testament emphasises heresy in particular,

because the unity in Christ is no indifferent, colourless unity, but always a unity in the truth. ... The relation between unity and truth can become so full of tension that a rupture is unavoidable. In the New Testament itself, this rupture means the expulsion of the heretics. The New Testament does not know the situation of a church in which error has obtained an official place. Yet it speaks to our situation, for it makes it abundantly clear that not all unity is naturally scriptural and that not all separateness is sinful. Everything depends on the answers to the questions: is it a unity in the truth? is it a separateness for the sake of the clear testimony of the Word of God?[512]

For ease of reference the Scripture texts of this paragraph have been included in an endnote.[513] The sole basis of biblical unity is union with Christ in the truth. The basis is doctrinal. Truth is one of the attributes of God (Ex 34.6; Rom 1.25, 3.7, 15.8). Christ is the truth (John 1.14, 14.6; Eph 4.21); the Holy Spirit is the Spirit of truth and he guides into all the truth (John 16.13). *Truth* in Scripture has an absolute and objective character. It is a corpus – the Word of God. (Ps 119.160; John 17.17; Eph 1.13) It is identified with the Christian faith (Rom 2.8; Gal 2.5, 5.7). People can know it (John 8.32), be led into it (John 16.13), be sanctified through it (John 17.17, 19), witness to it (John 18.37), obey it (Rom 2.8), state it openly (2 Cor 4.2), act for it (2 Cor 13.8), fasten it on like a belt (Eph 6.14), be saved through believing it (2 Thess 2.13), and walk in it (3 John 3-4). Conversely, people can act against it (2 Cor 13.8), fail to walk according to it (Gal 2.14), perish because they refuse to love it (2 Thess 2.10), be destitute of it (1 Tim 6.5), oppose it (2 Tim 3.8), and wander from it (Jas 5.19).

Paul stressed truth. The noun and its related words appear about 55 times in his letters; it appears in noun form in every letter except two. For Paul, truth is identified with God and his Word, the Gospel, the Church and the Christian life. That is its realm. It is a divine attribute, the basis of the Gospel of salvation, the rule of faith and life for the people of God. The church is the "pillar and ground of the truth" (1 Tim 3.15). Christ has given his church teaching gifts "for the equipping of the saints for the work of ministry, for the edifying of the body of Christ, till we all come to the unity of the faith". (Eph 4.12-13) Scripture emphasises unity in the church; it also emphasises truth, as it does love and other attributes. Each interacts with the others and the church must satisfy the requirements of each. Biblical unity must comply with the primary demands of truth. It is unity of the faith. "For I rejoiced greatly when brethren came and testified of the truth that is in you, just as you walk in the truth. I have no greater joy than to hear that my children walk in truth." (3 John 3-4)

A church must not only be determined to maintain its standards; it must also be willing for the cost of conflict over that maintenance, imposing discipline and accepting division if that is the cost. But whatever the issues that do arise in the life of the church, dealing with them requires diligence to keep the "unity of the Spirit". This does not preclude strong debate, an unyielding stand or personal accusation: "to whom we did not yield submission even for an hour" "I withstood him [Peter] to his face." (Gal 2.5, 11). Unity may not be the outcome nor is unity always the proper outcome: "They went out from us, but they were not of us" (1 John 2.19). But engagement in the right spirit is a servant of true unity. Greater unity was the outcome when Peter was at fault and Paul withstood him to his face before the Galatian church. The church likes peace, but it cannot isolate peace from the body of Christian standards. The obligation to be at peace is conditional: "If it be possible ... live peaceably with all men." (Rom 12.18) – the demands of truth and other duties may make it impossible. "But the wisdom that is from above is first pure, then peaceable ..." (Jas 3.17).[514]

The Imperfect Nature of the Church

Westminster 25.5 acknowledges: "The purest churches under heaven are subject both to mixture and error." Apostasy persisted for centuries in the Old Testament church. God responded with a succession of prophets to Israel and Judah and a high incidence of long-reigning 'good' Kings to Judah through whom he achieved reforms. Does this confirm that an imperfect church is the biblical norm? Comparison of a theocracy when God exercised forbearance because of ignorance (Acts 17.30; Rom 3.25), with the New Testament church when God has "spoken to us by His Son" (Heb 1.1-2), is of dubious validity. But the analogy fails in itself for God's response to OT apostasy included judgement which he carried out with strokes of varying severity before the ultimate blow of exile. There were secessions from Israel to Judah in the reigns of Rehoboam (2 Chron 11.13,16) and Asa (2 Chron 15.9) and Scripture commends the reforming kings. Some of them like Jehoshaphat were not thorough in their reforms and the response of the people was not always of the heart. Many key figures in Judah like Solomon, Asa, Joash, Amaziah, Uzziah, Ahaz and Hezekiah had serious lapses in their later years.

The New Testament presents the same principles. It does not hide the serious imperfections of the nascent first-century church. The Holy Spirit is concerned to present a true profile of the church – people called from the power of Satan unto God, again and again serving the Lord with sacrifice and distinction, communicating the Gospel, giving joy to the Apostles, struggling against persecution and every device of the evil one; but too often lacking in progressive sanctification, committing particular sins, remaining as children in the faith, susceptible to doctrinal lapse, vulnerable to deceit and infiltration, failing in standards of discipline. There were major doctrinal issues at Galatia, Thessalonica, Corinth and Colossae. Gaius and Diotrephes were apparently members of the same group of churches (3 John). Many features in the life and witness of the Seven Churches of Asia (Rev 2-3) were critically wrong.

Is this not the reality of the church in all ages? If the Apostles were willing to work with it, why not the future church? The fact is they were not willing to work with it as a norm. There was no acceptable level of error for them. Paul visited and wrote. Each of his letters dealt with problems, some of them, like the situation in Galatia, critical: "O foolish Galatians! Who has bewitched you that you should not obey the truth ... ?" (Gal 3.1). He confronted these issues because he saw their resolution as vital for the church's future. The situation in the Seven Churches of Asia evoked the Lord's specific condemnation, warnings and threats for five of the seven churches. There is no mention of unorthodoxy in Sardis and Laodicea. They needed revival. John was coming to deal with Diotrephes (3 John 10, 14). Conflict with false teachers, deceivers and antichrists was a dominant theme in 1 John. Throughout the church scene there was no accommodation with unbelief, but determined opposition to it as something that would destroy the church.

Paul and the other Apostles confronted these issues with doctrine, the objective criteria of belief. It was central to the corpus of letters to the churches, as well as the preaching and teaching of missionary journeys and pastoral visits. It was the same in the book of Acts in the period before the letters were written – "And they continued steadfastly in the apostles' doctrine" (Acts 2.42, cf 11.26, 13.1). A key feature of the Apostles' strategy was the appointment of qualified leaders. There is emphasis on their possession of the full range of Christian graces, but their aptitude for teaching was mandatory – "able to teach" (1 Tim 3.2). Titus 1.9 provides a fuller statement: "... holding fast the faithful word as he has been taught, that he may be able, by sound doctrine, both to exhort and convict those who contradict." So in the New Testament as well as in the Old, doctrinal mixture could not be accepted.

There is still the contention that there is no evidence of any New Testament church even considering the possibility of separation, although some faced serious issues. But this is superficial. The Scriptural position is that truth and error must always stand in opposite camps. They are two opposing and irreconcilable forces at work. Rehoboam's stupidity and arrogance triggered the split between Judah and Israel, but God had already ordained it for greater purposes: "for the turn of events was from the Lord, that he might fulfil His word ..." (1 Kings 12.15, cf v 24). The first act of Jeroboam, the new King of Israel, was to institutionalise idolatry in the form of two golden calves: "Here are your gods, O Israel, which brought you up from the land of Egypt!" (12.28). God had separated Judah from that powerful influence. He had earlier segregated Jacob and his family in Goshen, to separate them from harmful influences.[515]

In the conflict of 1 John, commendable separation had already taken place (2.18-19). Jude urged earnest contending for the faith "for certain men have crept in unnoticed" (Jude 4, cf Gal 2.4). They should have been kept out. Christ had a few things against Pergamos "because you have there those who hold the doctrine of Baalam ..." (Rev 2.14). They should not have been there! In Thyatira, the Lord's censure fell on the church for allowing Jezebel "to teach and beguile my servants ..." (2.20). He commends Ephesus for not allowing counterfeit apostles, wicked men, into the church; they had examined them and exposed them as liars (Rev 2.2). All the evidence points to disciplinary separation.

Some have found support for pluralism in the parable of the wheat and the tares (Matt 13.24-30, 36-43): "Let both grow together until the harvest ..."

(13.30). Without any doubt some "hypocrites and other unregenerate men" (WCF 18.1) infiltrate the "purest churches under heaven" (25.5) because fallible men judge their applications. But this parable does not address the composition of the organised church. It speaks of the make-up of God's Kingdom, the world, in which the people of God and the people of Satan will live together until he inaugurates "new heavens and a new earth in which righteousness dwells" (2 Pet 3.13): "The field is the world, the good seeds are the sons of the kingdom, but the tares are the sons of the wicked one." (Matt 13.38) Paul's practice of leaving the synagogue, shown in both Corinth and Ephesus, if the truth was rejected is important.

Internal Reformation of the Church
This is bound up with the view that the church must cope even with failures in doctrine and practice within it as part of its own imperfect nature. God endured the serious levels of apostasy in the Old Testament church for centuries but repeatedly called for internal reform. Theological aberration and its effects appeared in various New Testament churches, but the apostolic demand was for internal reform. So is internal reform not then the biblical procedure? The Presbyterian Bible Standards League took this view after the Heresy Trial in 1927. Accepting the need for internal reform in principle is one thing but dealing with it in church courts is another. In both Old and New Testament churches God dealt with it through sanctions.

A related view is long-term patience supported by faithfulness and prayer. Scattered throughout the history of the Church are notable examples of God bringing revival into situations of decline and darkness. Henry Cooke led reform in the Presbyterian Church in Ireland in the early 19th century which led to union with the Secession Church in the General Assembly of 1840. Since this is what God has done in the past, does this not teach patience until God in his sovereignty does it again? But that approach, in itself, is too simplistic. There should not be an assumption that God will keep doing it. Further questions need to be addressed. How pervasive and lasting has reform been? Was it just the momentum of a particular movement without a root and branch change? Did it eradicate error and enthrone a dynasty of truth? Was it more of the nature of the reforms under the 'good' kings of Judah, which temporarily reversed the progressive downward trend? What was the eventual outcome? What of the intervening period? Has the Church specified elements of reform and is there an agenda for dealing with them?

Those who take the pluralist position share in the corporate responsibility for whatever exists in the Church with regard to the faith, government, sacraments and discipline. Primary loyalty should never be to a church. Machen said of such at the first Assembly of the Presbyterian Church of America in 1936: "they are yielding to the most subtle of Satan's temptations, the temptation to do evil in order that good may come ..." The principles are still the same. It can be that the proponents of internal reform are just bonded to the 'Church of their fathers'.

There is little doubt that the internal reform philosophy has seriously limited the potential of corporate unity and witness of the Reformed Faith. The effectiveness of separate outside influence should not simply be disregarded.

Church Opportunity

Many who espouse reformed theology feel satisfied to be in mixed denominations because there is uninhibited opportunity to preach the Gospel and the reformed faith in the local congregation. The argument is heightened where the opportunity is seen to be much greater than it would be in a secession church with a lower profile and perhaps much smaller numbers. In addition, some genuinely feel the personal call of God to work and witness in the greater access situations and contribute to longer-term reform. Did not God in the 1920s, through W P Nicholson, favour with the blessings of salvation, at a level not since experienced, the Church which IEC founding fathers charged with departure from the faith? J G Vos again:

> These men feel no responsibility to separate from their modernistic denominations. They retain membership, with its benefits, while they disclaim responsibility for the corporate character of their denominations. They feel that as long as they are free to preach Christ in their own pulpit, they are not responsible for the modernism of their denomination as a whole ... Their position might perhaps be described as theological and religious isolationism. ... But their position is only possible to men holding the "low" view of the Visible Church. If they held the "high" view of the Visible Church, they would at once feel a corporate responsibility for conditions in their denomination. They would never rest till one or the other of two things had taken place; either the evils had been corrected or they themselves had been cast out of the Church. A man who holds the "high" view of the Visible Church could not sleep peacefully in his bed at night while knowing that modern unbelief is entrenched in high places in his denomination. He would feel keenly the guilt of compromise, and would not rest until he had cleared himself of all complicity in this compromise.[516]

It is always good when sinners hear the Gospel and especially when God uses it for conversions. He is sovereign and such is his compassion and mercy that he uses many kinds of situation and agency to make his Son's soul an offering for sin and to see his offspring. (Is 53.10) He sent Jonah to Nineveh. But this does not entitle the church to make its own rules. In particular, it is not a warrant to set aside the doctrine of the church. The doctrine of the church is what it all boils down to. There are church standards that God approves and with which he requires compliance.

Was IEC a Secession Church?

The answer may depend on the definition of secession. The word came to prominence in connection with the withdrawal of American States from the Union in the 1860s after Abraham Lincoln, a recognised opponent of slavery, was elected to office on 6 November 1860. Many in the southern states were afraid that he would curtail slavery or end it altogether, and consequently, on 20 December 1860, South Carolina was the first in a secession of states from the Union.[517] It resulted in the American Civil War. So secession is usually defined as something like "the act of formally withdrawing from an organisation". It usually means some kind of planned, corporate withdrawal.

The IEC founding fathers certainly saw their action in forming a new church organisation in secession terms even though they did not use the expression in their inaugural statement of 12 November 1927: "... and being convinced that however wise and useful it may be to remain in a church in the first stages of declension, after that the church has become corrupt there remains no other course in accord with the plain teaching of the Word of God than to 'come out of her'. In loyalty to the Head of the Church and for the maintenance of a testimony to His truth (we) do hereby unite in the purpose of forming a new spiritual organisation ..." They later used the term secession for their action quite freely.

Independent withdrawal by individuals who later decided to start another church does not quite fit classical secession norms. Plans for a new church were post-withdrawal although it must have been in the thinking of those who took the first steps. Some have suggested that the founding of IEC had negligible public impact. There is truth in that for there were no affiliated congregations or substantial numbers to start with in 1927 and it was not possible to have a high profile secession. However, the Conference series, 1928-31, operating with other factors did achieve awareness and the opening of 11 congregations in the first five years. As Rev. W J McDowell, an eyewitness of the events culminating in 1927, said in the April 1984 *Evangelical Presbyterian* in answer to comments in the February issue: "... the Evangelical Presbyterian church came into being because individuals seceded on account of the departure from true Christianity. I quite agree there ought to have been an organised secession – there was not, because many preferred peace to strife. Those individuals who seceded had to endure the cold shoulder and the pointed finger of scorn." But whatever the mismatch between the founding of IEC and the normal expectations of secession, all the core elements were and still are present.

The Internal Lessons

In addition to the recurrent lessons from the broader ecclesiastical scene, EPC must also seek to identify and apply particular lessons from its internal history. Many of them are encouraging. The Church has cause to be thankful for the courage, faithfulness, hard work, financial giving and obedience to the great commission at home and overseas that have characterised its witness from the beginning. God has used these things to progressively strengthen every aspect of the work and to increase its potential. Past years have demonstrated the reward of persevering through times of difficulty and discouragement. But there have failures too. W J Grier said in 1947: "We have not carried the flag to the top of the hill." Joseph McCracken said in 1957: "Let us not be continually harping on the shortage of man power but try attempting more with what is available. I believe this is the way to blessing. God will raise up other helpers as we attempt new things for Him." In 1967 W J McDowell commented that: "more regular attendance at all the means of grace, greater enthusiasm, and more zeal for the Lord's cause were pressing necessities."

The church in Thessalonica was born in affliction but Paul said of it: "For from you the word of the Lord has sounded forth, not only in Macedonia and Achaia, but also in every place…" (1 Thess 1.8). So has the Church's development and outreach been sufficiently purposeful? Has the burden for sinners been powerful enough to drive its people into their communities? To what extent has the Church traded with itself? Lack of resources curtailed the Church's expansion potential for significant periods but many more resources are available to it today. Advance brings its own special encouragement. The Church started with nothing but God provided and will always do so for the right things. There was the virtual absence of integrated development programmes in EPC until the late 1980s when the *Vision for the Nineties* Strategy Committee reported. One major result was a new church plant in Bangor in 1994, over 20 years ago. A 2008 Strategy Committee also recommended a new plant but it did not take place. Church planting is important for the Church's development programme but "He who observes the wind will not sow, And he who regards the clouds will not reap." (Eccles 11.4) It is periodically good to have a fresh look at the internal side too and this was the objective of a further strategy programme, 2012-14 which focused on the development of existing congregations. Strong congregations are among the factors which facilitate expansion.

Undoubtedly the greatest lesson is that of the calling of a confessional church through its leaders and members in terms of their doctrinal faithfulness, godliness of life and obedient, sacrificial diligence in the service of God: "and He died for all, that those who live should live no longer for themselves, but for Him who died for them and rose again." (2 Cor 5.15) The final chapter addresses this great lesson.

26

Living to the Standard

"Therefore, since all these things will be dissolved, what manner of persons ought you to be in holy conduct and godliness …" (2 Peter 3.11)

This amounts to nothing less than a call to radical discipleship. It calls for 'diligence' or concentrated effort. As we prepare to meet God on the day of Christ's return, we will make the knowledge of God the focus of our entire existence. Only when we are certain of our standing with him (1:10) ["be even more diligent to make your call and election sure"] can we live lives that will not only honour him, but will also enjoy his fullest blessing, in this world and the next.

Mark G Johnston, *Let's study 2 Peter and Jude*, pp 63-64

The constitution of the Evangelical Presbyterian Church sets out the Church's biblical standards, responsibilities, goals and procedures, but they need to be understood and applied pervasively in the practice of confessional church life.

The Confessional Church

As a starting point, a confessional church is commonly considered to be one which specifies one of the Reformation confessions of the 16th-17th centuries as its statement of faith. Presbyterian churches throughout the world usually choose the Westminster Confession of Faith, completed in 1646. Churches normally describe their confession as their 'subordinate standard' because the supreme standard is the Word of God. It is not just a particular church that makes this supreme-subordinate distinction. It is the prominent teaching of the Westminster Confession itself. Holy Scripture is the subject of its first chapter and it asserts: "The supreme Judge, by which all controversies of religion are to be determined … and in whose sentence we are to rest, can be no other than the Holy Spirit speaking in Scripture." (WCF 1.10)

Westminster was the last of the great post-reformation confessions and many regard it as their 'queen'.[518] There has been an encouraging upsurge of interest in it in recent years, much of it in the very readable category.[519] Westminster built on all the church's doctrinal statements before it; it expressed its teaching structurally and with precise language. It summarises the Bible's teaching on all its important doctrines and supports its findings with Scripture references. Such a confession greatly facilitates Bible study and is essential in establishing agreement within a church on what Scripture teaches.

WCF is a 'systematic' theology, having one chapter for each theological subject, helpfully divided into sub-sections. In addition, it is a 'system of theology'. In the first instance this is because its 33 chapters[520] are arranged logically in categories. One way of grouping related chapters together is:

God's Word, Existence and Nature (1-2)
God's Decrees of Creation and Providence (3-5)
Redemption (6-9)
The Order of the Steps of Salvation (10-18)
The Law of God and Living the Christian Life (19-24)
The Church (25-31)
The Last Things (32-33)

Secondly, and of great importance, WCF is a system of doctrine in that its teachings are structured around the sovereignty of God and covenants. In this context a covenant is an agreement between God and his people, which God has drawn up. The covenant of works and the covenant of grace (the first and second covenants) are the main WCF covenants and they link, in turn, to the first Adam and the last Adam, the Lord Jesus Christ. The Westminster Divines also published the Larger and Shorter Catechisms which apply the Confession's teaching in question and answer form. The Catechisms greatly expand the Bible's teaching on the commandments and on the Lord's Prayer. The Confession and the Catechisms together comprise the EPC subordinate standards.

Application of the Standards

But it is not sufficient simply to have confessional standards, however biblical, well-structured and precise they may be. The vital thing is their application and EPC does this in two main ways. First, it defines clearly the basis on which it accepts its confessional standards. EPC has amended the wording of the Confession at two points, each by an Amending Act, and has stated how it understands one other section, by a Declaratory Act. Second, there is a formula of subscription which contains a set of questions addressed to each man being ordained as a minister, elder or deacon. By answering these questions affirmatively, he declares that the confessional standards "as accepted by this Church" are his own personal confession of faith and this he does "without any reservations". Then he signs or subscribes the formula of subscription document which contains the questions and affirms his answers. These 'ordination vows' are made before witnesses. Through the formula, EPC ministers and elders commit themselves, through divine power, to adhere to the standards, to teach them and defend them to the utmost of their power against all error. In addition, EPC ministers and elders subscribe a document annually, renewing their commitment to the confessional standards and stating that they have refreshed their memories on their contents.

WCF and the Church

The whole of the Confession's teaching is necessary for the church, but the focus in this chapter is its section on the church – chapters 25-31. They deal with the doctrine of the church, its fellowship, sacraments, discipline and assemblies.

Chapter 25 is introductory and sets out some basic concepts. In one sense the church is 'invisible'. As such it comprises all God's chosen people in every age who are gathered into one under Christ its Head. Only God knows it in its totality. The 'visible' church consists of the people of every nation who profess faith in Christ and their children (Ezek 16.20-21; Acts 2.39). The baptism through which the children of believers are received into the visible church does not convey grace or automatically make them Christians but, since the promise is to believers and their children, the children are entitled to the seal of the covenant of grace. God brings them into his house and family, unites them with believers and gives them the outward privileges of the church. In this way he distinguishes them and sets them apart from the world.[521] The 'visible' church is the "Kingdom of the Lord Jesus Christ"; he only is its King and Head. It is also the house and family of God. It is not a physical building but is made up of "living stones" and built into a spiritual house, with Jesus Christ himself being the chief cornerstone. (1 Pet 2.4-10) Its members are the family who comprise this house. By free grace they are adopted sons and daughters of Jesus Christ, and Scripture applies the title Father almost exclusively to his children by adoption. (cf Heb 2.11, 1 John 3.1)

The ministry of the church is to gather and build up believers, and for these purposes Jesus Christ makes the Word of God effective by his presence and Spirit. There is no perfect church. Even the purest churches suffer from mixture and error; the purity of a particular church depends upon its commitment to teach and embrace the Gospel, its adherence to biblical worship, administration of the sacraments and discipline. People can come to faith outside the church but God normally brings salvation through his church.

Congregation and Presbytery
The foundation of the Presbyterian system is the local congregation and great privilege and responsibility rests on each. That is where the members are, where the denomination's membership declines or grows, where organisations function, where the Word is preached, where the resources come from. The congregation's court is the session, so called because its members sit like a court. It sends representatives to the upper court – the Presbytery, in EPC. These two courts have complementary roles. Presbytery leads the denomination. It sets identity, beliefs, standards, policies and procedures for the work at home and abroad. It addresses issues relating to its denominational effectiveness – its standing in the local church scene, how best to minister to local communities, to work overseas, to use resources, to lead the congregations. Its functions are *judicial* when it exercises discipline or adjudicates, and *administrative* when it co-ordinates and supports the whole of denominational life. It facilitates the sharing of interest, resources and abilities throughout the Church. Congregations share the ethos of the denomination.

Church Worship

WCF 21 – Religious Worship and the Lord's Day are placed within the Confession's section on the Law of God and Living the Christian Life, but are topics bound up with the church. WCF 25 – The Church, draws public worship within its scope. Worship can be given only to God through Jesus Christ, the only Mediator, and is the most elevated exercise that can engage the people of God. Believers must maintain holy fellowship and communion with God and with each other in the worship of God. (WCF 26) God specifies in Scripture how he is to be worshipped; everything else is forbidden. This is what is referred to as the Regulative Principle.

> Embedded in the Lord's instructions throughout Scripture is the idea that what we do in worship is actually limited. God has identified areas where we must go and some where we must not... Thankfully we do not need to guess these limits. Because he is not a capricious God, our Lord has revealed his will to us. We have such great imaginations, and we can generate so many devices for pleasing God (or pleasing ourselves) in worship, that God graciously gave his Word to be our guide and our boundary. ...
>
> God does not need us or our clever ideas (Acts 17.25), and neither does he need the worship we may devise in the hope of pleasing him. ...

When considering worship we also need to consider our temptation to false worship; for there is a tempter, one who is known to redirect worship away from God, and we are warned that he will continue this evil work of his until he is finally chained.[522]

WCF 1.6 (Scripture) includes a supplementary aspect: "there are some circumstances concerning the worship of God and the government of the church – circumstances common to human activities and societies – which are to be ordered by the light of nature and Christian prudence, according to the general rules of the Word, which are always to be observed."

Prayer
WCF 21.3 describes it, accompanied by thanksgiving, as "one special part of religious worship"; it should be offered with understanding, earnestness, perseverance and faith. It includes adoration, thanksgiving, communion, intercession and confession of sin. Prayers offered on behalf of the congregation in worship and those offered at the weekly prayer meeting are fundamental to the biblical requirement to pray "with and for others." (SC 100) In addition, there are times for special, prolonged corporate prayer as when Peter was about to be executed. (Acts 12) The Church was in prayer when the Holy Spirit separated Paul and Barnabas for the great missionary journeys. In more modern times people prayed for the revival which God sent in 1859. The EPC founding generation held whole nights or half nights of prayer. The practice of a week of prayer, usually at the beginning of the year, has continued in EPC congregations through the years. The subjects for prayer are vast in their scope "… for the whole church of Christ upon earth; for magistrates, and ministers; for ourselves, our brethren, yes, our enemies; and for all sorts of men living, or that shall live hereafter …" (LC 183) Prayer for revival may well be a long-term project but it is by revival that the Lord causes his church to forge ahead with renewed life and vigour.

The Other Elements
Having described prayer as a "special" part of worship in sub-section 3-4, WCF 21 then lumps all the other elements together in sub-section 5 as "all parts of the ordinary religious worship of God." These are Bible reading, preaching and hearing, singing and the administration and receiving of the sacraments.

Ministry of the Word: the Bible is to be read with godly fear and there is key emphasis on preaching along with the conscientious hearing of the Word with faith, reverence and understanding. Preaching imparts knowledge, commendation and encouragement, rebuke and warning, and is the normal means by which the church communicates the Gospel. "The Spirit of God makes the reading, but especially the preaching of the word, an effectual means of enlightening, convincing, and humbling sinners; of driving them out of themselves, and drawing them unto Christ." (LC 155) The whole "counsel" of God is the whole 'purpose' or 'plan' of God: "For I have not shunned to declare to you the whole counsel of God." (Acts 20.27) Paul here applies it to his own ministry, as Derek Thomas explains:

> What has God planned for this world and those who inhabit it? The forty-plus writers who produced the sixty-six books of Scripture saw themselves as caught up in the outworking of God's sovereign plan and purpose that entailed God's first creating, then rescuing, and finally re-creating, and eventually bringing to glory, a sin-infested, fallen world through a breath-taking scheme of redemption and restoration involving the commissioning, sending and incarnation of his Son. This would involve the birth, life, death, resurrection, ascension, and second coming of Jesus as the substitute and representative of God's elect children, who, in time, would be called, quickened, and saved through faith in Christ. Paul tirelessly preached this plan ...[523]

This is the great task. It covers the full revelation that God has given in Scripture. Carl Trueman asserts: "... if the preacher is to proclaim the whole counsel of God, then his preaching is never to be less than *doctrinal* in content. ... The basic distinctions necessary for understanding the world from a biblical perspective – that between creator and creature, between fall and redemption, between sin and obedience, between Adam and Christ – are all in essence doctrinal and need to be preached as such."[524]

Evangelism has a distinctive place within "the whole counsel". Christ commissioned his church to make disciples of all nations. The first word of this Great Commission is "Go". The 'going' pattern for the New Testament church was to build its base, spread increasingly into surrounding territories and then to the ends of the earth. EPC international mission is active today as it has been throughout the life of the Church. Prayer is required that God will give strategic direction to this great work and that he will always call people to serve him in it. The opportunities are greatly augmented today by the availability of global communication and travel, and by the many who now visit from overseas for studies and internships. At the same time, God continues to call men and women to long or short-term service in 'home' missions including the work of local outreach to communities, children and youth.

The Church needs wisdom, energy and determination in bringing the Gospel to bear in an age of change when indifference and opposition prevail. The church can preach the Gospel in response to its duty to do so but so much better when it is driven by the compassion the Saviour displayed when he saw people as helpless and sheep without a shepherd (Matt 9.35-38). The Saviour called the church to pray that the Lord will send labourers into such harvests. There can be few better factors motivating the Church's expansion.

Praise: the confession specifies "the singing of psalms with grace in the heart". Many Westminster churches, such as EPC, interpret this in the light of the "psalms, hymns and spiritual songs" of Ephesians 5.19, cf Colossians 3.16. J V Fesko concludes: "... the most likely scenario is that the Standards promote the inclusive use of psalmody in worship as a necessary element but are silent regarding the use of non-inspired scriptural songs in worship."[525] Aside from this discussion, the WCF section does promote essential elements – the congregational activity of singing, with the whole heart, by those who have experienced the work of redeeming grace.[526]

Baptism: It is the means of admission into the visible church, but its purposes are much wider and lasting. It is a sign and seal of the covenant of grace, of being engrafted into Christ, of regeneration and forgiveness of sins. Since the water of baptism symbolises cleansing, baptism speaks of submission to God, through Jesus Christ, to walk in holiness and newness of life. "The needful but much neglected duty of improving our baptism, is to be performed by us all our life long… to have our conversation in holiness and righteousness; as those that have therein given up their names to Christ; and to walk in brotherly love, as being baptised by the same Spirit into one body." (LC 167)

The Lord's Table: The purpose of the Lord's Supper is to commemorate his sacrificial death to the end of the world, to seal its benefits to all true believers, to nourish them spiritually, to express their renewed commitment to Christ, and to testify to the union and communion which they have with him and with one another in him. (WCF 29) The activity of faith is involved. The Larger Catechism asks some penetrating questions: How are they that receive the sacrament of the Lord's supper to prepare themselves before they come to it? (171) What is required of them that receive the sacrament of the Lord's supper in the time of the administration of it? (174) What is the duty of Christians, after they have received the sacrament of the Lord's Supper? (175)

The Lord's Day: believers are to keep it holy to the Lord "after due preparation of their hearts and arranging of their common affairs beforehand." They are to rest from all works, words and thoughts about day-to-day occupations and recreations and to devote the whole of the day to the public and private worship, and whatever necessity and mercy requires. (SC 60)

Giving: Giving is a Christian grace and an act of worship. Worshippers acknowledge that in giving to the work of the church they are giving to God what he has already given to them. God loves the cheerful giver (2 Cor 9.7) and believers are to excel in this grace. (2 Cor 8.7) WCF 21 does not include giving among its elements of worship, but 26.2 (The Communion of Saints) does relate the giving of material help to worship:

> It is the duty of professing saints to maintain a holy fellowship and communion in the worship of God and in performing such other spiritual services as help them to edify one another. It is their duty also to come to the aid of one another in material things according to their various abilities and necessities. As God affords opportunity, this communion is to be extended to all those in every place who call on the name of the Lord Jesus."

By grace, the Macedonian believers gave beyond their means in a situation of severe affliction. They did it only because they first "gave themselves to the Lord".

(2 Cor 8. 1-15, 9.1-15). That must underlie all true giving. Paul concludes: "Thanks be to God for his inexpressible gift."

Church Leaders

Leadership is a vital function in the church, its various offices being instituted by God himself (Eph 4.11-16, 1 Cor 12.28). This work is a calling of God to hold office and to serve in the church which Christ purchased with his own blood (Acts 20.28), and for which leaders will give an account. (Heb 13.17) EPC recognises this key arrangement in its constitution or 'Code' in providing separate chapters for minister, session and diaconate which set out the responsibilities of each at congregational level. Chapters on Presbytery and its functions extend the duties to that level for ministers and elders. One example is how the Code expresses the pastoral role of elders:

> The Ruling Elders shall join with the Minister in the government, nurture and discipline of the congregation. Upon them, equally with the Minister, devolves the responsibility of caring for the spiritual welfare of the people and the superintendence of all meetings and organisations within the congregation. It is the responsibility of Ruling Elders to pray with, and for, the congregation and to seek fruit among them. They are to visit the people, paying special attention to the sick, and to irregular attenders, and also to instruct the ignorant, comfort the mourner, warn the careless and nourish and guard the children of the Church.[527]

Deacons "assist the Session by administering the affairs of the congregation" in areas such as finance, premises, projects and ministering to those in need. "For those who have served well as deacons obtain for themselves a good standing and great boldness in the faith which is in Christ Jesus." (1 Tim 3.13)

The Lord provides all the Church's human resources, and leadership usually emerges at congregational level. The leaders of any organisation, including the church, must be proficient in their knowledge of its constitution and purposes. EPC acknowledges this need. It trains its ministers rigorously in accordance with its theological standards. The training of officebearers in the responsibilities of office is less well defined although development through doing the work, and attendance at Officebearers' conferences, is an effective part of it. Leadership collegiality is an important element in binding men together with singleness of purpose. In addition, leaders of the organisations, through which congregations do a great deal of outreach work, need training and support. The church must continuously look to God in prayer to qualify able, godly men to be ministers, elders and deacons and that he will give the church wisdom in identifying, developing and responding to them. (1 Tim 3.1-13, Tit 1.5-9, Heb 13.7, 17, 1 Pet 5.1-5)[528]

Church Members

The roles of leaders and members are distinct but there is continuous interaction between them in all that comprises church life. The leaders are themselves members. The people of God are, "strangers and pilgrims on the earth" (Heb 11.13) and elect exiles (1 Pet 1.1). God requires them to be holy: "as He who called you is holy, you also be holy in all your conduct, because it is written, 'Be holy for I am holy." (1 Pet 1.15-16) They should live to please God (1 Thess 4.1). As such they are to influence the world as its salt and light, maintaining their saltiness and shining their light before others to show the nature of their changed lives to the glory of God (Matt 5.13-16). As such they are to make disciples of all nations and teach them to obey all that the Lord has commanded. (Matt 28.19)

The whole of the Confession of Faith bears on living the Christian life although some of its chapters will often have particular influence, eg, Adoption, Sanctification, Good Works, Perseverance and Assurance. One great aspect is the Law of God and the duties it requires. The Catechisms treat this subject extensively in their sections on the moral law, ie, the ten commandments: LC, 91-149, SC 39-82. The following is a brief survey of rudiments of the Christian way of life. Acts 2.42 makes the main points: "And they continued steadfastly in the apostles' doctrine and fellowship, in the breaking of bread, and in prayers." Regular use of the confessional standards will bring their own rewards.

Graces: growth in grace is a major emphasis of the New Testament. Christian graces are inter-active, cumulative and essential for effective witness. Galatians 5.22-25 provides a comprehensive list: "But the fruit of the Spirit is love, joy, peace, longsuffering, kindness, goodness, faithfulness, gentleness, self-control … If we live in the Spirit, let us also walk in the Spirit." These graces were not in evidence as they should have been in Galatia. In biting and devouring one another they were in danger of consuming one another (5.15); "Let us not become conceited, provoking one another, envying one another." (5.26) It is not surprising that the same group of churches were distorting the Gospel and turning to another Gospel. (1.6-7) Peter's list is cumulative: "… giving all diligence, add to your faith virtue, to virtue knowledge, to knowledge self-control, to self-control perseverance, to perseverance godliness, to godliness brotherly kindness, and to brotherly kindness love. For if these things are yours and abound, you will be neither barren nor unfruitful in the knowledge of our Lord Jesus Christ." (2 Pet 1.5-8)

Love one another: speaking of gifts and graces Paul says: "The greatest of these is love." (1 Cor 13.13) Closely associated with it is peace, peace-making, unity, mutual sacrifice, sharing of gifts and service. Many churches experience internal conflict and EPC has too. It is not surprising because the church works partly in a supernatural arena. "For we do not wrestle against flesh and blood, but against … spiritual hosts of wickedness in the heavenly places." (Eph 6.12) Believers are to "love one another fervently from a pure heart." (1 Pet 1.22) The word 'fervently', is translated "earnestly" in Luke 22.44 to describe the intensity of the Saviour's prayer in Gethsemane: "He prayed more earnestly." Such love overcomes every potential deficiency as the church endeavours "to keep the unity of the Spirit in the bond of peace." (Eph 4.3)

Reading and study: spiritual growth is through "the diligent use" of "the ordinary means" – "especially the word, sacraments and prayer ..." (LC 153-154) It requires diligent, daily application for personal spiritual growth. The Christian life is a life of learning: "Come to me ... and learn from me...". (Matt 11.28-29) It requires time, priority, and fixed purpose for Christian service and integration with family life, employment and citizenship. Comparison of the hours spent on various pursuits with those on personal devotion is often a useful personal audit. The poetry of Psalm 1 expresses the delight which characterises the believer in mediating on the Word:

> *But his delight is in the law of the* L<small>ORD</small>,
> *And in His law he meditates day and night.*
> *He shall be like a tree*
> *Planted by the rivers of water,*
> *That brings forth its fruit in its season,*
> *Whose leaf also shall not wither;*
> *And whatever he does shall prosper.*

Fellowship: Through union with Christ all believers have fellowship with him in his graces, sufferings, death, resurrection and glory. Through union with each other in love, they share in each other's gifts and graces with the related duty to work, publicly and privately for one another's spiritual and practical good, everywhere where God enables.

Prayer: as with reading and study there is the personal side which the Westminster Confession is careful to include: "... as in private families, daily, and in secret each one by himself ..." (WCF 21.6). It is to be made with "understanding, reverence, humility, fervency, faith, love and perseverance ..." (WCF 21.3). Its perseverance and fervency should be expressed in wrestling like Jacob at Jabbok – "I will not let You go unless You bless me." (Gen 32.26) The subjects for prayer are extensive even in the context of families and individuals. Prayer for church leaders, their faithfulness, well-being and encouragement through conversions and growth in grace is an emphatic responsibility for themselves and church members.

Faithfulness: Scripture attributes it to God and to Jesus Christ. In the Christian life it is a fruit of the Spirit and refers to constant trustworthiness, reliability, integrity and obedience. Faithfulness is costly and many throughout the world today experience it acutely, as God calls some to be faithful unto death; for their faithfulness they receive "the crown of life"– the crown which is consummate eternal life. (Rev 2.10) It comes to expression in normal church life in love of the Church, faithful attendance at its services, promotion of the Church's identity and its great denominational 'distinctives' – the doctrine of the church, doctrinal integrity, the stand against pluralism, obedience to the Great Commission, and reformed worship.

Covenant Youth

David Watson, who has many years of across-the-board involvement in youth work, writes:

> An integral part of our confessional position is that God deals with us by covenants. These covenants with mankind are always gracious. One important aspect of covenant theology is that we believe the New Covenant, like the Old, embraces believers *and their children*. We believe our children are already part of the Church, the present as well as the future. The public profession made at the baptism of our children is, among other things, a pledge of our embracing the New Covenant in all its breadth. The promise by believing parents and the congregation to bring up our children in the nurture and admonition of the Lord is worked out on three levels – within the family, the congregation and the denomination, all harmoniously inter-linking.
>
> *Nurture within the Family*: Deuteronomy 6 and Psalm 78.1-8 ought ever to be ingrained in our hearts and minds. Samuel's parents (1 Sam 1.19-28) and Timothy's family (2 Tim 1.5) provide biblical examples. Family love, a father's teaching, a mother's knee, the family altar, travail in prayer and godly example all have a bearing towards spiritual birth and advance under the hand of God. Like Job, we must never allow our children out of our minds, hearts and prayers (Job 1.5). Children must see and understand what is meant by heart-felt love to God, serious adherence to the Scriptures, the supremacy of Jesus Christ in all walks of life, positive Sabbath observance, and concern for the unconverted. There is pressure today on Christian parents to let government schemes, secular education and godless morality mould their thinking and practice, rather than allowing God's Word to determine what is best for their families in terms of faith and practice. The influence and testimony of consistent, godly parents is therefore integral to the covenantal promises made, the ignoring of which will bring sorrow and loss as the Children of Israel found to their shame and hurt. We cannot convert our children; like Nicodemus, also a covenant child, they need the supernatural act of regeneration. Neither can we guarantee that our children will be converted, but, believing the promises of God, we expect them to be converted.
>
> *Nurture within the Congregation*: It goes without saying that Christian parents should formally belong to the local Church. More than that however, they will have a high view of church life as given from God, honouring those who teach, gladly submitting to church order and committing to love and serve one another. They count it a privilege to bring up their children among those who share their biblical world view and where the children see the Christianity that their parents profess lived out by others in the congregation. What a precious thing it is when fellow members embrace the children of the church in prayer, love and concern for their spiritual lives! With that in mind, Christian parents will make it a priority to have their children involved in church activities, even at the expense of other ambitions. Just as a child born into a Jewish Old Testament family was conscious of belonging to a

community of God's people distinct from the people around them, so our children should be conscious of being part of the community of Christ lived out on earth.

It follows that there is a duty on individual church members to be living examples of Christlikeness. We take very seriously Jesus's condemnation of those who put a stumbling block between children and the kingdom of God (Matt 18.6); who can measure the negative impact on a child of hypocrisy, jealousy or gossip in the congregation? Positively, children are welcomed in church services from their earliest days where they will be exposed to prayer, reading of the Scriptures, sound preaching, praise, administration of the sacraments and thanksgivings (see Confession of Faith Chapter 21), inculcating an understanding and sense of true worship. For that reason we do not favour the trend for children to leave the worship service to attend 'children's church'. It is a beautiful witness to see families worshipping together on the Lord's Day.

EPC congregations also provide a range of activities specifically for the young, so bringing biblical content and relevant application on each occasion. The young people are not there to be entertained, but to experience a reverence for God, leading to heart searching, repentance, faith and obedience. No-one should be in doubt that, whatever the activity, the message is: "we preach Christ crucified", with all that that involves.

Nurture within the Denomination: Nurture is particularly relevant here through teenage and student years. Where a congregation is small the young people may feel isolated, with few opportunities to talk through the issues specific to these years. With seemingly little to aspire to and limited opportunities to serve, discouragement can set in, resulting in a critical and lethargic attitude towards church life. Along with parental and congregational guidance, Presbytery has a role to play in addressing these matters. The needs of the YPA, camps, youth weekends, training seminars and outreach teams are to be constantly assessed and appropriately resourced. Thus the young people are guided against the evil practices, thought patterns and godless assertions of today and, as importantly, channelled, enthused and encouraged to positive witness and evangelism. This denominational involvement serves to strengthen the unity among the young people, congregations and Presbytery, and exposes covenant youth to the bigger church picture, remembering that Christ's kingdom is world-wide.

The three places of nurture will guide our young people towards whole hearted love for the Saviour. Our responsibility is to ensure that we do not stray from Christ and His Word, but remain clear on our distinctiveness from the world as a covenant people. By God's grace, we will be rewarded in seeing the generations to come walking in the fear of the Lord within God's glorious covenant church.

"Faith and Life"

The expression "faith and life" is taken from WCF 1.2: "Under the name of Holy Scripture, or the written Word of God, are all the books of the Old and New Testaments … All these are given by inspiration of God to be the rule of faith and life." The expression first appeared in EPC history in No 1 of the 1927 Articles of Faith where it referred to the Holy Scriptures as "the only rule of faith and practice." Chad van Dixhoorn said this:

> If this is God's Word, then little wonder that it is to be our rule of faith and life. Here we learn who and how to worship, who and how to trust for our salvation and all of our needs, and how to live our lives. It is for this reason that the whole Bible should be read frequently by all Christians, and should be at the centre of the Christian church. Those who ignore the Holy Scripture are doomed to stumble into ever deepening darkness. Those who embrace this Scripture, believe what it promises, and walk by its precepts, will never be without a guide or a light, and they will find their way to their Father's home.[529]

The Evangelical Presbyterian Church is called to safeguard diligently what God has given to it and is expressed in its supreme and subordinate standards. "O Timothy! Guard what was committed to your trust." (1 Tim 6.20-21) It cannot remain faithful without this diligence but it must ever do so in acknowledgement of its full dependence on God. Only his divine power working through the Church can ensure it:

> Now to him who is able to keep you from stumbling and to present you blameless before the presence of his glory with great joy, to the only God, our Saviour, through Jesus Christ our Lord, be glory, majesty, dominion, and authority, before all time and now and forever. Amen.
>
> Jude 24-25

Appendices

1   Heresy Trial: Charges

2   Articles of Faith of the Irish Evangelical Church (1927)

3   Form of Government (1930)

4   Ministers - Alpha

5   Ministers - Congregation

6   Ministers' Service Chart

7   Congregations Chart

8   Congregations-Ministers Chart

9   Office Bearers - Congregation

10   Membership-Attendance Statistics

11   **A** Member 'Long-Term' Missionary Service
       B Member Missionary Service Chart

12   Council-Presbytery Appointments

13   IEC-EPC Member Publications

14   Conferences

15   Autumn Evening Lectures

16   Sunday School Projects - Subject

17   YPA Projects

18   Camp Venues

APPENDIX 1 – Heresy Trial Charges

Charge 1 - Imputation

WHEREAS it is in accordance with the Word of God that He "pardoneth all our sin and accepteth us as righteous in His sight only for the righteousness of Christ imputed to us" (Shorter Catechism), inasmuch as "He was made sin for us who knew no sin, that we might be made the righteousness of God in Him" (2 Cor. v. 21), and it is a heinous offence to hold and teach what is contrary to this doctrine, we (the Accusers) charge the Rev. Professor Davey, of the Assembly's College, with holding and teaching what is contrary to the said doctrine, and we specify the following facts to sustain the charge:—

That in a publication issued by him, or by those acting under his authority and direction, entitled "The Changing Vesture of the Faith," he makes the following statements (page 73): "Salvation is usually connected with the historic fact of Christ's death rather than with the Divine-human character which it reveals, and we get such extreme statements as the notorious reply of an orthodox Protestant to a supposed legalist: 'Your religion is all doing, mine is all done.' In its relation to the forgiveness of sin this view is usually expressed in such terms as the following: 'My sins past, present, and to come, were laid upon Christ.' This baldly stated means that, even of my future sins, the guilt and punishment alike were expiated and borne by Christ on Calvary. The Apostle Paul was greatly troubled about the ethical deductions from such a theory, and whatever its values in the past or present, no one at any rate could accuse it of a primary regard for Christian morality." On page 76 of the same book he makes the statement: "Perhaps the weakest spot in the Protestant theory was the specific doctrine of imputation which underlay its theory of Justification. The theory in question rested on the assumption that God cannot forgive by grace upon change of heart. He must have some quantitative satisfaction for sin, and this was found in the positive righteousness of Christ, and in a definitive transference of man's guilt from his own shoulders to other shoulders, i.e., Christ's, which could bear it and bear it away." On page 78 of the same book he makes the statement, "But Protestantism has unwittingly done exactly the same thing. The centre of its orthodox system is a doctrine of atonement resting upon a theory of imputation which is only another form of transubstantiation. Guilt and righteousness are relative terms, which refer to the personal will and cannot be dissociated from it by any mental jugglery. Guilt is our obligation to have done otherwise than we did, righteousness is our voluntary acceptance of, and abiding in, the will of God. These words simply represent states of the consciousness, and are in no sense transferable. The effects of sin may, or might, be cancelled, but a man's guilt is merely a fact of the past which is as certain and inalienable as his birth; and again, no righteousness is of any real moral value which is not personal, appropriated, and voluntary." On page 80 of the same book he makes the statement: "God does actually take responsibility for all things past, present and to come, but imputation is not only an unsuitable word in virtue of its commercial derivation, but it stands for an absurd theory of what actually happens in experience; and it is almost an exact parallel to the Roman Catholic doctrine of transubstantiation, each of these two branches of Christendom positing the same irrationality at the very centre of its system of salvation. It is surely then not for us to sneer at others till at least our own house has been set in order."

That on the 9th day of January, 1926, when lecturing to his students, he then and there used the following words, or words to the following effect: "Paul's philosophy of sin is different from ours—physical taint—an impersonal thing which can be transferred—can be lifted off, an impossible thing. Treats it as impersonal and transferable. Sin cannot be transferable." Witness, W. J. Grier, B.A., Licentiate, 12 Hatfield Street, Belfast.

And we respectfully ask the Presbytery of Belfast to deal with the said Professor Davey according to the laws of the Church.

Charge 2 - Christology

WHEREAS it is in accordance with the Word of God that the character of our Lord was absolutely perfect, "all the fulness of the Godhead dwelling in Him bodily" (Col. 2:9), "doing always those things which please the Father" (John 8:29), "full of grace and truth" (John 1:14), of Whom the Father witnessed "This is My beloved Son in Whom I am well pleased" (Matt. 17:5), and it is a heinous offence to hold and teach what is contrary to this doctrine, we (the Accusers) charge the Rev. Professor Davey, of the Assembly's College, with teaching what is contrary to the said doctrine, and we specify the following facts to sustain the charge:—

That in a publication issued by him, or by those acting under his authority and direction, entitled "The Changing Vesture of the Faith," he makes the following statements (page 134): "Most of us have had our moments on the mountain top, moments of certainty, of exaltation, of self-forgetfulness, of mystery, of adoration, deep peace, or triumphant joy. But they do not stay; not even Paul, not even Christ Himself, had an unbroken sense of their abiding. The Gospels and the Epistles are full of the doubt, the depression, the stress, which are contrary to the human love of ease, but which make life great and heroic."

That in a publication issued by him, or by those acting under his authority and direction, entitled "Our Faith in God," on page 115 he makes the statement: "Whatever finality there may be about the revelation given us in Christ, it is not a finality of personality or of truth in toto. Even on the moral side finality must be sought in the spirit, not always or necessarily in the historical forms, of Christ's teaching or life." On page 116 he makes the statement: "It is not the Galilean Jew who is final, but something which tabernacled in Him, and expressed itself in the forms of the time, both in thought and practice." And on page 125 he makes the statement: "In Christ we have a perfect spirit, a perfect life, a final faith, in the imperfect vestments, social, historical, and intellectual, of a provincial Judaism, and an apocalyptic peasant piety; that is, we must penetrate beneath the clothes to the abiding reality for our filial faith. This finality lies, and will lie, so far as our mind can conceive the problem and the future at all, in the moral finality of His Spirit."

That on 5th December, 1925, when lecturing to his students, he then and there used the following words, or words to the following effect:—"Jesus was subject to variations of nervous system—like Paul, at one time sure of the end, and at others hope that might attain to the resurrection from the dead and not be a castaway." And on the same occasion he used words to the following effect:—"On the cross it was too late to retrace His steps, and there came the hour of physical exhaustion and nervous depression. All had gone. The kingdom had been injured, perhaps permanently, by His choice. He tasted death in the fullest sense because He felt that He had let down God. He had made the wrong choice. Christ knew He may have been mistaken. On the Cross He tasted that very experience. He knew that He had been mistaken and God had departed." And on 28th November, 1925, in lecturing to his students, he made use of words to the following effect:—"The innocent suffering for the guilty. Christ would not have put it that way. He would not regard Himself as innocent any more than good."

Witness, W. J. Grier, B.A., Licentiate, 12 Hatfield Street, Belfast.

That in lecturing to his students he made use of words to the following effect:—"On the cross it was too late to retrace His steps, The very thing that He had feared had come. He really tasted death. Did He feel then that He had made a mistake, and had let down God?" And that, in lecturing to his students, he made use of words to the following effect:—"Gethsemane was the greatest trial. He believed in His return—was that a matter of faith? Not of certainty? was His nervous system strained? was He hoping like Paul to attain to the resurrection of the dead? If He died He abandoned His work, which was important to Him, He abandoned it knowing that by His death was the way of the kingdom, but how He did not know. Was His reason in darkness?"

Witness, J. B. Wallace, M.A., Licentiate, 62 Cromwell Road, Belfast.

And we respectfully ask the Presbytery of Belfast to deal with the said Professor Davey according to the laws of the Church.

Charge 3 - Scripture

WHEREAS it is in accordance with the Word of God that the Holy Scriptures are "immediately inspired of God," and are "of infallible truth and of Divine authority" (Westminster Confession), and it is a heinous offence to hold and teach what is contrary to this doctrine, we, (the accusers), charge the Rev. Prof. Davey, of the Assembly's College, with teaching what is contrary to the said doctrine, and we specify the following facts to sustain the charge:—

That in a publication issued by him, or by those acting under his authority and direction, entitled "The Changing Vesture of the Faith," he makes the following statement on page 49: "Infallibility is the word most used in theology in this connection, and the quest of infallibility which has proceeded without intermission or diminution throughout the centuries in all branches of the Church, is the pursuit of the *ignis fatuus*, the will-o'-the-wisp of theology." And on page 50 he makes the statement: "Faith is one of the supreme requirements in true religion, and throughout all the search of man for external infallibility the heavens are as brass; and all the infallibilities which men have laboriously pieced together crumble away at the touch of criticism, that we may learn at long last that the true way is the way of dependence and trust, and that the only infallible guide is the living Spirit of God." On page 224 he makes the statement: "It is a remarkable thing, too, how the thought-currents of an age affect even the most determined of its opponents; the fourth Gospel, for example, is explicitly one of the most anti-gnostic writings in the New Testament, but it is also the most gnostic, so inevitable is this extraneous influence. No thought ever dominated Christianity like the thought of the person of Christ; yet dressed first in Jewish clothes, within a century it had changed them almost completely for the garments of the Hellenistic philosophy, with both loss and gain." And on page 230 of the same book he makes the statement: "Jewish eschatology in particular, with its whole apparatus of the two ages, and the great assize, with its programme of the 'day of the Lord' and its topography of the unseen world, and with all its unresolved differences of view regarding the resurrection, the intermediate state, and the like, still holds the imagination, and what is more serious, the theology of the Church in its grip. No one can deny that symbolically interpreted, the ideas have a considerable value; but as the expression of the Christian faith they are most inadequate and misleading. For example, they are full of such inconsistencies as the idea of two judgments—one at death, assigning souls to Paradise or Tartarus, and another on 'the day of the Lord,' when souls are apparently restored to their bodies and judged over again—such being the implication even of the Westminster Confession of Faith in its last two chapters." And on page 83 of the same book he makes the statement: "It is surely a great pity to find men thinking that their own safety lay in holding God to His Word rather than in a nature which is benevolence towards all men."

That in a publication issued by him, or by those acting under his authority and direction, entitled "Our Faith in God," he makes the following statement on page 99: "The Old Testament idea of God as the potentate who holds rebellious men in derision, the arbitrary and self-centred despot who seeks His own glory, is not the conception of God which Christ gave us, but something like its antithesis." On page 111 of the same book he makes the statement: "I know of no way of accepting truly the Christian faith which does not rest upon a willingness to change it any day for a better, if the other faith in question could be proved really more satisfactory, and more entitled to our acceptance." On page 114 of the same book he makes the statement: "Are Christ's theories of the authorship of Deuteronomy or of the 110th Psalm final for us, or His views about astronomy, or even about angels and demons?" On page 116 of the same book he makes the statement: "It is not the

Galilean Jew who is final, but something which tabernacled in Him and expressed itself in the forms of its time, both in thought and practice." On page 120 of the same book he makes the statement: "We may, perhaps, in some things be driven to modify or ignore certain views of Christ, e.g., in His theological or scientific statements, where they seem to conflict with His Spirit, or with investigated facts. If in points we must question the words of the historic Jesus, it is only to exalt the living and eternal Son of God, whose Spirit even yet leads us on into all truth, and still takes of the things of Jesus and interprets them to us." On page 127 of the same book he makes the statement: "Intellectually and aesthetically Christ is not our final revelation, though His Spirit is our greatest help towards the attainment of an ever greater truth, and beauty. And if in these spheres of mental activity Christ is not a final revelation still less are our Scriptures so."

That on the 9th January, 1926, lecturing to his students, he made use of the following words, or words to the following effect: "Pauline theology tended to one-sided emphasis. Pauline tendency to dehumanise Christ has its outworking in the fourth Gospel, and in many heresies which actually passed for orthodoxies till recently."

That on the 13th March, 1926, lecturing to his students, he made use of the following words, quoting Professor Peake with approval: "The Book of Revelation is not even a purely Christian product. It has pagan, Jewish, non-Christian elements. Sometimes the spirit of the book is not that of Christ at all. It represents the strength of paganism rather than Christian love."

That on 23rd January, 1926, when lecturing to his students, he made use of the following words, or words to the following effect: "The evangelist John interprets five statements of Christ, and every one he slightly misinterprets."

That on 12th November, 1925, he made use of the following words, or words to the following effect: "All the arguments are against Jeroboam's having made changes. He put himself forward as the defender of orthodoxy." That on 22nd October, 1925, he made use of the following words, or words to the following effect:

"Abraham, the one historical figure among the patriarchs, though I do not think his name was Abraham." "We have the story of the crossing of the Jordan, a very bad imitation of the crossing of the Red Sea." "Joshua's conquests not so very large. They are absurdly exaggerated in Joshua."

Witness, W. J. Grier, Licentiate, 12 Hatfield Street, Belfast.

That, lecturing to his students, he made use of words to the following effect: "The view that Jeroboam's calves, etc., were but a reaction against the innovation of David and Solomon. These judgments against Jeroboam said to be Deuteronomic; all the northern kings thus judged." Joshua—last part of the book said to be late. Judges more historical." "In some places the Book of Revelation is not Christian, but pagan. So we are told, although even that has value."

Witness, J. B. Wallace, M.A., Licentiate, 62 Cromwell Road, Belfast.

And we respectfully ask the Presbytery of Belfast to deal with the said Professor Davey according to the laws of the Church.

Charge 4 - Sin

WHEREAS it is in accordance with the Word of God that the "sinfulness of the first fall and of all other sins of angels and men proceedeth only from the creature, and not from God, who being most holy and righteous neither is nor can be the author or approver of sin" (Westminster Confession, Chap. V.), and it is a heinous offence to hold and teach what is contrary to this doctrine, we, (the Accusers) charge the Rev. Professor Davey with holding and teaching what is contrary to the said doctrine, and we specify the following facts to sustain the charge:—

That in a publication issued by him, or by those acting under his authority and direction, entitled "The Changing Vesture of the Faith," on page 80 he makes the statement: "God does actually take responsibility for all things past, present, and to come, but imputation is not only an unsuitable word in virtue of its commercial derivation, but it stands for an absurd theory of what actually happens in experience, and it is almost an exact parallel to the Roman Catholic doctrine of Transubstantiation." And in a book, entitled "Our Faith in God," issued by him or by those acting under his authority and direction, on page 53 he makes the statement:

"It is here that the belief in God becomes an essential to the best life and to the healing of the soul, for the Christian conception of God is that of a loving and omniscient Being, bearing Himself wittingly all the responsibility of man's transgressions, not merely their guilt but their consequences. Under the weight of conscious sin, I know of no sure escape for the rational, sensitive spirit of man from the burden of responsibility except the way of faith in God, whereby the man can roll the burden upon God, in the faith that God has actually borne the full responsibility of his sin, its guilt its venom and its consequences."

And we respectfully ask the Presbytery of Belfast to deal with the said Professor Davey according with the laws of the Church.

Charge 5 - The Trinity

WHEREAS it is in accordance with the Word of God that "the Son and the Holy Ghost are God equal with the Father, ascribing unto them such names, attributes, works, and worship, as are proper to God only" (The Larger Catechism), and it is a heinous offence to hold and teach what is contrary to this doctrine, we (the Accusers), charge the Rev. Professor Davey with holding and teaching that this doctrine is not thus taught in the Word of God, and we specify the following facts to sustain the charge:—That on the 31st October, 1925, when lecturing to his students he gave utterance to the following words or words to the following effect: "No clear Trinitarian conception in the New Testament. Only later that Trinitarian doctrine evolved." That on January 16th, 1926, when lecturing to his students he gave utterance to the following words or words to the following effect: "In the Fourth Gospel there is a conception of Binity not Trinity. The Fourth Gospel is not Trinitarian at all."

Witness, Wm. J. Grier, B.A., Licentiate, 12 Hatfield Street, Belfast.

That lecturing to his students he gave utterance to the following words or words to the following effect: "Athanasius was the creator of our Trinitarian doctrine." "We have two elements recognised, and even from the Synoptic Gospels onward we must recognise these two elements, and so we find that the Church developed along these two lines: (1) It had an adoptionist theology, (2) an Incarnation theology." "The doctrine of the Spirit said not to be Christian till the council of Nicea, and that in the New Testament it was a duality rather than the Trinity. The Trinitarian doctrine had to fight its way."

Witness, J. B. Wallace, M.A., Licentiate, 62 Cromwell Road, Belfast.

And we respectfully ask the Presbytery of Belfast to deal with the said Professor Davey according to the laws of the Church.

APPENDIX 2
ARTICLES OF FAITH of the Irish Evangelical Church

1. The Holy Scriptures, or the Word of God written, containing all the books of the Old and New Testaments, is of infallible truth and divine authority, and in its original languages is immediately inspired of God, and is the only rule of faith and practice.
2. It is most clearly set forth in Holy Scripture that there is but one living and true God, and that in the Godhead there are three Persons,—The Father, the Son, and the Holy Ghost, and that these three are one, the same in substance, equal in power and glory.
3. The second Person of the Holy Trinity, the eternal Son of God, was sent by the Father to be the Saviour of the world. He became man, being born of the Virgin Mary; He lived a perfect life of unapproachable holiness; He died on the cross as an atoning sacrifice for sin; He rose from the dead on the third day with that very body which had been laid in the tomb; He ascended into Heaven, and He will come again in glory to judge the living and the dead.
4. The Holy Spirit, whose personality and deity are plainly taught in Holy Scripture, is He through whom the soul is born again which repents and believes savingly in the Lord Jesus Christ: it is He in like manner through whom the saints are sanctified in the use of the truth of which He is the Author; and He it is who is the seal of our immortality, being the inspirer of all true assurance.
5. In the Justification of the sinner who believes in the Lord Jesus Christ, God reckons to him all the righteousness of Christ, and the efficacy of this imputation is such that the believer is fully accepted by God and may immediately rejoice in the hope of the glory of God.
6. Salvation being altogether through the free grace of God, and man being by nature fallen and corrupt, eternal life and glory cannot be merited by us, but are the gift of God in Christ; eternal death is the necessary consequence of the identification of the sinner with his sin, "He that is filthy being made filthy still;" and the faithful teaching and preaching of these doctrines are made fruitful of results by the Spirit of God, as also is the guilty silence in regard to them fraught with damage alike to the spirituality and the morality of a community.
7. Besides the Word of God and Prayer, the Lord has appointed as means of grace the Sacraments of Baptism and the Lord's Supper, in both of which the merits of Christ are set forth. In Baptism the Lord offers a seal of His acceptance, but this seal is not so attached to acceptance that the one may not exist without the other. Because the children of believing parents are called "holy" (1 Cor 7:14.), it is the evident will of God that they should share with the people of God in this means of Grace.

    The Lord's Supper has been appointed by Him for Remembrance of Him, and therefore it cannot itself be the Lord materially, and yet in a real though spiritual presence He is with such as communicate worthily.
8. The Lord's Day is hallowed by a perpetual command of God, and in it we celebrate the great miracles of the Resurrection of our Lord from the dead, and His creation of all things out of nothing, and a special blessing attaches to the land which keeps holy the Lord's Day.

APPENDIX 3
The Form of Government of the Irish Evangelical Church, 1930

1. That this Church be under the government of such members as have been baptised and are regular partakers of the Lord's Supper, and have subscribed to the first six articles of the Creed.
2. That the ordinances of Baptism and of the Lord's Supper be open to all who make a credible profession of faith in Christ as God the Son, and their Saviour.
3. That a congregation, for representation on the Central Council of the Church, have as a minimum membership on the Communion Roll twelve persons.
4. That each congregation, so far as its membership may justify, have certain persons elected to the positions of overseer (bishop, presbyter, elder or pastor) and deacon.
5. That all officebearers be chosen most of all because of their spiritual qualifications
6. That the ordained teacher or pastor in the congregation be *ex-officio* overseer.
7. That the overseer in the congregation in conjunction with the deacons, or if there be no overseer—the board of deacons, have to do with the admission or exclusion from the Sacraments of the Church, and with Church discipline, in necessary cases in conjunction with the Central Council.
8. That the deacons have to do with all monetary affairs and with the Church building, and assist the overseer in spiritual work, and that there be a triennial election of deacons.
9. That the Board of deacons present to the members annually a financial statement.
10. That the overseer, or if there be no overseer, the secretary of the board of deacons present annually a report to the congregation and to the Central Council.
11. That it be the duty of the board of deacons to see that the property of the congregation be so vested that there shall be no alienation from the doctrinal standards of the Church.
12. That each congregation have representation on the Central Council, at present an overseer or deacon for twelve to twenty communicating members, and another representative for every additional twenty or part of twenty.
13. That upon the Central Council of the Church devolve the fostering care of the congregations, the approval of deacons, colporteurs, theological teachers, evangelists, missionaries and pastors, as well as their demission when necessary, the power of confirming or vetoing the appointing of overseers, and the control of the finances of the central funds.
14. That in the Service of Ordination all persons to be ordained subscribe to the articles of the Creed, and that the form of ordination be by prayer and the laying on of hands, a suitable portion of Holy Scripture being read and instruction given on the essential elements of the Gospel, on the gift of the Holy Spirit for the fruitful exercise of office in the Church, and on the Power of the Spirit in the daily life of all members in Christ's body.

April 1930

APPENDIX 4 – Ministers Alpha

Atkinson, SGT

Richhill	Minister	05/09/1997	01/09/2000	3 year appointment
Knock	Int Mod	05/04/2000	05/02/2001	
Richhill	Int Mod	01/09/2000	19/03/2001	
Knock	Minister	21/03/2001	30/09/2004	To CWI

Mr Atkinson had ministerial standing as a member of Presbytery, 2004-2012, whilst CWI Deputation Secretary.

Ballantine, WCJ

Non-Cong	Licentiate	28/09/1988	02/12/1988	At Omagh
Lisburn Road	Minister	02/12/1988	31/12/1994	Ordination
Omagh	Int Mod	01/08/1989	17/11/1990	
Somerton Road	Int Mod	02/03/1993	05/12/1994	
Bangor-G'sport	Minister	04/01/1995	25/06/2006	Mission Church Status
Knock	Int Mod	05/02/2001	21/03/2001	
Dublin	Int Mod	31/07/2001	18/05/2002	
Groomsport	Minister	25/06/2006		
Crumlin	Int Mod	01/09/2008	02/04/2014	

Beckett, RC

Non-Cong	Licentiate	11/06/1981	07/10/1981	At Crumlin
Crosscollyer St	Minister	07/10/1981	03/01/1996	Ordination. North Belfast, 03/01/1996
Clintyfallow	Minister	17/10/1981	09/06/1985	Closure
Ballyclare	Int Mod	31/05/1986	23/03/1987	
Ballyclare	Minister	28/03/1987	03/04/1989	
Ballyclare	Int Mod	03/04/1989	12/01/1991	
North Belfast	Minister	03/01/1996		Joint, Crosscollyer Street-Somerton Road
Knock	Int Mod	01/10/2004	31/03/2007	

Burke, GN

Non-Cong	Licentiate	01/10/1984	17/11/1984	At Presbytery
Somerton Road	Minister	17/11/1984	03/04/1989	Ordination
Lisburn Road	Int Mod	01/09/1986	02/12/1988	
Knock	Minister	05/04/1989	05/04/2000	
Lisburn Road	Int Mod	04/01/1995	03/11/1999	
Stranmillis	Temp Min	01/08/1999	31/10/1999	
Stranmillis	Int Mod	01/11/1999	06/03/2000	
Stranmillis	Minister	05/05/2000		
Omagh	Int Mod	08/04/2002	24/03/2003	Rev W C J Ballantine, visitation
Knock	Int Mod	01/04/2007	02/01/2009	

Campbell, AA

Lisburn Road	Minister	05/05/1960	31/08/1984	Retired. D 01/10/1985
Clintyfallow	Int Mod	21/04/1961	17/10/1981	
Finaghy	Int Mod	01/06/1970	02/10/1970	
Finaghy	Int Mod	01/02/1978	07/04/1978	C E Hunter assisting
Stranmillis	Int Mod	08/06/1979	31/08/1979	

Appendix 4

Elliott, WL
O'seas Students	Co-ordinator	01/08/1997	13/06/2001	Part-time appointment
Lisburn Road	Minister	03/11/1999	19/03/2001	Part-time team appointment with Rev A J Lucas
Richhill	Int Mod	19/03/2001	13/06/2001	
Richhill	Minister	13/06/2001		
Lisburn Road	Int Mod	04/03/2002	01/11/2002	

Garland, CH
Non-Cong	Minister		28/09/1940	Ordination. At Botanic Ave
Crosscollyer St	Minister	16/11/1940	30/04/1955	
Crumlin	Minister	21/11/1942	02/12/1976	
Lisburn Road	Int Mod	01/05/1955	10/06/1955	
Clintyfallow	Int Mod	01/11/1955	11/05/1957	
Somerton Road	Minister	02/07/1957	31/12/1979	Retired. D 27/03/2003
Clintyfallow	Int Mod	21/03/1958	21/04/1961	Rev S Law assisting
Knock	Int Mod	28/02/1977	09/03/1977	

Garland, SJ
Non-Cong	Licentiate	13/01/1978	07/04/1978	At Council
Finaghy	Minister	07/04/1978	28/02/1987	Ordination
Ballyclare	Int Mod	01/02/1980	07/03/1981	
Somerton Road	Int Mod	01/01/1983	17/11/1984	

Mr Garland had EPC ministerial standing, 1990-2010, while released for missionary service in Nigeria.

Green, N
Omagh	Minister	03/04/1982	31/07/1989	Moved to Accrington
Accrington	Minister	01/09/1989	02/04/2001	Became Blackburn 06/06/1993; to EPCEW 02/04/2001

Grier, WJ
Shaftesbury Sq	Licentiate	11/12/1927	20/07/1929	
Lisburn Road	Licentiate	21/10/1928	20/07/1929	
Non-Cong	Minister	20/07/1929	20/07/1929	Ordination at Lisburn Road
Shaftesbury Sq	Minister	20/07/1929	03/08/1930	Cong. became Botanic Avenue
Lisburn Road	MinisFter	20/07/1929	20/03/1942	
Botanic Avenue	Minister	03/08/1930	31/10/1971	Cong. became Stranmillis
Knock	Int Mod	21/09/1951	18/09/1953	
Clintyfallow	Int Mod	23/10/1953	01/11/1955	
Lisburn Road	Int Mod	01/02/1958	05/05/1960	
Knock	Int Mod	01/10/1962	30/10/1964	
Seymour Hill	Int Mod	22/05/1970	20/11/1970	
Stranmillis	Minister	31/10/1971	08/06/1979	Retired. D 06/08/1983
Crumlin	Int Mod	02/12/1976	01/07/1977	

Hambleton, AM
Crumlin	Minister	02/04/2014		Ordination

Hobson, MP
Finaghy	Minister	03/05/2014		Ordination

Hunter, CE

Somerton Road	Student	01/04/1933	30/09/1933	
Crosscollyer St	Student	01/04/1934	01/09/1934	
Somerton Road	Student	01/04/1934	01/09/1934	
Ballyclare	Student	01/04/1935	29/06/1935	
Slatehill	Student	01/04/1935	29/06/1935	
Somerton Road	Student	01/04/1935	29/06/1935	
Non-Cong	Minister	29/06/1935	29/06/1935	Ordination at Botanic Avenue
Slatehill	Minister	29/06/1935	08/06/1939	
Somerton Road	Minister	29/06/1935	17/04/1942	
Ballyclare	Minister	29/06/1935	08/06/1939	
Clintyfallow	Minister	14/05/1939	22/03/1952	
Lisburn Road	Minister	08/05/1942	30/04/1955	
Crumlin	Int Mod	18/09/1942	21/11/1942	
Jocelyn Avenue	Int Mod	01/12/1944	01/03/1946	
Botanic Avenue	Int Mod	25/11/1949	31/03/1950	While W J Grier's ill
Finaghy	Int Mod	29/02/1952	03/04/1952	
Finaghy	Minister	03/04/1952	01/06/1970	Retired. D 07/02/1986
Crosscollyer St	Int Mod	01/05/1955	16/11/1956	
Crosscollyer St	Int Mod	01/02/1958	05/02/1960	
Crosscollyer St	Int Mod	01/11/1963	02/10/1970	
Seymour Hill	Minister	07/02/1965	01/06/1970	
Seymour Hill	Minister	20/11/1970	06/02/1972	Closure

Hunter, J

Knock	Minister	06/05/1928	20/09/1942	D 20/09/1942

Johnston, MG

Non-Cong	Licentiate	01/10/1984	10/11/1984	At Presbytery
Richhill	Minister	10/11/1984	01/03/1989	Ordination. Appointed to new work
Crumlin	Int Mod	02/02/1987	23/06/1989	
Richhill	Minister	01/03/1989	01/12/1994	Resigned. To London

Johnston, RJ

Non-Cong	Licentiate	18/09/2008		At Stranmillis
Knock	Minister	02/01/2009		Ordination
Finaghy	Int Mod	20/06/2012	03/06/2014	

Law, S

Knock	Minister	18/09/1953	30/09/1962	Returned to England
Somerton Road	Int Mod	20/11/1953	02/07/1957	

Leahy, FS

Finaghy	Asst Min	18/03/1949	15/10/1949	
Jocelyn Avenue	Asst Min	18/03/1949	21/10/1949	
Finaghy	Minister	15/10/1949	01/11/1951	Ordination
Jocelyn Avenue	Minister	21/10/1949	30/06/1953	To RPCI
Clintyfallow	Int Mod	22/03/1952	31/05/1952	
Clintyfallow	Minister	31/05/1952	30/06/1953	

Linkens, NJ

Non-Cong	Licentiate	20/11/1959	05/02/1960	At Council
Crosscollyer St	Minister	05/02/1960	31/10/1963	Ordination To PCI

Lucas, AJ

Ballyclare	Student	10/08/1997	10/08/1998	At Ballyclare	
Non-Cong	Licentiate	16/09/1998	03/11/1999	At Crosscollyer street	
Knock	Asst Min	01/08/1999	31/10/1999		
Lisburn Road	Minister	03/11/1999	14/04/2002	Ordination. Team ministry with Rev W L Elliott	
Omagh	Int Mod	01/07/2001	08/04/2002		
Dublin	Minister	18/05/2002	24/03/2007		
Omagh	Int Mod	01/04/2003	24/03/2007		
Omagh	Minister	24/03/2007			

Magee, B

Non-Cong	Licentiate	13/06/2006	11/06/2008	At Presbytery

McCracken, J

Slatehill	Student	17/03/1933	30/09/1933	
Ballyclare	Student	17/03/1933	30/09/1933	
Jocelyn Avenue	Student	16/03/1934	30/09/1934	
Ballyclare	Student	16/03/1934	30/09/1934	
Slatehill	Student	16/03/1934	30/09/1934	
Crosscollyer St	Student	01/04/1935	29/06/1935	
Jocelyn Avenue	Student	01/04/1935	29/06/1935	
Non-Cong	Minister	29/06/1935	29/06/1935	Ordination. Botanic Avenue
Crosscollyer St	Minister	29/06/1935	16/11/1940	
Jocelyn Avenue	Minister	29/06/1935	10/08/1944	To mission service South Africa, 3/11/1944
Knock	Int Mod	16/10/1942	30/10/1943	

McCully, W

Non-Cong	Licentiate	16/09/1998	16/09/1998	At Crosscollyer Street
Crumlin	Assistant	01/02/1999	31/05/1999	To EPCEW

McDowell, WJ

Non-Cong	Colporteur	14/02/1929	05/07/1935	Ordained IEC Missionary, Crosscollyer Street 06/06/1929
Ballyclare	Minister	08/06/1939	31/01/1980	Ordination. Retired. D. 02/12/1991
Slatehill	Minister	08/06/1939	19/01/1942	Closed 19 January 1942
Somerton Road	Minister	17/04/1942	25/09/1953	
Jocelyn Avenue	Int Mod	29/06/1953	09/10/1953	
Jocelyn Avenue	Minister	09/10/1953	29/05/1966	Closure
Knock	Int Mod	31/08/1965	04/11/1966	
Knock	Minister	04/11/1966	28/02/1977	

Morrison, HA

Crosscollyer St	Minister	22/08/1930	04/08/1933	'Associated' with Crosscollyer Street
Somerton Road	Minister	17/10/1930	04/08/1933	'Associated' with Somerton Road

Murphy, HH

Crumlin	Minister	28/01/1930	18/08/1933	Resigned. Crumlin withdrew from IEC
Jocelyn Avenue	Minister	30/01/1931	18/08/1933	Resigned.

Nisbet, WA

Somerton Road	Minister	13/01/1933	10/02/1933	Returned to Canada

Porter, WW

Lisburn Road	Minister	10/06/1955	31/01/1958	Ordination. To PCI
Crosscollyer St	Int Mod	16/11/1956	31/01/1958	
Clintyfallow	Minister	11/05/1957	31/01/1958	

Reid, NE

Non-Cong	Licentiate	17/07/1970	02/10/1970	At Council
Crosscollyer St	Minister	02/10/1970	28/02/1978	Ordination
Finaghy	Minister	29/10/1970	28/02/1978	
Dublin	Minister	01/03/1978	05/01/1980	New work in Dublin begins
Dublin	Minister	05/01/1980	26/05/1990	Mission Church
Dublin	Minister	26/05/1990	31/10/1998	Regular congregation; resigned - Dumisani
Non-Cong	Lecturer	01/07/1996	31/12/1996 to Dumisani	Temporary secondment
Non-Cong	Lecturer	12/12/1998	17/06/2011	Dumisani Theological Institute. Retired

Roger, JS

Ballyclare	Minister	12/01/1991		
Somerton Road	Int Mod	05/12/1994	03/01/1996	

Ross, JS

Knock	Minister	09/03/1977	31/08/1986	Ordination. To CWI
Crosscollyer St	Int Mod	01/03/1978	07/10/1981	
Ballyclare	Int Mod	01/01/1986	31/05/1986	

Thomas, DWH

Stranmillis	Minister	31/08/1979	18/08/1996	Ordination. To RTS, Jackson, Mississippi
Lisburn Road	Int Mod	03/09/1984	01/09/1986	
Knock	Int Mod	01/09/1986	05/04/1989	

Titcombe, EH

Knock	Minister	30/10/1943	21/09/1951	
Jocelyn Avenue	Int Mod	01/03/1946	22/10/1949	
Finaghy	Minister	01/11/1951	31/01/1952	Returned to England

Tracey, SJ

Non-Cong	Licentiate	03/09/1990	17/11/1990	At Presbytery
Omagh	Minister	17/11/1990	30/06/2001	Ordination. To OPC, Rockport, Maine
Dublin	Int Mod	01/07/1996	31/12/1996	N E Reid at Dumsiani, SA
Richhill	Int Mod	01/12/1996	09/06/1997	
Dublin	Int Mod	31/10/1998	31/07/2001	

Van Zyl, FWJ

Non-Cong	Licentiate	03/07/1964	30/10/1964	At Council
Knock	Minister	30/10/1964	31/08/1965	Ordination. Returned SA. D 11/11/1999

Appendix 4

Watson, S
Non-Cong	Licentiate	10/06/1977	01/07/1977	At Council
Crumlin	Minister	01/07/1977	02/02/1987	Ordination
Somerton Road	Int Mod	30/11/1979	31/12/1981	
Finaghy	Int Mod	01/03/1987	30/11/1987	
Finaghy	Minister	30/11/1987	20/06/2012	Retired
Somerton Road	Int Mod	03/04/1989	02/03/1993	
Stranmillis	Int Mod	18/08/1996	30/06/1999	
Stranmillis	Int Mod	06/03/2000	05/05/2000	
Lisburn Road	Int Mod	01/11/2002	30/06/2008	Merged, Finaghy 01/07/2008

Whitla, N
Ballyclare	Minister	07/03/1981	01/05/1986	To MERF
Somerton Road	Int Mod	01/01/1982	01/01/1983	

Woolsey, AA
Non-Cong	Licentiate	08/05/1989	23/06/1989	At Presbytery
Crumlin	Minister	23/06/1989	31/08/2008	Ordination. Retired
Richhill	Int Mod	01/12/1994	01/12/1996	

APPENDIX 5 – Ministers by Congregation

Accrington-Blackburn

Green, N	Minister	01/09/1989	02/04/2001	Blackburn 06/06/1993; to EPCEW 02/04/2001

Ballyclare

McCracken, J	Student	17/03/1933	30/09/1933	
McCracken, J	Student	16/03/1934	30/09/1934	
Hunter, CE	Student	01/04/1935	29/06/1935	
Hunter, CE	Minister	29/06/1935	08/06/1939	
McDowell, WJ	Minister	08/06/1939	31/01/1980	Retired. D 02/12/1991
Garland, SJ	Int Mod	01/02/1980	07/03/1981	
Whitla, N	Minister	07/03/1981	01/05/1986	
Ross, JS	Int Mod	01/01/1986	31/05/1986	
Beckett, RC	Int Mod	31/05/1986	23/03/1987	
Beckett, RC	Minister	28/03/1987	03/04/1989	
Beckett, RC	Int Mod	03/04/1989	12/01/1991	
Roger, JS	Minister	12/01/1991		
Lucas, AJ	Student	10/08/1997	10/08/1998	At Ballyclare

Bangor

Ballantine, WCJ	Minister	04/01/1995	08/05/2004	Appointed to Bangor Mission Church, opened 06/03/1994. To Groomsport, May 2004

Botanic Avenue

Grier, WJ	Minister	03/08/1930	31/10/1971	
Hunter, CE	Int Mod	25/11/1949	31/03/1950	While W J Grier's ill

Clintyfalllow

Hunter, CE	Minister	14/05/1939	22/03/1952	
Leahy, FS	Int Mod	22/03/1952	31/05/1952	
Leahy, FS	Minister	31/05/1952	30/06/1953	
Grier, WJ	Int Mod	23/10/1953	01/11/1955	
Garland, CH	Int Mod	01/11/1955	11/05/1957	
Porter, WW	Minister	11/05/1957	31/01/1958	
Garland, CH	Int Mod	21/03/1958	21/04/1961	Rev S Law assisting
Campbell, AA	Int Mod	21/04/1961	17/10/1981	
Beckett, RC	Minister	17/10/1981	09/06/1985	Closure

Crosscollyer Street

Morrison, HA	Minister	22/08/1930	04/08/1933	'Associated' with Crosscollyer Street
Hunter, CE	Student	01/04/1934	01/09/1934	
McCracken, J	Student	01/04/1935	29/06/1935	
McCracken, J	Minister	29/06/1935	16/11/1940	
Garland, CH	Minister	16/11/1940	30/04/1955	
Hunter, CE	Int Mod	01/05/1955	16/11/1956	
Porter, WW	Int Mod	16/11/1956	31/01/1958	
Hunter, CE	Int Mod	01/02/1958	05/02/1960	
Linkens, NJ	Minister	05/02/1960	31/10/1963	To PCI
Hunter, CE	Int Mod	01/11/1963	02/10/1970	
Reid, NE	Minister	02/10/1970	28/02/1978	To Dublin

Appendix 5

Ross, JS	Int Mod	01/03/1978	07/10/1981		
Beckett, RC	Minister	07/10/1981	03/01/1996	North Belfast, from 03/01/1996	

Crumlin

Murphy, HH	Minister	28/01/1930	18/08/1933	Resigned. Crumlin withdrew from IEC
Hunter, CE	Int Mod	18/09/1942	21/11/1942	
Garland, CH	Minister	21/11/1942	02/12/1976	
Grier, WJ	Int Mod	02/12/1976	01/07/1977	
Watson, S	Minister	01/07/1977	02/02/1987	
Johnston, MG	Int Mod	02/02/1987	23/06/1989	
Woolsey, AA	Minister	23/06/1989	31/08/2008	Retired
McCully, W	Assistant	01/02/1999	31/05/1999	
Ballantine, WCJ	Int Mod	01/09/2008	02/04/2014	
Hambleton, AM	Minister	02/04/2014		

Dublin

Reid, NE	Minister	01/03/1978	05/01/1980	New work in Dublin
Reid, NE	Minister	05/01/1980	26/05/1990	Mission Church
Reid, NE	Minister	26/05/1990	31/10/1998	Regular congregation. To Dumisani, SA
Tracey, SJ	Int Mod	01/07/1996	31/12/1996	N E Reid at Dumsiani, SA
Tracey, SJ	Int Mod	31/10/1998	31/07/2001	
Ballantine, WCJ	Int Mod	31/07/2001	18/05/2002	
Lucas, AJ	Minister	18/05/2002	24/03/2007	Closure

Finaghy

Leahy, FS	Asst Min	18/03/1949	15/10/1949	
Leahy, FS	Minister	15/10/1949	01/11/1951	
Titcombe, EH	Minister	01/11/1951	31/01/1952	Returned to England
Hunter, CE	Int Mod	29/02/1952	03/04/1952	
Hunter, CE	Minister	03/04/1952	01/06/1970	Retired. D 07/02/1986
Campbell, AA	Int Mod	01/06/1970	02/10/1970	
Reid, NE	Minister	29/10/1970	28/02/1978	
Campbell, AA	Int Mod	01/02/1978	07/04/1978	C E Hunter assisting
Garland, SJ	Minister	07/04/1978	28/02/1987	Began mission service with Qua Iboe, Nigeria
Watson, S	Int Mod	01/03/1987	30/11/1987	
Watson, S	Minister	30/11/1987	20/06/2012	Retired
Johnston, RJ	Int Mod	20/06/2012	03/06/2014	
Hobson, MP	Minister	03/05/2014		

Groomsport

Ballantine, WCJ	Minister	08/05/2004	25/06/2006	Appointed, Mission Church.
Ballantine, WCJ	Minister	25/06/2006		Full congregational status.

Jocelyn Avenue

Murphy, HH	Minister	30/01/1931	18/08/1933	Resigned
McCracken, J	Student	16/03/1934	30/09/1934	
McCracken, J	Student	01/04/1935	29/06/1935	
McCracken, J	Minister	29/06/1935	10/08/1944	To mission service SA 3/11/1944
Hunter, CE	Int Mod	01/12/1944	01/03/1946	
Titcombe, EH	Int Mod	01/03/1946	22/10/1949	
Leahy, FS	Asst Min	18/03/1949	21/10/1949	

Leahy, FS	Minister	21/10/1949	30/06/1953	To RPCI	
McDowell, WJ	Int Mod	29/06/1953	09/10/1953		
McDowell, WJ	Minister	09/10/1953	29/05/1966	Closure	

Knock

Hunter, J	Minister	06/05/1928	20/09/1942	D 20/09/1942
McCracken, J	Int Mod	16/10/1942	30/10/1943	
Titcombe, EH	Minister	30/10/1943	21/09/1951	
Grier, WJ	Int Mod	21/09/1951	18/09/1953	
Law, S	Minister	18/09/1953	30/09/1962	
Grier, WJ	Int Mod	01/10/1962	30/10/1964	
van Zyl, FWJ	Minister	30/10/1964	31/08/1965	Returned to SA. D 11/11/1999
McDowell, WJ	Int Mod	31/08/1965	04/11/1966	
McDowell, WJ	Minister	04/11/1966	28/02/1977	
Garland, CH	Int Mod	28/02/1977	09/03/1977	
Ross, JS	Minister	09/03/1977	31/08/1986	To CWI
Thomas, DWH	Int Mod	01/09/1986	05/04/1989	
Burke, GN	Minister	05/04/1989	05/04/2000	
Atkinson, SGT	Int Mod	05/04/2000	05/02/2001	
Ballantine, WCJ	Int Mod	05/02/2001	21/03/2001	
Atkinson, SGT	Minister	21/03/2001	30/09/2004	
Beckett, RC	Int Mod	01/10/2004	31/03/2007	
Burke, GN	Int Mod	01/04/2007	02/01/2009	
Johnston, RJ	Minister	02/01/2009		

Lisburn Road

Grier, WJ	Licentiate	21/10/1928	20/07/1929	
Grier, WJ	Minister	20/07/1929	20/03/1942	Ordained 20/07/1929
Hunter, CE	Minister	08/05/1942	30/04/1955	
Garland, CH	Int Mod	01/05/1955	10/06/1955	
Porter, WW	Minister	10/06/1955	31/01/1958	To PCI
Grier, WJ	Int Mod	01/02/1958	05/05/1960	
Campbell, AA	Minister	05/05/1960	31/08/1984	Retired. D 01/10/1985
Thomas, DWH	Int Mod	03/09/1984	01/09/1986	
Burke, GN	Int Mod	01/09/1986	02/12/1988	
Ballantine, WCJ	Minister	02/12/1988	31/12/1994	
Burke, GN	Int Mod	04/01/1995	03/11/1999	
Lucas, AJ	Minister	03/11/1999	14/04/2002	Team ministry with Rev W L Elliott
Elliott, WL	Minister	03/11/1999	19/03/2001	Part-time appointment with Rev A J Lucas
Elliott, WL	Int Mod	04/03/2002	01/11/2002	
Watson, S	Int Mod	01/11/2002	30/06/2008	Merged with Finaghy 01/07/2008

North Belfast

Beckett, RC	Minister	03/01/1996		Joint Charge: Crosscollyer Street-Somerton Road

Appendix 5

Omagh
Green, N	Minister	03/04/1982	31/07/1989	Moved to Accrington
Ballantine, WCJ	Int Mod	01/08/1989	17/11/1990	
Tracey, SJ	Minister	17/11/1990	30/06/2001	Call to OPC, Rockport, Maine
Lucas, AJ	Int Mod	01/07/2001	08/04/2002	
Burke, GN	Int Mod	08/04/2002	24/03/2003	Rev W C J Ballantine, visitation
Lucas, AJ	Int Mod	01/04/2003	24/03/2007	
Lucas, AJ	Minister	24/03/2007		

Richhill
Johnston, MG	Minister	10/11/1984	01/03/1989	New work
Johnston, MG	Minister	01/03/1989	01/12/1994	Resigned
Woolsey, AA	Int Mod	01/12/1994	01/12/1996	
Tracey, SJ	Int Mod	01/12/1996	09/06/1997	Commission oversight
Atkinson, SGT	Minister	05/09/1997	01/09/2000	Three year appointment
Atkinson, SGT	Int Mod	01/09/2000	19/03/2001	
Elliott, WL	Int Mod	19/03/2001	13/06/2001	
Elliott, WL	Minister	13/06/2001		

Seymour Hill
Hunter, CE	Minister	07/02/1965	01/06/1970	
Grier, WJ	Int Mod	22/05/1970	20/11/1970	
Hunter, CE	Minister	20/11/1970	06/02/1972	Closure

Shaftesbury Square
Grier, WJ	Licentiate	11/12/1927	20/07/1929	
Grier, WJ	Minister	20/07/1929	03/08/1930	Congregation became Botanic Avenue

Slatehill
McCracken, J	Student	17/03/1933	30/09/1933	
McCracken, J	Student	16/03/1934	30/09/1934	
Hunter, CE	Student	01/04/1935	29/06/1935	
Hunter, CE	Minister	29/06/1935	08/06/1939	
McDowell, WJ	Minister	08/06/1939	19/01/1942	Closed 19 January 1942

Somerton Road
Morrison, HA	Minister	17/10/1930	04/08/1933	'Associated' with Somerton Road
Nisbet, WA	Minister	13/01/1933	10/02/1933	Returned to Canada
Hunter, CE	Student	01/04/1933	30/09/1933	
Hunter, CE	Student	01/04/1934	01/09/1934	
Hunter, CE	Student	01/04/1935	29/06/1935	
Hunter, CE	Minister	29/06/1935	17/04/1942	
McDowell, WJ	Minister	17/04/1942	25/09/1953	
Law, S	Int Mod	20/11/1953	02/07/1957	
Garland, CH	Minister	02/07/1957	31/12/1979	Retired. D 27/03/2003
Watson, S	Int Mod	30/11/1979	31/12/1981	
Whitla, N	Int Mod	01/01/1982	01/01/1983	
Garland, SJ	Int Mod	01/01/1983	17/11/1984	
Burke, GN	Minister	17/11/1984	03/04/1989	
Watson, S	Int Mod	03/04/1989	02/03/1993	
Ballantine, WCJ	Int Mod	02/03/1993	05/12/1994	
Roger, JS	Int Mod	05/12/1994	03/01/1996	North Belfast, 03/01/1996

Stranmillis

Grier, WJ	Minister	31/10/1971	08/06/1979	Retired. D 06/08/1983
Campbell, AA	Int Mod	08/06/1979	31/08/1979	
Thomas, DWH	Minister	31/08/1979	18/08/1996	To RTS, Jackson, Mississippi
Watson, S	Int Mod	18/08/1996	30/06/1999	
Burke, GN	Temp Min	01/08/1999	31/10/1999	
Burke, GN	Int Mod	01/11/1999	06/03/2000	
Watson, S	Int Mod	06/03/2000	05/05/2000	
Burke, GN	Minister	05/05/2000		

Licentiates

Linkens, NJ	Licentiate	20/11/1959	At Council
van Zyl, FWJ	Licentiate	03/07/1964	At Council
Reid, NE	Licentiate	17/07/1970	At Council
Watson, S	Licentiate	10/06/1977	At Council
Garland, SJ	Licentiate	13/01/1978	At Council
Beckett, RC	Licentiate	11/06/1981	At Crumlin
Burke, GN	Licentiate	01/10/1984	At Presbytery
Johnston, MG	Licentiate	01/10/1984	At Presbytery
Ballantine, WCJ	Licentiate	28/09/1988	At Omagh
Woolsey, AA	Licentiate	08/05/1989	At Presbytery
Tracey, SJ	Licentiate	03/09/1990	At Presbytery
Lucas, AJ	Licentiate	16/09/1998	At Crosscollyer Street
McCully, W	Licentiate	16/09/1998	At Crosscollyer Street
Magee, B	Licentiate	13/06/2006	At Presbytery
Johnston, RJ	Licentiate	18/09/2008	At Stranmillis

Overseas Students

Elliott, WL	Co-ordinator	01/08/1997	13/06/2001	Part-time appointment

Others

McDowell, WJ	Colporteur	14/02/1929	05/07/1935	At Crosscollyer Street 06/06/1929
Reid, NE	Lecturer	01/07/1996	31/12/1996	
Reid, NE	Lecturer	12/12/1998	17/06/2011	Dumisani SA. Retired
Garland, SJ	Lecturer	28/02/1987	30/04/2010	Samuel Bill, Theological College of N Nigeria
Atkinson, SGT	Dep Secty	30/09/2004	11/06/2012	Irish Dep. Secty, CWI.

Appendix 6

APPENDIX 6 – Ministers' Service Chart

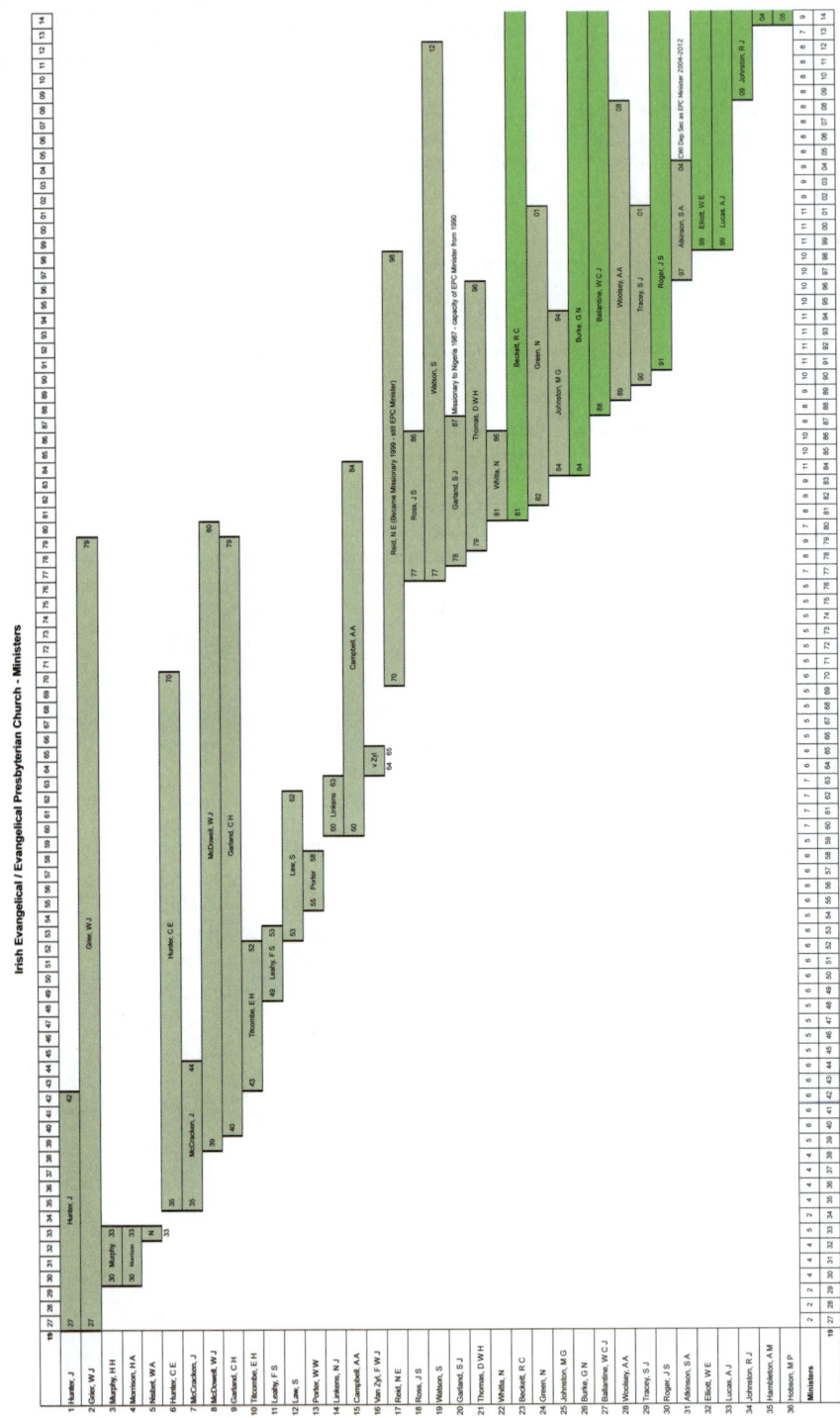

Appendix 7

APPENDIX 7 –
IEC-EPC Congregations Chart

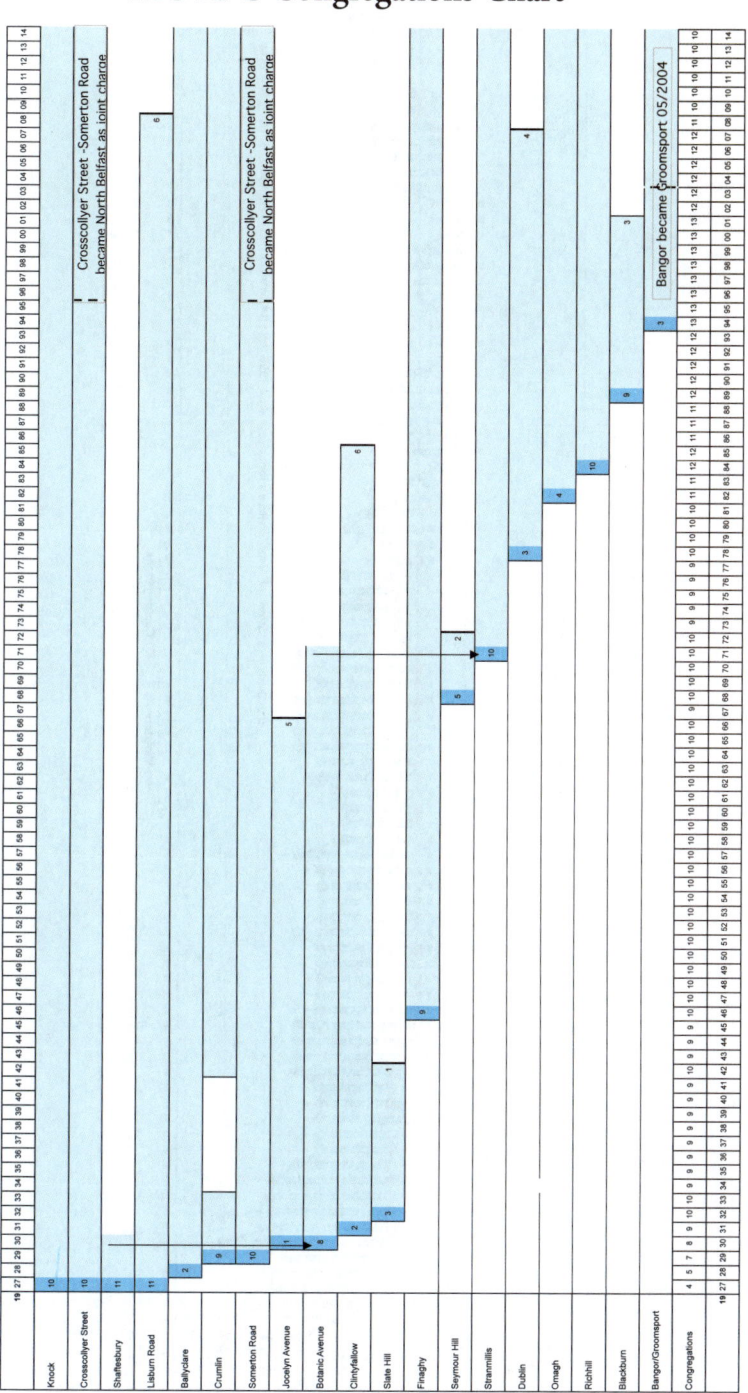

APPENDIX 8 – Congregation-Minister Chart

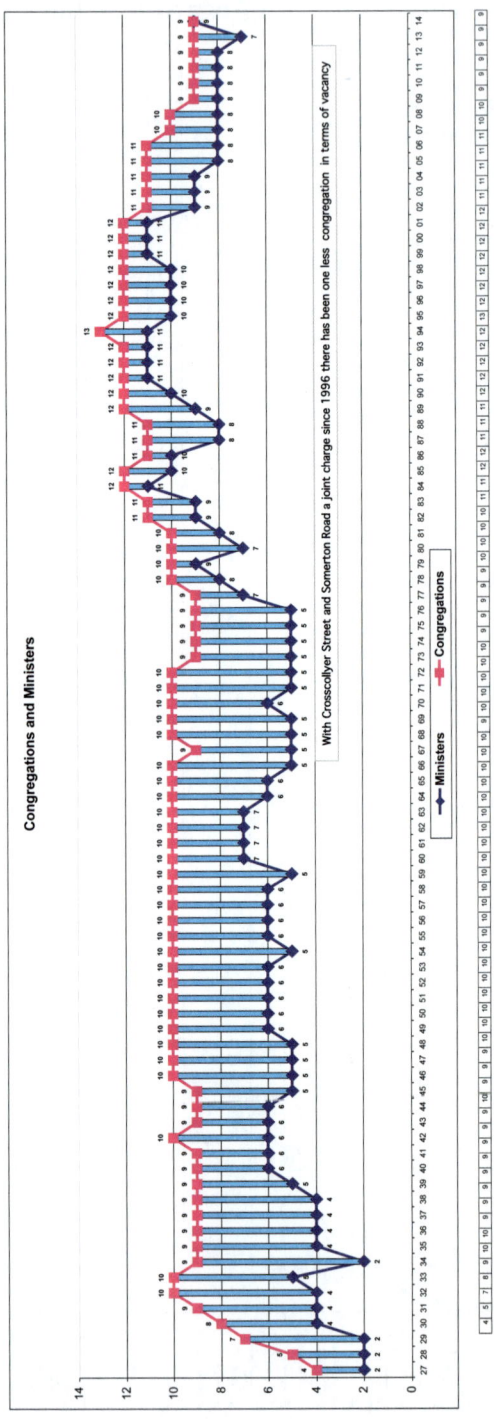

APPENDIX 9 – Office Bearers by Congregation

Ballyclare Deacons
Beggs, S	16/02/1957	10/04/1963
Hamill, I	23/01/1979	01/09/1981
Herron, WJ	02/03/1960	27/09/1969
Hoey, T	16/02/1957	27/09/1969
Logan, A	30/06/1987	31/12/2000
McConnell, J	16/02/1957	10/04/1963
McDonald, KA	16/12/1975	01/09/1981
McKenzie, D	08/11/1972	05/05/1982
McKenzie, RB	10/04/1963	08/04/1975
McKenzie, RT	16/02/1957	18/05/1966
McKinstry, J	16/02/1957	27/09/1969
Patton, TJ	12/01/1982	04/05/1987
Watson, D	18/05/1966	01/09/1981
Watson, JJ	02/03/1960	08/04/1975
Watson, P	09/01/2005	11/08/2013
Watson, S	27/09/1969	16/12/1975
Kelso, K	09/01/2005	
Logan, S	09/01/2005	
McFall, S	24/06/2001	
McMinn, AL	08/11/1972	
Roger, J	17/01/2010	
Schmidt, A	18/01/2015	

Ballyclare Elders
Hamill, I	01/09/1981	13/05/1991
McMullan, DH	08/04/1975	27/07/1978
Watson, JJ	08/04/1975	09/10/1998
Logan, A	31/12/2000	
McDonald, KA	01/09/1981	
McKenzie, RB	08/04/1975	
Watson, D	01/09/1981	

Bangor Deacons
Fullerton, L	19/05/2002	02/05/2004
Magee, B	19/05/2002	02/05/2004
Scott, KJ	19/05/2002	02/05/2004
Thompson, A	19/05/2002	02/05/2004

Bangor Elders
Kelly, TAD	07/10/2001	02/05/2004

Continued under Groomsport from 02/05/2004

Blackburn Deacons
Marshall, D	05/11/1995	02/04/2001
Neville, C	05/11/1995	02/04/2001
Nutter, P	05/11/1995	02/04/2001
Stevenson, D	05/11/1995	02/04/2001

Blackburn Elders
Ormerod, P	21/02/2001	02/04/2001
Riley, B	08/09/1995	02/04/2001

Botanic Avenue Deacons
Blair, JDP	12/04/1956	10/11/1957
Boyd, RJ	21/04/1960	30/10/1971
Brown, C	01/06/1950	10/11/1957
Brown, EC	01/04/1962	30/10/1971
Crooks, J	28/12/1969	30/10/1971
Grier, JG	03/03/1968	30/10/1971
Howard, RA	01/06/1950	19/10/1951
Kelly, TAD	28/12/1969	30/10/1971
Leahy, FS	23/05/1947	20/10/1949
McGurk, S	12/03/1947	11/03/1953
McIlrath, RC	01/04/1962	30/10/1971
Neill, WJ	11/03/1953	10/11/1957
Oliver, WM	12/03/1947	31/03/1960
Patterson, J	01/06/1950	06/04/1964
Stewart, WH	12/03/1947	01/04/1962

Botanic Avenue Elders
Blair, JDP	10/11/1957	30/10/1971
Brown, C	10/11/1957	30/10/1971
Neill, WJ	10/11/1957	28/06/1972
Sampson, WA	27/10/1966	30/10/1971
Woods, W	16/12/1962	22/08/1967

Continued under Stranmillis from 30/10/1971

Swann, T   12/03/1947   01/06/1975
Woods, W   11/03/1953   16/12/1962

Clintyfallow Deacons   **Clintyfallow Elders**
McNeill, JJ   09/12/1960   09/06/1985   McNeill, A   09/12/1960   09/06/1985
Reid, RJ   09/12/1960   09/06/1985   McNeill, J   09/12/1960   05/06/1961
Reid, W   09/12/1960   03/03/1978   Watson, JH   09/12/1960   17/03/1967

Crosscollyer Street Deacons   **Crosscollyer Street Elders**
Bellew, GM   09/03/1956   20/10/1957   Bellew, GM   20/10/1957   10/02/1997
Briggs, S   29/09/1982   27/09/1984*   Gilliland, JT   29/11/1995   03/01/1996
Currie, G   29/09/1982   18/03/1987*   Hamilton, A   29/11/1995   03/01/1996
Dunn, GW   09/03/1956   05/11/1957*   Johnston, A   01/02/1989   17/10/1994
Gilliland, JT   10/05/1992   29/11/1995   Simpson, J   20/10/1957   27/04/1975
Gordon, D   29/09/1982   03/01/1996
Hamilton, A   17/05/1987   29/11/1995
Hamilton, J   10/05/1992   03/01/1996
Johnston, A   17/05/1987   01/02/1989
McMullan, JC   09/03/1956   03/12/1980*   *Continued under North Belfast from 03/01/1996*
Simpson, J   09/03/1956   20/10/1957

Crumlin Deacons   **Crumlin Elders**
Beckett, W   29/06/1980   15/04/1984   Beckett, RC   01/12/1976   07/10/1981
Bell, E   01/12/1976   29/06/1980   Craig, DR   28/06/1992   02/04/2008
Brown, W   22/05/2005   19/06/2011   Livingstone, TJ 29/06/1980   11/01/1988
Craig, DR   01/12/1976   28/06/1992   Mackey, AP   01/12/1976   28/06/1991
Craig, HJ   01/12/1976   04/01/1978   Peacock, R   22/05/2005   19/12/2012
Doyle, S   01/12/1976   29/06/1980   Pinkerton, HE   29/06/1980   17/12/1993
Fleming, E   29/03/1998   22/05/2005   Bell, E   29/06/1980
Harkness, W   22/05/2005   19/11/2010   Woolsey, D   28/06/1992
Kilpatrick, J   22/05/2005   19/06/2011
Lucas, A   21/03/1993   01/03/1998
Moore, B   21/03/1993   22/05/2005
Park, D   01/12/1976   21/12/1998
Park, GE   01/12/1976   20/04/2000
Peacock, R   11/03/2001   22/05/2005
Pinkerton, B   01/12/1976   15/04/1984
Pinkerton, HE   01/12/1976   29/06/1980
Pinkerton, S   16/04/1989   03/06/1998
Wright, DJ   15/04/1984   16/04/1989
Lucas, A   19/06/2011

Dublin Elders
Brown, P   26/05/1990   30/04/2000
Somerville, I   26/05/1990   29/04/2007

Finaghy Deacons   **Finaghy Elders**
Lisburn Road continued under Finaghy from 01/07/2008
Allen, JP   07/11/1971   15/12/1986   Carlisle, G   31/05/1974   10/11/2004
Ashby, EA   25/10/1981   15/04/1993   Gilliland, JT   31/05/1974   15/08/1989
Bacon, WJ   07/10/1962   15/10/1971   McGurk, S   15/03/1957   16/05/1990
Ball, F   01/07/2008   21/10/2014   Quail, T   04/02/1990   06/08/2015
Ball, T   01/07/2008   11/07/2014   Shanks, SG   15/03/1957   29/12/1988
Carlisle, G   11/05/1956   31/05/1974   Gilliland, T   15/03/2015
Davison, H   29/09/1991   15/12/1994   Langtry, MC   13/01/1991

Office Bearers by Congregation

Elliott, E	07/11/1971	23/11/1975*	Tinsley, D	20/06/2008
Gibson, H	29/09/1991	15/04/1988	Williamson, HA	01/07/2008
Gilliland, JT	07/11/1971	31/05/1974		
Hagan, WM	11/05/1956	15/01/1964		
Kerr, E	31/07/1949	11/05/1956		
Langtry, MC	29/10/1978	13/01/1991		
Martin, D	21/12/1986	15/01/1994		
McGurk, S	02/04/1953	15/03/1957		
Miller, WJ	17/10/1965	07/11/1971		
Mitchell, R	11/05/1956	07/06/1959*		
Neill, T	17/10/1965	07/11/1971		
Phillips, S	23/11/1975	25/10/1981		
Quail, T	29/10/1978	04/02/1990		
Reid, Wm	29/10/1978	06/03/2011		
Shanks, J	31/07/1949	08/07/1953		
Shanks, SG	31/07/1949	15/03/1957		
Tinsley, D	29/09/1991	20/06/2008		
Gibson, J	09/12/2001			
Reid, Wd	29/09/1991			

Groomsport Deacons
Continued from Bangor from 02/05/2004

Groomsport Elders

Fullerton, L	02/05/2004	25/06/2006	Francey, S	25/06/2006	
Magee, B	02/05/2004	15/06/2013	Fullerton, L	25/06/2006	
Thompson, A	02/05/2004	23/04/2006	Kelly, TAD	02/05/2004	
Scott, KJ	02/05/2004	01/05/2011*			
Beattie, RIC	29/10/2006				
Glover, D	29/10/2006				
Macleod, A	01/05/2011				

Jocelyn Avenue Deacons

Jocelyn Avenue Elders

Brown, JR	14/04/1939	18/02/1944	Howard, RA	08/10/1954	11/10/1955
Higginson, H	09/02/1951	30/11/1951	Sampson, WA	08/10/1954	29/05/1966
Howard, RA	19/10/1951	08/10/1954			
Johnson, J	22/05/1936	03/01/1937			
Jones, J	09/02/1951	30/03/1954			
McBride, C	22/05/1936	14/04/1939			
Mills, S	22/05/1936	14/04/1939			
Morgan, T	09/02/1951	29/05/1966			
Porter, HG	30/03/1954	25/06/1960			
Porter, WW	30/03/1954	31/05/1955			
Sampson, WA	10/04/1936	18/02/1944			
Scott, JA	10/04/1936	14/04/1939			
Smiley, J	22/05/1936	25/10/1940			
Sullivan, J	09/02/1951	01/11/1951			

Knock Deacons

Knock Elders

Brand, NS	11/04/1947	06/02/1957	Amberson, WJ	03/06/1979	05/06/1989
Campbell, NA	02/04/2000	18/12/2004	Harper, F	03/06/1979	25/05/2006
Christie, J	07/11/1993	06/09/1995	Stephenson, JC	05/03/2000	
Connolly, DP	30/06/1957	25/04/1982	Thompson, W	02/07/1986	
Crozier, AJ	08/02/1987	18/08/1987			
Crozier, AJ	06/02/1991	06/10/1993			
Gillespie, JH	12/02/1932	25/02/1934			
Gillespie, JR	12/02/1932	29/07/1960			

Appendix 9

Gilliland, DG	07/11/1993	10/06/1998
Harper, F	13/04/1978	03/06/1979
Hind, P	22/04/1938	03/07/1946
Holmes, I	02/04/2000	26/09/2001
Houston, IJ	25/04/1982	13/05/1992
Hoy, WJ	12/04/1935	12/05/1976
Joyce, JW	22/04/1938	03/05/1958
Kell, JA	12/02/1932	02/06/1935
Kell, JA	11/04/1947	07/03/1952
Kerr, TH	24/03/1950	27/03/1953
Ladds, M	10/12/1997	17/10/2001
Leckey, WJ	13/04/1978	04/02/2004
Lindsay, HC	17/05/1935	22/04/1938
Lipsett, WE	23/06/1985	28/12/1995
McCluggage, D	12/02/1932	12/04/1935
McGreevy, J	31/03/1944	11/04/1947
McKibbin, G	04/06/1970	03/06/1979
Millen, RJ	31/03/1963	23/06/1985
Molyneaux, S	12/02/1932	04/06/1947
Montgomery, RH	12/04/1935	12/03/1950
Moody, A	02/04/2000	31/03/2007
Orr, G	11/06/1961	09/07/1967
Patterson, JJ	12/02/1932	15/01/1940
Porter, DC	27/03/1953	21/09/1960
Robinson, A	03/06/1979	25/04/1982
Ross, DC	27/05/1956	28/02/1979
Shanks, Jer	22/04/1938	17/09/1958
Sinclair, WS	27/03/1953	03/06/1953
Sinclair, WS	11/06/1961	20/04/1967
Smyth, C	03/06/1979	27/07/1988
Stephenson, JC	05/02/1997	05/03/2000
Thompson, W	23/06/1985	02/07/1986
Young, JS	27/05/1956	04/09/1957
Grier, JG	25/04/1982	

Lisburn Road Deacons

Bailie, TH	25/03/1949	06/08/1958
Ball, F	25/03/1949	01/07/2008
Ball, T	06/04/1960	01/07/2008
Campbell, NA	02/02/1975	18/06/1998
Gale, GI	19/03/1937	12/01/1951
Gilliland, J	08/05/1942	25/03/1949
Hawthorne, WJ	28/03/1958	07/04/1961
Jeffrey, T	08/05/1942	12/05/1944
Jennings, F	15/05/1983	24/06/1997
Kerr, E	25/03/1949	31/07/1949
Loney, A	25/03/1949	05/06/1964
Loney, C	02/02/1975	15/05/1983*
Martin, AH	19/03/1937	08/05/1942
Martin, T	25/03/1955	10/05/1955
Mason, EW	08/05/1942	26/03/1943
Mason, WJ	25/03/1955	28/03/1958
Millington, SH	08/05/1942	03/05/1950
Shanks, Jn	19/03/1937	31/07/1949
Shanks, SG	19/03/1937	31/07/1949

Lisburn Road Elders

Hawthorne, WJ	07/04/1961	24/03/1982
Johnston, S	07/04/1961	28/03/1962*
Loney, A	05/06/1964	08/07/1992
Walker, N	07/04/1961	22/12/1974*
Williamson, HA	02/02/1975	01/07/2008

Office Bearers by Congregation

Templeton, WJ 25/03/1949 07/04/1961
Turbitt, A 28/03/1952 25/03/1955
Turbitt, A 05/06/1964 15/05/1983*
Watson, Jas 07/04/1961 15/05/1983*
Continued under Finaghy from 01/07/2008

North Belfast Deacons
Continued from Crosscollyer Street and Somerton Road from 03/01/1996
Bolton, T 26/08/2001 15/04/2006
Coates, J 28/06/2006 31/08/2007
Donavon, J 26/08/2001 15/09/2007
Gordon, D 03/01/1996 26/08/2001
Hamilton, J 03/01/1996 22/09/1997
McMurray, WJ 03/01/1996 26/08/2001

North Belfast Elders
Gilliland, JT 03/01/1996 03/03/2014
Hamilton, A 03/01/1996 22/09/1997
Grier, J 03/01/1996

Omagh Deacons
Armstrong, W 26/03/1995 15/12/2002
Condy, K 20/02/2000 27/05/2012
Crawford, H 28/05/1991 03/05/1992
Crozier, AJ 03/04/1982 15/03/1985
Edgar, F 03/04/1982 07/08/1989
Harpur, A 28/05/1991 24/02/2013
Heatherington, G 03/04/1982 03/05/1992
McCain, R 28/05/1991 24/02/2013
Weir, D 04/06/2006 05/11/2007
Hamilton, J 24/02/2013
Johnston, D 24/02/2013
Johnston, W 24/02/2013
McConnell, D 28/05/1991
Orr, J 04/06/2006

Omagh Elders
Crawford, H 03/05/1992 20/06/2010
Gilmour, AR 14/03/1984 23/08/1988
Heatherington, G 03/05/1992 12/06/2000
Condy, K 27/05/2012

Richhill Deacons
Arthur, R 12/03/2006 17/10/2012
Boyd, P 27/06/1999 12/03/2006*
Douglas, T 19/06/1994 30/04/1996
Nicholson, T 25/06/1989 30/05/2004
Rees, M 27/06/1999 12/03/2006*
Wilson, S 27/06/1999 30/05/2004
Woolsey, D 25/06/1989 31/10/1990
Allen, J 25/06/1989
Dougan, D 12/03/2006
Henry, P 11/01/2015
Potts, J 11/01/2015

Richhill Elders
Dixon, J 13/12/1988 04/09/2000
Nicholson, T 30/05/2004 01/12/2008
Wilson, S 30/05/2004 06/06/2011
Wilson, W 13/12/1988 04/04/2011

Somerton Road Deacons
Beggs, DR 24/03/1953 21/08/1956*
Campbell, DE 14/04/1964 31/12/1964*
Corbett, H 14/06/1981 27/01/1986
Craig, W 28/04/1978 31/12/1982*
Crymble, D 08/06/1986 31/12/1982*
Dickson, T 29/06/1969 26/11/1972
Garland, SJ 26/11/1972 07/04/1978
Grier, J 08/06/1986 12/03/1989
Hogg, D 24/03/1953 20/12/1959*
Jones, VN 14/04/1964 29/06/1969

Somerton Road Elders
Grier, J 12/03/1989 03/01/1996

Appendix 9

Magee, R	28/04/1978	14/06/1981*
McMurray, WJ	20/12/1959	06/11/2009
Millar, J	14/04/1964	05/10/1967
Reid, R	14/06/1981	27/01/1984
Rennie, A	04/06/1961	31/12/1965*
Sands, S	24/03/1953	14/06/1981
Shannon, R	26/11/1972	16/12/1982

Continued under North Belfast from 03/01/1996

Stranmillis Deacons
Continued from Botanic Avenue from 30/10/1971

Beattie, RI	18/06/1989	21/11/2000
Beattie, RIC	20/06/1999	30/11/2003
Boyd, RJ	30/10/1971	20/06/1999
Brown, CE	19/06/1994	20/06/1999
Brown, EC	30/10/1971	02/11/1980
Carlisle, DF	18/06/1989	22/02/1995
Crawford, M	20/06/1999	14/12/2013
Crawford, R	18/06/1989	25/02/1994
Crooks, J	30/10/1971	24/01/1985
Dunlop, R	20/06/1999	14/12/2013
Gibson, H	20/06/1999	26/11/2000
Grier, J	01/06/1975	26/05/1985
Grier, JG	30/10/1971	16/04/1972
Harris, WA	31/05/1981	24/01/1985
Johnston, A	04/06/1978	21/02/1984
Johnston, R	20/06/2004	02/01/2009
Kelly, MT	18/06/1989	04/03/2007
Kelly, TAD	30/10/1971	02/09/1990
Logue, I	26/05/1985	02/09/1990
McClintock, PR	26/05/1985	20/06/1999
McClintock, R	31/05/1981	18/09/1988
McCormick, JR	04/06/1978	02/09/1990
McIlrath, RC	30/10/1971	19/08/1976
McMullan, C	18/06/1989	16/06/1991
Milburn, A	18/06/1989	31/10/1992
Moore, C	19/06/1994	26/11/2000
Scott, KJ	19/06/1994	12/03/1996
Stephens, J	18/06/1989	24/07/1994
Doherty, C	15/12/2013	
Fitzsimmons, R	15/12/2013	
Gaston, SA	19/06/1994	
Gordon, DE	20/06/1999	
Hanna, KJ	18/06/1989	
Johnston, A	15/12/2013	
Johnston, D	15/12/2013	
Kelly, K	18/06/1989	
Killen, NA	16/11/2008	
Nelis, P	20/06/2004	
Woolsey, S	16/11/2008	
Wright, I	15/12/2013	

Stranmillis Elders

Blair, JDP	30/10/1971	22/09/1987
Brown, C	30/10/1971	15/05/1992
Brown, EC	02/11/1980	07/06/2009
Kelly, TAD	02/09/1990	26/04/2001
Logue, I	02/09/1990	12/07/1999
McClintock, R	18/09/1988	13/09/2008
McCormick, JR	02/09/1990	05/09/2004
Sampson, WA	30/10/1971	28/09/1993
Stephens, J	24/07/1994	04/12/2000
Gibson, H	26/11/2000	
Kelly, MT	04/03/2007	
Moore, C	26/11/2000	

APPENDIX 10 – Membership-Attendance Statistics

31/12	Members	AM Attendance	New Members
1986	433		
1987	448	549	
1988	431		
1989	436	579	40
1990	438	598	34
1991	434	663	17
1992	428	679	24
1993	438	679	34
1994	465		
1995	458	662	21
1996	444	670	14
1997	453		
1998	443	641	25
1999	434	635	29
2000	430	624	27
2001	386	557	13
2002	416	541	39
2003			
2004	403		
2005	412	541	28
2006	388	511	9
2007	367	494	15
2008	352	483	9
2009	347	496	11
2010	346	478	9
2011	338	504	13
2012	341	495	13
2013	342	505	19
2014	350	518	21

APPENDIX 11A – EPC Long-term Member Missionaries

Co-operation with Free Church of Scotland
1937	1954	Dr H C Lindsay	Peru
1944	1974	Rev J & Mrs McCracken	South Africa
1944	1974	Miss A J Dunlop	India
1948	1953	Miss A Wilkinson	Peru
1951	1985	Miss F I Donaldson	Peru
1960	1963	W M Oliver	India
1999	2011	Rev N E & Mrs Reid	South Africa

Qua Iboe-Mission Africa and Partners
1987	2010	Rev Dr S & Mrs J Garland	Nigeria
2010-			Home based
2003-		P Gaiya née Johnston	Nigeria
		Stranmillis-Omagh	

AIM
1995	1998	A Moody	Uganda
		Richhill	

Korean World Mission
2004	2007	A & E Moody	Uganda
2007	2011	A & E Moody	Uganda
2013		A & E Moody	Uganda
		Knock (1999)-Stranmillis (2007)	

Christian Witness to Israel
2004	2012	Rev S G T Atkinson	Irish Deputation Secretary

SIM
2013		J Ray née Campbell	Ethiopia
		Stranmillis	

ReachAcross
2014

Wycliffe Bible Translators
2008-2012		E & K Underwood	Home based
		Stranmillis	

UFM One Hundred Fold Digital Technology
2012-

Appendix 11B

APPENDIX 11B – EPC Member Missionary Service Chart

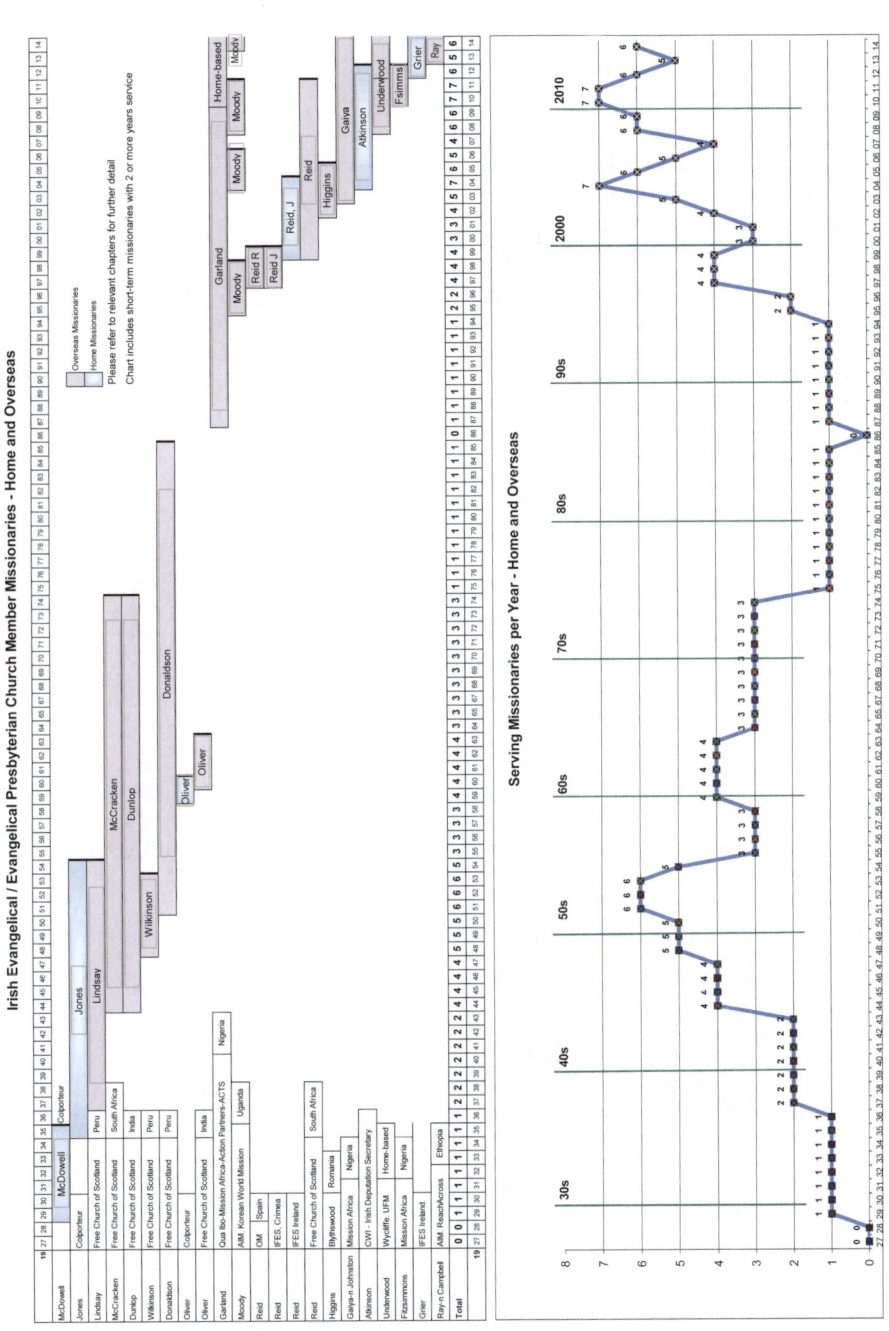

APPENDIX 12 – Council-Presbytery Appointments

Chair of Council

1927-42	Rev J Hunter	1961-62	Rev A A Campbell
1942-43	Rev W J Grier	1962-63	W A Sampson
1943-44	Dr J R Gillespie	1963-64	Rev W J Grier
1944-45	Rev C E Hunter	1964-65	Rev W J McDowell
1945-46	W A Sampson	1965-66	Rev C E Hunter
1946-47	Rev W J McDowell	1966-67	Rev C H Garland
1947-48	Rev C H Garland	1967-68	Rev A A Campbell
1948-49	Rev E H Titcombe	1968-69	W A Sampson
1949-50	Rev W J Grier	1969-70	Rev W J Grier
1950-51	Rev C E Hunter	1970-71	J D P Blair
1951-52	W A Sampson	1971-72	Rev W J McDowell
1952-53	Rev W J Grier	1972-73	Rev N E Reid
1953-54	Rev W J McDowell	1973-74	Rev C H Garland
1954-55	Rev C H Garland	1974-75	Rev W J McDowell
1955/9-56	Rev C E Hunter	1975-76	Rev W J Grier
1955-9/56	R A Howard.	1976-77	W A Sampson
1956-57	Rev W Porter,	1977-78	Rev W J Grier
1957-58	Rev W J Grier	1978-79	Rev A A Campbell
1958-59	Rev C E Hunter	1979-80	Rev W J McDowell
1959-60	Rev W J McDowell	1980	Rev J S Ross
1960-61	Rev C H Garland		

Notes

James Hunter last attended Council 24/11/1939. Rev W J Grier deputised until May 1942.

1942-43: chairman to be elected annually in May.
Dr J R Gillespie Vice Chair during Rev W J Grier's illness, 11/1949-04/1950.
1955-56: Rev S Law and S G Shanks declined on health grounds.
1955-56: R A Howard resigned 09/1956, emigrated to Rhodesia.
1956-57: 1958-59: Rev S Law declined nomination.
1962-63: Chairman of Council to preach in all congregations.
1963-64: Chairman's year of office now from April-March.

Moderator of Presbytery (Council became Presbytery in November 1980)

1980-81 Rev J S Ross
1981-82 E C Brown
1982-83 Rev S Watson
1983-84 Rev Dr R C Beckett
1984-85 Rev S J Garland
1985-86 Rev D W H Thomas
1986-87 Rev N E Reid
1987-88 E C Brown
1988-89 Rev Dr R C Beckett
1989-90 D Watson
1990-91 Rev G N Burke
1991-92 Rev M G Johnston
1992-93 Rev D W H Thomas
1993-94 Rev S Watson
1994-95 Rev W C J Ballantine
1995-96 Rev N E Reid
1996-97 Rev Dr A A Woolsey
1997-98 Rev S J Roger

1998-99 Rev S J Tracey
1999-00 Rev Dr R C Beckett
2000-01 M Langtry
2001-02 Rev G N Burke
2002-03 J Grier
2003-04 Rev S G T Atkinson
2004-05 Rev W C J Ballantine
2005-06 Rev W L Elliott
2006-07 K McDonald
2007-08 T Gilliland
2008-09 Rev A J Lucas
2009-10 Rev Dr R C Beckett
2010-11 H Gibson
2011-12 Rev G N Burke
2012-13 D Watson
2013-14 Rev N E Reid
2014-15 J Grier

Council-Presbytery Clerks

26/11/1927	29/05/1931	W J Grier
29/05/1931	29/03/1935	J A Kell
17/05/1935	05/071935	W J Grier, Temporary
05/07/1935	23/09/1955	S G Shanks
23/09/1955	22/05/1959	Rev W J McDowell, Assistant Secretary, acting
22/05/1959	20/05/1960	W A Sampson, Rev C E Hunter assist - Rev W J McDowell, Chair.
20/05/1960	26/03/1964	Rev W J McDowell. W A Sampson Assist Secretary, 20/05/1960.
26/03/1964	23/04/1965	W A Sampson during Chair of Rev W J McDowell
23/04/1965	31/08/1973	Rev W J McDowell
23/04/1971	21/04/1972	W A Sampson when Rev W J McDowell in Chair
01/09/1973	05/09/1983	Rev A A Campbell
05/09/1983	13/06/1994	Rev S Watson
13/06/1994	10/05/1999	Rev Dr R C Beckett
10/05/1999	01/09/2008	Rev J S Roger
01/09/2008	02/04/2012	Rev S Watson
02/04/2012	31/12/2012	W Thompson Interim appointment
01/01/2013		H Gibson

Notes
Various deputies during S G Shank's illness, March 1951-September 1955, mostly W A Sampson who was appointed Assistant Secretary March 1953

Editors Irish Evangelical-Evangelical Presbyterian

					Issues
Jun	1928	May	1981	Rev W J Grier	625
Jun-Jul	1981	Jul-Aug	1996	Rev D W H Thomas	141
Sep-Oct	1996	Nov-Dec	1996	Interim Arrangements	2
Jan-Feb	1997	Sep-Oct	2001	Rev S J Tracey	29
Nov-Dec	2001	Nov-Dec	2004	Rev S G T Atkinson	19
Jan-Feb	2005	Nov-Dec	2012	Mr H Gibson	48
Jan-Feb	2013	Mar-Apr	2015	Rev G N Burke	14

1928-1975   12 issues per year. Jun-Jul 1974 was a single issue
1976-1973   10 issues per year. Single issue for Jun-Jul and Aug-Sep
1994-2014   6 issues per year

Notes
Title changed to *The Evangelical Presbyterian* in June 1964
The original page size of 23x18 cm changed to A5 in Jun-Jul 1981 and to A4 Jan-Feb 2013.

FCOS Foreign-International Missions Board Representatives

1981-1985	Rev John Ross	1994-1997	Ernest Brown
1985-1989	Rev Derek Thomas	1997-1999	Rev Gareth Burke
1989-1991	Rev Norman Reid	1999-2011	Ernest Brown
1991-1994	Rev Robert Beckett	2012-2015	Rev Norman Reid

APPENDIX 13 – IEC-EPC Member Publications

Brown, Ernest C
Qualified Commissioned and Accountable
Studies in Eldership based on Acts 20.28
                              Evangelical Presbyterian Church
(Revised 2013)   Evangelical Book Shop   1994   PB   134pp

Service in a Sari
The Story of Nan Dunlop, Missionary in Central India
                              Evangelical Presbyterian Church
                              Evangelical Book Shop   1996   PB   176pp

Burke, Rev G N
Beginnings and Beliefs   1995   B'let   8pp
Some reflections on the history and beliefs of the EPC (1927-1997)

Burke, Ruth
Gowandale Adventure   DayOne Publications   2007   PB   96pp
and other stories for boys

Mystery at Ardfuar   DayOne Publications   2007   PB   96pp
and other stories for Girls

Mansoul   DayOne Publications   2013   PB   128pp
Based on John Bunyan's Holy War

Campbell, Rev A A
According to Purpose   N A Campbell   1988   PB   96pp

Manley Group
God's Providence as seen in the Book of Esther

EPC
The Way Ahead   Church Extension Committee   1991   PB   21pp
Popular version of Vision for the Nineties Strategy Paper

The Anatomy of a Church   Church Extension Committee   1991   Pamphlet

Garland, Rev S J
Abortion   EPC   1981   B'let   14pp
A Matter of Life and Death

The Christian and Alcohol   EPC   1981   B'let   10pp

Garland, Jean &   Africa Christian Textbooks   2005   PB   326pp
Dr Mike Blyth
AIDS is Real and it's in Our Church

Gillespie, Dr J H (Leloumenos)
FAITH in an Unchanging Vesture
An Exposure of Modernist Principles based on *The Changing Vesture of the Faith*
by Prof J E Davey, of the Presbyterian Assembly's College, Belfast

| | Wickliffe Press | 1927 | PB | 96pp |

Evangelical Book Shop

The Oxford Groups   Evangelical Book Shop   1934   Pamphlet

Stories of Christian Heroes   Morrison and Gibb   1937   PB   175pp
Liverpool Bible Depot and Evangelical Book Shop

Grier, Rev W J

The Momentous Event   Evangelical Book Shop   1945-1963 (5 Editions)
    Banner of Truth   1970   PB   128pp
A Discussion of Scripture Teaching on the Second Advent
First published in *The Irish Evangelical* 1944-45 as a series of 16 articles

The Origin and Witness of the Irish Evangelical Church
    Evangelical Book Shop   1946   HB   64pp
Re-published   Evangelical Book Shop   2009   PB   48pp

Errors and Fantasies of Russelism
    Evangelical Book Shop   1947   B'let

Who are Jehovah's Witnesses?   1949   B'let

The Irish Evangelical Church WHY?
    Evangelical Book Shop   1952   B'let   10pp
Semi-Jubilee Booklet

What is The Irish Evangelical Church?
What does it believe and Practise? Why does it Exist?
    Evangelical Book Shop   B'let   8pp

Unbelief of Barthianism   Evangelical Book Shop   1955   B'let

The Inspiration of the Holy Scriptures   1960   B'let

The True Catholic Faith   Evangelical Prot Society   PB   143pp
A Christian Correspondence Course in 18 Lessons
W J Grier contributed chapters.   1964 (second edition)

Protestants on Road to Rome   British Evangelical Council   1964   B'let   14pp

Huss and Farel   Evangelical Library   1965   B'let   24pp
Heroic Pioneers of the Reformation

An Accomplished Redemption   SGU   1966   B'let

Shall we Unite with Rome?   British Evangelical Council   1966   B'let   14pp

The Evangelical Presbyterian Church   1967   B'let   8pp
Why does it Exist? For what does it Stand?
40th Anniversary Booklet Evangelical Book Shop

The Best Books	Banner of Truth	1968	PB	176pp

A Guide to Christian Literature

After Upsala-Whither Bound? British Evangelical Council   1969   B'let
Trends in Ecumenical Thinking

The Importance, Doctrines and Lessons of the Reformation   1975   B'let   12pp
An Address delivered at Caxton Hall, Westminster on Reformation Day, 1975
The Protestant Truth Society

The Life of John Calvin   Banner of Truth   2012   PB   162pp
First published in *The Irish Evangelical* 1954-56 as a series of 23 articles

Harper, Frederick

A History of Knock Evangelical Presbyterian Church, 1927-2002
75 Years of Gospel Witness   Knock EPC Session   2002   PB   54pp

McDowell, Rev W J

Joseph … The Slave who became Governor		B'let	28pp

Proceeds for Ballyclare EPC Building Fund

Have we a Reliable Bible? 1949	B'let	
Is Bodily Healing in the Atonement?	1953	B'let
Should the Murderer be put to death?	1961	B'let
The Virgin Birth of our Lord	1966	B'let
The Baffling Mystery of the Godhead	1974	B'let
The Incomparable Book Banner of Truth	1988	B'let 14pp

Ross, Rev J S

Responsible Renewal   Ambassador   1986   B'let   32pp
Lessons from the life and Times of Henry Cooke

Stapleton, Timothy

In the Midst of Drowning   2011   B'let   29pp

Swann, Thomas

Water Baptism   Evangelical Book Shop   1935   B'let
What saith the Scriptures?

Thomas, Rev D W H

Serving the King   Evangelical Press   1989   PB   123pp
A Guide to Christian Usefulness

Wisdom
The Key to Living God's Way   Christian Focus   1990   PB   143pp

Help for Hurting Christians   Evangelical Press   1991   PB   160pp
Reflections on Psalms

God Delivers   Evangelical Press   1991   PB   415pp
Isaiah Simply Explained   Welwyn Commentary Series

God Strengthens	Evangelical Press	1993	PB	320pp
Ezekiel Simply Explained	Welwyn Commentary Series			
The Storm Breaks	Evangelical Press	1995	PB	352pp
Job Simply Explained	Welwyn Commentary Series			
Taken up to Heaven	Evangelical Press	1996	PB	144pp
The Ascension of Christ				

Watson, David
All the Way He Leads
Ballyclare EPC, A Brief History, 1928-1994

	Plantation Press	1994	PB	91pp
	Evangelical Presbyterian Church			

Woolsey, Rev Dr A A

Duncan Campbell	Houghton & Stodder	1974	PB	191pp
Reprinted as				
Channel of Revival	Faith Mission	1982	PB	191pp

Unity and Continuity in Covenantal Thought
A Study in the Reformed Tradition to the Westminster Assembly

Reformation Heritage		2012	PB	672pp

APPENDIX 14 – Conferences

Ministers' and Office Bearers' Conferences

1984 9-10 March   **Crumlin**   Rev D Paterson, FCOS
Togetherness

1985 1-2 March   **Belfast Bible College**   Prof A Loughridge, RPCI
Practical aspects of the Ministry – Family, Pastor, Devotion, Fellowship

1986 7-8 March   **Belfast Bible College**   Pastor Achille Blaize

1987 No Conference

1988 No Conference

1989 31 March-1 April **Lisburn Road**   Prof C Graham, FCOS
Marriage and Family – Principles and Problems

1990 20-21 April   **Ballyclare**   Prof H J Blair, RPCI

1991 12-13 April   **Stranmillis**   Prof A I MacLeod, FCOS
Prayer

1992 17-18 January   **Richhill**   Dr R B Gaffin, WTS
The Resurrection in Romans 6
Suffering in the Book of Hebrews

1993 9-10 October   **Richhill**   Dr S B Ferguson, WTS
Reaching our Preaching Standards
Pastoral Implications of the Marrow Controversy

1994 11-12 March   **Finaghy**   Rev G Thomas
The Stronger and Weaker Brother (Saturday)

1995 25-26 November   **Lisburn Road**   Prof A Loughridge, RPCI

1996 8-9 March   **Finaghy**   Rev Dr W Fleming, PCI
The Key to Spiritual Radiance and Vision (Prayer)

1997 14-15 February   **Crumlin**   Rev W Hughes
"Fellow-workers with Him" (2 Cor 6:1)

1998 13-14 February   **Ballyclare**   Rev J Cook, Barry
The Minister and his God, his Work, his Life
Elders, Deacons and their Work

1999 5-6 February   **Omagh**   Pastor J Hufstetler

2000 25-26 February   **Somerton Road**   Rev R J Johnston

2001 16-17 February   **Finaghy**   Rev I Hamilton
Preaching as a Conversion Ordinance (Friday)
Facing Sin's Reality (Friday)
The Spiritual Nurture of Young People in the Home and Church (Saturday)

2002 22-23 February **Stranmillis**   Dr D McKay, RPCI
Heaven and Hell
William Chalmers Burns

2003 28-29 March   **Somerton Road**   Rev M G Johnston,
                                                    Grove Chapel

2004 26-27 March   **Knock**   Rev Stephen Curry, B'money

2005 19-20 November **Groomsport**   Rev B Edwards
The New Hermeneutic (Friday)   *Christian Forgiving* (Friday)
Priorities in the Personal Life of a Christian Leader
William Tyndale, Character and Commitment in making an English Bible

2006 10-11 February **Richhill**   Dr John Scott
Responding to Contemporary Challenges

2007 2-3 March   **Ballyclare**   Rev J Magee, Erne West
Lessons found in Leviticus (Both days)

2008 22-23 February **Somerton Road**   Rev Richard Brooks, Matlock

2009 20-21 February **Omagh**
Dealing with Mental Illness in the Church - Friday   Rev Stephen McCauley
Marriage - Saturday   Dr Andrew Collins

2010   **Crosscollyer Street**   Rev Peter Naylor, EPCEW
Glories of Christ in a Time of Unbelief
Glory of God in the Church
What makes a Good Leader? Saving Faith

2011 04-05 March   **Stranmillis**   Rev David Meredith, FCOS
The Contemporary Church

2012 24 February   **Stranmillis**   Prof David McKay, RTC
(Ministers only on Friday. Saturday 25 02 2012 was Presbytery Strategy Day)
Open Theism
Calvin and Mission

2013 09 March   **Ballyclare**   Dr Carl R Trueman, WTS
Elders and Deacons – Structure and Authority in the Church
Martin Luther – Lessons for the Church to Learn

2014 21-22 March   **Stranmillis**   Dr Bob Akroyd, ETS
B B Warfield – 2 Addresses – Friday
The Gospel that Saves and the Gospel that Changes – 2 Addresses - Saturday

Presbytery Day Conferences
2009 Dr Derek Thomas   *Justification. Sanctification. Glorification*
2010 Prof Edward Donnelly *Called by Grace. Called to Glory*
2011 Rev Geoff Thomas   *The Beauty of Christ, The Joy of Christ*

2012	Pastor Achille Blaize		*Josiah's Reformation*
2013	Rev Iain D Campbell		*Living in the Light of our Hope*
			1 *Jeremiah buys a Field* (Jer 32)
			2 *Jars of Clay* (2 Cor 4)
2014	Rev David Court		*Living for Christ in a Hostile World* (2 Addresses)
2015	Rev Paul Levy		*Our Greatest Need, Why do we Suffer?*

ICRC General Conferences

1982	Gronigen	Netherlands	Rev D W H Thomas
1985	Edinburgh	Scotland	Rev D W H Thomas
1989	Vancouver	Canada	Rev N E Reid
1993	Zwolle	Netherlands	Rev Dr R C Beckett
			Rev M G Johnston

Cross-Fertilisation: Prophecy, Preaching, Wrath of God in Mission Work, Tolerance

1997	Seoul	Korea	Rev Dr R C Beckett
			Rev J S Roger

Reformed Missions, Women in Office, Church-State, Charismatic Challenges, To Asian Religions

2001	Philadelphia	United States	Rev G N Burke

Unity of the Church: A Reformed Perspective, In Westminster Tradition. Hermeneutics and the Bible

2005	Pretoria	South Africa	Rev N E Reid

The Lordship of Christ: In the Life of the Believer, In the Church, Proclaimed in the World

2009	Christchurch	New Zealand	Rev G N Burke

Vitality of the Reformed Faith: Facing the Challenge of: Charismatic Movement, Individualism, Islam

2013	Cardiff	Wales	Rev G N Burke	Rev A J Lucas
			J Grier	D Watson

Preach the Word: Necessity of Preaching, Nature of Preaching, Preaching in a Non-Literary Context

2017	Ontario	Canada	

APPENDIX 15 – Autumn Evening Lectures

1994   Revival: Principles of Scripture and Lessons from History
Revival – What Is It?
Revival in Wales – 1
Revival in Wales – 2
1859 Revival in Ulster
W P Nicholson and the 1920s
Duncan Campbell
Lewis Awakening
Revival Today?

1995   Reformation – Then and Now
The Dawn of Reformation
Martin Luther
John Calvin
Reformation in England
John Knox
The Reformation in Ireland
Catholic Reformation Today
Relevance of the Reformation Today

1996   Evangelism – Preaching the Gospel, Then, Now and How
George Whitefield
C H Spurgeon
C G Finney
D L Moody
Evangelism Today

1997   No Lectures

1998   Challenges facing the Church in the 21st Century
Evangelicals and their Historical Roots – John Grier
The Moral Condition of Society at the End of the 20th Century – Rev R C Beckett
New Forms of Worship – Rev Mark G Johnston
Developing a 'Quality' Church Membership – Rev J S Roger
Scriptural Interpretation in the New Millennium – Prof E Donnelly, RPCI
Missions in the 21st Century (Lectures 1-3 were repeated in Coleraine Town Hall)

1999   More Challenges to the 21st Century Church
The Relevance of Justification by Faith Alone
Challenges to our Young people (with particular reference to the Lord's Day)
Preaching to 21st Century Man
The Relevance of Genesis
The Danger of New Age Cults
The Relevance of the Second Coming

2000 Reaching 21st Century Man with the Gospel
Evangelism and the Reformation
Evangelism and the Sovereignty of God
Evangelistic Preaching
Youth Evangelism
Evangelism – Our Responsibility

2001 The Word of God and Prayer
The Place of the Word in Daily Life
The Place of the Word of God in Revival
The Relationship of the Word and Prayer
Lessons on Prayer from the Song of Solomon
The Place of Prayer in Revival
(Evangelical Book Shop 75th Anniversary Lecture)

2002 75th Anniversary Lectures
The Atonement
The Person and Work of Christ
Principled Secession

2003 "Where do we go from here?" Church Planting in the 21st Century
Church Planting and Justification by Faith
Church Planting in the Republic of Ireland
Resources for Church Planting
Church Planting in the United Kingdom
Church Planting in Revival
A Strategy for Church Planting

APPENDIX 16 – Sunday School Projects – Subject

From 1967-68 until 1979-80 Council appointed one Sunday School lesson to be devoted to one figure from Church History and one from Missionary Endeavour

1859 Revival	2008-09				
Augustine of Hippo	1981-82	2004-05			
Aylward, Gladys	2000-01				
Barnardo, Dr Thomas	1977-78				
Brainerd, David	1981-82	2001-02			
Bray, Billy	1979-80				
Bunyan, John	1977-78	1982-83	1988-89	2003-04	
Burnham, Martin & Gracia	2004-05				
Burns, William Chalmers	1972-73				
Calvin, John	1969-70	1980-81	2000-01	2008-09	
Carey, William	1970-71	1992-93			
Carmichael, Amy	1993-94	2004-05	2014-15		
Colegio san Andres, Lima	1988-89				
Columba, St of Iona	1997-98				
Corrie ten Boom	1995-96				
CWI	1990-91	1994-95			
Dunlop, Annie J	2013-14				
Elliott, Jim	1997-98	2006-07			
EPC History	2005-06				
Erickson, Joni	2002-03				
Fry, Elizabeth	1990-91				
Grenfell, Wilfred	2007-08				
Judsons of Burma	2002-03				
Khun, Isobel	2001-02				
Knox, John	1968-69	2014-15			
Lakhnadon Chr Hospital	1986-87				
Lewis, C S	2006-07				
Liddell, Eric	1985-86	1999-00	2011-12		
Livingstone, David	1968-69	1986-87	1998-99	2006-07	2013-14
Lloyd-Jones, Dr D M	2010-11				
Luther, Martin	1967-68	1974-75	1983-84	1996-97	
Martyn, Henry	1973-74	1989-90			
McCheyne, R Murray	1973-74	2002-03			
Moffatt, Robert	1996-97				
Muller, George	1998-99	2012-13			
Newton, John	1978-79	1993-94			
Paton, John G	1967-68	1978-79	2003-04	2012-13	
Patrick	1974-75				
Paul, Missionary Pioneer	1999-00				
Qua Iboe Fellowship	1989-90				

Roseavere, Dr Helen	2009-10		
Rutherford, Samuel	1992-93		
Slessor, Mary	1969-70	1980-81	2011-12
S Africa - Mission Work	1995-96		
Spurgeon, C H	1975-76	1991-92	
Studd, C T	1995-96	2010-11	
Taylor, Hudson	1991-92	2005-06	
Toplady, Augustus	1975-76		
Tyndale, William	1970-71	1994-95	
Wesley, John	1997-98		
Whitefield, George	1972-73		
Wilberforce, William	1979-80	2007-08	

APPENDIX 17 – YPA Projects

1966-67	India	Land Rover purchase	1,710
1969-70	Peru	Books for Colegio san Andrés Library	150
1970-71	S Africa	Literature	175
1972-74	Peru	New Church Building	398
1974-75	S Africa	Amatole Church rebuild	215
1975-76	Peru	Rev Pedro Arana	100
1976-77	Peru	New Sunday School Room	450
1979	India	Hospital Steriliser	1,500
1980	Dublin	Piano and Lectern	335
1981	S Africa	Joseph & Helen McCracken	1,000
1982	Peru	'Pay a Pastor' via David Ford	2,000
1983-84	India	Theatre Lights – Lakhnadon Hospital	2,000
1984-85	CWI	Pilgrim's Progress in Hebrew	1,500
1986-87	Peru	Minibus for Colegio san Andrés-with FCOS	1,000
1988	S Africa	Dumisani Bible School	1,350
1989	India	Emmanuel Peter, Ministry Student	615
	S Africa	Jeep purchase	615
	Peru	Bursary Scheme, Colegio san Andrés, Lima	615
1990-91	Peru	Bursary Scheme, Colegio san Andrés, Lima	1,000
	EEFC	Bibles for Ukraine Pastor	1,000
1992	S Africa	Dumisani Student Book Fund	
1993	Peru	Lima Evan Seminary: Student Book Fund	1,270
1994			
1995-96	India	Church building, Vijainagar, Jabalpur	1,000
1997	Nigeria	Garlands	
	Uganda	Andrew Moody	
1998	S Africa	Rebuilding storm-damaged Churches	3,000
1999	Peru	Work among children via Sandra Pepper	2,000
2000	Peru	Minibus Fund, Annie Soper School	1,600
2001	CWI	Children's Bible Project	2,150
2002	S Africa	Church repairs - Amathole and Mkhubiso	1,475
2003			
2004	Garlands	Publication of Aids is Real	
2005	Peru	Sports, Christian University, Moyobamba	1,645
2006	Uganda	Books for Pastors	2,500
2007	S Africa	Dumisani Theological Institute	1,300
2008	M East	Middle East Reformed Fellowship	1,500
2009	India	Chhapara Manse renovation	2,000
2010	CWI	Literature	1,581
2011	Uganda	Students for the Ministry	2,200
2012	S Africa	Dumisani Theological Institute renovations	2,930
2013	Spain	Spain Team	2,778
2014	Vietnam	Eric Magowan, OMF	1,200
	Cambodia		

APPENDIX 18 – IEC-EPC Camp Venues

From 1924-1929 a group of young men, most of whom joined the Irish Evangelical Church, camped at weekends. This planted the seed and provided the tent and other items of equipment for the first Boys' Camps. From 1930-1938 young men of the Church carried on the practice by camping from time to time.

Phase 1 - 1939-1952 - Boys Camps

	Boys
1939	Brown's Bay
1940-50	Venues not recorded. Brown's Bay frequent, 1940-1945
1951	Ballywalter
1952	Carnlough

Phase 2 - 1953-1968 - Boys and Girls Camps

	Boys	Girls
1953	Ballywalter	Ballyvester
1954	Ballyvester	Ballyvester
1955	Cloughey	Ballyvester
1956	Knockinelder	Ballyvester
1957	Tyrella	Tyrella, Rathmullan
1958	Kearney - 2 Camps	Ballyvester
1959	Tyrella	Tyrella, Rathmullen
1960	Knockinelder	Ballyvester
1961	Tyrella	Tyrella, Rathmullan
1962	Tyrella	Tyrella, Rathmullan
1963	Ballygalley	Brown's Bay
1964	Tyrella	Newcastle
1965	Tyrella	Newcastle
1966	Tyrella	Newcastle
1967	Dunseverick	Newcastle - 2 camps
1968	Tyrella	Newcastle - 2 camps

Phase 3 - 1969-1978 - Boys and Girls Camps with Inter-Camp Visits

	Boys	Girls
1969	Castlerock	Portrush - 2 Camps
1970	Castlerock	Portrush - 2 Camps
1971	Castlerock	Portrush
1972	Castlerock	Portrush, Glenmanus
1973	Castlerock	Portrush, Glenmanus
1974	Tollymore FP	Portrush, Glenmanus
1975	Dunseverick	Castlerock, Hazlett Primary
1976	Carnlough	Carnlough Primary School
1977	Carnlough	Castlerock, Hazlett Primary
1978	Ballycastle	Portrush, Ballywillan

Phase 4 - 1979-1985 - Joint Mixed Camps

1979	Westcoats, Lanarkshire
1980	Sligo
1981	Sligo
1982	Waterford
1983	Ecclefechan
1984	Sligo
1985	Dunblane

Phase 5 - 1986-1990 - Juniors and Seniors Camps

	Juniors	Seniors
1986	Dunblane	Elim Bible College, Surrey
1987	Berwick-U-Tweed	Paris
1988	Castle Douglas	Sunbury, Surrey
1989	Castle Douglas	Paris
1990	Sligo	Bryn-Y-Groes, Bala

Phase 6 - 1991 on - Juniors, Inters and Seniors Camps

	Juniors	Inters	Seniors
1991	Newcastle, Co Down	Alva, Clack'shire	Seven Oaks, Kent
1992	Bushmills, Co Antrim	Waterford	Paris
1993	Kilbroney, Rostrevor	Castle Douglas	Bala, North Wales
1994	Kilbroney, Rostrevor	Sligo	
1995	Kilbroney, Rostrevor	Ayr	Ayr
1996	Kilbroney, Rostrevor	Sligo	Bandon, Cork
1997	Kilbroney, Rostrevor	Ayr	Bandon, Cork
1998	Kilbroney, Rostrevor	Ayr	Ballyduff, Kerry
1999	Coleraine HS	Ayr	Middletown, Cork
2000	Coleraine HS	Avoca, Wicklow	Baambrugge, N'lands
2001	Coleraine HS	Avoca, Wicklow	Baambrugge, N'lands
2002	Coleraine HS	Arbroath, Angus	Coleraine
2003	Dunluce HS	Avoca, Wicklow	Greystones
2004	Dunluce HS	Newtownstewart	
2005	Dunluce HS, B'mills	Avoca, Wicklow	Stowmarket, Suffolk
2006	Dunluce HS, B'mills	Gartan, Donegal	Carrigart, Donegal
2007	Dunluce HS, B'mills	Rostrevor	Carrigart, Donegal
2008	Dunluce HS, B'mills	Bandon, Cork	Caraig Eden, Greystones
2009	Dunluce HS, B'mills	Castle Island, Erne	Castle Island, Erne
2010	Dunluce HS, B'mills	Coleraine,	Carrigart, Donegal
2011	Dunluce HS, B'mills	Moyallen, Portadown	Kinvara, Galway
2012	Dunluce HS, B'mills	Moyallen, Portadown	Rathdrum, Wicklow
2013	Dunluce HS, B'mills	Moyallen, Portadown	Carrigart, Donegal
2014	Dunluce HS, B'mills	Ballyclabber RPCI	Ballyclabber RPCI
2015	Dunluce HS, B'mills	Moyallen, Portadown	Newcastle, Co Down

Endnotes

Endnotes

[1] S W Murray, *W. P. Nicholson, Flame for God and Ulster*, The Presbyterian Fellowship, 1973, p 27.

[2] *Assembly's College* (now Union Theological College) was the most commonly used name for the College, the official designation being *The Presbyterian College, Belfast*. See Robert Allen, *The Presbyterian College Belfast*, Centenary Volume 1853-1953, William Mullan & Son Ltd, 1954, pp 298-299.

[3] The daughter of the Norman, Henry I, Matilda (Maud) married Geoffrey, Count of Anjou, France. Their son became Henry II. Geoffrey was called *Plantagenet* because he wore a sprig of the broom plant, *planta genesta*, in his cap. The Plantagenets ruled from 1154-1399.

[4] W J Grier, *The Origin and Witness of the Irish Evangelical Presbyterian Church*, pp 6-9.

[5] See Finlay Holmes, *Our Irish Presbyterian Heritage*, pp 62-63, for a treatment of the practice of the early Ulster Presbyteries on the matter of subscription.

[6] In the *Irish Evangelical* issues of February and March 1933, W J Grier presented Robert Blair's own account of the Lord's blessing on his ministry in Bangor and other places, and on that of his colleagues in the ministry.

[7] For an excellent summary of the Puritan movement see *The Story of the Puritans, Who were they? What did they accomplish? Why should we listen to them today?*, Erroll Hulse, Chapel Library, 30 pp.

[8] James VI of Scotland (1567-1625)

[9] See, for example, *www.bbc.co.uk/history/british/plantation/planters/es10.shtm*

[10] Cromwell's campaign in Ireland has generated much historical debate. A minority view is taken by the Irish author and columnist, Tom Reilly, in *Cromwell: an Honourable Enemy-the Untold Story of the Cromwellian Invasion of Ireland*, 1999, published to mark the 400th anniversary of Cromwell's birth. Reilly's "honourable" views have been rejected by various academics.

[11] James Edward failed to overthrow George I in the Jacobite Rebellion of 1715 and became known as the 'Old Pretender'. His son, Charles Edward – 'Bonnie Prince Charlie', the 'Young Pretender' also failed, in 1745-46. His final defeat was by the Duke of Cumberland at *Culloden*, 1746.

[12] Mary's sister Anne reigned 1702-1714. By 1700, Anne's only surviving child had died so the Act of Settlement, 1701, settled the succession to the English-Irish thrones on the House of Hanover, the nearest Protestant relatives of the Stuarts, and its non-Roman Catholic heirs. It was extended to Scotland in 1707. So, in 1714, the throne passed to George of Hanover, the great-grandson of James I. He became George I, the first Hanovarian monarch. Queen Victoria of the Hanovarian line married Prince Albert of Saxe-Coburg & Gotha in 1840. Their son reigned as Edward VII 1901-1910, the only Monarch of the Saxe-Coburg & Gotha line. His son, George V, changed the family name to the House of Windsor in 1917, during the first World War.

[13] *Filioque* (and the Son) was argued by Augustine and others on the basis that the Son was wholly consubstantial with the Father. It was added at the Synod of Toledo, Spain, in 589 AD and after it *filioque* began to appear in the text of the Nicene Creeds. The fuller Niceno-Constantinopolitan Creed with the *filioque* addition is often printed as the Nicene Creed. See Donald Macleod, *Shared Life*, Christian Focus Publications, PB, 1994, pp 37-45.

[14] The Glorious Revolution of 1689 leading to the *Revolution Settlement* for Scotland in 1690.

[15] *History of the Presbyterian Church in Ireland*, James Seaton Reid, D.D., M.R.I.A., Vol III, Second Edition, Tentmaker Publications, 1998, pp 155-156.

[16] *Ibid*, p 156.

[17] *Ibid*, pp 158-159.

[18] Rev. T Hamilton DD, *History of the Irish Presbyterian Church*, Special Edition 1887, p 116.

[19] Halliday said: "My refusal to declare my assent does not proceed from my disbelief of the important truths contained in the Westminster Confession, the contrary of which, by word and writing, I have often declared, as this venerable body can bear me witness; but my scruples are against the submitting to human tests of divine truth, when imposed as a necessary term

of Christian and ministerial communion, especially in a great number of extra-essential truths, without the knowledge or belief of which men may be entitled to the favour of God and the hopes of eternal life, and, according to the laws of the gospel, to Christian and ministerial communion." Webster's *History of the Presbyterian Church in America*, p 99.

[20] Rev. T Hamilton DD, *History of the Irish Presbyterian Church*, Special Edition 1887, pp 129-130.

[21] Rev. David Stewart, M.A., *A Short History of The Presbyterian Church in Ireland*, p 115.

[22] Arnold Dallimore, *George Whitefield*, Volume 1, Banner of Truth, Reprinted 1979, p 305

[23] Robert Buchanan, D.D., *The Ten Years' Conflict*, p 103.

[24] Robert Buchanan, D.D., *The Ten Years' Conflict*, pp 150-151, citing Rev. E Sydney's *Life of Sir Richard Hill (1733-1808), Tory Member of Parliament for Shropshire 1780-1806*. He was a supporter of George Whitefield and wrote religious tracts.

[25] Robert Buchanan did not favour this secession, essentially because the constitution of the church was sound and the grievances resulted from the mal-administration of the "prevailing party." Only some of the Evangelical party seceded. See *The Ten Years' Conflict*, pp 153 ff. Several Irish Presbyterian historians regard the work of Secession Ministers in Ireland very favourably.

[26] Finlay Holmes, *Our Irish Presbyterian Heritage*, p 69.

[27] "The lamentable divisions of Scottish Presbyterianism were beginning to heal. The Secession Church of 1733 had split over the Burgess Oath in 1747 into Burghers and Anti-Burghers. These bodies divided again, the Burghers, in 1799, into Auld Licht Burghers and New Licht Burghers; and the Anti-Burghers in 1806 into Auld Licht Anti-Burghers and New Licht Anti-Burghers. Now the movement went into reverse. The Auld Licht Burghers returned to the Church of Scotland in 1839, to become part of the Free Church of Scotland in 1843. The New Licht Burghers and New Licht Anti-Burghers came together in 1820 to form the United Secession Church. In 1847 the Relief Church and the United Secession Church joined as the United Presbyterian Church. In 1852 the majority of the Auld Licht Anti-Burghers who had stood out from the union of 1806 joined the Free Church of Scotland." G N M Collins, *The Heritage of our Fathers*, Chapter 11, Ebb-Tide Sets In.

[28] Rev. David Stewart, B.A., D.D., *The Seceders in Ireland*, PHSI, 1950, p 27.

[29] *Ibid*, p 65.

[30] *Ibid*, p 71.

[31] Rev. David Stewart, M.A., *A Short History of The Presbyterian Church in Ireland*, p101.

[32] William Thomas Latimer, *A History of the Irish Presbyterians*, 1902, pp 323-324

[33] For further information please see: www.rpc.org

[34] W J Grier, The Origin and Witness of the Irish Evangelical Presbyterian Church, p 8.

[35] See R. Finlay Holmes, *Henry Cooke*, p 1 for a brief discussion on Cooke's year of birth—1783 or 1788.

[36] I cannot trace the origin of this expression. Many connect with John 4:23, "But the hour cometh, and now is, ..." William Yancey is reported to have said about Jefferson Davis, President-elect of the Confederacy in 1861: "The man and the hour have met." Just an old English proverb?

[37] Finlay Holmes, *Henry Cooke*, Christian Journals Limited, 1981, p 22.

[38] There were prominent United Irishmen sympathies among the founders. The United Irishmen was a body formed in 1791 by Wolfe Tone and others to achieve Roman Catholic emancipation with Protestant cooperation. It desired complete independence from Britain and staged an unsuccessful rebellion in 1798. This was followed by the Act of Union in 1800.

[39] Finlay Holmes, *Henry Cooke*, Christian Journals Limited 1981, p 32.

[40] Rev. T Hamilton DD, *History of the Irish Presbyterian Church*, Special Edition 1887, p153.

[41] An anecdote from the period: in 1827, when the Cooke-Montgomery conflict was moving towards its climax, Dr John MacDonald, the 'Apostle of the North' from Ferintosh in Ross-shire, was preaching at Bandon, Co Cork. He came at the invitation of Episcopal clergy, who were keen for the Gospel to be preached in Gaelic. From his base at Bandon, Dr MacDonald went on two evangelistic tours, one to towns and villages within 20 miles, and the other to Bantry. Despite strong opposition from the priests, people crowded the churches, receptive to the message. Once, when preaching on the parable of the Good Samaritan, he said that he

would not at that time be dealing with the reason why the priest had passed the injured man by. However, a young man in the congregation stood up and supplied it: "It was because he knew that the thieves had left no money in his pocket"!

[42]Rev. David Stewart, M.A., *A Short History of The Presbyterian Church in Ireland*, p 122.

[43]*History of the Presbyterian Church in Ireland*, James Seaton Reid, D.D., M.R.I.A., Vol III, Second Edition, Tentmaker Publications, 1998, pp 489-490.

[44]President of the Faculty of Divinity since 1847, Cooke continued as President of the College until 1868. 'President' became 'Principal' in 1924.

[45]W J Grier, *The Origin and Witness of the Irish Evangelical Presbyterian Church*, Evangelical Book Shop, Belfast, 1945, p 9.

[46]W J Grier did a four-part series on the 1859 Revival in the *Irish Evangelical*, January-April 1959.

[47]Finlay Holmes, *Henry Cooke*, Christian Journals Limited, 1981, pp 21-22.

[46]*Record of the Trial of Rev. Prof. J. E. Davey*, p 197.

[49]Thomas Hamilton, *History of Presbyterianism in Ulster*, Abridged Edition, Mourne Missionary Trust, 1982, pp 149-150.

[50]Rev. T Hamilton DD, *History of the Irish Presbyterian Church*, Special Edition 1887, p 192.

[51]*History of the Presbyterian Church in Ireland*, James Seaton Reid, D.D., M.R.I.A., Vol III, Second Edition, Tentmaker Publications, 1998, pp 248-249.

[52]William Thomas Latimer, in *A History of the Irish Presbyterians*, 1902, p 342. I am greatly indebted to my 'kinsman' Peter Frizelle for drawing my attention to Latimer's prayer a number of years ago.

[53]David B Calhoun, *Princeton Seminary, The Majestic Testimony, 1869-1929*, Volume 2, p 395.

[54]Lefferts A Loetscher, *The Broadening Church*, University of Pennsylvania Press, Philadelphia.

[55]Stephen Tracey, minister of Rockmount, Maine, Orthodox Presbyterian Church, was minister of Omagh Evangelical Presbyterian Church 1990-2001.

[56]*Ibid*, p 131.

[57]*Ibid*, p 59.

[58]*Ibid*, pp 94 and 117.

[59]Broad Churchism and the Briggs Case, *Presbyterian Journal*, May 18, 1893, p 307, quoted by Loetscher, p 59.

[60]Following the Church of Scotland 'Disruption' in 1843 which brought the Free Church of Scotland into existence, The Free Church opened three colleges – Aberdeen in 1843, Edinburgh in 1846 and Glasgow in 1856. It relinquished the Aberdeen and Glasgow Colleges to the United Free Church as part of the 1909 settlement. See Endnote 66.

[61]Rev. W J Grier, *Origin and Witness of the Irish Evangelical Church*, p 10-11.

[62]Finlay Holmes, *Our Irish Presbyterian Heritage*, p 153. Holmes at this point refers by endnote to Allen, *The Presbyterian College*, p 187.

[63]James Montgomery Boice, *Foundations of the Christian Faith*, p 70.

[64]Robert Watts, D.D., Professor of Systematic Theology in the General Assembly's College, Belfast, *The Newer Criticism and the Analogy of the Faith*, p xiii-xiv.

[65]D K Paton described the mission of the Higher Critics like this: "Their work, briefly stated, is nothing less than an endeavour to prove that the Old Testament Scriptures—and these Scriptures are acknowledged to be the same now as in the time of our Lord—are unreliable; that they are largely composed of legend and myth; that the historical, prophetical, and other writings of the Book are full of mistakes and errors; and that in not a few instances the reputed authors of the books of the Old Testament are not the real authors. D K Paton, *The Higher Criticism: the Greatest Apostacy of the Age*, Passmore and Alabaster, p 10. Paton was a Presbyterian layman. His book received considerable acclaim and went to a "New and Larger Edition – Completing Twenty-Fourth Thousand" in 1898. Our copy bears the ownership signature of J H Gillespie, July 1927, and a Bible Standards League sticker.

R L Dabney concludes his *Refutation of Prof. W. Robertson Smith*, with a warning: "Finally, while we do not presume to question the personal sincerity of Mr. Smith's protestations of his own confidence in the substance of the Bible as containing a divine religion, we warn him that few who adopt his principles of criticism will think that they can consistently stop where he stops. The Germans whom he follows do not think so. Their first principle is, that the supernatural is incredible. The very aim of their policy in adopting a method so rash is, to be able thereby to eliminate this supernatural out of the Scriptures. And such will be the tendency wherever such methods are used. The result towards which they incline is virtual infidelity." *Refutation of Prof. W Robertson Smith*, Discussions of Robert Lewis Dabney, Volume 1, pp 438-439.

Professor Robert Dick Wilson of Princeton sums up his assessment of Higher Criticism: "Let us not grovel for the beetles and the earth worms of almost forgotten faiths which may perchance be discovered beneath the stones and sod of the Old Testament, while the violets and the lilies-of-the-valley of a sweet and lowly faith are in bloom on every page and every oracle revealed within the Word of God is jubilant with songs of everlasting joy. The true religion of Israel came down from God arrayed in the beautiful garments of righteousness and life. We cannot substitute for this heaven-made apparel a robe of human manufacture, however fine it be." Robert Dick Wilson, Ph.D., D.D., Professor of Semitic Philology in Princeton Theological Seminary, *Is the Higher Criticism Scholarly?*, pp 61-62.

[66] Magee also prepared students for the Presbyterian Ministry. "In 1845, Mrs Martha Magee endowed the College with her name and a substantial bequest to establish an institution in Ireland to prepare entrants for the Presbyterian ministry. The land was provided by the city of Londonderry. Twenty years later, Magee College opened the doors of the present elegant Gothic building (designed by the Dublin architect Gribben and built, on the expressed wish of the trustees, in Scottish freestone). ...
In 1880, new impetus was given to the educational provision at Magee College by its incorporation into the newly-formed Royal University of Ireland. Red brick professional houses, which 100 years later were to accommodate the work of the growing faculties, were added progressively to the site. Student numbers grew and by the turn of the century Magee College was, in terms of its student population, half the size of the then Queen's College, Belfast and larger than the Colleges at Cork and Galway. However, at that time the Royal University was replaced by the National University of Ireland, a watershed in the history of Magee College, bringing to an end its first flourishing phase of development. The College failed to join either the new institution or The Queen's University, Belfast, which was formed in 1908. Instead, Magee College established a relationship with [Trinity College Dublin by which] Magee students completed their third and fourth years of university at TCD and had conferred upon them degrees of Trinity College." Magee College was incorporated into the New University of Ulster in 1969. (http://library.ulster.ac.uk/magee/history.htm)
[67] Rev. W J Grier, *Origin and Witness of the Irish Evangelical Church*, pp 11-12.
[68] Dale Ralph Davis, *Joshua, No Falling Words*, Christian Focus Publications, 2000, p 135.
[69] In simple terms this meant that congregational property passed to the Free Church in cases where, at 30 October 1900 (the effective date of the Act), at least one third of the total members or adherents were members or adherents of the Free Church congregation. This effective date was greatly to the disadvantage of the Free Church for its membership had grown significantly since 1900, yet the settlement was not completed until 1909. The Free Church gave up its Colleges at Glasgow and Aberdeen to the United Free Church but claimed the historic and strategic New College building on the Mound in Edinburgh with its offices, assembly hall and college. The Commission resolved matters by allocating the offices to the Free Church for its college and offices, and the college and assembly hall to the United Free Church.
[70] Rev. W J Grier, *Origin and Witness of the Irish Evangelical Church*, p 15.
[71] Robert Allen, *The Presbyterian College Belfast 1853-1953* (1954), p 256.
[72] The statement was expanded in the 1948 Code: "The Presbyterian Church in Ireland has, under the guidance of the Holy Spirit, the inherent right, free from interference by civil authority, but under the safeguards for deliberate action and legislation provided by the Church itself, to frame or adopt its subordinate standards, to declare the sense in which it understands its Confession of Faith, to modify the forms of expression therein, or to formulate other doctrinal statements, and to define the relation thereto of its office-bearers and members, but always in agreement with the Word of God and the fundamental doctrines of the Christian faith contained in the said Confession, of which agreement the Church shall be the sole judge,

and with due regard to liberty of opinion in points which do not enter into the substance of the Faith."

[73] *Westminster Confession of Faith*, 1,10. The whole of Chapter 1 has a direct bearing on the issue. Section 4 reads: "The authority of the holy scripture, for which it ought to be believed and obeyed, dependeth not upon the testimony of any man or church, but wholly upon God, (who is truth itself,) the author thereof; and therefore it is to be received, because it is the word of God." The reference in Section 5 again links the Spirit with the Word: "the inward work of the Holy Spirit, bearing witness by and with the word in our hearts." See booklet by Rev. Warren W Porter, *Articles Declaratory – Some Questions and Answers*, 1971, Q & A 9, for a defence of the 1911 wording, whilst acknowledging that: "Undoubtedly the paragraph would be improved by some phrase which would make it clear that the "guidance of the Spirit of God" is to be found in Holy Scripture …".

[74] *The Code of the Presbyterian Church in Ireland* 1948, p 4.

[75] Finlay Holmes, *Our Irish Presbyterian Heritage*, p 155.

[76] The main sources for the O'Neill case are W J Grier, *Origin and Witness of the Irish Evangelical Church*, pp 18-23, and a paper on the case by Professor W P Addley, *The Heresy Hunt—Was O'Neill a Heretic?* from which most references to minutes and correspondence are taken.

[77] **1 Pantheism**

O'Neill: Out of Himself for a wise purpose God created men. Evil has its being in God's eternity. To use a partial illustration of this mystery, the plague bacillus comes straight from the same Father, from whose heart and mind are derived the science and the sacrifice that will in time without fail save life from its attacks.

Hunter's interpretation: All things are in God. Even evil may be said to have "its being in God's eternity." Man was made "out of" God. Hunter added that, "these are the tenets of pantheism, and in perfect consistency with it are the other positions of Mr. O'Neill."

2 The Estate of Innocency

O'Neill: Having risen out of a lower order of beings the condition of our life as rational creatures is moral conflict, and the fact of sin is universal. For, in order to become human, an ideal was required, which, being implanted within the framework of the lower nature, produced the law of sin in our members.

Hunter's interpretation: Man began his career on earth in a sinful condition, and not in a state of innocency.

3 Divine Vengeance

O'Neill: Can the horror of cruelty be overcome by a love which refuses to resist the evil? It is at any rate certain that there is no other way. Vengeance is out of place in the divine government. Not even the might of the worst man's fiendishness can for ever withstand the omnipotent attraction of His suffering love.

Hunter's interpretation: Towards unrepentant evil there is no vengeance in the Godhead. The impenitent have nothing to fear from God.

4 The Way of Salvation

O'Neill: How is the complete victory to be secured? The only answer to this supreme question is the command of Christ, "Resist not evil." There is the secret of the divine method. However limited the success hitherto attained by God through His Son's non-resistance of evil men, we are at least driven to admit that there is no other successful way.

Hunter's Interpretation: The way of salvation is not through our Lord suffering in the room of the sinner but only in His suffering at the hands of the sinner.

5 Christ's Infallibility

O'Neill: If the coming of the kingdom is sudden, we need not expect it to be universal. Had the kingdom come, as Christ perhaps anticipated, within a few years of His death … Christ's outlook was influenced by His environment. The religious Jews in despair of the unrighteousness of social arrangements, had pictured the overthrow of the present world-order and the establishment of a new earth by the intervention of God. This apocalyptic pessimism had a core of earnest faith. Jesus accepted the scheme as He found it, shaping His plans in accordance with it.

Hunter's interpretation: Our Lord Jesus Christ was not infallible. Even when we know His very words we cannot depend on them as an accurate presentation of spiritual things.

[78] The infant death of his nephew, John, born in Manchuria in 1905 would have given James Hunter a 'fellow feeling' with the experience of the O'Neills.

[79] See Robert Allen, *The Presbyterian College Belfast, Centenary Volume 1853-1953*, p 240.

[80] Rev. W J Grier, *Origin and Witness of the Irish Evangelical Church*, pp 21-23:

By appointment of the General Assembly of the Irish Presbyterian Church 15 lectures on "Comparative Religion and Christian Missions" were delivered by Mr. O'Neill during the session 1924-1925 to the students of the Belfast Presbyterian College. The bulk of the material of these lectures was issued in book form in 1925 under the title "The Quest for God in China." The first sentence of the preface of this book of Mr. O'Neill's is, "Those who are determined to find the beliefs of other people altogether wrong are recommended not to read this book." When brought to the test of Holy Scripture, Mr. O'Neill's beliefs as expressed in this book *are* "altogether wrong."

Mr. O'Neill pours scorn on the teaching of the Shorter Catechism about the Fall; pronounces a great panegyric on Gautama Buddha, founder of Buddhism, a man who propagated a faith which had no God, no prayer, no cheer, only austerities and at last annihilation; is very enthusiastic in wishing God-speed to Irish Priests and Christian Brothers, missionaries to China, in "winning 5,000,000 Chinese souls to the Roman Catholic Church"; tells how he had a Mahommedan Mullah (teacher) as speaker at a special evangelistic service in his church in Manchuria; quotes with approval a reference to Gandhi as "the greatest living Indian Christian"; tells that he addressed a Buddhist Conference for half an hour setting forth his beliefs and that the Buddhist chairman, in answer to his question if he had said anything unsuitable, replied "Not at all"; tells how the statue of the Buddhist goddess Kwanyin filled him with "great delight"; says that "the higher faiths of Asia are partial revelations of Eternal Reality" (as a sample of the higher faiths he gives Zoroastrianism, which teaches that the good Spirit is not really supreme, because from the beginning of time there existed a coequal evil Spirit); and takes his stand as an out-and-out pacifist glorying in the Copec reports of 1924, which, he says, opened a new era in the history of the church with the declaration that "all war is contrary to the Spirit and teaching of Jesus Christ."

Note especially the statement by Mr. O'Neill on page 260 of his book: "Now consider Jesus. When we say that He is God the Son, what do we mean? The core of the mighty affirmation made by the Council of Nicaea in A.D. 325, was strictly speaking, a statement of faith regarding the Divine Being, whom no man has ever seen."

Actually the core of the mighty affirmation of the Council of Nicaea was the true deity of Jesus Christ, *whom men have seen*. The Council was summoned just because of the controversy with the Arians as to the true deity of Jesus Christ. This was the question so warmly discussed at the meetings of the Council and this was the question with which their affirmation dealt. Here is their affirmation:—

"We believe in one God, the Father Almighty, Maker of all things visible and invisible. And in one Lord Jesus Christ, the Son of God, begotten of the Father, God of God, Light of Light, very God of very God, begotten, not made, being of one substance with the Father; by whom all things were made in heaven and on earth; who for us men, and for our salvation, came down and was incarnate and was made man; he suffered, and the third day he rose again, ascended into heaven; from hence he cometh to judge the quick and the dead. And in the Holy Ghost."

On page 262 Mr. O'Neill says, "The Father of Jesus is God and there is no other God." On page 260 he says, "Now consider Jesus. When we say that He is God the Son, what do we mean? ... We cannot prove that the unknown Source and Goal of all things lives and works with no other personality than that of Jesus Christ of Nazareth. We cannot prove it, but we can believe—can we really believe?—that God is like Christ."

These statements of Mr. O'Neill's might very well be from the lips of a present-day Unitarian. Yet though Mr. O'Neill's beliefs are "altogether wrong," the Irish Presbyterian Faculty considered him a man of pre-eminent attainments in Theology and gave him the degree of D.D. in 1933, and the General Assembly without a single dissenting voice appointed him its Moderator in 1936.

[81] Mark O'Neill, *Frederick – The Life of My Missionary Grandfather in Manchuria*, Joint Publishing (H.K.) Co., Ltd, pp 111-112.

[82] Robert Allen, *The Presbyterian College Belfast 1853-1953* (1954), p 256.
[83] *Ibid*, p 256.
[84] Our disagreement with aspects of FWS O'Neill's theology in no way detracts from his enormous contribution to China during the first half of the 20th century. We acknowledge also the personal and family cost he endured. The Chinese Government awarded him an Order of the Striped Tiger Medal for his work with the Chinese Labour Corps of 96,000 people who assisted the Allied Forces in France and Belgium from 1917 to 1919. His grandson, Mark O'Neill, handed it over to the Presbyterian Historical Society of Ireland in 2013.
[85] Presbyterian Church of England, Publication Department, [191-?]. There was a second impression in 1926. Mr McNeill was Minister of Claughton, Birkenhead before coming to Rostrevor – *A History of Congregations in the Presbyterian Church in Ireland 1610-1982*, p 430, 740. He published at least 3 other books of children's addresses, ibid, p 430.
[86] Rev. W J Grier, *Origin and Witness of the Irish Evangelical Church*, pp 28-29
[87] Finlay Holmes, *Our Irish Presbyterian Heritage*, p 153-154.
[88] See Robert Allen, *The Presbyterian College, Belfast, 1853-1953*, p 150.
[89] J H Gillespie wrote *Faith in an Unchanging Vesture* between the June 1927 Appeal to the General Assembly and the formation of *The Irish Evangelical Church* in October 1927. He used the chapter headings of the *Changing Vesture* as his own review structure. Referring in his Introduction to "the controversy which is found all over the world between 'new' and 'old' methods of thought" he goes on: "the present booklet brings, in simple non-technical language, concrete evidence of what is going on in the minds of the rival schools." The book does engage with Davey on the philosophical plane but majors on Scripture as it deals with a wide range of quotations from the chapters of the *Changing Vesture*.
[90] J E Davey, M.A., B.D., *The Changing Vesture of the Faith*, pp 37-38.
[91] *Ibid*, p 21
[92] *Ibid*, p 24.
[93] *Ibid*, pp 28-30.
[94] *Ibid*, p 25.
[95] *Ibid*, pp 7-8.
[96] *Ibid*, pp 35-37.
[97] Ibid, pp 245-246
[98] John Murray, *Collected Writings, Volume 1 – The Claims of Truth, The Redeemer of God's Elect*, Banner of Truth, 1976, p 29
[99] Donald Macleod, *Behold your God*, Christian Focus Publications, 1990, p 20-21.
[100] "In these addresses I have sought to show, in the first place, that it is reasonable to believe in God as Christ preached Him and believed on Him; reasonable to believe that He is one, rather than to accept the so-called atheism or agnosticism, but the actual polytheism, of modern unbelief, with its acceptance of a multitude of unsystematised principles, values, powers, and the like; reasonable to believe in His being, His personality, His goodness, His Fatherhood, His perfection and all-sufficiency, otherwise we discover our own actual or potential superiority to God, and invert our whole universe ...

"I have sought in the second place to show that the conception of God given us by Christ satisfies, and is necessary to satisfy, our thought, our aspirations, our spiritual, moral and physical needs, necessary for health of body, mind and soul, and necessary to the best life as fulfilling the true ideals of the gentleman or the sportsman ...

"I have sought, in the third place, to show that this faith in God through Jesus Christ is effective in practical life, that it works when actually tested, whether by Christ Himself, or the apostolic community, or by the martyrs and saints of the ages, or by ordinary men and women like ourselves; but I have tried to emphasise the view that a true faith will not merely ask, but venture, and that only in venture will real satisfaction and assurance be found ...

"And, finally, I have sought to show that this conception of God, given in and through Christ, is enough, and more than enough, for us to proceed with as the solution of all our problems, being not only the best we know, but the best we can conceive. Its finality lies in its potential universality, and in the spirit of Jesus Christ through which it found, and finds, expression. Not the forms but the spirit abides, and continual restatement and missionary work are both essential to its true finality and its ultimate victory, and to its actual power in any age

or environment. We must live our faith; there is no alternative for a living Church."
J Ernest Davey, M.A., B.D., *Our Faith in God Through Jesus Christ*, SCM 1922, pp 137-139

[101] William Thomas Latimer, in *A History of the Irish Presbyterians*, 1902, p 342.

[102] Robert Allen, *The Presbyterian College, Belfast, 1853-1953*, p 256.

[103] A small, brass-clip file has been preserved: "Testimonials of James Hunter MA, Minister of Dundela Presbyterian Church, Belfast." It contains: "Honours and Prizes gained during Academic Career" (nearly 30), and eight testimonials from: *Rev. H M Williamson*, Ex-Moderator of the General Assembly, 1896, *Matthew Leitch*, Assembly's College, 1897, *Robert Watts*, Assembly's College, *Rev. J L Porter*, President, Queen's College Belfast, 1887, *Hastings Crossley*, Queens' College (formerly of Royal University of Ireland), 1887, *Thomas W Dougan*, Queen's College, Belfast, *J MacMaster*, Magee College, 1887, *C D Yonge*, Queen's College, Belfast, 1887.

[104] In recent years it has been the premises of Hood & Co.

[105] John was born to John and Catherine in 1905 but died during his first year.

[106] Robert Allen, *The Presbyterian College Belfast 1853-1953* (1954), includes James Hunter in the Students of Theology for 1883 as MA, RU. (The RU certificates are BA in 1883 and MA in 1886).

[107] Professor of Hebrew at The Presbyterian College, Belfast, 1889-1929. Robert Allen says of him: "… he held and promulgated the very views which both Watts and Murphy (his predecessor) had spent their lives in impugning." Robert Allen, *The Presbyterian College Belfast*, 1853-1953. See Walker, Thomas - Index, p 354, for references.

[108] The *Irish Evangelical*, October 1942, p 1.

[109] Nelson Brown, *Knock Presbyterian Church 1872-1972*, pp 10-11.

[110] "Mr James Hunter crowned a very successful course at his College and University by taking his MA degree last July with First Class Honours in Ancient Classics." Written, 18 May 1887, from Magee College, Londonderry, by J MacMaster, Esq, D Lit, Professor of Latin and Greek, Magee College, Londonderry; Fellow of the Royal University of Ireland. Evidently Hunter took some part of the course at the Magee campus of the Royal University of Ireland.

[111] Robert Allen, *The Presbyterian College Belfast 1853-1953* (1954), p 256.

[112] Nelson Brown, *Knock Presbyterian Church 1872-1972*, p 10.

[113] *A History of Congregations in the Presbyterian Church in Ireland 1610-1982*, P.H.S.I., p 177.

[114] Nelson Brown, *Knock Presbyterian Church 1872-1972*, p 12.

[115] Presbyterian Church in Ireland, Mission Board Minutes, 14 May 1902.

[116] *A History of Congregations in the Presbyterian Church in Ireland 1610-1982*, P.H.S.I., pp 715-717.

[117] Makemie began studies at the University of Glasgow in 1675 and was ordained as an evangelist to the new world by the north Donegal Presbytery of Lagan, in 1682 in response to a call from Maryland for a Minister to settle there. In 1681 local Ministers were found guilty of holding a fast over the oppression of Presbyterians by the ecclesiastical hierarchy. They were confined until they would pay the huge fine of £20 each and sign an undertaking not to offend similarly again, but released after eight months notwithstanding their refusal to comply. It was during this situation that Makemie was ordained and commissioned. He preached in New England, Maryland, Virginia, North Carolina and Barbados. He founded the first Presbyterian congregation in America at Snowhill, Maryland in 1684 and in 1706 the first Presbytery - Pennsylvania. He was arrested in 1707 by the Governor of New York for preaching in a private home in Long Island without a licence. He successfully defended himself with an appeal to the English Toleration Act of 1689, but had to pay the substantial costs of his trial. The Republic of Ireland issued a commemorative stamp in 1982.

[118] "Queen's University (abbreviated to "QUB" and widely known as "Queen's") has its roots in the Belfast Academical Institution, which was opened in 1814 and remains as the Royal Belfast Academical Institution. The present university was first chartered as "Queen's College, Belfast" in 1845, when it was associated with the simultaneously founded Queen's College, Cork and Queen's College, Galway as part of the Queen's University of Ireland -- founded in 1845 to encourage higher education for Catholics and Presbyterians as a counterpart to the Trinity College, Dublin, then an Anglican institution. The Irish Universities Act, 1908

dissolved the Royal University of Ireland and created two separate universities - the current National University of Ireland and the Queen's University of Belfast. At its opening in 1849 as a Queen's College, it had 23 professors and 343 students." (http://en.wikipedia.org/wiki/Queen's_University_Belfast)

[119] S. W. Murray, *W. P. Nicholson, Flame for God in Ulster*, p 19.

[120] The December 1959 *Irish Evangelical*, page 6, carries an article: *The Home-Going of Rev. W P Nicholson* [29-10-1959]. In it W J Grier mentions the memorial service in Belfast, 9-11-1959, and notes: "At the request of the secretary of that organisation [Christian Workers' Union] the editor of this magazine gave a brief testimony. It was under the ministry of Mr Nicholson that the editor came to know the Lord in October 1922."

[121] Located in New York harbour about one mile southwest of Manhattan. It was a US immigration station from 1891-1954 and called "The Gateway to the New World." In 1965 the US Government made it part of the Statue of Liberty National Monument with the adjacent Liberty Island where the Statue of Liberty stands.

[122] 'A Testimonial' in *The Law and the Prophets*; Old Testament Studies in honour of Oswald T. Allis, J. H. Skilton, editor, 1974, p 33.

[123] David B Calhoun, *Princeton Seminary*, Volume 2, Banner of Truth, p 348. See also Ned B Stonehouse, *J Gresham Machen*, Banner of Truth, pp 356-360.

[124] Ned B Stonehouse, *J. Gresham Machen, A Biographical Memoir*, Banner of Truth, 1987, p 376.

[125] *The Law and the Prophets*, Old Testament Studies in honour of Oswald T. Allis, edited by John H. Skilton, Presbyterian and Reformed, 1974, p 13.

[126] Banner of Truth, May 1973, p 5.

[127] "The Separateness of the Church", a sermon preached on Matt 5.13 by J Gresham Machen and included in *God Transcendent* (a collection of Machen's addresses) as chapter 12, Banner of Truth, 1982, pb, p115.

[128] *Collected Writings of John Murray*, Vol 1, *The Banner of Westminster Seminary*, p 100.

[129] In addition there were 4 related items between Machen and others and the set of 13 letters between Grier and Prof. N B Stonehouse, 1948-62.

[130] Reference is to Judges 5:23 "'Curse Meroz,' said the angel of the LORD, 'Curse its inhabitants bitterly, Because they did not come to the help of the LORD, To the help of the LORD against the mighty.'" Deborah had pronounced a curse on the Merozites for not joining in the campaign against Sisera. The analogy must have been in use at this time, for Grier also mentioned Meroz in a letter to Machen, 10 May 1926.

[131] S W Murray, *W P Nicholson*, Flame for God in Ulster, p 22-23.

[132] Rev. Prof. Adam Loughridge, *Revivals in Ireland, Part 4*, The Evangelical Presbyterian, May 1983, p 4.

[133] W P Nicholson, *On Towards the Goal*.

[134] David N Livingstone and Ronald A Wells, *Ulster-American Religion*, Notre Dame, 1999, p 107.

[135] Ibid, p 136.

[136] From the Report of William Miller, Secretary, at CWU Annual General Meeting, 22 March 1945. On the history of the CWU he said: "Mr Nicholson's campaigns were held in 1921-22, and in 1923 the leaders of the various Christian Workers' Unions had a meeting and it was felt that the work should be consolidated by forming all the Unions into an Alliance, and its first meeting was held in Derry in 1923." The first extant minutes are of the Alliance Council Meeting, 13 August 1925. We acknowledge with gratitude the willingness of Mr Eric Patterson, a former Secretary, to allow us access to the CWU Minute Book.

[137] David N Livingstone and Ronald A Wells, *Ulster-American Religion*, Notre Dame, 1999, pp 114-115.

[138] J Austin Fulton, *Biography of J Ernest Davey*, p 33.

[139] David N Livingstone and Ronald A Wells, *Ulster-American Religion*, Notre Dame, 1999, p 133.

[140] Andrew Murray, *The Two Covenants and the Second Blessing*, pp 168-169.

[141] Stanley Barnes, *All for Jesus – The Life of W P Nicholson*, Ambassador, pp 23-29. Nicholson's own account that Barnes cites here from the Nicholson sermon *Born-Baptised-Filled*, is clear about Nicholson's distinction between the single 'baptism' and the plurality of 'fillings' of the Spirit, but in pp 28-29 Barnes appears to use both terms interchangeably, or 'filling' in the Nicholson sense of 'baptism', eg final paragraph: "William dated his own effectiveness in his Christian service to that night, seven months after his conversion when he surrendered fully, laid all on the altar of sacrifice and was filled with the Holy Spirit."

[142] In a mission Nicholson concluded in Botanic Avenue Irish Evangelical Church in 1946, since the YMCA Wellington Hall was not available for the second week, Rev. W J Grier obtained agreement from him that 'Second Blessing' teaching would not feature.

[143] J Austin Fulton, *Biography of J Ernest Davey*, p 32.

[144] Stanley Barnes, *All for Jesus*, The Life of W P Nicholson, p 42.

[145] Robert Allen, *The Presbyterian College*, p 256.

[146] For a discussion on Lightfoot's *morphe* argument see Donald Macleod, *The Person of Christ*, IVP, 1998, pp 212-213.

[147] Jim Grier lived at 12 Hatfield Street on the lower Ormeau Road from October 1925 until mid-1927. It later became the home of my maternal grandparents, and the address from which my mother was married. I too watched the cricket *gratis* – in the 1950s and 60s! Rugby was also on show in season.

[148] See, for example, *A New Systematic Theology of the Christian Faith*, Robert L Reymond, Nelson, 1998, pp 593-622.

[149] "At the end of his ministry at Knock [1924] Mr. Hunter joined Ravenhill where he became acquainted with William James Grier ... who attended the church..." (*Ravenhill Presbyterian Church 1898-1998 – Centenary History*, Ivan T Jess, 1997, p 38-39). See also W J Grier, *The Origin and Witness of the Irish Evangelical Presbyterian Church*, Evangelical Book Shop, Belfast, 1945, p 33.

[150] *Northern Whig and Belfast Post* 20 January 1932.

[151] James Hunter, *Five Years Ago and Today*, The Irish Evangelical, July 1932, p 1.

[152] W J Grier, *Irish Evangelical*, "Whose Faith Follow", October 1942, p 2.

[153] *The Presbyterian College Belfast*, Robert Allen, p 257.

[154] "The sub-committee ... had seven meetings, and carefully considered proposed changes: ... one member of the Sub-committee has not acted since February and did not join in the report, but the remaining five members ... submitted a unanimous report." Minutes of the General Assembly of the Presbyterian Church in Ireland, 1926, p 91. (The names listed show that the non-acting member was James Hunter).

[155] Grier said to Machen on 11 June 1926 of this vote: "It was lost by two votes and only for the mistakes of 4 or more commissioners in using wrong voting slips would have been carried."

[156] W J Grier, *Origin and Witness of the Irish Evangelical Church*, pp 30-32.

[157] Although the Liberalism in the PCUSA was forcing itself on to Princeton's agenda by 1926, the soundness of the Faculty and Princeton's Charter still made it the gold standard of orthodoxy. The reorganisation of Princeton was not until 1929.

[158] James Hunter, *Five Years Ago and Today*, The Irish Evangelical, July 1932, p 1. Grier said to Machen on 10 May 1926 about this refusal of Hunter's: "He intends promulgating his charges first."

[159] "A sub-committee of the College Committee held an investigation (!) on Monday, May 24th, 1926, seven students being cited to appear as witnesses. The post-card summoning the present writer was signed by the Rev. A. F. Moody, Convener of the Committee, and bore the words: 'Will you kindly meet the Committee in Room A, Church House, on Monday, 24th inst., at 11-30 o'clock, and bring your Notes of Prof. Haire's Class Lectures.'"

[160] "Dr. John Oman's *Grace and Personality* was the text-book used in Prof. Haire's class in the session 1925-26. Mr. Hunter in SOS No 1 referred to the statement made on page six of this book: 'Under this solvent (of historical investigation) all the infallibilities began to crumble. An infallible Orthodoxy followed an infallible Vicar of Christ, and infallible Scripture an infallible Orthodoxy, an infallible Christ an infallible Scripture.' The first statement made by Mr. Hunter in SOS. No. 1 was: 'Prof. Haire strives to have his students believe that the Bible is not infallible,

and that the Lord Jesus Christ was not infallible.'" *The Origin and Witness of the Irish Evangelical Church*, W J Grier, Evangelical Book Shop, 1945, pp 35-36.

[161] See *Northern Whig and Belfast Post*, Friday 4 June 1926.

[162] W J Grier, *Origin and Witness of the Irish Evangelical Church*, pp 34-37.

[163] James Hunter, *Five Years Ago and Today*, The Irish Evangelical, July 1932, p 1.

[164] Robert Allen, *The Presbyterian College*, p 257. See also Steve Bruce, *God Save Ulster*, p 21.

[165] David N Livingstone and Ronald A Wells, *Ulster-American Religion*, Notre Dame, 1999, p 62.

[166] *Comparisons between Doctrinal Positions of Professor Davey—and the Bible, and Standards of Irish Presbyterian Church.*

The Presbyterian Bible Standards League stands for the—Infallible Truth and Divine Authority of the whole Bible as the supernaturally-inspired Word of God, and for the maintenance of the present Doctrinal Constitution of the Irish Presbyterian Church intact. Its membership is open to all Communicants of that Church who accept and sign the articles of constitution. The minimum annual subscription is 2/6.

[167] See John M Barkley, *The Eldership in Irish Presbyterianism*, pp 111-115.

[168] Austin Fulton, *Biography of J. Ernest Davey* (1970), p 33.

[169] James Hunter, *Five Years Ago and Today*, The Irish Evangelical, July 1932, pp 1-2.

[170] Robert Allen, *The Presbyterian College Belfast*, Centenary Volume 1853-1953, William Mullan & Son Ltd, 1954, p 258, Note 1.

[171] *Record of the Trial of Rev. Prof. J. E. Davey*, p 210.

[172] Robert Allen, *The Presbyterian College Belfast,* Centenary Volume 1853-1953, William Mullan & Son Ltd, 1954, p 257.

[173] Charges 1 and 2 originally had 44 signatories and Charges 3, 4 and 5, 43. The non-signatories were two of the ministers, Rev. Samuel Hanna of Berry Street, Belfast who did not sign Charges 3 and 5, and Rev. John Ross of Ravenhill, Belfast who did not sign Charge 4. The picture is further complicated by deletion lines through the names of signatories tabled on 7 December 1926 and shown as such in the Trial Record: three from Charge 1, three from Charge 2, one from Charge 3, two from Charge 4 and two from Charge 5. Two of the three were the ministers, Hanna and Ross, and the deletions had the effect of removing them from the list of accusers altogether. However, at the first session Hanna complained that he had not given authority for his name to be deleted and the court agreed to rank him as an Accuser, presumably for the three Charges he had signed. Another of the three, an elder, W H Snoddy, complained similarly and was likewise reinstated as an Accuser, presumably, in his case, for all five Charges. Ross did not make a similar complaint at the first session; the attendance is not listed, and he may have been one of the six Witnesses or Accusers who sent apologies. But at the 11th session, dealing with Charge 2, the Court noted the deleting line through his signature on the tabled Charges, and unanimously agreed to treat him as one of the accusers, presumably for the four he had signed. He is listed among the Accusers present at the hearing for Charges 2-5. Another accuser who had come to regret his involvement was released from the proceedings in the first session, and another, one of the JPs, was released later in the course of the first Charge because of his business commitments. All this had the effect of reducing the full list of Accusers to 42.

[174] W J Grier, *The Origin and Witness of the Irish Evangelical Presbyterian Church*, Evangelical Book Shop, Belfast, 1945, p 38.

[175] There was only one quotation in the Charges from the Shorter Catechism. It was in Charge 1 and was extracted from the answer to Question 33, *What is Justification?* The extract in the Charge read: "pardoneth all our sin and accepteth us as righteous in His sight only for the righteousness of Christ imputed to us"; "sin" should have read "sins", and there should have been commas after "sins" and "sight".

[176] *Record of the Trial of Rev. Prof. J. E. Davey*, p 72.

[177] *Ibid*, p 93.

[178] *Ibid*, p 22.

[179] James Hunter, *Five Years Ago and Today*, The Irish Evangelical, July 1932, p 2.

[180] *The Witness*, Friday, June 17, 1927, p 9, column 2.

[181] *Record of the Trial of Rev. Prof. J. E. Davey*. See p 19, Eleventh Session, para 4; p 21, Thirteenth Session, para 3; p 22, Fourteenth Session, para 2 and para 10.

[182] The scope of "ours" is unclear. It certainly referred to Davey's own view but the expression indicates that he felt there was general agreement with him at least in his Church and College. When William Snoddy was examining J W Bruce, 22 02 1927, he asked: "Did he teach you Paul's philosophy of sin was different from his own?" *Record of the Trial of Rev. Prof. J. E. Davey*, p 49.

[183] James Hunter asked Grier: "Did Professor Davey say anything about the feelings and thoughts of our Lord in Gethsemane?" When he repeated the question after the Moderator had overruled an objection to it he substituted "Calvary" for "Gethsemane". Hunter followed with a question about Christ's deity on Calvary. Both Grier's answers related to Calvary but he brought in a Davey reference to the suffering at Gethsemane in the second. *Record of the Trial of Rev. Prof. J. E. Davey*, pp 24-25. It appears that Davey made similar statements about the suffering at both Gethsemane and Calvary. Grier wrote to Machen on 11 December 1925: "Our Professor of Biblical Literature has been giving us some lectures on Gethsemane. He was over at Cambridge recently and delivered a lecture there on the subject. His great contention is that 'if Christ were omniscient then Gethsemane was impossible, as it would be merely like the anaesthetic a patient takes, knowing he must come out all right.' I had a discussion with him afterwards and he said he recognised the consubstantiality of Christ with the Father, but distinguished between essence and attributes—i.e. having the same essence did not mean having the same attributes."

[184] For a discussion on Gethsemane-Calvary see *The Person of Christ*, Donald Macleod, IVP, 1998, pp 173-178.

[185] When the Court was reading back Grier's evidence about his notebook, the Moderator asked: "Mr. Corkey, you are the other man more particularly interested in this. Are you satisfied with the record?" *Record of the Trial of Rev. Prof. J. E. Davey*, p 111.

[186] *Record*, p 3. 'Transference' also appeared in the second and third of the four *Changing Vesture* extracts – see Charge 1, Appendix 1.

[187] J. Ernest Davey, M.A., B.D., *The Changing Vesture of the Faith*, James Clarke & Co, 1923, pp 78-79.

[188] "… if Christ was not our substitute, bearing our guilt and paying our dues, then every human being must carry his or her own sin. Much modern theology seems happy to accept this conclusion. Guilt, it is assumed, is not transferable. But if this is so, redemption is impossible." *Christ Crucified, Understanding the Atonement*, Donald Macleod, IVP, 2014, p 90. See also WCF 2.1, 6.3, 20.1.

[189] Op.Cit. p 80.

[190] The previous paragraph read:
"Yet Protestant theory has asserted that Christ can take our *sin, and* we can take His righteousness, in such a way that the substance of His good will can co-exist with the accidents of our guilt imputed to Him, and the substance of our evil nature co-exist with the accidents of His obedience and righteousness. Apart from the impossibility of thus dividing between substance and accidents, it is important to remember that it is the substance here which matters, and not the accidents. It is my nature, not my guilt for past sins, which most needs attention, not my *sins,* but my *sin,* for sins are but expressions of sin. All good is from God, and in that sense our righteousness must be His, but man's guilt cannot become God's. God may forgive our sin against Himself, *i.e.,* the suffering we have caused Him, He may overrule the effects of our sins for good, but He cannot take from our personalities the fact of our having done them, in which consists our guilt; this guilt He may overlook, but He cannot change it. Our sins may be made of no account for present and future, but they cannot be removed from the past as historical events, though I believe that some day they may cease to exist even for our memories. But if we think of *sin,* and not *sins,* we shall see that what matters is not what we have done, said, or thought, but the will which did these things; if that be regenerated, sin (not sins) may disappear as a fact of consciousness, because it has no further present existence as a state, but it disappears, not by imputation of our past to Christ, and His present to us, but by the simple process of change …"

[191] *Record of the Trial of Rev. Prof. J. E. Davey*, p 34; pp 209-210.

[192] Op. Cit. p 30.

[193] For a discussion of the 'quantitative' question see Donald Macleod, *Christ Crucified, Understanding the Atonement*, IVP, 2014, Crude commercialism?, IVP, pp 235-237: "… the right punishment is the one prescribed by the law, and while that punishment must be proportionate to the crime, it can seldom be its exact equivalent. In the case of sin, and by the decree of the Judge of all the earth, the punishment for sin is clear: 'the wages of sin is death' (Rom 6.23). This, in all its depth and awfulness, is what Christ suffered, and its 'value' lies not in the agonies of the cross being quantitatively equal to the pains of hell, but in the fact this this was the doom prescribed by the law. It was the statutory sentence."

[194] Charles Hodge, *Systematic Theology*, Vol 2, Eerdmans, 1960, pp 470-479.

[195] William Hendriksen, *Romans*, Banner of Truth, 1980, p 194.

[196] *Record of the Trial of Rev. Prof. J. E. Davey*, p 199.

[197] Charles Hodge, Systematic Theology, Volume 3, Eerdmans, pp 163-164.

[198] Charles Hodge: *The Epistle to the Romans*, Remarks, 4, Banner of Truth, 1972, p 76.

[199] An Arminian party in the Dutch Reformed Church. They were adherents of Jacobus Arminius, who died in 1609. They presented their articles of faith for Holland and West Friesland in a petition that became known as the Remonstrance. After a hearing at the Synod of Dort (1618-19), the orthodox position prevailed in the Church. In 1829, after the Cooke-Montgomery clash, the Unitarians of Ulster constituted themselves as the "Remonstrant Synod" which later became a constituent of the Non-Subscribing Presbyterian Church.

[200] Socinianism, after the Italian, Faustus Socinius (1539-1604) is one of the Unitarian Heresies. It patterned itself on the anti-Trinitarian views of Michael Servetus (1511-1553). It accepted the Scriptures as its authority, but by rationalistic interpretation of them, taught: Deity belonged only to God the Father; Jesus Christ was a sinless, outstanding man, divine, but not God; the Holy Spirit was a force or influence, but not a Person and not God. Salvation was effectively by works, imitating the example and ethical teaching of Jesus Christ. Socinianism began in Poland and Transylvania in the 16th century and at one stage is believed to have had a thousand students at its Academy in Racow, Poland. It became an issue in England in the 17th century and was seen to be within the latitudinarian grouping.

[201] Collected Writings of John Murray, 1: The Claims of Truth, Banner of Truth, 1976, p 313.

[202] *Truths we Confess, A Layman's Guide to the Westminster Confession of Faith*, R C Sproul, P&R 2006, Preface, p viii.

[203] THE MODERATOR— Is this the complete book?

MR. GRIER—I had also notes from Professor Davey on Old Testament Biblical Literature.

THE MODERATOR (handling book)— … Am I to understand that a considerable part of the book has been withdrawn from these rings?

MR. GRIER—There has nothing been withdrawn from Professor Davey's notes.

Has there been anything withdrawn since you gave evidence?—

(The witness did not answer).

THE MODERATOR—Answer the question at once and straight?

—(Mr. Grier did not reply).

THE MODERATOR—Has anything been withdrawn from these notes since you gave evidence? Can't you understand the meaning of the English language?

(Mr. Grier remained silent).

THE MODERATOR—I think you are only trifling with us. It is a most contemptible thing that you come to give evidence and cannot answer a question "yes" or "no."

MR. GRIER—I took out my notes on Professor Davey's Old Testament Biblical Literature.

THE MODERATOR—What has the Court to say in regard to these notes?

A MEMBER—Condemn them.

[204] *Record of the Trial of Rev. Prof. J. E. Davey*, p 89.

[205] *Ibid*, p 89.

[206] "Pauline Conception of Atonement. Pauline emphasis on Death of X. Death of X so dwarf the life in Pauline acct that have really a change from Gospel of J to Gospel about Jesus. Paul speaks of 'my Gospel'. Paul's G = Just. by act of acceptance – more an act of identification. This really = the use of word 'faith'. Salvation thro' (1) death to sin (identn + X's death to sin – a death in which we share) Paul had the idea that physical death = wages of human sin.

X in whom no sin died & so broke that law. If the death unto sin summed up by cross, life unto God summed up by resn & ascension. More than spiritual rising. Appears also for Paul's very peculiar conception of sin – physical. McGiffert Ch^{ity} of Ap. Age. Central thing for Paul – Ident-^{n} – not in legal but in concrete sense – mystical union.

"I in you and Christ in them. Paul's Gosp not to do with histal Jesus but et al mystical sacramental. A Christ who came to & departed from this earth – essential thing = union with Him. Not so much something did but something does.

"Paul not systematic. Very hard to fit in all passages + any one theory. Raised again for Justn. Justn bound up + Resn."

[207]REV. WM. CORKEY—You said in evidence that this paragraph —and you made a special point of stating it—that this paragraph was ipsissima verba of Professor Davey's lecture. Was it the ipsissima verba that you took down on that occasion, or was it the ipsissima verba that was corrected? There is a very vital word here "can't"—"can't be lifted off," and the "t" is scored out. Was that scored out in the class or has it been scored out since then?
MR. GRIER—I was in the habit of going through my lectures while my memory was still fresh, because being a fast writer I wanted to make sure that what I got was correct.
REV. WM. CORKEY—And so you wrote the word "can't" and changed it to "can" when your memory was still fresh?
MR. GRIER—I am not sure it was "can't."
THE MODERATOR—Do you mean it never was "can't?"
MR. GRIER—I don't remember that there ever was a "t" there.
REV. WM. CORKEY—Is that a "t" or not a "t?"
MR. GRIER—I cannot say at all.
REV. WM. CORKEY—Was that taken down in the class?
MR. GRIER—Yes.
REV. WM. CORKEY—Was that "t" scored out in the class.
MR. GRIER—No, it was scored out when I was going through it.
REV. WM. CORKEY—In other words the ipsissima verba here is not the ipsissima verba in the class?
MR. GRIER—I would not say that.
REV. DR. GEO. THOMPSON—Can we hear when he changed the "can't" into "can"?
MR GRIER—I would not say I changed it.
REV. WM. CORKEY—When was it changed?
MR. GRIER—I would not say it was "t." The quotation was accepted at the beginning as substantially correct.
REV. WM. CORKEY—There can be no doubt about it that it is "can't."
THE MODERATOR—As far as I can judge it was written "can't." I think two or three of you might see it. It belongs to the Court, not to me.
REV. WM. CORKEY—Have you any explanation, Mr. Grier, to give of these discrepancies?
MR. GRIER—I don't think there are any discrepancies at all.
[208]"Not helping the conservatives was the revelation that Grier had added comments to his notes on Davey's lectures, raising questions of whether the student had doctored the evidence." D G Hart, *Calvinism – A History*, Yale, 2013, p 268. We have no knowledge of Grier adding any comments to his Davey lecture notes and certainly not of a revelation about it. There was no accusation of it at the Heresy Trial of 1927. The 'can't' issue is the only one we are aware of and it was without significance for the outcome of the Trial. If this is what Hart is referring to it is strange that he should bring something so inconsequential into a history of Calvin. The Heresy Trial produced substantive Calvin-related issues but the 'can or can't' diversion was not one of them. W J Grier was a life-long devotee of Calvin and it is particularly regrettable that these inaccurate comments should appear in such a work.
[209]G N M Collins, *Principal John Macleod, D.D*, The Publications Committee of the Free Church of Scotland, 1951, pp 47-49.

After serving in the pastoral ministry of the Free Presbyterian Church until 1905, he [Macleod] moved to the Free Church of Scotland. He and others had dissented from the unwillingness of their own Synod to engage with the Free Church when key Free Church

legislation in 1905 had, in their view, opened the way for a negotiated healing of "the breach between the two branches of the Free Church of Scotland adhering to its Disruption position." (p 90). Macleod was Professor of New Testament at the Free Church College (1906-1913) and became Principal in 1927. He had retained his interest in the Ulster Presbyterian situation and would have known of James Hunter's pro-Free Church stand in 1900-05. "Macleod chose as his favourite mentor in the Gospel, Dr J. B. Stevenson, of the Botanic Avenue Reformed Presbyterian Church. ... Such was Principal Macleod's attachment to Botanic Avenue Church that he regarded the very fabric with affectionate interest. When it was purchased from the Reformed Presbyterians by the Irish Evangelical Church ... [in 1933] he expressed his pleasure that it was still to be a rostrum of the old Faith, and sent a subscription towards the cost of its purchase." (pp 48-49).
(As a result of a 10 year dispute over a Civil Magistrate issue, five ministers, 12 ruling elders and their congregations withdrew from the Reformed Presbyterian Synod of Ireland and formed the Eastern Reformed Presbyterian Synod in 1842. When it united with the General Assembly of the Presbyterian Church in Ireland in 1902, half of its congregations, Botanic Avenue included, returned to the RPCI Synod. So Rev. John Macleod attended Botanic Avenue during the tenure of the Eastern Reformed Presbyterian Synod. See *The Covenanters in Ireland*, Adam Loughridge, Cameron Press, 1984, pp 65-67 and *The Covenanters in Ireland, A History of the Congregations*, Cameron Press, 2010, pp 162-164.)

[210] The word Bolshevik comes from the Russian *bolshinstvo* meaning majority. Lenin led one of the two main groups into which the Russian Social Democratic Labour Party had split in the early 1900s. After his supporters gained a majority in 1903 Lenin began calling them *Bolshevik* and the opposing group *Menshevik* (minority). The Lenin faction became the All Russian Communist (*Bolshevik*) Party in 1918, and its adherents were known as *Bolsheviks* until the name was dropped in the 1950s. Samuel Hanna was here referring to the atheistic doctrines of Communism, known at that time in the English form, Bolshevism.

[211] The Modernist/Bolshevist analogy also appeared in Ulster Pamphlet No 6, page 2. This is one of the two that Hunter did not write. Is this a suggestion that Hanna wrote No 6? W J Grier wrote at length on the Ulster Pamphlets in the *Irish Evangelical*, February and March 1929, but he did not mention Nos 6 and 7.

[212] Ulster pamphlet No 7 is in a different format from the others, approx 3½" wide by 9" long. It was published by the "Spectator", Bangor. It is the address that S G Montgomery gave at a meeting on Tuesday 24 May 1927 in the King's Hall. The address majored on Imputation.

[213] This *No Middle Ground* section was also produced as a card by CSSM who acknowledged the *Moody Bible Institute Monthly* as its source.

[214] The information in this section for Machen's 1927 visit to Belfast is taken from: The Banner of Truth, Issue 235, April 1983: *J Gresham Machen in the United Kingdom: 3*, Geoffrey Thomas, p 28. En route to Belfast, Machen addressed the General Assembly of the Free Church of Scotland, 30 May 1927, on the subject, *What is Christianity?* After Belfast, Machen went to England where he gave 3 lectures to the Bible League of Great Britain, 10 June 1927, *What the Bible Teaches about Jesus*, *The Witness of Paul*, and *The Witness of the Gospels*. These addresses in Scotland and England were reprinted in *What is Christianity?* 1951, and in *J. Gresham Machen, Selected Shorter Writings*, edited by D G Hart, P & R Publishing, 2004.

[215] Grier to Machen 24 March 1927: "and on Lord's Day in one of the churches (Rev. Ross's)".

[216] *Record of the Trial of Rev. Prof. J. E. Davey*, p 168.

[217] *Ibid*, p 169-170.

[218] *Ibid*, p 170.

[219] *Ibid*, p 173.

[220] *Ibid*, p 174-175.

[221] *Ibid*, p 181.

[222] *Ibid*, p 199.

[223] *Ibid*, p 181.

[224] *Ibid*, p 184.

[225] *Ibid*, p 185.

[226] *Ibid*, p 186.

[227] *Ibid*, p 75.
[228] *Ibid*, p 103.
[229] *Ibid*, p 104.
[230] *Ibid*, p 155.
[231] *The Presbyterian College Belfast 1853-1953* (1954), p 260.
[232] Austin Fulton, *Biography of J. Ernest Davey* , 1970, p 31.
[233] *Record of the Trial of Rev. Prof. J. E. Davey*, p 187.
[234] *Ibid*, p 188.
[235] *Ibid*, p 198.
[236] This quotation is taken from Lord Alfred Tennyson's *The Grandmothers*: "That a lie which is half a truth is ever the blackest of lies; That a lie which is all a lie may be met and fought with outright; But a lie which is part a truth is a harder matter to fight."
[237] *Record of the Trial of Rev. Prof. J. E. Davey*, p 81.
[238] *Ibid*, p 85.
[239] *Ibid*, p 100.
[240] *Ibid*, p 187.
[241] *Ibid*, p 189.
[242] *Ibid*, p 192.
[243] *Ibid*, p 85.
[244] *Ibid*, p 97.
[245] *Ibid*, p 97: "But I verily believe some of my friends opposite hold the Nestorian heresy that in Christ's life you have two persons, a Divine Son of God and a human Jesus living in union—not really one person but two; others among them, of course, may hold the Docetic heresy of an unreal humanity—God pretending to be man but not really man. Others may hold the Apollinarian view that a Divine spirit took the place of the human soul, a view denied in our Catechism in the phrases 'taking to Himself a true body and a reasonable (or rational) soul.' But perhaps the commonest fundamentalist heresy is the Eutychian or Monophysite—that in Christ the human is lost in the Divine, and that only the Divine really matters—and references to Christ's omniscience and even omnipresence seem to mean either Monophysite or Nestorian views. What is true of Divine nature **in itself** is not necessarily true of Christ's personality if Incarnation demands a limitation."
[246] *Record of the Trial of Rev. Prof. J. E. Davey*, p 105.
[247] *Ibid*, p 192.
[248] *Ibid*, pp 83, 97, 109, 121, 123, 126, 128, 156, 188,189, 190,191.
[249] *Ibid*, p 189
[250] *Ibid*, p 209.
[251] *Ibid*, p 14.
[252] *Ibid*, p 193.
[253] *Ibid*, pp 209-210. See p 34 for the reference to formula, during examination of witness, W H Snoddy.
[254] *Ibid*. It is not clear whether Mr Corkey included the reference to page 16 of *The Record* in his speech or the reference was inserted by editors. In any case the unanimous decision of Presbytery recorded on page 16 of *The Record* that the case should not be discussed in public said nothing about *sub judice,* and appears to relate to the period of the Presbytery Trial. Presbytery passed a further resolution at the final sederunt of the Trial, recorded on page 23 of *The Record*, inhibiting public reference until after the appeal had been heard by the General Assembly, but it was not unanimous; it was by a very large majority.
[255] *Ibid*, p 203.
[256] *Ibid*, p 204.
[257] *Ibid*, p 187.
[258] *Ibid*, pp 210.
[259] *Ibid*, p 193.
[260] *Ibid*, p 194.
[261] J. Ernest Davey, M.A., B.D., *Our Faith in God*, p 115.
[262] *Record of the Trial of Rev. Prof. J. E. Davey*, p 122.

[263] Westminster Confession of Faith, 1.5. See also 1.6; 1.10.
[264] *Record of the Trial of Rev. Prof. J. E. Davey*, pp 126-127.
[265] "See endnote 236.
[266] *Record of the Trial of Rev. Prof. J. E. Davey*, p 206.
[267] *Ibid*, p 213.
[268] David N. Livingstone and Ronald A. Wells, *Ulster-American Religion*, Notre Dame, 1999, pp 62-63.
[269] Austin Fulton, *Biography of J Ernest Davey*, PCI, 1970, p 32.
Rev. David Stewart, Muckamore, produced *A Short History of the Presbyterian Church in Ireland* in 1936, "for the use of youth groups throughout the church". His penultimate chapter deals with 'Progress from the Union of the Synods' 1840-1936, and although he was publishing in 1936, and therefore writing in the aftermath of the Heresy Trial, he omits all reference to it and to the related events of the period. This is strange in the light of his interest in controversy shown by his treatment of the Arian dispute in the first half of the 19th century.
[270] See J Gresham Machen, *Christianity and Liberalism*, Victory Press, 1923, Introduction, eg, "But such changes in the material conditions of life do not stand alone; they have been produced by mighty changes in the human mind, as in their turn they themselves give rise to further spiritual changes. … In such an age, it is obvious that every inheritance from the past must be subject to searching criticism; and as a matter of fact some convictions of the human race have crumbled to pieces in the test. … So many convictions have had to be abandoned that men have sometimes come to believe that all convictions must go. If such an attitude be justifiable, then no institution is faced by a stronger hostile presumption than the institution of the Christian religion, for no institution has based itself more squarely upon the authority of a by-gone age."
[271] *The Derry Standard*, Bible Standards, April 1, 1927.
[272] Steve Bruce, *God Save Ulster, The Religion and Politics of Paisleyism*, Oxford, 1989, p 25.
[273] *Record of the Trial of Rev. Prof. J. E. Davey*, p 208.
[274] W J Grier, *The Origin and Witness of the Irish Evangelical Presbyterian Church*, Evangelical Book Shop, Belfast, 1945, p 50.
[275] The sermon was published as a pamphlet, price twopence. Mr Hanna gave this information about McKenzie: "At our last General Assembly in Derry, another of these men was brought over by aeroplane to tickle the ears and advance the destructive schemes of the modern junto in our church. Who was he, think you? No less than one of the famous 'shock-troops' who figured so conspicuously in Belfast 2 or 3 years ago—the Rev. Hamish McKenzie, Bridge of Allan. You may remember that we warned the Church and our fellow-citizens about those shock-troops, and you know how fruitless was their Mission, and no wonder for 'light can have no fellowship with darkness.' Last year this same Rev. Hamish McKenzie conducted a campaign in Rosemary St., under the euphonious title of 'Educational Evangelism.' I never heard of anyone who benefited by those meetings. The other day he addressed the Annual Meeting of the Scottish Sabbath School Union in Glasgow, and throwing off all disguise revealed himself in his true colours. He counselled teachers not to teach the Old Testament because it was 'unchristian, unintelligible and morally pernicious.' No wonder even Scots men are alarmed. Whenever you get a Scotsman excited, you may be sure there is something wrong. And so the Scottish papers are full of correspondence—some clamouring for Mr. McKenzie's head, and some trying to find an excuse for him. But the point of interest for us is: what does our Assembly think of itself to-day when it remembers that this same man was its honoured guest only a few months ago?"
[276] The *Irish Evangelical* of November 1950 had an article on the first issue of Biblical Theology, September 1950 – *Irish Barthians Start A New Journal*. The article concludes: "Two merits the journal has – it is well written and there is no mistaking where it stands."
[277] John Thompson became minister of Fortwilliam Park Presbyterian Church, Belfast on 12 January 1961. In 1974 he was awarded the degree of Doctor of Philosophy in the Faculty of Theology at Queen's University Belfast. His thesis was *Christological Perspectives in the Theology of Karl Barth*. In 1976 he was appointed Professor of Systematic Theology and Apologetics in the Presbyterian College Belfast. (*A History of the Congregations of the Presbyterian Church in Ireland 1610-1982*, page 169) He studied under J E Davey. He was a Barthian, and wrote a number of books, eg, *Christological Perspectives*. He retired in 1994. I went to see Dr Thompson

in his office in Union College some years ago. During the visit he expressed his delight that "Princeton is now the Barthian capital of the world".

[278] J Ernest Davey, *The Jesus of St John*, Lutterworth Press, 1958, p 15.

[279] Ibid. p 170.

[280] Ibid. p 170.

[281] This is the brief Summary of Charge 1 from the General Assembly Minutes, 9 June 1927. See Appendix 1 for the full wording. Strictly speaking the Charge was not that Professor Davey *denied*, but that he *taught* what was contrary to the Church Standards.

[282] *Shorter Catechism*, answer 33.

[283] John Calvin, *The Institutes of the Christian Religion*. (Battles Edition), Westminster Press 1960.

[284] J. Ernest Davey, M.A., B.D., *The Changing Vesture of the Faith*, James Clarke & Co, 1923, p 76.

[285] Ibid., p 78.

[286] For the fullest treatment, see Richard Muller, *The Unaccommodated Calvin* (Oxford University Press, 2000) and especially, *After Calvin* (Oxford University Press, 2003).

[287] Commentary on Romans 5:19.

[288] Commentary on 2 Corinthians 5:21.

[289] B. B. Warfield, *Modern Views of the Atonement*, Princeton Theological Review I (1903), pp 81-92, and reprinted in *The Person and Work of Christ* (Presbyterian and Reformed Publishing Company, 1970), pp 373-387.

[290] Ibid. p 387.

[291] R. A. Finlayson, *The Terminology of the Atonement*, in *Reformed Theological Writings* (Fearn: Christian Focus Publications, 1996), p 78.

[292] There have been theologians (Augustine, Anselm, Calvin and Rutherford, to name just four!) who have denied that this necessity is absolute. That is, they have argued that God could have pardoned sinners by divine fiat had he chosen to do so, but that once having committed himself to this God is bound by his decree. This makes imputation an issue of God's will rather than (strictly speaking), necessary justice. Among others, this view was upheld by the prolocutor of the Westminster Assembly, William Twisse, as well as by Samuel Rutherford and the early John Owen (later denied). See the relevant entries in John Macleod, *Scottish Theology* (Reformed Academic Press) and James Walker, *The Theology and Theologians of Scotland* (Knox Press). Calvin writes in the Institutes, 'If someone asks why [the atonement] is necessary, there has been no simple (to use the common expression) or absolute necessity. Rather, it has stemmed from a heavenly decree, on which men's salvation depended. Our most merciful Father decreed what was best for us.' The Institutes of the Christian Religion II.xii.1. See Robert L. Reymond, *A New Systematic Theology of the Christian Faith* (Nashville: Thomas Nelson Publishers, 1998), 664-67.

[293] Calvin's commentary on Luke 22:37. *A Harmony of the Gospels*, Volume III, St. Andrew Press, 1972.

[294] R A Finlayson, *The Terminology of the Atonement*, in *Reformed Theological Writings* (Fearn: Christian Focus Publications, 1996), p 78.

[295] J. McLeod Campbell, *The Nature of the Atonement* (Handsel Press, Carberry/Eerdmans, Grand Rapids: MI, 1996). Its reappearance in 1959 (London: James Clarke, 1959) coincided with the re-publication by the same publishers!—of another important work on the atonement by James Denney (United Free Church College), *The Christian Doctrine of Reconciliation* (London: James Clarke, 1959). Reviewing both of these books, R. A. Finlayson, of the Free Church College in Edinburgh, noted with respect to Denney's work, 'his exposition of the New Testament doctrine of reconciliation as achieved by Christ, is a complete answer to McLeod Campbell.' See *Christianity Today* 5:33 (Jan 2, 1961).

[296] *What St. Paul Really Said*, Lion UK: *Was Saul of Tarsus the Real Founder of Christianity?* (Forward Movement, 1997); *The Climax of the Covenant, Continuum: Christ and the Law in Pauline Theology* (Fortress Press, 1994). N T (Tom) Wright was the Bishop of Durham between 2003 and 2010. He is now Research Professor of New Testament and Early Christianity at St Andrews University. His earlier distinguished academic career at Oxford and Magill universities climaxed in the production by SPCK of his theological thought in the *Christian Origins and the*

Question of God series in 6 large volumes, of which 4 were out in early 2015, and the popular For Everyone series of 18 commentaries covering the entire New Testament. His views on the New Perspective and Justification by Faith have been critiqued by John Piper *The Future of Justification* (IVP) – see also endnote 294. (See also *The Westminster Confession into the 21st Century*, Ed Ligon Duncan, Vol 2, Mentor, pp 291-325: Donald Macleod, *The New Perspective: Paul, Luther, and Judaism*).

[297] His view has been labelled 'covenantal-nomism'. Briefly, a person is justified according to this view by aligning himself with the covenant community. It is, at root, an ecclesiastical understanding of justification in which baptism as the initiatory rite of entry into the covenant community plays a significant part. Needless to say, it is at polar opposite to the Reformational understanding of justification.

[298] This is the brief summary of Charge 2 from the General Assembly Minutes, 9 June 1927. See Appendix 1 for the full wording.

[299] Ibid, p 162

[300] J D G Dunn, *The Epistles to the Colossians and to Philemon*, NIGTC, Eerdmans/Paternoster, 1996.

[301] F F Bruce, *The Epistles to the Colossians, to Philemon and to the Ephesians*, NICNT, Eerdmans, 1984: "the adverb (meaning "corporeally") at the end of v. 9 no doubt implies His incarnation". Douglas J Moo, *The Letters to the Colossians and to Philemon*, Pillar NT Commentary (Eerdmans/ Apollos 2008) "the word "bodily" therefore suggests the idea of incarnation and, since the verb κατοικεῖ is in the present tense, also suggests that this indwelling of God in Christ is permanent."

[302] *Record of the Trial of Rev. Prof. J.E. Davey*, 1927, p 94.

[303] D A Carson, *Matthew*, Expositor's Bible Commentary with NIV, Vol 8, Zondervan, 1984, p 336.

[304] Donald Macleod, *The Person of Christ*, IVP 1998, pp 169-170.

[305] For a critique of the Kenotic Theory see Donald Macleod, *The Person of Christ*, IVP 1998, p 209ff

[306] *Record of the Trial of Rev. Prof. J.E. Davey*, 1927, p 100.

[307] J E Davey, *The Jesus of St. John*, 1958, p 165.

[308] Ibid, p 166

[309] Kenneth E Bailey, *Informal Controlled Oral Tradition and the Synoptic Gospels*, Themelios, 20.2, 1995.

[310] Richard Bauckham, *Jesus and the Eyewitnesses*, Eerdmans, 2006.

[311] John Calvin, *Harmony of the Gospels*, Vol 3, pp 150-151.

[312] *Ibid*. p 208.

[313] B B Warfield, Vol 10, *Reviews*, pp 260-261.

[314] This is the brief Summary of Charge 3 from the General Assembly Minutes, 9 June 1927. See Appendix 1 for the full wording.

[315] *Record of the Trial of Rev. Prof. J.E. Davey*, 1927, p 116.

[316] *Ibid*, p 115

[317] *Ibid*, p 115

[318] B B Warfield, *Works*, (10 vols), Oxford New York, 1927 and following, 1 229-280.

[319] J I Packer, *'Fundamentalism' and the Word of God*, IVP, 1958, p 82.

[320] *Record of the Trial of Rev. Prof. J.E. Davey*, 1927, p 115.

[321] This is the brief summary of Charge 4 from the General Assembly Minutes, 9 June 1927. See Appendix 1 for the full wording.

[322] Westminster Confession of Faith, 5.4.

[323] *Record of the Trial of Rev. Prof J.E. Davey*, 1927, p 142

[324] Ibid, p 188.

[325] For a discussion of the issues involved, as well as a thorough refutation of open theism, see J. Piper, J. Taylor, P. K. Helseth (eds), *Beyond the Bounds: Open Theism and the Undermining of Biblical Christianity*, Wheaton: Crossway Books, 2003.

[326] The words of Thomas Aquinas, quoted in *Catechism of the Catholic Church*, London: Chapman, 1994, p 93.

[327] J. Murray, 'The Theology of the Westminster Confession of Faith', in *Collected Writings*, Volume 4, Edinburgh: Banner of Truth, 1982, p 251.
[328] Charles Hodge, *Systematic Theology*, Volume 1, Michigan: Eerdmans, 1995 reprint, p 589.
[329] Murray, *Theology of the Westminster Confession*, p 252.
[330] This is the brief summary of Charge 5 from the General Assembly Minutes, 9 June 1927. See Appendix 1 for the full wording.
[331] Westminster Confession of Faith, 2.3.
[332] *Record of the Trial of Rev. Prof. J. E. Davey*. References of the paragraph up to this point are from p 147.
[333] *Ibid*, p 155.
[334] *Ibid*, p 147.
[335] *Ibid*, p 147.
[336] *Ibid*, p 148.
[337] *Ibid*, pp 147-148.
[338] *Ibid*, p 150.
[339] B B Warfield, *Biblical Doctrines*, (2nd vol. of *Works*, (1929)) Banner of Truth 1988, pp 147-167.
[340] *Record of the Trial of Rev. Prof. J. E. Davey*, p 155.
[341] *Ibid*, p 150.
[342] *Ibid*, p 155.
[343] *Ibid*, p 155; Austin Fulton, *Biography of J Ernest Davey*, PCI, 1970, p 123.
[344] *Record of the Trial of Rev. Prof. J. E. Davey*, p 155.
[345] David N. Livingstone and Ronald A. Wells, *Ulster-American Religion*, Notre Dame, 1999, p 62.
[346] *The Witness*, Friday, June 17, 1927, p 9, opening paragraph.
[347] Expression, "mob" taken from Austin Fulton, *Biography of J Ernest Davey*, 1970, p 36: "During the trial a series of interruptions was kept up by a mob in the gallery."
[348] *The Witness*, Friday, June 17, 1927, p 10-11.
[349] Geoffrey Thomas, *J. Gresham Machen in the United Kingdom: 3, The Banner of Truth*, Issue 235, April 1983, p 30. See also Rev. James Hunter, *Five Years ago and Today*, The Irish *Evangelical*, July 1932, p 2.
[350] Minutes of the General Assembly 1927, Eighth Session, 10 June 1927, pp 45-46.
[351] Report of the Commission on Reference from the Belfast Presbytery, Minutes of the General Assembly, 1928, p 73.
[352] Rev. Charles Hunter, the eldest of the Hunter family, was Minister of Ballyrashane Presbyterian Church, 1880-1928; he retired to Crieff where he died in 1929.
[353] Ivan T. Jess, *Ravenhill Presbyterian Church 1898-1998 – Centenary History*, 1997, pp 38-39.
[354] Fountain Street, Belfast, runs from Wellington Place to Castle Street. The 1790 map of Belfast marks the street as Stable Lane, but after a public fountain was set up in it, the name changed to Fountain Street. It is joined on the left by College Street, about half way along. Today, the addresses numbered 1-39 are on the far side of College Street, but in 1927 those numbered 29-39 comprised the Wellington Place end. This means that in 1927 *Le Chat Noir Café*, at no 33, was located about half way between Wellington Place and College Street, on the left, probably where Trailfinders is located in 2015. The re-numbering of the street, with College Street between 39 and 41, as it is today, appeared in the 1937 issue of the Belfast Street Directory.
The Proprietor of *Le Chat Noir*, was Mr S P Luke and he is designated as a Manufacturers' Agent, at the same address. *Le Chat Noir* was first listed in the Street Directory in 1927 and although Mr Luke returned to his native England in 1928, the café appeared in the Street Directory until 1935. It became *The Black Cat* in 1936 and was last listed in the 1937 issue. Opinions about black cats are quite polarised over whether they bring good luck or bad!
Cafés were evidently in vogue as a venue for meetings during the period. When students and friends gathered after the Heresy Trial to congratulate Professor and Mrs Davey on their recent marriage, they met in the *Merry Thought Café!* (*The Witness*, 17 June 1927, p 11)
[355] "Suggestions were made with regard to a union of Bible-believers from various churches and with regard to the support and encouragement of those taking the step spoken of by occasional

visitation by the ministers connected with the movement to administer the sacraments. ... It was then suggested that a deputation representative of those present should appear at the next meeting of Council of the Irish Alliance of Christian Workers Union on Wednesday 29th September at 4.30 pm to ask if that body was willing to take any definite steps towards the formation of a new church organisation and if this request was not acceded to—then to request the Council to recognise members of any such evangelical denomination as eligible for membership in IACWU." Minutes of first General Meeting, 17 September 1927.

[356] *The Dowry of the Past*, The Story of Berry Street Presbyterian Church, Belfast, p 42.

[357] The minute of the IACWU Council meeting of 28 September 1927 refers to "the new Evangelical Church" which was not constituted and given this title until 15 October 1927. It may be that the minute was not written until after 15 October 1927 when it would have been appropriate to use the title, "Evangelical Church".

[358] See Iain H Murray, *D. Martyn Lloyd-Jones, The Fight of Faith 1939-1981*, Banner of Truth, 1990, pp 473-567.

[359] J A Ross, *The Alliance News*, Vol 1, No 2, April 1926, p 2.

[360] On 28 September 1927 the Council did formulate a Notice of Motion for its next meeting: "that the rules of the Alliance be modified to admit and retain those who for conscience sake are obliged to sever their connections with the Modernist Churches." When the Motion came before the meeting of 15 December 1927, Article 1 of the Basis of Constitution was the point at issue: "That an Association of Christian Workers' Unions for the definite proclamation of the truth of the Gospel, in harmony with the Evangelistic Churches, be and is hereby formed." It was argued at the meeting that the words, "in harmony with the Evangelistic Churches" be deleted since "Evangelistic Churches, so called, were supporters of the Modernist cause and we should not as an Alliance be linked up in any way with them." The meeting was unable to reach agreement and remitted the issue to the Executive, which, on 26 April 1928, recommended no change to Article 1. It may be that "Evangelistic Churches" was being equated with the established denominations.

[361] IACWU Council Minutes 10 September 1925: "The matter of the founding and developing the new Bible School, formed in Belfast, was also considered. A report of which had already been done on this matter was presented by the Secretary, his statement being supported by the Rev. W P Nicholson. It was stated that the need for such a School was felt by many at the present time. Any of our young people desiring training, and there were very many such, either found it impossible to get the instruction sought for, or else found it necessary to cross to England or Scotland for it. And consequently it was decided, during Rev. Nicholson's mission in the Assembly Hall, that a beginning should be made in this direction under the auspices of the Alliance. The fact that the School was being formed was duly announced by Mr Nicholson at his meetings. And on Monday Sept, 31, [31 August 1925 was a Monday. Ed] the first meeting was held in the Minor Hall YMCA, Wellington Place. About 300 men were present. A statement as to the nature of the work being made by the Secretary of the Alliance, and the Rev. J Hunter, MA, having given a much appreciated address, Messrs R F Smith *(of address)* and A Graham *(of address)* [were] asked to act as Secretary and Treasurer respectively. This they kindly consented to do. At this meeting it was stated that the class, confined to men for the present, would be held on Fridays at 7.30 and would be conducted by Ministers interested in the work. It was stated that there would be a fee of 5 shillings charged and that classes would commence on September 11. The Council having been thus informed about what had been done and their approval and consent having been received, the question of finding a suitable place in which to hold the classes was next discussed. The securing of a hall which would be entirely in the hands of the Alliance it was felt would be a very desirable thing, as this would enable the work to be extended to women as well as men. And as a building had been found in a central position in town such as it was thought would be suitable for the work, namely an upper room in the Magdalene Schools, Shaftesbury Square, it was suggested that this hall should be taken for the year at a rent of £80. To this the Council agreed."

IACWU Council Minutes 15 October 1925: "The question of holding an inaugural meeting in connection with the Bible School in Belfast was also considered. And it was agreed that such a meeting should be held in the YMCA, Wellington Place, Belfast. ... Mr Nicholson was asked and kindly consented to give an address at this meeting. The Secretary was also asked to invite representatives from the various district councils to speak at this meeting."

IACWU Council Minutes 12 November 1925: "A brief report in connection with the inauguration meeting in connection with the Bible School was also given. This meeting was held in the YMCA as decided at last meeting of council. And whilst the attendance was not quite as large as had been anticipated, yet it was felt that the meeting had accomplished the desired end of making known the work of the Bible School. It was also stated that the secretary, in accordance with the decision of the council, had written to members of the various district councils asking them to take part at the meeting, but as these found it impossible to so take part the Rev. James Hunter MA was asked to speak along with Mr Nicholson."

[362]Mr Hunter's address was published as the leader in the Irish Evangelical October 1953 with the title, Be Courageous. The editor thanked the editor of the *Belfast Telegraph* for permission to publish the paper's report of the address.

[363]

	Article		Westminster
1	The Holy Scriptures or the Word of God written	1.2	Holy Scripture, or the Word of God written
	containing all the books of the Old and New Testaments	1.2	Are now contained in the Books of the Old and New Testaments
	is of infallible truth and divine authority	2.5	Of the infallible truth, and divine authority thereof
	And in its original languages is immediately inspired by God	2.8	The Old Testament in Hebrew … and the New Testament in Greek … being immediately inspired by God
	and is the only rule of faith and practice	2.2	To be the rule of faith and life
2	It is most clearly set forth in Holy Scripture that		
	there is but one living and true God	2.1	There is but one only living and true God
	and that in the Godhead there are three Persons—the Father, the Son and the Holy Ghost	SC	There are three persons in the Godhead: the Father, the Son, and the Holy Ghost;
	and that these three are one, the same in substance, equal in power and glory.	SC	and these three are one God , the same in substance, equal in power and glory.
3	The second Person of the Holy Trinity, the eternal Son of God	8.2	The Son of God, the second person in the Trinity, being very and eternal God
	was sent by the Father to be the Saviour of the world.		
	He became man, being born of the Virgin Mary;	8.2	Did … take upon him man's nature … being conceived … in the womb of the Virgin Mary
	He lived a perfect life of unapproachable holiness;	8.2,3	without sin … perfect … holy, undefiled
	He died on the cross as an atoning sacrifice for sin;	8.5 29.2	And sacrifice of himself The sacrifice of himself in his death … that one offering up of himself, by himself, upon the cross

	He rose from the dead on the third day with that very body which had been laid in the tomb;	8.4	On the third day he arose from the dead, with the same body in which he suffered;
	He ascended into Heaven	8.4	With which also he ascended into heaven
	and He will come again in glory to judge the living and the dead	8.4	and shall return to judge man and angels at the end of the world.

[364] WCF 1.4, 12.1, 13.1, 14.1, 15.2-3, and 18.2; Larger Catechism 11, 76, 80 and 81.

[365] James R Payton, Jr., *The Background and Significance of the Adopting Act, 1729*, Essay in *Pressing Towards the Mark*, OPC, 1986, pp 133-135, 143.

[366] W J Grier, *The Origin and Witness of the Irish Evangelical Church*, Evangelical Book Shop, Belfast, 1945, p 53. In writing about the demise of the Presbyterian Bible Standards League in *The Irish Evangelical*, October 1938, page 4, Grier stated, "When many of the members of the Irish Evangelical Church took their departure from the apostate Irish Presbyterian Church in 1927 …"

[367] Finlay Holmes, *Our Irish Presbyterian Heritage*, Publications Committee of the Presbyterian Church in Ireland, 1985, pp 154-155.

[368] E J Poole-Connor, *The Apostasy of English Non-Conformity*, London, 1933, p 9.

[369] *Ibid*, p 69.

[370] W J Grier, *Op cit*, Evangelical Book Shop, Belfast, 1945, p 63.

[371] By the end of 1931 the League had moved to a floor above the Evangelical Book Shop at 15 College Square East and then to 11-13 Bedford Street by August 1934. The *Belfast Telegraph* of 10 September 1938 carried an article under the heading: *Presbyterian Bible Standards League*, stating that the League had been discontinued by the consent of its members. The notice was signed by its President, Treasurer and Secretary. However, the local press of 13 September announced the reconstitution of the League under new office bearers. Principal F J Paul died on 3 July 1941 and in announcing his death the *Belfast Telegraph* noted his work in reconciling the Bible Standards League and the Assembly's college staff.

[372] *The Dowry of the Past*, The Story of Berry Street Presbyterian Church, Belfast, p 43.

[373] W J Grier, *The Origin and Witness of the Irish Evangelical Church*, Evangelical Book Shop, Belfast, 1945, p 53.

[374] Iain H Murray, *D Martyn Lloyd-Jones, The Fight of Faith 1939-1981*, Banner of Truth, 1990, p 545.

[375] *The Irish Evangelical*, January 1955, p 1.

[376] *Proximus ardet Ucalegon* - Neighbour Ucalegon is ablaze. (Virgil, *Aeneid*, Book 2, line 418). *Ucalegon* is a neighbour of Aeneas whose house is on fire. The root meaning of the name *Ucalegon* is What-me-Worry? The expression, not so much in vogue today, came to be used as a warning to a neighbour whose house is figuratively burning down or under the threat of it.

[377] Steve Bruce, *Paisley, Religion and Politics in Northern Ireland*, Oxford, 2007, p 21.

[378] Amy Wilson Carmichael, (1867-1951) grew up in Millisle, Co Down, a member of the Presbyterian Church. She arrived in India in 1895 and served for 56 years without a furlough. She founded the Dohnavur Fellowship in 1901 and was a prolific writer. See: *Amy Carmichael of Dohnavur*, Frank Houghton, CLC, USA; *A Chance to Die, The Life and Legacy of Amy Carmichael*, Elisabeth Elliot, Bethany Publishing (Baker) 2005; *The Wild-Bird Child, A Life of Amy Carmichael*, Derick Bingham, Ambassador, 2004; *At BBC Corner I Remember Amy Carmichael*, Margaret Wilkinson, 1996. *Amy Carmichael 'Beauty for Ashes'*, Iain H Murray, Banner of Truth 2015.

[379] *Char Noir* Minute.

[380] Ibid.

[381] Pace had been a missionary in the Philippines and is also associated with the production of Christian Cartoons.

[382] Dispensationalism has various categories. Essentially it is a doctrinal system which sees Israel and the church as two separate constituencies. God has distinct purposes for each and

he will restore national Israel under an earthly rule of the Messiah. The Scofield Bible lists seven dispensations or periods of time during which man's obedience is tested against particular revelations of God's will. See beginning of Chapter 19, "...and Experiencing Pain".

[383] *The Banner of Truth*, Issue 238, July 1983, p 26. The April 1983 issue carries a cover photograph of Dr Machen taken in the garden of 28 Knockdene Park South, Belfast, the home of W J Grier, during the June 1932 visit. During the 1932 visit to UK Machen gave 3 lectures to the Bible League of Great Britain, 17 June 1932: *Christian Scholarship and Evangelism, Christian Scholarship and the Defense of the Faith,* and *Christian Scholarship and the Building up of the Church*. These addresses were reprinted in *What is Christianity?*, 1951, and in *J. Gresham Machen, Selected Shorter Writings*, Edited by D G Hart, P & R Publishing, 2004.

[384] Slatehill, townland of Ballyfore, was between Carrickfergus and Ballynure. Ballyfore Mission Hall now stands on the site.

[385] John Bunyan, *The Pilgrim's Progress*, Banner of Truth, 1977, p1, p 25.

[386] In the opening address at the Leicester Conference 17 March 1975, Grier recalled that Rev. James Hunter preached on Job 19:25-27 at his ordination – "For I know that my redeemer liveth …".

[387] Steve Bruce, *God Save Ulster, The Religion and Politics of Paisleyism*, Oxford, 1989, p 25.

[388] Robert Allen, *The Presbyterian College, Belfast*, Centenary Volume 1853-1953, William Mullan & Son Ltd, 1954, p 4.

[389] See www.calvarychurch.ca/staff. Calvary began with Rev. William Nisbet accepting a call to remain in Canada and not return to his native Ireland ... The new church was called St. John's Evangelical Church, Independent. They first met on the last Sunday of May 1928 ... The church was greatly blessed under the ministry of William Nisbet and the congregation felt its loss when he accepted a call to a church in Northern Ireland in 1932. ... in 1934 Pastor Nisbet returned and his faithful ministry built a solid foundation for the future ... Pastor Nisbet retired in 1941.See internet also under 'Nisbet Lodge 2003, for more information and photograph'.

[390] The story of Lady Hayes' conversion appears with some biographical comment in the *Irish Evangelical*, October 1946, p 13 – *Life! Eternal Life!* She died 11 February 1943, aged 88. "Jesus, Thy blood and righteousness" was sung at her funeral. Mrs Margaret Leahy provided the following article for the *Banner of Truth,* with mention of her husband Prof. Fred Leahy, Reformed Presbyterian Church of Ireland: "On 15 September 2006, when Fred would have celebrated his 84th birthday, his brother wrote to me, enclosing an old little card, entitled "Our Baby Boy". The card was originally sent to his parents by his father's employer and her daughter, the Honourable Lady and Miss Hayes, of Donegal, Ireland, in 1922 on the occasion of Fred's birth. Although Lady Hayes was a member of the aristocracy, she was a true Christian, who was converted under the preaching of Canon Hay Aitken, a Church of England minister. Fred's father was originally from Dublin, and had served in the Irish Guards; although a regular church-goer, he did not know the Saviour. In 1919 he went to work on the Hayes estate in Donegal during a period of intense political and civil unrest in Ireland. Concerned about her employee's state of soul, Lady Hayes gave him a notable book to read, *Pardon and Assurance*, by W. J. Patton. It was to be the means of his conversion. In 1922, a baby boy was born into what was now a godly home, and the aforementioned card was sent to the new parents on that happy occasion. The verses on the card are remarkable, in that the prayers were amazingly answered in the fullness of time. How truly blessed is the baby for whom such prayers are offered! How truly blessed are those too, who see the links in the chain of Divine Providence in their lives!"

[391] This was the revised Irish Psalter of 1880 (the 1650 Scottish Psalter had been in use until then). The advertisements for some conferences, such as the one in Botanic Avenue in September 1931, included the words: "Revised Psalter will be used". The Psalter included 67 Paraphrases (1781); Isaac Watts (about 24 of them), Philip Doddridge, Michael Bruce and John Morison were the major authors. There were also five hymns bound in with the Paraphrases: 1-3 by Joseph Addison, 4 by Isaac Watts, and 5 Anon, but the use of these was extremely rare. The 1781 Paraphrases were an expansion and revision of the 1749 collection of 45. Some Scottish divines regarded a few in the new version as theologically inferior at points. See *Irish Evangelical*, February 1937, p 6.

[392] Scripture Union and CSSM published *Golden Bells*, or *Hymns for our Children*, in 1890. It was revised in 1925, with the subtitle *Hymns for Young People* and contained 703 items. It is the 1925 revision that Council adopted with some reservation in 1933-34. It was re-published with a Supplement (available separately) in the 1950s (in 1954 or earlier). The items in the Supplement were numbered 704 to 754.

[393] There are various forms of the Kenotic Theory, but essentially it affirms that in the incarnation Christ "emptied" himself, in some sense, of his deity. It was part of the Christological debate at the Heresy Trial, 1927. The kenosis of Phil 2:7, often translated as "emptying", means that Christ made himself nothing, or made himself of no account. *And can it be* appeared in the Golden Bells supplement of the 1950s.

[394] Dr. Robert L. Reymond, *A New Systematic Theology of the Christian Faith*, Nelson, 1998, pp 542-544. Regarding the first, Reymond argues that if Christ at His first coming offered to establish a literal millennium of Davidic reign, as Classic Dispensationalism teaches, "*Christ would have been justly executed under Roman law as an insurrectionist and a revolutionary!*" On the second, Reymond contends that under the Classic Dispensationalist scheme Christ first offered the Davidic kingdom to the Jews and that it was only after His rejection by the Jews that He began to teach that He must die for all men. "This interpretation implies that Jesus actually taught for a time (and that he also allowed the Jews to believe for a time) that if the nation of Israel would accept him as its King, he would forgive the nation of their sins on the basis of their faith in him as their messianic King and accordingly that he would not need to die for them. God would then have forgiven the Gentiles on some basis other than what we now know as the cross work of Christ. But on what other basis?"

[395] *The Momentous Event* was published in hardback by the Evangelical Book Shop and went through five editions of 1,000 copies each between 1945 and 1963. The Banner of Truth took over the publication in 1970 and has since printed five paperback editions of 10,000 copies each. The Banner has also published the four other-language editions. The Portuguese edition had been the most prominent of these, particularly in Brazil, where it has served as a reply to the dominant Dispensationalism.

[396] *The Irish Evangelical*, March 1936, p 11, reprinted from *The Gospel Witness*.

[397] His sister Catherine Gillespie was later President of the Ladies' Section.

[398] R L Dabney, *A Thoroughly Educated Ministry, Discussions*, Vol Two, Banner of Truth, 1982, p 676.

[399] P & R Publishing, 2007, p 4.

[400] Brother of Thomas Andrews, designer of the *Titanic*.

[401] Second world War in Northern Ireland. ww2ni.webs.com/informationother.htm

[402] The Dutch Reformed Church at Oosterbeek was destroyed during the fierce fighting that followed the airborne landings on 17 September 1944. In January 1946 the Oosterbeek Church wrote acknowledging the "noble gift" and describing the dreadful cost of war in their locality.

[403] The end of the 'Cold War' is usually marked by the opening of the Berlin Wall on 9 November 1989.

[404] See *The Westminster Confession into the 21st Century*, Volume 1, essay by Morton H Smith, *Theology of the Larger Catechism*, pp 101-122.

[405] Although there is diversity about which form of church government is the true biblical model there is general agreement that Scripture lays down form as well as principle. The *jure divino* principle states that church government and its form are established by *divine law*. Westminster sets out its case for the Presbyterian form in *The Form of Presbyterial Church-Government*, arguing for its system of ascending courts largely on the basis of Jerusalem and Ephesus, the two church complexes of the New Testament.

[406] Dr Carl McIntire graduated from Westminster Theological Seminary in 1931 and was a founder member of Machen's Independent Board for Presbyterian Foreign Missions. With Machen and others he was suspended from the ministry in 1935, and with them was a founder member of PCA (OPC) in 1936. He left the denomination in 1937, after Machen's death, over differences on millennial views and abstinence, and formed the Bible Presbyterian Church. He also opened Faith Theological Seminary with the assistance of Francis A Schaeffer, then a student. McIntire started the *Christian Beacon* magazine in 1936.

[407] Norman Porter was converted in 1933 and when Orangefield Baptist Church was formed in 1939 he became a foundation member, and later an officebearer. He became the Secretary of the Evangelical Protestant Society when it emerged from the National Union of Protestants in 1946, and in 1953 its Director. He was elected as an Independent Unionist MP for Belfast Clifton in 1953 and held the seat until 1958. He preached regularly in EP churches. His father was a member of the Jocelyn Avenue congregation. Norman Porter emigrated to Australia in 1970 where he pastored the Micham Baptist Church in Adelaide until 1979. He then moved to a Reformed Baptist church in Auckland, New Zealand where he spent three years. On his return to Northern Ireland in 1982 he became Pastor of Killycomaine Evangelical Church, Portadown. In 1986 he was called to Orangefield Baptist Church where he served until his sudden death at a Pastors' Conference in Portrush on 12 March 1991.

[408] For additional information on Dr Carl McIntyre and his role see *Between the Times*, The Orthodox Presbyterian Church in Transition, D G Hart, Index p 335.

[409] The RES became REC (Reformed Ecumenical Council) in 1988. Its current basis, revised in 2000, is: "The Basis of The Reformed Ecumenical Council shall be the Holy Scriptures of the Old and New Testaments, which bear witness to Jesus Christ, Savior and Lord, who is the foundation of the Church, and are in their entirety the infallible Word of the triune God, fully authoritative in all matters of faith and life; the subordinate standard founded on the Scriptures shall be the Reformed faith as a body of truth articulated in the Gallican Confession, the Belgic Confession, the Heidelberg Catechism, the Second Helvetic Confession, the Thirty-nine Articles, the Canons of Dordt, and the Westminster Confession."

[410] *The Irish Evangelical*, December 1947, Twenty Years Ago and Today, p 3.

[411] The Committee for the Historian of the Orthodox Presbyterian Church, 2011, p 53.

[412] The percentage time Mr Jones spent in each county was approximately

Antrim	30%	Fermanagh	8%
Armagh	6%	Londonderry	13%
Down	32%	Tyrone	11%

[413] *Irish Evangelical*, January 1940, p 3.

[414] *Irish Evangelical*, October 1930, p 5.

[415] Pastor Emile Guedj opened a new French Bible Mission Church in Colombes, North West Paris, in 1930 – in a very Roman Catholic area. He died in Colombes on 16 March 1977, aged 81. He provided an article for the magazine in May 1959: *Somewhat to Say*.

[416] The Reformation Translation Fellowship was formed at Canton, South China, in December 1948 through the efforts of Rev. Samuel E Boyle and J G Vos, (American Reformed Presbyterian missionaries), and Rev. Charles Chao of Manchuria. The British section began in 1954. Its doctrinal basis is the Westminster Confession of Faith. Its purposes include the translation and publication of Christian literature in Chinese, the publication of original Chinese theological works, and the promotion of original Chinese theological writing.

[417] 1958 has been Northern Ireland's first and best World Cup competition – the competition that saw the World Cup debut of the 17 year old Pele. Sweden hosted the finals. Northern Ireland's campaign was as follows:

Group A

Sunday	08 06 1958	Northern Ireland 1	0 Czechoslovakia
Wednesday	11 06 1958	Argentina 3	1 Northern Ireland
Sunday	15 06 1958	West Germany 2	2 Northern Ireland

Play-off

Tuesday	17 06 1958	Northern Ireland 2	1 Czechoslovakia

Quarter Finals

Thursday	19 06 1958	France 4	0 Northern Ireland

The following was dated 29 11 2007 on the IFA Official Website. "The Irish FA held an Extraordinary General Meeting last night during which proposed changes to the Articles of Association were discussed. ... the ban on Sunday Football was lifted after article 28 was carried. In order for a match to be played on a Sunday, the two clubs involved and the competition organisers must agree to do so. No sanction can be taken against anyone who does not agree to Sunday football." Northern Ireland's first Sunday home international took place at Windsor Park, Belfast, 29 March 2015. It was a Euro 2016 qualifier against Finland.

[418] The Banner of Truth Trust, 1988, 13 pages.
[419] See www.freepres.org/main.asp for an account of the work and witness.
[420] *Our Own Heritage*, A collection of articles dealing with the witness of the Free Presbyterian Church of Ulster from 1951-2002, Rev. Philip Kyle, 2002, published in association with Tavistock Free Presbyterian Church Devon.
"Some months after the constitution of Crossgar Free Presbyterian Church his own [Dr Paisley's] congregation in Ravenhill joined the new denomination as well. These folk had left the Presbyterian Church in Ireland many years prior to this to join the Irish Evangelical Church." (P 41) We are unable to identify any group who left PCI to join IEC and later became the 'Ravenhill' congregation. There was certainly a sizeable group who left PCI in 1935 and later formed the Ravenhill Evangelical Mission – see the following endnote. Through the years there have been membership transfers between IEC/EPC and FPCU.
[421] Ibid, pp 21 and 27. The FPCU *Revivalist*, editor Dr Ian R K Paisley MP, in its June 1987 issue presented a photograph of Rev. James Hunter on its front cover – the same photograph that W J Grier published in his *The Origin and Witness of the Irish Evangelical Church*, Evangelical Book Shop, Belfast, 1945. Pages 23-32 carried an article by the editor with the three-line title "1927 ... 1953 ... 1987. 60 YEARS ON. The Trial of Prof. J E Davey for Heresy". In the introductory paragraphs there is the statement in bold font: **The original elders of the Kirk Session of the Martyrs Memorial Free Presbyterian Church were amongst Davey's Accusers**. (The December 1994 *Revivalist*, under Editor's Note on Rev. James Hunter, p 28, also commented: "He was one of Professor Davey's accusers at the heresy Trial along with my first Kirk Session Members in Ravenhill). In a sermon 'The Trial of Prof. J. E. Davey', in 1983, Dr Paisley identified these men as Thomas H Watson, Alfred Carson and W L Harbinson, all elders in Ravenhill Presbyterian Church. Alfred Carson was one of the first group of signatories of the original Articles of Faith of the *Irish Evangelical Church* on 12 November 1927. He was appointed a member of Council and attended on three occasions – November 1927, December 1927 and January 1928. We do not have a record of his future Church affiliation and we are not aware of any association of Harbinson or Watson with *IEC*. The *Ravenhill Presbyterian Church, 1898-1998, Centenary History*, Ivan T Jess, 1997, has a section, 'Controversy and Split 1935', pp 47-50. The immediate issue concerned hair styles and head covering of some women in the choir and was referred to the Belfast Presbytery. One outcome was that a group, including four elders, left the Church and began to meet for worship locally. Later the group moved to a new building and became *Ravenhill Evangelical Mission*. In 1946 they installed I R K Paisley as their Minister. See Steve Bruce, *God Save Ulster!*, Oxford, 1986, pp 30-38.
Under the sub-heading, 'The Heresy Trial', the 1987 *Revivalist* article re-produced, with acknowledgement, W J Grier's "account of the trial and its appeal to the General Assembly". The 'Heresy Trial' chapter from *Origin and Witness* and the final paragraphs of the next chapter, 'The Teaching Approved by Presbytery and Assembly" were re-produced. The remaining pages of the article which are not from *Origin and Witness*, included an account of the FPCU protest over Principal J E Davey's induction as Moderator of PCI in 1953. 'The Leaflet Distributed' featured quotations from *Changing Vesture* and from the documents of the Heresy Trial sequence. The December 1994 *Revivalist* carried an article headed 'THE HERESY TRIAL OF 1927' which it described as "An address delivered by the late Rev. James Hunter MA in June 1932, five years after the decision of the General Assembly approving of Prof. Davey's apostasy." The same article had appeared three times in the *Irish Evangelical* - the Leader in the July 1932 with the title 'Five Years Ago and Today', the Leader, February 1946, under the title 'A Retrospect' and in November 1952 under the title, 'The Heresy Trial of 1927 An Address delivered by the late Rev. James Hunter, M.A., in June 1932'. James Hunter normally wrote the leading article. Perhaps the address was in connection with Machen's meetings in Belfast 25-26 June 1932.
[422] *Evangelical Presbyterian*, November 1967, p 11.
[423] J Claude MacQuigg, editor, *The Minnis Mills Tapestry*, 2005, p 83.
[424] *Whose Faith Follow*, 1943, was also the title of the book written by Rev. G N M Collins to mark the Free Church of Scotland's celebration of the Centenary of the Disruption of 1843.
[425] Murdo Nicolson joined the Presbyterian Church of Canada and ministered in Saskatoon, Vancouver and Calgary. He was Moderator in 1971. They had five children, four boys and one

girl. The eldest, a boy, died in infancy in Peru. They made regular visits to the UK, the last being in 1983. When Nicolson retired, they spent some months in his native island of Raasay, where the Free Church cause was very low. He took the services and raised quite a bit of money from his Canadian contacts, with which the church building was repaired and renovated. Nicolson died in Vancouver in 1985 and his wife in 1999. The Knock EPC register records the cessation of her membership as 18/10/1939.

[426] Fuller accounts of the four ministries appeared in *The Evangelical Presbyterian*, Jul-Aug – Nov-Dec 2013.

[427] For viewpoints: Wikipedia, *History of the Orange Institution*, www.grandorangelodge.co.uk, W P Malcomson, *Behind Closed Doors*, Evangelical Truth, 1999, pp 15-23.

[428] Mrs C R Grier provided an compelling account of the holiday in the *Irish Evangelical*, June 1950.

[429] The following recordings of W J Grier's addresses can be made available through *Evangelical Book Shop*, Belfast:

Treasure in Earthen Vessels	2 Corinthians 4:7	1968	Leicester
Come unto Me	Matthew 11:28-30	24 10 1971	Botanic Avenue
Heaven Opened	John 1:50-51	03 12 1972	Stranmillis
The New Covenant in My Blood	Matthew 26:28	07 10 1973	Stranmillis
The Christian's Attitude to Life, Death and Eternity	2 Corinthians 5:1-10	17 03 1975	Leicester
The Path of Prayer	Luke 11:1-13	01 08 1976	Stranmillis
Four Gospel Musts with statement on own call to the Ministry	Romans 10	06 11 1977	Stranmillis
The Boldness of the Righteous	Proverbs 28:1	1978	Leicester
The Need of Prayer	Ephesians 6:18	02 04 1979	Leicester
Retirement Statement	Romans 8	27 05 1979	Stranmillis
Pilgrim's Progress	Luke 15:11-32	03 06 1979	Stranmillis

[430] Frederick III commissioned this Catechism in 1559. It was written by Zacharias Ursinus, assisted by Caspar Olevianus and others, and published in Heidelberg in 1563. The third edition was divided into 52 sections to correspond with the weeks of the year. A large part of it expounds the Apostles' Creed. Questions 1-2: Introduction; 3-11: Sin and its Effects; 12-85 the Way of Salvation; 86-129: Living the Christian Life. The Catechism is particularly popular in the Netherlands where it is the second of the *Three Forms of Unity* – the other two being the *Belgic Confession* and the *Canons of Dordt*.

[431] Eg: The Challenges of our Time (April 1969), B B Warfield (February 1971), Boldness in the Work of the Ministry (April 1972), The Reformed Faith (May 1973), The Church at Prayer (May 1974), The Christian's Attitude to Eternity (June 1975).

[432] *The Best Books*, Banner of Truth Trust, 1968. Its 15 sections were: 1 Spiritual Classics, 2 Paperbacks, 3 Biography, 4 Church History, 5 Christian Doctrine – General, 6 Christian Doctrine – Particular Subjects, 7 The Christian Ministry, 8 The Bible – General, 9 The Bible – Commentaries and Expositions, 7 The Bible – Commentaries and Expositions, 10 The Bible – Specialist Studies, 11 Defence of the Faith, 12 Doctrinal Deviations and Cults, 13 Personal and Social Issues, 14 Books for Boys and Girls, Booklets and 15 Tracts.

[433] Shorter Catechism (April-May 1936), Commandments 5-10 (June 1938-February 1939), Momentous Event (March 1944-June 1945), John Calvin (June 1954-April 1956), Henry Cooke (May 1956-May 1957), 1859 Revival (Jan-April 1959), David Livingstone (April-May 1973).

[434] W J Grier wrote a series of 23 articles on Calvin in the *Irish Evangelical*, from June 1954 to April 1956. He used Calvin's foremost biographer, Emile Doumergue (1844-1937), as a major source. The 23 articles ran to almost 36,000 words. The Banner of Truth edited the original manuscript and published it in modern format in 2013: *The Life of John Calvin*, W J Grier.

[435] Simon J Kistemaker, 1 Corinthians, Baker, pp 587-588.
[436] Op. Cit. pp 33.
[437] Robert Allen, *The Presbyterian College Belfast*, Centenary Volume 1853-1953, William Mullan & Son Ltd, 1954, p 259.
[438] Austin Fulton, *Biography of J Ernest Davey*, PCI, 1970, pp 32-33.
[439] *Ibid*, p 33.
The Scopes Evolution Trial, often referred to as "The Monkey Trial", took place in Dayton, Tennessee, from 10-25 July 1925. In March 1925 the Tennessee courts had made it unlawful for teachers in publicly funded schools "to teach any theory that denies the story of the Divine Creation of man as taught in the Bible, and to teach instead that man has descended from a lower order of animals." John T Scopes and others agreed that Scopes, a biology teacher, would break the March 1925 law in order to set up a test case. The trial generated sensational public interest and reporters arrived from various parts of the world, making the trial one of the best known in American legal history. At the end of the dramatic proceedings the jury convicted Scopes of breaking the law and the Judge imposed the minimum fine of $100. A year later the Supreme Court of Tennessee reversed the decision on a technicality, namely that the jury, not the judge, must impose the fine if it was over $50, and dismissed the case. To have the appeal dismissed on a technicality was the last thing the defendants wanted—their goal was constitutional change, but the whole episode was an important setback for the creationist lobby.
[440] Ned B. Stonehouse, *J. Gresham Machen, A Biographical Memoir*, Banner of Truth, 1987, p 336. See pp 336-339.
[441] Rolland McCune, *Promise Unfulfilled, The Failed Strategy of Modern Evangelicalism*, Ambassador International, 2004, p 16. See discussion of Fundamentalism pp 15-26.
[442] Robin Chichester-Clark sent a formal acknowledgement; Mills, Cunningham, Pounder, Hamilton, Currie, and Clark sent replies.
[443] Strategy and longer-term outlook such as five and 10 year plans were fashionable in industry at that time and that played some part in EPC thinking on these lines.
[444] **Past and Present**
    A Memorable Stand
    Current Character
Vision for the Future
    Church Growth and Evangelism
    Helping Churches to Grow
    Planting New Churches
    Fellowship and Friendliness
    Communications and Public Image
    Foreign Missions
    Ministry and Administration
[445] In June 2000 Presbytery encouraged the Committee to explore interest by people in Dromara, Co Down, in starting meetings for the Dromara-Dromore-Moira area, but after some months of mid-week Bible Study it was decided that the opening could not be developed at this time.
[446] Until 1944 Council appointed Ministers to congregations, following consultation. And the 1944 ruling that a congregation could call its own Minister was only *in principle*—"application could not be made at present"! It was not until 1953 that the calls procedure was regularised by specific legislation.
[447] On this basis we invite delegates from: Affinity, Christian Reformed Church of the Netherlands, Congregational Union of Ireland, Evangelical Presbyterian Church of England and Wales, Free Church of Scotland, Free Church of Scotland Continuing, Orthodox Presbyterian Church USA, Reformed Churches in the Netherlands (Liberated), Reformed Presbyterian Church in Ireland.
[448] It is good that the chosen title *Book of Praise* has such a close link with the Psalter and with the Council's desire in 1933 for a church-wide "universal book of praise". *Book of Praise* is, however, far from unique as a title. It has been adopted by various bodies and publishers, of which probably the best known is *Book of Praise, Anglo-Genevan Psalter* published by the Canadian Reformed Churches in 1972. It is a book of Psalms with a selection of Hymns and Paraphrases,

incorporating the Three Forms of Unity, Ecumenical Creeds, Prayers and Liturgical Forms. It has gone through revisions and re-prints during the 1980s and 90s.

[449] Affinity.org.uk

[450] www.affinity.org.uk expresses this change as a asterisked footnote to its Doctrinal Belief: "Some members of Affinity believe that the visible church comprises baptised professors of the faith and their baptised covenant children."

[451] It is not our purpose to detail the case or to comment upon it. The case has attracted extensive comment including statements and articles by the Free Church of Scotland and the Free Church of Scotland (Continuing). Our purpose is to outline how the EPC Presbytery managed its effects within its own borders and how it has related to both bodies.

IEC/EPC has never had a formal relationship with the Free Church of Scotland in terms of the mutual eligibility of Ministers or members. Nevertheless the relationship has been by far our closest and has expressed itself in co-operation, support and friendship. James Hunter supported the Free Church case in the PCI courts, 1900-1905, and this brought him to some prominence in PCI. Rev. John MacLeod, later Principal of the Free Church College, came to speak in support of James Hunter during the pre-Assembly public campaign in 1927. A Free Church speaker featured at the conferences, 1928-1930, to launch the IEC and later at our 20th, 40th and 50th anniversaries. The Free Church has trained 11 of our Students for the Ministry since 1932 and we have co-operated with the Free Church in missions since 1937. The Free Church began sending a representative to our AGM in 1980 and in 1981 EPC began sending a representative to the Foreign Missions Board. Through the years Free Church Ministers have visited to provide pulpit supply, to speak at conferences and at mission occasions.

[452] At Presbytery's request an EPC delegation met with the FCoS Ecumenical Relations Committee in Ayr on 14 February 2000. In March 2000 Presbytery decided to exchange delegates with FCoS in the Spring of 2000 but when the Free Church (Continuing) sent a letter inviting an EPC delegate to its Assembly it re-opened that part of the discussion. The outcome was that Presbytery decided to send the Moderator and the Editor of the *Evangelical Presbyterian* as a 'Press Agent' to the FCoS Assembly and two observers to that of the FCC. The observers to FCC engaged in detailed discussions with FCC representatives during the visit.

On receiving reports from both visits Presbytery took the view that the Free Church situation was still evolving and decided to consider the matter again in December 2000, subsequent to the October 2000 FCoS Commission. Our December decision was to exchange a delegate with FCoS and an observer with FCC in 2011. The meeting also decided not to send Students for the Ministry to Scotland in view of the conflict situation that existed. The February 2001 meeting of Presbytery rescinded the December 2000 decision on 'Assembly' exchange and decided that it shall "in normal circumstances appoint the Moderator as a delegate to both purporting General Assemblies of the Free Church of Scotland and that we shall invite a delegate from each body to our APPR." It was also decided that it would not normally be permissible to raise the Scotland situation before the review date, the next one fixed for December 2003.

The December 2003 decisions extended the 'even-handed' treatment of both bodies until a December 2006 review, along with the ban on reference to the Free Church situation in Presbytery without sanction of the Presbytery Arrangements Committee, and all Presbyters were required to respect the convictions of their colleagues on the issue. In addition, EPC Mission Strategy was released from an earlier embargo. It was decided also to pray for the peace and prosperity of the two bodies and to write to each expressing our grief over their prospective actions in the secular courts.

[453] There were two 19th century secessions among the Dutch Reformed Churches - the Secession of 1834 and the Abraham Kuyper-led *Doleantie* of 1886. A process towards the end of the century reunited the great majority of the secession churches to form the Dutch Reformed Church (GKN). A section of CKGN felt it impossible, on Scriptural grounds, to join the merger and remained as CKGN. There was another split from GKN in 1944 over the Covenant of Grace and Infant Baptism. Opposing Ministers and elders were deposed and having liberated themselves from the GKN federation established GKNV.

[454] In 2015 congregations in Barry, Blackburn, Bury St Edmonds, Cambridge, Cardiff-Bethel, Cardiff-Immanuel, Chelmsford, Cheltenham-Naunton Lane, Cheltenham-North, Durham,

Gateshead, Hexham, Hull, Sheffield, Solihull, Evangelical Reformed Church in Sweden-Tranås and Stockholm.

[455] They began in 1987 and had reached Issue No 86 by the end of 2014. From 1987-1989 - *Letter from Nigeria*, 1989-1993 - *News to You from Bukuru*, 1993 on - *Garland Update*. ACTS eNews began in March 2004 and continues.

[456] Evangelical Book Shop Managers: W J Grier-1927-1951, S G Shanks-1951-1970 (WJG Superintendent 1951-1958), Samuel Watson (1970-1974), John Grier (1974-2012), Colin Campbell (2012-)

[457] *The Evangelical Presbyterian*, Jul-Aug 1999, pp 7-8.

[458] Steve Bruce, *Paisley, Religion and Politics in Northern Ireland*, Oxford, 2007.

[459] *Ibid*, p 26.

[460] Laurence Kirkpatrick, *Presbyterians in Ireland, An Illustrated History*, Booklink, 2006, pp 76-77.

[461] Not Rev. David Stewart, B.A., D.D., of Cregagh Presbyterian Church Belfast, who wrote *The Seceders in Ireland*, PHSI, 1950. He provides an excellent diagram of Irish Presbyterian History.

[462] *A History of Congregations in the Presbyterian Church in Ireland 1610-1982*, PHSI, 1982, p 665

[463] Austin Fulton, *Biography of J Ernest Davey*, PCI, 1970, p 32.

[464] Ed Maloney & Andy Pollak, *Paisley*, Poolbeg 1986, p 21.

[465] Steve Bruce, *God Save Ulster - The Religion & Politics of Paisleyism*, Oxford University Press, 1989, pp 23-24.

[466] David N. Livingstone and Ronald A. Wells, Ulster-American Religion, Notre Dam, 1999, p 68.

[467] Professor R F G Holmes, *Our Irish Presbyterian Heritage*, Publications Committee of the Presbyterian Church in Ireland, 1985, pp 153-155. See also *The Presbyterian Church in Ireland, A Popular History*, Columba Press, 2000, pp 130-132.

[468] One of the most influential books in 20th century economics, was, *Small is Beautiful*, 1973, by E F Schumacher. Over 700,000 copies across a range of languages were sold and it was republished in 1999 as a 25th Anniversary Edition. Comments about its value use expressions like prescient, universal, seminal, and almost timeless. Schumacher contends that the macro organisations and specialisation of the western world have far from been an unqualified success—they have serious downsides. He advocates smaller working units, regionally based and using local resources. There are important differences between the field of economics and the church, but the principle expressed in the universally known title of Schumacher's book should not be ignored. Sometimes "the sons of this world are more shrewd in their generation that the sons of light." (Luke 16.8)

[469] DGH is a religious and social historian and Visiting Professor of History at Hillside College, Hillsdale, Michigan. He has served as Dean of Academic Affairs at Westminster Theological Seminary, California, taught Church History and served as Librarian at Westminster Theological Seminary, Philadelphia, directed the Institute for the Study of American Evangelicals at Wheaton College and was Director of Partnered Projects, Academic Programs and Faculty Development at the Intercollegiate Studies in Wilmington, Delaware. He is a well-known author.

[470] J. Gresham Machen's Response to Modernism, 1993 Bethlehem Conference for Pastors.

[471] George Marsden, "Understanding J. Gresham Machen," in *Understanding Fundamentalism and Evangelicalism* (Grand Rapids: Wm. B. Eerdmans Publishing Co., 1991), p. 200.

[472] *The Gospel Magazine*, July 1967, p 315.

[473] *A Thoroughly Educated Ministry, Discussions*, Vol Two, Banner of Truth, p 675.

[474] Perhaps a version of "Those who cannot remember the past are condemned to repeat it", George Santayana (1905) Reason in Common Sense, p. 284, Vol 1 of The Life of Reason

[475] *The Heritage of our Fathers*, G N M Collins, Knox Press, 1974, Introduction, p v.

[476] Rev. David Stewart, B.A., D.D., in *The Seceders in Ireland*, PHSI, 1950, pp 32-33, gives a somewhat amusing account of changes that arrived with new thinking, but he is making a serious point:
New modes of thought were accompanied by new notions about other matters, such as dress, speech, and manner of living. In 1697 the Synod felt called upon to adopt means of checking

these extravagances, and accordingly recommended "that all ministers be grave and decent in their apparel, and that this be considered and inquired into by the respective presbyteries." Nor was the grandiloquence of certain ministers and probationers overlooked ...

Unhappily these admonitions fell upon deaf ears, for in 1700, just as the new century opened, the Synod found it necessary to adopt more stringent measures for the purpose of arresting these innovations. These peculiarities must have been very pronounced seeing the Synod could not tolerate them without a public revelation of their displeasure. Two overtures were passed "for reforming the levitees" [frivolities], the first of which dealt with apparel. "That there were some ministers, their wives and children, [who] are, too gaudy and vain in their apparel, and some too sordid, therefore, that it be recommended to the several presbyteries to reform these faults in themselves and theirs, and study decency and gravity in their apparel and wigs, avoid powderings, vain cravats, half-shirts, and the like." This was a brave attempt to find the golden mean, and secure uniformity in fashion as they hoped to do in doctrine. In one sense this enactment was a stimulus to trade by bringing the sordid up to the average, and in another sense it depressed business by suppressing extravagance. One would like to know where these dandies paraded in order to show off their finery, as at that date Belfast was little more than a village, and most of the other towns in Ulster were not even contemplated. It looks as if they were content to "waste their sweetness on the desert air."

The second overture was even more immoderate, as it was directed against gourmandizing, and was meant to correct the bill of fare. "That sumptuous dinners like feasts, on Mondays after communions, be forborne in ministers' houses, and none entertained that day but their guests who lodged with them; and also, that sumptuous prodigal dinners at ordinations be forborne."

[477] *History of Presbyterianism in Ulster*, Thomas Hamilton, Mourne Missionary Trust, 1982, p 116

[478] Ibid, p 116.

[479] *History of the Presbyterian Church in Ireland*, James Seaton Reid, D.D., M.R.I.A., Vol III, Chapter 25, Second Edition, Tentmaker Publications, 1998, p 156.

[480] Ibid, p 130.

[481] Ibid, p 159.

[482] *History of Presbyterianism in Ulster*, Thomas Hamilton, Mourne Missionary Trust, 1982, p 129.

[483] *Historical and Literary Memorials of Presbyterianism in Ireland 1731-1800*, Thomas Witherow, p 346.

[484] *The Code of the Evangelical Presbyterian Church* requires each minister and elder to reaffirm his subscription to the Confessional Standards annually (D1.4, F1.3,DSO 1). The annual Formula of Subscription includes the following clause: "In addition, I confirm that I have again familiarised myself with the contents of the Confessional Standards."

[485] Finlay Holmes, *Our Irish Presbyterian Heritage*, Publications Committee of the Presbyterian Church in Ireland, 1985, p 61.

[486] Lewis Carroll, *Through the Looking Glass*, 1872.

[487] Similar expressions are found in the writings of the Dutch reformed theologian, Gisbertus Voetius (1589-1676), a leading figure of the Synod of Dordt.

[488] G N M Collins, *The Heritage of our Fathers*, Knox Press, 1974, p 82

[489] J Gresham Machen, *Christianity and Liberalism*, Victory Press, 1923, p 7.

[490] Finlay Holmes, *Our Irish Presbyterian Heritage*, Publications Committee of the Presbyterian Church in Ireland, 1985, p 61.

[491] *Select Writings of William Cunningham, The Principles of the Reformation not the cause of Sects and Heresies*, John Hendryx, Editor, Kindle, 2012.

[492] The Roman Catholic Church has vested itself with infallible teaching authority, the Magisterium, through the Pope and the body of Bishops for whom it claims apostolic succession. Consequently it made submission to the Church's teaching in all matters of faith and practice conditional for salvation. Specifically, the Magisterium had authority to bind the conscience: "The Roman Pontiff, head of the college of bishops, enjoys this infallibility in virtue of his office, when, as supreme pastor and teacher of all the faithful – who confirms his brethren in the faith he proclaims by a definitive act a doctrine pertaining to faith or morals. The infallibility

promised to the Church is also present in the body of bishops when, together with Peter's successor, they exercise the supreme Magisterium, above all in an Ecumenical Council." (#891 Catechism of the Catholic Church)

Catholic apologists have attacked the right of private judgement from the Reformation to the present time. Regarding the word of the Apostles, John Henry Newman asserted in 1849: "Men were told to submit their reason to a living authority. Moreover, whatever an Apostle said, his converts were bound to believe; when they entered the Church, they entered it in order to learn. The Church was their teacher; they did not come to argue, to examine, to pick and choose, but to accept whatever was put before them. ... then there was no room whatever for what is now called private judgement." (*Faith and Private Judgement* from *Discourses addressed to Mixed Congregations*, www.newmanreader.org) And he added: "If you will not look out for a living authority, and will bargain for private judgement, then say at once that you have not the Apostolic faith." Catholic polemicists argue that private judgement is manifestly a failed philosophy, a licence for the development of heresy, a commentary on the sin of Adam and Eve. They point to the multiplication of Protestant denominations as a product of private judgement. Their scattered pronouncements are strong as they speak of the abyss of private judgement, of periodic 'reboots' of Christian theology. "Unfortunately, what Protestantism has done is to enshrine rebellious, fallen, private judgement as a dogma of the faith, and the consequences of it are manifest. It doesn't work!" "Nevertheless, private judgement at the end of the day is private judgement and will always be anathema in Catholic theology, a sure and very fast way to wash out into schism." "When Peter, the Rock, is rejected, Catholic unity dissolves into Protestant rivalry." (Stephen Hand, *"Traditionalists," Tradition And Private Judgement*, www.salbert.tripod.com/u1.htm

One strong emphasis is to see Protestant doctrines as re-inventions of the Magisterium: "Each group has its own Magisterium – its own teaching authority – but because they are rooted in the doctrine of private judgment, they encourage splits and end up operating in a capricious, careless manner in rank disregard for Christ's teachings and they actually encourage the tossing of believers to and fro with every wind of doctrine. ... By generating the winds of doctrine they are acting counter to the purpose for which Christ established a Magisterium in the first place, which was to prevent doctrinal confusion and give the ordinary people safety and security in their beliefs.

(The Roman Catholic Church divides the Magisterium into the Sacred Magisterium and the Ordinary Magisterium. The Sacred Magisterium comprises all the infallible teachings of the Church – those of the Pope speaking *ex cathedra*, the conciliar canons and decrees of Councils and the Ordinary Magisterium. The teachings of the Ordinary Magisterium are those without solemn definition such as those by local Bishops and are subject to possible revision.)

[493] *The Code of the Evangelical Presbyterian Church*, B1.2.

[494] For fuller discussion see *The Background and Significance of the Adopting Act of 1729*, James R Payton, Jnr, in *Pressing Towards the Mark*, Essays Commemorating Fifty Years of the Orthodox Presbyterian Church, 1936-1986, pp 131-145.

[495] Charles Hodge, *Reunion of the Old and New-School Churches*, The Princeton Repertory, July, 1867.

[496] David B Calhoun, *Princeton Seminary, The Majestic Testimony, 1869-1929*, Vol 2, Banner of Truth, 1996, p 349.

[497] *The Right of Private Judgement and Due Freedom of Enquiry*, Rev. Archibald Bruce (1746-1816), Secession Church, Linlithgow, and Professor of Divinity for the General Associate Synod.

[498] R L Dabney, *A Thoroughly Educated Ministry, Discussions*, Vol Two, Banner of Truth, 1982, p 676.

[499] Finlay Holmes, *Our Irish Presbyterian Heritage*, Publications Committee of the Presbyterian Church in Ireland, 1985, p 61.

[500] J E Davey used the expression: "... few can live at any considerable distance from the thought-currents of their age and environment". *The Changing Vesture of the Faith*, p 18.

[501] C S Lewis, *Surprised by Joy*, Geoffrey Bles, 1955, Harper Collins, 2002, pp 240-241.

[502] *The Story of Old Side Presbyterianism*, John R. Muether, Extracted from <u>Ordained Servant</u> vol. 5, no. 3 (July 1996).

[503] R Kent Hughes and Bryan Chapell, *1 & 2 Timothy and Titus,* Crossway 2000, P 66
[504] BEC debated Union and Separation at its 1985 Study Conference. See Foundations, A Theological Journal published by the British Evangelical Council, Issue No 15, Autumn 1985. Neil Richards concluded his report with Conclusions Drawn: "The continuing need for us to work for ways to express genuine evangelical church unity. The continuing need for us to remain separate from doctrinally-mixed denominations. The continuing need for us to grant each other liberty to pursue what each believes to be right within our common commitment to the aims of the BEC and to each other within the BEC family."
[505] Klaas Runia, *Reformation Today*, Banner of Truth 1968, p 111.
[506] *Ibid.* Quoted from the Report of the Leicester Conference, April 1965. The analogy of Spurgeon's stand in the Down-grade controversy is noted in the reference.
[507] The Unity of the Church was the theme of the 2001 General Conference of the International Conference of Reformed Churches, held in Philadelphia.
[508] Iain H Murray, *The Forgotten Spurgeon*, The Banner of Truth Trust, 1966, p150.
[509] David B Calhoun, *Princeton Seminary*, Vol 2, *The Majestic Testimony* 1869-1929, p 351
[510] Johannes G. Vos (1903-1983) served the Reformed Presbyterian Church of North America throughout his life. He was minister of two congregations and served as a missionary in Manchuria for 11 years. He then became a professor at Geneva College, USA from 1954 until his retirement in 1973. In 1946 he founded and edited the *Blue Banner Faith and Life*, a quarterly theological journal, and kept it going, single-handed, until 1979. His popular writing style and his ability to explain complexities simply earned him the accolade "The People's Theologian". His ongoing interest in mission work in China led to the co-founding with Rev. Samuel E Boyle and Dr Charles Chao of the *Reformation Translation Fellowship* which translates and publishes Reformed works for the Chinese Church.
[511] *The Irish Evangelical*, December 1953, p 15.
[512] *When is Separation a Necessary Duty?* was the leader in the EP, November 1967. It came soon after the 450th Anniversary of Luther's 95 Theses and the Lloyd-Jones call in 1966 for Evangelicals to leave the major denominations. It was based on two articles by Dr Klaas Runia, at the time at Reformed Theological College, Geelong, Victoria, Australia, which appeared in *Christianity Today* in June and July 1967, and in the *Christian*, July 1967. Klaas Runia's *Reformation Today*, was a more comprehensive statement of the issues, particularly Chapter 7 – *The Question of Separation.*
[513] **Exodus 34:6**: And the LORD passed before him and proclaimed, "The LORD, the LORD God, merciful and gracious, longsuffering, and abounding in goodness and truth …
Ps 119.160: The entirety of Your word is truth …
John 1.14: And the Word became flesh and dwelt among us, and we beheld His glory, the glory as of the only begotten of the Father, full of grace and truth.
John 8.32: And you shall know the truth, and the truth shall make you free.
John 14.6: Jesus said to him, "I am the way, the truth, and the life. No one comes to the Father except through Me."
John 16.13: However, when He, the Spirit of truth, has come, He will guide you into all truth
John 17.17, 19: Sanctify them by Your truth. Your word is truth … And for their sakes I sanctify Myself, that they also may be sanctified by the truth.
John 18.37: For this cause I was born, and for this cause I have come into the world, that I should bear witness to the truth. Everyone who is of the truth hears My voice.
Rom 1.25: who exchanged the truth of God for the lie, and worshipped and served the creature rather than the Creator, who is blessed forever. Amen.
Rom 2.8: but to those who are self-seeking and do not obey the truth …
Rom 3.7: For if the truth of God has increased through my lie to His glory, why am I also still judged as a sinner?
Rom 15.8: Now I say that Jesus Christ has become a servant to the circumcision for the truth of God, to confirm the promises made to the fathers …
2 Cor 4.2: by manifestation of the truth commending ourselves to every man's conscience in the sight of God.
2 Cor 13.8: For we can do nothing against the truth, but for the truth."

Gal 2.5: to whom we did not yield submission even for an hour, that the truth of the gospel might continue with you.
Gal 2.14: But when I saw that they were not straightforward about the truth of the gospel …
Gal 5.7: You ran well. Who hindered you from obeying the truth?
Eph 1.13: In Him you also trusted, after you heard the word of truth, the gospel of your salvation …
Eph 4.21: if indeed you have heard Him and have been taught by Him, as the truth is in Jesus…
Eph 6.14: Stand therefore, having girded your waist with truth …
2 Thess 2.10: and with all unrighteous deception among those who perish, because they did not receive the love of the truth, that they might be saved …
2 Thess 2.13: God from the beginning chose you for salvation through sanctification by the Spirit and belief in the truth …
1 Tim 6.5: useless wranglings of men of corrupt minds and destitute of the truth, who suppose that godliness is a means of gain. From such withdraw yourself.
2 Tim 3.8: Now as Jannes and Jambres resisted Moses, so do these also resist the truth: men of corrupt minds, disapproved concerning the faith …
Jas 5.19: Brethren, if anyone among you wanders from the truth, and someone turns him back
3 John 3-4: For I rejoiced greatly when brethren came and testified of the truth that is in you, just as you walk in the truth. ⁴ I have no greater joy than to hear that my children walk in truth.

[514] See John Murray, *The Epistle to the Romans*, Eerdmans, 1968, Vol 2, p 139.

[515] See Alfred Edersheim, *Old Testament Bible History*, AP&A, Hendrickson, 1995, Book 1, Chapter 22, p 75.

[516] J G Vos, *Religious Isolationism*, quoted in *IE*, December 1953, p 15.

[517] Alabama, Florida, Georgia, Louisiana and Mississippi followed in January 1861 and the six formed the Confederate States of America in February 1861. Later in 1861 five other states, Arkansas, North Carolina, Tennessee, Texas and Virginia seceded to the Confederacy.

[518] The Savoy Declaration of Faith and Order, 1658, is version of the Westminster Confession modified and adapted to suit Congregational church polity. The committee which drew up the declaration included Thomas Goodwin and John Owen. The Baptist Confession of Faith, 1689, is also an adaptation of Westminster to reflect Baptist views on baptism and church government.

[519] See: Ligon Duncan, Editor, *The Westminster Confession into the 21ˢᵗ Century*, Christian Focus Publications – Mentor, Vol 1 2003, Vol 2 2004, Vol 3 2009; R C Sproul, *Truths we Confess – A Layman's Guide to the Westminster Confession of Faith*, 3 Vols, P&R, 2007; J V Fesko, *The Theology of the Westminster Standards*, Crossway, 2014; Chad Van Dixhoorn, *Confessing the Faith – A reader's guide to the Westminster Confession of Faith*, Banner of Truth, 2014.

[520] As part of a drive within PCUSA for confessional revision the Church added two chapters (34-35) to WCF in 1903. D G Hart and John R Meuther comment in *Turning Points in American Presbyterian History, Part 8: Confessional Revision in 1903*: "In 1903 the church added two chapters on 'The Holy Spirit' and 'The Love of God and Missions.' Both were crafted with language that was vaguely biblical and not distinctively Reformed. In addition, the church revised chapter 16, article 7, which described the works of the unregenerate. Where these works were formerly described as 'sinful and cannot please God,' the revised language described them as 'praiseworthy.' Perhaps of greatest significance was the inclusion of a 'Declaratory Statement' that sought to explain the Confession's doctrine of election. In words that many accused of being deliberately ambiguous, the statement offered an 'avowal … of certain inferences' about predestination, softening the doctrine for those who found it offensive and contradictory to the doctrine of human freedom." (http://www.opc.org/new_horizons/NH05/08c.html)

[521] Westminster: *Directory for the Public Worship of God – Administration of the Sacraments*.

[522] Chad Van Dixhoorn, *Confessing the Faith – A reader's guide to the Westminster Confession of Faith*, Banner of Truth, 2014, pp 276-277.

[523] Derek W H Thomas, *Acts*, Reformed Expository Commentary, P&R Publishing, 2011, pp 580-581.

[524] Carl R Trueman, *The Preacher as Prophet: Some Notes on the Nature of Preaching*, The People's

Theologian, Writings in Honour of Donald Macleod, Mentor, Christian Focus Publications, 2011, p 212.

[525] J V Fesko, *The Theology of the Westminster Standards*, Crossway, 2014, p 360. See pp 357-361 for fuller discussion. See also R C Sproul, *Truths we Confess – A Layman's Guide to the Westminster Confession of Faith*, 3 Vols, P&R, 2007, Volume 2, pp 328-330, and Chad Van Dixhoorn, *Confessing the Faith – A reader's guide to the Westminster Confession of Faith*, Banner of Truth, 2014, p 285.

[526] See also: Ligon Duncan, Editor, *The Westminster Confession into the 21st Century*, Christian Focus Publications – Mentor, Vol 2, 2004, Douglas F Kelly, *The Puritan Regulative Principle and Contemporary Worship*, pp 63-98; Nick Needham, *Westminster and Worship: Psalms, Hymns? and Musical Instruments?*, pp 223-306.

[527] *The Code of the Evangelical Presbyterian Church*, D3.1.

[528] See Ernest C Brown, *Qualified Commissioned and Accountable – Studies in Eldership*, EPC, 1993, Revised 2013.

[529] Chad Van Dixhoorn, *Confessing the Faith – A reader's guide to the Westminster Confession of Faith*, Banner of Truth, 2014, pp 10-11.

Index

Index

The Contents (pages 6-10) provide a helpful main subject index
Endnote numbers are in italics, each list prefaced with *en*

1859, Revival, 53,476, 478, 485, *en 46*
1911, PCI Code, 66, 72
Aalders, G Ch, 290-291, 307
Abak, Nigeria, 373
Aberdeen, 61-62, 298, 485-486,
Abernethy, J, 39,396
Aberystwyth, 376
Abortion and Alcoholism, 341
Accrington, 337-338, 357, 444, 449, 452
Accusers, 133-135, 138, 140, 152, 160, 165, 167, 167-171, 174-175, 179, 182-183, 185, 188-189, 196, 224-225, 230, 237-238, 332, 335, 377-378, 434-436, 439, *en 173, 421*
Act of Uniformity, 35
Act of Union 1707, 42-43
Act of Union 1800, 49, 96, *en 38*
Action Partners, 374
Addis Ababa, 375, 386
Addison, J, *en 391*
Addley, WP, 18, 69, *en 76*
Adopting Act 1729, 60, 402, *en 365, 494*
Adoptionists, 211, 440
Affinity, 339, 345, 366, 368, *en 449, 450*
Africa Christian Textbooks, 373, 469
Africa Inland Mission, 16, 260, 374
After Calvin, en 286
AIDS is Real and it's in Our Church, 374
Akroyd, Bob, 474
Alabama, 517
Albania, 282
Albert Hall Belfast, 98
Albert Street, Belfast, 97-98
Alexander Hall, Princeton, 90
Alexander, Archibald, 87
Alexander's Hymns No 3, 245
Alice in Wonderland, 398
All for Jesus – the Life of W P Nicholson, 18, *en 141, 144*
Allen, R, 66, 69, 74, 78, 116, 132, 168, 331, *en 2, 62, 71, 79, 82, 88, 102, 106-107, 111, 145, 155, 164, 170, 172, 388, 437*
Allen S, 382
Alliance Hall Belfast, 108, 122, 232, 235-236, 249-250
Alliance News, 230-231, *en 359*
Allis, OT, 88-90, *en 125*
Almuñécar Spain, 363, 387
Alur language, 375
Amending Acts, 106, 401, 285, 404

American Civil War, 416
American Presbyterian Church, 60, 81, 178, 382, 401, 405, *en 519*
Amsterdam, 289-291
And can it be that I should gain, 260, *en 393*
Anderson, JT, 70
Anderson, R, 108
Andrews, JC, 254
Andrews, JM, 282
Andrews, T, *en 400*
Anglican, 36, 53, 80, 196, *en 118*
Anglo-Normans, 28-29
Annual Presentation of Presbytery Reports, 215, 340-341, 361
Annual Statistical Returns, 263
Anschluss, 282
Anselm, 194, *en 292*
Antiburghers, 43-44
Antinomianism, 142-145, 193
Antrim Monthly Meeting, 33
Anxious Bench, 406
Apollinarianism, *en 245*
Apostasy of English Non-Conformity, 237, *en 368*
Apostasy, 231, 236-237, 289, 315-316, 406, 412, 414, *en 366, 368*
Aquinas, *en 326*
Ardill, Mrs E, 269
Arianism, 38, 40-42, 48-55, 69, 88, 107, 147, 155, 178-179, 269, 379, *en 80, 269*
Aristotle, 209
Arkansas, *en 517*
Arminianism, 406
Armstrong, WP, 88
Arnhem, 283
Articles of Religion, 34
articulus stantis aut cadentis, 192
Asquith, H, 96
Associate Presbytery Scotland 1733, 43
Associate Synod Scotland, 43
Athanasius, 108, 269, 440
Atkinson, Basil C, 246
Atkinson, SGT, 213, 464, 467-468
Atlantic, 84, 92-93, 282
Atonement in the Light of History, 62
Atonement, 18-19, 62-63, 68, 136, 143, 145-148, 152, 160, 172, 175, 185-186, 193-196, 205, 403, *en 188, 193, 206, 289, 291, 292, 294, 295*

523

Auburn Affirmation, 402-403
Auld Licht Anti-Burghers, **en** *27*
Auld Licht Burghers, **en** *27*
Australia, 97, 182, 252, 254, 291, 307, 343, 350-351, 486-487, **en** *408, 512,*
Austria, 282
Authorised Version, 200, 315
Autumn Evening Lectures, 338, 364, 476
Bailey, KE, **en** *309*
Ballantine, WCJ, 213, 333, 467
Ballyclare, 128, 217, 245, 246, 248, 249, 251, 253, 257, 259, 287, 301, 345, 356, 361, 369, 371, 443, 444, 445, 446, 447, 448, 449, 457, 471, 472, 473, 474
Ballycoan, Belfast, 333
Ballyfore, **en** *384*
Ballymena, 41-42, 97, 258, 377
Ballynure, **en** *384*
Ballywalter, 303, 481
Balmoral Show, 219, 302, 326, 356-357
Banbridge, 70, 257, 314-315
Bandon, Cork, 482, **en** *41*
Bangor, Co Down, 20, 28, 31, 32, 33, 97, 100, 218, 287, 314, 324, 337, 355, 356, 357, 377, 417, 443, 449, 457, 459, **en** *6, 212*
Bann, 244, 358
Banner of Truth, 18, 19, 20, 131, 191, 246, 325, 327, 351, 470, 471, **en** *22, 98, 123, 126-127, 195, 198, 201, 214, 327, 339, 249, 358, 374, 378, 383. 385, 389, 395, 398, 418, 432, 434, 440, 473, 496, 498, 505, 508, 519, 522, 525, 529*
Baptism of the Spirit, 102-103, **en** *141*
Baptism, 315, 368, 399, 425, 441-442, 471, **en** *297, 518*
Baptism, Infant, 81, 421, 429, 441, **en** *453, 518*
Baptist Union, 293, 410
Barbican Mission to Jews, 266
Barkley,178, **en** *167*
Barnes, S, 102, **en** *141, 144*
Barth, C, 199, 500
Bauckham, R, **en** *310*
Beckett, RC, 213, 333, 350, 388, 466-468, 475-476
Beginnings of Life, 341
Behold your God, **en** *99*
Belfast Academical Institution, 48-49, 76, **en** *118*
Belfast Academy, 49
Belfast Assembly Hall Mission, 102
Belfast Bible College, 473
Belfast City Council, 310
Belfast Newsletter, 181, 224-225, 227, 332

Belfast Ropeworks, 244
Belfast Society, 38-40, 43, 396-397
Belfast Telegraph, 114, 156, 158, 164, 224, 226, 232, **en** *362, 371*
Belgian Gospel Mission, 260-261
Belgic Confession, 508, 510
Bellew, G, 236, 267
Bequest, 264, 302, 340, 358
Berkouwer, GC, 201, 291
Berry Street, 183, 238, 493, **en** *356, 372*
Best Books, 327, 471, **en** *432*
Between the Times, 295, **en** *408*
Bible Institute of Los Angeles (BIOLA), 97, 101
Bible League, 246-247, 252, 307, **en** *214, 383*
Bible Training Institute Glasgow, 97
Biblical Criticism, 60-61, 75
Biblical Doctrines, **en** *339*
Binitarianism, 211-212
Binity, 174, 212, 439
Biography of J. Ernest Davey, 186, 330, 332, **en** *168, 232*
Bismarck, 382,
Black Cat, **en** *354*
Black Man, 54
Black Oath, 34
Blackburn, 357, 370, 444, 449, 457, **en** *454*
Blair, Annie, 326, 339, 365, 385
Blair, G, 81
Blair, HJ, 81, 288
Blair, JDP, 214, 288, 297
Blair, Robert, 31-33, 34, 229, **en** *6*
Blaize, Achill,e 473, 475
Blitzkrieg, 282
Bloody Mary, 29
Blyth, M, 374, 469
Bodmer papyrus, 198
Boice, J M, 18, 62, 484, **en** *63*
Bolshevik, 158, **en** *210, 211*
Bonar, Andrew, 249
Bonnie Prince Charlie, 483
Book of Common Prayer, 36
Book of Kells, 28
Book *of* Praise, EPC, 266, 364-365, **en** *448,*
Book of Praise, Anglo-Genevan Psalter, **en** *448,*
Boru, Brian, 28
Botanic Avenue, 216, 233, 245, 246, 247, 249, 253, 254, 259, 262, 268, 269, 283, 287, 288, 291, 293, 294, 297, 298, 300, 304, 305, 306, 316, 317, 324, 325, 326, 334, 365, 392, 444, 445, 446, 449, 452, 453, 457, 462, 492, **en** *142, 209, 391, 429*
Botanic Avenue, RPCI, 233, **en** *209*
Boyle, SE, **en** *416, 510*

Boyne, Battle, 36
Boys' Brigade, 305
Brady, J, 162
Breach-ecclesiastical, 44-45, 141, 181, 208, *en 209*
Brice, Edward, 32
Briggs, CA, 60, *en 59*
Bristol, 40-41
British Council of Churches, 292, 346
British Evangelical Council, 292, 345, 351, 366-368, 470-471, *en 504*
British Israelites, 299
Britton, J, 235, 264
Broad(ening) Church, 14, 19, 23, 40, 56, 59-61, 63, 66, 68, 72, 74, 183, 399, 402, *en 59*
Broadening Church, 60, *en 54*
Broadisland, 32
Brookeborough, 315
Brooks, R, 474
Brown, H, 313
Brown, N, 78, 79, *en 109, 112, 114*
Brown's Bay, 303, 389, 481
Bruce, AB, 65
Bruce, Archibald, 403, *en 497*
Bruce, FF, 197, *en 301*
Bruce, JW, 494,
Bruce, M, *en 391*
Bruce, S, 116, 182, 242, 254, 378, 379, *en 164, 272, 377, 421, 458, 465*
Bruce, Wm, 49-50
Bube, M, 372
Buchanan, R, 42, *en 23-25*
Bukuru, Nigeria, 373, *en 455*
Bunyan, John, 250, 469, 478, *en 385*
Burgess Oath, 43-44, *en 27*
Burghers, 43-44, *en 27*
Burke, GN, 14, 213, 333, 356, 372, 467, 468, 475
Burke, R, 469
Butler Act, 314
Calhoun, DB, 60, 131, 410, *en 53, 123, 495*
Calvary, 136-137, 143-145, 195, 198, 208, 434, *en 183-184*
Calvin, J, 18, 19, 33, 47, 68, 140, 146, 147, 166, 168, 192, 193, 194, 195, 198, 233, 235, 307, 323, 327, 383, 471, 474, 476, 478, *en 208, 283, 292-293, 311, 432, 434*
Calvinism – A History, *en 208*
Calvinist, 170, 179, 253
Cambridge University, 101, 246
Campaigners, 305, 392
Campbell, AA, 126, 287-288, 308-309, 336, 344, 367, 466-467, 469
Campbell, CM, 14, 219, 376, *en 455*

Campbell, D, 476
Campbell, Duncan, 472, 476
Campbell, Iain D, 14, 192, 204, 475
Campbell, J, 375, 464
Campbell, JMcL, 195-196, *en 295,*
Camps EPC, 259, 267-268, 303-304, 322, 326, 347-348, 363, 388-392, 430, 481-482
Canada, 91-92, 108, 248, 321, 369, 446, 452, 475, *en 389, 424*
Canons of Dordt, *en 409, 425*
Cape Breton Island, 92, 325
Cape to Cairo Railroad, 97
Cape Town, 343
Cardiff, 475, *en 454*
Cardinal Hume, 346
Carey Lectures, 70, 100
Carlisle, J 51
Carmichael, Amy, 11, 244, 478, *en 378*
Carnlough, 303, 392, 481
Carrickfergus Castle, 29
Carrickfergus, 29, 32-33, 35, 97, 267, 301, *en 384*
Carroll, Lewis, *en 486*
Carson, Alfred, 235, *en 421*
Carson, DA, 197, *en 303*
Carson, Edward, 96, 165
Catechism of the Catholic Church, *en 326*
Cavan, 32, 256
Celts, 28
Cennick, J, 41-42
Central Fund EPC, 263-264, 302, 311
Cerinthus, 228
Ceylon and India General Mission, 260-261
Chafer, LS, 246, 272, 351
Chalcedon, 189, 198, 211
Chalmers, G, 42, 48
Change of heart, 70, 140, 142-143, 147, 193, 434
Change, 405
Changing Vesture of the Faith, 18, 70-74, 133, 139-140, 142-145, 147-148, 165, 167, 169, 171-172, 180, 193, 204, 241, 276, 434, 435-436, 439, 470, 489, *en 187, 284, 421, 500*
Chao, Charles, *en 416, 510*
Chapman, JW, 97
Charges, Heresy Trial, 23, 72, 73, 74, 117, 120, 132, 133, 134, 135, 139, 146, 149, 152, 153, 156, 159, 160, 161, 164, 166, 167, 169, 171, 172, 173, 175, 176, 179, 180, 184, 192, 205, 224, 225, 227, 316, 434, *en 158, 173*
Charismatic Gifts, 103
Charities Commission, 362
Charles I, 33, 35-36, 45

Charles II, 35-36, 316
Chelmsford, 370-371, *en 454*
Chi Rho, 247
Chichester, A, 32
Chichester, FR, 53
Child Evangelism Fellowship, 301
Child's Story Bible, 305, 348
Children's Special Service Mission, 16, 267, 305, *en 213, 392*
China (Inland Mission), 67-69, 80, 85, 231, 260-261, 283, 304, 313, 333, 488, *en 80, 84, 416, 509*
Christ - Active Obedience, 383
Christ – Deity, 38, 51, 68, 108, 136-137, 146, 161, 172, 197, 212, 441, *en 80, 183, 200, 393*
Christ – Divine-human character, 144, 146, 434
Christ – Emotions of, 198
Christ – Mediator, 147, 205, 208, 249, 422
Christ – Messiah, 78, 506, 409
Christ – 'Moral perplexity', 136
Christ - Omniscience, 73, 115, 136-137, 439, *en 245*
Christ – Perfection, 132, 168, 196, *en 100*
Christ - Two Natures, 189, 198, 212
Christ – 'Ideal Being', 136
Christ – Obedience, 140, 143-144, 194, 383, *en 190*
Christ – Union with, 146, 193-194, 411, 428, *en 206*
Christ and the Law in Pauline Theology, *en 296*
Christ Crucified, Understanding the Atonement, *en 188, 193*
Christchurch, 475
Christian Beacon, *en 406*
Christian Doctrine of Reconciliation, *en 295*,
Christian Endeavour Movement, 100, 324
Christian graces, 277, 350, 410, 413, 427-428
Christian Graduate, 327
Christian Hymns, 342, 365
Christian Institute, 363
Christian Liberty, 39, 55, 285, 298, 400-401, 403
Christian Reformed Church of America, 290
Christian Reformed Churches in the Netherlands, 370
Christian Scholarship ..., *en 383*
Christian Workers' Union, 100, 108-110, 230-232, 238, 245, 256, *en 120, 136, 355, 357, 361*
Christian Workers' Union (Alliance Hall) Bible School, 95, 108-109, 118, 122, 230, 232, 249, 252, 277, *en 361*

Christian Workers' Society, 100
Christianity and Liberalism, 89, *en 270, 489*
Christianity Today, *en 295, 511*
Christological Perspectives, *en 277*
Christology, 14, 23, 153, 159, 165, 168, 172, 192, 196, 197, 198, 285, 435
Christ's Crown and Covenant, 34, 45
Church and State, 45, 49, 63, 284
Church Councils, 210, 211
Church Development Committee, 358-359
Church Extension Committee, 334, 336, 338, 354, 358, 371, 469
Church Extension Fund, 312, 338, 355
Church Historian, 339
Church History Editorial Committee, 12
Church Holidays, 339
Church, Imperfect Nature, 412-414
Church, Internal Reformation, 407, 414-415
Church Leaders, 425, 428
Church Members, 237, 288, 323-324, 403, 426, 428-429, 476
Church Nurture, 295, 406, 426, 429, 430, 473
Church Opportunity, 415
Church of Scotland, 35, 42-43, 45, 51, 63-64, 242, *en 27, 60*
Church Sunday School Lesson Book, 304-305
Churches (Scotland) Act, 1905, 64
Churches Together, 346
Churchill, Sir W, 282, 396
Circuit of Ireland, 310
Civil Magistrate, 43, 285, *en 209*
Civil War, 11, 29, 35, 84, 96
Clare Co, 257
Clerks EPC, 467
Climax of the Covenant, 196, *en 296*
Clintyfallow, Co Tyrone, 217, 249, 251, 256, 287, 293, 335, 337, 357, 443-445, 447, 458
Clontarf, 28
Clowney, EP, 351
Co Antrim, 32, 42, 43, 48, 70, 133, 217, 249, 256, 257, 258, 300, 389, 392, 482
Co Armagh, 133, 218, 258, 323, 336
Co Down, 20, 28, 34, 48, 52, 97, 133, 218, 257, 259, 299, 300, 315, 337, 388, 389, 482, *en 378, 412, 445*
Co Fermanagh, 335
Co Londonderry, 48, 133, 388
Co Tyrone, 76, 133, 217, 249, 256, 357,
Code EPC, 261-262, 286, 338, 426, *en 484, 493, 527*
Code PCI, 66-68, 72, 118, 132, 134, 156, 170, 178-179-181, *en 72, 74*

Cold War, 284, *en 403*
Colegio Anglo-Puerano, Lima, 304
Colegio san Andrés, Lima, 321, 385, 478, 480
College Committee PCI, 106, 114-117, 132, 143, 492
Collins, A, 474
Collins, GNM, 59, 157, 223, 233, 253, 291-292, 298, 307, 316, 351, 399, *en 27, 209, 424, 488*
Collins, M, 11, 377-378
Colombes, Paris, *en 415*
Colossae, 412
Colportage, 20, 53, 246, 255-259, 262-264, 269, 298-301, 322, 442, 446, 453
Columba, 19, 28, 298, 327, 478
Columbanus, 28
Committed to Care, 363
Committee Structures, 338
Commonwealth and Protectorate, 35
Commonwealth of Nations, 282
Communion Wine, 283
Comparative Religion and Christian Missions, 68, *en 80*
Confederacy, *en 516*
Confederate States of America, *en 516*
Conferences EPC, 213, 236, 241,244-249, 251, 254, 269, 264, 276, 293, 298, 302-304, 306, 316, 334, 337, 350-351, 355, 362, 416, 426, 473-475, *en 391, 451*
Congregational Reports, 263
Congregational Union of Ireland, 288, 351
Conn, HM, 373
Connaught, 53
Conscience, 24, 45. 52, 237, 272, 400-401, 405, *en 360, 492*
Constitutionalist Party, 66
Cook, J 473
Cooke, H Statue, 54, 119
Cooke, H, 19, 32, 48-54, 74, 88, 95, 107, 112, 118-120, 155-156, 159, 178-179, 181, 229, 414, 471, *en 35, 37, 39, 41, 44, 47, 199, 433*
Cookstown, 50, 51, 358
Cooneyites, 299
Corinth, 409, 412, 414
Corkey, W, 54, 137, 142, 143, 147, 149, 150, 151, 152, 164, 166, 168, 169, 170, 171, 172, 173, 174, 175, 179, 181, 184, 185, 186, *en 185, 207, 254*
Cotswold Fellowship, 326
Council Committees, 308
Council of Churches for Britain and Ireland, 346
Council of Trent, 206, 402

Court, D, 475
Covenant of Grace, 234, 249, 273, 275, 410, 420-421, 424, *en 453*
Covenant youth, 428, 430
Covenantal-Nomism, *en 297*
Covenanter
Covenanters in Ireland, *en 209*
Covenanter, 241
Covenanters, 34, 45, 95, 229, 241
Covenanting Assembly, 34
Craigs, 258
Creation, 201, 249, 272, 291, 313, 331, 356, 406, 420, 441, *en 439*
Credal Subscription, 205
Cregagh Mission Hall, 232
Criminality, 138
Cromwell, O, 20, 35, 436, 438, 440
Cromwell: An Honourable Enemy, *en 10*
Cross and Its Meaning, 70
Cross, 137, 140, 143, 159, 172, 185, 195, 198, 205, 208, 245, 273, 289, 319, 436, 441, *en 193, 206, 363, 394*
Crosscollyer Street, 216, 245, 246, 249, 252, 253, 254, 255, 258, 259, 263, 287, 304, 305, 306, 330, 334, 335, 347, 359, 392, 446, 449, 453, 461, 474
Crossgar, 315, *en 420*
Crumlin, 192, 215, 217, 245, 249, 250, 252, 257, 258, 263, 274, 287, 296, 300, 306, 320, 358, 363, 443, 444, 445, 446, 448, 450, 453, 458, 473
Culloden, *en 11*
Culture, 29, 66, 90, 250, 324, 329, 368, 370, 398, 406
Cunningham, R, 32
Cunningham, Wm, *en 491*
Currie, J, 246, 251
Curry, S, 474
Czechoslovakia, 282, *en 417*
Dabney, RL, 18, 62, 395, 404, *en 65, 398, 498*
Dallas, 246, 252, 253, 254, 272, 275, 351
Dallimore, Arnold, *en 22*
Darby, JN, 272
D'Aubigné, M, 53
Davey, JE, 17, 18, 20, 23, 70, 71, 72, 73, 74, 100, 101, 107, 110, 114, 117, 132, 133, 134, 135, 136, 137, 138, 139, 140, 141, 142, 143, 144, 145, 146, 147, 148, 149, 150, 151, 152, 153, 158, 159, 160, 161, 164, 165, 166, 167, 168, 169, 170, 171, 172, 173, 174, 175, 176, 178, 179, 180, 182, 183, 184, 185, 186, 187, 188, 189, 192, 193, 194, 195, 196, 197, 198, 199, 200, 201, 202, 203, 204, 205, 207, 208,

209, 210, 211, 212, 224, 225, 226. 227, 238, 241, 247, 276, 330, 331, 332, 333, 377, 378, 379, 434, 435, 436, 438, 439, 440, 470, en *46, 89, 90-97, 100, 138, 143, 166, 168, 181-183, 185, 187, 203, 205, 207-208, 232, 261, 277-278, 281, 284, 307, 347, 354, 421, 438, 462, 500*
Davis, DR, en *68*
Days of His Flesh, 62, 70
Dayton, 330, en *439*
D-Day, 282
de Courcy, J, 29
de Gereformeerde Kerken in Nederland (Vrijgemaakt), 290, 344
Deacon, 42, 240, 261-262, 276, 286-287, 300, 311, 321, 336, 350, 370, 376, 405, 421, 426, 442, 457-462, 473-474
Dean Leslie of Down, 33
Dean of Edinburgh, 34
Deane, J
Death Penalty, 309
Declaratory Acts, 64, 106, 284-285, 401, 404, 421, en *73*
Democratization of American Christianity, 406
Denial, 188
Denney, J, 18, 97, 140, 141, 145, 211, 240, en *295*
Dereliction, 198
Derry Standard, 157, en *271*
Diotrephes, 412-413
Dispensational Premillennialism, 272-273
Dispensationalism, 206, 239, 272-273, 274, 275, en *382, 394-395*
Distinctives EPC, 382, 428
Docetism, 169, en *245*
Doctrinal latitude, 66, 396
Doctrinal mixture, 413
Doddridge, P, en *391*
Dods, M, 64, 66
Dohnavur, 11, en *378*
Doleantie, en *453*
Donaghadee, Co Down, 78, 301, 314
Donaldson, FI, 303-304, 326, 343, 385, 464
Donegal, 32, 81, 82, 83, 256, 257, 269, 299, 324, 334, 482, en *117, 390*
Donegore, 48
Donnelly, EA, 474
Douay New Testament, 256-257
Doumergue, Emile, 511
Down-Grade Controversy, 293, 410, en *506*
Dowry of the Past, 503, 505
Drift, 396-398
Drogheda, 35-36
Druids, 28

Dublin, 17, 28, 29, 33, 35, 38, 41, 42, 51, 66, 65, 96, 101, 108, 218, 287, 301, 324, 334, 335, 336, 347, 357, 387, 443, 446, 447, 449, 450, 458, 480, en *66, 118, 389*
Duke of Cumberland, 483
Dumisani Theological Institute, 374, 386, 480
Dunbar, G, 33
Duncan Campbell, 472
Duncan, J 'Rabbi', 310
Dundonald, 245, 320
Dundrum, Co Down, 29
Duneane, Co Antrim, 48
Dungannon, 156, 358
Dunlop, AJ, 303, 343, 385, 362, 366, 462, 464, 469, 478
Dunn, G, 304-305
Dunn, JDG, 197, en *300*
Dunn, Wm, 226
Dunnett, GC, 298
Dunse Law, 34
Dutch Republic, 36
Eaglewing, 34
East Lancashire Presbyterian Fellowship, 338
Easter Rising, 96
Eastern Reformed Presbyterian Synod, en *209*
Ecclesia reformata semper reformanda est, 398-399
Echlin, R, 33
Edersheim, Alfred, en *515*
Edgar, J, 156, 157, 161
Edinburgh Theological Seminary, 369
Edinburgh, 16, 34, 80, 97, 157, 250, 253-254, 258-259, 291-292, 298, 316, 325, 327, 345, 351, 360, 369, 370, 475, en *60, 69, 295*
Edward VI, 29
Edwards, B, 474
Edwards, J, 405
Egypt General Mission, 261
Egypt, 261, 269, 304, 406, 413
Elder (Eldership), 11, 18, 43, 52, 79, 113, 118, 133, 148, 157, 162, 171, 175, 188, 192, 214-215, 225, 228, 236, 240, 261, 287, 315, 321, 333, 336, 339, 350-351, 354, 359, 369-370, 376, 381-382, 401, 405, 421, 426, 442, 457-462, 469, 473-474, en *173, 209, 420-421, 484, 528*
Eldership in Irish Presbyterianism, 493
Elizabeth I, 29, 33
Elliott, Jim, 478
Elliott, WL, 213, 375, 467
Ellis Island, 84, en *121*
Emlyn, T, 38

English Prayer Book, 34
English Unitarian Fund, 48
Enquiry Rooms, 23, 98, 99, 100
EPC – Family Day, 362
EPC – Group Personal Pension Scheme, 334
EPC – *Anatomy of a Church*, 356, 469
EPC – Anniversaries, 13, 302, 307, 316-317, 351-352, 354, 356, 362, 381-382, 384, 470, 477, *en 451*
EPC – Articles of Faith, 210, 233, 235-236, 262, 273-275, 284-286, 310, 315, 321, 384, 441, *en 422*
Ephesus, 228, 380, 397, 413, 414, *en 405*
Episcopacy, 29, 33, 34, 45
Erdman, CR, 89, 410
Erskine, Ebenezer, 43Eschatology, 273, 437
Established Church, 44, 63
Establishment Principle, 63
Ethiopia, 375, 464
Ethos, 13, 82, 99, 234, 239, 248, 284, 422
EuCRC, 16, 369-370
European Alliance, 290
European Christian Mission, 260
European Missionary Fellowship, 16, 301
Eutychian, 498
Evangel, 258-259
Evangelical Alliance, 292
Evangelical Book Shop, 13, 14, 16, 18, 19, 192, 219, 247, 249, 257, 258, 259, 268, 269, 274, 301, 307, 317, 322, 325, 326, 327, 356, 376, 381, 469, 470, 471, 477, *en 395, 421, 429, 455*
Evangelical Lesson Book, 305, 348
Evangelical Library, 325, 470
Evangelical Party (Scotland), 63, 120, 178, 179, 242, 484, *en 25*
Evangelical Presbyterian Church – Why does it Exist? 317
Evangelical Presbyterian Church in England and Wales, 16, 357, 362, 368, 370-371, 474, *en 447*
Evangelical Protestant Society, 351, *en 407*
Evangelical Revival, 23, 41, 53, 63, 178
Evangelical Theological College, Dallas, 253
Evangelical Unity, 231-232, 292
Evangelicalism, 11, 19, 54, 80, 91, 163, 205, 368
Evangelism, 68, 97, 208, 301, 302, 346, 366, 369, 370, 374, 376, 410, 424, 430, 476, 477, *en 444*
Eve, 74, 313, 382, 407
Evolution, 291, 331, *en 439*
Exegetical method, 202
Exile, 406, 412, 426
Experience (JE Davey), 72-73, 113, 139, 145, 152, 166, 198, 209-210, 435

Faith and life, 173, 182, 203, 210, 411, 430-431, *en 363, 409*
Faith in an Unchanging Vesture, 18, 70, 276, 470, *en 89*
Faithfulness, 13, 36, 75, 296, 307, 310, 350, 378, 380, 383, 414, 416, 417, 427, 428
Fall, 38, 177, 181, 206, 228, 233, 234, 251, 326, 406, 424, 439
Federal Imputation, 195-196
Feed the Hungry Fund, 303
Fellowship of Independent Evangelical Churches, 16, 292, 293, 301, 367
Ferguson, SB, 473
Ferintosh, *en 41*
Ferrie, J, 51
Ferrier, HM, 298
FIFA World Cup, 310, *en 417*
Filioque, en 13
Finaghy, 217, 287, 296, 300, 304, 305, 334, 335, 357, 360, 363, 392, 443, 444, 445, 447, 448, 450, 451, 458, 461, 473
Finance Consultative Committee, 16, 338, 339, 340, 362
Finlayson, RA, 18, 195, 292, *en 291, 294-295*
Finney, CG, 405-406, 476
First Great Awakening, 405
Fisherwick PCI, 69, 76, 113
Fleming, W, 473
Fletcher, J, 102
Florida, 246, *en 517*
Ford, D, 292, 367, 480
Foreign Missions Committee, 260, 261, 303, 308, 342, 343, 366, 372, 375
Foreign Missions Day, 260
Foreign Missions, 52, 260, 261, 287, 290, 302, 303, 321, 327, 342, 343, 362, 372, *en 444, 451*
Foreordination, 206-208
Forgotten Spurgeon, 20, 111, *en 508*
Form of Government EPC, 24, 240, 261, 262, 263, 286, 287, 322, 442
Form of Presbyterial Church-Government, en 405
Formula of Subscription, 23, 39, 64, 106-107, 112-114, 116-117, 119, 139-140, 161-162, 170, 178, 235, 241, 273, 285, 286, 287, 397, 401, 404, 421, *en 253, 484*
Fosdick, HE, 89
Foundations of the Christian Faith, 18, *en 63*
Fountain Street Belfast, 230, 233, 236, 321, *en 354*
Foyle College, Londonderry, 82-83
France, 28, 31, 36, 96, 282, 283, 324, 369, *en 5, 84, 417*

Fraser, AR, 316
Free Church College, 16, 61, 97, 140, 157, 223, 241, 253-254, 261, 266, 316, 350-351, 358, 369, *en 209, 295, 451*
Free Church Defence Association, 64
Free Church of Scotland Continuing, *en 446, 452*
Free Church of Scotland, 14, 16-18, 59, 62-66, 69, 178-179, 192, 204, 233, 241-242, 246, 253-254, 261, 266, 288, 291-292, 294, 298, 302, 305, 307, 316, 321, 326, 342-344, 351, 358, 360, 364, 366, 369, 372, 374, 385, 464, 484-485, 496-497, 510-512, *en 27, 60, 69, 209, 214, 295, 424-425, 446, 451-452*
Free North, 157, 241
Free Presbyterian Church of Australia, 254
Free Presbyterian Church of Scotland, 64, 157
Free Presbyterian Church of Ulster, 16, 233, 315, *en 419-421*
French Bible Mission, 260, 261, 302, *en 415*
Fullerton, JA, 310
Fulton, AA, 18, 101, 103, 118, 153, 168, 169, 178, 186, 187, 330, 331, 332, 379, *en 138, 143, 168, 252, 269, 343, 347, 438, 462*
'Fundamentalism' and the Word of God, Packer, JI, *en 319*
Fundamentalism, 19, 20, 61, 89, 101, 169, 186, 330, 331, 332, *en 245, 319, 441, 471*
Fundamentalist-Modernist, 61, 331
Future of Justification, en 296,
Gaffin, RB, 473
Gaius, 412
Gaiya, M & P, 375, 386, 464
Galatia, 412, 413, 427
Galbraith, JP, 372,
Gale family, 303, 325, 366, 389
Galgorm Castle, 97
Gallery 'Mob', 225-226, 332-333, *en 347*
Galway, 486, 490, 301, 482
Gambling, 309, 362, 363, 370
Garland Update, en 454
Garland, CH, 126, 128, 236, 253-254, 259, 265, 269, 297-298, 308-309, 320, 322, 326, 333, 466
Garland, J, 128, 373, 386, 464, 469, 480
Garland, M, 128, 365, 366, 392
Garland, SJ, 128, 313, 333, 334, 341, 373-374, 386, 464, 467, 469, 480
Geddes, J, 34
Geelong, 291, *en 512*
Geneva Confession, 235
George of Hanover, 483

Georgia, *en 517*
German Rationalism, 59, 61, 119, 159
Germany, 59, 79, 282, 283, *en 417*
Gethsemane, 136, 137, 198, 427, 436, *en 183-184*
Giant's Causeway, 323
Gibson, AF, 345-346, 367
Gibson, D, 298
Gibson, H, 214, 467-468
Gibson, PG, 14
Gift Aid, 339
Gift Days, 264, 265, 309
Gillespie Family Tree, 86
Gillespie, Catherine R, 85, 306, 323, *en 397*
Gillespie, Catherine T, 84, 276, 320
Gillespie, G, 33
Gillespie, Harriet, 80
Gillespie, J H, 70, 85, 125, 214, 236, 248, 261, 269, 275-279, 320-321, 470, *en 65, 89*
Gillespie, J R, 76, 80-81, 86, 126, 214, 230, 235, 245, 247, 255, 264-265, 269, 277, 301, 311, 317, 321, 323, 324, 339, 382, 466
Gillespie, William, 80, 85
Girls' Own, 305
Giving, 425-426
Glasgow College, 40, *en 60*
Glasgow University, 33, 48
Glasgow, 33, 34, 40, 62, 92, 97, 293, 298, 347, 397, *en 60, 69, 117, 275*
Glendinning, J, 33
Glorious Revolution, 36, *en 14*
Go Teach, 305, 348
God Save Ulster, 18, 379, *en 164, 272, 387, 421, 465*
God Transcendent, 89, *en 127*
God-Breathed, 200-202, 204
Gog, 273
Golden Bells, 250, 266, 342, 364, 365, *en 392-393*
Golden Lampstand, 247
Goli Uganda, 375
Goligher, AT, 158
Goligher, J, 164-165
Gordon, RD, 158
Goshen, 415
Gospel Magazine, 258, *en 472*
Gospel Tent, 259
Gospel Trumpet, 259
Gospel, 11, 18, 28, 31, 34, 39, 41, 44, 56, 62, 83, 89, 91, 98, 99, 100, 102, 104, 105, 107, 108, 165, 174, 188, 198, 200, 201, 206, 208, 212, 232, 238, 240, 256, 257, 260, 261, 289, 291, 300, 301, 304, 305, 315, 322, 323, 326, 340, 361, 369, 370,

375, 376, 381, 384, 398, 400, 408, 409, 411, 412, 415, 422, 423, 424, 427, 435, 437, 438, 439, 440, 442, 471, 474, 476, 477, *en 19, 41, 206, 209, 214, 293, 360, 429*
Grace and Personality, *en 160*
Gracehill, 42
Graham, A, 109, 244, *en 361*
Graham, C, 473
Graham, JC, 156-158, 161
Grammar School Syllabus, 312-314, 351
Grand Rapids, 290-291, 307
Grandmother, *en 236, 265*
Granville, 335, 337
Great Commission, 260, 354, 407, 416, 424, 428
Great Depression, 244
Great Ejection, 35
Great White Throne, 148, 273
Green, N, 336-338
Green, WH, 90
Greene, WB, 60
Grier Family Tree, 86
Grier, Catherine, 121, 268, 305, 307-308, 323-324, 365-366, 428,
Grier, John Snr, 81
Grier, John, 13-14, 192, 196-199, 214, 219, 376, 381, 475-476, *en 455*
Grier, Julia, 14, 366, 367
Grier, Peter, 387
Grier, WJ, 3, 5, 14, 24, 32, 52, 61, 65, 68-69, 72, 81-86, 88-93, 101-102, 104, 106-110, 112-120, 121-126, 128, 131, 133, 135-139, 141-142, 146, 149-153, 156, 159, 160-161, 169, 171, 177, 183, 185-186, 188-189, 224, 227-230, 232-233, 235-241, 243, 245-249, 251-255, 259-262, 263-264, 266-269, 273-275, 277-278, 283, 288-294, 302-307, 311, 313-317, 320-327, 332-333, 343, 351-352, 364, 366-367, 378-379, 381-383, 417, 435-436, 438-439, 466-468, 470, *en 4, 6, 34, 45-46, 61, 67, 70, 76, 80, 86, 120, 129-130, 142, 147, 149, 152, 155-156, 158, 160, 162, 174, 183, 185, 203, 207-208, 211, 215, 274, 366, 370, 373, 383, 386, 421, 429, 434, 455*
Gronigen, 475
Groomsport, 34, 218, 287, 301, 355, 356, 357, 358, 443, 449, 450, 457, 459, 474
Growth in Grace, 427-428
Guedj, Emile, 261, 302, *en 415*
Guilt, 62, 138, 139, 144, 145, 146, 147, 172, 193, 194, 195, 208, 350, 400, 415, 434, 439, *en 188, 190*
Gutjahr, PC, 87

Haire, J, 112, 114, 115, 117, 132, 136, 142, 144, *en 159, 160*
Halliday, S, 40, *en 19*
Hall-Thompson, S, 314-315
Hamilton, I, 381, 473
Hamilton, T, 39-40, 43, 50, 55, 155, 396-397, *en 50*
Hampton Court Conference, 33
Hanna, RJ, 256, 298
Hanna, S, 133, 142-143, 146, 158, 161-162, 183, 226-227, 232, 238, *en 173, 210, 275*
Harland and Wolff, 244
Harmony of the Gospels, 18, *en 293, 311*
Harper, F, 355, 471
Hart, DG, 19, 295, 382, *en 208, 214, 383, 408, 520*
Hart's Loney, 268
Hatch, N, 406
Have we a Reliable Bible? 315, 471
Hawaii, 282
Hebrew, 49, 61, 70, 77, 81, 84, 90, 150, 174, 201, 322, 480, *en 107, 363*
Hedegard, D, 307
Hegel, F, 212, 396
Hegelianism, 187
Heidelberg Catechism, 326, *en 409, 430*
Hell, 98, 474, *en 193*
Help the Needy, 303
Hendriksen, W, 19, *en 195*
Henry I, 29, *en 3*
Henry II, 29, *en 3*
Henry VIII, 29
Heresy Trials, 60, 64, 211
Heritage of our Fathers, 18, 59, 233, *en 27*
Hezekiah, 412
Higher Criticism, 20, 61, 153, 165, 248, 312, *en 65*
Higher Life Movement, 102
Hill, R, 43, *en 24*
Hillside College, 469
History of the Congregations of the Presbyterian Church in Ireland, *en 277*
History of the Irish Presbyterian Church, 39, 483, *en 18, 20, 40, 50*
History of the Presbyterian Church in Ireland, 20, 38, *en 15, 43, 51, 479*
Hitler, Adolf, 282
Hodge, Charles, 11, 87-88, 140-141, 144-147, 166, 168, 172, 311, 401-402, 406, *en 194, 197, 198, 328, 495*
Hodge, CW, 88, 90
Holden, JS, 103
Holding Hands in the Dark, 346
Holiness Movement, 102

531

Holiness, 73, 147, 167, 198, 207, 400, 407, 410, 425, **en** *363*
Holland, 289, 307, 347, **en** *199*
Holmes, RFG, 19, 43, 54, 61, 67, 70, 233, 237, 379, 398, 399, 405, 460, **en** *5, 26, 35, 37, 39, 47, 62, 75, 87, 367, 467, 485, 490, 499*
Holocaust, 188
Holy Spirit, 37, 38, 50, 66, 102, 103, 112, 145, 166, 171, 174, 175, 176, 200, 202, 210, 233, 234, 239, 240, 247, 262, 319, 326, 350, 381, 400, 411, 412, 420, 423, 441, 442, **en** *72-73, 141, 200, 520*
Holywood, 32
Home Rule, 23, 76, 96
House of Lords, 64, 65, 66, 96
Houston, H, 365-366
Howard, Bertie, 323
Hufstetler, J, 473
Hughes, RK, 407
Hughes, W, 473
Hulse, E, **en** *7*
Human Agency, 406
Human Government, 272
Humanity, 168, 172, 188, 189, 198, **en** *245*
Humpty Dumpty, 398
Hungry Thirties, 244
Hunter Family Tree, 86
Hunter, Catherine Snr, 76
Hunter, Catherine T, 76, 80, 85
Hunter, CE, 125-126, 128, 235, 245-246, 253, 258, 263, 291, 298, 303, 309, 317, 320, 321-322, 326, 333, 466-467
Hunter, Charles Snr, 76
Hunter, Charles, 226, 333, **en** *352*
Hunter, J, 3-4, 13, 23-24, 54, 63-70, 74-86, 93, 95, 102, 104, 106, 108-110, 112-120, 122, 126, 132-136, 138, 142, 146-149, 151, 153, 156-161, 164, 166-167, 170-171, 174-175, 178-186, 205, 224, 226-233, 235-237, 239-242, 245-246, 249, 251, 253-254, 259-260, 262-263, 265-266, 268, 271, 273-277, 283, 301, 311-312, 315-319, 321, 325, 333, 351-352, 378-379, 382-383, 466, **en** *77-78, 103, 106, 110, 149, 151, 154, 158, 160, 163, 169, 179, 183, 209, 211, 349, 361-362, 386, 421, 451*
Hunter, John Robinson (Trust), 311-312
Hutcheson, F, 40, 62, 396
Hymns for our Children, **en** *392*
Hymns for Young People, **en** *392*
Hymns, 42, 78,156, 245, 249, 250, 251, 266, 299, 342, 365, 383, 424, **en** *391, 448, 526*
Hypocrisy, 71, 146, 429

Hypostases, 212
ICRC Regional Conference, 345
Ignite, 363
Imputation, 12, 23, 135, 139-140, 142, 144, 146-147, 149, 152-153, 159, 165, 172, 192-196, 204-205, 208, 233-234, 246, 434, 439, 441, **en** *190, 212, 292*
In Step, 345
Incommunicable Attributes, 73
Independent Unionist Party, 323
Independents, Civil War, 35
India, 11, 53, 80, 260-261, 303, 343, 372, 385, **en** *80, 378*
Indian Village Mission, 261
Industrial Revolution, 244
Inland South America Mission Union, 260-261
Innocence Dispensation, 272
Inspiration, God's concursive operation, 200
Institutes of the Christian Religion, 18, 47, **en** *283, 292*
Inter-Church Process, 16, 346
Inter-Church Relations, 241, 279, 288, 325, 338, 343-345, 366, 367, 371
Interim Moderator, 297, 321, 322, 333, 360,
International Conference of Reformed Churches, 16, 344-345, 366-371, 475, **en** *507*
International Council of Christian Churches, 16, 289-292, 344
International (Foreign) Missions Board (FCOS), 16, 67, 69, 339, 342-343, 372, 374, 468, **en** *451*
Interpretation, 44, 67, 106, 162, 164, 172, 175, 183, 185-187, 197, 202, 212, 223, 273, 285, 377, 397, 401-403, 405, 476, **en** *77, 200, 394*
Inter-testamental Pharisaism, 196
ipsissima verba, 136, 146, 150, **en** *207*
Irenaeus, 212
Irish Church Missions, 16, 53
Irish Education Inquiry, 50
Irish Evangelical Church – Why?, 316
Irish Evangelical, 247-249
Irish Famine, 53, 244
Irish Free State, 11, 23, 96, 257
Irwin, J, 144
Islandmagee, 303
Israel, 16, 242, 272, 273, 284, 318, 396, 397, 412, 413, 429, 464, **en** *65, 382, 394*
Italy, 79, 282
J. Gresham Machen in the United Kingdom, 246, **en** *214, 349*
Jabbok, 428
Jackson, P, 298

Jacob, 413, 428
Jacobite Rebellion, 483, *en 11*
James Francis Edward, 36
James I, 29, 33, *en 12*
James II, 36
Japan Evangelistic Band, 260
Japan Rescue Mission, 260
Jehoshaphat, 412
Jehovah, 150, 319
Jehovah's Witnesses, 256, 470
Jeroboam, 413, 438
Jerusalem Church, 236
Jerusalem, 163, 232, 236, 272, 409, *en 405*
Jess, IT, 228, 492, *en 149, 353, 421*
Jesus and the Gospel, 240
Jesus of St John, 188-189, *en 278, 307*
Jewish Monotheism, 211
Jezebel, 413
Joash, 412
Jocelyn Avenue, 245, 249, 252, 258, 259, 263, 287, 297, 445, 446, 447, 450, 459, *en 407*
Johnston (Gaiya) P, 375, 474
Johnston, JD, 351
Johnston, MG, 15, 213, 333, 337, 355, 367, 419, 467, 475-476
Johnston, RJ, 213, 361, 376, 473
Jones, J, 259, 260, 299-300, *en 412*
Jos Journal, 375
Judah, 412-414
Justification, 13, 23, 50, 70, 134, 136, 140, 142, 144, 146, 147, 150, 151, 152, 153, 160, 165, 167, 169, 171, 184, 185, 186, 187, 189, 192, 193, 234, 273, 370, 374, 434, 441, 474, 476, 477, *en 175, 296-297*
Kampen, 291
Kane, T, 361, 376
Keady, 258
Kell, JA, 245, 251, 467
Kelman, J, 171
Kenosis, 115, 197, 198, 266, *en 303, 305, 393*
Kerr, E, 290, 291, 298, 304-305, 326, 367, 392
Kerry, 257, 482
Keswick Convention, 79, 101, 230, 301
Kidner, D, 353
Kiev, 370
Kilkeel, 303
Kilkenny, 257
Killinchy, 32-33
Killing, 28, 35
Killycomaine Evangelical Church, *en 407*
Kilroot, 267
King William's Town, 374, 386

King, J, 109, 235
Kinghan, Wm, 245
Kingswood, Bristol, 41
Kingussie, 246, 298
Kirk of Shotts, 33
Kirkpatrick Church PCI, 79
Kirkpatrick, J, 396
Kirkpatrick, L, 19, 460
Kistemaker, SJ, 329, *en 435*
Klooster, F, 291
Knock (Dundela) PCI, 18, 64-65, 77-81, 106, 110, 164, 352, *en 103, 109, 112, 114, 149*
Knock EPC, 2, 126, 216, 245-246, 249, 261, 268, 276, 287, 311, 317, 320-321, 323, 356, 358, 363, 464, 471, 474, *en 425*
Knockdene Park South, 84, 269, 324, *en 383*
Knowles, J, 185-186
Knox, J, 33, 294, 384, 476
Korean World Mission, 375, 464
Kuiper, RB, 290
Kuluva, Uganda, 374
Kuyper, Abraham, 512
Kyle, P, 233, *en 420*
Labourers Together, 303
Ladies United Monthly Prayer Meeting, 17, 268, 284, 365-366
Ladies' Fellowships, 366
Lagan Presbytery, *en 117*
Lagan, 244, 324, 490
Lamb, R, 293, 351
Lanarkshire Christian Union, 97
Lanarkshire, 104, 482
Land Rover Ambulance India, 303
Langtry, M 214, 467
Laodicea, 413
Laois, 257
Larger Catechism, see Westminster
Latimer, WT, 19, 45, 56, 74, *en 32, 52, 101*
Latitudinarianism, 38, 55, 66, 402-403, 404-405, *en 200*
Laud, Wm, 33
Laud's Liturgy, 34
Law and the Prophets, *en 122, 125*
Law, S, 317, 351
Lawson's Shorter Catechism, 348
Le Chat Noir, 230-232, 236, 244, 260, 262, 316, *en 354*
Leahy, FS, 126, 333, *en 389*
Leahy, M, *en 389*
Lecture Notes, 110, 112, 133, 136, 138, 146, 149, 150, 179, 189, 211, *en 208*
Leeburn, WJ, 165
Leechman, 40, 62, 396

533

Legal Assessor, 133, 160, 180
Legerton, HJW, 310
Leicester Ministers' Conference, 325, *en 386, 429*
Leitch, Duncan, 294, 298
Leitch, M, 75, 77, *en 103*
Leitrim, 257-258
Leloumenos, 18, 70, 276, 470
Letter from Nigeria, *en 455*
Levy, P, 381, 475
Lewis, CS, 405, *en 501*
Liberalism, 19, 23, 24, 59, 60, 66-67, 69, 80, 85, 88-90, 101, 108, 212, 237, 302, 399, *en 157, 270, 489*
Liberty of Conscience, 400-401, 403
Life Here and the Life Hereafter, 69
Life of Reason, *en 474*
Lightfoot, J, 107, *en 146*
Lima, 304, 321, 478, 480
Limerick, 28, 257
Lincoln, Abraham, 416
Lindsay, 126, 261, 302, 304, 343, 385, 464
Linen Homelands, 244
Linen Mills, 244
Linkens, J, 445, 449, 453
Lisburn Road, 217, 244, 245, 246, 249, 251, 259, 262, 268, 287, 296, 304, 306, 313, 316, 323, 325, 326, 335, 357, 364, 375, 443, 444, 445, 446, 447, 448, 451, 458, 460, 473
Lisburn, 43, 97, 158, 161, 314, 358, 370
Livingstone and Wells, 99, 100, 101, 102, 116, 178, 224, *en 134, 137, 139, 165, 268, 345, 466*
Livingstone, J. 32, 33, 229
Livingstone, Wm, 43
Lloyd-George, D, 96
Lloyd-Jones, DM, The Fight of Faith 1939-1981, *en 358*
Loetscher, LA, 19, 60, *en 54, 59*
Log College, 406
Logos, 211-212
London, 41, 80, 103, 192, 276- 277, 293, 300-301, 322, 351, 367, 370- 371
Londonderry, 32, 36, 48, 62, 78, 82, 97, 108, 133, 153, 156, 157, 158, 160, 180, 256, 299, 388, *en 66, 110, 413*
Long Parliament, 34-35
Lord Protector, 35
Lord's Day Observance Society, 16, 310, 347, 362
Lord's Day, 233, 234, 250, 254, 260, 262, 298, 310, 311, 316, 317, 320, 335, 347, 349, 356, 362, 363, 422, 425, 430, 441, *en 215*

Lord's Supper (Table), 234, 261, 264, 276, 283, 297, 425, 441, 442
Los Angeles, 16, 97, 101
Loughridge, A, 98, 473, *en 152, 209*
Louis XIV, 36
Louisiana, *en 517*
Lower 'Textual' Criticism, 61
Loyal Orders, 323
Lucas, SM, 281
Luftwaffe, 282
Luke, SP, *en 354*
Lurgan Synod, 51
Lurgan, 97, 314
Luther, M, 33, 474, 476
Lylehill, 43
Lyons, J, 232
Lyons, RN, 232
MacDonald, J, 484
MacDougall, Archibald, 298
Macedonian Cry, 261
Machen, JG, 19, 20, 72, 87-93, 104, 107, 109-110, 112-114, 116-119, 153, 156, 159-161, 177, 228-230, 239-241, 243, 246, 247, 249, 252, 265, 268-269, 278, 290, 324-325, 351, 372, 382-383, 399, 403, 414, *en 123-124, 127, 129-130, 155, 158, 183, 214-215, 270, 349, 383, 406, 422, 440, 470-471, 489*
MacInnis, JM, 101
Mackay, Angus, 246
MacKay, Christina 304
MacKenzie, Alistair, 310
MacLeod, Alasdair I, 473
Macleod, D, 19, 197, *en 13, 99, 146, 184, 188, 193, 296, 304-305, 524*
Macleod, G, 322
Macleod, J, 18, 157, 223, 241-242, 266, *en 209, 292, 451*
MacMillan, D, 350
MacQuigg, JC, *en 423*
MacRitchie, M, 288
MacRury, H, 298
Magdalene School (IACWU), 108-109, *en 361*
Magee College, 32, 62, 78, 81, *en 66, 103, 110*
Magee, Bob, 267-268
Magee, J, 474
Maghera, 48
Magherafelt, 141, 256
Magill, G, 65
Magill, H, 235
Magisterium, *en 492*
Magog, 273
Majestic Testimony (Princeton), 18, 131, *en 53, 496, 509*

Major Bible Themes, 246
Makemie, F, 81, 123, *en 117*
Manchuria, 11, 20, 67, 68, 79, 80, 261, *en 78, 80-81, 416, 510*
Manchuria, Moukden, 80
Machurian Christian College, 80
Manton, T, 73, 105
Martyrs Memorial Free Presbyterian Church, *en 420*
Mary I, 29
May Street PCI, 52
McCauley, S, 474
McCormick, JR, 339
McCracken, J&H, 119, 126, 128, 247, 252-253, 258, 261, 267-268, 269, 277, 285, 291, 294, 296, 302-303, 305-307, 320-323, 326, 333, 343, 351, 374, 385, 417, 464, 480
McCrea, S, 310
McCully, Wm, 362
McCune, N, 341
McCune, R, 332, *en 441*
McDonald, K, 214, 467
McDowell, S, 366
McDowell, WJ, 126, 128, 246, 253, 255-259, 261, 263, 265, 267-268, 285, 288, 290-291, 293- 294, 297- 299, 303-306, 309, 314-315, 317, 320, 322, 326, 333, 352, 367, 416, 446, 449, 451-453, 466-467, 471
McEwan, WR, 307
McFadden, Alexander, 235, 264
McFetrich, D, 361
McIntyre, Carl, 290, 292, *en 408*
McKay, WDJ, 14, 199, 474
McKenzie, H, *en 275*
McNeill, Wm, 69, *en 85*
Melville, Andrew, 33
Members-Church, 427-428
Menshevik, *en 210*
Meredith, D, 474
Merozites, 95, *en 130*
Merry Thought Café, *en 354*
Mexico, 261
Michigan, 307, *en 469*
Milford, 81-83
Millar, WJ, 251
Millennium (Dispensationalism), 272-273, *en 394*
Miller (Anderson), Eileen, 300
Milligan, S, 351
Millisle, *en 378*
Ministers' and Office Bearers' Conference, 334, 350, 473
Ministers' and Office Bearers' Half Day of Prayer, 349-350
Minnis Mills Tapestry, 19, *en 425*

Miracle of the Kingdom, 67
'Mischievous Farce', 397, 401
Mission Africa, 373, 375, 386, 387, 464
Mission Awareness, 372, 374
Mission Box Secretary, 261, 342
Mission Boxes, 261, 302-303
Mission Legislation, 376
Mission to the World, 358
Missionaries, see Contents and Appendices
Missionary Committee, 260-261, 303, 308, 342-343, 355, 366, 372, 375, 468
Missionary Endeavour, 261, 348, 478
Missionary Enterprise, 303
Missionary Herald, 238
Missionary Representative, 343
Mississippi, 447, 453, *en 517*
'Moderate' Party, Scotland, 43, 63
Modern Views of the Atonement, *en 289*
Modernism (ist), 32, 61, 65-66, 69, 74, 87, 89, 101, 107, 113-114, 117-118, 119, 153, 154, 157, 158-159, 160-162, 165, 179, 183, 227-228, 230, 237, 248, 253, 265, 331, 366, 415, 470, *en 211, 360, 470*
Moloney, E, 379
Momentous Event, 19, 274, 324, 470, *en 395, 433*
Monaghan, 256
Monkey Trial, *en 439*
Monophysite, *en 245*
Monsma, M, 307
Montgomery, H, 50, 97, 98, 102, 147
Montgomery, SG, 164-165, 232, 246, *en 212*
Monthly Record (FCOS), 65, 241
Montreal, 307
Moo, D, 197
Moody Bible Institute Monthly, *en 213*
Moody Bible Institute, 246, *en 213*
Moody, A & E, 363, 374, 386
Moody, DL, 97, 476
Moorfields Tabernacle, 41
Moravians, 41-42
Morey, K, 367
Morocco, 324
Morphe, *en 146*
Morrison, HA, 252, 263, 272, 273, 274
Muckamore, 20, 40, 44, 257, 378, *en 269*
Muether, J, 406
Muller, G, 478
Muller, R, 19, *en 286*
Murdoch, E (Mrs Ardill), 269
Murphy, HH, 252, 263, 272, 273, 308
Murray, Andrew, 102, 249, *en 140*
Murray, IH, 15, 20, 88, 111, 351, 410, *en 358, 374, 378, 508*

Murray, J, 20, 73, 89, 90-91, 148, 191, 207, 324-325, 383, *en 98, 128, 201, 327, 329, 514*
Murray, SW, 20, 82, *en 1, 119, 131*
'Mutilated Statements', 224
Myth(ology), 150, 188, 312, *en 65*
National Covenant Scotland, 34, 45, 235
Nature of the Atonement, 18, 195, *en 295*
Naylor, P, 474
Nazi Germany, 282
Nehemiah, 239
Neo-orthodox, 196
Nestorian heresy, *en 245*
Netherlands, 16, 289, 291, 337, 344, 367, 370, 475, *en 430, 447*
New Covenant, 320, 368, 428, *en 429*
New England, 34, *en 117*
New Licht Anti-Burghers, 63, *en 27*
New Licht Burghers, 63, *en 27*
New Light, 32, 38, 39, 40, 49-50, 66, 155, 397
New Perspective, 82, 196, *en 296*
New School, 405, *en 495*
New Side, 405-406
New Systematic Theology of the Christian Faith, 20, 273, *en 148, 292, 394*
New Zealand, 307, 475, *en 407*
Newer Criticism, 20, 62, *en 64*
Newington PCI, 267
Newness of Life, 99, 100, 145, 425
Newry Synod, 49
Newry, 54, 77, 80, 301
News to you from Bukuru, en 455
Newtownards, 97, 98, 252
Newtownhamilton, 258
Newtownstewart, 76, 482
Nicea, Council of, 211, 440
Nicene Creed, 37, 78, 275, *en 13*
Niceno-Constantinopolitan Creed, 37
Nicholson, WP, 11, 18, 20, 23, 61, 82, 84, 95-109, 117, 119, 120, 137, 178, 183, 231, 249, 316, 330-331, 351, 415, 461, 476, *en 1, 119-120, 131, 133, 135, 141-142, 144, 361*
Nicolson, M, 321, *en 425*
Nigeria, 17, 128, 373, 374, 375, 386, 387, 444, 450, 453, 464, *en 455*
Nile Missions Press, 260
Nisbet, WA, 251, 254, 446, 452, *en 389*
Nonconformity, 20, 33, 237, *en 368*
Non-Secession, 237-239
Non-Subscribers, 40, 52, 54, 179
Non-Subscribing Presbyterian Church, 51, *en 199*
Non-Subscription, 32, 38-41, 43, 396-397
Norsemen, 28

North Africa Mission, 17, 260, 293, 324
North Belfast, 259, 267, 277, 443, 450-452, 458, 461-462, 330, 335, 359, 381
North Carolina, 490, *en 117, 517*
North Dakota, 382
Northern Ireland Office, 349
Northern Ireland Troubles, 330
Northern Ireland, 18, 23, 92, 96, 101, 133, 157, 282, 284, 299, 309, 310, 313, 314, 330, 341, 346, 349, 359, 362, 367, *en 377, 389, 401, 407, 417, 458*
Northern Whig and Belfast Post, 161, 224, *en 150, 161*
Nova Scotia, 92, 110
O'Neill, FWS, 67, 178, 180, 333, *en 76, 77-78, 80, 84*
O'Neill, Mark, 69, *en 81, 84*
Oberlin, 278
O'Dogherty, Sir C, 32
Office Bearers, 106, 228, 235, 261, 264, 286, 297, 334, 349-350, 374, 426, 442, 473
Old School, 38, 77, 87, 223, 256, 402, 405, 406, *en 495*
Old Side, 405, 406, *en 502*
Old Testament Bible History, 18, *en 515*
Olevianus, *en 430*
Oliver, WM, 290, 300, 303, 385, 464
Omagh Reformed Evangelical Church, 336
Omagh, 218, 287, 314, 336-338, 357-358, 443-444, 446-447, 452-453, 461, 464, 473-474, *en 55*
Oman, J, 492
On Being Presbyterian, 19, 281
On Towards the Goal, 20, 491
O'Neill, Con, 32
O'Neill, Phelim, 34
Onesimus, 194
Ontario, 475
Oosterbeek, 283, *en 402*
Open Theism, 20, 206, 474, *en 525*
Open-Airs, 251, 301
Oral Transmission, 198
Orange Order, 323
Orangefield Baptist Church, *en 407*
Ordinand, 61, 453
Origen, 108, 212
Origin and Witness of the Irish Evangelical Church, 19, 32, 116, 229, 237, 239, 324, 354, 315, 470, 483-489, 492-493, 499, *en 4, 34, 45, 61, 67, 70, 76, 80, 86, 149, 156, 160, 162, 174, 274, 366, 373, 421*
Original Secession Church, 43
Orr, J, 97
Orr, M, 304

Index

Orthodox Presbyterian Church, 17, 20, 266, 291, 343-344, 371-372, 383, 406, 447, 452, **en** *55, 363, 406, 408, 411, 467, 494, 520*
Our Faith in God, 70, 73, 74, 133, 165, 167, 173, 204, 435, 437, 439, **en** *100, 261*
Our Irish Presbyterian Heritage, 19, 233, 398, **en** *5, 26, 62, 75, 87, 367, 467, 485, 490, 499*
Our Own Heritage, 233, 315, **en** *420*
Overseas Students, 475, 453
Overseer, 262, 263, 442
Pace, EJ, 246, **en** *381*
Pacific Act, 39, 66
Packer, JI, 20, 200, **en** *319*
Paine, T, 299
Paisley, IRK, 18-19, 242, 313, 315, 378-379, **en** *272, 377, 387, 420, 458, 464-465*
Pale, The, 29
Palestine, 79, 125, 261, 269, 284
Paraphrases, 365, **en** *391, 448*
Pardon and Assurance, 256, 300, **en** *390*
Paris, 482, **en** *415*
Parkgate, Co Antrim, 48
Parliamentarians, 35
Pastoral Reports, 263
Paterson, D, 298, 350
Pathfinders, 304, 305, 392
Paton, DK, 20, 62, **en** *65*
Paton, JG, 478
Patrick, 27, 28, 29, 53, 478
Patronage Act, 43, 63
Patronage, 36, 42, 43, 45
Patterson, E, **en***136*
Patterson, JJ, 126, 251, 301, 321, 457, 460
Patterson, R, 321, **en** *425*
Patton, I, 43
Paul, FJ, 113, 136, 137, 139, 140, 142, 143, 144, **en** *371*
Payne, SJ, 165, 175, 183, 410
Payton, JR, 235, **en** *365, 494*
PCI: Book of Constitution, 66
PCI: Commission of Assembly, 24, 226-227,
Peace – Civil, 23, 34, 101, 283, 346
Peace – Ecclesiastical, 38, 41, 44, 80, 111, 114, 131, 154, 157, 167, 246, 407-408, 412, 415-416, 428, **en** *452*
Peace – Personal, 41, 102, 152, 298, 247, 277, 403, 427, 435
Pearl Harbour, 282
Penal(ty), 138, 141, 144, 194, 195-196
Pennsylvania, 19, 97, 485, **en** *117*
Pension Fund, 286, 297, 311, 334
Perrystown Community Centre, Dublin, 218, 335
Perrystown Evangelical Church, 336

Person and Work of Christ, 20, 477, **en** *289, Person of Christ*, 19, **en** *146, 184, 304-305*
Peru, 261, 302, 303, 304, 321, 343, 372, 385, 464, 480, **en** *425*
Petersen, J, 372
Philadelphia, 19, 87, 89, 92, 290, 307, 316, 351, 360, 373, 382, 402, 475, **en** *469, 507*
Philemon, 194, **en** *300*
Philo of Alexandria, 211
Pilgrim's Progress , 18, 249, 256, 300, 326, 480, **en** *385, 429*
Piper, J, 382, **en** *296, 325*
Plantagenet, 29, **en** *3*
Plantations, 29, 32, 35, 45, 472, **en** *9*
Plea (Statement) of Justification, 134, 152, 153, 160, 165, 166, 167, 184, 189, 196
Pluralism, 56, 296, 346, 369, 399, 410, 407, 413-414, 428
Pocket Testament League, 97
POCVA Board EPC, 363
Poland, 282, **en** *200*
Pollak, A, 19, 379, **en** *464*
Poole-Connor, EJ, 237, 293, 307, **en** *368*
Population, 34, 35, 53, 244, 335, 337
Populism, 99
Populist Ideology and Revivalism, 99
Port Talbot, 293
Portadown, 97, 133, 227, 246, 391, 482, **en** *407*
Porter, JL, 77, **en** *103*
Porter, N, 313, 315, 323, 351, **en** *407*
Porter, Wm, 51
Porter, WW, 126, 297, 301, 305, 333, 466, **en** *73*
Postmodernism, 204, 281
Potchefstroom South Africa, 291, 374,
Praise Committee, 364-365
Praise, 11, 55, 78, 104, 165, 250, 252, 255, 266, 277, 319-320, 323, 337-338, 342, 349, 364-365, 424, 429, **en** *448*
Prayer, 17, 31, 36, 45, 53, 55-56, 67, 74, 78, 99-100, 107, 118, 144, 165, 198, 204, 236, 238, 242, 245, 248, 250-253, 255-257, 263, 268, 277-278, 283-285, 303, 306, 309, 315, 319, 320, 322-324, 326, 333, 335, 337, 340-341, 346-347, 349-350, 355, 359, 361, 365-366, 369, 373-374, 380, 384, 414, 423-429, 441-442, 473, 477, **en** *52, 80, 390, 429, 431, 448*
Prayer, Days of, 283, 320, 349-350
Preaching, 33, 41-42, 44, 48-49, 53-54, 77-78, 83, 97-99, 155, 188, 232, 247, 251-253, 258, 277, 301, 322, 360, 374, 383, 398, 406, 413, 423-424, 429, 441, 473, 475-476, **en** *41, 117, 390, 524*
Premillennialism, 272

537

Premium Bonds, 309
Prenter, S, 65
Presbuteros, 312
Presbyterian (Assembly's) College: 18, 23, 52-53, 61-62, 66, 68, 70, 75, 77, 82, 100-101, 106-107, 109-110, 112-114, 116, 147, 156-157, 162, 183, 188, 237, 330, 360, 377-378, 434, 436, 470, *en 2, 62, 64, 71, 79, 82, 88, 102-103, 106-107, 111, 371, 142, 155, 164, 170, 172, 231, 277, 388, 437*
Presbyterian and Reformed, 20, 327, *en 125, 289*
Presbyterian Association in England, 17, 337, 357, 370
Presbyterian Bible Standards League, 17, 23, 92-93, 112, 116-120, 123-124, 138, 153, 156, 157-159, 161-162, 164, 230, 237, 246-248, 301, 315, 351, 379, 414, *en 65, 166, 366, 371*
Presbyterian Church in Ireland, A Popular History, 19, *en 467*
Presbyterian Church of America, 265-266, 358, 414
Presbyterian Church of Canada, *en 425*
Presbyterian Journal, *en 59*
Presbyterian Witness, 67, 225
Presbyterians in Ireland, 19, 378, *en 460*
Presbytery Arrangements Committee, 17, 338, 340, 350, 361, *en 452*
Presbytery Clerk, 339, 467
Presbytery Day, 213, 362, 474
Presbytery of Antrim, 39-43, 51-52, 55,
Presbytery of Dublin, 66
Presbytery Visitation, 361
Press Officer EPC, 339
Pressing Towards the Mark, 20, *en 365, 484*
Pretoria, 475
Pride, Colonel T Purge, 35
Princeton Repertory, *en 495,*
Princeton Theological Review, 63, 194, *en 289*
Princeton Theological Seminary, 60, 62, 77, 84, 87-93, 96, 101, 104, 107, 114, 131, 157, 194, 199-200, 246, 406, 410, *en 65, 157, 277*
Principled Presbyterianism, 382
Principles of the Reformation, *en 491*
Private Judgement – Right of, 106, 396-397, 399-401, 403, 405, *en 492, 497*
Private Spirits, 400
Promise Unfulfilled, 19, *en 461*
Protection of Children and Vulnerable Adults, 17, 363
Providence, 23, 32, 48, 53, 84, 96, 103, 104, 118, 174, 206, 207, 208, 259, 278, 289, 292, 301, 320, 330, 406, 420, *en 390*

Proximus ardet Ucalegon, 241, *en 376*
Psalms, 166, 250, 342, 364, 365, 424, 471, *en 448, 526*
Psalter, 78, 249, 250, 266, 322, 342, 364, *en 391, 448*
Public Meeting, 93, 109, 115, 119, 123, 137, 156, 159, 162, 180, 250, 314, 345
Public Morals Committee, 17, 340, 341, 349, 377
Public Questions Committee, 309, 340
Purce, AM, 225
Puritans, 19, 33, 35, 229, 294, *en 7, 526*
Qua Iboe Fellowship, 372-373, 375, 464, 478
Quantitative Satisfaction, 140-143, 147, 165, 172, 193, 434
Queen's County, 257
Queen's University Belfast, 17, 82, 276, 278, 323, 345, 375, *en 66, 118, 277*
Queen's University Bible Union, 82, 276, 278
Queensland, 252
Quest for God in China, 68, *en 80*
Quid pro quo, 141, 172
R Wright-Hay, 247
Racow, *en 199*
Radio Broadcasts, 356
Ramelton, 81, 82, 84
Rathbreasil, 29
Rathfriland, 257, 301, 323
Rathlin Island, 300
Rationalism, 62, 112, 119, 159, 162, 312, 330
Ravenhill Evangelical Mission, *en 421*
Ravenhill PCI, 19, 81, 84, 98, 109, 110, 228, *en 149, 175, 353, 421*
Ravenhill Presbyterian Church, (*Centenary History*), 228, 230, 340, 362, 442, *en 353*
Ravenhill Road FPCU, *en 420*
Ray, J, 375
Reading and Study, 427-428
Rebellion - Civil, 34, 35, *en 38*
Rebellion against God, 207
Record of the Trial of Prof J E Davey, 133-135, 143, 158-159, 164, 170, 172-173, 176, 181, 332, *en 48, 171, 173, 176, 181-183, 185-186, 191, 196, 204, 216, 233, 237-244, 246, 254-260, 262, 264, 266, 273, 302, 306, 315, 320, 323-324, 332-338, 340-343, 344*
Redemption Songs, 250
Redemption, 145, 250, 406, 407, 420, 423, 424, *en 188*
Reformation Settlement, 34
Reformation Standards, 239

538

Index

Reformation Today, 20, 476, **en** *505, 512*
Reformation Translation Fellowship, 302, **en** *416, 510*
Reformation, 20, 29, 34-35, 45, 53, 71, 119, 148, 162, 235, 239, 294, 302, 351, 397-400, 408, 414, 420, 470-472, 474, 476-477, **en** *297, 491-492*
Reformed Church in South Africa, 290
Reformed Churches in Spain, 17, 370
Reformed Churches of the Netherlands, Liberated, 337, 344, 370, **en** *447*
Reformed Ecumenical Synod, 290-292, 343
Reformed Presbyterian Church in Ireland, 15, 45, 81, 98, 192, 233, 241, 288, 301, 343-344, 349, 360, 370, 372, **en** *209, 390, 447*
Reformed Presbyterian Theological Hall, 81, 98
Reformed Presbyterian Witness, 241
Regiment Sessions PCI, 35
Regions Beyond Mission, 260
Regium Donum, 49
Rehoboam, 412-413
Reid, Angela, 374, 386
Reid, J, 387
Reid, JS, 20, 38-39, 48, 52, 55, 384, 396, **en** *15, 43, 51, 479*
Reid, NE, 213, 333-336, 369, 374, 386, 388, 464, 466-468, 475
Reid, R, 387
Reid, Stanford, 307
Reilly, T, **en** *10*
Religion & Politics of Paisleyism, 379, **en** *465*
Reminiscences of a Veteran Missionary, 253
Remonstrant Synod, 51, **en** *199*
Renwick, AM, 294
Resurrection, 69, 212, 275, 298, 310, 317, 320, 402-403, 424, 428, 436-437, 441, 473
Revised Psalter, 1880, 249, 266, 342, **en** *391*
Revivalist, **en** *421*
Reymond, RL, 20, 273, **en** *148, 292, 394*
Reynolds, H, 251
Richards, N, 345, **en** *504*
Richhill, 218, 287, 335-337, 355, 357-358, 374, 376, 443-445, 447-448, 452, 461, 464, 473-474
Richview PCI, 108, 119, 251, 252
Ridderbos, H, 291
Righteousness, 132, 138, 143-144, 147, 152, 192-194, 205, 276-278, 294, 340, 346, 369, 381, 414, 425, 434, 441, **en** *65, 77, 175, 190, 389*
Rio de Janeiro, 290
Roberts, JC, 351
Robertson, WM, 157-158
Rodgers, R, 351
Roger, J, 361
Roger, JS, 213, 356, 467, 475
Roman Catholic Church, 29, 206, 289, 346, 400, **en** *80, 492*
Romania, 367, 387
Rosemary Street PCI, 82
Ross, Charlie, 82, 84
Ross, J Allen, 84, 108-109, 231-232, **en** *359*
Ross, J, 84, 95, 109, 228, 230, 232, **en** *175, 215*
Ross, JS, 213, 336, 342, 466-468
Round Towers, 28
ROUTE, 370
Royal Belfast Academical Institution, 76, **en** *118*
Royal Black Preceptory, 299
Royal Ulster Agricultural Show, 302, 356
Royalists, 35
Ruling Elders' Union PCI, 118
Runia, K, 20, 291, 408, 410, **en** *505, 512*
Russelites, 256-257, 299-300, 470
Russia, 67
Russian Missionary Society, 260
Rutherford, S, 229, **en** *292*
Sabbath, 20, 276, 311, 348, 363, 429
Sabbaticals, 334
Sacraments, 71, 230, 233-235, 285, 297-298, 380, 414, 421-423, 427, 429, 441-442, **en** *355, 521*
Sacred Writings, 200
Salaries, 264, 297, 311, 340
Sampson, WA, 214, 265, 288, 290, 303, 305, 309, 322, 342, 466-468
Samuel Bill Theological College, 373
Sanballat, 239
Sanday, Wm, 198
Sandys Street, Newry, 77
Sardis, 413
Satan, 203, 273, 351, 412, 414-415
Sawyer J, 372
Schaeffer, FA, 290, **en** *406,*
Schism, 51, 185-186, 378-379, 407-408, **en** *492*
Schisma, Schismata, Schizo, 407-408
Schumacher, EF, **en** *468*
Scientific, 80, 90, 169, 201, 202, 438
Scofield, CI, 272, 275, **en** *382*
Scopes Trial, 330
Scott, Jas, 232, 277
Scott, Jn, 474
Scottish Reformation, 294
Scottish Theology, **en** *292*
Scripture – Authority, 61, 69, 71, 73, 117, 132, 157-158, 161, 166, 173-174, 202-204,

211, 313, 401, 436, 441, *en 72, 73, 166, 200, 363*
Scripture – Inerrancy, 117, 173, 201-202
Scripture – Infallibility, 38, 69, 100-101, 112-113, 115, 117, 132, 158-159, 161, 166, 173-174, 199-202, 204, 289, 291, 313, 436-437, 441, *en 160, 166, 363, 409*
Scripture – Obedience, 203, 242, 378, 408, 416, 424, 428, 430
Scripture – Organic Inspiration, 200
Scripture – Perspicacity, 400
Scripture – Self-attesting, 202
Scripture – Spiration, 200
Scripture Gift Mission, London, 260
Scripture Union, *en 392*
Seceders in Ireland, 20, *en 28, 461, 476*
Secession Church, 42-45, 56, 63, 74, 414-416
Secession, 43-45, 53, 56, 64, 11, 237, 345, 381, 407-416, 477, *en 25, 27, 453, 497*
Second Blessing, 19, 102-103, 182, *en 140, 142*
Second Coming, 272, 274, 275, 304, 407, 424, 476
Second Great Awakening, 405
Second Helvetic Confession, *en 409*
'Second Reformation', 53
Seeley, Sir J, 70
Selected Shorter Writings, 19, *en 214, 283*
Semi-Socinian, 66
Semper Reformanda, 396-399, 407
Seoul, 475
Separation - Ecclesiastical, 40, 48, 51-52, 231-232, 237, 246, 276, 296, 327, 332, 380, 407-408, 410, 413, *en 504, 512*
Separatism, 407-408
Servetus, M, *en 200*
Seven Churches of Asia, 412-413
Seventh Day Adventists, 299
Severance EPC, 226, 274
Seymour Hill EPC, 296, 334, 347
Shaftesbury Square IEC, 216, 249, 256
Shankill Road, 98
Shanks Family, 108
Shanks, J, ?36
Shanks, SG, 124, 125, 219, 255, 302, 303, 466, 467, *en 456*
Shannon, R, 236, 251
Shannon, R, 246
Shared life, *en 13*
Shaw, Bea, 323
Shawlies, 244
Shields, TT, 275, 290
Shiels, J, 141-143, 145, 172
Shipbuilding Belfast, 98, 100, 244, 282
Short and Harland, 282

Short History of the Presbyterian Church in Ireland, 20, 40, 378, *en 21, 31, 42, 260*
Short Stirling Bombers, 282
Shorter Catechism, see Westminster
Simson, J, 40, 62, 396-397
Sin – Paul's philosophy of, 136, 146, 435, *en 182*
Sin – Pre-forgiveness, 142, 144-145
Sin – God's liability for, 205
Sin – God's relation to, 208
Sing Psalms, 364
Singapore, 307
Sinless perfection, 102-103
Sixmilewater Valley, 33
Sixty Years of Evangelical Witness, 352
Size – EPC, 379-380
Skilton, JH, *en 122, 125*
Skinner's Alley Baptist Church, 41
Slatehill, 249, 253, 257, 258, 268, 296, 445, 446, 452, *en 384*
Sloat, L, 265, 316, 324
Small is Beautiful, *en 468*
Smallness, 379-380
Smethurst, J, 48, 49, 107, 155, 179
Smith, GA, 65, 66
Smith, WR, 60-61, 64
Smyrna, 228
Smyth, TAB, 186
Snoddy, WH, 138, 146, 158, 161, 164, 165, *en 173, 182, 253*
Society of Friends, 299
Socinianism, 66, 147, 148
Socinius, F, *en 200*
Soest, 370
Sola Scriptura, 400
Solemn League and Covenant, 35, 36, 45
Solomon, 323, 412, 438, 477
Somerton Road, 109, 217, 249, 252-254, 258, 263, 277, 287, 305, 330, 335, 347, 359, 363, 392, 443-448, 451-452, 461, 473, 474
Somme, 23, 96
SOS to Irish Presbyterians, 112-114, 117, *en 160*
Soudan Interior Mission, 260
South Africa, 247, 252-253, 255, 261, 277, 290-291, 296, 30-303, 305, 307, 322, 343, 351, 372, 374, 385-386, 446, 464, 475
South African Dutch Reformed Church, 102
South Belfast IEC, 108, 216, 245, 249, 269
South Carolina, 416
Soviet Union, 282, 284
Spain, 17, 261, 363, 370, 387, 480, *en 13*
Spanish Gospel Mission, 260
Speakers List IEC, 255

Speakers' Training IEC, 297-298
Speaking in Tongues, 103
Spears, T, 267
Special Committees, 338-339
Speers, K, 268, 366
Spiritual Songs, 365, 424
Sproul, RC, 148, *en 202, 519, 525*
Spurgeon, CH, 20, 111, 147, 293, 323, 410, 476, 479, *en 506, 508*
St George's Cross Tabernacle, 97
St Giles Kirk, 34
St John's Toronto, 254
Standard-Bearer, 237-238
Stapleton, T, 471
Stevenson, Rachel, 387
Stevenson, Ross, 89, 410
Stewart, ATQ, 399
Stewart, D, Cregagh, 44, *en 28, 475*
Stewart, D, Muckamore, 40, 44, 51, 378, *en 21, 31, 42, 269, 460*
Stirling, 43, 282
Stonehouse, NB, 290, 291, 307, 316, 324, 382, *en 123, 129, 440*
Stories of Christian Heroes, 278, 470
Story of Old Side Presbyterianism, en 502
Story of the Puritans, 19, *en 7*
Stott, J, 188
Strabane, 50, 76
Strafford, Earl, 33-34
Strang Millar, R, 307
Stranmillis, 83, 216-217, 334-335, 339, 349, 356, 358, 361, 364-365, 375-376, 443-445, 447-448, 453, 457, 462, 464, 473, 474, *en 429*
Strategy, 49, 118, 134, 156, 168, 230, 232, 236, 249, 263, 290, 311, 336-337, 345, 353-354, 358-359, 373, 413, 417, 469, 474, 477, *en 441, 443*
Strathpeffer Convention, 326
Stream, 367
Stuart monarchy, 33, 35, *en 12*
Student Notebooks, 146
Student population, 375, *en 66*
Sub judice, 158, 170, 181, *en 254*
Submission, church courts, 405, 411,
Subordinate Standards, 24, 93, 117-118, 186, 212, 240, 273-274, 315, 361, 401, 404-405, 421, 430, *en 72, 409*
Subscribers, 40, 41, 401, 404, 405
Subscription, 23, 38-41, 51-53, 60-61, 64, 67, 106, 112-114, 119, 140, 162, 178, 205, 228, 235, 241, 261-262, 273-275, 285-287, 320, 367, 396-397, 401-402, 404-406, 421, *en 5, 484*
Substitution, 136, 148, 194, 195, 196

Sudan Interior Mission, 17, 261
Suez Crisis, 284
Sunday School Project, 338, 341, 348, 478
Sunday School, 69, 108, 251, 267, 298, 301, 303-305, 336, 341, 348, 354, 373, 478, 480
Surety, 249
Surprised by Joy, en 501
Swann, T, 236, 325, 471
Swanwick Declaration, 346
Sweden, 307, 310, *en 417, 454*
Sword and Trowel, 410
Sydney, 95, 102
Synod of Dordt, 399, *en 409, 430, 487*
Synod of Kells, 29
Synod of Ulster, 38, 40, 42, 44, 49-50, 52-54, 56, 107, 396, 405
Synoptics, 212
System of Doctrine, 106, 274, 402, 420
Systematic Theology – Chair, 61-62, 89, 97, 112, *en 64, 277*
Systematic Theology – Subject, 90, 374
Systematic Theology – WCF, 420
Systematic Theology, Hodge, 141, 311, *en 194, 197, 328*
Tabernacle, 41, 97, 247
Taiwan, 351
Tallaght, Dublin, 335
Tape Library, 355
Templepatrick, 33, 43, 48
Ten Years' Conflict, 18, 42, *en 23-25*
Tennant, Wm, 406
Tennessee, 330-331, *en 439, 517*
Tennyson, AL, 174, *en 236, 265*
Terminology of the Atonement, en 291, 294
Tertullian, 163, 212
Texas, 246, *en 517*
Textual Variants, 201
Thatcher, Rt Hon M, 349
The Atonement in the Light of History and the Modern Spirit, 62
The Presbyterian, USA, 89
Theological College of Northern Nigeria, 17, 373
Theology and Theologians of Scotland, en 292
Theology of the Larger Catechism, en 404
Theology of the Westminster Confession, *en 327, 329*
Murray, *en 327, 329*
Theology Proper, 206
Theopneustos, 200
Thessalonica, 412, 417
Thiepval Wood, 96
Thirty-Nine Articles, 291, *en 409*
Thomas, DWH, 15, 88, 192-196, 213, 344, 381, 471-472, 474-475, *en 523*

Thomas, G, 246, 376, 474, *en 214, 349*
Thompson, DA, 307, 351
Thompson, G, 359
Thompson, Geo, 164, 171, 175, *en 207*
Thompson, H, 366
Thompson, J, 158, 161, 187, *en 277*
Thompson, S, 135
Thompson, W, 467
Thompson, WJ, 288
Thoroughly Educated Ministry, *en 398, 473, 498*
Thought for the Day, 356, 377
Titanic, 23, 244, *en 400*
Titcombe, EH, 126, 298, 306, 466
Todd, H, 236, 245, 248
Toombebridge, 48
Torbay, 36
Tories, 36
Toronto Blessing, 367
Torrey, RA, 97, 101
Tow, T, 307
Tracey, SJ, 14, 60, 213, 333, 467, 468, *en 15*
Training for the Ministry (and Admissions) Committee, 286, 308, 309, 333, 334, 338, 360, 364
Training for the Ministry Fund, 309, 361
Training of the Ministry, 84, 308-309, 339, 371, 397
Transcendence, 73, 167
Transubstantiation, 139, 147, 193, 234, 434, 435, 439
Traveller's Guide, 256-257
Treasurers EPC, 235-236, 297, 311, 317, 321, 339, 341
Trinitarianism, 210-211
Trinity College Dublin, 28-29, *en 66, 118*
Trinity Hymnal, 266, 342, 364, 365
Trinity, 14, 23, 47, 50, 72, 97, 112, 132, 147-148, 153, 159, 166, 174, 180, 192, 208-212, 233-234, 365, 439, 440, 441, *en 363*
Trinity, Philosophical Development, 212
Triunity, 211
Troup, J, 257
Trueman, CR, 15, 21, 424, 474, *en 524*
Trust Deeds, 302, 338
Truths we Confess, 20, *en 202, 519, 525*
Tudors, 28
Twisse, Wm, *en 292*
Two Covenants and the Second Blessing, *en 140*
Tyrconnell, 32
Tyrella Co Down, 259, 303, 304, 389, 388, 481
U-Boat War, 282

UFM OneHundredFold, 375
Uganda, 363, 374, 375, 386, 387, 464, 480
Ukraine, 370, 480
Ulster Automobile Club, 310
Ulster Covenant, 23, 323
Ulster Division, 23, 96
Ulster Hall, 160, 230
Ulster Pamphlets, 159, 230, *en 211, 242*
Ulster Volunteers, 96
Ulster-American Religion, 19, 99, 116, 379, *en 134, 137, 139, 165, 268, 345, 466*
Unaccommodated Calvin, 19, *en 286*
Understanding Fundamentalism and Evangelicalism, *en 471*
Underwood, E, 375, 386, 464
Union Church?, 230
Unionism, 54, 99
Unitarianism, 52, 210
United Free Church of Scotland College, 97, 140, *en 60, 69, 295*
United Free Church of Scotland, 62, 64-68, 97, 266, *en 60, 69*
United Irishmen, *en 38*
United Presbyterian Church, Scotland, 63-64, 67, *en 27*
Unity, 60, 70, 72, 101, 147, 175, 186, 210, 231-232, 292, 317, 323, 344, 346, 349, 368-369, 399-401, 407-412, 415, 427, 430, 472, 475, *en 492, 504, 507*
Urbanisation, 244
Ursinus, *en 430*
Uzziah, 412
Van Dyke, H, 89
Van Til, C, 89, 247
Van Zyl, FWJ, 126, 447, 451, 453
Vancouver, 475, *en 425*
VE-Day, 283
Venice, 269
Veto Act 1834, Scotland, 63
Viewers and Listeners Association, 309
Vikings, 28
Virginia, *en 117, 517*
Visible Church, 368, 408-410, 415, 421, 424, *en 450*
Vision for the Nineties, 354, 355, 359, 361, 372, 417, 469
Visitation, 256, 262-263, 298, 322, 348, 361, *en 355*
VJ-Day, 283
Voetius, Gisbertus, *en 487*
Voluntary Societies, 406
Vos, C, 348
Vos, GJ, 88, 96
Vos, JG, 410, 415, *en 416, 510, 516*
W. P. Nicholson, Flame for God and Ulster, *en 1, 119, 131*

Waddell, J, 69, 139
Walker, T, 61, 66, 77
Ward, R, 364
Warfield, BB, 20, 87-88, 115, 131, 194, 198, 200-201, 211-212, 382, 474, **en 289, 313, 318, 389, 431**
Was Saul of Tarsus the Real Founder of Christianity?, **en 296**
Watchword, 33, 64
Watson, Amy, 301
Watson, D, 13, 14, 381, 429
Watson, S, 14, 219, **en 456**
Watts, I, **en 391**
Watts, R, 61, 62, 77, 157, **en 64, 103, 107**
Way Ahead, 355-356, 469
Welch, J, 33
Wellhausen, 61, 312
Wellington Hall Belfast, 160, 161, 162, 246, 294, 313, 316, 351, **en 142**
Wentworth, 33-34
Wesley, Charles, 41-42, 266
Wesley, John, 41-42, 102, 479
Westbourne PCI, 252
Westminster Catechisms (LC, SC), 39, 48, 50, 60, 72-73, 106, 117-118, 133, 142, 148, 152, 159, 165, 171, 174, 228, 234, 238-240, 265, 273, 274, 275, 284, 285, 286, 294, 315, 348, 361, 384, 401, 402, 420, 421, 427, 434, 439, **en 80, 175, 245, 282, 364, 404, 433**
Westminster Confession into the 21st Century, **en 296, 404, 519, 526**
Westminster Confession of Faith, 24, 35-36, 38-41, 45, 48, 50-52, 54-55, 60-61, 63, 66-68, 72-74, 88, 106, 112, 117-118, 132, 140, 143, 146-149, 157, 159, 166-169, 172-174, 179, 183, 191-192, 194, 196, 199, 200, 204-206, 207-210, 212, 227-228, 234-235, 237, 239-241, 254, 265, 273-275, 284-286, 288, 291, 294, 297-298, 315, 361, 364, 368-369, 379-380, 382-384, 396-398, 401-406, 410, 412, 417, 420-423, 424, 427-429, 436-437, 439, 472, 475, **en 19, 72-73, 202,263, 292, 296, 322, 327, 329, 331, 363, 404-405, 409, 416, 484, 516-517, 519-521, 524-525, 528**
Westminster Divines, 35, 66, 72, 200, 265, 273, 274, 294, 384, 401, 420
Westminster Theological Seminary, 17, 87, 89, 92, 192, 246-247, 290, 307, 360, 373, **en 406, 469**
Wexford, 35
What is Christianity?, 160, 351, **en 214, 383**
What is the Irish Evangelical Church?, 317, 470

What St. Paul Really Said, 196, **en 296**
What the Bible Teaches about Jesus, **en 214**
Wheat and Tares, 414
Whigs, 36
Whitefield College of the Bible, 315
Whitefield, G, 18, 41, 405, 476, **en 22, 24**
Whitla, N, 213
Whole counsel of God, 105, 289, 294, 380, 423, 424
Whose Faith Follow, 18, 320, **en 152**
Whyte, A, 97
Whyte, Alexander, 97
Widows and Orphans Fund, 311
Wilkinson, Annie, 303, 326, 385
William of Orange, 36
William the Conqueror, 29
Wilson, RD, 62, 88, 89, 90, **en 65**
Wiltshire, 41
Witherow, T, 20, 32-33, 45, 48, 55, 397, **en 483**
Witness of Paul, **en 214**
Witness of the Gospels, **en 214**
Woolsey, AA, 14-15, 192, 208, 213, 239, 355, 363, 467, 472
World Council of Churches, 17, 289, 291, 292, 343
World Evangelisation Crusade, 260
World War I, 78, 96, 244
World War II, 282
Worship, 11, 39, 65, 71, 78-79, 173-174, 198, 238, 249-250, 290, 342, 351, 365, 381, 384, 401, 403, 422-425, 428-430, 439, 476, **en 421, 521, 526**
Wright, NT, 196, 246, 458, 462, **en 296**
Wright-Hay, R, 246-247
Wycliffe Bible Translators, 375, 386, 464
YMCA, Belfast, 101, 108, 114-115, 156-157, 162, 237, 244-246, 313, 349, **en 142, 361**
Young People's Association, 266, 267, 303, 306, 335, 347, 362
Young, EJ, 90, 316, 324
YPA Projects, 480
Yuile, J, 293
Zeitgeist, 407
Zwolle, 475

By Honour and Dishonour